KT-562-414

THE DEVELOPING CHILD

FIFTH EDITION THE DEVELOPING CHILD

Helen Bee

1817

HARPER & ROW, PUBLISHERS, New York

Cambridge, Philadelphia, San Francisco,
London, Mexico City, São Paulo, Singapore, Sydney

**DEESIDE COLLEGE
LIBRARY**

CLASS No. 159.922.7
ACCESS No. D66830

MULTIMEDIA LEARNING CENTRE
DEESIDE COLLEGE

Editor-in-Chief: Judith L. Rothman
Project Editor: Susan Goldfarb
Text Design: Lucy Krikorian
Cover Design: José R. Fonfrias
Cover Illustration: Artist—Mary Netzer-Schuman, Campus Laboratory School,
     University of Wisconsin, Oshkosh; teacher—Professor David
     Hodge
Text Art: J&R Art Services, Inc.
Photo Research: Cheryl Mannes
Production Manager: Willie Lane
Compositor: Arcata Graphics/Kingsport
Printer and Binder: Arcata Graphics/Kingsport
Cover Printer: Lehigh Press
Part-Opening Art: Part One: Kristine Koparanian; Part Two: Christine Malloy;
     Part Three: Lawrence Clayton; Part Four: Persia Lane; Part
     Five: Stephan Tchorbajian; Part Six: Samantha Tweedy

Picture credits begin on page 621.

The Developing Child, Fifth Edition

Copyright © 1989 by Harper & Row, Publishers, Inc.

All rights reserved. Printed in the United States of America. No part of this book
may be used or reproduced in any manner whatsoever without written permission,
except in the case of brief quotations embodied in critical articles and reviews.
For information address Harper & Row, Publishers, Inc., 10 East 53d Street, New
York, NY 10022.

Library of Congress Cataloging-in-Publication Data

Bee, Helen L., 1939–
    The developing child / Helen L. Bee. —5th ed.
      p.   cm.
    Includes bibliographies and indexes.
    ISBN 0–06–040604–6
    1. Child psychology. 2. Child development. I. Title. ·
    BF721.B336 1989   88–22813
155.4—dc19   CIP

89 90 91 9 8 7 6 5 4 3 2

Contents in Brief

To the Student   xiii
To the Instructor   xv

Part One   INTRODUCTION   1

Chapter 1   Basic Questions, Major Theories   3

Part Two   THE BEGINNINGS OF LIFE   35

Chapter 2   Prenatal Development   37
Chapter 3   Birth and the Newborn Child   75

Part Three   THE PHYSICAL CHILD   113

Chapter 4   Physical Development   115
Chapter 5   Perceptual Development   153

Part Four   THE THINKING CHILD   183

Chapter 6   Cognitive Development I: Cognitive Power   185
Chapter 7   Cognitive Development II: Structure and Process   225
Chapter 8   The Development of Language in Children   275

Part Five   THE SOCIAL CHILD   317

Chapter 9   Personality Development: Alternative Views   319
Chapter 10   The Concept of Self in Children   353
Chapter 11   The Development of Social Relationships   391
Chapter 12   Thinking About Relationships: The Development of
Social Cognition   433

Part Six   THE WHOLE CHILD   467

Chapter 13   The Ecology of Development: The Impact of Families, Schools, and Culture   469
Chapter 14   Atypical Development   509
Chapter 15   Putting It All Together: The Developing Child   543

Glossary   571

References   581

Picture Credits   621

Author Index   623

Subject Index   633

Detailed Contents

To the Student   xiii
To the Instructor   xv

Part One: INTRODUCTION   1

Chapter 1   BASIC QUESTIONS, MAJOR THEORIES   3

Describing and Explaining   5
The Key Questions   6
Theories of Development   12
Finding the Answers: Research on Development   25
Summary   31
Key Terms   32
Suggested Reading   33
Project: Observation of a Child   33

Part Two: THE BEGINNINGS OF LIFE   35

Chapter 2   PRENATAL DEVELOPMENT   37

Conception   38
The Basic Genetics of Conception   40
Development from Conception to Birth   45
Prenatal Sexual Differentiation   49
Explanations of the Normal Sequence of Development   50
Things That Can Go Wrong: Genetic Errors   52
Things That Can Go Wrong in the Environment: Disease, Drugs, and Diet   55
Other Characteristics of the Mother That Affect the Normal Sequence   63
An Overview of Risks and Long-Term Consequences of Prenatal Problems   68
Sex Differences in Prenatal Development   70

Social Class Differences in Prenatal Development   70
Summary   71
Key Terms   72
Suggested Reading   73

Chapter 3   BIRTH AND THE NEWBORN CHILD   75

Birth   76
What Can the Newborn Do?   91
The Daily Life of Infants   98
Individual Differences Among Babies   103
The Effects of the Infant on the Parents   106
Summary   107
Key Terms   109
Suggested Reading   109
Project: Observation in a Newborn Nursery   110

Part Three: THE PHYSICAL CHILD   113

Chapter 4   PHYSICAL DEVELOPMENT   115

Four Reasons for Studying Physical Development   116
Basic Sequences and Common Patterns   119
Development of Sexual Maturity   128
Using the Body: The Effects of Physical Changes on Behavior   132
Health and Illness in Childhood and Adolescence   136
Big or Fast Versus Slow or Small: Some Individual Differences in
  Physical Development   137
Determinants of Growth: Explanations of Physical Development   146
The Shape of Physical Development: A Last Look   149
Summary   149
Key Terms   151
Suggested Reading   151
Project: Plotting Your Own Growth   152

Chapter 5   PERCEPTUAL DEVELOPMENT   153

Some Basic Characteristics of Perceptual Development   154
Visual Development   155
Auditory Development   166
Development of Other Senses   168
Combining Information from Several Senses   169
The Basic Characteristics of Perceptual Development: A Second
  Look   170
Individual Differences in Perception   174
Answering the "Why" Questions: Explanations of Perceptual
  Development   178

Summary   179
Key Terms   181
Suggested Reading   181
Project: Development of the Object Concept   182

▬▬▬▬▬ Part Four: THE THINKING CHILD   183

Chapter 6   COGNITIVE DEVELOPMENT I: COGNITIVE POWER   185

Three Views of Intelligence   186
Measuring Intellectual Power: IQ Tests   188
What IQ Tests Predict   193
Stability of IQ Test Scores   198
Limitations of Traditional IQ Tests   199
An Alternative View: Sternberg's Triarchic Theory of Intelligence   201
Explaining the Differences: Factors Influencing IQ Test Scores   203
Influence of Heredity on IQ   203
The Influence of Environment on IQ   206
Group Differences in IQ: Race and Sex Differences   217
The Measurement of Intelligence: A Last Look   221
Summary   222
Key Terms   223
Suggested Reading   224

Chapter 7   COGNITIVE DEVELOPMENT II: STRUCTURE AND PROCESS   225

Piaget's Basic Ideas   226
The Sensorimotor Period: From Birth to 18 Months   230
Preoperational Thought: From 18 Months to 6 Years   233
Concrete Operational Thought: From 6 to 12 Years   242
Formal Operational Thought: From Age 12 On   247
Overview of the Stages of Cognitive Development   252
Criticisms of Piaget's Theory   253
Information Processing in Children   256
Putting the Three Approaches Together   264
Summary   268
Key Terms   270
Suggested Reading   270
Project: The Game of 20 Questions   271

Chapter 8   THE DEVELOPMENT OF LANGUAGE IN CHILDREN   275

What Is Language, Anyway?   277
The Early Steps   277

The Development of Grammar 284
The Development of Word Meaning 289
Using Language: Communication and Self-Direction 295
Explaining Language Development 297
The Influence of the Environment on Language Development 297
The Child's Role in Language Development 301
A Combined View 305
Individual Differences in Language Development 306
An Application of the Basic Knowledge: Learning to Read 309
Summary 311
Key Terms 313
Suggested Reading 313
Project: Beginning Two-Word Sentences 314
Project: Conversation Between Parent and Child 315

▰▰▰▰▰ Part Five: THE SOCIAL CHILD 317

Chapter 9 PERSONALITY DEVELOPMENT: ALTERNATIVE VIEWS 319

What Do We Mean by Personality? 320
The Major Alternative Views of Personality 322
A Biological Approach: Temperament 322
Learning Approaches to Personality 327
Psychoanalytic Theories 334
Freud's Theory 334
Erikson's Theory 339
A Tentative Synthesis 348
Summary 351
Key Terms 352
Suggested Reading 352

Chapter 10 THE CONCEPT OF SELF IN CHILDREN 353

The Concept of Self: Developmental Patterns 354
Individual Differences in the Self-Concept 364
The Self-Concept: A Summing Up 367
The Development of Gender and Sex-Role Concepts 368
Theories of the Development of Sex-Role Concepts and Sex-Role Behavior 374
Individual Differences in Sex Typing and Stereotypes 378
Some Real-Life Applications: Occupational Choices, Occupational Behavior, and Family Roles 383
Summary 386
Key Terms 388

Suggested Reading   389
Project: Sex Roles on TV   389

Chapter 11   THE DEVELOPMENT OF SOCIAL RELATIONSHIPS   391

Attachment and Attachment Behavior: Definitions   392
The Attachment Process: Parent to Child   394
The Attachment Process: Child to Parent   402
Attachments to Fathers and Mothers   407
Individual Differences in the Quality of Attachments   408
Beyond the First Attachment: Children's Relationships with Other
  Children   414
Positive Social Interactions Among Children: Developmental
  Patterns   414
Individual Differences in Positive Interactions: Popularity   421
Negative Social Interaction Among Children   423
Sex Differences in Social Interactions   425
Summary   427
Key Terms   429
Suggested Reading   429
Project: Observation of Children's Play Groups   430

Chapter 12   THINKING ABOUT RELATIONSHIPS: THE DEVELOPMENT OF SOCIAL COGNITION   433

Some General Principles and Issues   434
Thinking About Other People: Feelings, Qualities, Relationships   437
Thinking About What People *Ought* to Do   445
Social Cognition and Behavior   456
Social Cognition and General Cognitive Development   461
Summary   463
Key Terms   464
Suggested Reading   464
Project: Understanding of Friendship   465

■■■■■ Part Six: THE WHOLE CHILD   467

Chapter 13   THE ECOLOGY OF DEVELOPMENT: THE IMPACT OF FAMILIES, SCHOOLS, AND CULTURE   469

The Influence of the Family   471
Things That Can Affect Family Functioning   481

Beyond the Family: The Direct Influences of Other Institutions on
Children   491
A Final Point: Systems and Interpretations   503
Summary   504
Key Terms   506
Project: Television Aggression   506

Chapter 14   ATYPICAL DEVELOPMENT   509

Frequency of Problems   511
Mentally Atypical Development   512
Emotionally Atypical Development   521
Physically Atypical Development   530
Sex Differences in Atypical Development   532
The Impact of an Atypical Child on the Family   533
Interventions and Treatments   534
A Final Point   538
Summary   538
Key Terms   540
Suggested Reading   540

Chapter 15   PUTTING IT ALL TOGETHER: THE DEVELOPING CHILD   543

Ages and Stages   544
Returning to Some Basic Questions   559
Individual Differences   563
A Final Point: The Joy of Development   568
Summary   569
Suggested Reading   570

Glossary   571

References   581

Picture Credits   621

Author Index   623

Subject Index   633

To the Student

Hello and welcome. Let me invite you into the study of a fascinating subject—children and their development. This is a bit like inviting you into my own home, since I have lived in the world of the study of children for a great many years. Unfortunately, I cannot know each of you individually, but by writing this book as much as possible as if it were a conversation between you and me, I hope I can make the reading of this book, and the studying of this subject, as personal a process as possible.

Because such personal involvement is one of my goals, you will find that I often write in the first person and that I have included a number of anecdotes about my own life. (One of the amusing side effects of this style of writing is that I regularly meet students from around the country who, from having read this book, know all kinds of personal things about me and feel that they know me well.)

Welcome, too, to the adventure of science. From the very first edition of this book, one of my goals has been to try to convey the sense of excitement of scientific inquiry. I want each of you to take away some feeling for the way psychologists think, the kinds of questions we ask, and the ways we go about trying to answer these questions, as well as for the theoretical and intellectual ferment that is part of the process. Think of psychology as a kind of detective story—we discover clues after hard, often painstaking, work; we make new guesses or hypotheses; and then we search for new clues.

Of course, I also want you to come away from reading this book with a firm grounding of knowledge in the field. There is much that we do not yet know or understand. But a great many facts and observations have accumulated. These facts and observations will be of help to you professionally if you are planning a career with children (in teaching, nursing, social work, medicine, psychology, or the like); the information will also be useful in your likely eventual role as a parent. There is much to be learned. In the midst of all that learning, though, I hope you enjoy the reading as much as I have enjoyed the writing.

Helen Bee

To the Instructor

GOALS OF THE FIFTH EDITION

A major goal of any new edition of a text is to update the basic theories and research information. In a field changing as fast as developmental psychology, updating is no small task.

In addition, my personal goals since the first edition of this text have been several:

1. To find the often-elusive balance between theory and research on the one hand and practical application on the other. Both are important. The research and theory are certainly the core, not to be slighted. But—perhaps especially for beginning students—the ideas and findings need to be linked up to everyday issues, too. Among other things, I think it is important for students to understand just how difficult applications often are. To achieve this tricky balance, I have retained the strong theoretical flavor that has been characteristic of this book from the first edition, have used specific research illustrations throughout, and have introduced applications both in boxes and in the text itself.

2. To discuss child development in ways that are relevant to faculty and students in education, nursing, medicine, social work, and home economics as well as to those in psychology. Of course, it is impossible to meet all those needs in one book; but by including applied material that relates to school settings, to physical disabilities or disorders of development, and to family functioning, I have tried to link the core information with the practical issues of related fields.

3. To counteract the natural tendency toward ever-increasing length in revisions of texts, I have tried to keep this edition from expanding still further; indeed, I have tried to cut it slightly. The amount of information to convey seems to expand geometrically every four years, so it is hard to know what to cut or shorten. But neither student nor professor can cope with a thoroughly encyclopedic text. Once again I have aimed for a balance.

ORGANIZATION

The basic chapter organization introduced in the fourth edition remains the same in the fifth. The only significant overall organizational changes are the shifting of some topics from one chapter to another: the discussion of day care now appears in Chapter 13 (as part of the general discussion of "ecology"), and the treatment of reading and reading problems has been shifted from the perception chapter to the language chapter.

Before too many years (or editions) go by, no doubt the material on information processing will require a separate chapter. I debated reorganizing the material in such a way for this edition, but I concluded that, at least for now, Piaget's theory is still the dominant organizing theme. The coverage of information processing has been considerably expanded, however.

Within each chapter, the changes have been primarily of four kinds: factual updating, reorganization of information to improve clarity, expanded coverage of some topics, and introduction of new topics.

REORGANIZATION OF INFORMATION WITHIN CHAPTERS

The greatest single reorganization has been in Chapter 12, on social cognition. Selman's theory, which dominated this chapter in the fourth edition, has been moved off center stage, and a number of other views are included, such as Hoffman's theory of empathy development and Eisenberg's theory of prosocial reasoning.

Two chapters with significant but less sweeping reorganization are Chapter 5, which was restructured using several of Eleanor Gibson's concepts as a framework, and Chapter 1, which now includes an expanded discussion of major theories and omits the "research journey."

EXPANDED COVERAGE AND NEW TOPICS

Beyond the basic updating of *every* topic, certain topics have been significantly expanded or revised, and some new ones have been introduced. Some examples:

New Topics

Health and diseases of childhood (including eating disorders)
Teenage pregnancy and adolescent sexuality
Perception of patterns in infancy, along with crossmodal transfer
Sternberg's triarchic theory of intelligence
Language pragmatics and the use of language in self-control
Slobin's theory of language acquisition

Distinctions between radical behaviorism and social-learning theories

The impact of childhood sex-role development and self-concepts on adult occupations and adult family roles

The concept of the internal working model of attachment

Insecure/disorganized/disoriented category of attachment security

Eisenberg's theory of prosocial reasoning

Hoffman's theory of empathy development

The impact of parental work on family functioning and children's development

Delinquency

Depression in childhood and adolescence

Significantly Updated Topics

Phenotype and genotype

Smoking and pregnancy

Birth location and its impact

Effect of infant on the parents

Impact of early versus late puberty

Information processing

Strengths and weaknesses of Piaget's theory

Analysis of "motherese" and its role in language development

Temperament and behavior problems

Early differences in treatment of boys and girls

Cognitive views of aggression

Effects of TV on aggression and other behavior

CONTINUING STRENGTHS

In addition to these changes, of course, the strengths of the first four editions have been retained. The writing style is still personal; the descriptions of theory and research are clear; the topics flow smoothly from one point to the next. Students almost invariably report that they enjoy reading the book and that they learn from it.

SUPPLEMENTS

Instructor's Manual

The Instructor's Manual, which I prepared, contains fairly detailed suggestions about lecture material, good sources for further coverage of specific topics, and possible class projects and activities for each chapter. This material is both expanded and updated in this edition.

Test Bank

The Test Bank includes both multiple-choice and essay questions. Some of the questions (with minor changes) are carried over from the Test Bank from the fourth edition, but at least half are new. I wrote all of the essay questions; the multiple-choice questions were written partly by Robert Orr and Janet Orr, who prepared the test item file for the fourth edition; partly by me; and partly by Marité Rodriguez-Haynes of the Clarion University of Pennsylvania, who prepared enough additional questions especially for this edition to provide 100 questions for each chapter. The questions are available in book form and also on computer disk.

Harper Test

The Text Bank is now available on this highly acclaimed microcomputerized test generation system that allows instructors to create fully customized tests. It features full word processing capabilities, "help" screens for quick access to instructions, and a password option to protect data. Harper Test is free to adopters. It is available for Apple, IBM, and most compatibles.

Study Guide

The Study Guide has been thoroughly revised and rewritten to correspond with the fifth edition. A dual format allows for either traditional or programmed personalized system of instruction (PSI) review. Each chapter includes chapter objectives, key terms and concepts, a multiple-choice self-quiz, open-ended study questions, and an end-of-chapter programmed review unit.

ACKNOWLEDGMENTS

As in the past, my work has been greatly aided by the comments of excellent reviewers. Vernon Haynes, Youngstown State University; Philip Mohan, University of Idaho; and James Thomas, Northern Kentucky University, all reviewed the fourth edition and suggested revisions and updates. Michael Bergmire, Jefferson College; Vernon Haynes, Youngstown State University; Philip Mohan, University of Idaho; James Thomas, Northern Kentucky University; Amye Warren-Leubecker, University of Tennessee at Chattanooga; Richard Pare, University of Maine; and Dorothy Wedge, Fairmont State College, reviewed some or all of the chapters of the draft for this fifth edition and made unusually helpful comments. When I first started writing textbooks, I hoped that reviewers would be kind and not make many suggestions. Now I have learned that critical—even picky—comments are the most helpful. So I want to thank all of the reviewers for the brickbats as well as the occasional bouquets.

Finally, thanks go to the crew at Harper & Row, who carry through from manuscript to book, answering my questions, finding the right pictures, tracking down permissions, making sure that names are spelled the same way throughout the text, and adapting to my somewhat unusual schedule. They have all been remarkably efficient, even-tempered, and helpful.

Helen Bee

PART ONE

INTRODUCTION

1 Basic Questions, Major Theories

Describing and Explaining
The Key Questions
    What Should We Be Studying?
    What Are the Major Influences on Development?
    What Is the Nature of Developmental Change?
Theories of Development
    Biological Theories
    Learning Theories
Some Applications of Learning Principles to Child Rearing
    Psychoanalytic Theories
    Cognitive-Developmental Theories
    Contrasting the Theories
Finding the Answers: Research on Development
    Ways to Describe Behavior
    Ways to Describe Changes with Age
    Ways to Describe Relationships Among Variables
    Ways to Explain Development: Experiments and Quasi Experiments
Summary
Key Terms
Suggested Reading
Project: Observation of a Child

When I meet new people and they ask me what I do, I have to choose between several options. If I answer, "I'm a psychologist," a common reaction is a slight recoil. The person may take a small step backward, or laugh awkwardly, or say something like, "Well, don't psychoanalyze me!" But if I say, "I'm a child psychologist," the reaction is very different. If the person I am talking to has children, or expects to have children, the typical reaction is immediately to ask some practical question:

"My husband is from Italy; should we be speaking both English and Italian to our children?"

"Our first child is a year old, and my wife is planning to go back to work. How on earth do we find a good day-care situation for the baby? Is there such a thing as 'good day care,' anyway?"

"My wife and I are having an argument about how much TV we should let our kids watch. Is it really bad for them?"

"We're so proud of our little girl. She started to talk when she was only about 9 months old, and now that she's 2 she's chattering away in long sentences. Does this mean she's gifted? Are there good programs for gifted children around here?"

"I thought my baby was going to be placid and easygoing, but boy was I wrong! He's antsy, doesn't like to be held for very long, won't try anything new, screams if we leave him with a sitter. I'm at my wit's end."

Legislators, too, ask questions like these when they are faced with writing laws to protect or promote the health and welfare of children. And all of these people are genuinely concerned about their children, and about the impact on their children of a whole range of decisions and stresses that are part of adult lives.

Of course most people want an answer in 25 words or less: "Yes," or "No," or "Here's what you should do." Occasionally I can give an answer like that. To the question about raising bilingual children, I can say, "Yes, do speak both languages to your children, from the beginning" (though even this answer requires some elaboration, as you'll see in Chapter 8). Most often, I have to hedge a bit. Sometimes the difficulty is that we simply don't know anything, or not much. More often, we have a lot of research on a given subject, but the results don't add up to a simple answer. To give a really complete reply I would have to offer a short course in theories and data about children's development so that my answer could be embedded in the proper context. Few casual acquaintances would sit still for such a lecture!

It is precisely that context, though, that I can give you in this book. My purpose is not just to provide the framework on which you or I can construct answers to practical problems of child rearing or family life—though I hope I can do that. My purpose is also to convey to you my own conviction that the study of children and their development is fascinating in itself, whether it leads to clear practical applications or not.

To achieve both of those goals, we need to deal with two tasks: to *describe* development (*what* happens) and to *explain* development (*why* it happens the way it does).

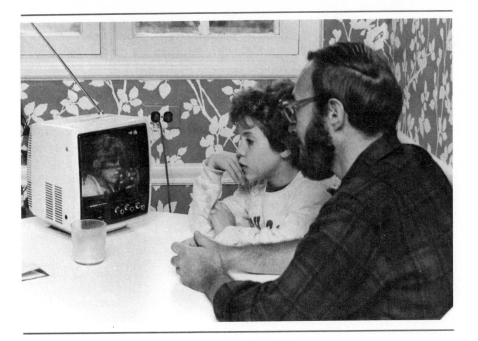

Figure 1.1   Should you let your children watch as much TV as they want, or should you set some limits? What limits make sense? Does it matter how old the child is? What about cartoons or educational programs? Many parents hope that psychologists can provide answers to questions like these. In this case, and for many other equally pressing practical problems, we do have some answers—although the answers are not always as simple or clear-cut as parents (or legislators) might like.

DESCRIBING AND EXPLAINING

The first task in any scientific endeavor is to *describe,* to answer the "what" question. Just what do we observe about children and the way they change (or stay the same) over the first 15 or 18 years of life? What is the "normal" or expected rate of growth? What are the patterns of changes in children's play or in their friendships? How wide a variation is there, for example, in the ages at which babies first crawl or toddlers first use two-word sentences? Which children are faster, which slower, and what else can we find out about those children?

What we need, in a word, are facts—about how children are the same, about how they change, and about how they differ from one another. The vast majority of research on children that I will be talking about throughout the book aims for just such basic description.

Good description is much harder to achieve than you probably imagine, and in many areas we are still a long way from even minimally good description. Even so, describing is not enough. The second major task is to answer the question "Why?" and to *explain* development. Why do children change in the ways they do, and why do children differ from one another? Such explanation is the role of theory. A good theory not only ties together many bits of descriptive information, it also proposes general principles. By using those principles, we may be able to predict patterns of behavior we have not observed before, or we may be able to devise ways to intervene effectively in the lives of children to avoid an unwanted outcome.

Theory and descriptive research are intimately linked. Researchers don't confine themselves to the realms of description for 20 or 30 years and then say one morning, "Well, I guess it's time to try to figure out why things are like that." Theory is present from the very beginning, sometimes as full-fledged models, sometimes as implicit or vaguely formed expectations or beliefs. In the field of developmental psychology, the work any one observer or researcher does is affected by his or her answers to a set of key questions.

THE KEY QUESTIONS

What Should We Be Studying?

The first key question concerns what we should be studying. Should we focus on developmental patterns that are common to all children, or on individual differences among children? As I pointed out earlier, both of these questions are possible aspects of the task of description, but individual researchers have tended to focus on one or the other, not both. As Eleanor Maccoby (1984) has pointed out, researchers who have studied social and personal behaviors have focused almost entirely on questions of individual differences, while those who have studied physical changes, language, perception, and major aspects of cognition have searched primarily for shared regularities—for ways in which children are the same and, in particular, for ways in which all children *change* or develop in the same sequences.

This rather uncomfortable split in the basic questions being asked means that rather different kinds of descriptive information are available about the various aspects of children's functioning. Fortunately, a few bridges are being built, as in the study of attachment (see Chapter 11) and in the exploration of information-processing approaches to cognition (see Chapter 7). But individual researchers still tend to lean toward one side or the other on this question.

What Are the Major Influences on Development?

The second key question is one of the central theoretical issues within developmental psychology. Are the changes we see in children over time due to *internal* influences or to *external* influences? That is, does the child develop the way he does because of some inner biological pattern built into the organism, or is the child shaped by the experiences he has had (such as loving or unloving parents, toys, school experiences, friendships, day care or home care)? This dispute is sometimes referred to as the **nature/ nurture controversy** or as the issue of **heredity versus environment.** For many years, psychologists argued this question as if the answer had to be one or the other, but not both. Few psychologists would cast the question in such black-and-white terms today. Instead, we have more recently become preoccupied with several important variations on the nature/ nurture theme.

Interaction and Transactions. For many researchers, the issue now is primarily to understand the relative contributions of internal and external influences on any given behavior and to understand the *interaction* between the two. There is now a good deal of evidence that internal and external influences do not merely add up—they combine in quite complex ways. The same experience may have a quite different effect on children with different inherited patterns or on children of different ages.

A particularly elegant example of the way internal and external influences might interact has been suggested by Frances Horowitz (1982, 1987). Her model is shown in Figure 1.2. She argues that we can categorize infants or young children simultaneously along an internal and an external dimension. The internal dimension she calls *vulnerability,* which refers to the general physical robustness of the infant at birth. A prematurely born infant, for example, would be highly vulnerable. The external dimension is the degree of richness or facilitative quality of the environment, such as loving and responsive parents and the availability of appropriate toys and materials. Horowitz proposes that the outcome for the child is not simply an additive sum of the internal and external influences but a more complex interaction. An "invulnerable" or "resilient" child will do quite well even in relatively unstimulating environments. And even the most vulnerable children will reach nearly optimum development in really facilitative environments. But vulnerable children in inadequate environments will be markedly worse off than any other group.

In fact, as we'll see throughout the book, there is a growing body of research that shows precisely this pattern. For example, low-birth-weight infants are more likely to have very low IQ scores in later years if they are reared in poverty-level families than if they are reared in middle-class families (Werner, 1986).

Other models of complex interactions have emerged from studies of the child's impact on the environment around him. A cranky or difficult baby calls forth different behaviors from her parents than does an easygoing child; a child who complies right away to requests or demands develops a very different relationship with his parents than a child who is more defiant. Thus the child is a dynamic partner in the environmental system. Indeed, as Scarr and McCartney (1983) have pointed out, to a considerable degree a child chooses or selects her own environment. The child selects a "niche,"

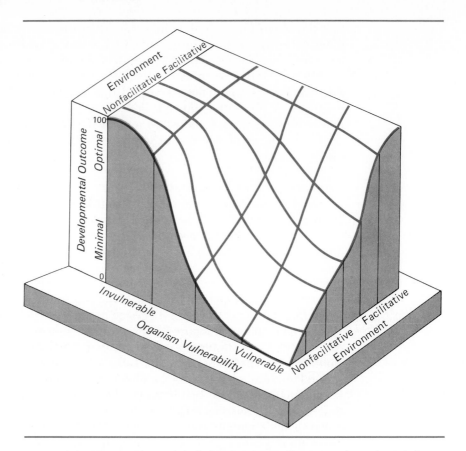

Figure 1.2 Horowitz's model of the interaction between the vulnerability of the child and the quality of the environment. The height of the surface is the "goodness" of the developmental outcome (like later IQ scores or language skills or social skills). The higher the surface, the better the outcome. As you can see, Horowitz proposes that a vulnerable infant in a nonfacilitative environment will have by far the worst outcome—worse than the simple summing of the effects would predict. (*Source:* Adapted from Horowitz, 1982, Figure 2.1, p. 28.)

choosing the types of experiences that may be most stimulating or compatible. For example, a child with good natural coordination is likely to spend much more time in active physical play than a less-coordinated child. The resulting form of the child's development is thus not at all a simple sum of environment and heredity but some very complex transaction or process.

Timing of Experience.   Another question currently being asked about environmental influences is whether it matters *when* a child has any particular experience. For example, suppose a mother decides she must go back to work, but she could choose to go back when her baby is 6 months old or wait until the child is 3 years old. Would it matter? Interest in this question was stimulated by research on other species, which showed that specific experiences had quite different or much stronger effects at some points in development than at others. For example, baby ducks will become *imprinted* on (become attached to and follow) any duck or any other quacking, moving object that happens to be around them 15 hours after they hatch. If nothing is moving or quacking at that critical point, they don't follow anything (Hess, 1972). So the period just around 15 hours after birth is a **critical period** for the duck's development of a proper following response.

Critical periods of this same very precise type are hard to find in human development (Colombo, 1982). Some events in prenatal development do fit this definition—for example, the timing of a mother's contracting rubella (German measles) while pregnant. If the rubella virus enters the mother's system during a narrow range of days in the first three months of pregnancy, some damage or deformity occurs in the fetus. Infection with the same virus at a later time has no such effect.

Although strict critical periods may not be common, many psychologists have adopted the broader, looser concept of a **sensitive period**—months or years during which a child may be particularly responsive to specific forms of experience or particularly influenced by their absence. So, for example, the period from 6 to 12 months of age may be a sensitive period for the formation of a core attachment to the parents. Other periods may be particularly significant for intellectual development or language. More generally still, some psychologists assume that the whole first five or six years of life form a kind of sensitive period; emotional patterns or skill levels established during these years are thought to be highly resistant to later change.

On the other end of the continuum are psychologists—perhaps most notably Jerome Kagan (1984)—who argue that children are far more resilient than that, that there is a potential for *plasticity* (change or growth) throughout the life span. Abused infants, in this view, are not necessarily warped or damaged forever. If their environment is changed, they can change, can recover.

I can hear both of these positions when I listen to parents. On the one hand, I hear parents worrying that something they have done (or not done), like going back to work "too soon," will somehow have a permanent negative effect on their child. On the other hand, most of us seem to believe in the benefits of remedial action, too. If you're out of shape, exercise; if a child has developed a speech problem, hire a speech therapist; if poverty-level environments do not provide enough intellectual stimulation in the first years of life, then create programs like Head Start or Follow Through for children or education programs for their parents. Among psychologists, these issues are also a point of dispute.

Figure 1.3 More and more infants are being placed in day care within the first year of life. Some theorists argue that this is a very risky trend, since the first year is a sensitive period for the establishment of key attachments and of basic cognitive skills. Others think children are much more resilient than that. Of course, the *quality* of the day care, as well as (or instead of) the timing, may be the critical factor.

Context: How Broad an Environment Should We Study? Still another question about the environment is how widely we should cast our net in examining children's environments. Until quite recently, most developmental psychologists cast a rather narrow net. We focused almost exclusively on family interactions (mostly *mother*-child interactions at that), perhaps on playmates, and on some inanimate sources of stimulation such as toys. If we looked at the larger family context at all, it was usually in terms of the general wealth or poverty of the family.

Recently, however, there has been a strong push to widen our scope. Urie Bronfenbrenner has been the strongest voice for such a broader contextual approach (1977, 1979, 1983); he is joined by a chorus of others (e.g., Horowitz, 1987; Lerner, 1986; Pederson, 1981; Sameroff, 1982). Bronfenbrenner argues that if we are to describe development properly, we need to describe the total setting, or *system,* in which it occurs. Each child grows up in a complex social environment with a distinct cast of characters: brothers, sisters, one or both parents, grandparents, baby-sitters, pets, schoolteachers, friends. And this system is itself embedded in a larger social system: the parents have jobs which they may like or dislike; they may have close supportive friends or they may be quite isolated. My own children,

Figure 1.4 Children reared in poverty like this have few toys and possibly less consistent or less stimulating environments. They may also live in an entirely different family system, with different relationships between parents, different sources of family strain, and different links between the family and the larger society. Theorists like Bronfenbrenner insist that if we are to understand the impact of the environment on the child, we have to study the entire system and not just its parts.

for example, spent six years of their early lives with both parents working at home. They attended a small rural school on an island isolated from the mainland by an hour's ferry ride. The family configuration included not only the usual uncles and aunts but also four sets of grandparents and many step-relatives. To call this entire configuration "the environment" or "sources of stimulation" is to grossly oversimplify the process. But researchers still disagree on how broadly we need to define the environment, how large a context we need to examine to understand a child's development.

What Is the Nature of Developmental Change?

The third key question on which researchers (and theorists) differ concerns the nature of developmental change itself: Is a child's expanded ability just "more of the same," or does it reflect a new kind of activity? For example, a 2-year-old is likely to have no individual friends among her peers and an 8-year-old is likely to have several. We could think of this as a *quantitative* change (a change in amount) from zero friends to some friends. Or we could think of it as a *qualitative* change (a change in kind or type) from disinterest in peers to interest, or from one *sort* of relationship to another. Where a given researcher or theorist stands on this question has a profound effect on the way he or she perceives children and their behavior. Does development simply consist of becoming more of *x* or *y*? Does a child get better and better at certain things? Are the *processes* the same and only the efficiency or the speed different, or are there different processes at different ages? For example, do older children and younger children learn things in the same way, following the same rules, or do older children simply approach new tasks in a different way?

Stages and Sequences.   A very important related question concerns the presence or absence of *stages* in the course of development. If development consists only of additions (quantitative change), then the concept of stages is not needed. But if development involves reorganization or the emergence of wholly new strategies or skills (qualitative change), then the concept of stages may become attractive. Certainly we hear a lot of "stagelike" language in everyday conversation about children: "He's just in the terrible twos," or, "It's only a stage she's going through."

Psychologists have had a good deal of trouble defining just what a "stage" is (Lerner, 1986). Generally, when a child shifts from one stage to another, there is thought to be a change not only in skills or physical characteristics but also in underlying *structure*. The child approaches tasks differently, sees the world differently, is preoccupied with different issues.

You will see as we go through this book that there are many stage theories of development. The concept of stages seems at first blush to be a tidy way of organizing information, a simple way of describing changes with age. But as you will also see—particularly when we get to the discussion of cognitive development—it has turned out to be a rather slippery concept.

THEORIES OF DEVELOPMENT

Each of the many logical combinations of answers to the key questions I have been raising might form the basis of a theory of development. Of those possible combinations, four have been most influential: biological theories, learning theories, psychoanalytic theories, and cognitive-development theories. Since you will meet these four again and again throughout the book, let me describe them to you briefly here and point out the ways in which they differ in their answers to the key questions.

Biological Theories

The most basic proposition of biological theories of development is that both our common patterns of development and our unique individual behavioral tendencies are programmed in the genes or influenced by such physio-logical processes as hormone changes. Biologically oriented theorists do not argue that environment is unimportant—no one takes such an extreme position. But genetic programming is seen by many psychologists as a power-ful framework, affecting both shared and individual patterns of development.

The Concept of Maturation.   The theorist who most emphasized the biological underpinnings of common developmental patterns was probably Arnold Gesell (1925). He introduced the concept of **maturation,** which we might define as *genetically programmed sequential patterns of change* in such physical characteristics as body size and shape, hormone levels, or coordination. You can probably remember your own physical changes during adolescence. The timing of pubertal changes differs from one child to the next (I remember being the tallest child in the school at age 11), but the basic sequence is the same for us all. These developmental se-quences, which begin at conception and continue until death, are shared by all members of our species. The "instructions" for these sequences are part of the specific hereditary information that is passed on at the moment of conception.

In its pure form, maturationally determined development occurs re-gardless of practice or training. You don't have to practice growing pubic hair; you don't have to be taught how to walk. But such changes do not occur in a vacuum. These powerful "automatic" maturational patterns can be disturbed by environmental conditions such as malnutrition or accidents. Even the physical changes at adolescence can be altered in extreme circum-stances, particularly by malnutrition. Severely undernourished girls do not menstruate, for example.

I need to touch on one other possible point of confusion about the term *maturation.* It is often used as a synonym for *growth,* but the terms do not mean exactly the same thing. *Growth* refers to some kind of step-by-step change in quantity, as in size. We speak of the growth of the child's vocabulary or the growth of the body. Such changes in quantity *may* be the result of maturation, but not necessarily. A child's body might change in size because of a change in diet, which is an external effect, or because muscles and bones have grown, which is probably a maturational effect. To put it another way, the term *growth* is a *description* of change, while the concept of maturation is one *explanation* of that change.

Temperament and Other Inherited Differences.   Another group of biological theorists have focused not on shared patterns but on the influ-ence of heredity upon unique individual characteristics. Arguments about the origins of differences in intelligence have always included a strong heredity position (as you'll see in Chapter 6). Recently, several influential theories about the origins of **temperament** or *personality* (those unique or characteristic styles each of us has in responding to individuals and objects) have incorporated ideas from the geneticists.

For example, Arnold Buss and Robert Plomin (1984, 1986) suggest that there are three central dimensions of temperament: emotionality (the tendency to get distressed or upset easily); activity (the tendency toward vigorous, rapid behavior); and sociability (the tendency to prefer the presence of others to being alone). These theorists, along with several others (e.g., Thomas & Chess, 1977, 1986), argue that, to at least some degree, an individual's position along these temperamental dimensions is inherited and persists throughout life.

Looking back at the key questions, we can see that biological theorists are attempting to explain both common patterns of development and individual differences. Although they acknowledge the role of environment, they strongly emphasize the "nature" side of the nature/nurture dispute. In addition, they emphasize quantitative rather than qualitative change. Gesell, of course, talks about *sequences* of maturational changes, but he does not describe separate, qualitatively different stages. Biological theories of development have been enjoying a considerable revival in recent years, so you will encounter several variations on these themes in the chapters to come.

Learning Theories

Learning theorists have started from the other end of the nature/nurture argument. A leading theorist, Albert Bandura, puts it this way: "Except for elementary reflexes, people are not equipped with inborn repertoires of behavior. They must learn them" (Bandura, 1977, p. 16). Biology is not rejected here. Bandura goes on to point out that hormones or inherited propensities can affect behavior, but specific experiences with the world around you are the stuff of which development is made.

This emphasis on the importance of the environment, and on the central processes of learning, is common to all the theorists in this group. But it is important to distinguish between two subvarieties of learning theorists. The most extreme environmental position, which was influenced strongly by the work of B. F. Skinner, might be called a *radical behaviorist* view. Donald Baer (1970), for example, in his "age-irrelevant concept of development," assumes that the basic principles of learning are the same no matter how old the learner may be. What we call "development," in this view, is really just a long sequence of individual learning experiences. Children may appear to "develop" in similar ways, but this is only because they are likely to have similar learning experiences. Baer thinks that if we could devise the right sequence of experiences, a 2-year-old should be able to learn tasks we normally think of as demanding a 10-year-old's skills.

Few developmental psychologists today would take such an extreme position. But nearly all would agree on the importance of the two fundamental learning processes that are central to the learning-theory approach: classical conditioning and operant conditioning. You may already have encountered these concepts in psychology classes, but let me review them quickly.

Classical Conditioning. This type of learning involves the acquisition of new signals for existing responses. If you touch a baby on the cheek, he will turn toward the touch and begin to suck. In the technical terminology of **classical conditioning,** the touch on the cheek is the **unconditioned stimulus;** the turning and sucking are **unconditioned responses.** The baby is already programmed to do all that; these are automatic reflexes. But suppose that the sound of the mother's footsteps and the feeling of being picked up always come just before the baby is touched on the cheek. Now what happens? The sound and the feelings eventually "trigger" the responses of turning and sucking. They have become **conditioned stimuli.** The steps in the process are described in Figure 1.5.

This might seem a relatively minor sort of learning, but it is particularly important in the child's developing emotional responses. Things or people that are present when you feel good come to be associated with "feeling good." Those that are associated with uncomfortable feelings may later trigger fear or anxiety or embarrassment. Since a child's mother or father is present so often when nice things happen—when the child feels warm, comfortable, and cuddled—mother or father usually comes to be a conditioned stimulus for pleasant feelings. A tormenting older sibling, however, may come to be a conditioned stimulus for angry feelings, even after the sibling has long since stopped the tormenting.

Sometimes it can take only one occasion to create an emotional conditioned response. I remember an occasion at least 20 years ago when I was invited to give a talk to a group of psychologists in a town near my home. It turned out to be one of the worst talks I have ever given. I was embarrassed. Ever since then, every time I even drive by that particular town on the freeway, I feel embarrassed. The sight of the place has become

Step 1		Step 2		Step 3	
Stimulus	Response	Stimulus	Response	Stimulus	Response
Touch on the → Head turn cheek (Unconditioned (Unconditioned stimulus: UCS) response: UCR)		Touch on the → Head turn cheek (UCS) (UCR) | Mother's voice (Conditioned stimulus: CS)		Voice (CS) →	Head turn (CR)

Figure 1.5 The three steps in the development of a classically conditioned response. In step 1, the unconditioned stimulus automatically triggers the unconditioned response. In step 2, some additional stimulus occurs at the same time as the unconditioned stimulus. In step 3, the additional stimulus—called the conditioned stimulus—is also able to trigger the original response.

a conditioned stimulus for my discomfort. The feeling has weakened over the years, but it is still there.

The important point here is that from the earliest months of life, children learn new cues through classical conditioning, particularly cues for emotional responses.

Operant Conditioning.

Operant conditioning—a type of learning also called *instrumental conditioning*—results from the consequences of a person's behavior. The basic principles are these:

Any behavior that is reinforced will be more likely to occur again in the same or in a similar situation. There are two types of reinforcements. A **positive reinforcement** is any event which, following some behavior, increases the chances that that behavior will occur again in that situation. Typically such pleasant consequences as praise, a smile, food, a hug, or attention serve as positive reinforcers, although that may not be true for every individual or every situation.

A second major type of reinforcement is a **negative reinforcement.** This term has been used in a variety of ways over the years, so there is some confusion about the meaning (Maccoby, 1980a). The definition I am giving you here, however, is the most widely used. Negative reinforcement occurs when something an individual finds *unpleasant* is *stopped.* An example will make this clearer. Suppose your little boy is whining and begging you to pick him up. At first you ignore him, but finally you do pick him up. What happens? He stops whining. So your picking-up behavior has been *negatively reinforced* by the cessation of his whining, and you will be *more* likely to pick him up next time he whines. At the same time, his whining has probably been *positively reinforced* by your attention and picking up, so he will be more likely to whine on other occasions.

Both positive and negative reinforcements strengthen behavior. **Punishment,** in contrast, is intended to weaken some undesired behavior. Sometimes punishments involve eliminating nice things (like "grounding" a child, or taking away TV privileges, or sending her to her room—things you probably remember from your own childhood); often they involve administering unpleasant things (such as scolding or spanking).

This use of the word *punishment* fits with the common understanding of the term and shouldn't be too confusing. What *is* confusing is the fact that punishments don't always do what they are intended to do. For example, your child may have thrown his milk glass at you to get your attention, so spanking him may be a positive reinforcement instead of the punishment you had intended. Punishment—as you'll see more fully in Chapter 13—is definitely a two-edged sword.

Another basic law of learning is that if you reinforce someone part of the time for some behavior, but not all of the time—a procedure called **partial reinforcement**—it will take longer for the person to learn the particular behavioral pattern, but then the pattern will be much harder to get rid of. If you smile at your daughter only every fifth or sixth time she brings a picture to show you (and if she finds your smile reinforcing), she'll keep on bringing pictures for a very long stretch, even after you quit smiling altogether. In the technical words of learning theory, the partially reinforced response is highly "resistant to extinction."

These basic principles of operant conditioning have direct relevance for day-to-day child-rearing practices. Some of the applications are discussed in the box on page 18.

Social-Learning Theory. The second major tradition within learning theory is usually called *social-learning theory.* The key figure here is Albert Bandura (1977, 1982), a major theorist whose views have undergone some interesting changes over the years. Bandura accepts the importance of classical and operant conditioning, but he makes several additional assertions.

First, he argues that reinforcement is not always necessary for learning to occur. Learning may also occur merely as a result of watching someone else perform some action. Learning of this type, called **observational learning** or **modeling,** is involved in a wide range of behaviors. Children learn ways of hitting from watching other people in real life and on TV. They learn generous behavior by watching others donate money or goods. They learn physical skills such as bike riding or skiing partly from watching other people demonstrate them. They are also affected by the rewards or punishments they see someone else receive, a process usually referred to as **vicarious reinforcement.**

Second, Bandura calls attention to a class of reinforcements called **intrinsic reinforcements** (also called *intrinsic rewards*). These are within the person rather than external—for example, the pleasure a child feels when she finally figures out how to draw a star, or the sense of satisfaction you may experience after strenuous exercise. Pride, discovery, that "aha" experience are all powerful intrinsic reinforcements.

Interestingly, there is now some evidence that the intrinsically reinforcing quality of some experience may be *reduced* by external positive reinforcers. If you watch to see what toys children choose to play with spontaneously and then give them praise or "good work" certificates for playing with those toys, the children will continue playing with the toys as long as the reward lasts. Later, however, they are *less* likely to choose those toys in spontaneous play (Danner & Lonky, 1981; Lepperd, 1980). So although rewards (positive reinforcements) "work," there are some hidden costs.

Third, and perhaps most important, Bandura has gone far toward bridging the gap between learning theory and cognitive-developmental theory by emphasizing important *cognitive* elements in learning. For example, observational learning is not automatic. What we learn from observing someone else is influenced by what we pay attention to, by our ability to

SOME APPLICATIONS OF LEARNING PRINCIPLES TO CHILD REARING

All parents, whether they are aware of it or not, reinforce some behaviors in their children by praising them or by giving them attention or treats. And nearly all parents attempt to discourage unpleasant behavior through some kind of punishment. Often, however, parents (myself included) think they are rewarding behaviors they like and ignoring those they don't like, yet the results don't seem to meet their expectations. When this happens, it may be because more than one learning principle is operating at once or because we have misapplied those principles.

For example, suppose you have a favorite armchair in your living room that is being systematically ruined by the dirt and pressure of little feet climbing over the back of the chair. You want the children to *stop* climbing on the chair. So you scold them. After a while you may even stoop to nagging. If you are really conscientious and knowledgeable, you may carefully try to time your scolding so that it operates as a negative reinforcer, by stopping your scolding when they stop climbing. But nothing works. They keep on leaving those dirty footprints on your favorite chair. Why? It could be because the children *enjoy* climbing up the chair. So the climbing is intrinsically reinforcing to the children, and that effect is clearly stronger than your negative reinforcement. One way to deal with this might be to provide something *else* for them to climb on.

A second example of the complications of applying learning principles to everyday dealings with children is what happens when you inadvertently create a partial reinforcement schedule. Suppose your 3-year-old son repeatedly demands your attention while you are fixing dinner (a common state of affairs, as any parent of a 3-year-old can tell you). Because you don't want to reinforce this behavior, you ignore him the first six or eight times he says "Mommy" or tugs at your clothes. But after the ninth or tenth repetition, with his voice getting louder and whinier each time, you can't stand it any longer and finally say something like, "All right! What do you want?" Since you have ignored most of his demands, you might well be convinced that you have not been reinforcing his demanding behavior. But what you have actually done is to create a partial reinforcement schedule; you have rewarded only every tenth demand or whine. And we know that this pattern of reinforcement helps to create behavior that is *very* hard to extinguish. So your son may continue to be demanding and whining for a very long time, even if you later succeed in ignoring it completely.

Because many parents have difficulty with situations just like this and have trouble seeing exactly what it is they are reinforcing, many family therapists ask families to keep detailed records of their child's behavior and their responses to it. Gerald Patterson, in his book *Families* (1975), lays out a plan for families to follow in doing this. He has used such strategies with good success in treating families with highly aggressive or noncompliant children, and you may find it helpful as well. When you see, through your own records and observations, just what it is you are doing to reinforce whining or noncompliance or destructive behavior (or whatever), it is much easier to change your pattern of response.

make sense out of what we saw and to remember it, and by our actual capacity to repeat the observed action. I will never become an expert tennis player merely by watching Martina Navratilova play!

Bandura introduces other cognitive components into the process of operant conditioning, too. In learning situations, children and adults set goals, create expectations about what kinds of consequences are likely, and judge their own performance. The addition of concepts like these make Bandura's learning theory an *age-relevant* theory. If we assume, for example, that children of different ages observe or notice different things and that they analyze or process those observations differently, then learning is going to vary systematically by age. As Bandura says, "Thought mediates reinforcement effects" (1982, p. 13); to the extent that thought differs at different ages, so will reinforcement processes.

To summarize, and to return to the key questions I discussed earlier, learning theorists—particularly the more radical behaviorists—focus on environmental influences and on individual differences. They see developmental change as primarily quantitative, without stages. Current forms of social-learning theory, though, have softened many of these fairly extreme positions by emphasizing the child's own role in interpreting and organizing the information given by reinforcements.

Psychoanalytic Theories

In contrast, psychoanalytic theorists emphasize sequential (often stagelike) qualitative change, and they assume that internal processes are as important as external experience in shaping behavior.

Sigmund Freud (1905, 1920) is usually credited with originating the psychoanalytic approach, and his theory of development continues to be of some importance. Among current theorists in this tradition, Erik Erikson (1950/1963, 1959/1980) is probably the most influential.

Freud's interest in development arose from his desire to explain the origins of deviant behavior among adults. Since he was mostly observing disorders of personality in adults, he focused on the process of personality development. Other theorists, such as Erikson, place more emphasis on the development of cognition, but Freud's emphasis on personality remains a strong bias in this particular theoretical approach.

Freud saw personality as emerging from important *instinctive* biological roots. Each individual, he thought, is basically focused on gratification of a set of instincts, of which the "sexual" instinct (understood more generally as a "pleasure-seeking" instinct) is the most central. The specific form of gratification sought and the strategies used to obtain it change with age, but the inner push to obtain gratification remains constant over the lifetime.

All the major psychoanalytic theorists propose that development of the personality occurs in a series of steps or stages. Freud described five *psychosexual stages*. I'll be discussing these in some detail in Chapter 9. For now, the key idea is that at each stage, sexual energy (which Freud called the **libido**) is invested in a single part of the body called an **erogenous zone.** Freud believed that the order in which the erogenous zones become paramount is governed by maturation. The infant first focuses on stimulation in the mouth because that is initially the most sensitive part of the body. Later, when neurological development has progressed, other parts of the anatomy become more sensitive and the child's focus of sexual energy shifts—first to the anus, then to the genitals.

Erikson, too, proposes a series of stages, which he calls *psychosocial stages.* Unlike Freud, Erikson emphasizes the conscious self as much as unconscious instincts. He sees development over the life span as a prolonged search for a mature *sense of identity.* In the process, Erikson thinks, a person moves through a fixed sequence of tasks or dilemmas, each centered on the development of a particular facet of identity. For example, Erikson

Figure 1.6 Erikson proposes that each child must move through a series of dilemmas or tasks, the first of which is to establish a sense of basic trust. The child in the photo on the left seems to have established such trust with his parent. In contrast, the child on the right may have developed mistrust instead— although, of course, it is difficult to tell with just one picture.

proposes a first dilemma that is central in the first 12 to 18 months of age: the development of a sense of *basic trust*. If the child's caregivers are not responsive and loving, however, the child may instead develop a sense of *mistrust,* which will affect her responses to all the later stages.

Freud and Erikson share some important common assumptions. They both see development as resulting from the interaction of the child's instincts or physical qualities with the responses of those around him. Basic trust cannot be developed unless the parents (or other caregivers) respond to the infant in a loving, consistent manner. The oral stage cannot be fully completed unless the infant is given sufficient gratification of the desire for oral stimulation. Freud and Erikson also agree that "leftover" or unresolved issues from early stages will be carried forward and will affect the person's ability to deal with subsequent stages. So a young adult who developed a sense of mistrust in the first years of life may have a more difficult time establishing secure intimate relationships with a partner or friends. It is this collection of "excess baggage" that leads to abnormal or deviant personality patterns in the child or the adult.

Returning to the key questions I discussed earlier, you can see that these psychoanalytic theorists started out trying to explain individual differences, particularly individual differences in abnormal personality. But the theories they propose to account for deviance include, as central elements, descriptions of the typically shared *normal* sequence too. They take an intermediate position on the nature/nurture question, emphasizing the importance of inborn instincts, of appropriate environmental supports, and of the child's own processing of the experience. Development itself they see as primarily qualitative change, in distinct stages.

Cognitive-Developmental Theories

All the psychoanalytic explanations of development share an emphasis on the relatively greater importance of relationships with people rather than interactions with objects and on the development of personality rather than thinking. Cognitive-developmental theorists reverse this order of dominance and place greatest emphasis on the development of thinking and on the importance of the child's interaction with the inanimate as well as the animate world. Further, cognitive-developmental theories assume that there is spontaneous activity on the part of the individual. Thus the cause of change is internal as well as external.

The central figure in cognitive-developmental theory is Jean Piaget (1952, 1970, 1977; Piaget & Inhelder, 1969), a Swiss psychologist whose theories have shaped the thinking of a whole generation of developmental psychologists. Piaget, along with other early cognitive theorists such as Lev Vygotsky (1962) and Heinz Werner (1948), was struck by the great regularities in the development of children's thinking. He noticed that all children seemed to go through the same kinds of sequential discoveries about their world, making the same sorts of mistakes and arriving at the same solutions. For example, 3- and 4-year-olds all seem to think that if you pour water from a short, fat glass into a tall, thin one, there is now more water, since the water level is higher in the thin glass than it was in the fat glass. But most 7-year-olds realize that there is still the same amount of water in either case. If a 2-year-old loses her shoe, she may look for it briefly and haphazardly, but she is unable to undertake a systematic search. A 10-year-old, in contrast, is likely to use such good strategies as retracing her steps or looking in one room after another.

Piaget's detailed observations of such changes in the abstractness and complexity of the child's thinking led him to several assumptions, of which the most central is that it is the nature of the human organism to *adapt* to its environment. This is an active process, not a passive one. In contrast to many learning theorists, Piaget does not think that the environment *shapes* the child. Rather, the child (like the adult) actively seeks to understand his environment. In the process, he explores, manipulates, and examines the objects and people in his world.

The process of adaptation, in Piaget's view, is made up of several important subprocesses—*assimilation, accommodation,* and *equilibration*—all of which I will define fully in Chapter 7. For now, the key idea is that the child's exploration of the environment leads, in turn, to a series of fairly distinct "understandings" or "theories" about the way the world works. Since Piaget thought that virtually all infants begin with the same skills and built-in strategies, and since the environments children encounter are highly similar in important respects, the sequences of "understandings" they develop are also similar. Thus Piaget proposed a fixed sequence of four major stages, each growing out of the one that preceded it, and each consisting of a more-or-less complete system or organization of concepts, strategies, and assumptions.

Contrasting the Theories

No doubt by now your head is swimming with theories. To help you sort out the similarities and differences, I have summarized the several positions on the key questions in Table 1.1. In this table, and in my description of the theories, I have intentionally made the contrasts as great as possible to help you keep the alternatives clearly separate. But what you will find as we go along, in fact, is that many current theories involve very interesting mixtures of these approaches. Bandura's current theory, for example, has acquired some strong flavors of a cognitive-developmental approach. At the same time, the newest information-processing models of cognitive development (which I'll introduce in Chapter 7) offer ways of thinking about cognitive development that explain both common sequences and individual differences with the same concepts. The newer theories of the child's attachment to her parents also combine several threads, introducing some distinctly cognitive elements into an otherwise psychoanalytically oriented

Table 1.1

A Summary Comparison of Several Theories of Development on Some of the Key Questions About Development

		Theories			
		Learning			
Issue/question	Biological	Radical	Social	Psychoanalytic	Cognitive-developmental
What should we study: shared patterns or individual differences?	Both	Individual differences	Individual differences	Both	Shared patterns of development
What are the major influences on development: nature or nurture?	Primarily nature	Primarily nurture	Primarily nurture	Both	The child's own internal processing of experience
What is the nature of developmental change: qualitative or quantitative?	Both	Primarily quantitative	Both; learning occurs, but child's interpretation and understanding change	Qualitative	Qualitative
Are there stages or sequences?	Maturational sequences but not stages	No	No stages, but perhaps sequential changes	Definitely stages	Definitely stages

Figure 1.7 The four theoretical approaches offer quite different explanations of this child's angry or aggressive outburst. Biological theorists might argue that the child inherited the genes for a "difficult" temperament and simply shows more of this kind of behavior. Learning theorists would say that this child has been reinforced for such behavior in the past. Psychoanalytic theorists would emphasize the child's inborn aggressive instincts, not yet controlled at this age. Cognitive-developmental theorists—who have had little to say about such social behaviors—might describe it in terms of previous assimilations or explorations of the environment.

approach. Throughout, a return to an emphasis on biological roots can be found. Having distinctly separate theories may be tidy, but I find the new blends, the new syntheses, far more intriguing.

But before we can begin to look at these newer theories and at the current descriptions of all aspects of children's development in more detail, I need to give you one more tool—some basic knowledge about the way in which research in this field is done.

▬▬▬▬▬▬▬▬▬ ## FINDING THE ANSWERS: RESEARCH ON DEVELOPMENT

How do we set about the task of describing or explaining the changes (or the continuities) that we see in children as they grow? How do we try to answer the "what" and the "why" questions?

Ways to Describe Behavior

The most basic need for any research on development is to be able to describe children's actual behavior accurately. How does a 2-year-old or a 4-year-old react to the presence of a strange adult? What are the physical skills of an 8-year-old? What is the vocabulary of a 10-year-old?

Observation. One very basic way to answer questions like these is simply to watch people, although, as you might guess, it is more complicated than that! Before you begin observing, you have to make a whole series of decisions. First of all, should you try to watch *all* the behavior you see, or should you focus your attention on only specific aspects of the behavior of children or adults? You can try to record each action by a child and describe its context (*very* hard work, by the way, as you'll see if you try the project for this chapter), or you can count smiles or aggressive behaviors or the number of children in play groups or whatever specific behavior may interest you. Obviously, there are both benefits and drawbacks to each choice.

A second decision is whether you are going to observe in a natural setting or whether you are going to set up special conditions or a controlled setting in which to observe. After years in which most observation was done in artificial settings (which gives you good control), there is presently a strong push to move back to natural settings, where we can gain a better understanding of the complex dynamics of real-life interactions.

Questionnaires and Interviews. Because observation is a very time-consuming procedure, researchers sometimes try a shortcut: they ask people about themselves, using written **questionnaires** or **interviews.** Questionnaires are not often used with young children, but interviews with older children are quite common, as are questionnaires with parents or teachers.

Ways to Describe Changes with Age

A special problem facing developmental psychologists is to describe changes over age. Two basic research designs have been devised to solve this problem: cross-sectional and longitudinal research.

Cross-Sectional Research. If we want to know whether 4-year-olds can learn some particular concept in the same way as 8-year-olds or to answer any one of hundreds of equivalent descriptive questions about development, the simplest and least time-consuming strategy is to study *separate groups* that differ in age. Such comparisons of age groups are called **cross-sectional studies.** You will encounter dozens of examples as you read through the book: comparisons of the generosity of 4-year-olds and 8-year-olds, comparisons of the self-knowledge of 18-month-olds and 3-year-olds, and the like.

Cross-sectional research can obviously be highly useful. It is relatively quick to do, and it shows age differences quite well. But this design also has distinct limitations. First of all, it cannot tell us anything about *sequences* of development, such as the sequence of concepts children have about their own gender. We might be able to show that 2-year-olds have a different idea of gender than 4-year-olds by doing a cross-sectional comparison, but that won't tell us whether there are steps in between or whether every child acquires the concept in the same sequence. Similarly, cross-sectional studies are not useful if we are interested in the consistency of individual behavior over time, such as whether a temperamentally difficult infant remains crankier than average at school age.

Finally, cross-sectional studies have the serious limitation that the subjects in each group may differ in more than just age. Each broad age group is typically called a **cohort** (roughly similar to a generation, though a cohort can cover a smaller span of years), and each cohort lives through a specific set of experiences at a specific time in their lives. When we are comparing age groups, we are also comparing cohorts, and the differences we see in behavior or skill may be due to the individuals' differing life experiences and not just to age. In studies of children this is not typically a major problem, since we can assume that when the age groups being compared are relatively close together, all the children have grown in similar life circumstances. In studies of adults, though, this *is* a major problem, since adults now in their sixties or seventies grew up in a distinctly different world than the one we now inhabit.

Longitudinal Research. To answer questions about sequence or consistency, we have to study the *same* group of individuals over time. This is called a **longitudinal study.** Short-term longitudinal studies, in which groups of children are studied for a period of several years, have become fairly common in recent years. There are also some famous long-term longitudinal studies—such as the Fels study in Ohio (Kagan & Moss, 1962), the Kauai study in Hawaii (Werner, Bierman, & French, 1971; Werner, 1986), and the Berkeley Growth Study in California (Macfarlane, Allen, & Honzik, 1954; Block, 1971)—in which groups of children have been followed from infancy through adolescence or even into adulthood. These sets of observations have yielded very rich veins of information about development.

Longitudinal designs obviously help to get around the "cohort problem" that is built into cross-sectional comparisons. But there is still a problem: each longitudinal study follows only a *particular* group, born at a particular time in history. We cannot be sure that another group of children, studied longitudinally at another time, would show the same patterns of development. Think, for example, of all the ways in which life is different for a child growing up today than for one growing up in the Great Depression of the 1930s (a time when the subjects in several of the major longitudinal studies were born). Among other differences, more mothers now work, divorce rates are markedly higher, and television has become a fact of life. Might these changes affect the patterns of development we see? Individual longitudinal studies cannot tell us that. Only repeated longitudinal studies, of children growing up in different times and environments, can begin to answer such questions.

Ways to Describe Relationships Among Variables

Another central task for developmental psychologists is to describe the *relationships* between variables: What sorts of behaviors go together? Which features of the environment are associated with rapid or slow development or with one pattern of development or another? The most common way to describe relationships of this kind is with a statistic called a correlation. I will mention this statistic repeatedly through the book, so you should know a bit about how to interpret it.

A **correlation** is simply a number, which can range from −1.00 to +1.00, that describes the strength of a relationship between two variables. A zero correlation indicates that there is no relationship between those variables. You might expect, for example, to find a zero or near-zero correlation between the length of big toes and IQ. People with toes of all sizes have high IQs, and those with toes of all sizes have low IQs, too. The closer a correlation comes to −1.00 or +1.00, the stronger the relationship being described. The length of big toes is probably correlated both strongly and positively with shoe size, for example. Height and weight are also strongly positively correlated, as are the weekly hours of exercise you engage in and your aerobic capacity.

A *negative correlation* describes a relationship in which a lot of one thing is associated with a low amount of something else. There is a negative correlation between the amount you eat when you are on a diet and the number of pounds you lose; there is a negative correlation between the amount of disorder and chaos in a family and the child's later IQ (more chaos goes with lower IQ).

Perfect correlations (−1.00 or +1.00) do not happen in the real world, but correlations of .80 or .70 do occur, and correlations of .50 are common in psychological research. Remember that you can judge the strength of the relationship between two things by the size of the correlation. But keep one more thing in mind: correlations are primarily useful for describing. It is far more difficult (although sometimes it is necessary) to try to use correlational research to answer "why" questions. Ordinarily, correlations tells us only that two things happen together, not *why* they go together. Knowing that families with high levels of noise and confusion are more likely to have children with lower IQs does *not* tell us that quiet and orderliness *cause* better intellectual development. Such a causal connection may exist, but other explanations are possible. Fortunately, powerful new analytical methods that use correlations as a starting point can help us to get around this limitation, but the best general rule is still to remember that correlations do not prove causal connections.

Ways to Explain Development: Experiments and Quasi Experiments

The traditional way to approach the task of explanation is to shift from observing naturally occurring events to introducing some intentional variations or controlling the situation systematically. That is, we do experiments.

In an **experiment** there are at least two groups, to which subjects are assigned *randomly*. One group (usually called the **experimental group**) is given some special experience. For example, one group of preterm infants (those born before the normal end of the 40-week gestation period) might be given a special massage three times a day in addition to the normal hospital routine. A second group, usually called the **control group,** receives only the normal routine care. Then later we test both groups of infants in a common way and see whether they differ. In this case we might weigh and measure them all three weeks later, or three months later, to see whether the infants who had received the massage (the experimental group) had gained weight faster than those who were not given the massage (the control group). If the two groups differ on such a measure (called the *dependent variable*), we can be fairly sure that the difference has been caused by the particular experience we provided.

One of the critical elements of an experiment is that subjects are assigned randomly to the different groups. If we put only the sickest preterm infants in the massage group, for example, we would not be able to interpret the results. If there was no difference in weight gain between the massage group and the control group, it could be because sicker preterm infants simply gain weight more slowly anyway; and if we did find a difference in weight gain favoring the massaged group, we couldn't be sure whether this same effect would occur with less-sick preterm infants. Random assignment of subjects to groups is a way around this problem; it allows much more unambiguous conclusions.

Problems with Experiments in Studying Development. Rigorous experiments have been done in some areas in developmental psychology. But there are two special problems in studying children and their development that limit the use of experimental designs.

First, many of the questions we want to answer have to do with the effects of particular unpleasant or stressful experiences on children—abuse, prenatal influences such as the mother's drinking or smoking, low birth weight, poverty, rejection by peers. For obvious ethical reasons, we simply cannot manipulate those variables. We cannot ask some pregnant women to have two alcoholic drinks a day and others to have none; we cannot assign some children to poverty environments and some to middle-class families. So, to study the effects of such negative experiences, we must rely on various forms of correlational designs, including longitudinal studies.

Second, *we cannot assign subjects randomly to age groups.* If we want to compare the ways in which 4-year-olds and 6-year-olds approach some particular task, such as searching for a lost object, we can compare the two groups—but the children differ in a host of ways in addition to their ages. Older children have had more and different experiences (the "cohort problem" again). Thus, unlike psychologists studying other aspects of behavior, developmental psychologists *cannot* systematically manipulate many of the variables we are most interested in, such as age or many environmental features.

To get around this problem, we can use any one of a series of strategies that are sometimes called *quasi experiments,* in which we compare groups without assigning the subjects randomly. Cross-sectional comparisons (comparing different age groups) are quasi experiments. So are studies in which we select naturally occurring groups that differ in some dimension of interest, such as children with prenatal malnutrition as opposed to those without it or children whose parents choose to place them in day-care programs as opposed to children whose parents rear them at home.

Such comparisons have built-in problems, since groups that differ in one way are likely to be different in other ways as well. For example, families who place their children in day care, compared to those who rear them at home, are also likely to be poorer, may more often be single-parent families, and may have different values or even different religious backgrounds. If the children differ, is it because they have spent their daytime hours in different places or because of these other differences in their families? We can sometimes make such comparisons a bit clearer if we match the two groups on other variables (like income or marital status), but quasi experiments, by their very nature, will always be more complicated to interpret and understand than completely controlled experiments.

All these strategies are common in developmental research. Explaining developmental sequences is a complex and difficult task, and researchers have had to become increasingly inventive to devise ways of sorting out the alternative possibilities.

I do not expect you to become experts in analyzing research strategies. But I do hope that you will develop some skill in judging the quality of research. Table 1.2 gives you a checklist you might use as a starting point in making a judgment about research.

This checklist should be particularly helpful when you come across reports of research in magazines and newspapers. For example, you should be cautious about reports based on "reader surveys" (such as when readers of the *Ladies' Home Journal* or *Psychology Today* are invited to respond to a questionnaire printed in the magazine). These samples are self-selected and highly biased. You should even be skeptical about statements in newspaper articles, like "Research shows that pregnant women who drink coffee have smaller babies." Ask yourself what kind of research would have to be done to support that particular point and whether the evidence given really is good enough. Remember that not everything you read is true!

Table 1.2
▬▬▬▬▬

A Checklist of Things to Look For in Evaluating Research

Clarity	Can you understand what was done and what was found?
Importance of findings	Does the study have some obvious practical relevance? Does it help to untangle a theoretical puzzle? Does it advance our understanding of some problem?
Promotion of new ideas	Good research should lead to new ideas, new theoretical insights, and new questions as well as answer old questions. Does this study do that?
Consistency	Are the findings from this study consistent with the results of other research? Are they consistent with your own experience? This may be hard for you to judge, since you don't know all the other research on a given question, but it is important to keep it in mind if you can. Don't throw out inconsistent results, but look carefully at any study that doesn't fit with other evidence.
Replicability	If the same research were done again, would the same result occur? Exact replications aren't often done in social science research, but they probably ought to be done more often.
Choice of subjects	Were all the children or families studied middle-class? Or were they all from poverty environments? Did all the subjects volunteer? Can we generalize the results to apply to other groups?
Appropriateness of method	Was the method chosen for the study consistent with the questions being asked? For example, is the researcher using a cross-sectional design to study consistency of behavior? If so, it's the wrong design for that question.

━━━━━━ ## SUMMARY

1. The study of child development may lead to answers to important practical questions, but such answers are likely to be complex and embedded in theory.

2. In understanding development, there are two major tasks: describing developmental sequences and processes and explaining the patterns we see.

3. Differing answers to several key questions lie behind many of the differences between theories.

4. The first key question is, what should we be studying—shared patterns or common regularities, or individual differences?

5. The second key question is, what are the major influences on development—internal factors such as heredity or other biological differences, or external influences such as environmental variations?

6. An alternative view, dominant at present, is that development results from complex interactions of the effects of internal and external influences.

7. To understand external influences properly, we must pay attention both to the timing of particular experiences and to the broader environmental context, including not just the family but also the larger society as it affects the family and the child.

8. The third key question is, what is the nature of developmental change? Is it primarily quantitative change, or is there qualitative change?

9. A subquestion is, is it meaningful or helpful to describe qualitative change (if it does indeed occur) as taking place in structurally distinct stages?

10. Four major theoretical approaches reflect varying combinations of answers to the key questions.

11. Biological theorists generally assume that the most significant influences on development are internal and that developmental change is primarily quantitative.

12. Arnold Gesell's maturational theory focuses on the impact of genetic programming on shared, unfolding patterns of development. Other biological theorists, such as those studying temperament, focus on genetic contributions to individual differences.

13. Learning theorists generally place strongest emphasis on environmental influences, thought to produce largely quantitative change. Radical behaviorists take the most extreme position, arguing that the basic laws of learning can be used to account for all of what we think of as development. More cognitively oriented social-learning theorists argue that the child's interpretation of learning situations also has an effect.

14. Three major types of learning occur: classical conditioning, operant conditioning, and observational learning.

15. Psychoanalytic theorists have primarily studied the development of personality, emphasizing the interaction of internal instincts and envi-

ronmental influences that produces shared stages of development as well as individual variations.

16. Cognitive-developmental theorists emphasize the child's own active exploration of the environment, a critical ingredient leading to shared stages of development. They strongly emphasize qualitative change.

17. Newer theories have combined many of the features of these four positions.

18. Research to describe and explain development requires accurate and detailed observation of children's behavior in various settings.

19. Both cross-sectional studies (of different people of different ages) and longitudinal studies (of the same people at several ages) can be used to study age changes; each method has certain benefits and disadvantages.

20. To describe the relationships among variables, the correlation statistic is normally used. It can range from +1.00 to −1.00.

21. Explaining development ordinarily requires an experiment or a quasi experiment. In an experiment, the researcher controls (manipulates) one or more relevant variables and assigns subjects randomly to different treatment and control groups. In a quasi experiment, subjects are not randomly assigned to the experimental and control groups. Quasi experiments are needed in developmental research because subjects cannot be randomly assigned to age.

▰▰▰▰▰▰▰ **KEY TERMS**

classical conditioning One of three major types of learning. An automatic unconditioned response such as an emotion or a reflex comes to be triggered by a new cue, called the conditioned stimulus (CS), after the CS has been paired several times with the original unconditioned stimulus.

cohort A group of persons of approximately the same age who have shared similar major life experiences, such as cultural training, economic conditions, or type of education.

conditioned stimulus In classical conditioning, the stimulus that, after being paired a number of times with an unconditioned stimulus, comes to trigger the unconditioned response.

control group The group of subjects in an experiment that does *not* receive any special treatment.

correlation A statistic used to describe the degree or strength of a relationship between two variables. It can range from +1.00 to −1.00. The closer it is to 1.00, the stronger the relationship being described.

critical period A period of time during development when the organism is especially responsive to and learns from a specific type of stimulation. The same stimulation at other points in development has little or no effect.

cross-sectional study A study in which different groups of individuals of different ages are all studied at the same time.

erogenous zones Portions of the body that in Freudian theory are thought to be sequentially the seat of heightened sexual awareness: the mouth, the anus, and the genitals.

experiment A research strategy in which the experimenter assigns subjects randomly to groups and controls or manipulates a key variable of interest.

experimental group The group (or groups) of subjects in an experiment that is given some special treatment intended to produce a specific consequence.

heredity versus environment A classic "argument" within psychology, in which two major sources of potential influence on behavior are contrasted.

interviews A broad category of research strategy in which people are asked about themselves, their behavior, and their feelings.

intrinsic reinforcements Those inner sources of pleasure, pride, or satisfaction that serve to strengthen the likelihood of the behavior that triggered the feeling.

libido The term used by Freud to describe the pool of sexual energy in each individual.

longitudinal study A study in which the same subjects are observed or assessed repeatedly over a period of months or years.

maturation The sequential unfolding of physical characteristics, governed by instructions contained in the genetic code and shared by all members of the species.

modeling A term used by Bandura and others to describe observational learning.

nature/nurture controversy A common description of the classic argument between the advocates of internal and external influences on development.

negative reinforcement The strengthening of a behavior by the removal or cessation of an unpleasant stimulus.

observational learning Learning of motor skills, attitudes, or other behaviors through observing someone else perform them.

operant conditioning A learning process in which the probability of a person performing some particular behavior is affected by positive or negative reinforcements.

partial reinforcement Reinforcement of behavior on some schedule less frequent than every occasion.

positive reinforcement Strengthening of a behavior by the presentation of some pleasurable or positive stimulus.

punishment Unpleasant consequences administered after some undesired behavior by a child or adult, with the intent of extinguishing the behavior.

questionnaire A pencil-and-paper assessment of one or more variables, using standardized questions.

sensitive period Similar to a critical period, but broader and less specific. A time in development when a particular type of stimulation is particularly important or effective.

temperament An individual's unique collection of typical responses or styles of response to experiences. Temperament may be genetic in origin and is somewhat stable over time.

unconditioned response In classical conditioning, the basic unlearned response that is triggered by the unconditioned stimulus.

unconditioned stimulus In classical conditioning, the cue or signal that automatically triggers (without learning) the unconditioned response.

vicarious reinforcement The strengthening of some behavior through observing someone else be reinforced for that behavior. Thus children who observe others being praised for some behavior may be more likely to perform that behavior themselves.

SUGGESTED READING

Achenbach, T. M. (1978). *Research in developmental psychology: Concepts, strategies, methods.* New York: Free Press.
This is a difficult book but an excellent source for more detailed information about developmental research. The author also includes information about topics such as the ethics of research.

Miller, P. H. (1983). *Theories of developmental psychology.* New York: Freeman.
A good introduction to the major theoretical approaches outlined in this chapter.

PROJECT: OBSERVATION OF A CHILD

I have several purposes in suggesting this project. First, many of you will have had relatively little contact with young children and need to spend some time simply observing a child to make other sections of the book more meaningful. Second, I think it is important for you to begin to get some sense of the difficulties involved in observing and studying children. So I am suggesting here, as a preliminary step, that you keep an observational record, noting down each thing that the child does or says. You will find, I think, that the task is less straightforward than it seems, but this type of observation is the best place I know to begin.

- *Step 1.* Locate a child between 18 months and 6 years of age; age 2, 3, or 4 would be best.
- *Step 2.* Obtain permission from the child's parents for observation. Tell them that it is for a course assignment, that you will not be testing the child in any way but merely want to observe a normal child in the child's normal situation.
- *Step 3.* Arrange a time when you can observe the child in his or her "natural habitat" for about one hour. If the child is in nursery school, it's all right to do your observation there as long as you get permission from the teachers. If not, you should observe the child at home or in some other familiar situation. You must not baby-sit during the observation; you must be free to be in the background and cannot be responsible for the child during the observation.
- *Step 4.* When the time for the observation arrives, place yourself in as unobtrusive a place as possible. Take a small stool with you if you can so that you can move around as the child moves. If you are in the child's home, the child will probably ask what you are doing. Say that you are doing something for school and will be writing things down for a while. Don't invite any kind of contact with the child; don't meet his or her eyes; don't smile; and don't talk except when the child talks directly to you, in which case you should say that you are busy and will play a little later.
- *Step 5.* For one hour, write down everything the child does, insofar as possible. Write down the child's speech word for word. If the child is talking to someone else, write down the other person's replies, too, if you can. Describe the child's movements. Throughout, keep your description as free of evaluation and words of intent as you can. Do not write, "Sarah went into the kitchen to get a cookie." You don't know why she went. What you saw was that she stopped what she had been doing, got up, and walked into the kitchen. There you saw her getting a cookie. Describe the behavior that way rather than making assumptions about what is happening in the child's head. Avoid words like *try, angrily, pleaded,* and *wanted.* Describe only what you see and hear.
- *Step 6.* When you have completed the observation, reread what you wrote and consider the following questions: Did you manage to keep all description of intent out of your record? Were you able to remain objective? Were you able to write down all that the child did? If not, what sorts of things were left out? What kinds of information about this child could be extracted from your record? Could anyone get a measure of the child's level of activity or count the number of times the child asked for attention? What changes in this method of observation would you have to introduce in order to obtain other sorts of information? What do you think was the effect on the child of your presence?

PART TWO | THE BEGINNINGS OF LIFE

2 Prenatal Development

Conception
The Basic Genetics of Conception
  Germ Cells
  Genes
  Males and Females
  Twins and Siblings
  Genotypes and Phenotypes
Development from Conception to Birth
  The Period of the Ovum
  The Embryonic Period
  The Fetal Period
Prenatal Sexual Differentiation
Explanations of the Normal Sequence of Development
Things That Can Go Wrong: Genetic Errors
  Chromosomal Problems
  Single-Gene Defects
  Diagnosing Chromosomal Anomalies and Single-Gene Defects
Genetic Counseling: Better Information Brings Difficult Decisions
Things That Can Go Wrong in the Environment: Disease, Drugs, and
    Diet
  Diseases of the Mother
  Drugs Taken by the Mother
  The Mother's Diet
Diet and Exercise During Pregnancy
  Other Teratogens
Other Characteristics of the Mother That Affect the Normal Sequence
  The Mother's Age
  Number of Pregnancies
  The Mother's Emotional State
An Overview of Risks and Long-Term Consequences of Prenatal Problems
Sex Differences in Prenatal Development
Social Class Differences in Prenatal Development
Summary
Key Terms
Suggested Reading

Several years ago, while my large extended family was gathered for our traditional Christmas celebration, my four-months-pregnant sister-in-law Nancy complained of a headache. Having heard warnings about the possible ill effects of various kinds of drugs during pregnancy, she was very reluctant to take any aspirin. She tried all the usual home remedies (shoulder rubs, warm baths, herb tea) but the headache persisted. Finally she took a nonaspirin pain medicine, which did the trick.

This incident brought home to me how very far we have come in this country in increasing women's awareness of the potential hazards associated with drugs or other outside agents during pregnancy. I was impressed by Nancy's determination to avoid doing anything harmful, but I was also struck by how long the list of "don'ts" had become and by how hard it is for a conscientious woman to be sure about what is okay and what is not. I certainly did not have all the answers for her. Still, our knowledge has increased greatly in the past decades.

In this chapter I want to explore what physicians, psychologists, and biologists have discovered about the basic processes of development from conception to birth. What does normal prenatal development look like? What are the forces that shape that development? Equally important, we need to look at the factors that can influence or alter those normal patterns. How much can the mother's health practices, such as drugs or diet or exercise, help or hinder the process? Do other characteristics of the mother, such as her age, her level of anxiety, or her general health, make a difference? These questions have great practical importance for those of you who expect to bear (or father) children in the future. But they are also important basic issues as we begin the study of the developing child.

CONCEPTION

The first step in the development of a human being is the moment of conception, when a single sperm cell from the male pierces the wall of the ovum of the female. That sounds simple when it is put into one sentence; but since the sperm and the ovum both have to be in the right place at the same time, it is far more complicated than it sounds.

Ordinarily, a woman produces one **ovum** (egg cell) per month, from one of her two ovaries. This occurs roughly midway between two menstrual periods. If it is not fertilized, the ovum travels from the ovary down the **fallopian tube** toward the **uterus,** then gradually disintegrates and is expelled as part of the next menstruation.

When a couple have intercourse, millions of sperm are deposited in the woman's vagina. They travel through the cervix and the uterus, and several thousand of them survive to make their way up the fallopian tubes. If there is an ovum in the fallopian tube (which typically happens only during a few days of each menstrual cycle), then one of the sperm may manage to penetrate the ovum, and a child will be conceived.

Figure 2.1 The nine months of a pregnancy may be a time of delighted anticipation, as it seems to be for these parents. It is also a time in which the genetic patterning for the child (the genotype) is already established and complex maturational sequences are unfolding.

Once conception has occurred, the fertilized ovum continues on its journey down the fallopian tube. Then, instead of disintegrating, it implants itself in the wall of the uterus. Figure 2.2 shows part of this sequence of events in schematic form.

This description may leave you with the impression that virtually all fertilized ova eventually progress through the full sequence of prenatal development. In fact, that is far from true. Perhaps as many as 50 percent of all fertilized ova are spontaneously aborted during the first weeks, usually without the mother even knowing she was pregnant at all. Of those that survive the first three to four weeks of development, perhaps another 10

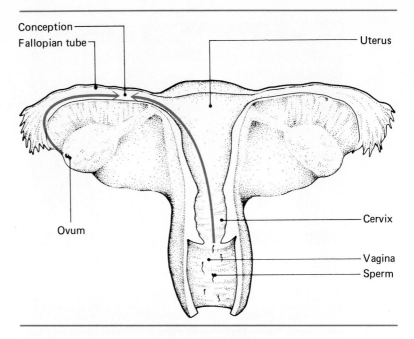

Figure 2.2 Schematic diagram of the female reproductive system showing how conception occurs. The ovum has traveled from the ovary partway down the fallopian tube. There it is met by one or more sperm, which have traveled from the vagina through the cervix and the uterus.

to 25 percent are subsequently spontaneously aborted—an event usually called a *miscarriage* in everyday language (Tanner, 1978; Smith & Stenchever, 1978). So considerably fewer than half of all fertilized ova eventually result in living children.

THE BASIC GENETICS OF CONCEPTION

As most of you no doubt know from biology courses, the nucleus of each cell of our bodies contains a set of 46 **chromosomes,** arranged in 23 pairs. These chromosomes include all the genetic information for that individual. They control the development of unique physical characteristics; shared growth patterns; and possibly temperament, intelligence, and other individual qualities.

Whenever a new cell is needed for growth or tissue replacement, an existing cell divides, in a process called **mitosis.** Just before the division, the chromosomes are duplicated, so that when the division is complete, both the old cell and the new cell have the full set of 23 pairs of chromosomes.

Germ Cells

The process of cell division differs only in the case of the sperm and the ovum, which are called **germ cells.** In the early stages of their development, germ cells divide by mitosis, just as other cells do. But the final step, called **meiosis,** is different. In meiosis, the chromosomes do *not* duplicate themselves before cell division occurs. Instead, both the old cell and the new cell receive one chromosome from each of the 23 pairs. The sperm and ovum, then, each have only 23 chromosomes instead of 46. Thus, when a child is conceived, the 23 chromosomes in the ovum and the 23 in the sperm combine to form the 23 *pairs* that will be part of each cell in the newly developing body.

This process allows for a vast number of possible combinations of chromosomes in the fertilized ovum. In meiosis itself, there are approximately 8 *million* possible combinations of chromosomes, drawing one chromosome from each of the 23 pairs. Since the ovum and sperm may each reflect any of 8 million combinations, the potential number of combinations of 46 chromosomes in the fertilized ovum is approximately 70 *trillion*.

Even this immense variability is further augmented by a process called **crossing over:** At one point in meiosis, before the cell divides, the two chromosomes that make up each pair line up directly opposite one another, and some portions of each chromosome may be exchanged between the members of the pair. In this way the chromosomes themselves are altered, thus increasing still further the number of possible different combinations of chromosomes in the germ cells.

Genes

The 23 pairs of chromosomes are themselves made up of many thousands of **genes,** which are even tinier particles. A gene controls a specific aspect of an individual characteristic or developmental process. At a still finer level, we find that the genes are composed of molecules of a chemical called **deoxyribonucleic acid** (DNA). James Watson and Francis Crick (1953) deduced that DNA is in the shape of a *double helix*, a kind of twisted ladder. The remarkable feature of this ladder is that the rungs are made up in such a way that the whole thing can "unzip," and then each half can guide the duplication of the missing part. It is this characteristic of DNA that makes it possible for the chromosomes contained in the fertilized ovum to duplicate during mitosis so that each cell in the developing embryo will then contain a full set.

Each chromosome is linear—made up of a long string of genes. A particular gene is located not only on a specific chromosome, but in a specific spot (called a *locus*) on that chromosome. The locus of the gene that determines whether you have type A, B, or O blood is on chromosome 9; the locus of the gene that determines whether you have the Rh factor in your blood is on chromosome 1 (Scarr & Kidd, 1983).

It may already have occurred to you that since each individual inherits *two* copies of each chromosome (one from the mother and one from the father), the genetic instructions at each gene locus may be contradictory. For example, if you get a gene for blond hair from your mother and one for black hair from your father, or a blue-eye gene from one parent and a brown-eye gene from the other, what happens? What are the possibilities?

Sometimes the end result is some intermediate blending of the two characteristics, which seems to be what happens in the case of height. Less often the child develops *both* characteristics; for example, people with type AB blood express the blood-type genes from both of their parents. And sometimes only one gene is expressed—one of the two genes is *dominant* over the other. The "weaker" gene is called a *recessive* gene. For example, the gene for brown eyes is dominant over the gene for blue eyes. Thus if a particular fertilized ovum carries a brown-eye gene on one chromosome and a blue-eye gene on the other at the locus that determines eye color, the child will have brown eyes. Note, though, that this child will continue to carry the blue-eye gene. It is present, although it is not expressed. But he can still pass that gene on to his children, since half his sperm will carry the chromosome with the blue-eye gene.

This description may leave you with the impression that all genetic characteristics are determined by the operation of single genes. Such single-gene effects do operate for a number of physical traits, as well as for some inherited diseases, as you'll see shortly. But by far the most common form of genetic influence seems to be *polygenic*. That is, a pattern or trait (such as temperament, IQ, or rate of physical development) is governed by more than a single gene, and the combined expression of those many genes is clearly far more complex than is true of simple recessive and dominant genes.

Males and Females

Still another complexity comes from the fact that there are actually two types of chromosomes. In 22 of the pairs, called **autosomes,** the members of the pair look alike and contain exactly matching genetic loci. But one pair, called the **sex chromosomes,** is unique. The two quite different-looking sex chromosomes are referred to by convention as the X and Y chromosomes. A normal human female has two X chromosomes (an XX pattern), while a normal human male has one X and one Y (an XY pattern). There are genetic loci on each sex chromosome that are not matched on the other, and the large X chromosome carries many more genes than the much smaller Y.

Two implications of this difference are particularly important and intriguing. First, the sex of the child is determined by the X or Y chromosome from the sperm. Since the mother has *only* X chromosomes, every ovum carries an X. But the father has both X and Y chromosomes. When the father's germ cells divide, half the sperm will carry an X, half a Y. If the sperm that fertilizes the ovum carries an X, then the child inherits an XX pattern and will be a girl. If the fertilizing sperm carries a Y, then the combination is XY and the infant will be a boy.

It thus appears, contrary to common historical belief, that it is the father, not the mother, who determines the sex of the child. But even that is too simple a statement for this splendidly complicated process. It turns out that the mother really does have an effect, since the relative acidity or alkalinity of the mucus in the vagina (which varies from one woman to the next and in all women over the course of their monthly cycle) affects the survival rates of X-carrying and Y-carrying sperm. So the woman's chemical balance can sharply alter the probability of conceiving a child of a particular gender, even though it is still true that the X or Y in the sperm is the final determining factor.

A second important consequence of the difference between X and Y chromosomes is that, because the X chromosome contains more genetic material than the Y, a boy inherits many genes from his mother on his X chromosome that are not matched by, or counteracted by, equivalent genetic material on the Y chromosome. Since the X chromosome contains the loci for genes that, when abnormal, cause specific diseases, such as hemophilia and muscular dystrophy, a boy may inherit these if his mother carries the (recessive) gene for the disease. (A girl, in contrast, could not inherit such a disease unless she received the gene signaling that disease on both of her X chromosomes, one from her mother and one from her father.) Such *sex-linked* inheritance patterns occur for other characteristics besides diseases. Interestingly, the difference in the amount of genetic material in the X and Y chromosome may help to account for the greater general physical vulnerability of males—a point I will be returning to later.

Twins and Siblings

Given what I have said so far, I am sure it is clear to you why brothers and sisters are not exactly like one another: each has inherited a unique combination of genes from mother and father.

The exception to this rule is the case of identical twins, who come from the *same* fertilized ovum. In such cases the ovum divides into two distinct entities *after* it has been fertilized by the sperm. Each of the two developing organisms then has the same genetic material in the same combination, and the two children should turn out to be alike in all those areas affected by heredity.

Fraternal twins, in contrast, develop from separate fertilized ova. This can happen if the woman ovulates more than once in a given month (fairly common in women taking fertility drugs). Because two separate combinations of chromosomes are involved, fraternal twins don't even need to be of the same sex (as you can see in Figure 2.3), while identical twins are always same-sex pairs.

Figure 2.3 Identical twins, like the ones above, come from the same fertilized ovum and have exactly the same heredity. They look alike and frequently act alike, too. Fraternal twins, like the ones below, come from two separately fertilized ova and are no more like each other than any other pair of brothers or sisters.

Genotypes and Phenotypes

With all this emphasis on genes as causes of physical patterns, disease, or other characteristics, I may well have given you a misleading impression about the unchangeability of genetic effects. In fact, no geneticist today would assert that the inherited combination of genes *determines* the outcome for any given individual. Geneticists (and psychologists) make an important distinction between the **genotype** (the specific set of "instructions" contained in a given individual's genes) and the **phenotype** (the actual observed characteristics of the individual). The phenotype is a product of three things: the genotype, all the environmental influences from the time of conception onward, and the interaction between the environment and the genotype.

Let me give you an example. The well-known disorder phenylketonuria (PKU) is caused by a defective gene that prevents the individual from processing a particular amino acid (phenylalanine) in the normal way. Toxins accumulate, interfering in brain development, damaging the central nervous system, and resulting eventually in mental retardation. This disease is clearly inherited; geneticists have even located the specific recessive gene involved. However, there is a highly effective treatment: an infant whose blood test shows she has PKU is simply put on a diet that contains little or none of this amino acid (no small task, but manageable). The child does *not* become retarded. In adulthood, these individuals can even eat a full range of food without difficulty (except for pregnant women, who must temporarily follow the diet again in case the baby has PKU). Thus, while the person still *has* the disease in the sense that the genotype still contains the defective gene, the disease is not *expressed* in the phenotype.

This distinction between the genotype and the phenotype is an important one. Genes are not irrevocable signals for this or that pattern of development, this or that disease. Genetic predispositions are all affected by the specific experiences the individual may have from conception onward.

▬▬▬▬▬ **DEVELOPMENT FROM CONCEPTION TO BIRTH**

The period of gestation for the human infant is usually given at 280 days, or 40 weeks, counting from the first day of the last menstrual period. The actual conception, however, normally takes place about 2 weeks after the last menstrual period, so the actual period of gestation from conception to delivery is about 265 days, or 38 weeks. In the discussion that follows, I will be counting from the presumed time of conception, rather than from the final menstrual period. Within those 38 weeks, three subperiods of gestation are usually distinguished: the period of the ovum, the embryonic period, and the fetal period.

The Period of the Ovum

Sometime during the first 24 to 36 hours after conception, mitosis begins. The DNA ladders making up the chromosomes "unzip" so that each chromosome can duplicate. Then the single cell splits in two. The two new cells each contain a set of the full 23 pairs of chromosomes. The process continues, and within two to three days there are several dozen cells and the whole mass is about the size of a pinhead.

You can see the steps in this process in Figure 2.4. In the early stages, there is an undifferentiated mass of cells. But within about four or five days, several different types of cells appear. Fluid appears in the ball of cells, separating the mass into two parts. The outer cells will form the placenta and the inner mass will form the embryo. When it touches the wall of the uterus, the outer shell of cells breaks down at the point of contact. Small tendrils develop and attach the cell mass (called a **blastocyst** at this stage) to the uterine wall. At the time of implantation—one to two weeks after conception—there are perhaps 150 cells in the blastocyst (Tanner, 1978).

The Embryonic Period

The second major phase of prenatal development lasts from implantation until about eight weeks after conception. During this period, rapid cell division continues and more and more cells differentiate into various types,

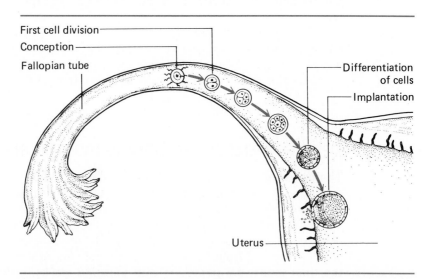

Figure 2.4 The normal progression of development from conception to implantation, which covers approximately the first 10 days of gestation. (*Source:* Smith & Stenchever, 1978, p. 43.)

such as nerve cells or bone cells. Some cells also form a saclike series of membranes around the embryo. The embryo floats inside in a liquid (the amniotic fluid) and is attached to the enveloping sac by the umbilical cord.

The umbilical cord, in turn, is attached to the **placenta,** a remarkable organ that develops gradually during the embryonic period. The placenta, which lies next to and is attached to the uterus, serves essentially as liver, lungs, and kidneys for the developing baby. It provides oxygen, and beginning at about two weeks after conception, it provides nutrition.

The placenta also serves a critical filtering function. The mother's bloodstream does not connect directly to the embryo's separate circulatory system. Instead, her blood passes through several membranes in the placenta. Nutrient substances, such as proteins, sugars, and vitamins, are small enough to pass through these filtering membranes into the baby's blood; however, many (but not all) harmful substances, such as viruses, are too large and are filtered out, as are most of the mother's hormones. Most drugs and anesthetics, however, do pass through the placental barrier (Smith, 1978), and so do some disease organisms—as we'll see in more detail shortly. You can see the placenta and other organs in Figure 2.5.

Growth during the embryonic period is extremely swift. By eight weeks' gestation, the embryo, now about 1½ inches in length, has eyes; the beginnings of ears; a mouth that opens and closes; a nose; hands and feet (though the fingers and toes are still webbed together); arms with elbows and legs

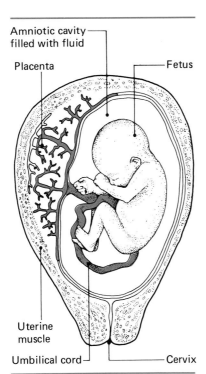

Amniotic cavity filled with fluid

Placenta

Fetus

Uterine muscle

Umbilical cord

Cervix

Figure 2.5 The organization of body structures during the fetal period. Note especially the placenta and the umbilical cord and the fact that the fetus floats in the amniotic fluid.

with knees; a primitive circulatory system, including a heart that beats; some kidney and liver function; and a spinal cord.

The Fetal Period

From about eight weeks' gestation until birth, the developing organism is referred to as the **fetus.** As you could tell from the list of characteristics of the embryo at eight weeks' gestation, virtually all major organs, parts of the body, muscles, and nerves are present in at least rudimentary form very early. The remaining seven months involve primarily a process of refining what has already begun. It's a bit like the process of building a house. You put in the foundation first, then the framework for the walls and roof. The plumber and the electrician do their work early, too, while the framework is still open. The house takes its full shape; you can see where the windows and doors will go, how big the rooms will be, how the roof will look. This stage is reached quickly, but after that there is a very long process of filling in around the form already established. So it is with the embryo and the fetus. At the end of the embryonic period, the main parts are all there in at least some basic form; the next seven months are for the finishing process. Table 2.1 lists some of the milestones of fetal

Table 2.1

Major Milestones of Fetal Development

Gestational age	Major new developments
12 weeks	Sex of child can be determined; muscles develop more extensively; eyelids and lips are present; feet have toes and hands have fingers.
16 weeks	First fetal movement is usually felt by the mother at about this time; bones begin to develop; fairly complete ear is formed.
20 weeks	Hair growth begins; child is very human-looking at this age, and thumb sucking may be seen.
24 weeks	Eyes are completely formed (but closed); fingernails, sweat glands, and taste buds are all formed; some fat is deposited beneath skin. The infant is capable of breathing if born prematurely at this stage, but survival rate is low for infants born this small.
28 weeks	Nervous system, blood, and breathing systems are all well enough developed to support life; premature infants born at this stage have poor sleep/wake cycles and irregular breathing, however.
29–38 weeks	Interconnections between individual nerve cells (neurons) develop rapidly; weight is added; general "finishing" of body systems takes place.

development. (The whole prenatal process can be seen very vividly in the first of four color photo essays in this book.)

Analogies like this can be very useful, but I want to be careful about pushing this particular one too far. A house is full-sized as soon as the framing is completed; and all the wiring is in place when the electrician is finished. Neither of these things is true for the embryo or fetus.

The nervous system is barely sketched in at eight weeks' gestation. Only a small part of the brain and only the suggestion of a spinal cord have developed. Nerve cells, called *neurons*, continue to be added rapidly until about the seventh or eighth month of gestation. The brain develops from the inside outward, with the outer layers developing last. Then, at about seven months' gestation, the neurons begin to develop branches (called *dendrites*), which in turn begin to connect one neuron with another at points called *synapses*. They continue their rapid and extensive development during the first few years after birth (Parmelee & Sigman, 1983).

Similarly, the major growth in size occurs late in the fetal period; the gain in length occurs earlier than the major gain in weight. The fetus is about half her birth length by about 20 weeks' gestation, but she does not reach half her birth weight until nearly three months later, at about 32 weeks.

PRENATAL SEXUAL DIFFERENTIATION

I've already said that the sex of the child is determined at the moment of conception by the XX or XY combination of chromosomes. You'd think that was the end of the story, but it is not. As I pointed out in the discussion of genotypes and phenotypes, the basic genetic patterning does not *guarantee* a particular outcome. In this case it does not guarantee that the newborn infant will have the appropriate sexual characteristics or that he or she will have the behaviors and sexual preferences typical for his or her genetic pattern.

Gender differentiation is also significantly influenced prenatally by the action of a series of hormones (Hines, 1982). Simplifying a bit, it seems that for the development of a male child, both the genetic programming (XY) *and* a particular pattern of hormone action are required for normal gender development. Sometime between four and eight weeks after conception, the hormone *testosterone* begins to be secreted by the rudimentary testes in the male embryo. If this hormone is not secreted or is secreted in inadequate amounts, the genetically XY embryo will be "demasculinized," to use John Money's term (Money, 1987), even to the extent of developing female genitalia. Normal development of the girl does not require any additional hormonal input, but the accidental presence of testosterone (because of heightened levels in the mother, for example, perhaps from some drug she has taken) at the critical time acts to "defeminize" or masculinize the female fetus, possibly resulting in malelike genitalia.

Even more interesting is the fact that there is now growing evidence, particularly from studies of other animals, that such prenatal hormones affect not just the development of genitalia but also the pattern of brain development (Hines, 1982), influencing such functions as the pattern of growth-hormone secretions in adolescence and the relative dominance of the right and left hemispheres of the brain. Most speculatively, John Money (1987) has suggested that the sexual orientation of the developing child and adolescent may also be partially influenced by the prenatal hormonal environment. In lower species, prenatal hormones appear to permanently affect later male or female sexual behavior. In humans, prenatal hormones are only part of the picture; the child's experiences in the early years of life are also critical influences. But Money argues that it is possible that the pattern of prenatal hormones may help to create a propensity toward heterosexual, bisexual, or homosexual orientations at later ages.

EXPLANATIONS OF THE NORMAL SEQUENCE OF DEVELOPMENT

One of the most important points about the child's prenatal development is how remarkably regular and predictable it is. If the embryo has survived the early, risky period, development usually proceeds smoothly, with the various changes occurring in what is apparently a fixed order, at fixed time intervals. To be sure, things can go wrong. But in the vast majority of instances (perhaps 90 percent of recognized pregnancies), the entire process runs in a predictable, fixed pattern.

We don't have to look far for an explanation. Whenever there is that much regularity in a fixed sequence, maturation seems the obvious answer. The fetus doesn't learn to grow fingernails. It doesn't have to be stimulated from the outside to grow them. Rather, the development of fingernails, along with all the other parts of the complex system, is controlled by the instructions contained in the genes. This normal sequence of development is not immune to modification or outside influence, but it takes a fairly sizable intervention to make very much difference.

Another important point about development is that the effect of any outside influence depends heavily on its *timing* (that is, there is a *critical period,* or *sensitive period,* as I described in Chapter 1). The general rule is that each organ system—nervous system, heart, ears, reproductive system, and so on—is most vulnerable to disruption at the time when it is developing most rapidly (Kopp & Parmelee, 1979). At that point it is maximally sensitive to outside interference, whether that be from a disease organism that passed through the placental barrier, from inappropriate hormones, or from drugs or some other agent. Since the most rapid development of most organ systems occurs during the embryonic and early fetal periods (up to about 12 weeks' gestation), this is the period of greatest risk. Figure 2.6 shows the maximum times of vulnerability for different parts of the body.

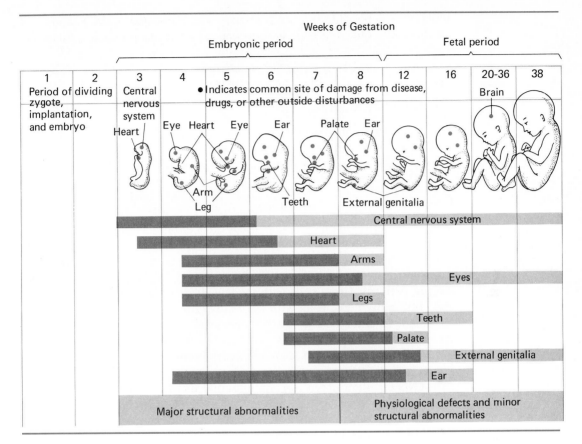

Figure 2.6   Critical periods in the prenatal development of various body parts. The darker portion of each line signifies the period during which any external insult—such as drugs, a disease in the mother, or chemicals in the environment—is likely to produce a major structural deformity in that particular body part. The lighter part of the line shows the period in which more minor problems may result. You can see which body parts are most vulnerable to outside interference during a given week. The embryonic period is the time of greatest vulnerability for most body structures. (*Source:* Moore, 1982, Figure 8-14, p. 152.)

Before I begin talking about the things that can go wrong, I want to reemphasize that the maturational sequence is really quite robust. Normal prenatal development requires an adequate environment, but *adequate* seems to cover a fairly broad range. *Most* children are quite normal. The list of things that *can* go wrong is long (and is getting longer as our knowledge expands), but many of these possibilities are quite rare. More important, a very great number of them are partially or wholly preventable, and many of the remaining problems do not appear to have permanent consequences for the child. As I go along, I'll try to point out the sort of preventive action that is possible in each instance; and at the end of the chapter, I'll return to the question of long-term consequences of prenatal difficulties.

THINGS THAT CAN GO WRONG: GENETIC ERRORS

The first thing that can go wrong is the genetic material itself. Either the chromosomes can divide improperly during meiosis, or a gene that causes a specific disease or physical problem can be passed on to the child.

Chromosomal Problems

Chromosomal anomalies can take the form of either too many chromosomes or too few. The creation of germ cells by meiosis actually involves two chromosomal divisions in sequence. At both points, any one chromosome may fail to divide properly, so there are a very large number of possible deviant patterns. Germ cells with too few chromosomes usually fail to survive, but many germ cells with too many chromosomes do survive. Such anomalies in chromosome number appear to occur in 3 to 8 percent of all fertilized ova (Kopp, 1983), but perhaps as many as 90 percent of these abnormal conceptuses are spontaneously aborted. Only about 1 percent of live newborns have such abnormalities.

Over 50 different types of chromosomal anomalies have been identified, many of them very rare. The most common is **Down's syndrome** (also called *mongolism* and *trisomy 21*). It occurs in approximately 1 out of every 600 to 700 live births (Reed, 1975). Down's syndrome is caused when the two copies of chromosome 21 fail to separate during meiosis. When the germ cell (either ovum or sperm) with the extra copy of chromosome 21 combines with a normal germ cell at conception, the fertilized egg contains three instead of two copies of chromosome 21 (hence the label *trisomy 21*). Children with Down's syndrome have distinctive facial features (as you can see in Figure 2.7); they often have heart defects or other internal malformations and are usually mentally retarded.

The risk of this deviant pattern is greatest for mothers over 35 (although there is also a heightened risk for teenage mothers). Among women 35 to 39, the incidence of Down's syndrome is about 1 in 280 births; among those over 45, it is as high as 1 in 50 births (Kopp, 1983; Mikkelsen & Stone, 1970). The father, too, can contribute to this defect: in about a third of the cases, the original improper cell division is in the sperm and not the ovum (Magenis, 1977). This defect *may* occur more often among older fathers, but that possibility is still in dispute (Kopp, 1983).

Sex-Chromosome Anomalies. Other types of genetic anomalies are caused by an incomplete or incorrect division of the sex chromosomes. An XXY pattern causes Klinefelter's syndrome, which may occur as often

Figure 2.7   A Down's syndrome child. Note the
distinctive eye characteristics and the flattened face.

as 1 in 500 births (Kopp, 1983). This pattern produces boys who often
have very long legs, poor coordination, and poorly developed testes, and
who sometimes are mildly mentally retarded. The XYY pattern is not quite
as common. These boys typically are unusually tall and are mildly retarded.
A single-X pattern (XO, which causes Turner's syndrome) and a triple-X
pattern (XXX) may also occur. Girls with Turner's syndrome are exceptions
to the rule that embryos with too few chromosomes do not survive. These
girls show stunted growth, are usually sterile, and often perform particularly
poorly on tests that measure spatial ability. Turner's syndrome girls perform
at or above normal levels on tests of verbal skill, however (Scarr & Kidd,
1983). Girls with an XXX pattern are of normal size but are slower than
normal in physical development. They also have markedly poor verbal abilities (Rovet & Netley, 1983).

Fragile-X Syndrome.   A quite different type of genetic anomaly, which
has received a good deal of attention lately, involves not an improper amount
of chromosomal material, but rather some kind of weakness or fragility in
an X chromosome. Both boys and girls may have a fragile X, but boys—

lacking the potentially overriding influence of a normal X—are much more susceptible to the negative intellectual or behavioral consequences. The affected boy appears to be at a considerably heightened risk for mental retardation or for a form of seriously disturbed behavior called *autism* (which I'll describe in Chapter 14).

Single-Gene Defects

Another type of genetic problem can occur if a child inherits the gene for a specific disease. When the gene is dominant, the disease occurs if the child inherits the gene from *either* parent. (In such instances, of course, the parent who passes along the problem *also* has the same disorder.) A particularly ugly problem of this type is Huntington's disease; symptoms do not appear until midlife, and the victim then suffers a rapid loss of both mental and physical functioning.

Fortunately, dominant-gene defects, although numerous in variety, are not all that common, in part because many people who inherit serious dominant-gene defects do not have children and so do not pass the problem on to the next generation. Thus, over time, these genes decline in frequency.

The situation is quite different in the case of recessive-gene diseases like cystic fibrosis and PKU. According to some estimates (e.g., Scarr & Kidd, 1983), the average adult carries genes for four different recessive diseases or abnormalities. But since these diseases are expressed only if both members of a chromosome pair carry the defective gene, you don't ordinarily know that you could pass on the hidden problem. If you marry someone else who (also unknowingly) carries that same defective gene, your children will have a one-in-four risk of inheriting the gene from both of you and thus exhibiting the disease.

If a recessive gene signaling some disease is sex-linked (carried on the X chromosome), however, the risks are somewhat different, as I explained earlier. In this case, a girl will have the disease only if she inherits the gene from both parents, but a boy will have the disease even if he inherits the gene just from his mother.

There are many recessive-gene and sex-linked diseases. I have listed a few of the better-known ones in Table 2.2.

Diagnosing Chromosomal Anomalies and Single-Gene Defects

It is now possible to diagnose many of these anomalies and diseases very early in pregnancy. This has in turn made it possible to reduce the number of children born with crippling problems. But the new technology also forces couples—and the rest of society—to deal with a wide range of extremely difficult personal and moral issues, some of which I have discussed in the box on pages 56–57.

Table 2.2

Some of the Major Inherited Diseases

Phenylketonuria	A disorder that prevents metabolism of a common amino acid (phenylalanine). Treatment consists of a special phenylalanine-free diet. The child is not allowed many types of food, including milk. If not placed on the special diet shortly after birth, the child usually ends up very retarded (IQs of 30 and below are not uncommon). Affects only 1 in 8000 children. Diagnostic tests for this disorder are now routinely given at birth; cannot be diagnosed prenatally.
Tay-Sachs disease	An invariably fatal degenerative disease of the nervous system. Virtually all victims die within the first three to four years. This gene is most common among Jews of Eastern European origin, among whom it occurs in approximately 1 in 3500 births. Can be diagnosed prenatally.
Sickle-cell anemia	A sometimes fatal blood disease, with joint pain, increased susceptibility to infection, and other symptoms. The gene for this disease is carried by about 2 million Americans, most often blacks. Can be diagnosed prenatally.
Cystic fibrosis (CF)	A fatal disease affecting the lungs and intestinal tract. Children with CF now live into their twenties. The gene is carried by over 10 million Americans, most often whites. Carriers cannot be identified before they have an affected child. If a couple has had one CF child, they know that each subsequent pregnancy carries a risk of another affected child. Cannot be diagnosed prenatally.
Muscular dystrophy (MD)	A fatal muscle-wasting disease, carried on the X chromosome, which is found almost exclusively among boys. The gene for the most common type of MD, Duchenne's, has just been located, so prenatal diagnosis may soon be available.

THINGS THAT CAN GO WRONG IN THE ENVIRONMENT: DISEASE, DRUGS, AND DIET

So far I have talked only about the sorts of genetically caused deviations from normal development that are set in motion at the moment of conception. But the environment in which the embryo and fetus grows for the rest of prenatal life also has an impact. Any environmental agent that can cause malformation or deviation in the development of the embryo or fetus is called a **teratogen.** The list of teratogens is long, but the critical ones can be classified as the "three Ds": disease, drugs, and diet.

GENETIC COUNSELING: BETTER INFORMATION BRINGS DIFFICULT DECISIONS

Not so many years ago, when a child was conceived, that child was born with whatever good or bad qualities happened to come along. The parents had no choices. That is no longer true. New scientific advances now give parents many options, some of which may require extremely difficult decisions. There are basically two sources of information: prepregnancy genetic testing of the parents and several forms of tests available during pregnancy to diagnose abnormalities in the fetus directly.

Prepregnancy Genetic Testing

Before conceiving, you and your spouse can have blood tests that will tell you whether you are carriers of genes for some specific diseases, such as Tay-Sachs or sickle-cell anemia or Huntington's disease. Since not all the genes for inherited diseases have been located, carriers of many diseases (such as cystic fibrosis) cannot yet be identified in this way. But geneticists discover the locations of additional diseases yearly. The gene for Duchenne's muscular dystrophy, for example, was recently identified (Kunkel et al., 1986).

It may seem a routine matter to have such tests done, but there are some very tricky circumstances. Take the case of a young adult whose parent is going through the prolonged and agonizing physical and mental deterioration of Huntington's disease. Recall that this genetic disease, controlled by a *dominant* gene, is expressed only in midlife. The young adult has a 50:50 chance of carrying the gene and thus of developing the disease in midlife. If you

were this person, you would presumably not wish to pass this gene on to a child. But if you have the test done and find out you are carrying the gene, you know you are facing a dreadful disease. Would you want to know? Many adults with Huntington's disease in their families have elected *not* to have the test done.

For most of us, the decision to have prepregnancy testing is simpler. But if you find that you and your spouse both carry a recessive gene for a serious problem, the decisions get harder. You could decide to have no children at all or to adopt children. Or you could count on the fact that you have a three-out-of-four probability of having a normal child and take a chance (since the child would suffer from the recessive-gene disease only if he received the gene from both parents, and that would happen, on average, only 25 percent of the time). Or you could conceive and then use any of several new techniques for diagnosing disease or abnormality prenatally. If such techniques reveal a problem, you could choose to abort the fetus. The options are clear, but the choices are immensely hard.

Prenatal Diagnosis of the Fetus

Three prenatal diagnostic strategies are now available. The safest of the three is *ultrasound,* which involves the use of sound waves to provide an actual "moving picture" of the fetus. Some kinds of spinal cord abnormalities can be diagnosed with ultrasound, for example, as can other major physical defects. The procedure is not painful, and it gives parents an often delightful chance to see their unborn child moving, but it cannot provide information about the presence of chromosomal anomalies or inherited diseases. If you want such information, you have two choices: **amniocentesis** or *chorionic villus sampling* (CVS). In both cases, a needle is inserted and cells are taken for diagnosis. In amniocentesis, the cell sample is taken from the amniotic fluid; in CVS, the sample is taken from what will become the placenta.

Both amniocentesis and CVS will provide information about any of the chromosomal anomalies and about the presence of genes for many of the major genetic diseases. Each technique has its own advantages and disadvantages. Amniocentesis was developed earlier and is the more widely used of the two. Its major drawback is that because the amniotic sac must be large enough to allow a sample of fluid to be taken with very little danger to the fetus, the test cannot be done until the sixteenth week of gestation. If the test reveals an abnormality, the parents must decide whether they want to abort at that stage of pregnancy. CVS, in contrast, is done between the ninth and eleventh weeks of gestation. The major drawback is that CVS is much riskier than amniocentesis. In 3 to 5 percent of cases, CVS causes a miscarriage; the equivalent risk for amniocentesis is about 0.5 percent. Not an easy set of choices.

Further Choices and Dilemmas

Suppose you use one of these diagnostic techniques and it reveals a physical abnormality or chromosomal anomaly or genetic disease. What do you do? Are you prepared to abort? Many people have very strong feelings about the morality of abortion. Others have equally strong feelings about the morality of bringing handicapped individuals into the world, especially those who require long-term care.

And what about the case—which happened to some friends of mine—in which the amniocentesis shows a chromosomal anomaly, but one so rare that the physicians cannot provide any information about likely outcomes?

Or what if you learn that your child will have a disease that can occur in mild or moderate as well as severe forms, such as sickle-cell anemia? The tests will not tell you how severely the child will be affected. How do you choose? In the same vein, we may eventually have genetic tests that will be able to tell us whether an unborn child has a high risk of developing emotional disturbances, such as depression or schizophrenia, or early heart disease. Would you want to know that? Would test results affect your decision to have a child?

And perhaps most troubling of all (to me at least), what about the use of amniocentesis or CVS to determine the sex of the fetus? Is it morally legitimate to choose to abort a fetus because it is not of the desired gender?

Many of us are used to thinking of scientific knowledge as morally neutral. But these few examples show clearly that it is not. As genetic counseling becomes more common, as diagnostic techniques become still more sophisticated, these will become compelling questions for many couples—including many of you.

Diseases of the Mother

Many disease organisms contracted by the mother cannot be passed through the placental membrane to the embryo or fetus. But others, particularly viruses, can attack the placenta, reducing the nutrients available to the embryo, or they can attack the embryo or fetus directly. The organisms that cause rubella and rubeola (both forms of measles), syphilis, diphtheria, influenza, typhoid, serum hepatitis, and chicken pox all may be passed to the child in this way, as apparently can the viruses that cause AIDS and another illness called CMV. In addition, it is possible for the child to contract other diseases (such as genital herpes) during birth itself, when the fetus comes into contact with the mucus membranes in the birth canal.

In all cases, as I indicated earlier, the timing of the infection is critical in determining the degree of effect. If an infection occurs during the first months of gestation, there may be major malformations; if it occurs later, there may be some growth retardation but the effects are often less pervasive.

Of the diseases on this list, the riskiest for the child are rubella, CMV, herpes, and AIDS.

Rubella.   **Rubella** (also called German measles) is most damaging during the first month of gestation. Half of infants exposed in this time show abnormalities, while only a quarter of those exposed in the second month show effects (Berg, 1974; Kopp, 1983). The particular organ systems most affected by rubella are the eyes, heart, and ears, with deafness a common outcome.

Fortunately, rubella is preventable. Vaccination is available and should be given to all children as part of a regular immunization program. Women who were not vaccinated in childhood can be vaccinated later, but it must be done at least three months before a pregnancy. (Those women among you who wish to have children and who have not been vaccinated for rubella should be checked for immunity. If you are not immune, you should be vaccinated, but only if you are sure you are not pregnant at the time of vaccination.) Rubella vaccine uses a live virus that can cross the placenta, so vaccination during the first three months of a pregnancy might have the same effect on the embryo/fetus as does the disease itself—although this is now in dispute among epidemiologists.

CMV.   *Cytomegalovirus (CMV)* is a common disease-causing virus in the herpes group. As many as 3 percent of pregnant women may be infected (Kopp, 1983), although the disease has so few symptoms that it is quite possible to have it and not know it. Current estimates are that somewhere between 1 in 100 and 1 in 1000 infants is infected prenatally. Many (but not all) have fairly serious problems later, with damage particularly to the brain and nervous system. *Microcephaly* (abnormally small head) is one fairly common result, as is deafness (Hanshaw, 1981).

Herpes Simplex. Infection by this virus (also known as *genital herpes*) has received a great deal of press attention lately, so most of you know that this disease is not curable (at least not at the present state of medical science). If a pregnant woman is in the active phase of the disease during delivery, it is possible that the child will contract it during birth. Not only will the child then experience the skin sores periodically, but other complications are also possible, most notably meningoencephalitis (a potentially serious inflammation of the brain and spinal cord). Because of this risk, physicians generally recommend surgical delivery (cesarean section) if the mother has herpes, although vaginal delivery may be possible if the disease is inactive. I should point out that *oral* herpes (often shown by cold sores on or around the mouth) has no known detrimental effect on the developing fetus.

Drugs Taken by the Mother

Try sitting down and making a list of all the drugs you have taken in the past month or the past year. I'm not talking here about such illegal drugs as marijuana or cocaine (although they, too, affect the developing infant) but about everyday legal drugs like aspirin, decongestants, vitamins, sleeping pills, and tranquilizers. Equally common in the everyday lives of most of us are alcohol, tobacco, and caffeine. Ours is a drug-taking culture, and this is no less true of pregnant women. Ten or fifteen years ago, the average woman took six or seven prescribed drugs and another three or four over-the-counter drugs (such as aspirin) during the course of her pregnancy (Stewart, Cluff & Philp, 1977). Today that number is doubtless lower, but it is not zero. And many pregnant women also smoke, drink alcohol, and drink coffee, tea, and other caffeine-containing beverages. What are the effects of these drugs on the embryo or fetus?

This turns out to be a harder question to answer than you might suppose. Because a woman may take several different drugs, the effects of a specific drug are often hard to identify. Furthermore, the effects may be subtle; long-term learning problems, for example, may not show up for many years. Still another difficulty is that the same drug may have many different effects. Thus a child exposed to a drug may be at increased risk for having *some* kind of problem but not necessarily for a *particular* problem (Jacobson et al., 1984a). J. G. Wilson (1977) estimates that 4 to 5 percent of observable physical defects in infants are caused by known drugs. Given the difficulties in pinning down the outcomes, this may be a low estimate.

Some drugs prescribed specifically for pregnant women have later been found to have significant negative effects. *Thalidomide,* for example, was a tranquilizer prescribed fairly often during the early 1960s. Later it was found that this drug, if taken during the first 52 days of pregnancy, greatly increased the risk of a particular physical deformity in which the infant was born with foreshortened or missing limbs. Another drug, *diethyl-*

stilbestrol (DES), was commonly prescribed during the 1940s and 1950s to help prevent miscarriages (although it was later found to be ineffective for this purpose). No obvious deformity was seen at first in the offspring of women who received DES during their pregnancies, but a number of subtle long-term effects have appeared, including increased risk of vaginal cancer among girls and increased risk of sterility among boys whose mothers received DES during their pregnancies (Henley & Altman, 1978).

Current findings suggest that antibiotics like tetracycline, anticoagulants, insulin, amphetamines, and tranquilizers may also have negative effects on the developing embryo or fetus, as may lithium carbonate, a drug now prescribed often for serious depression (Kopp, 1983). Even caffeine has come under suspicion lately, although the findings on this one are mixed. Obviously, given this list, any pregnant woman would be well advised to consult her physician before taking *any* medication, including common over-the-counter drugs.

On a day-to-day basis, though, the drugs we have most contact with are not antidepressants or anticoagulants but alcohol and nicotine. Should a pregnant woman drink or smoke?

Smoking. The most consistently observed effect of smoking on prenatal development is reduced birth weight of the infant (Jacobson et al., 1984b; Werler, Pober, & Holmes, 1985). On average, the difference is about 200 g (a bit less than half a pound)—quite a lot when you consider that a baby weighs only a few pounds at birth. This reduced weight seems to result from lowered placental blood flow (nicotine constricts the blood vessels, so the fetus suffers from a loss of nutrition). In addition, women who smoke also increase their risk of premature delivery. In one very large study involving over 30,000 women, for example, Patricia Shiono and her colleagues (Shiono, Klebanoff, & Rhoads, 1986) found that compared to pregnant women who did not smoke, those who smoked a pack a day or more had a 20 percent greater chance of delivering their baby at 37 weeks' gestation or earlier and a 60 percent greater chance of delivering at 33 weeks' gestation or earlier. Both low birth weight and premature delivery increase infant mortality.

Long-term consequences for the infants of mothers who smoke have been much harder to pin down. Several longitudinal studies point to higher rates of learning problems in school-age children whose mothers smoked during pregnancy (Nichols, 1977; Fogelman, 1980; Dunn et al., 1977), but other researchers have not found such effects (Lefkowitz, 1981). Thus, while we know that infants born to mothers who smoke have lower survival rates in the early months of life, we do not yet know whether those who survive have increased long-term risks.

Despite the inconsistencies in the studies on long-term effects, though, the moral to be drawn from this research seems clear: Do not smoke during pregnancy. If you cannot quit entirely, then at least cut back, since all these studies show a relationship between the *dosage* (the amount of nicotine you are taking in) and the severity of consequences for the child.

Drinking. An equally clear moral emerges from a look at the recent work on the effects that maternal alcohol ingestion has on prenatal and postnatal development.

In the early 1970s, Kenneth Jones and his colleagues (1973) identified a syndrome characteristic of children born to alcoholic mothers, which they labeled **fetal alcohol syndrome (FAS).** Infants with FAS are generally smaller than normal and have smaller brains. They frequently have heart defects, their faces are distinctively different (as you can see in Figure 2.8), and they ordinarily show mild to moderate mental retardation.

Since the first identification of FAS, extensive evidence has accumulated showing that alcoholism or regular heavy drinking has major negative effects on the child's development (Rosett & Sander, 1979; Abel, 1984). The recent evidence also shows that more moderate drinking has at least some effects too. In a series of comprehensive and well-designed studies, Ann Streissguth and her colleagues (1980a, 1981, 1984) have found that women who average 1 ounce of absolute alcohol per day (or more) during pregnancy (the equivalent of about two beers, one and a half 6-ounce glasses of wine, or two 1-ounce drinks of liquor) are more likely to have sluggish,

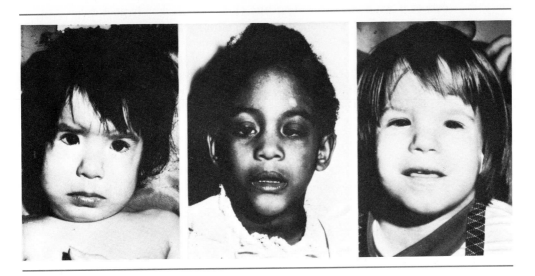

Figure 2.8 These three children, from three racial backgrounds (from left: American Indian, black, and white) have all been diagnosed as having fetal alcohol syndrome (FAS). All are mentally retarded and have relatively small heads. Note the short nose and low nasal bridge typical of FAS children. (*Source:* Streissguth et al., *Science, 209* [July 18, 1980]: Figure 2, p. 355; copyright 1980 by the American Association for the Advancement of Science.)

hard-to-arouse babies, often of lower birth weights. In later months and years, small but consistent differences persist. These infants score lower on developmental tests at 8 months of age and have a poorer attention span at age 4. Other researchers have also observed that children whose mothers drank moderate amounts during pregnancy have poorer language skills at age 2 than do children whose mothers did not drink—and this was true even when the two groups were matched as well as possible on many other variables (Morrow-Tlucak et al., 1987).

Whether there is any safe level of alcohol consumption during pregnancy I can't tell you, given the evidence we have today. My hunch is that we will find that (as with nicotine) there is a fairly straightforward relationship between risk and dosage, that there is some increased risk even at low dosage. Probably it also matters when in the pregnancy the drinking occurs and how much you drink on any one occasion. The *safest* course is not to drink at all.

The Mother's Diet

Just as drugs matter, so too does a mother's diet, although no one knows *exactly* what is the best diet or what are the precise effects of too much or too little of a particular nutrient. I've explored some of what we know about a good diet in the box on pages 64–65. The other half of the question concerns what we know about the effects of unusually poor diets.

Severe malnutrition during pregnancy leads to greatly increased risks of stillbirth, low birth weight, and infant death during the first year of life (e.g., Stein et al., 1975). The effects seem to be worse when malnutrition occurs during the last half of pregnancy, particularly in the last three months. Babies whose mothers suffer severe malnutrition during the final trimester are lighter at birth and have a greatly increased risk of dying during the first year. When you think back to the general rule I gave earlier—that interference in prenatal development has the biggest effect during the time of maximum growth of any system—this pattern makes good sense. The major gain in weight occurs during the final three months, so we'd expect these babies to be small, as they are, and perhaps therefore more vulnerable to disease.

The final trimester is also a time of rapid growth of the connective links between nerve cells. Malnutrition during these months seems to cause a reduction in the number of connective links between the nerve cells in the brain, and it slows development of the myelin sheaths around the nerve fibers in the fetus (Lewin, 1975).

Other Teratogens

The list of other potential environmental hazards is very long indeed, including some chemicals, such as pesticides. One chemical about which we have relatively good information is lead.

In most industrialized countries, adults are exposed to fairly high amounts of lead, although the introduction of unleaded gasoline and elimination of lead-based paint have lowered the dosages. Disturbingly, however, researchers are beginning to find that even quite low levels of lead in the blood of the newborn—levels classified as "safe" by current federal guidelines—are associated with slightly lower IQ scores at later ages than scores of children with still lower lead levels (Bellinger, 1987; Dietrich et al., 1987).

OTHER CHARACTERISTICS OF THE MOTHER THAT AFFECT THE NORMAL SEQUENCE

Beyond the factors I have been describing—diet, drugs, and diseases—three other maternal characteristics seem to make a difference in prenatal development: the mother's age, the number of children she has already had, and her overall emotional state during the pregnancy.

The Mother's Age

One of the particularly intriguing trends in modern family life is the increasing likelihood that women will postpone their first pregnancy until their late twenties or early thirties (Giele, 1982). Of course, there are many reasons for such decisions, chief among them being the increased need for second incomes in families and the desire of many young women to complete job training and early career steps before bearing children. For our purposes in this chapter, though, the key question is the impact of maternal age on the mother and on the developing child.

The evidence tells us that the optimum time for childbearing is in a woman's early twenties. Mothers in their teens and those over 30 (particularly over 35) are at increased risk for several kinds of problems.

Older Mothers.   To get the most depressing news over with first: women over 30 or 35 do run a slightly higher risk of death during pregnancy or delivery (Buehler et al., 1986), although the good news is that the mortality rate for pregnant women over 35 was halved between 1978 and 1982. The older mother is also much more likely to conceive an infant with Down's syndrome—a pattern I already discussed. (The link between maternal age and this particular anomaly is so well established that women over 35 are now routinely urged to undergo amniocentesis to check for the presence of an extra chromosome 21.) For a *first* pregnancy in women over 35, there are also increased risks of stillbirth and longer labor (Kessner, 1973).

It is important to emphasize that, except for Down's syndrome, these increased risks are more likely for older mothers from poverty environments. This suggests that age is not the only factor. Rather, the mother's overall

DIET AND EXERCISE DURING PREGNANCY

Life-styles have been changing; slimness and fitness in women are perhaps more highly valued now than before, especially among younger women of childbearing age. And every woman wants to give her unborn child the best possible start in the world. So questions about weight gain, diet, and exercise during pregnancy are of vital concern. The evidence is not of the highest quality in every case, but at least there are a few facts and a few suggestions that I can pass on to you.

Weight Gain

For many years, physicians thought that the fetus acted as a sort of "parasite" on the mother's body, taking whatever nourishment it needed, even at the expense of the mother. Research by Pedro Rosso (1977a, 1977b), however, has challenged this assumption as well as other customs about nutritional needs in pregnancy.

Rosso's research shows that if the mother is even a little underweight or malnourished, the fetus may not compete successfully for nourishment and may be born underweight, with increased risk of disease or disorders. The old rule of thumb was that a woman should gain 2 pounds per month during pregnancy. Rosso's work indicates that this is not nearly enough. The current advice is that a woman who is at her normal weight before pregnancy should gain 25 to 30 pounds, and a woman who is underweight before pregnancy should gain slightly more. Even overweight women need to gain at least 20 to 24 pounds in order to support the optimum development of the infant. Infants born to women who gain less than this may suffer from some fetal malnutrition and are often born underweight for their gestational age (Winick, 1980; Brown, 1983).

Furthermore, it matters *when* the weight is gained. During the first three months, the woman needs to gain only a minimal amount (2 to 5 pounds). But during the last six months of the pregnancy, the woman should be gaining at the rate of about 14 ounces (350 to 400 g) per week in order to support fetal growth (Pitkin, 1977; Winick, 1980). One practical consequence of this is that a woman who has gained 20 pounds or so during the first four or five months should *not* cut back in order to hold her weight gain to some magic total number. Restricting caloric intake during those final months is exactly the wrong thing to do.

A Good Diet

Pure poundage is not enough to ensure optimal development for the child. It also matters *what* the mother eats. Caloric requirements go up 10 to 20 percent (perhaps 300 calories a day beyond your maintenance level), but protein needs appear to go up much more markedly. The current recommendation (Winick, 1980) is that a pregnant woman age 19 or older needs to take in 1.3 g of protein daily per kilogram (2.2 pounds) of her weight. For example, a woman weighing 125 pounds requires about 75 g of protein per day. Because they are still growing, the protein requirement for teenagers is still higher—perhaps 1.5 or 1.7 g per day per kilogram of weight. (Since an egg has about 7 g and a cup of cottage cheese has 33 g of protein, even this heightened requirement is not difficult to meet.) Requirements for most vitamins and minerals also increase during pregnancy. Calcium needs rise 50 percent, from 800 mg to 1200 mg daily, and iron requirements also increase, to perhaps 75 mg daily (Winick, 1980).

Exercise

Two questions about exercise during pregnancy are relevant: Is it safe for the fetus, and does it make labor and delivery easier? The tentative answer to both questions seems to be "yes," but I am not satisfied that we have nearly enough research on these questions yet.

Since blood oxygen levels appear to remain fairly constant in exercising pregnant women, the fetus does not appear likely to suffer from any oxygen deprivation. Furthermore, the few existing studies comparing babies born to mothers who exercised and those who did not show no differences in birth weight, length, or healthiness at birth (Leaf, 1982). However, this is true *only* if the exercising woman gains a sufficient amount of weight. Not long ago I read a letter to the editor in *Runner's World* magazine from a man who bragged that his wife maintained a schedule of running 30 to 40 miles per week during her pregnancy and gained only 2 pounds in nine months! Such low weight gain is *not* desirable. So if you plan to exercise regularly while you are pregnant, you will need to make sure you have enough caloric intake to compensate for the calories burned during exercise.

The general rule of thumb now used by most physicians and midwives is that a woman can (or even should) maintain whatever level of exercise was typical for her before she became pregnant. Large increases in exercise level are not recommended. Furthermore, some kinds of complications of pregnancy may preclude exercise. So before embarking on or continuing with a vigorous program of exercise, a pregnant woman would be wise to consult her physician or midwife.

Aside from maintaining physical fitness during pregnancy, the main argument for exercise is that it *may* shorten labor to some degree (Leaf, 1982). I say "may" because the evidence here is scanty. I do not offer guarantees!

It is heartening to have at least some research on questions like these. But the answers are still tentative, and each pregnant woman will need to make the best decision she can, given the information.

physical health is probably critical. Older mothers, particularly if they live in poverty, are likely to be less healthy. But older women who maintain good physical fitness appear to be able to reduce the risks of pregnancy considerably. So if you are going to have a late baby, the message seems to be, "Stay in shape."

Young Mothers.   At the other end of the age range, there are also added risks of a low-birth-weight infant, stillbirth, or difficulties during delivery (Kessner, 1973; Monkus & Bancalari, 1981). These effects are particularly evident for mothers 15 or younger. You can see the relationship between maternal age and the likelihood of a low-birth-weight infant or a stillbirth in Figure 2.9.

Teenage pregnancies represent a large percentage of all births in the United States (Scott, 1979). Something on the order of 17 to 20 percent

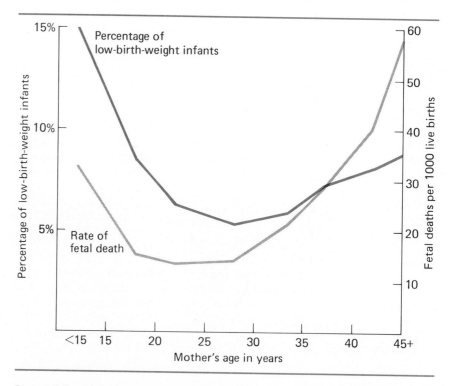

Figure 2.9   Both younger and older mothers are more likely to have low-birth-weight infants or to have infants who die within a year of birth, as you can see clearly from these curves. But a great deal of this pattern is caused by the facts that younger mothers receive poorer prenatal care and older mothers are likely to be generally less healthy. (*Sources:* Reproduced from D. Kessner, *Infant death: An analysis by maternal risk and health care,* 1973, p. 100, with the permission of the National Academy of Sciences, Washington, D.C.)

of all births are to teenagers, of which about a third are to girls under 17. Perhaps 10,000 babies are born each year to girls 15 or younger. Given the fact that a very young mother has not completed her own growth and thus has extra nutritional needs of her own, we should probably not be surprised that such pregnancies are at higher risk for low birth weight or fetal death.

But as is true for pregnancies in older women, teenage pregnancies appear to be risky mostly because teenagers who get pregnant are more likely to be poor (and thus probably have poor nutrition) and because teenagers are less likely to get decent prenatal care. Except for those who are under 15 when they give birth, among whom the risks are slightly higher regardless of prenatal care, teenagers who have good diets and adequate prenatal care are no more likely to have problems with the pregnancy or delivery than are women in their twenties (Robertson, 1981; Strobino, 1978).

So while the mother's age can help us to predict problems in a pregnancy, age itself is probably not the critical factor in most difficulties; rather, it is the general physical and nutritional condition of the mother that matters the most.

Number of Pregnancies

As a general rule, women who have had more than four pregnancies are at greater risk (as are their offspring) than are women who have had fewer. Their babies are more likely to be stillborn and to be smaller at birth (Kessner, 1973). Eleanor Maccoby and her colleagues (1979) have also found that any child after the first, especially if the pregnancies are closely spaced, has lower levels of hormones in the blood at birth. In particular, firstborn boys in this study had much higher levels of testosterone (the male hormone) at birth than did later-born boys. We don't know yet what the implications of such a difference may be for development, but this study does point to the possibility of some kinds of physical "depletion" in the mother as a result of pregnancy, which can affect the physical development of later-born children.

The Mother's Emotional State

Finally, the mother's state of mind during the pregnancy seems to have some effect on the outcome. Arnold Sameroff and Michael Chandler (1975) have concluded that a woman who experiences prolonged or severe anxiety during her pregnancy—for whatever reason—has increased risk of a difficult pregnancy, including more nausea and vomiting, miscarriage, premature delivery, and longer and more difficult labor.

It doesn't seem quite fair that the women who are the most anxious are more likely to have their worst fears confirmed, but that's the way it seems to work. Furthermore, the mother's nervousness or anxiety also seems to affect the infant after birth. Infants born to tense or anxious mothers are more irritable, cry more, and are more likely to spit up or have intestinal problems—a pattern called *colic* (Lakin, 1957). There may be a kind of "self-fulfilling prophecy" here—mothers who expect to have more trouble with their infants may in fact have more troublesome babies because of the way they respond to their children. But the connection may be physiological rather than purely psychological. Prolonged anxiety during the pregnancy changes the chemical composition of the mother's blood, which may have some effect on the developing fetus that would account for the baby's later irritability.

AN OVERVIEW OF RISKS AND LONG-TERM CONSEQUENCES OF PRENATAL PROBLEMS

Every time I rewrite this chapter I am aware that the list of things that can go wrong seems to get longer and longer and scarier and scarier. Physicians, biologists, and psychologists keep learning more about both the major and the subtle effects of prenatal environmental variations, so the number of warnings to pregnant women seems to increase weekly. One of the ironies of this is that too much worry about such potential consequences can make a woman more anxious, and anxiety is on the list of warnings! So before you begin worrying too much, let me try to put this information into perspective.

First, let me say again that *most* pregnancies are normal, and most babies are healthy and normal at birth.

Second, there are specific preventive steps that any woman can take to reduce the risks for herself and her unborn child. She can be properly immunized; she can quit smoking and drinking; she can watch her diet and make sure her weight gain is sufficient; and she can get early and regular prenatal care. It is *very* clear from many studies that mothers who receive adequate prenatal care reduce the risks to themselves and their infants. In addition, she and the child's father can have genetic counseling.

Third, if something does go wrong, chances are good that the negative consequences to the child will be short-term rather than permanent. And many physical defects can be treated successfully after birth.

Of course, some negative outcomes *are* permanent and have long-term consequences for the child. Chromosomal anomalies, including Down's syndrome or deviations in sex-chromosome patterns, are permanent and are nearly always associated with mental retardation or school difficulties (Pennington et al., 1982). Some teratogens also have permanent effects— for example, fetal alcohol syndrome, deafness resulting from rubella, or limb defects from thalidomide. And as you'll see in Chapter 3, *very* low-birth-weight infants (those under about 1500 g, about $3\frac{1}{2}$ pounds) have an increased risk of persistent long-term learning problems or low IQ, regardless of the richness of the environment in which they are reared.

But many of the effects I have talked about in this chapter may be detectable only for the first few years of the child's life, and then only in certain families. The relationship between prenatal problems and long-term outcomes, in fact, is a perfect example of the kind of interaction effect I talked about in Chapter 1 (recall Figure 1.2). As Horowitz (1982) points out, low-birth-weight infants or those with poor prenatal nutrition, higher lead exposures, or other difficulties are likely to show persisting problems if they are reared in unstimulating or unsupportive environments. The same children reared in richer and more varied environments typically catch up to their peers by school age, if not before. So it is not the prenatal problem by itself that is the cause; it is the combination of a prenatal problem and a relatively poor early environment that seems to produce long-term negative effects.

Let me give one specific example. Philip Zeskind and Craig Ramey (1981) have studied a group of 10 infants, born to poverty-level mothers, who were extremely thin at birth—a sign of prenatal malnutrition. Half of these babies had been assigned randomly to a special enriched day-care program beginning when they were 3 months old. The other five babies received nutritional supplements but were reared at home, in much less stimulating circumstances. Other children in the day-care center were of normal weight at birth, as were other home-reared children included in the study. Table 2.3 gives the IQ scores of these four groups of children when they were 3 years old. As you can see, the results match Horowitz's model very well. Prenatally malnourished infants did well in the stimulating environment of the day-care center but extremely poorly in a less-supportive environment. Well-nourished infants also did better in the day-care environment than at home, but the difference is not nearly so large.

Studies like these persuade me that problems experienced by the embryo or fetus may make an infant more vulnerable to later stresses or problems or may mean that the child requires a better family environment to develop normally. But in many cases such normal development *is* possible. So don't despair when you read the long list of cautions and potential problems. The story isn't as gloomy as it first seems.

Table 2.3

IQ Scores of 3-year-old Children

	Prenatal nutritional status	
Experience after birth	Malnourished	Well nourished
Enriched day care	96.4	98.1
Home-reared	70.6	84.7

Source: Based on data from Zeskind & Ramey, 1981, p. 215.

SEX DIFFERENCES IN PRENATAL DEVELOPMENT

Since nearly all prenatal development is controlled by genetic maturational instructions that are the same for all members of our species—male and female alike—there aren't very many sex differences in prenatal development. But there are a few, and they set the stage for some of the physical differences we'll see at later ages.

- As I've already pointed out, boys secrete testosterone during the early months of gestation. This leads to the "fixing" of the brain so that the proper male hormones are secreted at the right moment later in life. Girls do not secrete any equivalent hormone prenatally.
- Girls are a bit faster in some aspects of prenatal development, particularly skeletal development. They are one to two weeks ahead in bone development at birth (Tanner, 1978).
- Despite the more rapid development of girls, boys are heavier and longer at birth (Tanner, 1978).
- Boys are considerably more vulnerable to all kinds of prenatal problems. Many more boys than girls are conceived—on the order of 120 to 150 male embryos to every 100 female—but more of the males are spontaneously aborted. At birth, there are about 105 boys for every 100 girls. Boys are also more likely to experience injuries at birth (perhaps because they are larger), and they have more congenital malformations (Zaslow & Hayes, 1986).

The striking sex difference in vulnerability is particularly intriguing, especially since it seems to persist. Older boys are more prone to problems as well—a pattern I'll discuss more thoroughly in Chapter 14. One possible explanation for this, as I suggested earlier, may lie in the basic genetic difference. The XX chromosome combination affords the girl more protection against fragile-X syndrome and against "bad" genes that may be carried on the X chromosome. In particular, a gene affecting susceptibility to infectious disease is carried on the X chromosome (Brooks-Gunn & Matthews, 1979); boys are at much higher risk of having such susceptibility.

SOCIAL CLASS DIFFERENCES IN PRENATAL DEVELOPMENT

I will be talking much more fully about social class differences in development in Chapter 13, but I cannot leave this chapter without saying a word about the impact of social class on the risks of pregnancy and birth.

The basic sequence of fetal development clearly does not differ, whether children are born to poor mothers or to middle-class mothers. But many of the problems that can affect prenatal development are more common among the poor. For example, mothers who have not graduated from high school are about twice as likely as mothers with a college education to have a low-birth-weight or stillborn infant (Kessner, 1973). Poor women are also likely to have their first pregnancy earlier and to have more pregnancies overall, and they are less likely to be immunized against such diseases as rubella. Perhaps most critically, poor women generally seek prenatal care much later in their pregnancies—and are more likely to have no prenatal care at all.

We know that the lack of prenatal care is one of the keys, because when low-cost or free prenatal care is made easily available to the poor, the infant mortality rate drops sharply (Kessner, 1973). If we are willing to devote the resources needed for such an effort, we can significantly reduce the rates of infant death, physical abnormalities, and perhaps even mental retardation. To my mind, this is a goal worth striving for.

SUMMARY

1. Conception occurs when the man's sperm penetrates the woman's ovum, ordinarily in the fallopian tube.

2. At conception, the 23 chromosomes from the sperm join the 23 from the ovum to make up the set of 46 that will be reproduced in each cell of the new child's body.

3. Chromosomes, which are made up of deoxyribonucleic acid (DNA), carry genes in a particularly linear sequence.

4. The child's sex is determined by one of the 23 pairs of chromosomes, XX for a girl and XY for a boy.

5. Geneticists distinguish between the genotype, which is the pattern of inherited characteristics, and the phenotype, which is the set of characteristics of an individual that emerges when the genotype interacts with specific experience.

6. During the first days after conception, the initial cell divides (mitosis), travels down the fallopian tube, and is implanted in the wall of the uterus.

7. Over the next weeks, cell differentiation takes place, and the placenta, umbilical cord, and amniotic cavity all form.

8. The developing organism is first called the ovum; then the blastocyst; then (beginning at about two weeks after gestation) the embryo. After eight weeks it is called the fetus.

9. Most organ systems develop in rudimentary form during the embryonic period; enlargement and refinements take place during the fetal period.

10. During the embryonic period, the XY embryo secretes the hormone testosterone, which stimulates the growth of male genitalia and shifts the brain into a "male" pattern. Without that hormone, the embryo would develop as a girl, as do normal XX embryos.

11. Normal prenatal development seems heavily determined by maturation sequences—a "road map" contained in the genes. Disruptions in this

sequence can occur; the timing of the disruption determines the nature and severity of the effect.

12. Problems in prenatal development can begin at conception if a chromosomal abnormality, such as Down's syndrome, occurs or if the child receives genes for specific diseases.

13. Prior to conception, it is possible to test whether the parents carry genes for many inherited diseases. After conception, several diagnostic techniques may be used to determine whether the developing fetus carries some genetic diseases or anomalies.

14. Some diseases contracted by the mother may affect the child, including rubella, AIDS, CMV, and genital herpes. These may result in disease or physical abnormalities in the child.

15. Both alcohol and nicotine have harmful effects on the developing fetus; the greater the dosage, the greater the potential effect appears to be.

16. The mother's diet is important. If she is severely malnourished, there are increased risks of stillbirth, low birth weight, and infant death during the first year of life.

17. Older mothers and very young mothers, along with those who have borne four or more children, also run increased risks, but these risks are greatly reduced if the mother is in good health and receives adequate prenatal care.

18. Among other teratogens, prenatal lead exposure has been shown to be associated with lower IQs in infancy and early childhood.

19. The mother's emotional state may also affect the developing child. The more anxious the mother, the more difficult her pregnancy and delivery and the more irritable her infant is likely to be.

20. Some difficulties in prenatal development can produce permanent disabilities or deformities, such as Down's syndrome or deafness from rubella. Some produce other lasting problems, as in the case of very low birth weight. But many disorders associated with prenatal problems can be overcome if the child is reared in a supportive and stimulating environment.

21. Sex differences in prenatal development are few in number. Boys are slower to develop, are bigger at birth, and are more vulnerable to most forms of prenatal stress.

22. Nearly all problems in prenatal development are more common among poor women, but these increased risks can be greatly reduced with good diet and adequate prenatal care.

■■■■■ KEY TERMS

amniocentesis A medical test for genetic abnormalities in the embryo/fetus that may be done at about 16 weeks' gestation.

autosomes The 22 pairs of chromosomes in which both members of the pair are the same size and carry parallel information.

blastocyst The name used for the small mass of cells that implants itself into the wall of the uterus about two weeks after conception.

chromosome The structure in each cell in the body that contains genetic information. Each chromosome is made up of many genes.

crossing over   The process that occurs during meiosis in which genetic material may be exchanged between the members of a chromosome pair.

deoxyribonucleic acid (DNA)   The chemical of which chromosomes are composed.

Down's syndrome   A genetic anomaly in which every cell contains three copies of chromosome 21 rather than two. Children born with this genetic pattern are usually mentally retarded and have characteristic physical features.

embryo   The name given to the organism during the period of prenatal development from about two to eight weeks after conception, beginning with implantation of the blastocyst into the uterine wall.

fallopian tube   The tube down which the ovum travels to the uterus and in which conception usually occurs.

fetal alcohol syndrome (FAS)   A pattern of physical abnormalities, including mental retardation and minor physical anomalies, found often in children born to alcoholic mothers.

fetus   The name given to the developing organism from about eight weeks after conception until birth.

gene   A uniquely coded segment of DNA in a chromosome which affects one or more specific body processes or developments.

genotype   The unique pattern of characteristics and developmental sequences mapped in the genes of an individual. Will be modified by individual experience into the phenotype.

germ cells   Sperm and ova. These cells, unlike all other cells of the body, contain only 23 chromosomes rather than 23 pairs.

meiosis   The process of cell division that produces germ cells, in which only one member of each chromosome pair is passed on to the new cell.

mitosis   The process of cell division for all cells other than germ cells, in which both new cells contain 23 pairs of chromosomes.

ovum   The germ cell produced by a woman, which, if fertilized by a sperm from a male, forms the basis for the developing organism.

phenotype   The expression of a particular set of genetic information in a specific environment; the observable result of the joint operation of genetic and environmental influences.

placenta   An organ that develops during gestation between the fetus and the wall of the uterus. The placenta filters nutrients from the mother's blood, acting as liver, lungs, and kidneys for the fetus.

rubella   A form of measles that, if contracted during the first three months of pregnancy, may have severe effects on the developing baby.

sex chromosomes   The X and Y chromosomes, which determine the sex of a child. In humans, XX is the female pattern, XY the male pattern.

teratogen   Any outside agent (such as a disease or a chemical) that significantly increases the risk of deviations or abnormalities in prenatal development.

uterus   The female organ in which the blastocyst implants itself and within which the embryo/fetus develops. (Popularly referred to as the *womb*.)

▬▬▬▬   **SUGGESTED READING**

The Boston Women's Health Collective. (1984). *The new our bodies, ourselves: A book by and for women* (2nd ed.). New York: Simon & Schuster.
This relatively recent revision of a popular book is focused on the adult female's body rather than on prenatal development, but it has an excellent discussion of health during pregnancy and good descriptions and diagrams showing stages of prenatal development. You may not be entirely in sympathy with all of the political views expressed, but this volume is nonetheless a very good compact source of information on all facets of pregnancy, including prenatal diagnosis of anomalies and diseases.

Nilsson, L. A. (1977). *A child is born.* New York: Delacorte Press, Seymour Lawrence.
This book is full of marvelous photographs of the embryo and fetus. It also has a good basic text describing prenatal development and problems of pregnancy.

3 Birth and the Newborn Child

Birth
  The Normal Process
  The First Greeting: Parents and Newborns
  Conditions During Birth: Where, Who, and What
Gentle Births: Are They Important?
  Cesarean-Section Delivery
  Problems at Birth
What Can the Newborn Do?
  Reflexes
  Perceptual Skills: What the Infant Sees, Hears, and Feels
  Motor Skills: Moving Around
  Learning and Habituation
  Social Skills
The Daily Life of Infants
  Sleeping
  Crying
  Eating
Breast-Feeding Versus Bottle-Feeding
Individual Differences Among Babies
  Temperament
  Sex and Social Class Differences in Infants
The Effects of the Infant on the Parents
Summary
Key Terms
Suggested Reading
Project: Observation in a Newborn Nursery

I magine (if you can) that you are a woman nine months pregnant with your first child. The long months of prenatal life are nearly over, and the baby is about to be born. If you are like many of today's mothers, you and your partner have looked into alternative locations or "styles" of delivery; both of you may have taken prenatal classes; and you have tried to prepare yourselves for what the baby will be like and how the advent of this new member of the family will change your life. You are a little apprehensive about the process of delivery and a bit uncertain about what to expect from the baby and about your own abilities to cope, but you are eager for the whole adventure to begin.

In this chapter I want to try to answer some of the questions that new parents reasonably ask about birth and about newborn babies. Does it make a difference whether the baby is born in a hospital or at home? Does it matter whether the father is present or not? What happens if the birth is too early or if something else goes wrong? I also want to describe the beginnings of the child's independent life so that you can be clearly aware of the starting point for the long developmental journey. In the past few decades, researchers have discovered a great many things about newborns, and we now realize that these apparently helpless creatures really have a wide range of quite remarkable abilities. This knowledge has not only changed the information given out to new parents; it has also changed our theories of development.

BIRTH

The Normal Process

Labor progresses through three stages of unequal length.

The First Stage of Labor. Stage 1 covers the period during which two important processes occur: dilation and effacement. The cervix (the opening at the bottom of the uterus) must open up like the lens of a camera (**dilation**) and also flatten out (**effacement**). At the time of actual delivery of the infant, the cervix must normally be dilated to about 10 cm (about 4 inches), as you see in Figure 3.1. This part of labor has been likened to putting on a sweater with a neck that is too tight. You have to pull and stretch the neck of the sweater over your head in order to get it on. Eventually the neck is stretched enough so that the widest part of your head can pass through.

A good deal of the effacement may actually occur in the last weeks of the pregnancy, as may some dilation. It is not uncommon for women to begin labor 80 percent effaced and 1 or 2 cm dilated. The contractions of stage 1 of labor, which are at first widely spaced and later more frequent and rhythmic, serve to complete both processes.

Customarily, stage 1 is itself divided into phases. In the *early* phase (also sometimes called the *latent* phase), contractions are relatively far

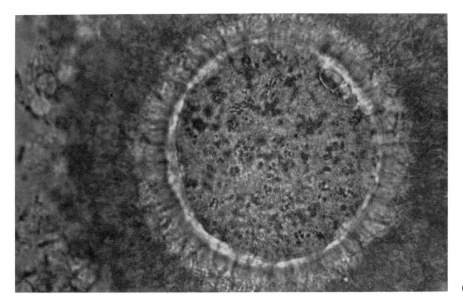

(1)

Nothing can convey prenatal changes more
graphically than photographs. Here, in Figure 1, you
can see the ovum just after it has been fertilized. In
Figure 2 you can see the embryo 28 days later, vastly
more complex but with little humanlike form as yet.

(2)

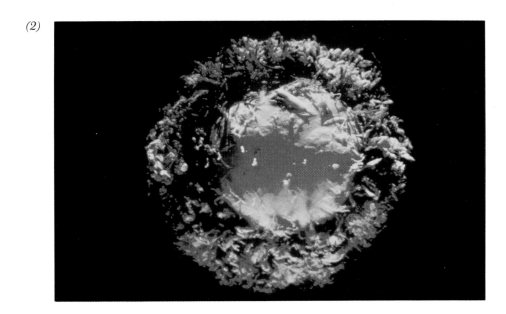

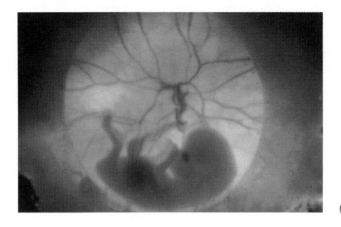

(3)

Early in the fetal period many physical features are already present. Figure 3 shows a fetus at 9–10 weeks; Figure 4, a fetus of 14–16 weeks. Fingers and toes are clearly present, as are many facial features.

(4)

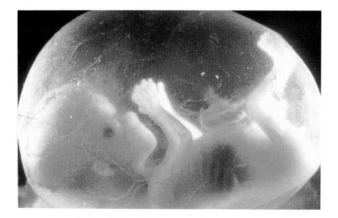

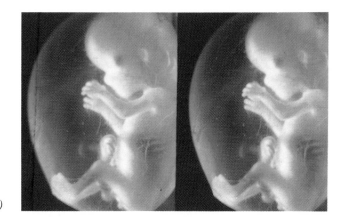

(5)

(6)

In the middle of the fetal period changes are gradual. Figure 5 is a photo of a fetus at about 16–18 weeks. Figure 6 was taken only slightly later, at perhaps 18–20 weeks, and Figure 7 was taken at about 22 weeks. Infants this small can now sometimes be saved if born prematurely.

(7)

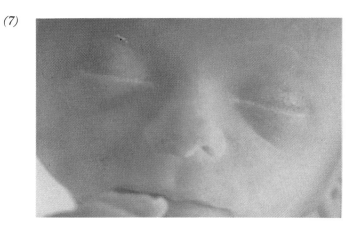

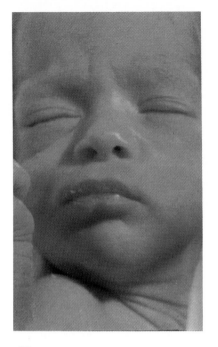

By the seventh month (Figure 8) the features are clearly much more complete; most infants born at this age now survive, although the lungs and nervous system are still quite immature. The nearly full term infant in Figure 9 is more mature in both respects, in addition to being heavier and longer. Finally the process is done and the full-term infant is born (Figure 10).

(8)

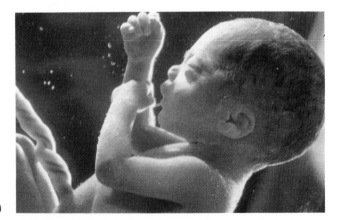

(9)

(10)

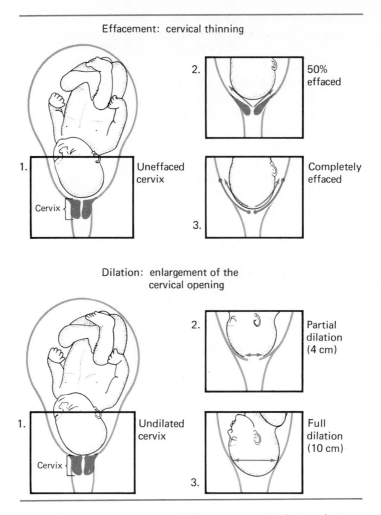

Figure 3.1 The processes of effacement and dilation during labor. (*Source:* Stenchever, 1978, Figure 5-4, p. 84).

apart and are typically not too uncomfortable. In the *late* phase, which begins when the cervix is about halfway dilated (5 cm), contractions are closer together and are more intense. This phase continues until the cervix is dilated to 8 cm. Finally, the last 2 cm of dilation are achieved during the *transition* phase. It is this phase, in which the contractions are closely spaced and strong, that women typically find the most painful, but transition is also typically the shortest phase. Following transition comes the urge to help the infant out by "pushing." When the birth attendant (physician or midwife) is sure the cervix is fully dilated, she or he will encourage this pushing, and the second stage of labor begins.

The length of stage 1 varies widely from one woman to the next. In a woman having her first infant, the average length is about 12 hours. In the late phase and in transition, the dilation occurs, on average, at the rate of 1.2 cm per hour (Stenchever, 1978).

The Second Stage of Labor. Stage 2 is the actual delivery, when the baby's head moves past the stretched cervix, into the birth canal, and finally out of the mother's body. Most women find this part of labor markedly less distressing than the transition phase because it is here that they can assist the delivery process by pushing. Stage 2 typically lasts from a half hour to two hours.

Most infants are delivered head first. A few babies are born feet first or bottom first (called *breech* presentations), and in these deliveries the birth attendant must often take a more active role, perhaps using medical instruments to aid the baby's descent. Often a physician must deliver the infant by cesarean section.

The Third Stage of Labor. Stage 3 is the delivery of the placenta (also called the *afterbirth*) and other material from the uterus. You can see all these stages of labor schematically in Figure 3.2.

The First Greeting: Parents and Newborns

The brief description I've just given does not begin to convey the emotional impact of the experience of childbirth for the mother, or for the father if he is present. For many women there is a time of intense joy as they greet the infant for the first time: laughter, exclamations of delight at the baby's features, first tentative and tender touching. Here's an excerpt from one mother's greeting (Macfarlane, 1977, pp. 64–65):

> She's big, isn't she? What do you reckon? (Doctor makes a comment). Oh look, she's got hair. It's a girl—you're supposed to be all little. Gosh. Oh, she's lovely. Oh, she's opened her eyes (laughs). Oh lovely (kisses baby).

Most parents are intensely interested in having the baby look at them right away. They are delighted if the baby opens her eyes, and they will try to stimulate her to do so if she doesn't. The parents' first tentative touches also seem to have a pattern to them: the parent first touches the infant rather gingerly with the tip of her or his finger and then proceeds gradually to stroking with the full hand (Klaus & Kennell, 1976; Macfarlane, 1977).

Several researchers have argued that real deviations from this acquaintanceship pattern may signal potential problems in the parents' future interactions with the infant. Ruth and Henry Kempe (1978), for example, noted that mothers and fathers who showed little pleasure on seeing the baby, who did not speak positively about or were actually critical of the child's

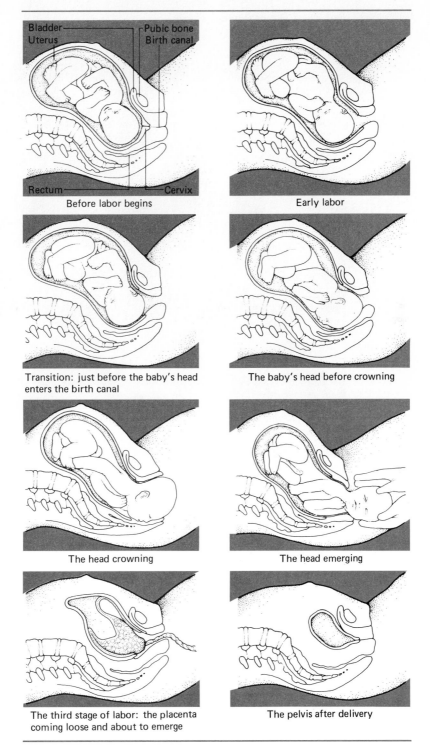

Figure 3.2 The sequence of steps during delivery is shown clearly in these drawings. You can see the dilation phase, transition, the delivery itself, and the delivery of the placenta.

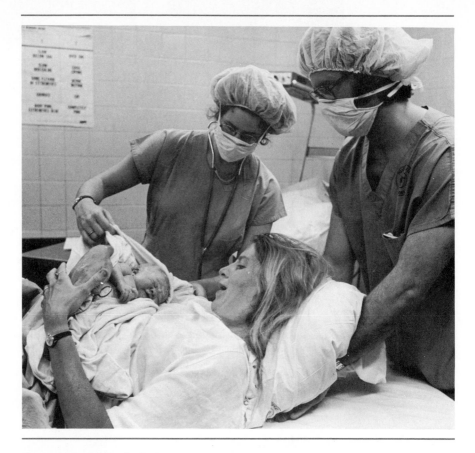

Figure 3.3   Hello, baby!

appearance, who turned away or did not smile at the infant, or who poked or pinched the newborn rather than stroking, were parents who later were more likely to be abusive or neglectful of the child. Thus these first encounters are intense—usually tender and full of amazement, but sometimes revealing of other emotions, too.

Conditions During Birth: Where, Who, and What

In the majority of all births (75 to 80 percent), the delivery occurs with few or no complications. The whole process is normal and satisfying to the mother, and the infant emerges from the process looking quite healthy. Still, there are many decisions about the delivery that can affect the child's health or the mother's satisfaction with the delivery. These decisions are made by a variety of people in the system—the parents, the birth attendant, the hospital staff, to name just a few. Since many of you will face these decisions at some point in the future, I want to give you the best current information I have.

Drugs During Delivery.   One key decision concerns the use of drugs during delivery. Three types of drugs are commonly used: (1) *analgesics* (such as Demerol), given during stage 1 of labor to reduce pain; (2) *sedatives* or *tranquilizers* (such as Nembutal, Valium, or Thorazine), given during stage 1 to reduce anxiety; and (3) *anesthesia,* given during transition or stage 2 of labor to block pain, either totally (general anesthesia) or in portions of the body (local anesthesia). Many women receive all three types of drugs; others may receive none or only one or two of them.

Despite a move toward "natural" (largely drug-free) childbirth among some groups of women, the use of drugs is still the norm rather than the exception. Brackbill (1979) estimated that in the late 1970s approximately 95 percent of deliveries involved some drug administration. A decade later, the percentage has probably declined, but some drug usage is still normative—for the simple and persuasive reason that drugs help to control the pain of childbirth.

Nonetheless, there are some unanswered questions, primarily about the potential effects of such drugs on the newborn. Because of the wide variability of drug combinations and dosages (and because women cannot be assigned randomly to drug or dosage groups), it has proved extremely difficult to design research that sorts out specific effects of specific drugs. The research is, in a word, messy. But a few facts or general trends have emerged.

First, nearly all drugs given to the mother during labor pass through the placenta and enter the fetal bloodstream. So the infant is obviously going to show some short-term effects. Infants whose mothers have received any type of drug are ordinarily found to be more sluggish, to suck less vigorously, to gain less weight in the days and weeks immediately after delivery, and to spend more time sleeping (Brackbill, 1979). Several observers have found differences in the infants, or in the infant-mother interaction, persisting a month or two after birth. Ann Murray and her colleagues (1981) found that mothers who had received anesthesia thought their 1-month-olds were harder to care for and less sociable than did mothers who had received no anesthesia. Another study found that the higher the level of medication at delivery, the less the mother smiled at her baby during feeding a month later (Hollenbeck et al., 1984).

Whether these effects persist past the first month we simply don't know. A few studies show persisting effects (Brackbill, 1979; Sepkoski, 1987); others do not. If there is a lasting effect, it is probably an indirect rather than a direct effect. That is, the mother who is given medication during delivery finds herself becoming acquainted with a less-responsive baby. Many mothers will adapt to these qualities in their babies, but a few mother-infant pairs, as a result of the greater difficulty of their early encounters, may develop long-term patterns of interaction that are less optimal. The infant's development may be affected as a result. Note that none of the effects is large. We are talking here about possible subtle, not major, differences.

What does all this mean for you as the individual mother? I think it means two things. First, the most cautious choice is to have as little medication as possible during delivery—consistent with your level of tolerance. Second, if you have received medication, particularly anesthesia, bear in mind that the child is also drugged and that this will affect her behavior in the beginning. If you *allow* for this effect, and realize that it will wear off, the chances seem to be very good that your relationship with your child will not be significantly altered.

The Location of Birth: Four Alternatives.   A second decision parents must make has to do with *where* the baby is to be born. These days, most parents have four choices: (1) a traditional hospital maternity unit; (2) a hospital-based birth center, which provides a more homelike setting where family members can be present during labor and delivery; (3) a freestanding birth center, where delivery is typically attended by a midwife rather than (or in addition to) a physician; and (4) home delivery.

At the turn of the century, only about 5 percent of babies in the United States were born in hospitals; now the figure is closer to 99 percent if you include birth centers as hospital deliveries (U.S. Bureau of the Census, 1985). In many European countries, however, home delivery is still a common alternative (e.g., Tew, 1985). In the United States, home deliveries have not increased in recent years, but birth-center deliveries seem to be increasingly popular. Freestanding birth centers in particular have multiplied rapidly in the past decades.

The arguments made for home or birth-center deliveries are primarily that they are more natural, that they treat pregnancy and delivery as a normal process (rather than as an illness), and that the birth is less likely to be traumatic if the mother is in a comfortable or familiar setting. The counterargument (particularly against home deliveries) is that they are less safe. If anything should go wrong, full hospital facilities may not be available quickly enough.

The importance of this consideration is underlined by the fact that, although only women at low risk for problems are admitted to freestanding birth centers, between 15 and 25 percent of women who begin labor in such a center are subsequently transferred to a hospital because of complications (Baruffi, 1982). Obviously a hospital birth center is an attempt at a middle ground in this controversy.

When you make your own decision about delivery, the questions of both safety and psychological comfort are likely to be of central concern to you. As a developmental psychologist, I also want to know whether the location or conditions of the delivery may have a direct or indirect impact

Figure 3.4   More homelike birth settings like this one, which might be in a freestanding birth center or in a birthing room in a hospital, are becoming increasingly common as mothers and birth attendants search for alternatives with both the safety of a hospital or clinical setting and some of the comforts and flexibility of a home delivery. The father is usually present at such deliveries, and so also may be friends, older children, and parents.

on the long-range development of the child. As in the case of drug effects, though, we have only preliminary answers.

The safety issue has been the center of the greatest controversy. Women who have not had good prenatal care or who are at high risk for complications are clearly less safe delivering at home than in a hospital. But women who show no signs of difficulties during pregnancy seem to be as safe delivering in nonhospital settings (including freestanding birth centers) (Baruffi, 1982). This is particularly clear in statistics from Great Britain and Holland, where nonhospital deliveries are more common (Tew, 1985).

Some people who advocate delivery at home or in freestanding birth centers insist that babies born in such settings are better off than those born in hospitals—not just physically but also psychologically. If the parents' birth experience is more positive, the argument goes, then their bond to the infant may be stronger and their initial and continuing interactions may be more positive.

This is a very difficult assertion to test, in part because women who choose to deliver at home or in a freestanding birth center are different in other ways from women who opt for the hospital. They may use fewer drugs during pregnancy, eat differently, or have different attitudes about delivery and motherhood. If we find later that non-hospital-delivered infants have different types of interactions with their parents or score higher on tests of development, we can't be sure that the cause was the delivery location and not one of these other differences. Still, it is a question worth pursuing. One fragment of evidence comes from Aiden Macfarlane, who reports that women who deliver at home are less likely to be depressed in the days after giving birth than women who deliver in a hospital (1977). But whether the depression that can follow hospital delivery is long-lasting, and whether it has any long-term effect on the mother's relationship with her infant, we do not know. Given all this ignorance, and barring any signs of trouble in the pregnancy, the decision about the location of the delivery seems to be very much a matter of personal choice. If there *are* any indicators of increased risk in pregnancy, however, hospital delivery is the safest alternative.

The Who of Delivery: The Presence of Fathers.

A third important decision has to do with who should be present at the delivery. In particular, how important is it that the father should be present?

Participation by fathers in the delivery room—as "coach" or merely as observer or emotional supporter of the mother—is clearly on the increase. In the United States as recently as 1972, only about one-fourth of hospitals permitted the father to be present in the delivery room, but by 1983 virtually all of them did (Allen, 1983).

Three arguments are given in favor of the father's presence: (1) he can provide psychological support for the mother; (2) through coaching or other assistance, he can help her control the pain she experiences; and (3) he will become more strongly attached to the infant by being present at the birth. There is at least some evidence in support of the first two of these arguments, but there are highly mixed findings regarding the third.

When fathers are present during labor and delivery, mothers report lower levels of pain and receive less medication (Henneborn & Cogan, 1975). And when the mother has a coach (the father or someone else), the incidence of problems in labor and delivery (such as cesarean births) goes down, as does the duration of labor (Sosa et al., 1980). Furthermore, at least one study shows that women are more likely to report that the birth was a "peak" experience if the father was present (Entwisle & Doering, 1981).

What we do not know is whether the father's relationship with his infant is affected positively if he is present at delivery, or if he has an opportunity for early contact with the infant. Assertions about such positive benefits were made quite widely by both psychologists and pediatricians in the 1970s (e.g., Macfarlane, 1977; Greenberg & Morris, 1974) and seem to have been accepted by many parents. (It is now very difficult, for example, to find fathers who are willing to be assigned randomly to a nonparticipation group in an experiment.) Those fathers whose birth experience has been particularly positive show signs of greater attachment to their infant throughout the first year (Peterson, Mehl, & Leiderman, 1979), but fathers as a group show no magical effect. Palkovitz (1985) reviewed all the evidence and concluded that the father's presence may enhance the marital relationship but is neither necessary nor sufficient for the father's emerging attachment to his infant.

All of this is not intended as an argument against fathers' participation, by the way. Fathers' own reported delight at being present at the birth of their children is reason enough. And the facts that the father's presence seems both to help the mother—she controls her pain, requires less medication, and has a shorter labor—and to enhance the husband-wife relationship seem to be compelling reasons for continuing the move toward greater participation.

Other Elements of the Conditions of Birth. There are other elements in the complex of decisions surrounding delivery, many of which parents are now negotiating with their birth attendants. Is the infant kept in a separate newborn nursery, or does the baby stay with the mother full time (this is called *rooming in*)? Are the birth conditions "gentle," following the suggestions of Frederick Leboyer, or are more traditional practices followed? (I have discussed the question of gentle births in the box on pages 86–87.) Each prospective parent needs to give these choices some careful thought.

Cesarean-Section Delivery

So far I have been discussing the process of normal vaginal delivery. In some cases, however, such as when the fetus is in a breech presentation, when the mother has an active case of genital herpes (see Chapter 2), or when fetal monitors show that the fetus is experiencing distress during delivery, the baby may be delivered through an abdominal incision rather than vaginally. This is called a **cesarean section** (C-section for short).

The frequency of C-sections has quadrupled since 1968. Today, at least 20 percent of all deliveries are by this method (U.S. Bureau of the Census, 1985). In some hospitals the rate is well above 30 or 35 percent. Obstetricians are in the midst of a major debate about causes and consequences of this remarkable increase in C-sections (Gleicher, 1984; de Regt et al., 1986). The argument often made is that new diagnostic techniques like fetal monitoring have made it possible to identify more infants who may be at risk; C-section delivery thus may save babies or lead to healthier

GENTLE BIRTHS: ARE THEY IMPORTANT?

Still another new direction in childbirth procedures has been suggested by a French obstetrician, Frederick Leboyer (1975). Leboyer is convinced that the process of birth is extremely traumatic and painful for the baby. He describes the experience as "hell and white-hot" because of the bright lights, noise, and rough handling. He argues that physicians need to try to reduce the stress as much as possible. Deliveries done using the **Leboyer method** are usually referred to as "gentle births"; they involve a number of changes from typical delivery procedures.

In a birth by the Leboyer method, no pressure is placed on the head during stage 2 of labor, while the head is being delivered. The room is darkened as much as possible, and the birth attendants speak quietly or in whispers. Sometimes soothing or quiet music is played. After the baby is delivered, she is placed on the mother's abdomen immediately. No effort is made to stimulate the infant's crying or breathing, except that the infant's mouth and nose are cleared if they are blocked. The umbilical cord is clamped only after the baby begins to breathe on her own and after the cord has stopped pulsing. A few minutes later, the baby is placed in a deep, warm bath, where she remains for five to six minutes. This recreates the sensations of the warm liquid she has been accustomed to in utero and soothes the infant still further.

Many physicians, while agreeing that births can and probably should be made more gentle, do not buy all of Leboyer's arguments and do not think that every change he suggests is essential. (For example, the environment in utero is actually very loud and noisy. So why the need for quiet during delivery?) For prospective parents, who are searching for the conditions of delivery that seem best, there are some important questions embedded in the debate.

First of all, is the baby really traumatized at birth? Opinions differ. Some psychoanalytically oriented theorists, such as Otto Rank (1929), have been convinced that birth is traumatic. Rank went so far as to suggest that "birth trauma" left an emotional scar that lasted throughout life. Other observers, including Macfarlane (1977), have been struck instead by how capable and adaptable the newborn is. The baby seems to adjust rapidly to the demands of the environment he finds himself thrust into. Obviously, this is a difficult question to study systematically, so opinions are about all we will have to go on.

babies. The counterargument, made recently by Kenneth Leveno and his colleagues (1986), is that fetal monitoring has led to many unnecessary C-sections, particularly in otherwise low-risk pregnancies. Some of the current findings may lead to a decrease in the rate of C-sections, but they will doubtless remain common (possibly in part because of the fear of malpractice suits; doctors are less and less willing to take any risk).

Problems at Birth

Soon after birth, most medical attendants give the baby a quick examination and rate the infant from 0 to 2 on each of the five "signs" that make up

A second important question is whether the gentle method is as safe for the infant as conventional delivery procedures. On the basis of limited experimental evidence, the answer seems to be "yes." For example, in one small study, Kliot and Silverstein (1984) found no differences on such measures as heart rate, temperature, and Apgar score between a group of 79 babies delivered with Leboyer methods and a comparison group of 12 infants delivered in the conventional way. Scores for both groups were within the normal range on all physiological measures. Many other obstetricians report that they have used aspects of the Leboyer method without detrimental effects (e.g., Grover, 1984).

The most interesting question from my perspective is whether there are any longer-lasting effects of such birth practices. Do "Leboyer children" turn out better in later months or years? Do they respond differently to their parents?

There has been remarkably little decent research aimed at answering this question. Several small studies show Leboyer-birth infants to be more relaxed and alert immediately after delivery, with their eyes open for more of the time (e.g., Oliver & Oliver, 1978). But I know of only one longer-term experiment in which subjects were assigned at random to Leboyer or conventional deliveries (Nelson et al., 1980; Saigal et al., 1981). These researchers found no differences between Leboyer-delivered babies and babies who experienced moderately gentle normal hospital deliveries on any measures up through eight months of life.

Despite this scarcity of evidence, I suspect that at least some of Leboyer's methods, such as placing the infant on the mother's stomach immediately or delaying the cutting of the cord, will become fairly widely accepted. Leboyer's arguments called attention to the *possible* impact of some accustomed practices, and many physicians and midwives have consequently taken another look at the conditions of birth. Then, too, many parents find these conditions soothing, and that is no small argument. Were I giving birth today, I would certainly search for a birth attendant who was sensitive to these questions. But since I am not convinced that the full Leboyer method is critical for the child or the parent, I would not search high and low for that rare birth attendant who follows the entire Leboyer procedure. You will have to make your own choice.

the **Apgar score** (named after Virginia Apgar, the prominent physician who developed the scoring system). The criteria used are listed in Table 3.1 (Apgar, 1953). The maximum score is 10, although this score is actually unusual; most infants are still somewhat blue in the fingers and toes in the first minutes after birth. Nonetheless, 85 to 90 percent of infants do score 9 or 10 on this scale five minutes after birth, meaning that they are getting off to a good start (National Center for Health Statistics, 1984). A baby can score low for any number of reasons, most commonly reduced oxygen supply or low birth weight.

Extremely low Apgar scores are associated with very high rates of infant death. But, like many of the prenatal problems I mentioned in the

Table 3.1
■■■■■■■■■

Evaluation Method for Apgar Scoring

Aspect of infant observed	Score assigned		
	0	1	2
Heart rate	Absent	<100/min.	>100/min.
Respiratory rate	Absent	Weak cry	Good strong cry
Muscle tone	Limp	Some flexion of extremities	Well flexed
Response to stimulation of feet	None	Some motion	Cry
Color	Blue; pale	Body pink, extremities blue	Completely pink

Source: After Robinson, 1978, Table 5-2, p. 102.

■■■■■■■■■

last chapter, Apgar scores in the range of 5 to 8 are associated with long-term risk primarily when the infant grows up in nonoptimal circumstances. Most children with low Apgar scores appear to develop normally when they live in stimulating and supportive environments (Breitmayer & Ramey, 1986). This is still further support for the Horowitz model (remember Figure 1.2).

Anoxia: Lack of Oxygen.   Reduced oxygen supply is called **anoxia.** Anoxia may occur during the period immediately surrounding birth, because the umbilical circulation fails to continue the supply of blood oxygen until the baby breathes or because the umbilical cord has been squeezed in some way during delivery. Perhaps as many as 20 percent of newborns experience some degree of anoxia.

Long-term consequences of anoxia are very difficult to check. *Prolonged* anoxia is often associated with such major consequences as cerebral palsy or mental retardation. But we simply do not know what more subtle effects (if any) there may be on brain structure or function from briefer periods of oxygen deprivation.

Low Birth Weight.   Another potentially serious complication is to have an infant born weighing less than the normal or optimum amount, a condition generally labeled **low birth weight.** The cutoff point for this designation is generally 2500 g (about 5.5 pounds). Those below 1500 g (about 3.3 pounds) are usually described as **very low birth weight.** The incidence of low birth weight has declined in the past decade, but it is still high: In 1983, nearly 7 percent of all newborns weighed less than 2500 g and 1.2 percent weighed less than 1500 g (U.S. Bureau of the Census, 1985).

All low-birth-weight infants used to be lumped into a single group, often called *premature* infants. It is now clear, though, that it is very important to distinguish between several groups or types of low-birth-weight infants. Some infants have low birth weights because they are born too soon; these are usually called **preterm** infants. (Any birth before 37 weeks' gestation is usually considered preterm.) A second important type of low-birth-weight infant is the **small-for-date** baby. These infants are unusually light, given the number of weeks of gestation they have completed. They may even have completed the full 38 weeks' gestation but weigh under 2500 g. Infants in this group appear to have suffered from some kind of significant problem prenatally—malnutrition or constriction of blood flow (from the mother's smoking, among other things)—while the preterm infant is merely born early and may be developing normally in other respects (Tanner, 1978).

Birth weight is one of the best predictors of infant mortality. Still, with recent enormous improvements in medical knowledge and technology, some astonishingly small infants now occasionally survive. As many as 50 percent of infants as small as 500 to 1000 g at birth (1 to 2 pounds) now survive in some hospitals, and perhaps 80 percent of low-birth-weight infants over 1000 g survive. (You can get some sense of what these very tiny babies look like from Figure 3.5.)

All low-birth-weight infants share some characteristics, including markedly lower levels of responsiveness at birth and in the early months of life (DiVitto & Goldberg, 1979; Barnard, Bee, & Hammond, 1984a). They are also all at higher risk of experiencing respiratory distress in the early weeks, and they may be slower in motor development than their normal-weight peers.

When we look at really long-term consequences of low birth weight, however, distinctions between the several subvarieties of low-birth-weight infants become important. Preterm infants above 1500 g who are normal-sized for their length of gestation generally catch up to their normal peers within the first few years of life, particularly if they are reared in stimulating and supportive families. But both very low-birth-weight and small-for-date infants show much higher rates of long-term problems, including lower IQs, smaller size, and more problems in school (Kopp, 1983; Hittelman, Parekh, & Glass, 1987). In one large longitudinal study of very low-birth-weight infants, for example, Jane Hunt (1981) found that 46 percent showed some form of learning disability when they started school.

Let me emphasize two points about what we know now concerning the consequences of low birth weight. The bad news is that some of the negative outcomes are simply not apparent until past infancy or at school age. A child may appear to be okay at age 1 or 2 but may show problems at 3; she may seem to have caught up by 4 but may still show some kind of learning disability later. Hunt, for example, found that as the children progressed further in school (confronting more and more complex tasks), the percentage who showed some kind of problem increased. The good

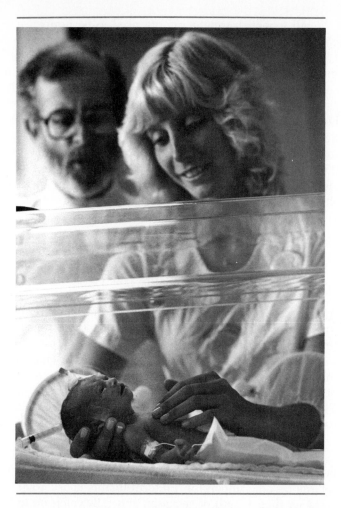

Figure 3.5   Very low-birth-weight babies, like this one, are not only quite amazingly small; they are also skinny and wrinkly because they lack most of the layer of fat under the skin that you see in a full-term newborn. Many infants this small do survive.

news is that even among very low-birth-weight infants, many show no long-term disability at all, and low-birth-weight infants born recently show lower rates of problems than those born a generation ago. Regrettably (and perhaps surprisingly), we are not yet able to predict which children will do well. We do know that low-birth-weight children who are reared in middle-class or more highly stimulating families do better than those reared in poorer environments (e.g., Pederson et al., 1987). We also know that very low-birth-weight infants and those who are sicker at birth (requiring more help with breathing, for example, or suffering brain hemorrhage) have poorer outcomes. But even among these children there are some who develop normally. We simply do not know all the risk factors yet.

One other piece of good news is that we do now know something about treatments that seem to improve the long-term chances of good functioning for low-birth-weight infants. Several kinds of special rhythmic stimulation, including rocking beds, heartbeat sounds, and body massage, given regularly to preterm infants while they are still in the hospital, seem to improve alertness, weight gain, and even later IQ (e.g., Barnard & Bee, 1983; Scafidi et al., 1986).

WHAT CAN THE NEWBORN DO?

The baby has been born. He cries, breathes, looks around a bit. But what else can he do in the early hours and days? On what skills does the infant build?

Reflexes

Infants are born with a large collection of **reflexes,** which are automatic physical responses triggered involuntarily by specific stimuli. Many of these reflexes are still present in adults, so you should be familiar with them—the knee jerk the doctor tests for, your automatic eye blink when a puff of air hits your eye, or the involuntary narrowing of the pupil of your eye when you're in a bright light.

In addition to these persisting reflexes, the newborn has a special set of low-level or rudimentary reflexes, some of which are useful for his survival. I've listed some of the more helpful and interesting reflexes in Table 3.2, and you can see pictures of one of these in Figure 3.6.

Clearly, the rooting, sucking, and swallowing reflexes are essential if the baby is to get fed, and the Moro reflex could help the baby move away from unpleasant things. The Babinsky and grasp reflexes, though, are less useful. These two reflexes are governed by the medulla—the part of the brain that develops earliest. Both of these drop out at about 6 months or so, when the more complex parts of the brain begin to dominate. If present *past* this age, however, such a rudimentary reflex may be a sign of some neurological difficulty. Tests for these reflexes are thus often used in older infants, children, or adults as part of diagnostic neurological examinations.

Perceptual Skills: What the Infant Sees, Hears, and Feels

I've summarized what we know about the abilities of the newborn in Table 3.3. When I look at the summary, several points stand out.

First of all, newborns are remarkably good at many perceptual skills—contrary to the beliefs of most parents and many psychologists until a few

Table 3.2

Major Reflexes in the Newborn Baby

Reflex	Description
Rooting	An infant touched on the cheek will turn toward the touch and search for something to suck on.
Sucking	When the infant gets her mouth around something suckable, she sucks.
Swallowing	This reflex is present at birth, though it is not well coordinated with breathing initially.
Moro	This is also called the *startle reflex*. You see it in an infant when she hears a loud noise or gets any kind of physical shock. She throws both arms outward and arches her back (see Figure 3.6).
Babinsky	If you stroke an infant on the bottom of his foot, he first splays out his toes and then curls them in.
Grasp	A baby will curl his fingers around your hand or any graspable object. The signal for this is a touch on the palm.
Stepping	If you hold a very young infant up so that her feet just touch the ground, she will show movements similar to walking, stepping her feet alternately.

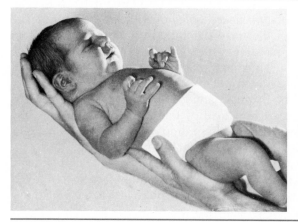 

Figure 3.6   These two photos show the Moro reflex very well. In the left-hand photo the baby is fairly relaxed, but when the adult suddenly drops the baby (and catches him again), the baby throws his arms out in the first part of the Moro reflex. This baby will later close his fingers, too. This reflex may be left over from our ape ancestry: when its mother lets go briefly, a young monkey grabs hold of a bunch of fur and thus clings. Although this reflex has little usefulness for human babies, it can be seen for the first six months or so.

Table 3.3

Perceptual Skills of the Newborn

Sense	What the baby can do
Sight	Focuses both eyes on the same point; the best focus point is about 8 inches away (Haynes, White, & Held, 1965). Follows a moving object with the eyes; this skill is not well developed at birth but improves rapidly (Kremenitzer et al., 1979). Discriminates some colors; this can clearly be done by 2 weeks (Chase, 1937, a classic study) and *may* be possible earlier (Bronstein & Teller, 1982).
Sound	Responds to various sounds, particularly those in the pitch and loudness range of the human voice. Discriminates between slightly different linguistic sounds, like *pah* and *bah* (Morse & Cowan, 1982). Locates the source of a sound (Clifton et al., 1981). If already crying or fussing, may respond to rhythmic sounds like heartbeats by being soothed (Salk, 1960). Discriminates the mother's voice from other voices on the first day or within a few days of birth.
Smell	Reacts strongly to some smells, such as ammonia or anise (licorice). Discriminates the smell of the mother from that of a strange woman, beginning in the first week of life (Cernoch & Porter, 1985).
Taste	Discriminates between salty and sweet tastes and prefers sweet tastes. Discriminates between sour and bitter (Jensen, 1932, another classic study).
Touch	Responds to touches over most of the body, especially on the hands and in the mouth.

years ago. The senses of hearing and smell seem to be particularly well developed at birth.

Even more striking is how well adapted the baby's perceptual skills are for the interactions he will have with the people in his world. He hears best in the range of the human voice; he can discriminate his mother (or another regular caregiver) from others on the basis of smell or sound very early (visual discrimination comes later); he can focus his eyes best at a distance of about 8 inches, which is just about the distance between the infant's eyes and the mother's face during nursing.

Newborns are also soothed by sounds and movements that are easily made by mothers and fathers, especially those that are something like the sounds or movements the baby experienced prenatally. For example, Lee Salk first reported in 1960 that babies were soothed by the sound of a heartbeat, perhaps because it was like the sound or the rhythm heard in the womb. More recently, Rosner and Doherty (1979) have reported that recordings of intrauterine sounds (including heartbeat but also sounds of digestion) were soothing to crying newborns. (Note, though, that these sounds have to be quite *loud* to have such a soothing effect, presumably because the heartbeat and other intrauterine sounds were loud for the fetus.) Rocking motions also appear to be soothing, again perhaps because they are like the movements the baby experienced before birth when the mother walked.

Mothers and other caregivers have certainly known about these soothing actions for centuries. Rhythmic sounds and movements—lullabies and rocking, for example—are often used to soothe babies who are distressed. Heartbeat sounds or uterinelike sounds may be equally effective for that purpose.

Motor Skills: Moving Around

In contrast, the motor skills of the newborn are not very impressive. A newborn infant can't hold up her head; she can't coordinate her looking and her reaching yet; she can't roll over or sit up. The newborn baby does *move* a lot, but we don't know whether these movements of the arms and legs and head are attempts by the baby to explore the world around her or whether they are more like reflexes—automatic movements in response to sounds or sights or other stimulation.

During the early weeks, there are fairly rapid improvements in motor ability. By 1 month, for example, the baby can hold her chin up off the floor or mattress (Figure 3.7). By 2 months, she is beginning to swipe at

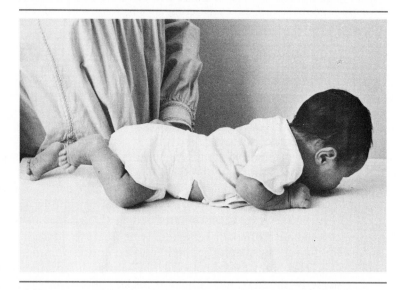

Figure 3.7 Newborn infants have very poor motor control. Their heads must be supported when they are held; they cannot even raise their heads off a mattress. This baby, who is about 1 month old, has just developed enough muscular strength to lift his head a little bit.

objects near her with her hands. Still, compared to perceptual abilities, the baby's motor abilities are primitive and develop only slowly during the first years of life.

Learning and Habituation

Both the perceptual abilities and the child's motor skills seem to be heavily influenced by maturation. At birth, seeing and hearing have matured, while the neurological structures and muscles required for moving have not. But what about learning? How early can the baby learn from her environment? For the theorist, these are important questions because they touch on the general issue of maturation versus learning. For the parent, they are equally important. The baby begins to learn such things as the sound of the mother's voice before birth (DeCasper & Spence, 1986), and then learns very rapidly after birth. Given this capacity, it makes sense to talk to and try to stimulate the baby—to give her things to learn from and learn about.

Classical Conditioning. Researchers are still arguing about whether newborn infants can be classically conditioned (e.g., Sameroff & Cavanaugh, 1979). My own conclusion from this research is that the newborn can be classically conditioned but that it is very hard to do. By 3 or 4 weeks of age, though, classical conditioning is quite easy to demonstrate in an infant. This means that the conditioned emotional responses I talked about in Chapter 1 may begin to develop as early as the first weeks of life.

Operant Conditioning. There is no disagreement about whether newborns can learn through operant conditioning. They can and do. In particular, the sucking response and head turning have both been successfully increased by the use of reinforcements such as sweet-tasting liquids (Sameroff & Cavanaugh, 1979) or the sound of the mother's voice or heartbeat (DeCasper & Sigafoos, 1983).

The fact that conditioning of this kind can take place means that whatever neurological "wiring" is needed for learning to occur is present at birth.

Schematic Learning. The fact that babies can recognize voices and heartbeats in the first days of life is evidence that another kind of learning is going on as well, sometimes referred to as *schematic learning*. The concept of a *schema* emerged from Piaget's theory. The baby is organizing her experiences into expectancies, into "known" combinations. These schemas or expectancies are built up over many exposures to particular experiences and thereafter help the baby to distinguish between the familiar and the unfamiliar. Carolyn Rovee-Collier (1986) has recently suggested that we might think of classical conditioning in infants in much the same way. When a baby begins to move her head as if to search for the nipple when she hears her mother's footsteps coming into the room, this is not just some kind of automatic classical conditioning, but the beginning of the development of expectancies. From the earliest weeks, the baby seems to begin to "map" links between events in her world—between the sound of her mother's footsteps and the feeling of being picked up, between the touch of the breast and the feeling of a full stomach. Thus early classical conditioning may be the beginning of the process of cognitive development.

Habituation.   A related concept is that of **habituation.** Habituation is the automatic reduction in the strength or vigor of an unreinforced response to a repeated stimulus. An example would probably help: Suppose you live on a fairly noisy street. The sound of cars going by is repeated over and over during each day. But after a while, you not only don't react to the sound, you quite literally *do not perceive it as being as loud.* The ability to do this—to dampen down the intensity of a physical response to some repeated stimulus—is obviously vital in our everyday lives. If we reacted constantly to every sight and sound and smell that came along, we'd spend all our time responding to these repeated events and we would not have energy or attention left over for things that are new and deserve attention.

The ability to *dishabituate* is equally important. When there is some change in a habituated stimulus—say there's an extra-loud screech of tires on the busy street by your house—you again respond fully. Thus the reemergence of the original response strength is a sign that the perceiver—infant or child or adult—notices some significant change.

It turns out that the capacity to both habituate and dishabituate is present in the newborn (Lipsitt, 1982). She will stop looking at something you keep putting in front of her face; she will stop showing a startle reaction (Moro reflex) to loud sounds after the first few presentations but will again show a startle response if the sound is changed. Habituation itself is not a voluntary process; it is entirely automatic. But in order for it to work, the newborn must be equipped with the capacity to "recognize" familiar experiences. That is, she must develop schemas of some kind.

The existence of these processes in the newborn has an added benefit for researchers: it has enabled them to figure out just which things an infant responds to as if they were "the same" and which things are responded to as "different." If a baby is habituated on some stimulus, such as a sound or a particular picture, the experimenter can then present slight variations of the original stimulus to see the point at which dishabituation occurs. In this way, researchers have begun to map the normal pattern of schemas of the newborn or very young infant.

Social Skills

All the skills of the newborn I have described so far are important for the baby's comfort and survival. But human newborns, unlike those in many other species, are a very long way from being independent. If they are to survive, someone must provide consistent care over an extended period. So the infant's capacity to entice others into the caregiving role is critical. It is here that the "social" skills of infants come into play.

When you think about a newborn baby, you probably don't think of him as particularly social. He doesn't talk. He doesn't flirt. He smiles, but not often during the first weeks and not in response to social stimuli. Normal newborns nonetheless have a collection of behaviors that are remarkably effective for attracting and keeping the attention (and attachment) of adults. What's more, as I have just pointed out in talking about the baby's perceptual skills, the social interaction process is very much a two-way street: adult faces and voices are remarkably effective for attracting and keeping the

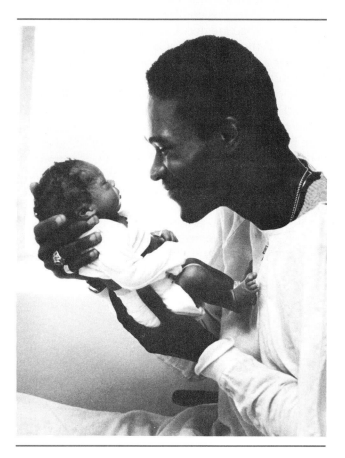

Figure 3.8　Newborn babies are very skilled at attracting and keeping the attention of adults (this Dad seems clearly captured!)—a useful trait, since they need to be cared for continuously. A baby can meet your gaze after the first few weeks and can smile, "take turns" during feeding, snuggle, be consoled, and cry.

baby's attention, too. There is even some intriguing (although controversial) evidence that newborn babies actually may be able to imitate the facial expressions or gestures of adults—particularly expressions that involve movement of some kind, such as sticking out the tongue and opening and closing the mouth (Meltzoff & Moore, 1983; Vinter, 1986). It would seem from all this that the adult and the baby are programmed from the beginning to join in a crucial social "dance," one which forms the root of the developing relationship between parent and child and which is critical for the formation of the parent's attachment to the child.

The baby's repertoire of social behaviors is quite limited, but these few behaviors appear to be very effective in eliciting care. He cries when he needs something, which ordinarily brings someone to him to provide care. And then he responds to that care by being soothed, which is very reinforcing to the caregivers. He adjusts his body to yours when you pick him up; after the first few weeks, he gets quite good at meeting your eyes in a mutual gaze and at smiling—both of which are very powerful "hooks" for the adult's continued attention.

One other thing the baby does from the beginning, which seems to be critical for any social interaction, is to take turns. As adults, we take turns in a range of situations, including conversations and eye contacts. In fact, it's very difficult to have any kind of social encounter with someone who does *not* take turns. Kenneth Kaye (1982) argues that the beginnings of this "turn taking" can be seen in very young infants in their eating patterns. As early as the first days of life, the baby sucks in a "burst-pause" pattern. He sucks for a while, pauses, sucks for a while, pauses, and so on. Mothers enter into this "conversation" too, often by jiggling the baby during the pauses. The eventual conversation looks like this: suck, pause, jiggle, pause, suck, pause, jiggle, pause. The rhythm of the interaction is really very much like a conversation and seems to underlie many of the social encounters among people of all ages. The fascinating thing is that this rhythm, this turn taking, can be seen in an infant one day old.

THE DAILY LIFE OF INFANTS

What an infant can see and hear, what she can do, are probably more interesting to psychologists than to parents. To the parent, the key question is really what the baby does with her time. How is the infant's day organized? What sorts of natural rhythms occur in the daily cycles? What can you expect from the baby as you struggle to adapt to and care for this new person in your life?

Researchers such as Heinz Prechtl and his colleagues (e.g., Prechtl & Beintema, 1964), who have studied newborns, have described five differ- ent **states of consciousness**—states of sleep and wakefulness in infants, which I've summarized in Table 3.4. You can see that the baby spends more time sleeping than doing anything else; and of the time awake, only about two to three hours is "quiet awake" or unfussy, active awake.

Table 3.4

The Basic States of Infant Sleep and Wakefulness

State	Characteristics	Average no. of hours spent in state	
		At birth	At 1 month
Deep sleep	Eyes closed, regular breathing, no movement except occasional startles.	16–18 hr	14–16 hr
Active sleep	Eyes closed, irregular breathing, small twitches, no gross body movement.		
Quiet awake	Eyes open, no major body movement, regular breathing.	6–8 hr	8–10 hr
Active awake	Eyes open, with movements of the head, limbs, and trunk; irregular breathing.		
Crying and fussing	Eyes may be partly or entirely closed; vigorous diffuse movement, with crying or fussing sounds.		

Sources: Based on the work of Prechtl & Beintema, 1964; Hutt, Lenard, & Prechtl, 1969; Parmelee, Wenner, & Schulz, 1964.

The five main states tend to occur in cycles, just as your own states occur in a daily rhythm. In the newborn, the basic period in the cycle is about one and a half or two hours. Most infants move through the states from deep sleep to lighter sleep to fussing and hunger and then to alert wakefulness, after which they become drowsy and drop back into deep sleep. This sequence repeats itself about every two hours. Before very long, though, the infant can string two or three of these periods together without coming to full wakefulness, at which point we say that the baby can "sleep through the night." One of the implications of this rhythm, by the way, is that the best time for really good social encounters with a young infant is likely to be just after she is fed, when she is most likely to be in a quiet awake state.

Let me take a somewhat more detailed look at the major states.

Sleeping

Sleeping may seem like a fairly uninteresting part of the infant's day. Parents obviously find the child's sleep periods helpful, particularly as they develop into a pattern with a long nighttime sleep. But there are two other aspects of an infant's sleep that are intriguing to psychologists.

First, irregularity in a child's sleep patterns may be a symptom of some disorder or problem. For example, babies born to drug-addicted mothers seem unable to establish a pattern of sleeping and waking. Brain-damaged infants have the same kinds of difficulties in many cases, so any time an infant fails to develop clear sleep/waking regularity, it *may* be a sign of trouble.

The other interesting thing about sleep in newborns is that they show the external signs that signify dreaming in older children or adults: a fluttering of the eyeballs under the closed lids, called **rapid eye movement (REM)** sleep. Interestingly, newborn infants show a bigger percentage of REM sleep than do adults (Roffwarg, Muzio, & Dement, 1966). Whether this means that the newborn is actually dreaming in the way an adult dreams, I haven't the faintest idea. But some sort of very busy activity seems to be going on during the baby's sleep time.

Crying

For many parents, the infant's crying may be mainly a disturbing or irritating element, especially if it continues for long periods and the infant is not easily consoled. But crying can serve important functions for the child, for the physician or psychologist, and for the parent-child pair.

Newborns actually cry less of the time than you might think. Anneliese Korner and her colleagues (1981) monitored all the crying and noncrying activity of a group of normal newborns in the first three days of life and found that they cried only 2 to 11 percent of the time.

To be sure, there are quite wide individual differences in crying patterns. In particular, about 15 to 20 percent of infants develop a pattern called *colic,* which is a pattern of daily, intense crying (three or more hours a day) that appears at about 2 weeks of age and then disappears spontaneously at 3 or 4 months of age. The crying is generally worst in late afternoon or early evening (a particularly inopportune time, of course, since it is usually when the parents are tired and need time with one another, too). Physicians do *not* know the cause of colic. It is a difficult pattern to live with, but it *does* go away.

Normal physical development seems to require at least some crying. Crying helps to improve lung capacity (since the baby gulps in more air between cries) and helps to organize the workings of the heart and respiratory system. The actual sound quality of the baby's cry may also turn out to be a useful diagnostic sign for the physician or psychologist. A number of very intriguing recent studies have shown that babies with some kinds of physical problems—small-for-date babies, preterm infants, babies who experienced complications at delivery—have more piercing, grating, unpleasant cries than do physically normal infants (Zeskind & Lester, 1978, 1981; Friedman, Zahn-Waxler, & Radke-Yarrow, 1982). So it isn't necessarily the parents' imagination that some babies' cries are especially hard to take. Eventually, it may be possible for physicians to use the presence of such a grating or piercing cry as a signal that there may be some underlying physical problem with the infant.

The most important function of the baby's cry, though, is as a signal of distress. For caregivers, it is absolutely vital to know when the child is in need in some way, and most babies are very good at passing on this information in the form of a cry.

Most parents quite naturally respond quickly to these signals, feeding the baby, changing diapers, holding and cuddling the infant. But there is a dilemma, too, for many parents. If you pick up your baby immediately every time she cries, will you be reinforcing crying? Or is such quick responding essential if the child is to learn, in some way, that her needs will be met? (See Figure 3.9.)

There has been a long, wordy, and inconclusive theoretical and empirical dispute about this question in the child development literature (e.g., Ainsworth, Bell, & Stayton, 1972; Gewirtz and Boyd, 1977; Hubbard & van Izendoorn, 1987). Five years ago, both theorists and researchers seemed to agree that infants who are picked up or cared for quickly when they cry, cry *less* than do infants whose caregivers delay in responding. Now even this conclusion is in some dispute. It does seem clear that responding quickly to those intense infant cries that signal real distress or pain leads to less crying overall. But immediately responding to milder crying, or whimpering—the sort of crying a baby may do when she is put down for a nap, for example—seems to be less critical in affecting crying. In children

Figure 3.9   What to do?

BREAST-FEEDING VERSUS BOTTLE-FEEDING

Many people get pretty heated over the question of breast-feeding versus bottle-feeding. Advocates of breast-feeding argue that it is the only "natural" way to feed a baby. Those who prefer bottle-feeding may be just as passionate in defense of their choice. Statistically, breast-feeding is the option of choice for the majority of women. In developing countries, 90 percent or more do so, and in the United States and in Western Europe over 50 percent do so for at least a few months—a number that has been rising in recent years (U.S. Bureau of the Census, 1985). For the mother, the decision has important practical ramifications. For me, as usual, the key questions concern the potential effects of the type of feeding on the baby and on the interaction of the infant and the mother. Some of the answers to these questions may help you make your own decision when the time comes.

Effects on the Baby

There are several potent arguments in favor of breast-feeding. First and foremost, breast milk seems to provide important protection for the infant against many kinds of diseases. The baby receives antibodies from the mother—antibodies that he can't produce himself but that help to protect him against infections and allergies. For example, breast-fed infants have fewer respiratory and gastrointestinal infections than do bottle-fed babies (Marano, 1979).

Second, breast milk is easier for the baby to digest than cow's milk or formula based on cow's milk. In particular, the fat in breast milk is almost entirely absorbed by the baby, while only about 80 percent of the fat in formula is absorbed. This is particularly relevant for low-birth-weight infants, who have difficulty digesting fats. The high-cholesterol fats in breast milk may also have a long-lasting benefit. Isabelle Valadian (cited in Marano, 1979) has found that adults who were exclusively breast-fed for at least two months have lower cholesterol levels than those who were given formula.

Third, there *may* be a slightly higher risk of obesity or overweight in bottle-fed babies (Taitz, 1975). The most likely explanation of any such connection is that the breast-fed infant has more control over the

over 18 months or 2 years, in fact, rapid response to any crying may even be linked to higher rates of crying—an example of a reinforcement effect. All in all, parents who are *sensitive* to and responsive to their child's signals have children who cry less than do parents who are less sensitive or responsive. Furthermore, the more responsive parent doubtless also helps to foster a sense of trust in the infant, an outcome of greater significance than is rate of crying.

Eating

Eating is not a "state," but it is certainly something that newborn babies do frequently! Given the approximately two-hour state-change cycle, babies may eat as many as 10 times a day. By 1 month, though, the average number is about five and a half feedings, which drops to about five per

amount that he eats. When he is no longer hungry, he stops sucking. The mother doesn't really know how much milk he's taken, but she watches for the cues he gives her that he's had enough. The mother of the bottle-fed baby, on the other hand, may feel that the baby should take all the milk in the bottle and keep urging him to continue even though he's giving signals that he's no longer hungry. So bottle-fed babies—at least in some mother-infant pairs—may be more often overfed.

Mother-Infant Interaction

While the physical effects on the infant argue in favor of breast-feeding, no such advantage seems to be found when we look at patterns of mother-infant interaction. Bottle-fed babies are held and cuddled in the same ways as are breast-fed babies, and mothers who bottle-feed appear to be just as sensitive and responsive to their babies as mothers who breast-feed. Tiffany Field (1977), for example, looked at the kind of "turn taking" that Kenneth Kaye describes

(and that I discussed in the section on social skills in infants). Field found that both breast-feeders and bottle-feeders entered into the dialogue equally well.

Advice?

The dietary evidence argues for breast-feeding if it is at all possible and if the mother remains in good health and continues to eat a good diet. Many pediatricians are now urging this choice on their patients. But for some mothers this option is not possible. They may need to be away from their infant for long stretches each day, may be in poor health, or may want to share the feeding with the infant's father to encourage his participation in the child's care. If any of these reasons is true in your own case, you should know that your infant can receive his basic dietary requirements from formula and that your relationship with your infant will not be adversely affected. When circumstances or philosophy permit, however, breast-feeding seems to be the best option for the child's short-term, and perhaps long-term, health.

day by 4 months (Barnard & Eyres, 1979). From the parents' perspective, one of the critical decisions about feeding is whether to breast-feed or bottle-feed. I have summarized the arguments on both sides in the box above.

INDIVIDUAL DIFFERENCES AMONG BABIES

Most of my emphasis in the past few pages has been on the ways in which infants are alike. Barring some kind of physical damage, all babies have similar sensory equipment at birth and can experience the same kinds of happenings around them. But babies differ, too, in important ways. One of the key ways is in those aspects of behavior and responsiveness psychologists call *temperament.*

Temperament

Babies range from placid to vigorous in their response to any kind of stimulation. They also differ in their rates of activity, in their emotional dispositions (irritable or sunny), in their preference for social interactions or solitude, in the regularity of their daily rhythms, and in many other ways. I'll be talking about temperament at greater length in Chapter 9, but at this point it is important to introduce some concepts and terminology.

Psychologists who have been interested in these differences have proposed several different ways of describing the key dimensions of temperament. Buss and Plomin, for example, argue that there are only three dimensions: emotionality, activity, and sociability, or EAS (1986). Thomas and Chess (1977) describe nine dimensions, which they organize into three types: the easy child, the difficult child, and the slow-to-warm-up child.

It is not yet clear just how this theoretical debate is going to turn out. What is clear is that the Thomas and Chess formulation, particularly their description of the difficult child, has been most influential. So for now let me use their designations and describe the three basic types for you.

The Easy Child. Easy children approach new events positively. They try new foods without much fuss, for example. They are also regular in biological functioning, with good sleeping and eating cycles; they are usually happy; and they adjust easily to change.

The Difficult Child. By contrast, the difficult child is less regular in body functioning and is slow to develop regular sleeping and eating cycles. These children react vigorously and negatively to new things, are more irritable, and cry more. Their cries also have a more "spoiled," grating sound than do the cries of easy babies (Boukydis & Burgess, 1982). Thomas and Chess point out, however, that once the difficult baby has adapted to something new, he is often quite happy about it, even though the adaptation process itself is traumatic.

The Slow-to-Warm-Up Child. Children in this group are not as negative in responding to new things or new people as is the difficult child. They show instead a kind of passive resistance. Instead of spitting out new food violently and crying, the slow-to-warm-up child may let the food drool out and may resist mildly any attempt to feed her more of the same. These infants show few intense reactions, either positive or negative, although once they have adapted to something new, their attitude is usually fairly positive.

Although Thomas and Chess found that only 65 percent of the children they studied could be clearly classified into one of these three types, such temperamental differences can often be seen in very young infants (as

Table 3.5

Consistency of Temperament Over Time: Correlations Between Scores on a Measure of Easiness/Difficultness on the Same Children at Different Ages

Ages	Correlation
1 and 2	.42[a]
2 and 3	.37[a]
3 and 4	.29[a]
4 and 5	.44[a]
1 and 5	.05
1 and early adulthood	.17
3 and early adulthood	.31[a]
4 and early adulthood	.37[a]
5 and early adulthood	.15

[a] Correlation is larger than could occur by chance more than 5 times in 100 such samples (in statistical terms, p = <.05).
Source: After Thomas & Chess, 1986, Table 4.3, p. 45.

any parent of two or more children can tell you). Furthermore, the patterns are at least somewhat persistent throughout childhood. In particular, difficult infants tend to be still rated as somewhat difficult two to three years later, and difficult 3- or 4-year-olds are somewhat more likely to show signs of a difficult temperament in adulthood (Thomas & Chess, 1986). Some of the specific research findings are listed in Table 3.5; you can see that the correlations are not large, but they are consistently positive and beyond chance in most instances.

I am not arguing here (nor are Thomas and Chess or other psychologists who study temperament) that these individual differences are absolutely fixed at birth. Like the genotype, inborn temperament is affected—shaped, strengthened, bent, or counteracted—by the child's relationships and experiences. But you should be aware that not all babies respond in the same ways to the world around them.

Sex and Social Class Differences in Infants

I need to look at least briefly at two other kinds of individual differences among infants—sex differences and differences associated with social class.

The very first thing we ask about a new baby is its sex, as if gender were the single most important thing: "Is it a boy or a girl?" Given that preoccupation with gender, it may surprise you to know that there are remarkably few sex differences among young infants. As was true at birth, girls continue to be a bit ahead in some aspects of physical maturity, and boys continue to be more vulnerable. For example, more boys die during the first year of life. Male infants also have more muscle tissue than do girls, and they seem to be slightly more physically active (Eaton & Enns, 1986). But boys and girls do not seem to differ on the temperamental dimensions Thomas and Chess have described: boys are not more often "difficult" in temperament and girls are not more often "easy," even though that is what our stereotypes might lead us to expect.

When we compare infants born to middle-class and poor families, we again find fewer differences than you might expect. It is true that children of poor mothers are more likely to be of low birth weight and to have more problems at birth—that's one of the problems I mentioned in Chapter 2. But if we look just at healthy babies, there are no differences between poor and middle-class babies in perceptual skills, motor development, or learning.

THE EFFECTS OF THE INFANT ON THE PARENTS

Before leaving this discussion of birth and infancy, I think it is important to come back to a point I made in Chapter 1—namely, that what happens in the child's development is an interactive, or a transactional, process. The child influences the environment, particularly the parents, in highly significant ways. We can already see that influence clearly in the first weeks of life. Let me give you three examples.

The Infant's Influence on the Marriage Relationship. Any new parent can tell you that the mere arrival of the first child—never mind the infant's individual qualities—has a powerful effect on the nature and quality of the parents' relationship with one another. Sociologists have known for years that marital satisfaction typically goes down in the first months and years after the first child is born (e.g., Rollins & Feldman, 1970). For most couples, it is the sense of lost time with one another, as well as a sense of ignorance and strain about caring for the child, that is the core of the change (e.g., Belsky, Spanier, & Rovine, 1983). When the infant's temperament is difficult, the strain on the parents' relationship to one another is even greater (Sirignano & Lachman, 1985).

The Effect of Infant Temperament. The infant's temperament also has at least some effect on the way the parents treat the child. For example, Michael Rutter (1978a) finds that temperamentally difficult children are more often criticized by their parents, presumably because the child's behavior *is* more troublesome.

Even this effect of the child, however, is by no means inevitable. A skilled parent (especially the parent who correctly perceives the child's "difficultness" as a temperamental quality and not as something caused by the parent's ineptness or by some willfulness of the child) can avoid some of the pitfalls and can handle the difficult child more adeptly. But as Susan Crockenberg's work shows (1986), in order to achieve such an optimum result, the parent of a difficult child needs more support from the spouse, more optimum circumstances. Thus a temperamentally difficult child strains the entire family system. Family systems with fewer resources will be less able to respond adaptively.

The Impact of a Low-Birth-Weight Infant. Low-birth-weight infants also strain the family system (as do other infants with abnormalities or illness). Such babies are remarkably hard to "read"; they do not enter well into the "dance" of interaction. As a result, parents have to struggle to maintain their emotional involvement with the child. Several observers (including my colleagues and I) have noted that in the first months after the baby has come home from the hospital, mothers of low-birth-weight infants interact *more* with their babies than do mothers of full-term infants, as if they were trying extra hard to stimulate and relate to the babies. But if you check again 10 or 12 months later, you find that the mothers of the low-birth-weight infants show lower levels of interaction with their babies, as if the infant's unresponsiveness was so unreinforcing that the mother had backed away, at least a little (e.g., Barnard, Bee, & Hammond, 1984).

The variations in mother-infant interactions that result from these differences in infant characteristics are not huge, and they do not occur in precisely the same way in every mother-infant (or father-infant) pair. Nor are the "interactional trajectories" established in the first months of life necessarily permanent. Both parent and child change, as does their interaction. But the infant's qualities do matter, do enter into the complex equation of the entire family system.

SUMMARY

1. The normal process of labor and birth has three parts: dilation, delivery, and placental delivery.
2. The first "acquaintance" process after delivery may be an especially important one for parents. Most parents show an intense interest in the baby's features, especially the eyes.
3. Most drugs given to the mother during delivery pass through to the infant's bloodstream. They have short-term effects on infant responsiveness and on feeding patterns. They may have some long-term effects as well.
4. The location of the delivery (hospital versus birth center) *may* make some difference, but we know little yet about the effects of location on the baby or on the parent-infant bond.

5. The presence of the father during delivery appears to help reduce the mother's discomfort, but it is not clear whether his presence also enhances the father's attachment to the infant.

6. Perhaps one-fifth of all deliveries in the United States today are by abdominal incision (cesarean section) because of indications of fetal distress or other specific problems.

7. Several types of problems may occur at birth, including reduced oxygen supply (anoxia) to the infant and low birth weight.

8. Low-birth-weight infants have higher risk of death during the first year of life, but if they survive, many catch up developmentally to full-sized peers by school age. Those with birth weights below 1500 g or who are very small for date are more likely to show lasting problems.

9. The newborn has far more skills than most physicians and psychologists had thought, including excellent reflexes, good perceptual skills, and effective social skills.

10. The important infant reflexes include feeding reflexes, such as rooting and sucking, and the Moro reflex.

11. Perceptual skills include focusing both eyes; tracking slowly moving objects; some color vision; discrimination of sounds and sound direction; and responsiveness to smells, tastes, and touch.

12. Motor skills, in contrast to perceptual skills, are only rudimentary at birth.

13. Social skills, while rudimentary, are sufficient to bring people close for care and to keep them close for social interactions. The baby can meet a gaze and smile within the first month of life.

14. Newborns can learn from the first days of life, most easily by operant conditioning but possibly also through classical conditioning.

15. Newborns also habituate to repeated stimulation.

16. Young infants spend most of the day sleeping and are in an awake and alert state only a fraction of the time. Rhythms and daily cycles of sleeping, waking, crying, and eating are established early.

17. Babies differ from one another on several dimensions, including vigor of response, general activity level, restlessness, and irritability. These temperamental dimensions, which Thomas and Chess have grouped into "difficult," "easy," and "slow-to-warm-up" types, appear to be at least somewhat stable.

18. Male and female babies differ at birth on a few dimensions. Girls are more mature physically. Boys are more active, have more muscle tissue, and are more vulnerable to stress. No sex differences are found, however, on temperamental dimensions.

19. No consistent differences between middle-class and poor infants are found on the usual measures of infant development.

20. From the beginning, the infant is part of a transactional system, influencing the parents as well as being influenced. For example, marital satisfaction typically declines after the birth of the child; the child's

temperament affects the parents' responses to the child; and low-birth-weight infants call forth different patterns of parental interaction.

▬▬▬▬▬ ## KEY TERMS

anoxia A shortage of oxygen. Prolonged anoxia can result in brain damage. This is one of the potential risks at birth.

Apgar score An assessment of a newborn's condition. Scores of 0, 1, or 2 are summed for five criteria at one and five minutes after birth.

cesarean section Delivery of the child through an incision in the mother's abdomen.

dilation The first stage of childbirth, when the cervix opens sufficiently to allow the infant's head to pass into the birth canal.

effacement The flattening of the cervix, which, along with dilation, allows the delivery of the infant.

habituation An automatic decrease in the intensity of a response to a repeated stimulus, which enables the child or adult to ignore the familiar and focus attention on the novel.

Leboyer method A "gentle" birth method proposed by Frederick Leboyer, which includes dimmed lights and quiet, slow-paced birth.

low birth weight The phrase now used (in place of the word *premature*) to describe infants whose weight is below the optimum range at birth. Includes infants born too early (preterm, or short-gestation, infants) and those who are small-for-date.

preterm infant Descriptive phrase now widely used to label infants born before 37 weeks' gestational age.

rapid eye movement (REM) One of the characteristics of sleep during dreaming. REM occurs during the sleep of newborns, too.

reflexes Automatic body reactions to specific stimulation, such as the knee jerk or the Moro reflex. Many reflexes remain in the adult, but the newborn also has some additional low-level or rudimentary reflexes that disappear as the cortex develops fully.

small-for-date infant An infant who weighs less than is normal for the number of weeks of gestation completed.

states of consciousness Five main sleep/wake states have been identified in infants, from deep sleep to active awake states.

very low-birth-weight infants Infants who weigh 1500 g ($3\frac{1}{3}$ pounds) or less at birth.

▬▬▬▬▬ ## SUGGESTED READING

Brackbill, Y., Rice, J., & Young, D. (1984). *Birth trap: The legal low-down on high-tech obstetrics.* St. Louis: Mosby.

A strong book written for parents facing all the decisions about childbirth I have discussed in this chapter. Brackbill is a psychologist and refers often to the available research.

Brazelton, T. B. (1983). *Infants and mothers: Differences in development* (rev. ed.). New York: Delta/Seymour Lawrence.

An update of an excellent book, written by a remarkably observant and sensitive physician. It describes the first year of life in some detail and also chronicles the progress of several infants who differ in basic temperament.

Leach, P. (1983). *Babyhood* (2nd ed., rev.). New York: Knopf.

A detailed look at the first two years of life, written for a lay audience but based very thoroughly on research. Very readable and practical.

McCall, R. (1979). *Infants: The new knowledge.* Cambridge, MA: Harvard University Press. Not new, but an excellent description of the abilities and characteristics of infants, written in an easy style. McCall describes a fair amount of research but does so in a manner that is readily understood by nonscientists.

Pines, M. (1982, February). Baby, you're incredible. *Psychology Today*, pp. 48–52.

A lively description of some of the skills of newborns, written by one of the best science writers around.

Restak, R. M. (1982, January). Newborn knowledge. *Science 82*, pp. 58–65.

Another good brief description of some of the skills of newborns. Very nice pictures, too.

PROJECT: OBSERVATION IN A NEWBORN NURSERY

Despite the changes in birth practices, most hospitals still have newborn nurseries, and you can go and look through the window at the infants. However, you *must* obtain permission before you do so; newborn nurseries are complex, busy places, and they cannot tolerate additional people crowding around the window. If your instructor has assigned this project to the whole class, he or she will need to schedule times with the hospital administration and the nursing staff in the newborn nursery. If you are going on your own, you should check with the hospital office first to determine whether they have any standard procedure for obtaining permission to observe. If they do, then follow their procedure. If they have no procedure, you must at the least contact the head nurse in the obstetrics and newborn section of the hospital.

Once you have obtained the required permission and arranged a time that will be least disruptive of the hospital schedule, I would like you to observe the infants (through the window) for approximately half an hour. Proceed in the following way:

	Baby's state				
30-second intervals	**Deep sleep**	**Active sleep**	**Quiet awake**	**Active awake**	**Crying, fussing**
1					
2					
3					

1. Set up a score sheet that looks something like the one shown above, continuing the list for sixty 30-second intervals.
2. Reread the material in Table 3.4 until you know the main features of the five states of infant sleep and wakefulness as well as possible. You will need to focus on the eyes (open versus closed and rapid eye movement), the regularity of the baby's breathing, and the amount of body movement.
3. Select one infant in the nursery and observe that infant's state every 30 seconds for half an hour. For each interval, note on your score sheet the state that best describes the infant over the preceding 30 seconds. Do *not* select an infant to observe who is in deep sleep at the beginning. Pick an infant who seems to be in an in-between state (active sleep or quiet awake), so that you can see some variation over the half-hour observation.
4. If you can arrange it, you might do this observation with a partner, each of you scoring the same infant's state independently. When the half hour is over, compare notes. How often did you agree on the infant's state? What might have been producing the disagreements?

5. When you discuss or write about the project, consider at least the following issues: Did the infant appear to have cycles of states? What were they? What effect, if any, do you think the nursery environment might have had on the baby's state? If you worked with a partner, how much agreement or disagreement did you have? Why?

You may find yourself approached by family members of babies in the nursery, asking what you are doing and why you have a clipboard and a stopwatch. Be sure to reassure the relatives that your presence does not in any way suggest that there is anything wrong with any of the babies—you are doing a school project on observation. You may even want to show them the text describing the various states of consciousness.

MULTIMEDIA LEARNING CENTRE
DEESIDE COLLEGE

PART THREE

THE PHYSICAL CHILD

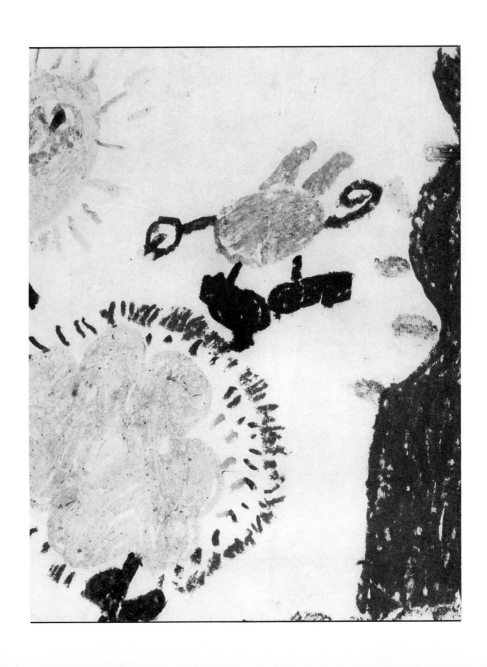

4 Physical Development

Four Reasons for Studying Physical Development
    The Child's Growth Makes New Behaviors Possible
    The Child's Growth Determines Experience
    The Child's Growth Affects Others' Responses
    The Child's Growth Affects Self-concept
Basic Sequences and Common Patterns
    Height and Weight
    Shape
    Bones
    Muscles
    Fat
    The Nervous System
    Hormones
Development of Sexual Maturity
    Sexual Development in Girls
    Sexual Development in Boys
    Other Changes in Puberty
Using the Body: The Effects of Physical Changes on Behavior
    Motor Development in the Early Years
Motor Development and Toys
    Adolescent Sexuality
Health and Illness in Childhood and Adolescence
Eating Disorders: Obesity, Bulimia, and Anorexia
Big or Fast Versus Slow or Small: Some Individual Differences in Physical
    Development
    Differences in Rate
    Sex Differences in Physical Growth
    Social Class and Racial Differences
Determinants of Growth: Explanations of Physical Development
    Maturation
    Heredity
    Environmental Effects
The Shape of Physical Development: A Last Look
Summary
Key Terms
Suggested Reading
Project: Plotting Your Own Growth

Some years ago, when my daughter was about 8½, a lot of well-rehearsed family routines seemed to unravel. She was crankier than usual, both more assertive and more needful of affection, and alternately compliant and defiant. What on earth was happening? Had I done something dreadfully wrong? Was there something going on at school? I mentioned my problems to several colleagues and began to hear tales from other parents about the special difficulties they had had with their daughters between ages 8 and 9.

Nothing in any of the developmental research or theory I had ever read suggested this ought to be a particularly stressful time. But I began, slowly, to put some faith in my observations and to search for an explanation. Having been trained with a heavy emphasis on environmental influences on development, I always look there first. But that didn't offer me much in the way of answers. The 8- or 9-year-old has been in school for at least two or three years, and no major new adaptation is being demanded. It was only when, belatedly, I began to think about physical changes that an explanation occurred to me: Girls of 8 or 9 are actually beginning **puberty** (the changes of adolescence). The first hormone changes begin at about this age, and many of the inconsistent and uncomfortable behaviors I was seeing could easily be a response to the changing hormones in the system.

It may amuse you to think of the clever psychologist being stumped by something so obvious. But in fact, developmental psychologists have often placed too little emphasis on physical growth. We describe it briefly and then take it for granted. But I am convinced, both by the research literature on the effects of physiological change and by my observations as a parent, that an understanding of physical development is an absolutely critical first step in understanding children's progress, for at least four reasons.

FOUR REASONS FOR STUDYING PHYSICAL DEVELOPMENT

The Child's Growth Makes New Behaviors Possible

Specific physical changes are needed before the infant can crawl or walk; others are needed for an older child's growing skill at running, kicking a ball, or jumping rope; and at adolescence, the development of full reproductive capacity is based on a complex sequence of physical changes.

The flip side of this is that the *lack* of a particular physical development may set limits on the behaviors a child is capable of performing. An infant of 10 months cannot be toilet trained, no matter how hard parents may try, because the anal sphincter muscle is not yet fully mature. Toddlers cannot easily pick up raisins or Cheerios from their high chair trays until the muscles and nerves required for thumb-forefinger opposition have developed.

It seems to me that such limits deserve far more attention than they normally receive—by parents, teachers, and others. Think, for example, about children who participate in Pee Wee League football or Little League baseball. I have several times watched coaches reduce their young charges to tears by demanding levels of coordination and skill that 5- and 6-year-olds (or 10- and 11-year-olds) can only rarely (if ever) achieve.

The Child's Growth Determines Experience

A child's range of physical capacities or skills can also have a major indirect effect on cognitive and social development by influencing the variety of experiences she can have. For example, an infant who cannot crawl can explore only the things that are brought to her or are within easy reach. When she begins to crawl, her experiences are greatly expanded. Similarly, a child who learns to ride a bike widens her horizons still further as she explores her neighborhood on her own, perhaps for the first time.

The Child's Growth Affects Others' Responses

These changes in the child's skills affect both his experiences and the way the people around the child respond to him. For example, parents react quite differently to an infant who can crawl than to one who cannot. They begin to say "no" more often, put things out of reach, or put the baby in a playpen more of the time. Such restrictiveness, particularly if it continues into the second year of life, may have long-term consequences for the child's intellectual development. In one longitudinal study I have been involved with, for example, we found that those children who had been most restricted at age 2 had lower IQ scores at age 4 and 8 than did those who had been less restricted (Barnard, Bee, & Hammond, 1984).

Adults' expectations are also affected by children's size and shape, attractiveness, and physical skills. Children who are pretty or tall or well coordinated are treated differently from those who are homely or petite or clumsy (Brackbill & Nevill, 1981; Lerner, 1985). A Little League baseball coach may be more supportive of a child with advanced large-muscle coordination (good for home runs), while a classroom teacher may be especially appreciative of children with superior small-muscle coordination (used for writing and drawing). As a general rule, the larger or more developed a child, the more "adult" his behavior is expected to be.

Both adults and children are also biased in favor of some specific body types. In the terminology introduced by Sheldon some years ago (1940), the most favored type is the **mesomorphic** (well-muscled and square in build). Both **endomorphic** (rounded) and **ectomorphic** (thin, tall, bony) body types are less preferred by both children and adults (Lerner, 1985, 1987). Thus individual differences in physical patterns or speed of growth can have profound effects on children's early experiences.

Figure 4.1   As soon as babies are able to scoot or crawl, they begin to explore much more widely—which inevitably takes them into some potentially dangerous places, like this one. Parents deal with the child's newfound skill in lots of different ways. Some child-proof the house as much as possible; others restrict the child, perhaps by putting her in a playpen. Some restriction seems to be okay, but research shows that overrestrictiveness can affect the child's intellectual development. Thus a fairly simple change like the child's new ability to crawl can have long-range repercussions.

The Child's Growth Affects Self-concept

The final reason for us to pay close attention to physical development is that physical skills (or lack of them) can have a profound effect on a child's self-concept (which I'll be talking about much more fully in Chapters 9 and 10). A personal example may help emphasize this point. As a child, I was unusually tall for my age. I was nearly 5 feet 6 inches tall at age 12, and when I finally stopped growing I was just under 6 feet. There are some distinct advantages to being that tall: I can see over people at movies;

Figure 4.2 These children are the same age, but you'd never guess it by looking at them. Most adults will automatically assign the larger child more complex tasks, will expect more of her, and may even talk in a more adult way to this child.

I can reach the tops of cupboards and bookcases. But at age 12, the advantages weren't so obvious. I felt gawky and conspicuous and socially inept, all of which became parts of my self-concept (35 years later I describe this as my "moose" feeling). Now I wouldn't trade an inch, but my self-concept, and my behavior as a consequence, were greatly affected for many years by experiences resulting from my physical growth in the early years.

For all these reasons, I think it is important to begin our exploration of development with a fairly detailed look at physical growth and change.

BASIC SEQUENCES AND COMMON PATTERNS

Height and Weight

The most obvious thing about children's physical development is that they get bigger as they get older. But even this simple statement may conceal some surprises. The biggest surprise for most people is the fact that at birth an infant is nearly one-third of his final height; by age 2 he is about half as tall as he will be as an adult. Another surprise is the fact that growth from birth to maturity is neither continuous nor smooth. You can

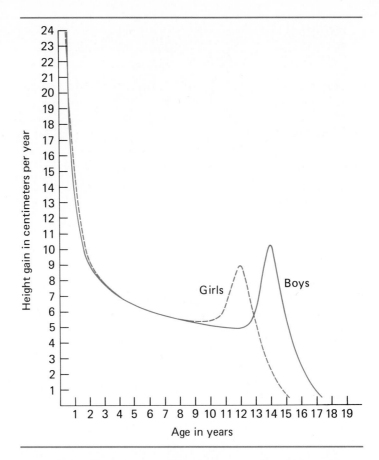

Figure 4.3 These curves show the gain in height for each year from birth through adolescence. You can see the very rapid growth in infancy, the slower growth in the preschool and elementary-school years, the growth spurt at adolescence, and the cessation of growth at adulthood. (*Source:* Tanner, 1978, p. 14. From Tanner, Whitehouser, & Takaishi [1966]. *Archives of diseases in childhood,* Fig. 8, p. 466. London: British Medical Association House.)

see in Figure 4.3, which shows the growth patterns for height for boys and girls, that there are four different parts or phases.

The first phase lasts for about the first two years. During this time, you can see from the figure that the baby gains in height very rapidly, adding 10 to 12 inches in length in the first year. The baby gains weight at an equally rapid rate. An infant will normally double his birth weight by 5 months and triple it in the first year. After this rapid growth during the first two years, the second phase begins, when the child settles down to a slower but steady addition of 2 to 3 inches and about 6 pounds per year until adolescence.

The third phase begins with the dramatic adolescent "growth spurt" (shown clearly in Figure 4.3), when the child may add 3 to 6 inches per year for several years. After the growth spurt, in the fourth phase, the teenager again adds height and weight slowly until her or his final adult size is achieved.

Shape

At the same time, the shape and proportions of the child's body are changing. In an adult, the head is about one-eighth or one-tenth of the total height. But the toddler isn't built like that at all. In the 2-year-old, the head is about one-fourth of the total body length.

Individual body parts do not all grow at the same rate, either. This is particularly striking at adolescence. A teenager's hands and feet grow to full adult size earliest, followed by the arms and legs; the trunk is usually the slowest part to grow. We often think of an adolescent as "awkward" or uncoordinated. That turns out to be an inaccurate description. I think what people see as awkwardness in teenagers is just the asymmetry of the different body parts. The adolescent's body looks "leggy" and has proportionately large hands and feet. (My daughter, at age 12, had feet as large as mine, even though she was nearly a foot shorter.)

Children's hands and faces also change from infancy through adolescence. The size and shape of a child's jaw change when the permanent teeth come in (during the elementary-school years mostly) and again in adolescence, when both jaws grow forward and the forehead becomes more prominent. This often gives teenagers' (especially boys') faces an angular, bony appearance quite unlike their earlier look—as you can see in the set of photographs of one boy in Figure 4.4.

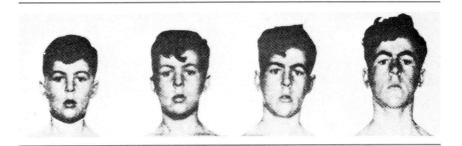

Figure 4.4 In these photos of the same boy before, during, and after puberty, you can see the striking changes in the jaws and forehead shape that dramatically alter appearance in many teenage boys. The same changes occur in girls but are not as dramatic. (*Source:* Tanner, 1962, Plate 1, p. 17.)

Bones

The observable changes in size and shape are the result of changes on the inside in bones, muscles, and fat. Bones change in three ways with development: They increase in number, become longer, and grow harder.

Number of Bones. Bones increase in number in the hand, wrist, ankle, and foot. For example, in an adult's wrist there are nine separate bones. In the 1-year-old, there are only three. The remaining six develop over the period of childhood, with complete growth by adolescence.

In one part of the body, though, the bones fuse rather than differentiate. The skull in the infant is made up of several bones separated by spaces called **fontanels.** Fontanels allow the head to be compressed without injury during the birth process, and they also give the brain room to grow. In most children, the fontanels are filled in by bone by about age 2, creating a single connected skull bone (although the originally separate parts of the skull retain distinctive names).

Hardening of Bones. All of the infant's bones are softer and have a higher water content than adults' bones. The process of bone hardening, called **ossification,** proceeds steadily from birth through puberty. Bones in different parts of the body harden in a particular sequence; the bones of the hand and wrist harden before those in the feet, for example.

You may well be thinking, "Why do I have to know about bone hardening?" But think about the fact that infants' bones are soft and that they have fewer bones in some parts of the body. This makes babies very flexible—an important characteristic if they're going to fit into the cramped space of the uterus. It also makes them quite floppy, which is one of the reasons babies cannot walk or even sit up right away. As the bones stiffen, the baby becomes able to manipulate his body more surely, which increases the range of exploration he can enjoy.

Increased Size of Bones. While the composition of the bones changes and their number increases, their shapes are also changing. This is particularly noticeable in the long bones of the leg and arm, which get steadily longer throughout the years of childhood. Growth of these bones stops only when the ends of the bones (called *epiphyses*) finally harden completely in the middle or late teens.

Muscles

Although the bones are not all formed at birth, the newborn baby has virtually all the muscle fibers she will ever have (Tanner, 1978). But like the infant's bones, these early muscle fibers are small and watery. As the child grows, the muscle fibers get longer, thicker, less watery. Like bones and height, muscle tissue develops at a fairly steady rate until adolescence;

then there is a kind of growth spurt in muscles as well. One of the clear results of this rapid increase in muscle tissue is that adolescents become quite a lot stronger in just a few years. Both boys and girls gain muscle mass and strength, but as you can see in Figure 4.5, the gain is much greater in boys. In men, about 40 percent of the body mass is muscle, while in women, only about 24 percent is muscle.

Some of you may be asking yourselves at this point whether this is an inevitable physiological difference. Could it be that the greater level of physical exercise typical of teenage boys (from sports and simply more body movement) contributes to their greater growth of muscle tissue, and hence greater strength? Is part of the strength difference due to lack of

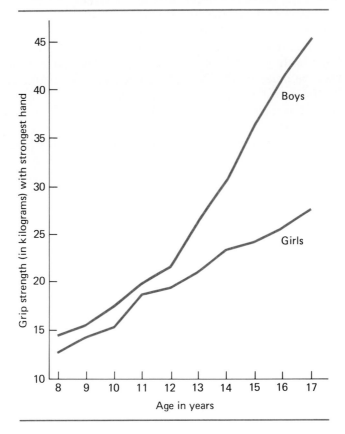

Figure 4.5 Both boys and girls gain strength over the years of childhood and adolescence, but boys gain much more, particularly at puberty. Some of this might be caused by greater exercise by boys at this age, but a good portion of this difference seems to be due to the impact of increases in male hormone at adolescence in boys. (*Source:* Adapted from Montpetit, Montoye, & Laeding, 1967, Tables 1 and 2, p. 233.)

muscular fitness in girls? Until comparisons of equally fit teenagers are made, we won't know for sure. But the sheer amount of muscle tissue appears to be a real physiological sex difference, generated by differing amounts and patterns of hormones in the blood. Even extremely fit teenage girls or adult women appear to have less muscle tissue than equally fit males.

Fat

Another major component of the body is fat, most of which is stored immediately under the skin. This *subcutaneous fat* (sometimes called "baby fat") is first laid down beginning at about 34 weeks' gestation. There is an early peak at about 9 months after birth; the thickness of this layer of fat declines until about age 6 or 7, then rises until adolescence.

Again, though, there is a very large sex difference in these patterns. From birth, girls have slightly more fat tissue than boys do, and this difference becomes gradually more marked during childhood. At adolescence the difference becomes particularly striking. In girls, about 20 to 24 percent of body weight is made up of fat at the beginning of puberty, and this *rises* to perhaps 28 percent at age 17; in boys, in contrast, only about 17 to 20 percent of body weight is made up of fat at the beginning of puberty, and this *declines* to perhaps 10 to 12 percent at age 17 (Chumlea, 1982; Forbes, 1972). At this age, girls have more fat cells and the cells are larger than are boys'.

Of course, as with muscle tissue, this sex difference in fat may be partially a life-style or activity-level effect; girls and women who are extremely athletic (long-distance runners, ballet dancers, and the like) typically have much lower body fat levels (perhaps as low as the average boy). But very fit boys have still *lower* fat levels.

The Nervous System

Growth in height and weight involve changes you can see. Even the changes in muscles, bones, and fat can be detected in the child's longer legs, greater strength, or softness or leanness of body. But there are two enormously important types of developmental changes in the body that are not so easy to perceive. The first of these is change in the nervous system.

Brain Development. At birth, the two most fully developed parts of the brain are the **medulla** (or hindbrain) and the **midbrain.** The medulla, in the lower part of the skull, regulates such basic things as suckling, breathing, heart rate, body temperature, and muscle tone. The midbrain governs attention and habituation, sleeping, waking, and elimination—all things the newborn does well.

The least-developed part of the brain at birth is the **cortex,** which is the convoluted gray matter that is involved in perception, body movement, and all complex thinking and language. As I mentioned in Chapter 2, most of the neurons (nerve cells) in the brain are present at birth, but the neurons of the cortex are not well connected. Over the first two years of life, the number and density of dendrites and nerve synapses increase rapidly, along with the size of individual neurons and the total weight of the brain. Between birth and adulthood, brain weight increases from about 350 to about 1350 g, and the great majority of that growth occurs in the first two to three years of life (Nowakowski, 1987).

Dendritic branching and synapse formation continue fairly rapidly in the first months after birth, and may continue at a slower rate until adolescence. Recent research by anatomists, however, suggests a curious reversal of this growth process at about age 2. At that point there appears to be a *pruning* of the synapses, as if redundant or unneeded links have to be eliminated before maximum efficiency can be achieved (Goldman-Rakic, 1987; Huttenlocher et al., 1982). There may be another pruning of synapses in adolescence.

Myelinization. Another important process is the development of sheaths that insulate nerve fibers from one another and make it easier for them to conduct impulses. The nerve sheath is made of a material called **myelin;** the process of developing the sheath is called **myelinization.** At birth, the spinal cord is not fully myelinized, which is one of the reasons for the slower development of muscular control over the lower trunk and legs. Myelinization of the nerves leading to and from the brain proceeds rapidly during the early months and is almost complete by the time the child is 2. In the brain itself, however, both myelinization and growth of connective tissues continue up to adolescence.

To understand the importance of myelin, it may help you to know that *multiple sclerosis* is a disease in which the myelin begins to break down. The individual with this disease gradually loses motor control; the specific symptoms depend on which portions of the nervous system are affected by the disease.

Hormones

A second less-visible set of changes we need to look at is in *hormones*— secretions of the various **endocrine glands** in the body. Hormones govern growth and physical changes in several ways, which I've summarized in Table 4.1.

Of all the endocrine glands, the most critical is the **pituitary,** since it provides the triggers for release of hormones from other glands. For example, the thyroid gland secretes thyroxin only when it has received a signal to do so in the form of a specific thyroid-stimulating hormone secreted by the pituitary.

The role hormones play in physical development is perhaps most striking at adolescence, but it is significant at earlier stages as well.

Table 4.1
▬▬▬▬▬

Major Hormones Involved in Physical Growth and Development

Gland	Hormone(s) secreted	Aspects of growth influenced
Thyroid	Thyroxin	Affects normal brain development and overall rate of growth.
Adrenal	Adrenal androgen	Involved in some changes at puberty, particularly the development of secondary sex characteristics in girls.
Testes (in boys)	Testosterone	Crucial in the formation of male genitals prenatally; also triggers the sequence of changes in primary and secondary sex characteristics at puberty in the male.
Ovaries (in girls)	Estradiol	Affects development of the menstrual cycle and breasts in girls, but has less to do with other secondary sex characteristics than testosterone does in boys.
Pituitary	Growth hormone	Affects rate of physical maturation.
	Activating hormones	Signals other glands to secrete hormones.

Prenatal Hormones. Thyroid hormone (thyroxin), which appears to be involved in stimulating normal brain development, is secreted by the fetus from about the fourth month of gestation. The pituitary also begins to produce growth hormone very early, beginning as early as 10 weeks after conception. Presumably this helps to stimulate the very rapid growth of cells and organs of the body. And as I mentioned in Chapter 2, the testes of the developing male produce testosterone, which influences the development of both male genitals and some aspects of the brain.

Hormones Between Birth and Adolescence. The rate of growth between birth and adolescence is governed largely by the thyroid hormone and by the pituitary growth hormone. Thyroid hormone is secreted in greater quantities for the first two years of life, then falls to a lower level and remains steady until adolescence (Tanner, 1978). This pattern of high early hormone production followed by slower and steadier production levels obviously matches the pattern of change in height and weight that I already described.

Secretions from the testes and ovaries, as well as adrenal androgen, remain at extremely low levels until about age 7 or 8. Then adrenal androgen begins to be secreted—the first signal of the changes of adolescence, and no doubt one of the sources of the changes I observed in my 8-year-old daughter (Shonkoff, 1984).

Hormones in Adolescence. The early rise in adrenal androgen is only the first step in a complex sequence of hormone changes at adolescence. To help you sort it out (and to help *me* sort it out), I've put together a chart showing the hormones involved and their effects (Figure 4.6).

The key is again the pituitary. At some point in late childhood (the age varies a lot from one child to the next), the pituitary gland (at a signal from another gland, the *hypothalamus*) begins secreting increased levels of **gonadotropic hormones** (two in males, three in females). These in turn stimulate the development of the testes and ovaries, which begin then to secrete more hormones (testosterone in boys, a form of **estrogen** called *estradiol* in girls). Over the course of puberty, testosterone levels increase 18-fold in boys and estradiol levels increase 8-fold in girls (Nottelmann et al., 1987). At the same time, the pituitary also secretes three

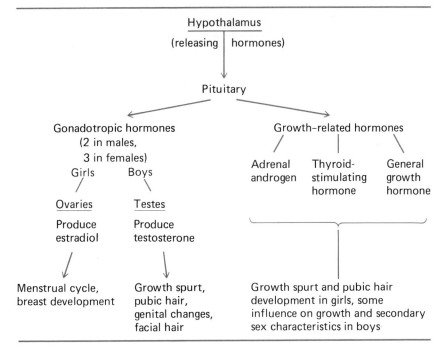

Figure 4.6 The action of the various hormones at puberty is exceedingly complex. This figure oversimplifies the process but gives you some sense of the sequence and the differences between the patterns for boys and girls.

other hormones that affect growth and that interact with the specific sex hormones.

As you can see in Figure 4.6, hormone interactions differ in boys and girls. In particular, the growth spurt and pubic hair development in girls are less influenced by estrogen and more influenced by adrenal androgen. Curiously, adrenal androgen is chemically very similar to testosterone, so it takes a "male" hormone to produce the growth spurt in girls. Adrenal androgen is less significant in boys, presumably because they already have male hormone in the form of testosterone floating about in their bloodstreams.

It is somewhat misleading, by the way, to talk about "male" and "female" hormones. In fact, both males and females have at least some of each (estrogen or estradiol, and testosterone or adrenal androgen); the difference is essentially in the relative proportions of the two. These proportions differ among individuals of the same gender as well. Some males produce relatively more testosterone or less estrogen, while others may produce more balanced amounts. Similarly, some girls may have a pattern of hormones that includes relatively more adrenal androgen while others may have relatively little.

Just how this hormonal process is turned off (or toned down) at the end of puberty is much less clear (Dreyer, 1982). But in some fashion the levels of both growth hormones and gonadotropic hormones produced in the pituitary drop, and the rate of body change gradually tapers off.

DEVELOPMENT OF SEXUAL MATURITY

The visible results of the hormonal changes that take place during puberty are not only a spurt in height but, more important, a set of physical changes that bring about full sexual maturity. These changes are normally divided into two groups: the primary and secondary sex characteristics. **Primary sex characteristics** are those necessary for reproduction, such as the testes and penis in the male and the ovaries, uterus, and vagina in the female. **Secondary sex characteristics** are those that are not necessary for reproduction, including breast development, body and facial hair, and lowered voice pitch.

Each of these physical developments follows a specific sequence. The progress of an individual teenager can then be described as a point along that sequence. Following the work of J. M. Tanner (1978), these sequences are customarily divided into five stages; stage 1 always represents the preadolescent stage, stage 2 the first signs of pubertal change, stages 3 and 4 the next steps, and stage 5 the final adult characteristic. (To give you a more concrete sense of these stages, Table 4.2 describes the steps in pubic hair development.) These stages have proven to be extremely helpful not only in describing normal progress through puberty but also in identifying the rate of development of individual youngsters.

Table 4.2

The Five Stages of Pubic Hair Development

Stage 1	There is no pubic hair at this first stage. (In all of Tanner's series of five stages, stage 1 represents the *pre*pubertal level.)
Stage 2	A few pubic hairs appear. They are usually long and slightly pigmented, either straight or slightly curly. This first growth is normally at the base of the penis or along the labia.
Stage 3	Pubic hair in stage 3 is not only denser but darker, coarser, and more curled. It is also spread over a larger area.
Stage 4	The pubic hair now resembles that of an adult in quality but covers a smaller area. There is no spread to the thighs, nor is the full triangle completed.
Stage 5	Adult pattern of pubic hair, in both distribution and quality.

Source: After Petersen & Taylor, 1980.

Sexual Development in Girls

In girls, the sequence of observable changes often begins with the growth spurt, accompanied by the first changes in breasts. The first menstruation (called **menarche** and pronounced "*men*-ar-kee") is fairly late in the sequence, typically two years after the first visible pubertal changes. You can see this sequence clearly in Figure 4.7.

Menarche is a clear single event that is often taken as a measure of sexual maturity. In fact, however, although some girls do conceive shortly after menarche, most girls do not produce any ova during the first several menstrual cycles. Then, for a while, only some cycles are fertile, until full fertility is achieved about a year after menarche. For most girls in the United States and Western Europe, the average age of menarche is between $12\frac{1}{2}$ and 13; and 95 percent of all girls experience this event between the ages of 11 and 15 (Garn, 1980; Tanner, 1978).

Sexual Development in Boys

In boys, there are major changes in reproductive organs beginning at about age 11 to 12. The testes and scrotum enlarge first, and the penis begins to enlarge a little later. Unlike the girls' pattern, in boys the height spurt comes somewhat later in the sequence, peaking at about the time that the genital development is complete. Among the last changes for boys are the development of facial hair and the lowering of the voice. You can see some parts of this sequence in Figure 4.8 and compare it to the girls' sequence in Figure 4.7.

Precisely when in this sequence the boy achieves reproductive maturity

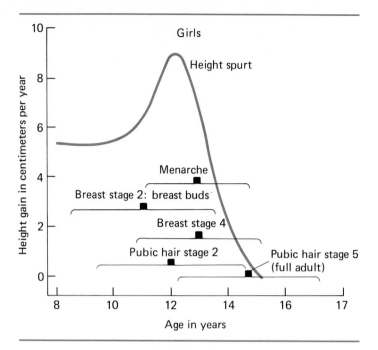

Figure 4.7 This figure, which shows the pubertal changes for girls, should give you some sense of the most common sequence of events. The box on each line represents the average age at attainment of that change, and the line indicates the range of normal times. Note the *wide* range of normality for all of these changes. (*Sources:* Tanner, 1978; Garn, 1980; Chumlea, 1982.)

is very difficult to determine. The first nocturnal emission is a private event (unlike menarche, which normally occasions both discussion and assistance), and it is hard to tell just when the seminal fluid begins to contain viable sperm. For most boys, real fertility seems to occur sometime between 12 and 16.

Two things are particularly interesting about these sequences. First, if you compare Figures 4.7 and 4.8, you will see that girls are about two years ahead of boys in their pubertal development. Most of you remember that period at age 11 or 12, in late elementary school or junior high, when all the girls were suddenly taller than the boys and the girls began to show secondary sex characteristics while the boys were still definitely prepubertal (a painful time for a lot of us).

A second intriguing thing about these sequences of development is that while the order of development seems to be highly consistent *within* each sequence (such as breast development or pubic hair development), there is quite a lot of variability *across* sequences. A boy may be in stage 2 of genital development but already in stage 5 of pubic hair development.

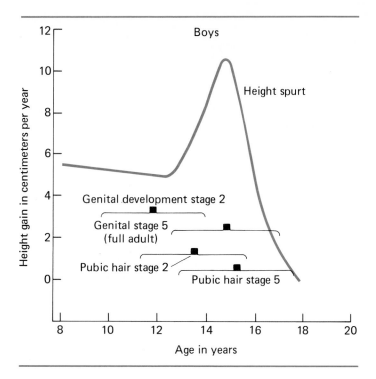

Figure 4.8 The sequence of pubertal changes for boys. If you compare this figure with the pattern for girls (at left), you can see clearly that all the changes are about two years later for boys. (*Sources:* Tanner, 1978; Chumlea, 1982.)

And different young people may experience the set of changes in somewhat different orders. So far physiologists have not figured out why this occurs. I've given you the averages in the tables and figures, but if you are trying to predict the development of an individual child, you should remember that the pattern may be quite different from the norm.

Other Changes in Puberty

Aside from the changes in primary and secondary sex characteristics and in height, musculature, and fat, other important changes in the body organs also seem to be triggered by the same hormones that produce pubertal changes. In particular, the heart and lungs increase considerably in size and the heart rate drops. Both of these changes are more marked for boys than for girls—another of the factors that increases the capacity for sustained effort for boys relative to girls. Before about age 12, boys and girls have similar physical strength, speed, and endurance; after puberty, boys have more of all three.

USING THE BODY: THE EFFECTS OF PHYSICAL CHANGES ON BEHAVIOR

Obviously, children's bodies change enormously over the first 15 years of life. The brief picture I have provided of these changes should give you some sense of the alterations in muscles, fat, internal organs, and nervous system. But what this description does not tell you is how the changes affect the way the child can *use* her body—to crawl, walk, run; to catch, throw, or kick balls; or even to become sexually active or pregnant. How, in other words, do all the physical changes show up in behavior? Answering that question could take volumes, but I can at least explore two examples: early motor development and adolescent sexual activity.

Motor Development in the Early Years

Psychologists usually use the phrase **motor development** to describe the complex changes in the child's body activities and movements. For parents or teachers, this is often the most noticeable part of physical development. The baby's first step, after all, is a big milestone, as is the child's first bike ride. These milestones are, in turn, built on all the changes in bones and muscles and nervous system I have been describing.

Robert Malina (1982) suggests that we can divide the wide range of motor skills roughly into three groups: *locomotor* patterns, such as walking, running, jumping, hopping, and skipping; *nonlocomotor* patterns, such as pushing, pulling, and bending; and *manipulative* skills, such as grasping, throwing, catching, kicking, and other actions involving receiving and moving objects. Nearly all the *basic* skills in all three areas are complete by about 6 or 7 years of age. After that, change is mostly improvement in performance as the child refines the basic skills and integrates them into more and more complex movement sequences. So 6- and 7-year-olds can run, and they can probably dribble a basketball, but they can't yet do both at the same time.

The Development of Walking: An Example. Since most motor behavior is easier to picture than to describe in words, you will want to take a look at the photos in the second color photo essay, which depicts the changes in motor skill from early infancy through the period of late preschool or early elementary school. A closer look at the shift from standing to walking is shown in Figure 4.9. This wondrous set of changes, when the infant finally learns to walk unaided, is watched with particular eagerness (and some trepidation) by parents. But it is not at all a simple process. It involves an immensely complex set of changes in muscles, bones, and nervous system. Esther Thelen points out, for example, that the infant's large head, narrow shoulders, and short legs are "hopelessly designed for upright stability" (1984, p. 234). The changes in body proportions that

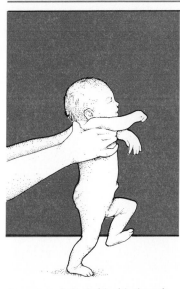

A newborn baby held with the sole of the foot on a table moves his legs in a reflex walking action.

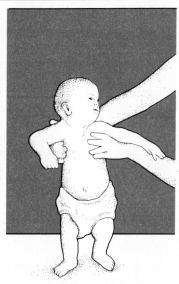

At 8 weeks the baby briefly keeps his head up if he is held in a standing posture.

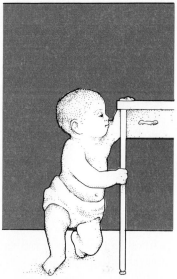

By 36 weeks he can pull himself up and remains standing by grasping hold of furniture.

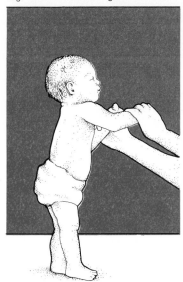

By 48 weeks he can walk forward if both hands are held (or sideways, gripping furniture).

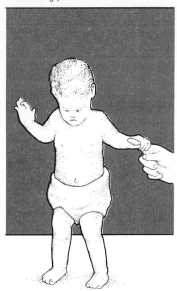

At 1 year the child walks forward if someone holds one of his hands.

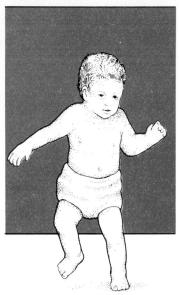

By 13 months the child has become capable of walking without help.

Figure 4.9 These drawings show one of the key locomotor skill sequences, from standing to walking. (*Source:* The Diagram Group, *Child's body: An owner's manual.* New York: Paddington Press, 1977, section D-13.)

MOTOR DEVELOPMENT AND TOYS

If you have ever tried to buy a toy for a child, you know how bewildering it can be to walk into a store and see aisles and aisles of bright, attractive items. You want to find something that is right for the child's skills, but how do you know what makes a good toy and what toys are good at what ages? The answers to these questions can come partly from what we know about a child's motor development.

Birth to 6 Months

Little babies use their hands and their eyes to play, so a good choice is something that is bright and safe to hold on to that can be hooked to the crib so it won't fall. Mobiles and "crib gyms" fit the category, and so do soft toys that tie to the sides of the crib.

6 to 12 Months

Older babies are more mobile and are interested in toys that let them try out their new large-muscle skills. These babies enjoy jumping in sling seats that hang from doorways, and they like to move around the house in "walkers" (similar seats set on wheeled frames). Probably the best thing for a child this age is to childproof your house, removing hazards like sharp objects and poisons so the child can explore freely. Using playpens (now usually called *play yards*) is probably not as good, although they may sometimes be necessary for safety reasons.

Infants of this age also enjoy stacking and nesting toys. Measuring cups and pots and pans are often better for this than expensive baby toys.

Second Year

Give a toddler an expensive toy and chances are she will show at least as much interest in the box it came in. (Big boxes that can be crawled into are usually a particular hit.) At the other end of the size scale, smaller objects (but not so small that they can be swallowed) are often favorites, since the child can now pick things up with his thumb and forefinger.

Toddlers like toys with wheels, but *push toys* are better than *pull toys* because the child can see the object while it moves. Near the end of the year, toward the second birthday, the child can sometimes handle a big crayon or pencil and may enjoy "drawing." For obvious reasons, washable colors are preferred!

Third Year

When in doubt, get something with wheels. Kiddie cars, tricycles, and other riding toys are favorites among large toys, and cars and

take place during the first year of life all improve the balance by shifting the child's center of gravity downward. Growth of muscle tissue in the ankles, the legs, and the abdomen are also important underpinnings of walking, as is the myelinization of the nervous system. The infant also must learn to control his posture by paying attention to the visual and body cues that signal swaying or other body movement. All these complex developments converge by the end of the first year, enabling the child to begin walking—unsteadily, to be sure, but independently.

The child's changing motor skills have many practical ramifications for parents, one set of which—selecting appropriate toys—I have explored

trucks (for both sexes) among small ones. Building toys start to be interesting, especially those with many possibilities like large wooden blocks (homemade ones are just as satisfactory as expensive sets from a store).

Coloring and drawing are usually great favorites, as are those messy classics, painting and Play Doh. As with younger children, "washable" is an important label to look for.

Fourth to Seventh Year

Small-muscle coordination develops rapidly during this period, and the child can manage toys like beads (to be strung on a string) and more accurate cutting (although typical children's scissors are too dull for much accuracy; a sharp pair of scissors is a great gift for a child old enough to use them safely).

Large-muscle skills are improving too, and smaller balls (baseball- or tennis-size) can be used as well as large ones. By the end of this period, the child can often manage a bicycle or at least start on one with training wheels.

Elementary School

Coordination is well developed by this age. Seven- and eight-year-old children can usu-

ally ride a bicycle easily and can skip rope and play most games that require hitting, kicking, or throwing a ball. I should emphasize that children as young as 3 can do most of these things, too, *if* you provide a large enough ball, a wide enough hockey stick, or a light enough racket. From age 3 through at least age 10, the development of play and athletic skills is more one of degree than of kind. So if you are interested in having your child develop specific abilities needed for later organized sports, you can begin quite early, as long as the materials are sized properly for the child's ability and you do not press for perfect coordination too early.

Practice in small-muscle coordination over the earlier years also makes the elementary-school-age child much more skillful with model building, arts and crafts, and even sewing—all of which may make excellent toys/games/gifts for children this age.

As a general rule, at every age steer clear of expensive, complex toys that do only one or two things (especially all those wretched toys that require batteries!). I am thinking here of toys like robots that whirr and walk. Children are intrigued for a while, but they rapidly lose interest, and such toys are not adaptable to other forms of play.

in the box above. The child's growing physical independence also has a major effect. It is a remarkable day when your child first hops on her bike and casually announces, "I'm going to ride over to Julie's house to play." Things are never quite the same again!

Adolescent Sexuality

Another obvious place to look at the impact of physical changes on behavior is adolescence, when the body changes bring about sexual fertility. Do teenagers become sexually active at the same time?

Obviously, some do. Adolescent sexual activity has increased dramatically in the past decades. The most recent evidence (e.g., Dryer, 1982; Darling, Kallen, & Van Dusen, 1984; Stark, 1986) shows that in the United States today, about half of all the boys and about a third of all the girls aged 15 to 17 are sexually active. The rates are considerably higher among 18- and 19-year-olds and among black teenagers of every age.

Despite these heightened levels of sexual activity, and despite the greater acceptance of teenage sexuality among both teens and their parents, it is remarkable how little teenagers know about physiology and reproduction. At best, only about half of white and a fifth of black teenagers can describe the time of greatest fertility in the menstrual cycle (Morrison, 1985). Many girls are convinced they cannot get pregnant because they are "too young." Perhaps in part because of such ignorance, only 14 percent of teenage girls use contraceptives the first time they have intercourse (Stark, 1986).

Given both of these trends, we shouldn't be surprised that the rate of teenage pregnancy is high. Approximately 1 million teenage girls become pregnant every year (roughly 1 in 10 girls), and about half carry their pregnancies to term. Perhaps 10,000 babies are born every year to girls under 15. The most striking of these statistics is that, by at least some estimates, fully 44 percent of all teenage girls will become pregnant at least once before the age of 20 (Hofferth, 1987a).

What will surprise you—especially in light of the alarmist articles in the popular press in recent years—is that the rate of teenage births has actually been declining slightly in recent years, in large part because abortion has become much more common. Still, the fact that the problem is not getting worse is no reason for cheer. By any standards, this is a lot of teenage pregnancies. And since many teenagers do not get adequate prenatal care, the risk for themselves and their infants is markedly increased. What's more, the later life pattern of a teenage mother is greatly changed. She finishes fewer years of school, has poorer-paying jobs later on, has more children, and is more likely to be divorced (e.g., Moore et al., 1981; Hofferth, 1987b). To help these teenagers avoid some of these unpleasant consequences, we may need to rethink our attitudes about the timing and importance of sex education in the schools.

HEALTH AND ILLNESS IN CHILDHOOD AND ADOLESCENCE

The health or illness of a child is of central concern to parents (as well as to pediatricians, epidemiologists, and society in general). Children do get sick—often. In the United States, children between ages 1 and 3 get sick eight or nine times a year, mostly with colds or other upper respiratory illnesses, ear infections, and the like. Preschoolers and elementary-school children get sick less often but still perhaps six times a year (Parmelee, 1986). Most of these illnesses are quite brief. More lasting disorders (called *chronic* illnesses), including such things as diabetes, asthma, and ulcers, are found in perhaps 1 in 10 youngsters at some time during their childhood (Starfield & Pless, 1980).

One of the most interesting findings on childhood illness is that a pattern of repeated illness in childhood—even just unusually frequent colds—seems to be associated with higher rates of illness in adolescence and poorer health in adulthood (Starfield & Pless, 1980). This link is not at all invariable, of course. Many "sickly" children are quite healthy as adults. But a pattern of frequent early illness increases the probability of health problems later.

Another danger for children is accidents. In fact, for children past age 1 in the United States, accidents are the major cause of death. Automobile accidents are the most common cause of fatality, accounting for 36 percent of deaths in teenagers and young adults and 20 percent of deaths in children between 1 and 14 (National Center for Health Statistics, 1984b). Suicide is also an increasing risk among teenagers. Rates have tripled since 1960 and now represent about 12 percent of teen deaths—about 15 deaths per 100,000 teenage males per year (Hawton, 1986).

Still another potential problem among children and adolescents is poor health habits, including too little exercise and poor food. Perhaps the most troubling are the various *eating disorders*—obesity, bulimia, and anorexia nervosa—which I have discussed in the box on pages 138–140. But more generally, researchers are finding that the sedentary, high-calorie life-style of American youngsters not only contributes to current physical problems—it may also create significantly higher risk of later disease. By some reports, for example, 40 percent of adolescents have at least one risk factor associated with heart disease—high blood cholesterol, overweight, or high blood pressure (Harvard Education Letter, 1987). It is clear that regular exercise can help to prevent heart problems and can improve school performance (Kolbe et al., 1980), but teenagers in recent years exercise less rather than more.

It is clear that all children get sick at least some of the time; a minority are sick fairly regularly. Such regular or persistent sickness can have long-term implications for a child's physical and emotional development, as can poor health or exercise habits.

BIG OR FAST VERSUS SLOW OR SMALL: SOME INDIVIDUAL DIFFERENCES IN PHYSICAL DEVELOPMENT

So far I have been concentrating on sequences of development—on patterns of physical development that are common to virtually all children. But I am sure you have gathered from several brief comments (as well as from your own observation of children) that there are wide individual differences in the *rate* and *timing* of the physical changes I have been describing as

EATING DISORDERS: OBESITY, BULIMIA, AND ANOREXIA

Among the many health hazards for children and adolescents, some of the most common are those that have something to do with food, collectively called *eating disorders*. The most frequent of these is obesity. Using one definition of obesity (to be more than 20 percent heavier than the normal weight for your height), 15 to 20 percent of children and teenagers are obese. Both boys and girls are counted in the ranks of the obese. In contrast, two other eating disorders, bulimia and anorexia nervosa, are found almost exclusively in girls.

Bulimia (also sometimes called *bulimia nervosa*) is a pattern of uncontrollable binge eating (such as consuming 50 candy bars or several pizzas at one sitting) sometimes followed by purging—either by laxatives or by self-induced vomiting. National statistics are not available, but two recent large studies of high school and college girls, each including more than 1000 students (Johnson et al., 1984; Pyle et al., 1983), suggest that perhaps as many as 5 percent of girls between ages 14 and 22 would meet the requirements for a clinical diagnosis of bulimia. In the high school sample Johnson studied, for example, more than half said that they had had at least one eating binge, 8.3 percent had binged frequently, and 4.9 percent had binged on at least a weekly basis. One percent reported both weekly binge eating and weekly purging. College students in Pyle's sample reported equivalent frequencies: 4.5 percent of the women reported at least weekly binges, and 1.9 percent reported at least weekly purges.

Anorexia nervosa is less common (affecting perhaps 1 in 250 girls), but it is potentially more deadly. The main symptom is the refusal (or perhaps more accurately, the inability) to eat normally. Often the girls have gone on a diet to lose weight and then continued to limit their food intake drastically. Some girls literally starve themselves to death.

Let me look a bit further at what we know about the causes of each of these three problems.

Obesity

Obesity is a significant long-term health problem. Obese adults have shorter life expectancies and higher risks of heart disease and high blood pressure. We also know that there is a link between fatness in childhood and obesity in adulthood. Obese *infants* have only a slightly higher risk of obesity in adulthood compared to leaner babies. But obesity in older children—beginning perhaps at age 4 to 6—is quite strongly predictive of adult fatness (Roche, 1981; Grinker, 1981).

To oversimplify a bit, there seem to be three causes for childhood obesity: heredity, exercise or activity level, and diet. The first point is that children clearly seem to inherit a tendency toward fatness or leanness. Jean Mayer (1975) found in one study that only 7 percent of children with normal-weight parents were obese, but 80 percent of those with two obese parents were themselves seriously overweight. Adopted children raised by obese parents, in contrast, are less likely to be overweight.

The second contributor is exercise (or the lack of it). Again some of the most interesting research comes from Jean Mayer. He found that obese children simply don't move as much, even while doing the same things thinner children do. Just why some children move less vigorously is not so clear. It may be a basic temperamental difference; it may reflect differences in basic body type;

or it may be that already-heavy bodies simply require more effort to move around, so the overweight child moves less and less vigorously. Whatever the reason, lack of exercise appears to be an important element in overweight in children and in adults.

The third element in the equation is obviously the child's diet, along with the family's eating patterns. In some few cases, parents may simply overfeed a child. More often, the pattern is probably considerably more complex. Erik Woody and Philip Costanzo (1981) suggest, for example, that a child may initially become overweight because of overfeeding or the ad lib availability of rich food or snacks. But parents may then react to that overweight (particularly in girls) by becoming extremely restrictive about food. This external restriction, in turn, may have the negative consequence of reducing the child's need to develop self-control about eating.

In other cases, a sedentary life-style, combined with high rates of junk food intake, may be the culprit. One group of researchers estimates, for example, that the prevalence of obesity increases approximately 2 percent for each additional hour of TV viewing per day (Harvard Education Letter, March, 1987). In most obese children, probably all three elements—genetic predisposition, low levels of activity, and overeating patterns—combine to increase the risk of obesity.

Bulimia

We know much less about the causes of bulimia, in part because recognition of the disorder is much more recent. But it seems to be centrally a response by some girls and women to a currently intense cultural emphasis on thinness. Girls (much more than boys) are taught—explicitly and implicitly—from very early on that it matters if they are pretty or attractive and that thinness is one of the critical variables in attractiveness. (As I write this, I am aware of the fact that out of all the interesting questions about children's health I could have chosen to discuss, I picked one that deals with food and thinness. I, too, am hooked!)

Those girls who most fully accept and internalize this model of beauty are most prone to develop bulimia. So, for example, bulimia is more common among girls and women in the middle and upper classes, in which the ideals of fitness and thinness are particularly emphasized. Ruth Striegel-Moore and her colleagues (Striegel-Moore, Silberstein, & Rodin, 1986) have also found that bulimic girls and women are more likely than are nonbulimics to agree with statements like "Attractiveness increases the likelihood of professional success."

Bulimia seems to develop in adolescence, and not before that, precisely because one of the effects of puberty is to increase the amount of fat in the girl's body. This is particularly true of early-developing girls, who characteristically acquire and retain higher fat levels than do later-maturing girls. Thus an early-developing girl who deeply believes that thinness is essential for beauty and that beauty is essential for happiness seems at particularly high risk for developing bulimia (Striegel-Moore, Silberstein, & Rodin, 1986).

Anorexia Nervosa

Many of the same causal factors are probably at work in girls who develop anorexia—a powerful drive to be thin and an equally strong desire to be in control of their bodies. Not eating, or eating only stringently limited amounts (such as one Cheerio for breakfast), is one way to achieve such control. Anorexic women also have startlingly abnormal body images, perceiving themselves as fat even when they are gaunt and emaciated.

Clearly there is much we do not know about either of these disorders. Are all three of these eating problems—obesity, bulimia, and anorexia—facets of some underlying disorder? Why would an intense passion for thinness lead one girl to stop eating and another to binge and purge? We do not know. But given the increasing prevalence of these two problems among today's teenagers, these are questions researchers need to try to answer in the coming years.

well as in children's physical shape and skills. Not only are these differences interesting in their own right; they also may affect a child's relationships with her peers or her general contacts with the world around her.

Differences in Rate

Children vary *widely* in the speed with which they go through all the body and motor changes I have described. Some children walk at 7 or 8 months, others not until 18 months. Some are skillful soccer players at 5 or 6, others not until much later (if at all). These differences are most striking at puberty, when young people of the same age may range from stage 1 to stage 5 in the steps of sexual maturation—as you can see very vividly in Figure 4.10.

As a general rule, a particular child is consistently early, average, or slow in physical development. The child whose bone development is slower probably also walks later, shows slower motor development, and goes through puberty later (Tanner, 1978). Similarly, tall infants tend to become taller teenagers and taller adults. There are exceptions to both of these generalizations, but what Tanner calls the *tempo of growth* is a powerful element in development.

Effects on Mental Development.   These differences in rate of physical development appear to have at least some small link to a child's mental development, too. The general rule is that children whose physical development is rapid are also slightly ahead in mental development. So if we compare children of the same age, those with the "oldest" skeletal or pubertal development or the best motor coordination are also likely to score higher on an IQ test or to do slightly better in school (e.g., Tanner, 1978; Pollitt, Mueller, & Leibel, 1982). It is also true that taller children of any given age tend to score higher on IQ tests than shorter children of the same

Oh, the joys of motor development! In early infancy changes can be observed almost daily, as the baby first lifts her head off the mattress, then begins to swat at things with her hands, and later lifts her whole head and chest up. Only a few months later the baby is creeping and crawling, and walking with help. Once she can manage that, stairs are not far behind, with big-wheeled trikes a year or two down the road. By age 4 or 5, children are remarkably well coordinated, running and playing with ease and freedom. And by 5 or 6 they can begin to do such complex things as jumping rope—albeit imperfectly at first.

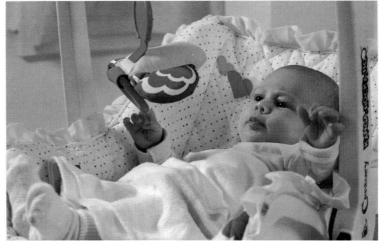

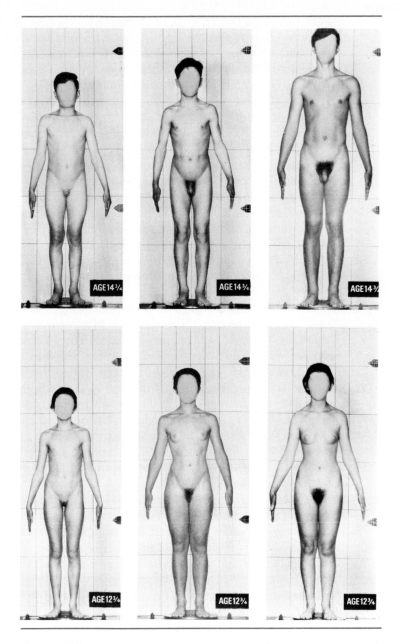

Figure 4.10   Teenagers vary enormously in the timing and speed of pubertal changes, as you can see very graphically from these photographs. Each of the three boys is the same age, as is each of the three girls, but the children range from Stage 2 to Stage 5 of pubertal development. (*Source:* J. M. Tanner, Growth and endocrinology of the adolescent. In L. J. Gardner [Ed.], *Endocrine and genetic disease of childhood and adolescence,* 2nd ed., © 1975 by W. B. Saunders Co., Philadelphia, PA., p. 28.)

age (Humphreys, Davey, & Park, 1985; Dornbusch et al., 1987). None of these differences is terribly large. The correlation between height and IQ is only about .20 or .30, and in actual IQ points, the difference between the tallest and the shortest is probably no more than 5 to 10 points (Tanner, 1978). Still, the relationship is found consistently.

Some of this relationship between growth rate and mental development may be due to the direct impact of brain growth; some may reflect differences in diet or differences in confidence or self-esteem between larger, fast-developing children and the slower developers. And some may be due to differences in the responsibilities or opportunities offered by the people around the child or in the expectancies of the adults or the child. Interestingly, these differences persist into adulthood. That is, adults who were early developers as children still have a slight intellectual advantage over their slower-developing peers, even though the latter group has caught up in height, brain growth, and physical skill. Presumably this carryover into adulthood is a consequence of the psychological effects of "earliness" or "lateness" rather than of the physiological effects.

Effects on Personality.   When we look directly at these psychological effects, some interesting things emerge. Most of the research on this set of questions has focused on the impact of early versus late puberty on teenagers' mental health or self-image. What happens to a girl who begins to menstruate at 10, or to a boy who does not go through a growth spurt until age 16? Do they turn out differently from children who are more "on time"?

A whole burst of recent research on this question has led to an interesting, complex hypothesis. The general idea, proposed by a number of psychologists—including Mary Faust (1983), Richard Lerner (1985, 1987), and Anne Petersen (1987)—is that each young child or teenager has some *schema,* some internal model about what is "normal" or "right" about puberty. Each girl has an internal model about the right age to develop breasts or to begin menstruation; each boy has an idea or image about when it is right to begin to grow a beard or for his voice to get lower. According to this hypothesis, it is the discrepancy between this expectation and what actually happens that determines the psychological effect. Those whose development occurs outside the desired or expected range are likely to think less well of themselves, perhaps to have fewer friends or to experience other signs of distress.

In our culture today, most young people seem to share the expectation that pubertal changes will happen sometime between ages 12 and 14; anything earlier is seen as "too soon," and anything later is thought of as "late." If you compare these expectations to what I have already said about the actual average timing of pubertal changes, you'll see that such a norm includes girls who are average in development and boys who are *early.* So we should expect that these two groups—normal-developing girls and early-developing boys—should have the best psychological functioning. Early-

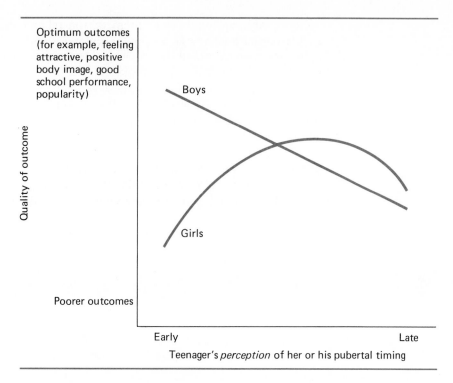

Figure 4.11 A theoretical model describing the effects of early and late puberty for boys and girls. According to this model, the best position for girls is to be "on time," while for boys the best position is to be "early." But for both sexes, it is the *perception* of earliness or lateness, and not the actual timing, that is probably critical. (*Source:* Adopted from Tobin-Richards, Boxer, & Petersen, 1983, p. 137.)

maturing boys are also more likely to be of the mesomorphic body type (broad-shouldered and well-muscled). Since, as pointed out earlier, this body type is consistently preferred at all ages, and since boys with this body type tend to be good at sports, the early-developing boy should be particularly advantaged.

Figure 4.11 shows the specific predictions graphically. Early boys should be best off, followed by average boys and girls. The least well off should be late-developing boys and early-developing girls. And in fact that is generally what the newer research shows. Girls who are early developers (before 11 or 12 for major body changes) show consistently more negative body images—they think themselves too fat, for example (Tobin-Richards, Boxer, & Petersen, 1983; Petersen, 1987a; Simmons, Blyth, & McKinney, 1983). These girls are also more likely to get into trouble in school and at home (Magnusson, Stattin, & Allen, 1986). And there are hints that for girls, very late development is also somewhat negative, but the effect is not so striking as that in later-developing boys.

Among boys, as Figure 4.11 predicts, the relationship is essentially linear. The earlier the boy's development, the more positive his body image, the better he does in school, the less trouble he gets into, and the more friends he has (e.g., Duke et al., 1982).

In nearly all these studies, earliness or lateness has been defined in terms of the actual physical changes. But if you think back to the basic hypothesis, you'll remember that the key is thought to be the young person's expectation, or model, of how things ought to be. A very interesting study of ballet dancers makes it clear that it is the expectation, and not the actual rate of development, that is critical. In this study, Jeanne Brooks-Gunn (Brooks-Gunn & Warren, 1985; Brooks-Gunn, 1987) studied girls from 14 to 18 years old, some of whom were highly serious ballet dancers

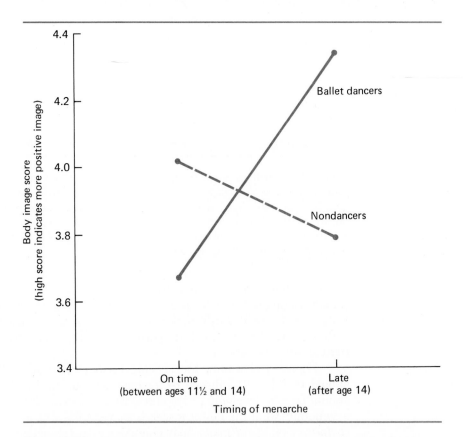

Figure 4.12 Serious ballet dancers, for whom a very lean, prepubescent shape is highly valued, clearly prefer to have a very late puberty. Those dancers whose menarche was "on time" by ordinary standards actually had poorer body images than did those who were objectively quite late, while the reverse was true for nondancers. This shows nicely that the critical variable is not the actual earliness or lateness of puberty but the adolescent's perception of what is normal or desirable. (*Source:* Adapted from Brooks-Gunn & Warren, 1985, Table 1, p. 291.)

studying at a national ballet company school. In this group, a very lean, almost prepubescent body is highly desirable. Given this, we would expect that dancers who were very late in pubertal development would actually have a better image of themselves than those who were "on time." And that is exactly what was found, as you can see in Figure 4.12. Among nondancers the same age, normal-time menarche was associated with a better body image than late menarche, but exactly the reverse was true for the dancers.

Thus it seems to be the discrepancy or mismatch between the desired pattern and any given child's actual pattern that is critical, not the absolute age of pubertal development. Because the majority of young people share similar expectations, we can see common effects of early or late development. But to predict the effect of early or late development in any individual teenager, we would need to know more about her or his internal model.

Sex Differences in Physical Growth

I've mentioned a number of sex differences in physical growth as I've gone along in this chapter, but let me pull together all the bits and pieces for you here. Table 4.3 summarizes the major findings.

Table 4.3
▬▬▬▬▬

Summary of Sex Differences in Physical Growth

Characteristic	Nature of difference
Rate of maturation	Girls are on a faster timetable throughout development; this difference amounts to about two to four weeks at birth and about two years at adolescence.
Predictability or regularity of maturation	Girls' physical growth is more regular and predictable, with fewer uneven spurts. It is easier to predict the final height of a girl, for example, than that of a boy.
Strength and speed	There is little difference until adolescence, but after puberty, boys are stronger and faster.
Heart and circulation	At adolescence, boys develop a larger heart and lungs and a greater capacity for carrying oxygen in the blood than do girls.
Fat tissue	Girls from birth onward have a thicker layer of fat tissue just below the surface of the skin, and after puberty a larger percentage of their body weight is composed of fat.
Motor skills	In the preschool years, girls are better at tasks requiring jumping, hopping, rhythmic movement, and balance. In elementary school and later, boys are better at activities requiring running, jumping, and throwing, while girls are better at hopping.

Sources: Tanner, 1978; Archer, 1981; Malina, 1982.

As you'll see from the table, most physical differences between males and females become more pronounced after puberty. Preadolescent girls and boys are about equal in strength and speed. One of the implications of this is that a 12-year-old girl is probably just as strong and just as good at throwing balls and stealing bases as a 14-year-old boy, since they are both at about the same point in pubertal development. At this age, girls should be able to compete effectively in Little League or other sports. A few years later, though, boys will become stronger and faster, as well as larger. It will be the unusual girl who is able to compete successfully with boys in sports that call for considerable strength or speed. This is not an argument against athletics for girls. On the contrary. Everything I know about the effect of maintaining fitness for adult health and longevity points to the importance of encouraging both boys and girls to develop athletic interests and skills that will carry forward into adult life. But it *is* an argument against mixed-sex competitive teams in high school.

Social Class and Racial Differences

As a group, poor children grow a bit more slowly and are a bit shorter than middle-class children, most probably because of dietary differences. Menarchal age is also about six months later in girls growing up in less-affluent homes than in girls in middle-class homes (Garn, 1980).

Different racial groups, too, show somewhat different rates or patterns of development. Of course, in the United States, in which minority racial status and poverty so often coexist, some of the apparent racial differences may well be caused by the underlying economic differences. But there appear to be some genuine racial differences as well.

Black infants and children appear to be slightly ahead of white children in some aspects of physical development. In fact, the gestational period of the black fetus seems actually to be slightly shorter than that of the white fetus (Smith & Stenchever, 1978). Black babies also show somewhat faster development of motor skills such as walking, and they are slightly taller than their white counterparts, with longer legs, more muscle, and heavier bones (Tanner, 1978). At puberty, black girls have slightly earlier menarche as well (perhaps three months, on average). Thus the tempo of growth appears to be slightly faster in black than in white children.

Asian children also have a relatively rapid tempo of growth but are smaller, with long upper bodies but shorter final height.

DETERMINANTS OF GROWTH: EXPLANATIONS OF PHYSICAL DEVELOPMENT

So far I have been answering "what" questions. I have been describing common developmental patterns and individual differences in rate or pattern. But "why" questions are equally important. Why does physical development occur as it does, and what can affect it?

Maturation

It seems very clear that some set of internal signals governs most of the growth patterns I have described. While the *rate* of development varies from one child to the next, the *sequence* is virtually the same for all children, even those with marked physical or mental handicaps (Kopp, 1979).

In infancy, the sequences have recurrent themes. In particular, physical development tends to follow both a **cephalocaudal** pattern (from the head downward) and a **proximodistal** pattern (from the center outward). Thus, muscles in the neck and trunk develop before muscles in the legs and arms, myelinization proceeds from the top downward, and so forth. Interestingly, at adolescence this pattern is somewhat reversed, since final adult size is reached first by the feet and hands and only last by the trunk.

The precise mechanisms that control such regular sequences of development are not fully understood. We presume that the signals are contained in the genetic code.

Heredity

Our genetic heritage is individual as well as species-specific. In addition to being programmed for the basic developmental sequences, each of us also receives genetic instructions for unique growth tendencies. Both size and body shape seem to be heavily influenced by specific inheritance. Tall parents tend to have tall children; short parents tend to have short children (Garn, 1980). And there are similarities between parents and children in such things as hip width, arm length (some ancestor certainly passed on a gene for long arms to me!), and sitting height (long or short trunk).

Rate or tempo of growth seems to be an inherited pattern as well. Parents who were themselves early developers, as measured by such things as bone ossification or age of menarche, tend to have children who are faster developers too (Garn, 1980).

Environmental Effects

But, as usual, nothing is completely one-sided. There are potent external influences on physical growth as well.

Practice.   First of all, practice matters, even for the development of basic skills like crawling or walking. Twenty years ago, the conventional wisdom was that maturationally determined skills didn't need practice. Psychologists thought that when the child's muscles and bones and nervous system were "ready" to support some skill, it would simply appear. That is partly true, but now we know it isn't that simple. For instance, when opportunities to practice certain motions are greatly restricted, children's motor development is retarded.

A study by Wayne Dennis (1960) of children raised in Iranian orphanages is a good example. The babies in one of the institutions were routinely placed on their backs in cribs with very lumpy mattresses. They had little or no experience in lying or moving on their stomachs as a normal baby would, and they even had difficulty rolling over because of the hollows in the mattresses. These babies almost never went through the normal sequence in learning to walk—presumably because they didn't have enough opportunity to practice those precursors of the skill that begin in a prone position, such as creeping and crawling. They did learn to walk eventually, but they were about a year late.

It would appear from this and other research (e.g., Razel, 1985) that for the development of such universal basic skills as crawling or walking, some minimum amount of practice is needed just to keep the system working as it should. For more complex combinations of basic actions, such as those required for kicking or throwing objects, practice is essential for skill development. It is even possible that in infancy and childhood, opportunities to move and practice individual movements are necessary to stimulate brain development, particularly nerve myelinization. That is, the effects may work both ways—from brain development to better motor skill and from practicing movements to faster brain development.

Diet. A second major influence on physical growth is the child's diet. Poorly nourished children grow more slowly and don't end up as large. More important, malnutrition in the early years may have a permanent effect on some parts of the brain and nervous system.

As I pointed out earlier, the period of maximum brain growth is the final three to five months of pregnancy and the first two to three years after birth (particularly the first six months after birth). Severe malnutrition during that time, even if the child later has an adequate diet, may still cause a lasting slow rate of physical and motor development (Malina, 1982). Such children may show some catch-up in height or growth rate, but they are typically shorter and slower than their peers. Research with animals (and some parallel studies of the brains and nervous systems of malnourished children who have died) shows that the main physical effects of malnutrition are to reduce the number of dendrites and synapses between individual neurons and to slow the rate of myelinization (Dickerson, 1981; Ricciuti, 1981). As a consequence, the cortex does not become as heavy. If the child's diet continues to be bad for the first two or three years, the effects appear to be permanent.

The effects of milder malnutrition, or *subnutrition,* are harder to detect and have not been widely studied. We really don't know how poorly the child must be nourished before we see the effects in growth rate or motor coordination. It does appear, however, that chronic subnutrition affects the child's level of energy, which in turn can affect the nature of the interactions the child has with both the objects and the people around him (Barrett, Radke-Yarrow, & Klein, 1982).

Illness. A third type of experience that can affect a child's growth is long-term illness. Usually a child grows more slowly during illness, perhaps because she is less active, because her diet has changed, or because of the operation of the disease itself. But after she recovers, her growth jumps ahead, and she shows something Tanner calls "catch-up" (Tanner, 1970, 1978). He describes the case of one child who had a tumor on the adrenal gland from ages 1 to 3 (Prader, Tanner, & Von Harnack, 1963). By age 4, the child was only the size of an average 2-year-old. When the tumor was removed, however, the child shot up. She grew about eight inches in the next two years, and by adolescence she was within the normal range. She was still smaller than average, so the catch-up wasn't total. But after several years of rapid growth, she returned to the *pace* of development she had shown before her illness.

    Generally speaking, the earlier in a child's life an illness or malnutrition occurs, the more lasting the effect and the less successfully the child catches up to fully normal development. This is another example of a *sensitive period* of the kind I discussed in Chapter 1.

THE SHAPE OF PHYSICAL DEVELOPMENT: A LAST LOOK

Of all the facets of development I'll describe in this book, physical development is probably least influenced by specific experience and most governed by underlying maturational patterns. But it is a mistake to conclude that environment has only minor effects. The strength and coordination required to throw a basketball high enough to reach the basket undoubtedly develop in predictable ways over the early years without much intervention. But the skill needed to get the ball through the hoop with regularity, from different angles and distances, develops only through continual practice. The development of really smooth, coordinated skill in virtually all complex motor tasks requires practice. It also requires decent health and an adequate enough diet to maintain the system. More important, the rate and pattern of the child's physical development also affect his self-image, his personality, his interactions with the world around him. So physical development influences experience as much as the reverse.

SUMMARY

1. It is important to know something about physical growth and development because specific new behaviors are triggered by physical changes, because physical skills affect the kinds of experiences the child can

have, and because her feelings about her own body can affect self-concept and personality.

2. Changes in height and weight are rapid during the first year, then level off to a steady pace until adolescence, when there is a sharp "growth spurt."

3. Bones develop in a similar pattern, with rapid early growth and another rapid growth spurt at adolescence. Bones increase in number and harden slowly.

4. Muscle tissue increases in density and muscle fibers get longer. These increases at adolescence are much larger in boys than in girls.

5. Fat cells are added in the early years and then again rapidly at adolescence, in this case more in girls than in boys.

6. The brain is not fully developed at birth; over the first two years, dendrites, synapses and the myelin sheaths covering the nerve fibers develop.

7. Hormones are vital influences throughout growth, particularly during adolescence. The pituitary gland secretes triggering hormones at the beginning of puberty, which stimulate the production of sex hormones. These, in turn, trigger the development of primary and secondary sex characteristics.

8. Pubertal changes begin as early as age 8 or 9 in girls and continue until the midteens. The changes start about two years later in boys. In both sexes, the physical changes proceed in reliable sequences: secondary sex characteristics begin to appear, the growth spurt follows, and reproductive maturity arrives late in the sequence.

9. Developing motor skills—walking, running, bending, picking things up, throwing, and the like—reflect all the underlying physical changes. The child has acquired most basic motor skills by about age 6.

10. Physical changes are also reflected in adolescent sexual behavior, which has increased in recent decades. Perhaps half of teenage boys and a third of teenage girls are sexually active, and 10 percent of teenage girls become pregnant each year.

11. Illness is a normal part of a child's early life; some kind of illness occurs six to nine times each year, on average. Chronic illness is less common. Repeated or frequent illness in childhood is associated with poorer health later on.

12. Children differ markedly in the rate at which developmental changes take place. In general, rapidly developing children have advantages over slower-developing children in intellectual skill. Personality effects are more complex. In general, children whose physical development is markedly earlier or later than they expect or desire are likely to show more negative effects than do those whose development is "on time."

13. Girls and boys differ in both rate and pattern of physical development. Among other differences, girls begin puberty earlier, and adolescent boys develop more muscle tissue and a larger heart and circulatory system than do girls.

14. Some social class and racial differences can also be detected, with children from poverty-level environments developing more slowly. Both black and Asian children show a more rapid tempo of development than do white children.

15. Maturation is the most important process underlying physical growth and development. Most maturational sequences require only minimal environmental support. However, specific heredity, diet, and illness affect both the rate and pattern of development in individual children.

▬▬▬▬ KEY TERMS

cephalocaudal From the head downward. Describes one pattern of physical development in infancy.

cortex The convoluted gray portion of the brain which governs most complex thought, language, and memory, among other functions.

ectomorphic Body type defined by bone length. An ectomorphic individual is tall and slender, usually with stooped shoulders.

endocrine glands Glands (including the adrenals, the thyroid, the pituitary, the testes, and the ovaries) that secrete hormones governing overall physical growth and sexual maturing.

endomorphic Body type defined by amount of body fat. An endomorphic individual is soft and round in shape.

estrogen The female sex hormone secreted by the ovaries.

fontanels The "soft spots" in the skull present at birth. These disappear when the several bones of the skull grow together.

gonadotropic hormones Hormones produced in the pituitary gland which stimulate the sex organs to develop.

medulla A section of the brain in the lower part of the skull. It develops earlier than the cortex and regulates basic functions such as suckling, breathing, heart rate, and muscle tone.

menarche Onset of menstruation in girls.

mesomorphic Body type characterized by amount of muscle mass. A mesomorphic person is square-chested, broad-shouldered, and muscular.

midbrain A section of the brain below the cortex. It develops earlier than the cortex and regulates attention, sleeping, waking, and other "automatic" functions.

motor development Growth and change in ability to perform physical activities, such as walking, running, riding a bike.

myelin The material composing the sheaths around most of the nerves of the body. Myelin sheaths are not completely developed at birth.

myelinization The process by which myelin sheaths are formed around nerve fibers.

ossification The process of hardening by which soft tissue becomes bone.

pituitary gland One of the endocrine glands. It plays a central role in controlling the rate of physical maturation and sexual maturing.

primary sex characteristics Sexual characteristics related directly to reproduction, including the uterus and testes.

proximodistal From the center outward. With cephalocaudal, describes the pattern of physical changes in infancy.

puberty The collection of hormonal and physical changes at adolescence that bring about sexual maturity.

secondary sex charactersitics Sexual characteristics not directly involved in reproduction, including breast and body hair development and changes in body size and proportions.

▬▬▬▬ SUGGESTED READING

The Diagram Group. (1977). *Child's Body.* New York: Paddington Press.
  Although not new, this is an excellent book, designed as a parents' manual and full of helpful information about physical development, health, and nutrition.

Petersen, A. C. (1987, September). Those gangly years. *Psychology Today,* pp. 28–34.
A nice, brief current report on many of the latest findings on the effects of puberty on children and on their families.

Stark, E. (1986, October). Young, innocent and pregnant. *Psychology Today,* pp. 28–35.
An excellent discussion of the who and why of teenage pregnancy and contraceptive use (or nonuse).

Tanner, J. M. (1978). *Fetus into man. Physical growth from conception to maturity.* Cambridge, MA: Harvard University Press.
A detailed, very thorough, and remarkably understandable small book that covers all but the most current information about physical growth.

PROJECT: PLOTTING YOUR OWN GROWTH

This project will work only if your parents are among those who routinely stood their children up against a convenient doorjamb for measuring—and they still live in the house with the marked-up doorjamb. But those of you who can meet both conditions might find it interesting to go back and plot your rate of growth over the years of childhood. Calculate the number of inches you grew each year (estimating when needed), and draw a curve similar to the one in Figure 4.3.

How does your curve compare to the averaged data in the figure? When was your maximum height spurt (the year in which you grew the most inches)? During elementary school, did you grow about the same number of inches per year? If you are female, add to the graph a point that represents your first menstruation (to the best of your recollection). Where did menarche fall on the curve? Does it match the pattern shown in Figure 4.7—that is, did menarche occur *after* your major growth spurt?

If you do not have access to such data for your own growth, you may want to inquire among your friends or neighbors to see if someone else has doorjamb data you can use.

5 Perceptual Development

Some Basic Characteristics of Perceptual Development
Visual Development
  Acuity
  What Babies and Children Look At
  Making Discriminations
  Ignoring Visual Cues: The Perceptual Constancies
  The Object Concept
Auditory Development
  Acuity
  Detecting Locations
  What Infants and Children Listen To
  Discriminating Individual Voices
Development of Other Senses
  Smell and Taste
  Touch
Combining Information from Several Senses
Blind Babies Can "See" with Their Ears
The Basic Characteristics of Perceptual Development: A Second Look
Individual Differences in Perception
  Perceptual Styles
  Sex Differences
  Social Class Differences
Answering the "Why" Questions: Explanations of Perceptual
    Development
  Arguments for Nativism
  Arguments for Empiricism
Summary
Key Terms
Suggested Reading
Project: Development of the Object Concept

Several years ago, I went sailing for the first time. In the beginning, everything was extremely strange and difficult. I kept calling things "ropes" only to be told that they were not ropes but "lines" or "sheets" or "halyards" or something else complex or obscure-sounding. I had to learn to notice the differences so that I could tell what to reach for when I was given an instruction. I had to learn to read all the various gauges and other markers, too, and how to figure out what was important to watch for in the waves. And I had to learn what I could safely ignore, such as the colors of the various ropes (oops, I mean lines). Obviously, in one afternoon, I learned only a fraction of what I would need to know to be a good sailor, but I did begin to learn what to pay attention to, which discriminations were important and which irrelevant. My first sailing experience is a good example of both perception and perceptual learning. Psychologists use the word **perception** to describe the active process of obtaining information about the world through stimulation (Gibson & Spelke, 1983), and they use the term **perceptual learning** to describe the improvements in a person's ability to extract relevant or needed information from the environment.

My problems with sailing pale by comparison with the tasks facing an infant. The newborn is bombarded with stimulation, all of it essentially unfamiliar, which must be attended to, sorted out, understood, and eventually ignored. Furthermore, since the baby is not a passive creature, she seeks out still more stimulation by moving her eyes and body, turning her head to hear sounds, and the like. Coordinating all this information is a formidable task of perceptual learning.

Just how does the infant accomplish this enormous task? With what perceptual skills does she start, and how does she proceed? What does an infant pay attention to, and how does that change over time? What and how does she learn about the world that comes to her through her senses?

As we search for answers to these questions, it may help to begin by laying out some general principles that seem to describe perceptual learning in the early years of life. These principles can then serve as a framework on which you can hang the many specific facts I will be describing.

SOME BASIC CHARACTERISTICS OF PERCEPTUAL DEVELOPMENT

Eleanor Gibson, one of the major theorists in this field, points out that perceptual development does not appear to occur in stages. There are, however, some fundamental dimensions on which change occurs (Gibson, 1969; Gibson & Spelke, 1983), four of which are helpful for this discussion.

1. *Purposefulness of perceptual activity.* Even as recently as a decade ago, many psychologists thought that the young infant was "captured" by stimulation—that the baby was a relatively passive recipient of stimulation. As William James put it, the baby was surrounded by a "blooming,

buzzing confusion." Now we know that even the newborn explores the world around him using some rules, some strategies. As the child gets older, his rules become more flexibly applied, more intentional, more adaptive to the setting.

2. *Awareness of the meaning of perceptual information.* If you were to see a ball that reflects back the light, you would guess that the ball would feel smooth; you also recognize that round things can be held easily in the hand and thrown. Probably a newborn is not aware of all these things. But infants quickly come to react to the potential actions, qualities, or meanings of their experiences. Gibson calls these qualities of objects *affordances*. An object affords the opportunity for certain actions. With development, the infant and the child gradually learn the links between how objects appear and what those objects can do or be used for.

3. *Degree of differentiation.* Initially, the baby focuses on fairly big chunks or on prominent features. With development, the child focuses on more and more detail, on finer gradations, on more difficult discriminations.

4. *Ignoring the irrelevant.* The child gradually becomes more efficient, focusing only on those critical things that are essential in some situations and ignoring the rest. A child in a noisy classroom, for example, must learn to focus his attention on the teacher's voice and ignore the voices of the children around him. Children become steadily better at identifying what is irrelevant and then ignoring it.

I am sure that all of this sounds quite abstract to you at this point. To put some flesh on these theoretical bones, let me get down to the basic task of description. What do we know about children's seeing, hearing, touching, tasting, and smelling? What skills are present at birth, what strategies or rules does the child begin with, and how do those perceptual strategies or skills change with age?

I should alert you ahead of time to the fact that there is more to say about the development of visual skills than about the other sense modalities. This is partly because visual information appears to be a highly significant source of data for infants and partly because researchers figured out fairly early on how to study vision in infants. And for every modality, we know a lot more about the changes that occur in infancy than those that occur later. One reason is that psychologists have been intrigued with the way perceptual skills change very rapidly in the early months of life. This does not mean that perceptual learning does not occur in later childhood or adulthood. Clearly it does, as my experience on the sailboat shows. But the basic processes seem to be laid down early, and it is the basic processes I want to describe.

VISUAL DEVELOPMENT

Let me begin at the most basic point. Just what is an infant physically capable of seeing? What is her visual acuity?

Acuity

Acuity refers to how well or how clearly you can perceive something. When you go to apply for a driver's license, you take the "eye test" that involves reading the letters on one line of a large chart; that's a test for visual acuity. The usual standard for visual acuity in adults is "20/20 vision." This means that you can see and properly identify something twenty feet away that the average person can also see at 20 feet. A person with 20/100 vision, in contrast, has to be as close as 20 feet to see something that the ordinary person can see at 100 feet. In other words, the higher the second number, the poorer the person's visual acuity.

Newborn babies have quite poor acuity, perhaps as poor as 20/800 (which is legal blindness) (Dobson & Teller, 1978), but it improves rapidly during early infancy. Most 4-month-olds have acuity in the range of 20/200 and 20/50, and acuity improves steadily thereafter (see Figure 5.1). Most children reach 20/20 by about age 10 or 11.

The fact that the newborn sees so poorly is not so negative a thing as it might seem at first. Of course, it does mean that she can't see things that are far away; she probably can't see well enough to tell if a tall object 10 feet away is a person or a lamp. But she sees quite well close up. She focuses her eyes particularly well at a distance of about 8 inches, which

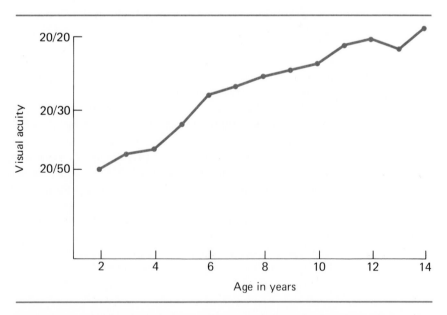

Figure 5.1   Children's visual acuity improves over the first 10 to 15 years. Children younger than age 2 have still poorer acuity—20/800 at birth, improving to 20/100 by about 4 months. (*Source:* Weymouth, 1963, pp. 132 & 133.)

is just about the usual distance between the baby's eyes and the mother's face during feeding.

What Babies and Children Look At

Of perhaps greater interest is just what the baby looks at. Does the child scan objects systematically? Does she prefer to look at some kinds of objects rather than others? Just how does she use her eyes to examine her world?

Researchers have become extremely clever at devising ways of discovering what babies look at. Robert Fantz (1956) is credited with a strategy called the *preference technique,* in which infants (propped up in infant seats) are shown two pictures or objects that vary in some interesting dimension, like shape or size or symmetry or number of edges. The babies' eye movements are then watched carefully to see which of the two pictures or objects each baby looks at the most. Another strategy takes advantage of the processes of habituation and dishabituation (described in Chapter 3). An infant is shown a particular figure over and over until he stops examining it (habituation). Then he is shown another picture that varies in some fashion from the original to see if he exhibits renewed interest (dishabituation). If the baby shows interest in this new picture, you know he perceives it as "different" in some way. Using these strategies, researchers have been able to figure out what "rules babies look by" (to use Marshall Haith's phrase, 1980). Some interesting conclusions have emerged.

Scanning and Attention in Newborns.   The general rule of thumb—suggested by several researchers, such as Gordon Bronson (1974) and Philip Salapatek (1975)—is that for the first six to eight weeks of life the baby's visual attention is focused on *where* objects are in his world. Marshall Haith (1980) has even shown that newborns exhibit visual search in the dark. In the dark, babies open their eyes widely and scan the whole area, as if looking for light or for some object. If the lights are on, the baby searches until he finds an edge—some place in his range where there is a big contrast between light and dark. Once he finds such an edge, he stops searching and moves his eyes back and forth across and around the edge. Babies will also follow moving objects with their eyes.

The same rules seem to apply even when the baby is looking at a human face. Up to about 6 weeks of age, when babies look at faces they look mostly at the edges (Haith, Bergman, & Moore, 1977). If they do look at features, they are most likely to look at the eyes—not surprising when you think about it, since the eyes have a good deal of light/dark contrast and move as well. The only other part of the face very young infants seem to look at is the mouth, and then only when it is moving. We know for sure that even newborns look at moving mouths, because we know that they will imitate certain mouth movements, like mouth opening or tongue protrusion, as you can see in Figure 5.2 (Meltzoff, 1985; Field, 1982).

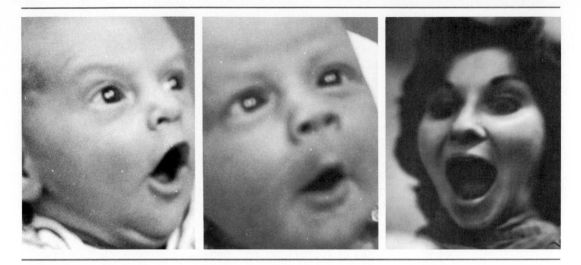

Figure 5.2 When newborn babies look at faces, they most often look at the edges of the face, or at the eyes. But they also look at things that move, like this adult's mouth. What is amazing is that they not only look at the mouth—they actually imitate the adult's mouth movement, which is a remarkable ability when you think about it. (*Source:* T. M. Field, Social perception and responsivity in early infancy. In T. M. Field, A. Huston, H. C. Quay, L. Troll, & G. E. Finley [Eds.], *Review of human development.* Copyright 1982 by John Wiley & Sons, New York, p. 26.)

This ability to imitate facial expressions in the first days after birth is a remarkable skill. The baby must not only focus on the other's mouth movements but must match his own movements to the other's simply on the basis of feedback from his own muscle movements (after all, the baby can't see his own face). Equally remarkable are the recent findings that even newborns are responsive to *patterns* in or *relationships* among stimuli.

In one study, for example, Sue Antell and Albert Caron (1985) habituated newborn babies to a picture of a square below a cross. When they then showed the babies the same square and cross, but this time with the cross below the square, the babies showed renewed interest, indicating that they had perceived the difference. Findings like these make it look as if from the very beginning, the baby is programmed to look in certain ways and to pay attention to certain relationships.

The Shift at 2 Months of Age. At about 8 weeks of age, after the cortex has developed more fully, we see some major shifts in the ways babies examine their world visually. The baby's attention now shifts to *what* an object is rather than merely where it may be located. To put it another way, the baby seems to move from a strategy designed primarily to *find* things to a strategy designed primarily to *identify* things.

What is amazing in all of this is the degree of detail the infant now seems to be able to take in and respond to. Not only do babies now look at eyes and other facial features more than at edges; they also look at and take in many more details. They notice whether two pictures are placed horizontally or vertically (Linn et al., 1982); they can tell the difference between pictures with two things in them and pictures with three things in them; and they clearly notice patterns. Whereas the newborn saw the difference between "square over cross" and "cross over square," the 2- or 3-month-old seems to notice even more generalizable patterns, such as "big over small."

In one experiment, Albert and Rose Caron (1981) chose stimuli like those in Figure 5.3. The babies were first shown pictures like the ones on the left, which shared some particular relationship ("small over big" or alternating pictures, in these examples). After a baby habituated (i.e., stopped looking), she was shown a figure like those on the right-hand side of Figure 5.3, which either followed or did not follow the same pattern. If the baby had really habituated to the *pattern* of the original pictures (e.g., "small over large"), she should show little interest in the pattern in column A but should show renewed interest in the pattern in column B. Caron and Caron found that 3- and 4-month-old infants did precisely that,

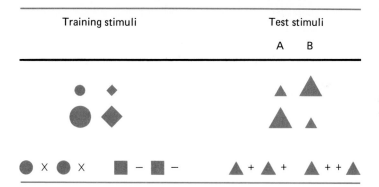

Figure 5.3 These are examples of the stimuli Albert and Rose Caron used in their study of infants' responses to visual patterns. They first showed the baby a series of training figures like the ones on the left. One baby might see a whole series of pictures with a small figure on top of a larger one; another baby might see alternating figures like the circle and the X. After the baby had habituated (stopped looking), she was then shown each of two test stimuli. Stimuli in column A followed the same pattern as the training figures; those in column B followed a different pattern. In these studies, 4-month-old babies showed renewed interest in column B patterns (indicating that they thought of these new figures as "different") but not in column A patterns. (*Source:* Caron & Caron, 1981, p. 227.)

which indicates that even at this early age, babies are finding and paying attention to patterns and not just to specific stimuli.

Making Discriminations

By paying attention to such detail, the infant learns to make *discriminations* (tell the difference) between rather complex objects, such as faces. From the parents' perspective, the most important discrimination is for the baby to be able to tell the difference between Mom and Dad or between either parent and a stranger. There is some dispute about just how early babies can make this discrimination. Tiffany Field and her colleagues (Field et al., 1984) have found that some babies as young as 2 days old respond differently to their mothers' faces than to the face of a stranger. The more common finding is that babies can consistently discriminate the parent's face from other faces by about 3 months of age (Zucker, 1985). And by 5 or 6 months of age, most infants can discriminate between different emotional expressions, such as sadness or fear or joy (Schwartz, Izard, & Ansul, 1985).

Catalogues of perceptual abilities like these may seem rather dry and irrelevant to the real world. But I hope it is clear that these rapidly emerging skills are a vital part of the baby's social repertoire and that they affect her responses to those around her as well as their responses to her. For example, the ability to discriminate one emotion from another in the parent's face is necessary for a process called *social referencing,* in which the infant or toddler (or older child or adult) judges the value, importance, or desirability of some new object or experience by checking to see how other people are reacting to it. If a 1-year-old is confronted with a new toy, for example, he will usually look first at his mother, checking her facial expression. If her face shows fear, the infant will stick closer to her than if her face shows joy (Klinnert, 1984; Zarbatany & Lamb, 1985). Such social referencing would not be possible if the infant were not already capable of making quite fine discriminations between facial expressions or between other subtly different cues.

Ignoring Visual Cues: The Perceptual Constancies

I have been describing what the infant and young child pays attention to, but there is an equally important set of cues that the child must be able to ignore. Specifically, the child must acquire a set of rules we call **perceptual constancies.**

When you see someone walking away from you, the image of the person actually becomes smaller on your retina. But you don't see the person as getting smaller. You see him as the same size but moving farther away. When you do this, you are demonstrating **size constancy;** you are able to see the size of an object as constant even when the retinal image becomes smaller or larger.

Other constancies include **shape constancy** (the ability to recognize that the shape of an object remains the same when you look at it from different angles) and **color constancy** (the ability to recognize that colors are constant even though the amount of light or shadow on them changes).

Taken together, the several specific constancies add up to the larger concept of **object constancy,** which is the recognition that objects remain the same even when they appear to the eye to change in certain ways. The evidence we have suggests that babies may be born with rudimentary forms of several constancies but that the constancies become more fully established over the first several years.

Size Constancy. In infants, the most-studied aspect of size constancy is **depth perception.** For example, when you see a man walking away from you, in order to maintain size constancy you have to be able to judge how far he has gone; this requires depth perception. For the infant, depth perception is obviously not only an essential ingredient in size constancy; it is also essential for other everyday tasks, like aiming the hands properly to reach a toy or a bottle. Can the baby judge depth?

One of the earliest (and still one of the cleverest) studies of infant depth perception was the work of Eleanor Gibson and Richard Walk (1960), who built an apparatus called a *visual cliff.* You can see in Figure 5.4 that it consists of a large glass table with a sort of runway in the middle. On one side of the runway there is a checkerboard pattern immediately below the glass; on the other side—the "cliff" side—the checkerboard is several feet below the glass. If a baby has no depth perception, she should be equally willing to crawl on either side of the runway, but if she can judge depth, she should be reluctant to crawl out on the cliff side. From the baby's perspective, the cliff side would indeed look like a cliff and she should stay away.

The original study by Gibson and Walk used babies 6 months old and older (since they had to be able to crawl at least a bit to be tested on this apparatus). By and large, these infants did *not* crawl out on the cliff side, but they were quite willing to crawl out on the shallow side. In other words, 6-month-old babies have depth perception.

But what about younger infants? The traditional visual cliff procedure can't give us the answer, since the baby must be able to crawl in order to "tell us" whether she can judge depth. But two other lines of evidence, including a modified visual cliff study, suggest that some depth perception is present as early as 2 months of age. Joseph Campos and his colleagues (Campos, Langer, & Krowitz, 1970) attached equipment to young infants that allowed the recording of their heart rates while the babies were on the visual cliff apparatus. He observed that babies' heart rates went down slightly when they were out on the cliff side but did not do so when they were on the noncliff side. This difference in response, which suggests that some discrimination took place, occurred in infants as young as 2 months but *not* in still younger babies.

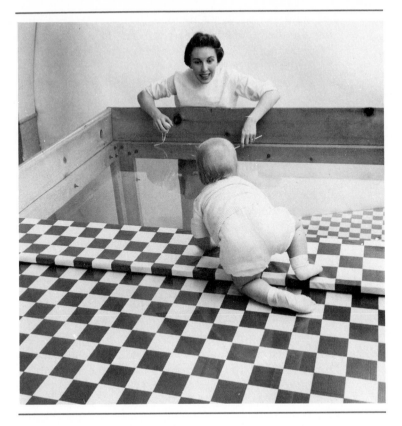

Figure 5.4 The "visual cliff" apparatus used by Gibson and Walk in their studies of depth perception in infants. In this photo, the mother is trying to coax the baby out onto the "cliff" side. (*Source:* Gibson & Walk, 1960, p. 65.)

Another procedure for studying depth perception in very young infants is to see how they react when an object (or a film of an object looming) approaches them as if on a collision course. If the infant has some depth perception, he should flinch, move to one side, or blink as the object appears to come very close. In fact, that is what a number of researchers have observed young babies doing. Such avoidance responses are fairly well established by 2 months of age (Bornstein, 1984), indicating at least some depth perception at that age.

Shape Constancy. Shape constancy, too, is extremely important for the baby. She has to realize that the bottle is still the bottle even though it is turned slightly and thus presents a different shape and that her toys remain the same when they are in different positions. Current research indicates that at least rudimentary shape constancy is present by 2 or 3 months of age (e.g., Cook & Birch, 1984; Bower, 1966). In Thomas Bower's classic study (1966), 2-month-old infants responded to a tilted or turned rectangle as if it were the same as the original rectangle, even though the retinal image cast by such a tilted rectangle was actually a trapezoid.

One of the ironies about perceptual development is that at a later age, when learning to read, a child has to *unlearn* some of these shape constancies. For the first four to five years of life, the basic rule is that an object is the same whether you see it right side up, upside down, or turned around to the left or to the right. But when you learn to read, that old rule has to be modified. Letters like *b* and *d* are the same shape—except with the direction reversed. The letters *p* and *q* are the same kind of pair, and *p* and *b* are the same except that one is upside down. So in order to read (at least the Latin alphabet), the child must now pay attention to something she'd learned to ignore—namely, the rotation of the letter in space.

Of course, there is a good deal more to learning to read than simply ignoring shape constancy. But we do know that 5-year-olds who have difficulty discriminating between mirror images of shapes also have more difficulty learning to read (Casey, 1986).

Color Constancy. Results from studies by Marc Bornstein and his colleagues (Bornstein, Kessen, & Weiskopf, 1976), similar in design to Bower's studies of shape constancy, make it clear that most babies have at least some color constancy by the time they are about 4 months old, and perhaps sooner.

Taken together, the evidence indicates that by 4 months (and possibly much sooner), infants have mastered the basic elements of object constancy. That is, they can judge depth to some degree and thus can achieve size constancy, and they can use color and shape constancy in their perceptions of objects in their worlds. All these constancies improve over the first year of life, but it is extremely interesting to find such complex responses present as early as 2 or 4 months of age.

The Object Concept

A related development is the extension of the various constancies to a broader understanding of the invariance of objects, including objects which may not be currently visible. This understanding is called the **object concept.** One aspect of the object concept is the understanding that objects continue to exist even when the infant can't see them any longer. For example, even when the mother goes out of the room, she still exists. That understanding is usually referred to as **object permanence.** The other aspect of the object concept is the understanding that individual objects retain a unique identity from one occasion to another. That is, mother is the same mother no matter when you see her, the rattle you are holding in your hand is the same rattle you held yesterday, and so forth. This is referred to as **object identity.** Both aspects of the object concept seem to develop over the first year or two of life.

Object Permanence. Jean Piaget was the first to describe the emergence of object permanence. According to his observations, replicated frequently by later researchers, there are a series of steps in the child's emerging understanding.

The first sign that the baby is developing object permanence comes at about 2 months of age. Suppose you show a toy to a child of this age, then put a screen in front of the toy and remove the toy. When you then remove the screen, the baby shows some indication of surprise, as if she knew that something should still be there (Piaget, 1954; Gratch, 1979). The child thus seems to have a rudimentary schema or expectation about the permanence of an object. But an infant of this age shows no signs of searching for a toy if he drops it over the edge of the crib or it disappears beneath a blanket or behind a screen (as you can see in Figure 5.5).

Six- or eight-month-old babies, however, *will* look over the edge of the crib for the dropped toys. (In fact, babies of this age may drive their parents nuts playing "dropsy" in the high chair.) Infants this age will also search for partially hidden objects. If you partially cover a favorite toy with a cloth, the infant will reach for the toy, which suggests that in some sense the infant "recognizes" that the whole object is there even though she can see only part of it. But if you completely cover the toy with the cloth, the infant will stop looking at the cloth and will not reach for the toy, even if she has seen you put the cloth over it.

This changes again somewhere between 8 and 12 months. Infants this age will reach for or search for a toy that has been covered completely by a cloth or hidden by a screen (Dunst, Brooks, & Doxsey, 1982). Further refinements of object permanence appear during the second year of life, but by 12 months most infants have at least a preliminary grasp of the basic fact that objects continue to exist even when they are no longer visible.

Object Identity. Object identity, in contrast, does not seem to be part of the child's understanding even in rudimentary form until perhaps 5 months of age. One approach to studying this, developed by Thomas Bower (1975), is to violate the principle of object identity and see if the infant shows surprise. Bower used mirrors to give the impression that several mothers were standing in front of the infant. Infants younger than about 5 months showed no surprise at this—in fact, they seemed to view the idea of multiple mothers with some pleasure. Infants older than 5 months, though, were very upset by the multiple mothers, suggesting that they realized that there should be only one mother—evidence for object identity.

I have discussed object constancy and the object concept in some detail because they form a sort of bridge between perception and early cognitive development and because they have such obvious practical rele-

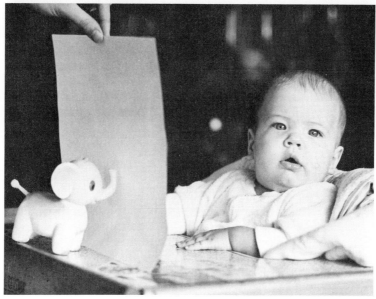

Figure 5.5   These photos show the response of a 5- to 6-month-old infant in an object permanence test. The baby stops reaching for or searching for the toy when it is hidden from her. An older baby would keep searching or push the screen aside to reach for the toy.

vance to the emergence of the child's attachment to the caregiver. In particular, some kind of object permanence may be required before the baby can become attached to an individual person, such as his mother or father. Babies younger than 6 months may be more sootheable by someone familiar with their habits and may smile more at Mom and Dad than at strangers;

but the full-fledged attachment of the baby to a single other person (which I'll describe in more detail in Chapter 11) doesn't seem to emerge until about 5 or 6 months, just about the time that the child begins to understand that Mom continues to exist when she is out of sight.

AUDITORY DEVELOPMENT

Acuity

Although children's hearing improves up to adolescence, newborns' auditory acuity is much better than their visual acuity. Current research evidence suggests that within the general range of pitch and loudness of the human voice, newborns hear as well as adults do, although adults have better hearing of quiet and low-pitched sounds (Olsho, 1985).

Detecting Locations

Another basic auditory skill that improves with age is the ability to determine the location of a sound. You can tell roughly where a sound is coming from in large part because your two ears are separated from one another, so the sound arrives at one ear slightly before the other. If the sound comes from a source equidistant from the two ears (the *midline*), then the sound arrives at the same time at the two ears. We know that newborns have some primitive ability to judge the general direction from which a sound has come because they will turn their heads toward a noise. This skill improves rapidly, and by 6 months, most infants are quite good at making judgments of this kind (Bower, 1977a).

What Infants and Children Listen To

As was true with vision, if we are to understand the child's auditory develop-ment we have to go beyond basic acuity and ask what aspects of sounds the infant or child seems to pay attention to, what discriminations he can make.

What we find is that very young infants seem to be capable of extremely fine discriminations. For example, as early as 1 month, babies can discrimi-nate between speech sounds like *p* and *b* or *d* and *t* (Trehub & Rabinovitch, 1972). More interesting, they can also tell the difference between syllables such as *bah* and *pah*. By perhaps 6 months of age, they can discriminate between two-syllable "words" like *bada* and *baga;* and they can even respond to a syllable that is hidden inside a string of other syllables like ti*bati* or ko*bako* (Morse & Cowan, 1982; Goodsitt et al., 1984; Kuhl, 1987). It doesn't even seem to matter what voice quality the speech sound is made in. By 6 months, babies respond to individual sounds as the same whether they are spoken by male or female voices or by an adult's or a child's voice (Kuhl, 1983).

What is even more intriguing to me is that, as with vision, there is evidence that infants pay attention to *patterns* of sounds from the very beginning. One particularly striking demonstration of this comes from a study by Anthony DeCasper and Melanie Spence (1986). They had pregnant women read a particular children's story (such as Dr. Seuss's *The Cat in the Hat*) out loud each day for the final six weeks of the pregnancy. After the infants were born, the researchers played recordings of the mother reading either this same story or a previously unheard story. The newborns clearly preferred the sound of the story they had heard in utero. Not only does this study demonstrate that the auditory system is well developed some weeks before birth; it shows that even before birth, infants are paying attention to and discriminating among complex patterns of sounds.

Further evidence for the same point comes from the observation that babies as young as 6 months listen to melodies and recognize the patterns. Sandra Trehub and her colleagues (Trehub, Thorpe, & Morrongiello, 1985; Trehub, Bull, & Thorpe, 1984) trained 6-month-old babies to turn their heads toward a loudspeaker for a particular six-tone melody, then tested the babies with melodies that varied in a number of ways. Babies responded to new melodies as the same if they had the same contour (notes going up and down in the same sequence) and were in approximately the same range. They responded to them as different if the contour changed or if the notes were much higher or much lower. Thus, as with vision (recall Figure 5.3), it is apparently the pattern and not just the specific sounds that the child is paying attention to.

Discriminating Individual Voices

Since babies' auditory acuity is better than their visual acuity at birth, they are able to tell the difference between two particular voices earlier than they can discriminate between two faces—possibly as early as the first day of life. DeCasper and Fifer (1982) have found that the newborn can tell his mother's voice from another female voice (but not his father's voice from another male voice), and he prefers the mother's, possibly because he has become familiar with the mother's voice while still in utero. By 6 months, babies even know which voice is supposed to go with which face. If you put an infant of this age in a situation where he can see both his father and mother and can hear a tape-recorded voice of one of them, he will look toward the parent whose voice he hears (Spelke & Owsley, 1979).

Collectively, the research on auditory development tells us that babies can do a pretty good job of hearing what is said around them and to them and that they are paying attention both to sound patterns and to very detailed features of the sounds they hear—all of which is obviously critical for language development. It also tells us that it really is worthwhile to start talking to babies from birth. In fact, as you'll see in Chapter 8, parents who begin talking to their infants very early have children whose language development is more rapid.

DEVELOPMENT OF OTHER SENSES

Smell and Taste

The senses of smell and taste have been studied much less, but we do have some basic knowledge. As in adults, the two senses are intricately related—that is, if you cannot smell for some reason (like when you have a cold), your taste sensitivity is also significantly reduced. The taste buds on the tongue detect four basic tastes: sweet, sour, bitter, and salty. The mucous membranes of the nose register smell, which has nearly unlimited variations.

Newborns appear to respond differentially to all four basic flavors (Crook, 1987). Some of the clearest demonstrations of this come from an elegantly simple set of studies by Jacob Steiner (1979; Ganchrow, Steiner, & Daher, 1983). Newborn infants who had never been fed were photographed before and after flavored water was put into their mouths. Steiner

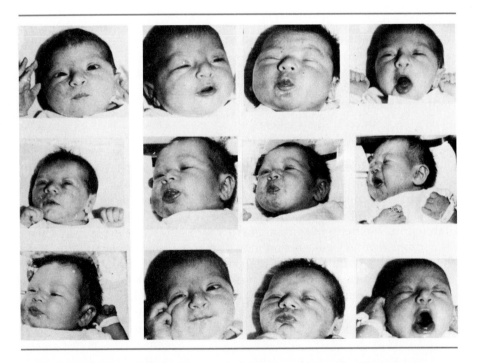

Figure 5.6 These are three of the babies Steiner observed in his experiments on taste responses of newborns. The left-hand column shows each baby's normal expression. You can see how that expression changed when the babies were given a sweet taste, a sour taste, and a bitter taste. (*Source:* J. E. Steiner, Human facial expressions in response to taste and smell stimulation. In H. W. Reese & L. P. Lipsett [Eds.], *Advances in child development and behavior,* Vol. 13. New York: Academic Press, 1979, Figure 1, p. 269.)

could determine whether the babies reacted differently when he varied the flavor. As you can see in Figure 5.6, babies respond to the sweet-tasting liquid with a relaxed face and an expression that looks a lot like a smile. They respond to the sour liquid with pursed lips and to the bitter liquid with an arched mouth and an expression resembling disgust. The fact that the babies showed such distinctive expressions tells us that different flavors do indeed taste different to the infant.

Babies as young as 1 week old can also tell the difference between their mother's and other women's smells—although this seems to be true only for breast-fed babies, who spend quite a lot of time with their noses against their mother's bare skin (Macfarlane, 1975; Cernoch & Porter, 1985). Thus far, there is no indication that young infants identify their fathers only by smell.

Touch

If you think back to the list of reflexes in the newborn I gave you in Table 3.2, you'll realize that the newborn has at least some sensitivity to touch. A touch on the cheek triggers the rooting and sucking reflexes; a touch on the bottom of the foot triggers the Babinsky reflex. Babies appear to be especially sensitive to touches on the mouth, the face, the hands, the soles of the feet, and the abdomen; they are less sensitive in other parts of the body. Probably the sense of touch becomes more finely tuned over the early years of life and the child becomes able to detect and respond to more subtle differences in the form or location of stimulation, but that is mostly supposition, since there has been less research on touch perception in infants or children than on other aspects of perceptual sensitivity (Reisman, 1987).

COMBINING INFORMATION FROM SEVERAL SENSES

I have been talking about each sense separately, tracing the development of each set of perceptual skills. But if you think about the way you receive and use perceptual information, you'll realize quickly that you rarely get information through only one sense at a time. Ordinarily you have *both* sound and sight, or touch and sight, or still more complex combinations of smell, sight, touch, and sound. Adults coordinate this information in complex ways. For example, if you have seen an object but have not touched it, you can usually still pick it out from a batch of objects using only touch cues (that is, you know what it *ought* to feel like on the basis of what you saw). And if you see a drum being beaten in a particular rhythm, you expect to hear that same rhythm. Amazingly enough, it now seems that quite young babies can integrate information across senses in this same way, again apparently by paying attention to the underlying pattern and searching for the same pattern in another modality.

For instance, in several delightfully clever experiments, Elizabeth Spelke (Spelke & Owsley, 1979) has shown that 4-month-old infants can connect sound rhythms with movement. She showed babies two films simultaneously. One film showed a toy kangaroo bouncing up and down and the other a donkey bouncing up and down, with one of the animals bouncing at a faster rate. From a speaker located between the two film screens, the infant heard a tape recording of a rhythmic bouncing sound that matched one of the two rates. In this situation, babies spent more time watching the film whose rhythm matched the sound they were hearing, a result I find remarkable.

Equally notable is the observation that 4-to-5-month-old babies will look longer at a face of a person mouthing a vowel they are hearing over a loudspeaker than at the face of a person mouthing another vowel (Kuhl & Meltzoff, 1984). Already at this age babies have hooked up sound with vision, and they expect the patterns from the two sources to match.

Connecting information from touch and vision seems to come a bit later (Brown & Gottfried, 1986; Spelke, 1987). Only at about 4 or 5 months do infants consistently reach for things they see (whereas from the first days of life they look at things they hear), and only between 6 and 12 months do infants begin to be able to identify by sight objects that they have previously explored only tactually or vice versa.

A really lovely example of the ability of infants to use information from one modality to replace information from another comes from a series of studies of blind infants by Thomas Bower (1977b), in which the infants were equipped with special ultrasonic devices (see Figure 5.7). The study is described in the box on pages 172–173.

All of this burgeoning (and I think fascinating) research on combining of information from several senses has raised some important theoretical questions. Piaget, in particular, proposed that such intermodal integration of information was simply not possible in early infancy, that infants developed knowledge about the world separately in each modality and only later were able to combine them into more coordinated schemas. Research like Spelke's and a whole host of similarly inventive studies show that this is simply not the case (Gibson & Spelke, 1983).

THE BASIC CHARACTERISTICS OF PERCEPTUAL DEVELOPMENT: A SECOND LOOK

Before going on to talk about individual differences, let me pause for a moment to go back to the four basic trends in perceptual development I laid out at the beginning of this chapter and see what evidence we have for each one.

Purposefulness of activity does seem to increase with age. Although

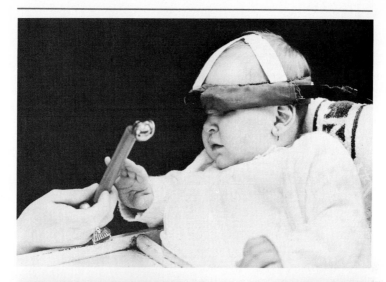

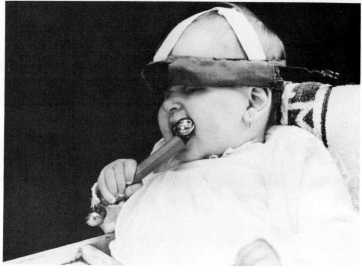

Figure 5.7 A blind baby using the special sonic guide Bower has studied (see box on pp. 172–173). Notice how she reaches accurately for the object, much as a sighted infant does using visual cues. (*Source:* Bower, Blind babies see with their ears. *New Scientist, 1977, 73,* p. 255, photographs by Ric Gemmel.)

even the newborn has a pattern, has "rules" by which she operates perceptually, the transition at about 2 months seems to involve a shift into another gear, in which the infant explores visually and with other senses in a more systematic way. This transition is not complete by 2 months of age, though. For example, Brian Vandenberg (1984) gave children aged 4 through

BLIND BABIES CAN "SEE" WITH THEIR EARS

One of the most fascinating—and practically relevant—sets of studies of infant perception I have seen in recent years is a series of observations T. G. R. Bower made of blind infants who have been equipped with a special ultrasonic device that allows them to perceive the world around them. Figure 5.7 on page 171 shows what the apparatus looks like.

The ultrasonic device works in a way that is similar to echolocation in dolphins or bats. The transmitter continuously bombards the environment with high-frequency sound waves, which bounce off of the objects—toys, walls, people—around the baby. The bounced-back sound is received by the headset and transmitted to the infant's ears through the speakers. Qualities of the reflected sound provide the baby with information about variations in the shape, distance, and size of objects.

- The pitch of the sound the baby hears tells her how far away the object is. Low pitch signals a nearby object and high pitch signals a farther-away object.
- The loudness of the sound tells the baby how big the object is. Loud sounds signal large objects and softer sounds signal smaller objects.
- The clarity of the sound tells the baby something about the texture of the surface. Very clear sounds indicate hard surfaces and fuzzy sounds indicate soft surfaces.
- The right/left location of the sound tells the baby where the object is located in space. The two ears receive signals at different times, depending on the object's location; so objects on the right make sounds that arrive at the right ear fractionally sooner than at the left ear while objects on the left do the reverse.

Bower reports on tests of this apparatus with six blind babies ranging in age from 5 to 16 months. The results are fascinating. First of all, even the 5-month-old baby was able to learn to use this device very quickly—within hours or days. Babies using the equipment quickly began to reach accurately for objects, to crawl or walk through doorways, even to hold out their hands and move them around in order to listen to the reflected sound. The babies accompanied these actions with signs of great joy and delight.

All these behaviors are strikingly similar to what we see in sighted infants, who begin reaching for objects within the first 2 to 3 months and show visual regard of the moving hand in the early months as

12 a series of toys to play with, including many novel toys. The younger children tended to have their attention "captured" by one particular toy and to stay with that toy for most of the session. The older children typically looked at and explored all the toys first and then went back to the ones of special interest. Thus, as the child gets older he explores more systematically, more intentionally—he is less likely to be controlled by some dominant stimulus.

The child's increased awareness of meaning is also clear from all the bits and pieces I have been describing. It is striking that almost from the first day of life the infant seems to pay attention not just to the specific properties of a stimulus but also to underlying patterns or *information*

well. What Bower's experiments show is that blind infants can glean essentially the same information about the environment from auditory cues that sighted infants get from visual cues. I am sure that these early experiments will be followed by widespread use of such devices for blind babies—a wonderful breakthrough for these handicapped infants, thanks to new techniques developed by engineers and to knowledge of perceptual development gained by developmental psychologists.

But there are some equally fascinating theoretical implications. Bower has found that the younger babies actually have an easier time learning to use this apparatus than the older babies. And adults have a very difficult time with it—taking weeks or months to learn what an infant learns within a few hours or days. Why might this be so?

Bower argues that the very young infant is really not treating the stimulus input as "sound." Rather, he is treating it as a description of the world around him, much as sighted people perceive light. Light is a background variable that gives us information, but it is not usually a property of objects. Blind infants treat the sounds the same way—as if they tell about the physical qualities of the world "out there." This suggests that for the infant, auditory and visual information is essentially interchangeable.

But, like the adult, the older infant—starting as early as about 12 months of age—perceives the sounds as *part of* the objects in some way. So the 13-month-old baby Bower tested with the apparatus kept putting the toys and objects up to her ear, as if the sound were being made by the object rather than informing her about the object's location. This older infant and the adults who have been tested appear to treat sound and sight as distinct sources of information rather than as interchangeable sources.

On the basis of evidence like this, Bower argues that babies are operating on very abstract perceptual principles. Over time, however, perceptual information becomes more and more specific, more and more differentiated. Obviously we need to use perceptual information in such differentiated ways in order to make discriminations, to recognize objects and people. But one of the prices of that developmental "advance" is that we lose the baby's ability to use the information interchangeably. The practical implication of this finding is that blind babies should begin training with the ultrasonic device as early as possible.

given in that stimulus (Pick, 1986). Although this ability seems to be present very early in life, it clearly increases during infancy. By 6 or 12 months of age, babies can connect sound and sight patterns, can recognize things visually that they have only experienced before by touch, and can recognize melodies and many other patterns. Beyond the first year of life, the child of course continues to show development in this domain as she discovers more subtle, more complex, or more superordinate meanings or affordances (to use Gibson's term).

The degree of differentiation in perceptual skill and discrimination abilities also clearly increases with age. Newborns pay attention to only a few dimensions, such as movement or the edges of things; older babies attend to many more properties of objects, including texture, color, shape, and density. In each of these areas, the child's discriminations become still more subtle in the preschool and later years.

Ignoring the irrelevant, too, is something we can already see in young infants, although I have talked least about this dimension of change. The various object constancies, which all require the child to ignore certain perceptual changes, develop gradually in the first year of life. We see this same trend in later years as children become less and less distractible. In one study, for example, Higgins and Turnure (1984) gave preschoolers, second-graders, and sixth-graders easy and difficult learning tasks while music played in the background at either a low or a very high sound level. Preschoolers were much more disrupted by the sound than were older children. In fact, the sixth-graders actually performed better when there was music playing, as if the distraction forced them to focus their attention more fully on the task.

All in all, research on perceptual development in the early years of life has called into question a whole series of previously cherished beliefs about infants and their abilities. Despite their many limitations, infants seem to approach and respond to the world around them in a much more organized and sophisticated way than most psychologists had thought even a decade ago. And the fact that babies respond to patterns of stimulation, to underlying information, and not just to the surface sensory input, means that the infant is capable of far more complex cognitive processes than we had given her credit for.

INDIVIDUAL DIFFERENCES IN PERCEPTION

Perceptual Styles

So far I've talked as if all infants and children are pretty much alike in the way they perceive things. That's true. But it is also true that there are some fascinating differences in the *style* in which people (including infants) examine the world around them.

Reflection Versus Impulsivity. One dimension of individual differences is simply the speed or care with which a person examines objects or situations, a dimension Jerome Kagan calls **conceptual tempo** (Kagan et al., 1964; Kagan, 1971). The two ends of this dimension are usually called **reflection** and **impulsivity.**

Evidence of conceptual tempo can be seen in quite young infants (Kagan, 1971). A slower-tempo baby will remain still and look at something new with fixed concentration, while the faster-tempo baby will thrash around, become excited, gurgle, and look away after only a short period of examination. In preschool and school-age children, the task most often used to measure tempo is a picture-matching game, using pictures like the one in Figure 5.8. The child's job is to find which of the six pictures

Figure 5.8 A sample item from Kagan's test of "reflection versus impulsivity." The child taking the test must try to select the picture from among the bottom six that exactly matches the figure at the top. (*Source:* Kagan, Rosman, Day, Albert, & W. Phillips. Information processing in the child: Significance of analytic and reflective attitudes. *Psychological monographs,* 1964, *78* [1, Whole No. 578], p. 23. Copyright 1964 by the American Psychological Association. Reprinted with permission.)

at the bottom *exactly* matches the picture at the top. A *reflective* child looks carefully at all the alternatives before making a choice. Not surprisingly, he makes few errors. An *impulsive* child, on the other hand, looks over the options quickly and chooses one—which is frequently inaccurate.

Not all children fit neatly into this category system. Some, often called *fast accurates,* work quickly but still make few errors. Others, called *slow inaccurates,* take a lot of time but still end up making mistakes. Very little research has been addressed to these groups of children. In most cases, only the slow accurate (reflective) and fast inaccurate (impulsive) children have been contrasted.

This dimension of style is at least somewhat stable during childhood. In one longitudinal study, Kagan and his colleagues Deborah Lapidus and Michael Moore (1978) compared children's tempo measured at 8 months and again at 10 years and found a significant (though not very large) correlation. That is, reflective infants were somewhat more likely to become reflective children and impulsive infants to become impulsive children. Kagan has also found that reflective children have a somewhat easier time learning to read, which makes sense when you think about the sort of careful examination of letter forms that is needed in the early stages of reading (Kagan, 1965). Other school tasks may also demand reflective skill, so reflectives are often found to do slightly better in school (e.g., Haskins & McKinney, 1976).

But don't jump to the conclusion that reflectiveness is always best. Many (if not most) tasks in everyday life do not require careful examination or search. A quick look is enough, and someone with a reflective style may take far longer than the task requires. If you're driving down a street looking for a sign that says "Connecticut Avenue," you don't need to stop at every corner and carefully examine the street sign. You can tell just by the length of the name whether it could be "Connecticut" or not. In other words, any time a simple glance is enough, the impulsive person will be more efficient. It is only when a detailed examination is needed to make a discrimination or a judgment that the reflective style is helpful.

Field Dependence and Independence. Another categorization of perceptual styles, emerging originally from studies of adults, has been suggested by H. A. Witkin and his associates (1962). Witkin was intrigued by the fact that some people's perceptions seemed to be heavily influenced by the background environment while other people's did not. People who could ignore the irrelevant background material, who could break apart a stimulus and look at only part of it, Witkin called **field-independent,** and those who were more influenced by the context or who focused on an entire situation he called **field-dependent.**

In children, field dependence/independence has most often been measured with the *Embedded Figures Test.* In this task, the subject is shown a simple figure, such as a square or a pie shape, and is then asked to find a figure exactly like that in a complex drawing. The subject must ignore the other features of the drawing (the field) and pay attention only to the abstract shapes. (You might want to see how good you are at this yourself. One of the items from a children's version of the Embedded Figures Test is shown in Figure 5.9. The adult version is considerably harder.)

Generally speaking, children become more and more field-independent

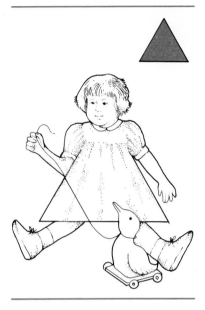

Figure 5.9　A sample item from the Coates Preschool Embedded Figures Test, a measure of field dependence versus field independence. The simple figure at the upper right must be located in the complex figure below. How long does it take you to find it? (*Source:* Coates, 1973.)

as they get older, at least until adolescence (Kogan, 1983); this is certainly what we'd expect in view of the basic developmental changes in perceptual learning strategies I've described so far. But at any given age, there are still individual differences; some children are more field-independent, others more field-dependent.

Field dependence/independence has proven to be an extremely interesting dimension of individual difference. For example, field-independent children seem generally to focus their attention on objects or tasks, while field-dependent children focus more on people. The field-dependent child's very reliance on outside cues, on the context, may help her to learn better social skills. In contrast, the field-independent child, perhaps because of her greater ability to "disembed" parts from wholes, tends to be better at certain cognitive tasks, such as those that require spatial visualization.

The research on both reflection/impulsivity and field dependence/independence is full of contradictions and confusions. Neither style is as consistent or as pervasive as theorists at first proposed. But all of this work points to the possibility that there may be underlying differences in the ways in which infants and children examine and understand their worlds. Such differences in style may cut across our traditional categories of analysis. For example, might these differences in perceptual or conceptual style be related to temperament differences?

Sex Differences

As nearly as I can determine, there are fewer sex differences in perceptual skills than in any other area of development. Boy babies and girl babies do not seem to differ in levels of acuity or in discrimination ability. And they do not appear to differ in the rate of acquisition of such basic concepts as object identity or object permanence.

Measures of field independence/dependence, however, commonly do show a sex difference: boys are more field-independent and girls more field-dependent. Possibly this difference is found because many measures of this dimension involve some aspect of spatial visualization. (Boys as a group are generally better at such tasks—more about that in Chapter 6.) On tests of conceptual tempo (reflection versus impulsivity), in contrast, no consistent sex differences have been found.

Social Class Differences

There are no consistent social class differences that I know of in the basic maturation of perceptual skills. Middle-class children do not shift from looking at contours to looking at the middle of pictures any sooner than do poor children, for example. But in older children, there are differences in conceptual tempo; poor children are more often impulsive and middle-class children are more reflective, which may be one of many factors explaining why poor children have more difficulty learning to read.

ANSWERING THE "WHY" QUESTIONS: EXPLANATIONS OF PERCEPTUAL DEVELOPMENT

Theories of perceptual development have been dominated from the beginning by one of the key theoretical issues I raised in Chapter 1, namely, the nature/nurture controversy. In studies of perception, this is cast as nativism versus empiricism. The question is surely familiar by now: Are the child's perceptual skills built in or emergent with maturation (the **nativist** position), or are they the result of learning, of interaction with the environment (the **empiricist** position)? Or, to put it another way, does the infant perceive the world in generally the same way as an adult does, using the same strategies and abilities, or does the infant perceive the world quite differently and have to learn the more complex perceptual skills of an adult?

Such either/or, black/white statements of theoretical dilemmas can be (often are) helpful, but the truth usually turns out to be more the color of an elephant—gray. Still, it is helpful to see just what shade of gray our elephant may be this time.

Arguments for Nativism

In the case of perceptual development, the arguments on the nativist side are quite powerful. The more skillful researchers have become in figuring out ways to test infants' perceptual skills, the more skillful the newborn appears to be. Babies have considerable perceptual acuity, some depth perception, and some rudimentary constancies. More important, babies do not have to be taught what to look at. There are "rules" for looking (and presumably for listening and touching, too) that can be detected at birth. As Kagan puts it: "Nature has apparently equipped the newborn with an initial bias in the processing of experience. He does not, as the nineteenth-century empiricists believed, have to learn what he should examine" (Kagan, 1971, p. 60). These "biases" change with age, but later changes, too, seem to be strongly related to maturation of the nervous system. The shift in visual attention patterns at 2 months, for example, occurs at about the same time as a parallel change in the visual perception area of the cortex.

Arguments for Empiricism

On the other side of the ledger, however, a great deal of evidence from research in other species argues that some *minimum level* of experience is necessary to *maintain* the perceptual systems. Animals deprived of light show deterioration of the whole visual system and a consequent decrease in perceptual abilities (e.g., Hubel and Weisel, 1963, whose study was one of the first). Wayne Dennis's study of orphanage babies in Iran (1960), which I've touched on before, suggests that the animal research may be generalizable to human subjects as well. The infants (who didn't have a chance to look at things, to explore objects with hands and eyes and tongue, and who were deprived of the opportunity to move around freely) were retarded in the development of both perceptual and motor skills.

Juri Allik and Jaan Valsiner (1980) suggest an interesting analogy to computer hardware and software. The perceptual hardware—specific neural pathways, rules for examining the world, a bias toward searching for patterns, and the like—may be preprogrammed. But the software—the program for the child's response to a particular real environment—depends on specific experience. A child is *able* to make visual discrimination between people or objects within the first few months of life. That's built into the hardware. But the specific discriminations she learns, and the number of separate objects she learns to recognize, will depend on her experience. The basic system is thus adapted to the specific environment in which the child finds herself.

━━━━━　## SUMMARY

1. Perceptual development generally follows four patterns of change: increased purposefulness, increased awareness of meaning of perceptual information, increased differentiation of focus, and increased ability to ignore the irrelevant.

2. Visual acuity is quite poor at birth but improves rapidly in the first few months.

3. Visual attention appears to follow definite rules, even in the first hours of life. Newborns search for objects and focus on edges or on movement. They also show some sensitivity to pattern or relationship among visual cues.

4. At about 2 months of age, babies focus more on *what* the object is, examining the middle as well as the edges and attending to more complex relationships and patterns.

5. Babies can discriminate the parents' faces from other faces by 3 or 4 months, perhaps earlier, but visual discrimination may lag behind olfactory and auditory discrimination.

6. By 2 months of age, babies show some signs of the perceptual constancies of size, color, and shape.

7. Object identity and object permanence are other properties of objects the child must learn in the first several years. By 12 months of age, most children have the rudiments of object permanence and realize that objects continue to exist even when they are out of sight.

8. Object identity—the realization that an object is the same from one encounter to the next—is evident in at least beginning form by about 5 months.

9. Auditory acuity is better at birth than is visual acuity. Shortly after birth, babies are good at hearing sounds in the range of the human voice, at detecting the location of sounds, and at making fine discriminations between individual speech sounds. After a few months, they also attend to patterns of sounds and melodies.

10. Smell and taste sensitivities are also present in very young babies, as is response to tactual stimulation. As with all perceptual skills, however, the infant's acuity and discrimination ability increase over the early years of life.

11. Infants appear to be able to combine information from vision and hearing from the earliest months; integration of tactual and visual information comes later.

12. Individual differences in perceptual style include the dimensions of reflection versus impulsivity (tempo) and of field independence versus field dependence.

13. No sex differences are consistently observed in basic perceptual skills, although girls are frequently found to be more field-dependent than are boys.

14. Social class differences in perceptual abilities are rare, although poor children tend to have a faster conceptual tempo (to be more impulsive in style) than are middle-class children.

15. Both the empiricists and the nativists are correct to some extent about the origin of perceptual skills. Many basic perceptual abilities, including strategies for examining the objects around one, appear to be built into the system at birth or develop as the brain develops over the early years. But specific experience is required both to maintain the underlying system and to learn fundamental discriminations and patterns.

■■■■■■■■■■■ **KEY TERMS**

acuity Sharpness of perceptual ability—how well or clearly one can see or hear or use other senses.

color constancy The ability to see the color of an object as remaining the same despite changes in illumination or shadow. One of the basic perceptual constancies that make up object constancy.

conceptual tempo A dimension of individual differences in perceptual/conceptual style, suggested by Kagan. It describes the general pace at which objects (or people) are examined or explored.

depth perception The ability to judge the distance of an object from the body on the basis of a number of cues.

empiricism The opposite of nativism. The theoretical point of view that all perceptual skill arises from experience.

field dependence One end of a dimension of individual difference in perceptual style, proposed by Witkin. Field-dependent individuals are heavily influenced by the context in which objects appear.

field independence The other end of the field-dependence dimension. Field-independent individuals can ignore the context or distracting cues around objects.

impulsivity One end of the continuum of conceptual tempo described by Kagan. Impulsive individuals examine objects or arrays quickly, making rapid scans, and they may make more errors if fine discriminations are required.

nativism The opposite of empiricism. The view that perceptual skills are inborn and do not require experience to develop.

object concept A general term including the concepts of object permanence and object identity.

object constancy The general phrase describing the ability to see objects as remaining the same despite changes in retinal image.

object identity Part of the object concept. The recognition that objects remain the same from one encounter to the next.

object permanence Part of the object concept. The recognition that an object continues to exist even when it is temporarily out of sight.

perception The process of obtaining information about the world through stimulation.

perceptual constancies A set of skills, including shape, size, and color constancy, that permit us to recognize that an object stays the same even when it appears to change.

perceptual learning An increase in the ability to extract information (via the senses) from the environment as a result of practice or experience.

reflection One end of the tempo dimension of perceptual style. Reflective individuals examine objects or arrays very carefully and slowly. They normally perform better than impulsive individuals when fine discriminations are required.

shape constancy The ability to see an object's shape as remaining the same despite changes in the shape of the retinal image. A basic perceptual constancy.

size constancy The ability to see an object's size as remaining the same despite changes in the size of the retinal image. A key element in this constancy is the ability to judge depth.

■■■■■■■■■■■ **SUGGESTED READING**

There are not many good nontechnical sources on perceptual development. If you are interested in further detail, two moderately technical sources are Linda Acredolo and Janet Hake (1982) and Bornstein (1984), both listed in the references at the end of the book. The following sources are intended for the nonprofessional reader.

Bower, T. G. R. (1977). *The perceptual world of the child.* Cambridge, MA: Harvard University Press.
This brief book (about 85 pages) covers in readable fashion most of the major aspects of perceptual development during the early years. A great deal of fascinating research has been done in the years since this book was written, particularly the work on the infant's attention to pattern and meaning. Still, this is a good general source.

Lamb, M. E., & Campos, J. J. (1982). *Development in infancy.* New York: Random House. This more recent general text on infancy contains a clear chapter on perceptual development.

PROJECT: DEVELOPMENT OF THE OBJECT CONCEPT

For this project, you will need to locate an infant between 6 and 12 months of age. Obtain permission from the baby's parents, assure them that there is nothing harmful or difficult in the activities you will be doing, and ask that one of the parents be there while you're presenting the materials to the baby.

Obtain from the parents one of the baby's favorite toys. Place the baby in a sitting position or on his or her stomach close enough to reach the toy easily (see Figure 5.5). Then perform the following steps:

- *Step 1.* While the baby is watching, place the toy in full view and within easy reach. See if the infant reaches for the toy.
- *Step 2.* In full view of the infant, cover part of the toy with a cloth, leaving part visible. Does the baby reach for the toy?
- *Step 3.* While the infant is reaching for the toy (you'll have to pick your moment), cover it completely with the cloth. Does the baby continue reaching?
- *Step 4.* In full view of the child, while the child is still interested in the toy, cover the whole toy with the cloth. Does the baby try to pull the cloth away or search for the toy in some way?

You may need to use more than one toy and/or spread the tests over a period of time in order to keep the baby's interest.

When the toy is partly covered (as in steps 2, 3, and 4 above), the baby's reaching actions should develop in the order listed. Jackson, Campos, and Fischer (1978) report that step 2 (reaching for the partly covered toy) is "passed" at about 26 weeks, step 3 (continuing to reach after the toy is fully covered) at about 28 or 29 weeks, and step 4 (reaching for the fully covered toy) at about 30 or 31 weeks. The closer to this age range your subject is, the more interesting your results are likely to be.

Did your subject's performance conform to those expectations? If not, why do you think it might be different? You might read the paper by Jackson, Campos, and Fischer and consider the reasons they give for differences in results in several studies. For example, do you think is was important to use a familiar toy? Did it matter that a parent was present?

THE THINKING CHILD

6 Cognitive Development I: Cognitive Power

Three Views of Intelligence
Measuring Intellectual Power: IQ Tests
   The First IQ Tests
   Modern IQ Tests
   Achievement Tests
   The Wechsler Intelligence Scale for Children
   IQ Tests in the Schools
What IQ Tests Predict
   School Performance
   Later Job Success
Stability of IQ Test Scores
Limitations of Traditional IQ Tests
An Alternative View: Sternberg's Triarchic Theory of Intelligence
Explaining the Differences: Factors Influencing IQ Test Scores
Influence of Heredity on IQ
   A Journey into Some Classic Research
The Influence of Environment on IQ
   Differences in Environment Between Families
   Differences in Environment Within Families
   School Experiences and Special Interventions
Group Differences in IQ: Race and Sex Differences
   Racial Differences in IQ
   Sex Differences in IQ
The Measurement of Intelligence: A Last Look
Summary
Key Terms
Suggested Reading

For the past several years, I have been rather halfheartedly trying to teach myself German. At times this feels like a hopeless task, since languages have never been my strong suit. (I had four years of French in high school and college and have never been even remotely fluent.) But I have persisted with German in an on again, off again sort of way. One of the problems is just to get the vocabulary into my brain. There are lots of ways of doing that—using flash cards, repeating a word over and over and using it in many sentences, associating a German word with the English one by making a little sentence or using some kind of mental picture. I have tried all of these at times and am slowly acquiring at least a basic vocabulary.

In our everyday lives, each of us faces myriad tasks that call for the same kinds of skills. We learn new things, analyze, remember, plan, organize—studying for exams, trying to remember what to buy at the grocery store, organizing our finances, balancing the checkbook, remembering phone numbers, using a map. Not all of us do these things equally well or equally quickly. But all of us perform such activities every day of our lives.

These activities are all part of what we normally describe as *cognitive functioning* or "intelligence." What I will be exploring in Chapters 6 and 7 is how we have all acquired the ability to do all these things. One-year-olds cannot use maps or balance a checkbook. How do they come to be able to do so? And how do we explain the fact that not all children learn these things at the same rate or become as skilled?

Answering questions like these turns out to be remarkably complicated, in part because there are really three different theories or views of cognition or intelligence, each of which has led to a distinct and huge body of research and commentary. Blending the three is a tricky task—one that I don't want to attempt until I have first presented each view separately.

THREE VIEWS OF INTELLIGENCE

Historically, the first approach to studying cognitive development or intelligence was focused on individual differences. The incontrovertible fact is that people differ in their intellectual skill—their ability to remember lists for the grocery store, the speed with which they solve problems, the number of words they can define, their ability to analyze sequences or complex situations. When we say someone is "bright" or "very intelligent," it is just such skills we mean, and our label is based on the assumption that we can rank-order people in their degree of "brightness." It was precisely this assumption that led to the development of intelligence tests, which were designed simply to give us a way of measuring such individual differences in **intellectual power.**

This "power" definition of intelligence held sway for many years. But it has one great weakness—it does not deal with the equally incontrovertible fact that "intelligence develops: Behavior becomes increasingly complex

Figure 6.1 Tests of intellectual performance, like the achievement test these children are taking, have become an inescapable part of the lives of youngsters today. Such tests reflect an "intellectual power" view of cognitive development.

and abstractly organized with age" (Butterfield, Siladi, & Belmont, 1980). If you give a 5-year-old a mental list of things to buy at the grocery store, not only will she have trouble remembering more than a few of them, she will also not use many good strategies to aid her memory, such as rehearsing the list or organizing the items into groups. An 8-year-old would remember more things and probably would rehearse the list under his breath or in his head as he was walking to the store. So not only does the child's skill (intellectual power) increase with age; the mental strategies, techniques, and types of logic he applies to the problem also change as the child gets older.

This inescapable fact forms the foundation of the second great tradition in the study of intelligence, the *cognitive-developmental* approach of Jean Piaget and his many followers. The focus here is on the development of cognitive **structures** rather than on power, on patterns of development that are *common* to all children rather than on individual differences.

These two traditions have lived side by side for some years now, rather like not-very-friendly neighbors who smile vaguely at one another when they meet but never get together for coffee. In the past few years, though, the two have developed a mutual friend—a third approach that at least partially integrates the first two. Proponents of this third view—such as Robert Sternberg (1985), Earl Butterfield (Butterfield, Siladi, & Belmont, 1980), and Robert Siegler (1986; Siegler & Richards, 1982)—argue that what is needed is an understanding of the fundamental processes or strategies that make up all cognitive activity. What are the building blocks, the underlying elements (such as memory processes or planning strategies)? Once we have identified such basic processes, we can then ask if or when they change with age (a link to Piaget's theory) and whether people differ in their speed or skill in using them (a link to the traditional individual-differences view). This third approach has come to be called **information-processing** theory, and it is very much the new (and biggest) kid on the block.

Each of these three views tells us something useful and different about intelligence or cognitive development, so we need to look at all three. In other chapters, I nearly always begin by talking about developmental changes (changes in structure) and then turn to a discussion of individual differences (power). But in this case, I will follow the historical pattern and begin by describing the oldest of these three traditions—the measurement of intelligence. In Chapter 7 I'll talk about Piaget's views of developmental changes in intellectual structure and about information processing.

MEASURING INTELLECTUAL POWER: IQ TESTS

Intelligence tests have a certain mystique about them, and most of us have a greatly inflated notion of the permanence or importance of an IQ score. If you are going to acquire a more realistic view, it's important for you to know something about what such tests were designed to do and something about the beliefs and values of the men and women who devised them.

The First IQ Tests

The first modern intelligence test was published in 1905 by two Frenchmen, Alfred Binet and Theodore Simon. It was written at the request of the French government, which sought a way to identify children who would be likely to have trouble in school. Thus, from the beginning, the test was based on the assumption that individuals differed in mental ability. Equally important, from the beginning the test had a practical purpose, which was to predict school success. For this reason, and because Binet and Simon defined intelligence as including judgment, comprehension, and reasoning, the tests they devised were very much like some school tasks, including measures of vocabulary, comprehension of facts and relationships, and mathematical and verbal reasoning. Can the child describe the difference between wood and glass? Can the young child touch his nose, his ear, his head? Can the child tell which of two weights is heavier?

Similar types of tests were later used by Lewis Terman and his associates of Stanford University (Terman & Merrill, 1937) when they translated and revised the test for use in the United States (a test referred to as the **Stanford-Binet**). It consisted of a series of individual tests for children of each age. There were six tests for 4-year-olds, six tests for 5-year-olds, and so on. A child taking the test was given these age tests beginning below his actual age and continuing "upward" until a level was reached at which he failed them all.

This procedure led to a score called the **intelligence quotient (IQ),** which was computed by comparing the child's chronological age (in years and months) with her **mental age** (the level of questions she could answer correctly). A child who could solve the problems for a 6-year-old but not those for a 7-year-old would have a mental age of 6. The formula used to calculate the IQ was

$$\frac{\text{Mental age}}{\text{Chronological age}} \times 100 = \text{IQ}$$

This resulted in an IQ above 100 for children whose mental age was higher than their chronological age and an IQ below 100 for children whose mental age was below their chronological age.

This old system for calculating the IQ is not used any longer, even in the modern revisions of the Stanford-Binet. Nowadays IQs from any type of test are calculated by a direct comparison of a child's performance with those of a large group of other children the same age. But an IQ of 100 is still average, and higher and lower scores still mean above- and below-average performance. The majority of children achieve scores that are right around the average of 100, with a smaller number scoring very high or very low. Figure 6.2 shows the distribution of IQ scores that we would see if we gave the test to hundreds or thousands of children, along with the labels typically attached to different ranges of scores. You can see that two-thirds of all children will achieve scores between 85 and 115.

Modern IQ Tests

The tests used most frequently by psychologists today are the Revised Stanford-Binet and the Wechsler Intelligence Scale for Children (Revised). The second test, usually called the **WISC-R,** was developed by David Wechsler (1974). Because the Binet has items designed for testing preschool-age children and the WISC-R does not, the Binet is more often used with 3- to 6-year-olds. Both the WISC-R and the Revised Binet are used with older children. To give you some idea of the sorts of items included in

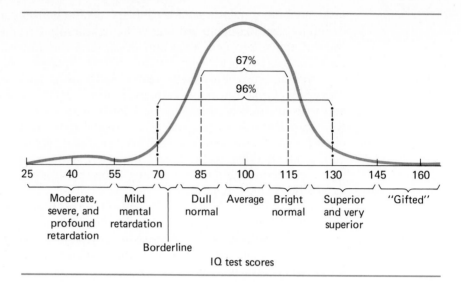

Figure 6.2   The approximate distribution of scores on most modern IQ tests. The tests are designed so that the average score is 100 and two-thirds of the scores fall between about 85 and 115. Because of brain damage and genetic anomalies, there are slightly more low-IQ children than there are very high-IQ children.

tests like these, I've described the WISC-R in some detail in the box on the opposite page.

Infant Tests.   Neither the Binet nor the WISC-R can be used with infants much younger than about 3. Infants and toddlers don't talk well, if at all, and the usual childhood tests rely heavily on language. So how do we measure "intelligence" in an infant? This becomes an important question if we want to be able to identify, during infancy, those children who are not developing normally, or if we want to predict later intelligence or school performance.

Nearly all infant tests are constructed to be very like the later IQ tests—they include a series of items of increasing difficulty that are intended to tap or demand basic cognitive processes. The most widely used such test today, the **Bayley Scales of Infant Development** (developed by Nancy Bayley, 1969), yields separate scores for mental development and motor development. Included among the mental items are such tasks as reaching for a dangling ring (3 months), uncovering a toy hidden by a cloth (8 months; obviously measuring an aspect of object permanence), putting cubes in a cup on request (9 months), or building a tower of three cubes (17 months).

Although infant tests were originally designed to tap the same basic intellectual processes as the tests for older children, in fact the scores on infant tests do not predict later IQ scores at all well—a point I will return to shortly. As a result, scores on tests like the Bayley are used today primarily

THE WECHSLER INTELLIGENCE SCALE FOR CHILDREN

Unlike the Binet, which has separate tests for children of each age, the WISC-R uses the same ten types of problems for all children. Each type of question runs from very easy to very difficult items. The 10 subtests are divided into two groups: those that rely heavily on verbal abilities and a group called performance tests, which involve less language ability and test the child's perceptual skills and nonverbal logic. Here is a list of the 10 types of tests, with examples similar to actual items.

Verbal Tests

- *General information.* "How many eyes have you?"
- *General comprehension.* "What is the thing to do when you scrape your knee?"
- *Arithmetic.* "James had ten marbles and he bought four more. How many marbles did he have altogether?"
- *Similarities.* "In what way are a pear and an orange alike?"
- *Vocabulary.* "What is an emerald?"

Performance Tests

- *Picture completion.* The child is shown pictures of familiar objects in which a part has been left out. He has to identify the missing part, such as a tooth missing from a comb.
- *Picture arrangement.* Pictures like the frames of a comic strip are laid out in the wrong order in front of the child. The child has to figure out the right order to make a story.
- *Block design.* Sets of special blocks (red, white, or half red, half white on the different sides) are given to the child. Using these blocks, she has to copy designs. The first problems involve only four blocks; harder problems include nine blocks.

- *Object assembly.* Large pictures of familiar objects like a horse or a face have been cut up into pieces—rather like jigsaw puzzles, but in bigger pieces. The child has to put them together in the correct configuration as rapidly as possible.
- *Coding.* A series of abstract symbols like balls and stars or curved lines are shown in pairs. The child must learn which symbols go together, because he is given several rows of boxes that show only one of each pair, and he must fill in the paired symbol in each box as quickly as possible.

Uses of Scores on the WISC-R

One of the reasons many educators prefer the WISC-R to the Stanford-Binet is that it allows them to look at the variation in a child's performance. Gifted children typically do well on all the tests. Very retarded children typically do poorly on all the tests, although they may do a little better on the performance tests than on the verbal ones. But children with some kind of learning disability or brain damage may show a lot of variability. For example, children who have difficulty learning to read nearly always do better on the performance tests. But they may often do quite well on the vocabulary subtest and very poorly on the coding subtest (Sattler, 1974). So it isn't just words that are the problem.

The key point is that significant *unevenness* in a child's performance on the WISC-R (or on any other IQ test) may alert the teacher to a specific learning problem. Two children with the same total IQ scores may have very different patterns of test performance and may need very different kinds of special help.

to identify children who may have significant developmental problems and not to predict later IQ.

Achievement Tests

Thus far in this catalogue of common tests, I have omitted the one kind of test with which you are likely to be personally most familiar, namely, the **achievement test.** Nearly all of you have taken these tests in elementary and high school. They are designed to test *specific* information learned in school, using items like the ones in Table 6.1. The child taking an achievement test doesn't end up with an IQ score, but his performance is still compared to that of other children in the same grade across the country. Often the scores are reported in *percentiles*. A child who does just as well as the average child in her grade would be at the fiftieth percentile; one who did better than 90 percent of the other children would be at the ninetieth percentile; and so forth.

Table 6.1

▬▬▬

Some Sample Items from a Fourth-Grade Achievement Test

Vocabulary

jolly old man
1. angry
2. fat
3. merry
4. sorry

Language expression

Who wants _____ books?
1. that
2. these
3. them
4. this

Mathematics

What does the "3" in 13 stand for?
1. 3 ones
2. 13 ones
3. 3 tens
4. 13 tens

Reference skills

Which of these words would be first in ABC order?
1. pair
2. point
3. paint
4. polish

Spelling

Jason took the *cleanest* glass.
right __ wrong __

Mathematics computation

79	149	62
+14	−87	× 3

Source: From Comprehensive Tests of Basic Skills, Form S. Reprinted by permission of the publisher, CTB/McGraw-Hill, Del Monte Research Park, Monterey, CA 93940. Copyright © 1973 by McGraw-Hill, Inc. All rights reserved. Printed in the USA.

How are these tests different from an IQ test? The original idea was that an IQ test measured the child's basic capacity, her underlying **competence,** while the achievement test was supposed to measure what the child had actually learned (her **performance**). This is an important distinction. Each of us presumably has some upper limit of ability—what we could do under ideal conditions, when we are maximally motivated, well, and rested. But of course everyday conditions are rarely ideal, so we typically perform below our hypothetical ability.

Unfortunately, it is not possible to measure competence. We can never be sure that we are assessing any ability under the best of all possible circumstances. We *always* measure performance. The authors of the famous IQ tests believed that by standardizing the procedures for administering and scoring the tests, they could come close to measuring competence. Certainly it is good practice to design the best possible test and to administer it carefully. But it is important to understand that a test never really measures underlying competence; it only measures today's performance.

If you follow this logic to the end, you realize that, in some sense, all intelligence tests are achievement tests. The difference between tests called IQ tests and those called achievement tests is really a matter of degree. The intelligence tests include items that are designed to tap fairly fundamental intellectual processes like comparison or analysis (and they *may* come close to measuring maximal performance); the achievement tests call for specific information the child has learned in school or elsewhere. College entrance tests, like the Scholastic Aptitude Tests (SATs, which many of you have taken recently) fall somewhere in between. They are designed to measure fairly basic developed abilities, such as the ability to reason with words, rather than just specific knowledge. All three types of tests, though, measure aspects of a child or young person's performance and not competence.

If that's so, why bother with IQ tests at all in the schools? Educators and psychologists are still arguing about this question. I've explored some of the uses of IQ tests in the schools, along with some of the reservations about them, in the box on pages 194–196.

WHAT IQ TESTS PREDICT

The fact that IQ tests do not fully measure basic ability or competence, as they were originally intended to do, does not mean that they are useless. For most psychologists, the critical question is what the tests predict. If IQ test scores can help us make predictions about future problems or success, then such tests may still be useful tools.

School Performance

Psychologists have most often used IQ test scores to predict school performance. After all, Binet designed the first tests specifically to predict school

IQ tests were originally designed for use in the schools, and they are still used more in that setting than in any other. Lauren Resnick (1979) argues that there are three basic school-related uses of the tests: sorting, accountability, and legitimizing educational practices.

The Sorting Function

When Binet designed the first tests, it was with precisely this purpose in mind—to be able to sort children into groups that would or would not benefit from particular levels or kinds of instruction. This is clearly the dominant use of IQ tests in schools today.

A child who seems to be learning slowly in class may be given an IQ test to see if he might be retarded. The test score would then be one of several pieces of information used to decide if the child should be in a special class. Or a child who is having difficulty learning to read but is otherwise doing okay may be given a test like the WISC-R or other special tests designed to diagnose specific learning disabilities or brain damage. At the other end of the scale, IQ tests are quite routinely used to identify children who might be eligible for special programs for the gifted.

IQ tests are also sometimes used before school starts as a type of "readiness" test. When my daughter was not quite 5, she was given an IQ test because we wanted her to enter school at an age a few months younger than the official school cutoff point. The school psychologist used the IQ test to help him determine if she would be able to handle the work of kindergarten.

All these uses of the tests are for diagnosis and sorting. They help the teacher or the school to learn which children need special help (either because of poor performance or very high performance), and they help to pin down the sort of help that may be most useful.

The Accountability and Legitimizing Functions

More recently, IQ tests are beginning to be used in another way as well—to justify educational practices to the public. *Accountability* is becoming a watchword in public life, and public schools are affected by the need to justify their actions, just as are other government groups. In many states, achievement tests are being used for this purpose. All the children in one or more grades may be given the same test, and then the results are made public. If the children in a given state are doing well by national standards, then all the educators pat themselves on the back. But if the children do poorly, what happens?

Poor performance by a group of children in a given class or a given school might come about because the school or the teacher just isn't doing a very good job. That's what parents are likely to conclude if they see low test scores, and they may pressure the schools to improve. In the face of pressure like this, some educators have fallen back on the IQ test as a measure of competence. If the children in a school have been given IQ tests and have performed relatively poorly, then how can the school be expected to teach them as readily?

It should be obvious from what I've already said that I think this is fallacious reasoning. But I know it happens because I have seen it in the small school district on whose school board I served for several years. In one year, our fourth-graders did poorly on the statewide achievement tests. The school psychologist suggested that we give them all IQ tests to see if they were "really" not very bright. The school board did not take his advice, but I suspect this use of IQ tests, as justification or legitimization of school policy, will become more prominent as schools come under increasing pressure.

The Arguments Against Using IQ Tests in Schools

Over the years, many voices have been raised against using IQ tests in schools in either of these ways. There are several arguments.

First of all, while the tests do measure the sorts of intellectual skills needed in schools, they simply do not tap a whole host of other skills which may be equally (or more) important for success outside of school. By using IQ test scores, we may not only label a child as "slow" or "retarded"; we may ignore important compensatory skills. According to this argument, too much emphasis on IQ scores risks reinforcing the already widespread belief that what IQ tests measure are the defining characteristics of "intelligence."

Second, the tests may simply be biased in such a way that some subgroups of children are more likely to score high or low on the tests than are other subgroups. Black children, for example, may do less well on the test simply because there are some items that are not equally accessible to blacks and whites. Williams (1970) gives an example: an item on the earlier version of the Stanford-Binet required the child to answer the question "What's the thing for you to do if another child hits you without meaning to do it?" Maximum credit was given if the child responded "Walk away" or some equivalent. But in many black (or poor) neighborhoods, staying and confronting the other child may be the only reasonable alternative. In the earlier version of the test, the child who answered the test question by saying "Hit him back" received no

credit on the Binet, even though that is a reasonable response within his own culture.

Such obviously biased items have been carefully eliminated from the tests in recent revisions. But it is still true that when IQ tests are used for sorting functions such as identifying children to be placed in special classes, proportionately many more black children than whites end up being classified as slow or retarded. In 1979, this fact led a federal judge in California to prohibit the use of standardized IQ test scores for placement in special classes. Judge Peckham assumed that there was no underlying difference in ability between black and white children, so the tests must clearly be biased. He has recently reaffirmed his ruling and has been upheld by the U.S. Court of Appeals. Whatever one feels about the court rulings—and there are many who feel that the alternative methods for identifying children for special classes are as bad or worse—all would agree that IQ tests, as currently designed and administered, require knowledge, motivation, and test-taking skills that may not be part of the repertoire of many minority group children (Zigler & Freedman, 1987).

Finally, there is the problem of the self-fulfilling prophecy of an IQ test score. Since many people, including both parents and teachers, still believe that IQ scores are fixed, once a child is labeled as "having" a particular IQ, that label tends to stay attached to the child and to be difficult to remove later. In a classic (but controversial) study, Robert Rosenthal (1966) showed that when told that a group of children were likely to show more rapid intellectual development, elementary-school teachers treated those children differently from the way they treated a group of children they were told were not likely to be so bright. Thus, assigning a child a particular IQ score carries risks as well as potential benefits.

My own conclusion from all this is that widespread use of IQ tests (such as for accountability) in the schools is not warranted. There is no reason that every child should be given such a test. But I still think that selective, careful use of IQ tests and other tests of cognitive functioning can be a helpful part of a method for selecting children for special programs. The key word in that sentence is *careful.*

success. The research findings on this point are quite consistent: the correlation between a child's test score and her grades in school or performance on other school tests is about .60 (Sattler, 1974). Since school performance is affected by many factors other than intelligence, such as motivation and past achievement, this strong but by no means perfect correlation is about as high as we can expect. It tells us that on the whole, children with top IQ scores will also be among the high achievers in school and those who score low will be among the low achievers. Still, some children with high IQ scores don't do all that well in school and some low-IQ children do well.

IQ scores not only relate moderately well to *current* grades—they can also predict future grades. Preschool children with high IQ scores tend to do better when they enter school than those with lower scores; children who test well in fourth or fifth grade are likely to perform well in high school.

There is also a consistent finding that the higher a child's IQ, the more years of school she's likely to complete (Brody & Brody, 1976). Children with lower scores are more likely to drop out of high school or to complete high school but not go on to college. And of the young people who *do* decide to try college, those with lower IQ scores have more trouble finishing. So the test scores do predict school performance reasonably well.

I am *not* saying here that IQ *causes* good or poor performance in school—although that is one possibility, and one that has been widely believed. All we know is that the two events—high or low IQ scores and high or low school performance—tend to go together, so we can use one to predict the other.

Later Job Success

Once a person gets out of school, does his or her IQ still predict anything important? Do people with higher IQs get better jobs, or do they do better in the jobs they hold? Yes and no.

There is a relationship between IQ and the types of jobs people hold as adults. Most doctors and lawyers, for example, have fairly high IQs, while cooks and salesclerks have lower average IQs (Brody & Brody, 1976). This happens partly because occupations like medicine or law have "entrance requirements," including IQ-like tests, while jobs like mechanic, cook, or salesclerk do not. So jobs in the latter group are open to people with less training or lower achievement. Even with entrance requirements, though, the relationship between IQ and occupation is far from perfect. In one longitudinal study, Dorothy Eichorn and her colleagues (Eichorn, Hunt, & Honzik, 1981) found that IQ scores obtained for a group of 117 men at age 17 to 18 were correlated only .46 with the status of the men's occupations when they were in their forties. So there are quite a lot of people with high IQs who don't end up in high-level jobs and quite a few with lower IQs who do.

Furthermore, once a person is in a particular job or occupation, her

Figure 6.3 The job of secretary is one for which the IQ score predicts success. The job has no "entrance requirements"—that is, you don't need a high IQ to get into this occupation. Once in it, however, adults with higher IQs are more successful than those with lower IQs.

IQ doesn't tell us very much about how well she will succeed. Doctors with IQs of 150 don't make more money or have more satisfied patients than doctors with IQs of 120. And high-IQ carpenters don't hammer straighter nails than low-IQ carpenters. Only in those occupations that have no entrance requirements but do make intellectual demands, such as secretarial work or bookkeeping, does IQ predict performance.

STABILITY OF IQ TEST SCORES

One of the bits of folklore about IQ tests is that a particular IQ score is something you "have," like blue eyes or red hair. This notion is based on the assumption that IQ scores remain stable over time—that a child who achieves a score of, say, 115 at 3 years of age will continue to score in about the same range at age 6 or 12 or 20. The fact that IQ scores can predict future school performance certainly tells us that there is *some* stability, but scores on IQ tests are less stable than you probably think.

First of all, as I already pointed out, scores from infant IQ tests given in the first 12 or 18 months of life have only a limited resemblance to scores on tests given to the same children later (Kopp & McCall, 1982).

Let me give you a concrete example from some research of my own (Bee et al., 1982). My colleagues and I have studied a group of 193 families since before the birth of their first child through the child's eighth year. Among many other things, we administered the Bayley test of infant mental development when the children were 12 months old and again at 24 months. At age 4 we tested them with the Stanford-Binet, and at age 8 we gave them the WISC-R. When we looked at the correlations between the early infant IQ test scores and later IQ scores, we found the results in Table 6.2. As you can see, the test score at 12 months was only very weakly correlated to later test scores, so many children who had done poorly at 12 months later performed much better and vice versa.

Past about age 2 or 3, the consistency of performance on IQ tests becomes considerably better. If two tests are given within a fairly short space of time—say a few months or a year apart—the scores are likely to be very similar. The correlations between adjacent-year IQ scores in middle childhood, for example, are typically in the range of .80 (Honzik, 1986). This high level of predictability, however, masks an interesting fact: most children show quite wide fluctuations in their scores. Robert McCall and his colleagues (McCall, Appelbaum, & Hogarty, 1973), for example, looked at the test scores of a group of 80 mostly middle-class children who had been given IQ tests at regular intervals from the time they were $2\frac{1}{2}$ until they were 17. The *average* amount of variation in IQ score in this group (the difference between the highest and lowest score achieved by each child) was 28 points, and one child in seven showed a shift of more than 40 points. Thus, a child might achieve a test score in the "dull normal"

Table 6.2

▬▬▬▬▬▬

Relationship Between Infant IQ Test Scores and IQ at Ages 4 and 8

	Infant IQ test scores (Bayley)[a]	
IQ predictions	At 12 months	At 24 months
4 years (Binet)	.21[*][b]	.53[*][b]
8 years (WISC-R)	.15	.39[*][b]

[a] The sample included children from working-class and middle-class families. The higher the correlation, the stronger the relationship. Thus, the infant IQ test score at 12 months is only very weakly related to later IQ measures, while the 24-month score is more strongly related.

[b] Asterisk indicates that the correlation is statistically significant. In this instance it means that a correlation this large could occur by chance only 1 out of 100 times in a sample this size.

Source: From Bee et al., 1982, and unpublished data for eight-year WISC-R scores.

▬▬▬▬▬▬

range in one year and test at a "superior" level at another age. You can see several examples in Figure 6.4.

Such wide fluctuations are more common in young children. The general rule of thumb is that the older the child, the more stable the IQ score becomes, although even in older children, scores may fluctuate in response to major stresses or to positive changes in family circumstances.

The fact that such wide variations can occur calls into question a common school practice of using a fixed cutoff score to determine eligibility for special programs (such as those for gifted or retarded children), particularly if only a single test score is used. For example, if the cutoff for eligibility for a gifted program is an IQ of 135, a child might obtain a score of 130 at one testing and be declared ineligible. The child might not be tested again later, even though she might score above 135 on another occasion.

LIMITATIONS OF TRADITIONAL IQ TESTS

I have been pointing out some of the limitations of the traditional tests as I go along. But let me pause for a moment to summarize and to talk a bit further about what IQ tests do *not* do.

They do not measure underlying competence. Thus, an IQ score cannot tell you (or a teacher or anyone else) that your child has some specific, fixed, underlying ability.

The scores are not etched on a child's forehead at birth, never to change. IQ scores become quite stable in late childhood, but individual children can and do shift, particularly in response to any stress in their lives.

MULTIMEDIA LEARNING CENTRE
DEESIDE COLLEGE

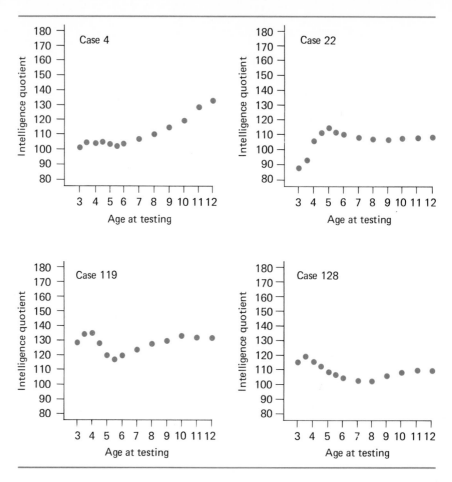

Figure 6.4 Some examples of the changes in IQ scores that can occur with age. These four cases represent children in the Fels longitudinal study, who were all tested repeatedly from early childhood through adolescence. Case 4 showed an unusually large increase in IQ; case 22 did not vary as much but showed a very rapid rise in IQ in the preschool years (a fairly common pattern, by the way); case 119 showed a more variable pattern; and case 128 showed a slight overall decline (also fairly common). These four cases are not necessarily typical or average, but they do show the kinds of variation that can occur. (*Source:* Sontag, Baker, & Nelson, 1958, Appendix, pp. 58, 61, 77, 79. © The Society for Research in Child Development, Inc.)

Perhaps most important, traditional IQ tests simply do not measure a whole host of skills that are likely to be highly significant for getting along in the world. IQ tests were originally designed to measure only the specific range of skills that are needed for success in school. This they do reasonably well. What they do not tell us is how well a particular person may be at other cognitive tasks requiring skills such as creativity, insight, "street smarts," reading social cues, or understanding spatial relationships.

In the past decade, a number of psychologists have been particularly struck by these limitations of traditional tests and by traditional ways of thinking about intelligence. Howard Gardner (1983), for example, suggests that there are six separate types of intelligence (linguistic, musical, logical-mathematical, spatial, bodily-kinesthetic, and personal), only two of which are actually measured on traditional IQ tests. Another current view, which I find particularly intriguing, is the triarchic theory proposed by Robert Sternberg.

AN ALTERNATIVE VIEW: STERNBERG'S TRIARCHIC THEORY OF INTELLIGENCE

In his **triarchic theory of intelligence,** Robert Sternberg argues that there are three aspects or types of intelligence. The first, which he calls **componential intelligence,** includes what we normally measure on IQ or achievement tests or SATs. All of what we call *analytic* thinking—planning, organizing, remembering facts and applying them to new situations, and the like—are parts of componential intelligence.

The second aspect he calls **experiential intelligence.** A person with well-developed intelligence of this type is creative, can see new connections between things, can relate to experiences in insightful ways. A graduate student who is good at this, for example, is one who can come up with good ideas for experiments, who can see how a theory could be applied to a totally different situation, or who can synthesize a great many facts into a new organization. (I use some of this ability when I decide how to organize the material in any chapter in this book. I read a whole lot and then look for a pattern, an organization, that will make sense out of the disparate pieces.) You might like to try your hand at some of the kinds of tests Sternberg has devised to measure this kind of ability, shown in Table 6.3 (the answers are at the bottom of the table in case you are stumped—as many people are).

The third aspect Sternberg calls **contextual intelligence** (sometimes also called "street smarts"). People who are skilled in this are able to manipulate their environments, to see how they can fit in best, to know which people to cultivate and how to cultivate them, to adapt themselves to their setting or the setting to themselves. In college we see this form of intelligence in a student who is particularly good at figuring out what the professor wants in any given course, who goes regularly to office hours to talk to the professor, who chooses paper topics he knows the professor prefers. This is not just manipulation. It requires being attuned to a variety of fairly subtle signals and then acting on the information. Good salespeople, for example, have a high level of contextual intelligence.

If you think about the people you know, you can probably come up with some individuals who are highly intelligent in all three ways. But

Table 6.3

Some Samples of Insight Questions from Sternberg's Tests of Experiential Intelligence

1. Aeronautical engineers have made it possible for a supersonic jet fighter to catch up with the bullets fired from its own guns with sufficient speed to shoot itself down. If a plane, flying at 1000 miles an hour, fires a burst, the rounds leave the plane with an initial velocity of about 3000 miles an hour. Why won't a plane that continues to fly straight ahead overtake and fly into its own bullets?

2. If you have black socks and brown socks in your drawer, mixed in a ratio of 4 to 5, how many socks will you have to take out to make sure of having a pair of the same color?

3. In the Thompson family, there are five brothers, and each brother has one sister. If you count Mrs. Thompson, how many females are there in the Thompson family?

In solving the following analogies, assume that the statement given before the analogy is true, whether it actually is true or not, and use that assumption to solve the analogy.

4. LAKES are dry.
   TRAIL is to HIKE as LAKE is to:
   a. swim
   b. dust
   c. water
   d. walk

5. DEER attack tigers.
   LION is to COURAGEOUS as DEER is to:
   a. timid
   b. aggressive
   c. cougar
   d. elk

The following problems require detecting the relationship between the first two items and finding a parallel relationship between the second two. In answering, explain what those relationships are.

6. VANILLA is to BEAN as TEA is to LEAF.

7. ATOM is to MOLECULE as CELL is to ORGANISM.

8. NOON is to EVE as 12:21 is to 10:01.

Answers: 1. Gravity pulls the bullets down. If the plane continues to fly a level course, it cannot shoot itself. 2. Three (the proportion of black and brown socks is irrelevant). 3. Two, the mother and her daughter, who is sister to each brother. 4. d. 5. b. 6. Vanilla comes from a bean, tea from a leaf. 7. Atoms combine to form molecules, cells combine to form an organism. 8. Each of the terms is the same forward as backward.

Source: From *Intelligence Applied* by R. J. Sternberg, copyright © 1986 by Harcourt Brace Jovanovich, Inc. Reprinted by permission of the publisher.

you can probably also think of some people who are much more intelligent in one of these ways than in the other two. Sternberg's point is not just that standard IQ tests have omitted many of these kinds of items, but that in the world beyond the school walls, experiential or contextual intelligence may be required as much or more than is the type of intelligence measured on an IQ test.

Thus, while the standard IQ tests do measure a significant aspect of intellectual ability, they do not measure *all* significant aspects of intellectual skill. It is important to keep this limitation in mind as we move on to questions about the origins of individual differences in IQ. What I will be talking about is the origins of only one aspect of intelligence—the kind of intelligence demanded in school.

EXPLAINING THE DIFFERENCES: FACTORS INFLUENCING IQ TEST SCORES

So far, I have been answering "what" questions: What are the tests like? How much variation do we see in children's scores? What do the tests predict? The tougher job is to answer the "why" or "how" questions: Why does one child obtain higher scores than another? Are these differences genetic? Are they environmental? Are they some combination of the two?

INFLUENCE OF HEREDITY ON IQ

When Binet and Simon wrote the first IQ test, they did not assume that IQ was fixed or inborn. But many of the American psychologists who revised and promoted the use of the tests *did* believe that intelligence was inherited and fixed at birth. Those who took this view and those who disagreed have been arguing about the heritability of IQ for at least 60 years. Although there is still not complete consensus, theorists agree that there is at least *some* genetic influence on measured IQ scores. The arguments now are really about just how large the genetic contribution may be. To give you some of the flavor of this fascinating body of research, and to make it clear why definite answers to the questions involved are so hard to come by, let me take you on a brief journey.

A Journey into Some Classic Research

There are two basic ways of searching for a genetic influence on IQ (or on any other trait, for that matter). You can study identical and fraternal twins or you can study adopted children. As I explained in Chapter 2, identical twins share exactly the same genetic patterning, while fraternal twins do not. So if identical twins should turn out to be more like one another in IQ than fraternal twins, that would be evidence for a genetic influence on IQ.

In the case of adopted children, the strategy is to compare the child's IQ to that of her *birth* (biological) parents (with whom she shares genes but not environment) and to that of her adoptive parents (with whom she shares environment but not genes.) If the child's IQ should turn out to be more similar to or better predicted by her *birth* parents' IQs, that would again be a point for the influence of heredity.

Twin Studies. The results of many studies over the past 50 years show consistently that the IQ scores of identical twins are more alike than the scores of fraternal twins (Loehlin & Nichols, 1976; Segal, 1985; Wilson, 1977, 1978, 1983). Robert Plomin (Plomin & DeFries, 1980), combining the results of all the major studies of IQs in twins, estimates that the correlation between the IQ scores of identical twins who have grown up together is .86 (a *very high* correlation), while the correlation between scores of same-sex fraternal twins reared together is about .60 (lower, but still fairly substantial). Score one point for heredity.

But wait a minute. Isn't it possible that identical twins are *treated* more alike than are fraternal twins? Maybe they are dressed alike, spend more time together, are disciplined alike, have more similar toys, and so on. In fact, this does seem to be true (Lytton, 1977), which means that at least some of the similarity between twins that has been ascribed to heredity may really be caused by the environment.

The logical way to check out this possibility is to look at the IQ scores of identical twins who were not reared together, perhaps because they were separated by adoption at an early age. If such twins are *still* like each other in IQ, even though they have not been reared together, that would surely show a hereditary effect.

As you might imagine, there aren't many pairs of identical twins who have been reared in different families. But there are a few, and psychologists who have studied them (e.g., Shields, 1962) have generally found that the twins' IQ scores are still quite similar (the average correlation is .75 in Plomin and DeFries' 1980 analysis of combined data). But more detailed analyses of these cases also show that the less similar the environments in which the twins were reared, the less alike their IQ scores are (Bronfenbrenner, 1975; Kamin, 1974; Farber, 1981). Thus, the twin data, which first appear to show an extremely strong hereditary influence on IQ, are not as clear-cut as they seem.

Adoption Studies. Results from adoption studies are also two-sided. The most common finding is that adopted children's IQs can be predicted better from knowing the IQs or the level of education of their birth parents than from knowing the IQs or education of their adoptive parents (Horn, 1983; Scarr & Weinberg, 1983; Plomin & DeFries, 1983, 1985a; Skodak & Skeels, 1949). Again that sounds like a clear point for a genetic influence, but again there are some signs of environmental influences.

First of all, there is typically at least *some* correlation (in the range of .20) between the IQs of the adoptive parents and that of the adopted child. Second, several investigators have found that when two unrelated children are adopted into the same family, their IQs turn out to be more similar than you'd expect by chance, even though they have *no* shared inheritance at all (e.g., Scarr & Weinberg, 1977). (Interestingly, this seems to be true only for young children's IQ scores. By adolescence, two adopted

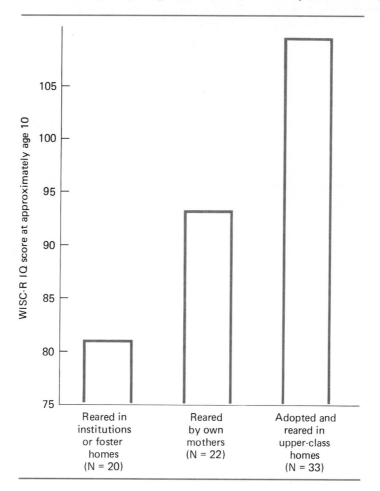

Figure 6.5 Dumaret compared the IQ scores of three groups of French children. One group had been adopted shortly after birth and reared in upper-class families; another group were full or half-siblings of the first group, but they had been reared at home by their birth mothers; and still another group were siblings of the first group who had been reared in institutions or foster homes. You can see that the average IQ of the children who had been reared in more advantaged homes was 16 points higher than the average IQ of those who had been reared at home, and both were markedly higher than the IQs of their brothers and sisters reared in institutions. (*Source:* Dumaret, 1985, Table 2, p. 562.)

children reared in the same family have IQs that are uncorrelated [Scarr & Weinberg, 1983; Willerman, 1987]). Third, and perhaps most important, adopted children born to mothers from relatively poor or uneducated backgrounds typically have IQs 10 or 15 points higher than those of their birth mothers (Scarr & Kidd, 1983; Skodak & Skeels, 1945).

A similar difference is apparent when adopted children's IQs are compared to the scores obtained by their siblings who were reared by their birth mothers; Figure 6.5 (page 205) shows the results of Dumaret's (1985) study in France.

Summing Up the Journey.   There is no easy resolution of these findings. On the one hand, as Sandra Scarr says, "the evidence for some genetic individual differences in behavior is simply overwhelming" (1978, p. 336). On the other hand, I am convinced that the genetic component in measured IQ is far smaller than the 80 percent suggested by the most adamant geneticists (such as Jensen, 1980) and much more like the 35 to 50 percent suggested by Sandra Scarr (Scarr & Kidd, 1983). In sum, we do appear to inherit particular characteristics or skills that have a significant influence on the speed or efficiency with which we can perform those intellectual tasks included on IQ tests. The specific environment in which we grow up has a significant effect as well. To be sure, there are limits to the degree of influence any environment may have. As Scarr and Carter-Saltzman (1982) put it, "two intellectually gifted parents could not adopt any 'normal' infant in the expectation that that child would intellectually match an offspring of their own." But it is important to examine just what it is about environments that makes a difference.

THE INFLUENCE OF ENVIRONMENT ON IQ

As you might imagine, an enormous amount of research has been addressed to this question, all of it beginning to converge on several common findings.

Differences in Environments Between Families

Most of the research has been aimed at describing the cultural position or family life of children who score higher on IQ tests compared to those who score lower.

Social Class Differences.   One of the most consistent findings is that children from poor or working-class families or from families in which the parents are relatively uneducated have lower average IQs than do children from middle-class families. This relationship is vividly illustrated in Figure 6.6, which is based on data from a huge national study of over 50,000 children born in 12 different hospitals around the United States between 1959 and 1966 (Broman, Nichols, & Kennedy, 1975). I have given

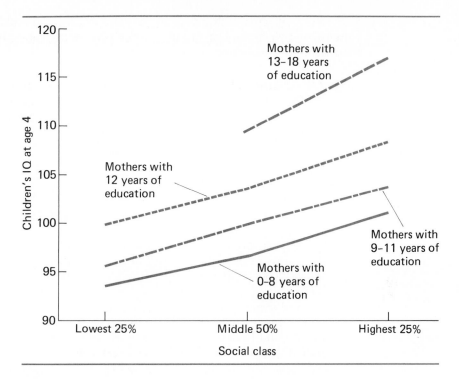

Figure 6.6 These results from a very large national study of test scores of 4-year-old children show very clearly that IQ is related to the social class of the child's family (measured by the family income and the occupations of the adults) and by the education of the child's mother. Each line represents the scores for children of mothers at a particular education level, living in three different social class environments. (There were too few low-social-class mothers with 13 to 18 years of education in this sample, though, so there are no data for this point.) Higher social class and higher education in the mother are each related to higher IQ in the child. (*Source:* Broman, Nichols, & Kennedy, 1975, p. 47).

you the results only for white children who were tested with the Stanford-Binet at age 4, a total sample of over 11,800 children. As you can see in the figure, the average IQ of the children rises as the social class rises and as the mother's education rises.

These differences are *not* found in infancy (Golden & Birns, 1983), but after age 2½ or 3 they appear to widen steadily with age (Farran, Haskins, & Gallagher, 1980). This increasing IQ gap is sometimes called a **cumulative deficit.**

Findings like these could be the result of genetic influences (brighter parents presumably have more education and earn more money and also pass on their "bright" genes to their children). They could also be due to differences in prenatal risks, in diet, or in general health. Neither of these factors, however, is likely to account for all the IQ differences we see.

There are also real differences in the ways infants and children are treated in these two groups of families, which are independently important in cognitive development.

Specific Family Characteristics and IQ.   When we look at individual families, watching the ways in which they interact with their children, and then follow the children over time to see which ones later have high or low IQs, we can begin to get some sense of the kinds of specific family interactions that foster higher scores. My reading of the rich array of such research has led me to these five general characteristics of families whose children achieve higher IQ scores:

1. *They provide appropriate play materials for the child.*   It is not the sheer quantity of play materials that is significant; rather, it is the appropriateness of the play materials for the child's age and developmental level that seems to be critical. A set of nesting pots or pans to play with is just as good as an expensive toy, so long as the child has access to them.

2. *They are emotionally responsive to and involved with their child.*   They spend time with the child, encourage her play and problem solving, and respond to her questions, actions, and activities. They smile at the child and speak warmly to her and about her.

3. *They talk to their child.*   They use language that is descriptively rich and accurate.

4. *They avoid excessive restrictiveness, punitiveness, or control.*   Instead, they give the child room to explore, even opportunities to make mistakes.

5. *They expect their child to do well and to develop rapidly.*   They emphasize and press for school achievement.

Of all the studies I have drawn on in reaching these conclusions, the most influential and interesting are probably those of Bettye Caldwell and her colleagues Robert Bradley and Richard Elardo (Elardo, Bradley, & Caldwell, 1975; Bradley & Caldwell, 1976, 1984; van Doorninck et al., 1981).

Caldwell has devised a measure of the environment she calls the HOME Inventory (Home Observation for Measurement of the Environment). An interviewer/observer visits a home, talks with the parent about a typical day in the family, and observes the kinds of materials available to the child and the kinds of interactions the parent has with the child. The observer then scores "yes" or "no" for each of a series of specific items about that family. Some items from this scale are listed in Table 6.4.

In the original study, Elardo, Bradley, and Caldwell observed the homes of 77 children from poor and working-class families. The homes were first observed when the children were 6 months old and again at 24 months. The children's IQs were tested at age 3 and again at $4\frac{1}{2}$. The researchers

Figure 6.7 A child reared in a family with this kind of enrichment—with parents who are responsive to her, involved with her, who talk to her and allow her to experiment, even with precious objects like a piano—is likely to have a higher IQ than if she had been reared in a less stimulating or more restrictive home.

Table 6.4

Some Sample Items from the HOME Inventory

The mother spontaneously vocalizes to the child at least twice during the visit (excluding scolding).	Yes ___	No ___
When speaking of or to child, mother's voice conveys positive feeling.	Yes ___	No ___
Mother does not shout at child during visit.	Yes ___	No ___
Child gets out of house at least four times a week.	Yes ___	No ___
Child has push or pull toy.	Yes ___	No ___
Family provides learning equipment appropriate to age—mobile, table and chairs, high chair, playpen.	Yes ___	No ___
Mother structures child's play periods.	Yes ___	No ___
Mother reads stories at least three times weekly.	Yes ___	No ___

Source: Caldwell & Bradley, 1978.

found that the HOME inventory scores and the children's IQs were correlated, as you can see in Table 6.5: mothers who were emotionally responsive to their 6- or 24-month-old infants, provided appropriate play materials, spent time with their infants, and provided variety in the children's experience had children who later had higher IQs. The correlations are by no means perfect. Some mothers who do these things have children with moderate IQ scores, and some mothers who do not do these things have children who test well. But the relationship is remarkably strong, considering how little time was spent observing each family.

My colleagues and I at the University of Washington (Barnard, Bee, & Hammond, 1984b) have replicated these findings in the longitudinal study I mentioned earlier. In still a third parallel study, Craig Ramey and his colleagues at the University of North Carolina (Ramey, Farran, & Campbell, 1979; Yeates et al., 1983) have also partially replicated Caldwell's results. In Ramey's research and in our own, the mother's level of punishment and restriction emerged as a more critical ingredient in the "environmental recipe" than was true in Caldwell's study. Mothers who were more physically restrictive and more punitive toward their children, especially right around 24 months of age, had children who had *lower* IQs later on.

In what I have just said about specific family characteristics, I have implied that these are *causal* relationships—that appropriate toys, involved parents, complex and accurate language all *cause* higher IQ. And that is one possibility. But other interpretations are possible, too. For example, bright children may elicit more stimulation from their environments, and brighter parents are likely to provide a richer, more responsive, more verbal environment for their child as well as passing on "good IQ genes" to the child. We could look at the impact of environment without the confounding effect of parental genetic contribution by studying family interactions in *adoptive* families. In the one such study I know of (Plomin, Loehlin, &

Table 6.5
▬▬▬▬▬▬

Correlations of the Caldwell HOME Inventory and the Child's IQ Scores

HOME inventory	Correlations with IQ	
	At 3 years	At $4\frac{1}{2}$ years
Scored at 6 months	.50[*a]	.44[*a]
Scored at 24 months	.70[*a]	.57[*a]

[a] Asterisk indicates that the correlation is statistically significant. In this instance it means that a correlation this large could occur by chance only 1 out of 100 times in a sample this size.
Source: Elardo, Bradley, & Caldwell, 1975, pp. 73–74; Bradley & Caldwell, 1976, p. 1173.

DeFries, 1985), the same key environmental variables emerged. The predictions of later IQ were weaker but still significant. Thus, we can be reasonably certain that these features of the environment have a significant causal impact on children's intellectual competence or performance.

Differences in Environments Within Families

Within families, the experiences of individual children also differ in ways that affect IQ. Being the oldest of a large family, for example, is a very different experience from being the youngest or being in the middle; being the only girl in a family of boys is different from being a girl with only sisters. Psychologists are just beginning to study these within-family variables. Thus far, we have been looking mostly at fairly obvious differences, like how many children there are in a family and a particular child's position within the family. Both of these variables seem to be at least slightly related to the child's IQ. On average, the more children there are in the family, the lower the average IQ of the children. And if the children are closely spaced, firstborn children have the highest IQs, with average IQs declining steadily as you go down the birth order (e.g., Zajonc & Marcus, 1975; Zajonc, 1983). One set of data that shows this effect quite clearly is in Figure 6.8. Such a pattern has not been found in every study, but the finding is common enough to require explanation.

One current explanation, offered by Robert Zajonc, is called the **confluence model.** Zajonc argues that the birth of each succeeding child "dilutes" the intellectual climate of the home. The oldest child initially interacts only with his parents and thus has a maximally complex and enriching environment. After siblings are born, he may also have the opportunity to "tutor" a younger sibling, a form of interaction that has been shown to be intellectually stimulating for the tutor. The second- or later-born children, in contrast, from the beginning experience a lower average intellectual level in the family, simply because they interact with both other children and adults. A later-born child *may* have an advantage if the children are very widely spaced, since then she is interacting entirely with others (parents and much older siblings) who are intellectually advanced.

The oldest child doesn't have all the benefits, however. Robert McCall (1984), for example, has found that firstborn children typically show IQ drops of 10 points after the birth of a younger brother or sister. This decline is made up by the time the child is 17, but it is evident in the earlier years. From Zajonc's point of view, of course, this would make sense, since the average intellectual climate of the home is diluted for the older child when the younger one is born.

The confluence model has prompted a good deal of debate and criticism (e.g., Rogers, 1984). Family *size* does seem to have a small, fairly consistent relationship to IQ, with lower scores for children from bigger families (Steelman, 1985). But comparisons of firstborns and later-born siblings have simply not yielded such clear results. Furthermore, while the predictions

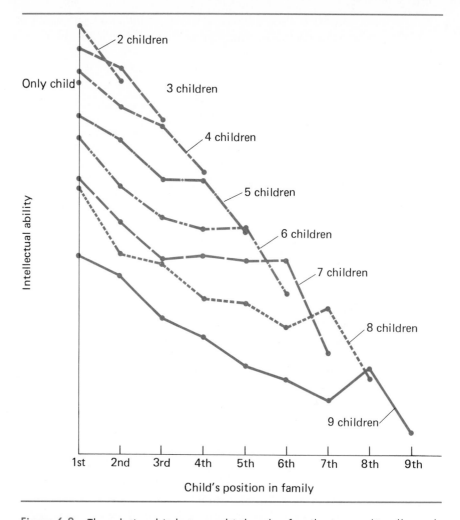

Figure 6.8 The relationship between birth order, family size, and intellectual ability is shown clearly in these findings from a very large study of over 400,000 young men in Holland who were tested when they began their military service. Each line represents a family of a particular size, and each dot represents the average intellectual ability of the young men who were the first, second, third, or *n*th child in a family of that size. (The test used in this case was the Raven Progressive Matrices, a test that correlates highly with the more familiar IQ tests.) Clearly, the larger the family, the lower the scores for all the offspring. And later children in families of any size have lower scores than those born earlier. Zajonc estimates that the difference between the highest point here (the oldest of two) and the lowest (the youngest of nine) is 10 IQ points. (*Source:* Zajonc, 1975, p. 43. Reprinted from *Psychology Today Magazine.* Copyright © 1975, Ziff-Davis Publishing Company.)

from this model work fairly well for large groups, they don't do so well when we look at individual families. It seems clear that a child's placement within the structure of the family has some impact, but whether the confluence model is the best description of the nature of the effect is still an open question.

School Experience and Special Interventions

Obviously, family experiences affect the child's intellectual development. But children also spend an enormous amount of time in school, in preschool, in day care, or in other group settings. How much effect do these environments have on the child's intellectual growth? Do children who have been to preschool do better on IQ tests?

Most of our answers to the first question come from a series of studies of specially enriched preschools in which children from poverty environments have been enrolled. Since we know that children from such backgrounds are likely to show a "cumulative deficit" in IQ scores (or school achievement), many researchers and policymakers in the early 1960s conceived the idea of special preschools for such children. Several other researchers argued that if preschool was a good thing, then perhaps enriched environments for poor children beginning in infancy would be even better.

Preschool Interventions.　 Early results from Head Start and from more experimental preschool programs were somewhat discouraging. Children who had been enrolled in such programs at age 3 or 4 showed IQ gains of about 10 points during the preschool year, but the effect seemed to fade once they were in regular schools (Klaus & Gray, 1968; Bissell, 1973; Weikart, 1972). More recent news, though, has been more positive. There seems to be a "sleeper effect" in the impact of enriched preschool programs: if you keep track of the children into late elementary school or junior or senior high school, you find that those who attended the special preschool are doing better than children from similar backgrounds who did not have the preschool experience.

This conclusion emerges from a combined analysis by Irving Lazar and Richard Darlington (1982) of the results of 12 different longitudinal studies of children who had been in specially enriched preschool programs. The "experimental group" children (those who had been in the special preschools), compared to the "control group" children (those without the preschool experience), showed higher mathematics achievement test scores and somewhat higher reading achievement. (You can see the achievement test results from one of these 12 projects in Figure 6.9.)

Lazar and Darlington also found that children who had had preschool experience were less likely to be assigned to special remedial classes or to be held back a grade. For example, over the 12 studies, only about 13 percent of the experimental group children were placed in special education classes, compared to nearly 30 percent among the control groups. So al-

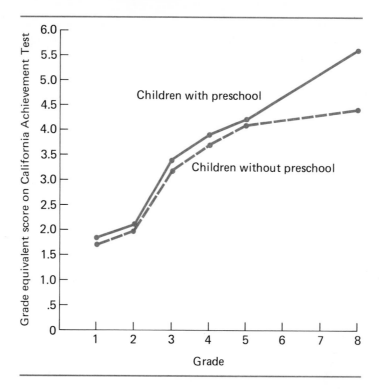

Figure 6.9 The effect of a preschool enrichment program on children's performance in grade school. Note that the children who have attended preschool are very slightly ahead on achievement test scores all along, but the difference increases from sixth grade on. This is the "sleeper effect" of preschool. (*Source:* Bulletin of the High/Scope Foundation, 1977, p. 5. Reprinted with permission of High/Scope Educational Research Foundation, 600 N. River St., Ypsilanti, MI 48197.)

though the children with preschool experience don't *test* a whole lot higher (and do *not* differ in IQ), they *function* better in school.

Infancy Interventions. Even bigger environmental effects, including apparently lasting increases in IQ, have been found when researchers have provided highly enriched environments beginning in early infancy for children from poverty families. The best-designed and most meticulously reported of the infancy interventions has been carried out by Craig Ramey and his colleagues at North Carolina (Ramey & Haskins, 1981a, 1981b; Ramey, Yeates, & Short, 1984; Ramey & Campbell, 1987), a study I mentioned in passing earlier. Infants from poverty-level families whose mothers had low IQs were enrolled in a special day-care program, eight hours a day, five days a week. The children attended the program from 6 to 12 weeks of age until age 5, when they began kindergarten in the public school. The program was both cognitively rich and emotionally warm—

Figure 6.10 Preschool experience, especially if it includes cognitive enrichment like this, has a clearly beneficial effect on a child's intellectual performance, especially in the case of children from poverty-level environments, who may not receive this kind of enrichment at home.

very much the kinds of "optimum" stimulation for children that I described in the section on specific family characteristics and IQ. At the same time, Ramey studied a randomly assigned control group of infants from highly similar backgrounds, who did not receive the special enriched program but did receive nutritional supplements and medical treatment while being reared largely at home.

The IQ scores of the children at various ages are shown in Figure 6.11. You can see that the children who had been enrolled in the special program had significantly higher IQ scores than the control children, even a year and a half after the end of the enrichment program. They also performed better on achievement tests in first grade and were less likely to be held back for a second year in kindergarten (over 30 percent of the

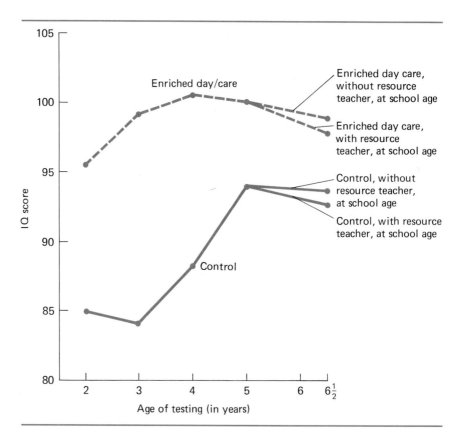

Figure 6.11 You can get some sense of the impact of special intervention programs begun in infancy from the results of the Ramey study. Up through age 5, the children either attended a special enriched day-care program (the experimental group) or were reared by their parents (the control group). At kindergarten age, half of each group received additional support in the form of a resource teacher assigned to their families. The other half of each group received no special treatment during kindergarten. The assistance of a resource teacher at school age made no significant difference in IQ scores (in fact, the children with resource teachers did slightly worse, although the difference is not statistically significant). However, the difference between children who had attended the enriched preschool and those who had not remained statistically significant even after 18 months of regular school. (*Source:* Ramey & Campbell, 1987, Figure 3, p. 135.)

control group children repeated kindergarten). Many of the children from the control group families were performing at a level that would be considered subnormal or retarded. Very similar results come from a study in Wisconsin by Rick Heber (Heber, 1978; Garber & Heber, 1982), who found that even at age 9, the enriched-care children scored significantly above the control children on an IQ test.

These results do *not* mean that all mental retardation could be "cured" by providing children with heavy doses of special education in infancy. They do show that the intellectual power of those children who begin life with few advantages (poverty environment, less-stimulating parents) can be significantly increased if richer stimulation is provided.

▬▬▬▬▬ ## GROUP DIFFERENCES IN IQ: RACE AND SEX DIFFERENCES

So far, in talking about individual differences in intellectual power, I have sidestepped two "hot" issues—namely, racial and sex differences in IQ or cognitive power. The honest truth is that I would rather sidestep them completely (some things are nearly too hot to handle). But that is not fair to you. You need to see what we know, what we don't know, and how we are trying to explain both kinds of differences. But since I do not want to place too much emphasis on this topic, I will be brief.

Racial Differences in IQ

A number of racial differences in intellectual performance have been found. There are hints, for example, that Chinese and Japanese children may score higher on cognitive tests than white children, particularly on tests of mathematical skill (e.g., Stevenson et al., 1985). But the basic finding that has given researchers and theorists the most difficulty is that in the United States, black children consistently score lower than white children on measures of IQ. This difference is *not* found among infants, by the way. Black children show somewhat faster motor development in infancy, and there are no differences in total scores on IQ tests until about age 2 or 3.

Some scientists have argued that these findings reflect basic genetic differences between the races (e.g., Jensen, 1980). Other scientists, after reviewing the evidence, concluded that either an environmental or a genetic argument was possible, that we simply didn't know enough yet (e.g., Loehlin, Lindzey, & Spuhler, 1975). But several recent studies by Sandra Scarr and her colleagues (Scarr & Kidd, 1983) and by Moore (1986) show powerful environmental influences at work.

For example, Scarr has found that black children adopted into white middle-class families, and thus reared in the environment for which the tests are most valid, score as well as do white children adopted into the same families. In another study of adopted black children, Moore (1986) found that those who had been reared in white families not only had higher IQ scores than those adopted into black families (117 versus 103), they also approached the IQ testing situation quite differently. They stayed more focused on the task, were more likely to try some task even if they didn't think they could do it. Black children adopted into middle-class black families did not show this pattern of persistence and effort. They asked for help more often and gave up more easily when faced with a difficult task. When Moore then observed each adoptive mother teaching her child several tasks, he could see parallel differences. The white mothers were more positive, more encouraging, and were less likely to give the child the answer than were the black mothers.

Findings like these show that the IQ difference we see is probably primarily a reflection of the fact that the tests, and the schools, are designed by the majority culture to promote a particular form of intellectual activity (Sternberg's componential intelligence) and that many black or other minority families rear their children in ways that do not maximize (or emphasize) this particular set of skills. Sternberg has recently argued (Sternberg & Suben, 1986) that in fact, in some black subcultures, it is contextual intelligence that is particularly emphasized and trained. The IQ differences between blacks and whites then appear to reflect not a fundamental genetic difference but rather a cultural difference. The difficulty for many black children (and any children reared in poverty) is that they are later educated in, and must make their way as adults in, a culture that particularly values the very kinds of intellectual ability that an IQ test measures. The fact that we may be able to account for the racial differences in IQ by appealing to cultural or subcultural variations does not make the IQ difference disappear, nor does it make it trivial. But it does put it into a different—perhaps less explosive—framework.

Sex Differences in IQ

In contrast to comparisons of racial groups, comparisons of total IQ test scores of boys and girls do *not* reveal consistent differences. It is only when we break down the total score into several separate skills that some patterns of sex differences emerge. I've summarized the major findings in Table 6.6.

Two crucial points need to be made about the differences described in the table. First, these are *average* differences. On *every* measure, there is a great deal of overlap between the scores of males and females. There are many girls good at spatial visualization and many boys good at verbal reasoning.

Second, *the absolute size of the differences is very small*. For example, even though it is true that girls typically do better on measures of verbal skill, sex accounts for only about *1 percent* of the variation in scores. So knowing a child's gender tells you very little about her likely performance

Table 6.6

A Summary of Sex Differences in Intellectual Abilities

Type of ability	Nature of the difference
Spatial visualization. Ability to manipulate abstract shapes, to visualize three-dimensional spaces from two-dimensional drawings, and so forth. (Some items that measure this ability are shown in Figure 6.12.)	Boys are quite consistently better at this, beginning as early as age 10 and continuing in adolescence and adulthood.
Arithmetic computation. Basic adding, subtracting, and counting.	Young girls (up to about age 8) are slightly better at this.
Mathematics. More-complex problems; high-school math.	Boys score higher on standard measures of math achievement given in high school or college; more boys are identified as highly gifted in mathematics, too.
Numerical reasoning. Word problems involving numbers.	Boys again have a slight advantage.
Verbal abilities.	Girls are a bit more talkative and use slightly longer sentences in very early language and to some extent in later language.
Verbal reasoning. Anagrams, for example.	Girls are a bit better, beginning at about adolescence.

Sources: Maccoby & Jacklin, 1974; Linn & Petersen, 1985; Halpern, 1986; Johnson & Meade, 1987.

on a test of verbal skill. The largest differences are found on measures of spatial visualization, where perhaps 5 to 10 percent of the variation among high-school or college students' performance can be accounted for by gender (Halpern, 1986).

The large overlap in the distributions and the small absolute size of the differences mean that these differences have little practical importance for such real-life situations as job qualifications. But the consistency of the findings still leaves us with something to explain. Probably there are both biological and environmental forces at work.

Biological influences are clearest in the case of sex differences in spatial abilities (see Figure 6.12 for tests that measure this ability). In particular, there are hints that delayed or late puberty is associated with particularly good spatial abilities in both boys and girls, possibly because late puberty is associated with somewhat different organization of the left and right sides of the brain. Since girls as a group go through puberty earlier than boys, on average they are going to have poorer spatial ability. Deborah Waber first observed this in 1977, and a number of other investiga-

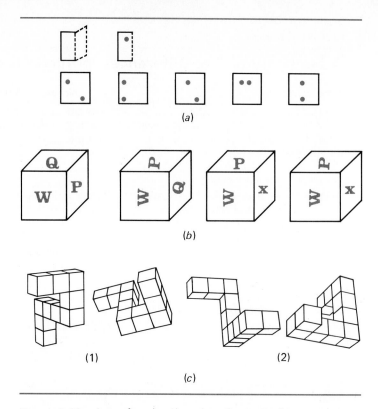

(a)

(b)

(1)   (2)

(c)

Figure 6.12 It is often hard to describe just what is meant by the term *spatial ability*. So here are three items like ones used on tests of spatial ability. Each requires a slightly different aspect of the skill. (*a*) Spatial visualization. Imagine folding and unfolding a piece of paper. The figure at the top represents a square piece of paper being folded. A hole is punched through all of the thicknesses of the folded paper. Which figure shows what the paper looks like when it is unfolded? (*b*) Spatial orientation. Compare the three cubes on the right with the one on the left. No letter appears on more than one face of a given cube. Which of the three cubes on the right could be a different view of the cube on the left? (*c*) Mental rotation. In each pair, can the three-dimensional objects be made congruent by rotation? (*Source:* Halpern, 1986, Fig. 3.1, p. 50, & Fig. 3.2, p. 52.)

tors have replicated the finding since then (e.g., Sanders & Soares, 1986). But this pattern has not been observed consistently, and researchers are still puzzling over what seems to be a complex set of hormonal and brain influences on spatial ability.

In contrast, there appear to be no reasonable biological explanations of the small sex differences in mathematical or verbal reasoning. In the case of mathematics, particularly, there is considerable evidence that girls' and boys' skills are systematically shaped by a series of factors (Chipman, Brush, & Wilson, 1985; Harvard Education Letter, 1986):

- Boys take more math courses than girls do. When the amount of math is held constant, the sex difference in test scores becomes much smaller.
- Parental attitudes about mathematics are markedly different for boys and girls. Jacquelynne Parsons and her colleagues (Parsons, Adler, & Kaczala, 1982), for example, found that parents of fifth- to eleventh-graders thought their daughters were less good at math and had to work harder to achieve well in math than their sons, despite the fact that the students did not actually differ in math achievement. Similarly, Susan Holloway and Robert Hess (1985) have found that mothers of mathematically skillful elementary-school girls attribute their daughters' success to effort and good teaching; mothers of equally skilled boys attribute their sons' success to ability. When daughters did poorly in math, though, mothers attributed this to lack of ability, while for sons, the explanation of poor performance was that the boys were not working hard enough.
- Girls and boys have different experiences in math classes. In elementary school, teachers pay more attention to boys during math instruction (and more attention to girls during reading instruction), and in high school, math teachers direct more of their questions and comments to boys, even when girls are outspoken in class.

The cumulative effect of these differences in expectation and treatment show up in high school, when sex differences on standardized math tests become evident. In part, then, the small sex differences in test scores appear to be perpetuated by subtle family and school influences on children's attitudes. Whether these differences can explain the greater percentage of boys than girls who show real giftedness in mathematics is not so clear. But environmental factors appear to be the best explanation of the sex difference in average test scores.

THE MEASUREMENT OF INTELLIGENCE: A LAST LOOK

One of the questions that students often ask at about this point is whether, given all the factors that can affect a test score, it is worth bothering with IQ tests at all. I think that these tests do assess some important aspects of children's intellectual performance and that they can be helpful in identifying children who may have difficulties in school. (Certainly the IQ test is a *better* method of selecting such children than are the strategies that would replace the tests—most particularly teacher evaluations, which are more subject to bias than the tests are.) But it is worth emphasizing again that they do *not* measure a lot of other things we may be interested in, including all the facets of intelligence Sternberg describes. An IQ test is a specialized tool, and like many such tools, it has a fairly narrow range of appropriate use. I don't want to throw out this tool, but we have to keep its limitations very firmly in mind when we use it.

SUMMARY

1. When we study the development of intelligence, we need to distinguish between measures of intellectual power and measures of intellectual structure. IQ tests are intended to measure "how much" intelligence a child or adult has. They tap individual differences in intellectual power.

2. The most commonly used individually administered tests are the Stanford-Binet and the Wechsler Intelligence Scales for Children (WISC-R). The most common infant IQ test is the Bayley Scales of Infant Development.

3. All current IQ tests compare a child's performance to that of others her or his age. Scores above 100 represent better-than-average performance; scores below 100 represent poorer-than-average performance.

4. Both IQ tests and school achievement tests measure a child's performance, not capacity or underlying competence. Achievement tests, however, test much more specific school-related information than do IQ tests.

5. IQ test scores are quite good predictors of school performance and number of years of school completed; they are much less good predictors of later success in the work world.

6. IQ scores are quite stable from one testing to the next, and this becomes more and more true the older the child gets. But individual children's scores still may fluctuate 20 or 30 points or more over the course of childhood.

7. IQ tests do not measure many other facets of intellectual functioning in which we might be interested, including what Sternberg calls experiential and contextual intelligence.

8. Studies of identical twins and of adopted children show clearly that there is at least some genetic influence on measured IQ. Current estimates are that perhaps 35 to 50 percent of the variation in individual IQs may be attributed to heredity.

9. Environmental influence, however, is also substantial. Poor children consistently test lower than do children from middle-class families; firstborn and early-born children have higher scores, on average; and families that provide appropriate play materials and encourage intellectual development have children who score higher on IQ tests.

10. Environmental influence is also shown by improved test performance among children who have been in special enriched preschool or infant day-care programs.

11. A consistent difference of about 10 points on IQ tests is found between

white and black children. It seems most likely that this difference is due to environmental and cultural differences between the two groups, such as differences in health and prenatal care and in the types of intellectual skills trained and emphasized at home.

12. Males and females do not differ on total IQ test scores but do differ in subskills. Males are better at spatial visualization and mathematical reasoning; females are better at verbal reasoning and some other verbal tasks.

KEY TERMS

achievement test A test, usually given in schools, designed to assess a child's learning of specific material, such as spelling or arithmetic computation.

Bayley Scales of Infant Development The best-known and most widely used test of infant intelligence.

competence The behavior of a person as it would be under ideal or perfect circumstances. It is not possible to measure competence directly.

componential intelligence One of three types of intelligence in Sternberg's triarchic theory of intelligence. This is the type of intelligence typically measured on IQ tests: analytic thinking, remembering facts, organizing information.

confluence model Zajonc's term for his explanation of family-size and ordinal position effects on IQ. Assumes that a child's IQ is partially determined by the average intellectual level of the family members with whom the child has contact.

contextual intelligence One of three types of intelligence in Sternberg's triarchic theory of intelligence. Often called "street smarts," this type of intelligence includes skills in adapting to an environment and in adapting an environment to one's own needs.

cumulative deficit Any difference between groups in IQ (or achievement test) scores that becomes larger over time.

experiential intelligence One of three types of intelligence described by Sternberg in his triarchic theory of intelligence. Includes creativity, insight, seeing new relationships among experiences.

information processing A way of looking at cognition and cognitive development that emphasizes fundamental processes: memory strategies, problem-solving strategies, planning, and basic functions such as noticing differences and similarities.

intellectual power That aspect of intellectual skill that has to do with how well or how quickly a child can perform cognitive tasks. A dimension of individual difference in intellectual skill.

IQ Intelligence quotient. Originally defined in terms of a child's mental age and chronological age. IQ is now computed by comparing a child's performance with that of other children of the same chronological age.

mental age A way to describe the level of mental tasks a child can perform. A child who can perform tasks normally done by 8-year-olds but not tasks done by 9-year-olds has a mental age of 8.

performance The behavior shown by a person under actual circumstances. Even when we are interested in competence, all we can ever measure is performance.

Stanford-Binet The best-known American intelligence test. It was written by Louis Terman and his associates, based upon the first tests by Binet and Simon.

structure That aspect of intellectual skill that changes with age and is shared by all children. Focus is on *how* the child arrives at a particular answer rather than on the correctness of the answer.

triarchic theory of intelligence A theory proposed by Sternberg, proposing the existence of three types of intelligence: the componential, the contextual, and the experiential.

WISC-R The Wechsler Intelligence Scale for Children (Revised). Another well-known American IQ test that includes both verbal and performance (nonverbal) subtests.

▬▬▬ SUGGESTED READING

Gallagher, J. J., & Ramey, C. T. (1987). *The malleability of children.* Baltimore: Paul H. Brookes.

If you are interested in the impact of special programs on IQ, this is the most recent and readable source I know. Included are papers by several of the researchers involved in major intervention studies (including Ramey), as well as reviews of this research by other key figures, such as Bettye Caldwell.

Jensen, A. R. (1980). *Bias in mental testing.* New York: Free Press.

Jensen has been the most consistent spokesperson for a hereditary position on IQ differences. This is a massive and technically detailed book, but it is the very best source for understanding this viewpoint.

Ramey, C. T., & McPhee, D. (1986). Developmental retardation: A systems theory perspective on risk and preventive intervention. In D. C. Farran & J. D. McKinney (Eds.), *Risk in intellectual and psychosocial development.* Orlando, FL: Academic Press.

An excellent current review of the biological and environmental factors that cause mental retardation, including a good discussion of the culture of poverty and its effect on IQ.

Trotter, R. J. (1986, August). Three heads are better than one. *Psychology Today,* pp. 56–62.

A wonderful description of Sternberg's triarchic theory, in nontechnical language.

Zajonc, R. B. (1975, January). Birth order and intelligence: Dumber by the dozen. *Psychology Today,* pp. 37–43.

A brief account of Zajonc's argument concerning birth order and IQ.

7 Cognitive Development II: Structure and Process

Piaget's Basic Ideas
  Development as Adaptation
  The Functional Invariants
  The Starting Point for Development
  Stages of Development
The Sensorimotor Period: From Birth to 18 Months
  Piaget's View of the Sensorimotor Period
  Current Work on the Sensorimotor Period
  Overview of the Sensorimotor Period
Preoperational Thought: From 18 Months to 6 Years
  Piaget's Views of the Preoperational Period
  Current Work on the Preoperational Period
  Overview of the Preoperational Child
Young Children's Play
Concrete Operational Thought: From 6 to 12 Years
  Piaget's Views of Concrete Operations
  Current Work on the Concrete Operations Period
  Overview of the Concrete Operational Child
Piaget's Theory and Early Education
Formal Operational Thought: From Age 12 On
  Piaget's View of Formal Operational Thought
  Current Work on the Formal Operations Period
Overview of the Stages of Cognitive Development
Criticisms of Piaget's Theory
  The Timing of Developments
  The Role of Specific Knowledge or Expertise
  Are There Stages?
Information Processing in Children
  Developmental Approaches to Information Processing
  Changes in Processing Strategy: A Summary
  Individual Differences in Information Processing
Putting the Three Approaches Together
Summary
Key Terms
Suggested Reading
Project: The Game of 20 Questions

Imagine the following scene: Your 5-year-old, John, and your 8-year-old, Anne, come into the kitchen after playing outside, both asking for juice. With both children watching, you take two identical small cans of juice from the refrigerator and pour each into a glass. Since one of the glasses is narrower than the other, the juice rises higher in that glass. The 5-year-old, having been given the fatter glass, complains, "Anne got more than I did!" To which Anne replies (with the wonderful grace of the 8-year-old to her sibling), "I did not, you dummy. We both got the same amount. The two cans were just alike." To restore family harmony, you get out another glass identical to Anne's and pour John's juice into this new glass. The level of the liquid is now the same, and John is satisfied.

If this were an item on an IQ test, we'd say that Anne was "right" and John was "wrong." But such an emphasis on rightness or wrongness misses an essential point about this interchange: there seems also to be a *developmental* change, a shift in the way the child sees or understands the world and the relationships of objects. John is not being pigheaded or "dumb." He is merely operating with a different kind of reasoning than Anne's. A year or two from now, John will sound the way Anne does now.

If we are to understand children's thinking, we need to understand these changes in the *form* or *structure* of their thinking as well as differences in *power*. How do children come to understand the world around them? What assumptions do they make? What kind of logic do they use, and how does it change over time?

These were precisely the kinds of questions that Jean Piaget asked in his many years of research on children's thinking. His work has influenced several generations of psychologists. Today it would be more accurate to say that he is no longer the intellectual "father" of current researchers but their "grandfather" or "great-grandfather." The family resemblance is still visible, but a whole lot of other influences have entered the picture. To do justice to both Piaget's theory and the current variations, I will use Piaget's ideas as a basic framework, but I will also describe the current work and the criticisms of the theory that have emerged in recent years.

PIAGET'S BASIC IDEAS

Piaget's early training and professional work was in biology, but he later became interested in philosophy and psychology and worked briefly for Alfred Binet on the development of some of the early IQ tests. His job for Binet was to give the same IQ test items to a whole series of children and to score the correctness of each child's answer. But Piaget soon found he was much more interested in the children's wrong answers than their right ones. It seemed to him that there were some important patterns in the kinds of errors children made, with children of similar ages making similar mistakes. The critical issue, he thought, was not whether children got the right answers but how they *arrived* at their answers, how they think.

Following these beginning observations, Piaget's early work led him to a series of basic assumptions or propositions about the development of thinking in the child.

Development as Adaptation

First, for Piaget, cognitive development is, in part, the result of *active, voluntary exploration* by the child. For infants, this may mean watching, listening, and putting things in their mouths; for preschoolers, it may mean making mud pies or playing with blocks; for older children, asking questions and doing science experiments. The child is attempting to adapt to his world, to find meaning, to understand.

The Functional Invariants

Second, Piaget proposes that this adaptational process can be broken down into three subprocesses (collectively called the *functional invariants*)— namely, assimilation, accommodation, and equilibration. (These terms may be unfamiliar, but the concepts are not inherently any more difficult than ideas such as reinforcement or classical conditioning.)

Assimilation. Each time we encounter some object, some person, some experience, we "assimilate" it in some way. **Assimilation** means that we notice it, "recognize" it, take it in, hook it up with earlier experiences or categories. For example, you are assimilating as you read this paragraph, hooking this information onto the closest concept you already have. Or suppose you are trying to learn how to bake bread and you watch a friend kneading dough. You will assimilate parts of what he is doing—those parts that you notice and understand.

This is not a passive process. Assimilation is not simply taking pictures like a camera and storing them in mental slots. Assimilation is selective, and it involves modification of information as it is assimilated. For example, if I see a friend wearing a new dress in an usual color of orangish red, I may label the color "red" in my mind (thus assimilating it to my "red" category) even though it is not precisely red. Later, when I remember the dress, I will remember it as being redder than it really is. The process of assimilation, then, has changed the perception as well as categorizing it.

Accommodation. The complementary process, **accommodation,** involves changing the mental categories or actions or concepts, all of which Piaget calls, collectively, **schemes.** After seeing my friend's dress, my "red" scheme may be expanded somewhat to include this unusual new variation. My bread-kneading scheme will be significantly changed after watching an expert at work.

With any new experience, then, we take in (assimilate) new information and hook it onto the closest previous experience or action for which we have an existing scheme. When the fit is not very close, we adapt (accommodate) our scheme, changing it or creating new schemes to handle the assimilated information.

Equilibration.   The third part of the adaptation process is **equilibration.** It is the basic self-regulatory process Piaget postulated, resulting from a fundamental motive in each of us to stay "in balance." The child is always striving to achieve an overall understanding, an overall mental structure that fits the experience she has had. A scientist shows a kind of equilibration when she tries to make sense out of all the facts she has learned. She tries to fit the facts into her theory (assimilate them); she makes adjustments in the theory so that the facts fit better (accommodation). But sometimes the accumulation of facts just can't be made to fit, and a new theory is needed.

This process of changing the basic assumptions, the basic theory, is similar to what Piaget has in mind with the concept of equilibration. He sees the child as constructing a series of "theories" about the world. Each theory seems adequate initially but is eventually given up in the face of new experiences and new information, until at adolescence the child finally arrives at a theory, a model, that works for nearly all experiences.

The Starting Point for Development

A third basic assumption Piaget made is that the infant begins the process of cognitive development already possessing certain inborn strategies (schemes) for interacting with and exploring the environment. As I have already described in Chapter 5, the newborn can see, hear, touch, suck, and grasp. More important, from the beginning the baby's use of these skills appears to follow basic rules, such as the "look at the edges" rule that seems to dominate children's visual searching in the early days of life. These early schemes or rules then undergo systematic change in predictable sequences, as a result of assimilation, accommodation, and equilibration.

Stages of Development

Piaget's fourth point was that because the child strives for coherence in her understanding at any given age, she has a more or less unified cognitive system (a structure) with its own unique form and rules (which is why children the same age often give the same "wrong" answers to questions). But because the child has new experiences all the time, these structures eventually change (equilibrate), giving way to new ones. It is this orderly progression of structures that creates the *stages* that are a key feature of Piaget's theory (listed in Table 7.1). The transition from one stage to the next may be gradual (and the ages may vary from one child to the next),

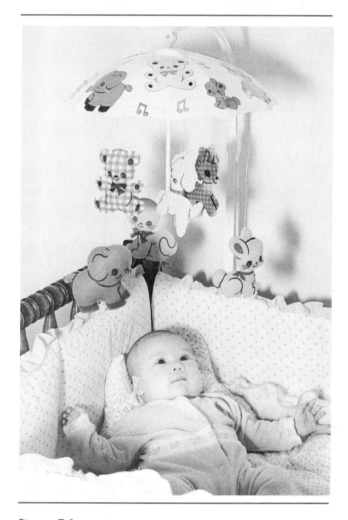

Figure 7.1 Babies appear to be born with a collection of basic strategies for exploring the world around them. For example, very young infants, like this one, use a "search for objects and scan the edges" strategy. These strategies—or *schemes*, to use Piaget's word—are the starting point of the long process of cognitive development.

but each stage is qualitatively different from the preceding one, and each is thought to be internally consistent. Thus, a 3-year-old thinks quite differently from an 8-year-old, and both think differently from a 13-year-old.

All of that probably sounds quite abstract. The best way for me to make it concrete is to go through the four stages Piaget proposed and tell you what Piaget thought about the logic characteristic of each—as well as what some of the more recent research is telling us.

Table 7.1

Piaget's Stages of Cognitive Development

Stage	Age	Description
Sensorimotor	Birth–2 years	The baby "understands" the world in terms of what she can do with objects and of her sensory information. A block is how it tastes, feels to grasp, looks to the eye.
Preoperational	2–6 years	By about 18–24 months, the child can represent objects to himself internally and begins to understand classification of objects into groups and to be able to take others' perspectives. Fantasy play appears, as does primitive logic.
Concrete operational	6–12 years	The child's logic takes a great leap forward with the development of powerful new internal mental operations, such as addition, subtraction, and class inclusion. The child is still tied to specific experience but can do mental manipulations as well as physical ones.
Formal operational	12 years +	The child becomes able to manipulate ideas as well as events or objects in her head. She can imagine and think about things that she has never seen or that haven't yet happened; she can organize systematically and exhaustively and think deductively.

THE SENSORIMOTOR PERIOD: FROM BIRTH TO 18 MONTHS

Piaget's View of the Sensorimotor Period

The key features of the **sensorimotor stage,** according to Piaget, are as follows: (1) The infant's response to the world is almost entirely sensory and motor. (2) The infant functions in the immediate present, responding to whatever stimuli present themselves. (3) The infant does not plan or intend. (4) The infant has no internal representation of objects—no mental pictures, or words, that stand for objects and that can be manipulated mentally. (Piaget thought that such internal representations did not develop until about 18 to 24 months.)

John Flavell summarizes all this very nicely:

[The infant] exhibits a wholly practical, perceiving-and-doing, action-bound kind of intellectual functioning; she does not exhibit the more contemplative, reflective, symbol-manipulating kind we usually think of in connection with cognition. The infant 'knows' in the sense of recognizing or anticipating familiar, recurring objects and happenings, and 'thinks' in the sense of behaving toward them with mouth, hand, eye, and other sensory-motor instruments in predictable, organized, and often adaptive ways. . . . It is the kind of noncontemplative intelligence that your dog relies on to make its way in the world. (Flavell, 1985, p. 13)

Piaget thought that sensorimotor intelligence developed through a series of six substages, which I've sketched very briefly in Table 7.2. You

Table 7.2
████████████

Substages of the Sensorimotor Period Proposed by Piaget

Substage	Age	Piaget's label	Characteristics of the stage
1	0–1 month	Reflexes	Almost entirely practice of built-in reflexes, such as sucking and looking. These reflexes are modified (through accommodation) as a result of experience.
2	1–4 months	Primary circular reactions	The infant tries to make interesting things happen again with her body, such as getting her thumb in her mouth. Visual and tactual explorations are more systematic. But infants in this stage still do not appear to distinguish between body and outside objects or events. They do not link their own actions to results outside themselves.
3	4–10 months	Secondary circular reactions	The infant tries to make external interesting things happen again, such as moving a mobile by hitting it intentionally. He also begins to coordinate information from two senses and develops the object concept. He understands, at some level, that his own actions can have external results.
4	10–12 months	Coordination of secondary schemes	The infant begins to combine actions to get things she wants, such as knocking a pillow away in order to reach for a toy. She uses familiar strategies in combination and in new situations.
5	12–18 months	Tertiary circular reactions	"Experimentation" begins; the infant tries out *new* ways of playing with or manipulating objects. Improved motor skills make wider exploration possible, too.
6	18–24 months	Beginning of thought	Internal representation is now readily apparent; the child uses images, perhaps words or actions, to stand for objects. Really the beginning of the next stage, the preoperational stage.

may notice that the shift from substage 1 to substage 2 sounds a good deal like the transition at about 2 months of age I described in Chapter 5, when the infant shifts from examining edges and movement (*where* an object is) and focuses more on the internal features of objects (*what* an object is). You will also see that the object concept develops in substage 3.

In Piaget's view, all these substages gradually build toward the key accomplishment of this period, namely, internal representation at about 18 months. It is only then, he thought, that the child can both form and manipulate mental images.

One of Piaget's observations of his own daughter, Lucienne, illustrates this transition. At the time of this observation, Piaget was playing with Lucienne and had hidden his watch chain inside an empty box. He describes what happened then:

> I put the chain back into the box and reduce the opening to 3 mm. It is understood that Lucienne is not aware of the functioning of the opening and closing of the match box and has not seen me prepare the experiment. She only possesses two preceding schemes [strategies]: turning the box over in order to empty it of its contents, and sliding her fingers into the slit to make the chain come out. It is of course this last procedure that she tries first: she puts her finger inside and gropes to reach the chain, but fails completely. A pause follows during which Lucienne manifests a very curious reaction. . . . She looks at the slit with great attention; then, several times in succession, she opens and shuts her mouth, at first slightly, then wider and wider! [Then] . . . Lucienne unhesitatingly puts her finger in the slit, and instead of trying as before to reach the chain, she pulls so as to enlarge the opening. She succeeds and grasps the chain. (Piaget, 1952, pp. 337–338)

What an enormous discovery this child seems to have made! Faced with a new situation, instead of going immediately to trial and error, she paused and appeared to discover the solution through some kind of analysis. Piaget saw this behavior as a sign of the very beginning of the child's ability to manipulate and combine, to experiment and explore, with *mental* images instead of real objects or actions.

Current Work on the Sensorimotor Period

Many of Piaget's observations about the young infant were made before the development of newer, more sophisticated research techniques for studying babies. These newer techniques, many of which I described in Chapter 5, reveal that newborn and very young infants are far more cognitively skillful than Piaget had supposed. A couple of examples:

• *Imitation.* You'll see from Table 7.2 that Piaget thought infants could not distinguish between their own body and other things until substage

3, at perhaps 4–5 months of age or older. If that's true, then infants should not be able to imitate other people's gestures or facial expressions until at least that age; such imitation seems to imply a distinction between "you" and "me." But in fact, as I pointed out in Chapter 5, babies *do* show such imitation—particularly of facial movements like tongue protrusion—as early as two or three days of age (e.g., Meltzoff & Moore, 1983; Meltzoff, 1985).

• *Internal representation.*   Many of the studies I talked about in Chapter 5, particularly those showing cross-modal transfer during the first year of life, seem to point to the presence of internal representation far earlier than 18 months. For instance, infants can recognize by feel things that they have seen, and link the sight of something with its expected sound. All of these accomplishments seem to require the baby to create a fairly complex and abstract mental image. Note, though, that even though the infant may create quite sophisticated mental representations, that does not mean that he can *manipulate* these images in his head. The sensorimotor-stage infant still has to try things out with hands or tongue or eyes.

Overview of the Sensorimotor Period

In a number of important respects, Piaget seems to have underestimated the ability of infants to store, remember, and organize sensory and motor information. Babies pay much more attention to patterns, to sequence, to prototypical features than Piaget thought. At the same time, many of the sequences Piaget described, such as the sequence of development of the object concept, have held up well to close research scrutiny. Furthermore, his image of the infant as a "little scientist" building theories about the world is very much in keeping with the recent evidence. The infant assimilates information to his existing schemes (actions, skills, "prototypes") and modifies (accommodates) the schemes as he goes along. By the time the infant has reached the age of 18 or 24 months, his perceptions and actions are already quite well organized.

PREOPERATIONAL THOUGHT: FROM 18 MONTHS TO 6 YEARS

In Piaget's view, the radical change that occurs at about age 18 months or 2 years, the beginning of the **preoperational stage,** is that the child is now able to use symbols—images or words or actions that *stand for* something else. We see this in children's pretend play, which I have talked about in the box on pages 234–235. At age 2 or 3 or 4, a broom may become a horsie or a block may become a train. We can also see such symbol use at about the same time in the emergence of language (which I'll describe in Chapter 8). And we see the child's improving ability to manipulate these symbols internally in such things as her improving memory or in her ability to search more systematically for lost or hidden objects.

YOUNG CHILDREN'S PLAY

Go to a preschool some time and watch the children during an unstructured time— when they are not eating or napping or being "organized" by the adults. What are the children doing? They are building towers out of blocks, moving dolls around in the doll house, making "tea" with the tea set, racing toy trucks across the floor, dressing up in grown-up clothes, putting puzzles together. They are, in a word, *playing*. This is not trivial or empty activity; it is the stuff on which much of cognitive development seems to be built.

Any parent who has watched the development of his or her child during the preschool years knows that play changes in very visible ways during the years from 1 to 7 (as you can see yourself in the photos in the third color photo essay). When psychologists attempt to describe these changes, a series of "steps" or "stages" emerge (Rubin, Fein, & Vandenberg, 1983). These changes flow together; children show several of these kinds of play at any one time. But we can still see at least the following seven different kinds of play, in something like this order.

Sensorimotor play. The child of 12 months or so spends most of her play time exploring and manipulating objects, using all the sensorimotor schemes in her repertoire. She puts things in her mouth, shakes them, stacks them, moves them along the floor. In this way she comes to understand what objects can do. Older children continue to show this kind of play with *new* toys or objects, but this type of play diminishes in frequency some time in the second year of life.

First pretend play. The first sign of pretend play is usually something like a child using a toy spoon to "feed" himself or a toy comb to comb his hair. The toys are still used for their actual or typical purposes (spoon for feeding) and the actions are still oriented to the *self*, but there is pretend involved.

Elaboration with objects. Between 15 and 21 months, there is a shift: the recipient of the pretend action now becomes another person or a toy. The child is still using objects for their usual purposes (such as drinking from a cup), but now she is giving the pretend drink to a doll instead of herself. Dolls are especially good toys for this kind of pretend, since it is not a very large leap from doing things for or to yourself to doing things for or to a doll. So children dress and undress dolls, feed them imaginary food, comb their hair.

Substitute pretend play. Between 2 and 3 years of age, children make another big change in their play and begin to use objects to stand for something altogether different.

Despite the child's enormous achievement (which John Flavell, one of the current major theorists and observers, describes as "nothing short of miraculous" [1985, p. 82]), Piaget's description of this second stage was oddly negative in tone. He focused mostly on all the things the preschool-age child still *cannot* do. More recent research has given us a much more positive view. I can contrast the two views most clearly by describing several key dimensions of the toddler's thinking, first through Piaget's eyes and then through the eyes of recent researchers.

They may comb the doll's hair with a baby bottle while saying that it is a comb or use a broom to be a horsie or make "trucks" out of blocks. The earlier forms of play, in which toys are used for their "real" purposes (such as using blocks to build towers), does not disappear. But among 4- and 5-year-olds, as much as 20 percent of free play involves this new, complicated kind of pretending (Field, De Stefano, & Koewler, 1982). And children who show more of this kind of play are also seen by their teachers as having more general social competence and are more popular and less egocentric (Connolly & Doyle, 1984). Just what is causing what here is not so clear, but it is at least plausible that elaborated pretend play helps promote cognitive advances.

Sociodramatic play. At about age 4 or 5, children also begin to play parts or take roles. They play "daddy and mommy" or "cowboys and Indians" or "doctor and patient" or "train conductor and passengers." Sometimes the stories that are acted out are very elaborate, and children clearly get great delight out of these fantasies. Equally important, by playing roles, pretending to be someone else, they also become more and more aware of how things may look or feel to someone else, and their approach to the world becomes less egocentric.

Awareness of the roles. Six-year-olds not only create elaborate "dramas," they will also describe or label the roles they are playing. They plan the play ahead of time or assign people to different roles rather than merely drifting into a new set of roles in the process of play. This change seems to reflect a cognitive advance and is not actually seen until about age 6 or later—at about the time that we see the transition to concrete operations.

Games with rules. At elementary-school age, pretend play begins to wane and is replaced by complex games with specific rules—jacks or marbles or baseball or "kick the can" or the equivalent. Earlier forms of play may involve spontaneously created rules, but in elementary school, children more and more play games that have persisting, agreed-upon rules.

As adults, most of us associate the word *play* with "goofing off" or nonproductive activities. But in some very real ways, play is children's "work." Opportunities to manipulate and experiment with objects, pretend with them, play parts and roles—all seem to be important ingredients in the child's cognitive and social development (Rubin, Fein, & Vandenberg, 1983; Piaget, 1962). The key point is that children need to have *time* for play—time when they are not watching TV, not organized, not required to do anything "constructive."

Piaget's View of the Preoperational Period

Perspective Taking: Egocentrism. Piaget pointed out that children in the preoperational stage look at things entirely from their own perspective, from their own frame of reference—a quality Piaget called *egocentrism* (Piaget, 1954). The child is not being selfish; rather, she simply thinks (assumes) that everyone sees the world her way.

Figure 7.2 shows a classic experiment illustrating this kind of egocen-

Figure 7.2 This kind of experimental situation has been used to study egocentrism in children. The child is asked first to pick out the picture that shows how the two mountains look to him, then to pick out the picture that shows how the mountains look to the little clay figure. Preschool children typically pick the same picture both times—the one that shows how it looks from their perspective.

trism. The child is shown a three-dimensional scene with mountains of different sizes and colors. From a set of drawings, he picks out the one that shows the scene the way he sees it. Most preschoolers can do this without much difficulty. Then the examiner asks the child to pick out the drawing that shows how the little doll figure or the examiner sees the scene. Here preschool children have difficulty. Most often they pick the drawing that shows their *own* view of the mountains (e.g., Gzesh & Surber, 1985; Flavell et al., 1981).

In Piaget's view, one of the key tasks of the preoperational period is for the child to become "decentered"—to shift from the self as the only frame of reference. As Herbert Ginsburg and Sylvia Opper put it:

> The [preoperational] child decenters his thought just as in the sensorimotor period the infant decentered his behavior. The newborn *acts* as if the world is centered about himself and must learn to behave in more adaptive ways. Similarly, the young child *thinks* from a limited perspective and must widen it. (Ginsburg & Opper, 1979, p. 111)

Understanding Identities.

In a similar way, Piaget sees a new level or layer of understanding of the identity of objects that must be addressed by the preschool child. The sensorimotor infant eventually understands that objects continue to exist even when they are out of sight. But there are other aspects of objects that also remain constant despite apparent changes—that are *conserved,* in Piaget's language—and this **conservation** baffles the preschool child. For example, the number of buttons you have is not changed if you move them around in different arrangements; an amount of lemonade is not changed if you pour it into a different container.

One classic experiment about conservation, which is illustrated in Figure 7.3, uses two equal-sized lumps of clay (Inhelder & Piaget, 1958). The experimenter takes one lump and—in full view of the child—squashes

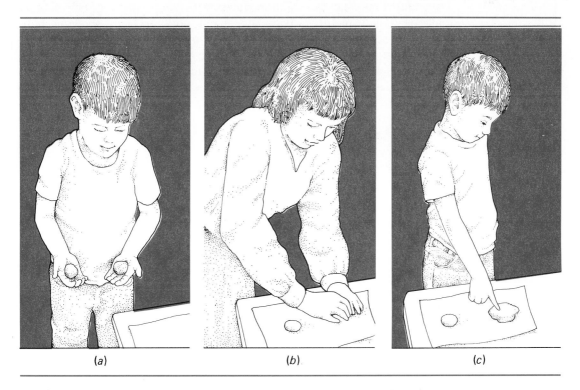

(*a*)　　　　　　　　(*b*)　　　　　　　　(*c*)

Figure 7.3　In the classic conservation experiment using balls of clay, the child first holds both and agrees they are the same (*a*). The experimenter then squishes one of the balls into another shape (*b*) and asks the child whether they are the same or different (*c*).

it like a pancake. The question for the child is, "Is there the same amount here [pointing to the pancake] as there is here [pointing to the ball]? Or is there more here, or more here?" Preschoolers nearly always think the amount of clay is different after it has been squished (most think the pancake has more), but by age 6 or 7, children will nearly always tell you that the two are still the same.

It was a problem of conservation that confronted Anne and John and their juice glasses. John—aged 5—had not yet achieved a full understanding of conservation of quantity, while Anne had. Instead, John's attention was focused on the height of the liquid in the glass, which is a classic "error" for the preschooler.

Classification.   Another area Piaget describes is the child's ability to classify objects—to put things in sets or types and to use abstract or formal properties such as color or shape or even verbal labels as a basis for such classification. Piaget studied this by giving young children sets of objects or picture cutouts of people, animals, or toys and asking them to put together the things that "go together" or "are similar" (Piaget & Inhelder, 1959). Two- and three-year-old children, faced with such an array, will usually make designs or pictures. At perhaps age 4, children begin showing more systematic sorting and grouping of objects, using first one dimension (e.g., shape, such as round things versus square things) and later two or more dimensions at once (e.g., size *and* shape: small round things versus small square things and large round things versus large square things).

Despite this big advance, there is still some distance to go. In particular, the preoperational child still does not grasp the principle of **class inclusion:** he does not understand that some classes are fully contained within other classes. Dogs are part of the larger class of animals, roses are part of the class of flowers, and so forth.

For a child to show that she understands class inclusion, it is not enough for her simply to use words like *animal* to refer to more than one kind of creature. She must also understand the logical relationships. Piaget usually studied this by having children first create their own classes and subclasses and then asking questions about them. One 5½-year-old child, for example, had a set of flowers made up of a large group of primroses and a smaller group of other mixed flowers (Piaget & Inhelder, 1959, p. 108):

> *Piaget:* "If I make a bouquet of all the primroses and you make one of all the flowers, which will be bigger?"
> *Child:* "Yours."
> *Piaget:* "If I gather all the primroses in a meadow will any flowers remain?"
> *Child:* "Yes."

The child understood that there are other flowers than primroses but did *not* yet understand that all primroses are flowers—that the smaller, subordinate class is *included in* the larger class. Piaget thought this understanding did not come until about age 7.

Reasoning. Piaget's daughter Lucienne announced one afternoon when she had not taken her nap, "I haven't had my nap so it isn't afternoon." This is a very good example of the kind of reasoning you'll hear in the preschool-age child. Lucienne knew that afternoon and nap usually go together, but she had the relationship between them wrong. She thought that the nap "caused" the afternoon. The basic characteristic of this type of reasoning, which Piaget called **transductive reasoning,** is that the child sees that two things happen at the same time and assumes that one is the cause of the other. (A lot of superstitious behavior in adults is based on the same type of logic. If a baseball manager wore green socks the day his team won a key game, he might wear the same green socks for every game after that "for luck"; if so, he's showing a kind of transductive reasoning.)

Preoperational children's thinking is also rigid. They see things in black and white, in terms of good and bad. Rules of games are absolute and cannot possibly be changed; the more toys you break, the "worse" the action, regardless of whether you did it on purpose or not. More important, Piaget concluded that young children do not yet have the ability to *examine* their own thoughts, conclusions, or strategies.

Current Work on the Preoperational Period

As was true for the sensorimotor period, the current work on the preoperational period shows us that children in the 2 to 6 age range are probably a good deal more skillful than Piaget supposed.

Perspective Taking. I'll be talking more about current research on perspective taking in Chapter 12, but let me just say here that there is now a great deal of evidence that children as young as 2 and 3 have at least *some* ability to understand that other people see things or experience things differently.

John Flavell has devised a number of clever ways to show this (Flavell et al., 1981). Suppose you make up a card with a picture of a dog on one side and a picture of a cat on the other. You show the child both sides and then hold the card vertically between you, so the child can see either the cat or the dog and you see the other animal. You ask the child which animal you are looking at. Three-year-old children have no trouble understanding that you see something different from what they see. Children of this same age also talk in simpler sentences when they talk to a 2-year-old or to a handicapped child than when they talk to an adult (Guralnick & Paul-Brown, 1984; Shatz & Gelman, 1973), which again shows that they have some awareness of the different needs of the listeners.

But if you are *both* looking at the *same* thing from different angles, those same 3-year-olds have a much harder time understanding that you have a different viewpoint. For example, Flavell put a picture of a turtle down on the table between the child and himself, with the head toward the child and the tail toward the experimenter. The child had to say whether the experimenter saw the turtle "right side up" or "upside down." Most 3- and 4-year-olds could *not* answer this correctly.

The preoperational child thus seems to be less egocentric than Piaget thought, but she is still considerably more tied to her own perspective than will be true a few years later.

Understanding Identities.

Here, too, researchers have found signs of conservation earlier than Piaget suggested. For example, Rochel Gelman (1973), in an influential study, showed that children as young as 3 could display a form of number conservation. She showed 3-year-olds two plates, one with a row of three toys (e.g., two mice and a truck) and one with a row of two toys. On each trial, the plates were shuffled, and the child had to pick one plate as "the winner." The child had to learn that the plate with three toys was always "the winner."

After the child had learned this, the experimenter rearranged the three toys so that they were pushed together and presented the two plates again. What Gelman found was that the 3-year-olds still picked the three-toy plate as "the winner," showing that they realized the arrangement of the toys on the plate did not change the number. But children of the same age cannot do Piaget's typical conservation of number experiment, which involves larger numbers of M&M's or poker chips in rows. Why the difference?

Part of the difference seems to lie in how many objects there are (Wellman, 1982). Three-year-olds can count to 3, and they already understand that if you count two sets of things and arrive at the same number, they are the same. But they aren't good at counting to higher numbers and have not yet grasped the basic *principle* that shifting things around doesn't *ever* change the number. Thus, their judgment of equality or inequality is still based on counting rather than on the principle of conservation. What Gelman has shown, then, are some of the first steps that build toward a more general concept of conservation.

In general, researchers have found that 3-year-olds can display some early versions of conservation and that 4- and 5-year-olds, under supportive conditions, can often give quite clear conservation responses.

Classification Skills.

This ought to sound like a familiar refrain by now: young children classify better than Piaget thought, particularly if you simplify the task or if you make it clear that you want them to use some kind of superordinate category for classifying. For example, Sandra Waxman and Rochel Gelman (1986) told 3- and 4-year-olds that a puppet really liked pictures of food (or animals or furniture). The children were then given 12 pictures and asked to put the ones the puppet would like in one bin and the ones the puppet would not like in another bin. When they were given the category label in this way, these young children could quite easily classify the pictures into food and nonfood categories or furniture and nonfurniture categories.

Even 2-year-olds may be capable of such classification. Sugerman (1979, cited in Gelman & Baillargeon, 1983) found, for example, that toddlers of this age, if given two groups of objects (such as four dolls and four rings), tended to move them into separate piles or areas during play.

All in all, this research shows that the basic understanding that things-go-together-in-groups is present by at least age 2 (and perhaps earlier). But whether the child can display this understanding will depend on the way you set up the task. Piaget happened to pick a relatively difficult version of the task, so he ended up underestimating the child's understanding.

Class inclusion, however, is another matter. Recent research by Ann McCabe and her colleagues (1982) shows that real understanding of class inclusion does not appear until age 7 or 8, just as Piaget originally suggested.

Reasoning. In this area, too, we hear the same song: children at ages 2 to 6 are not consistently as primitive in their logic as Piaget thought.

Figure 7.4 Even children as young as 2 or 3 show some signs of classification in their play with toys—putting things the same shape together, for example. But they do not do so systematically until somewhat later.

For example, Merry Bullock and Rochel Gelman (1979) have shown that children as young as 3 understand that a cause has to come *before* an effect rather than after it—a remarkably sophisticated level of logical understanding at so early an age. Still, Piaget was quite correct in saying that 4-year-olds are less skillful in their logic than 7-year-olds.

Overview of the Preoperational Child

If we add up the different bits of information I've just given you, two points seem clear. First of all, Piaget underestimated the preoperational child. Preschool children are capable of forms of logic that Piaget thought impossible at this stage. They can solve some conservation problems, show some awareness of others' perspectives, understand the beginnings of causal relationships. To be sure, in order for the preschool child to demonstrate these relatively advanced forms of thinking, you have to make the task quite simple, eliminate distractions, or give special clues. But the fact that they can solve these problems at all is both striking and troublesome for Piaget's theory.

An equally important point, though, is that Piaget seems to have been quite correct in saying that preschool children think differently from older children. The very fact that they can perform certain tasks *only* when the tasks are made very simple or undistracting is evidence for such a difference. Their attention is more likely to be captured by obvious changes (such as on conservation tasks). In general, they have difficulty distinguishing between appearance and reality—between how things seem or look and how they "really are" (Flavell, 1986a, 1986b; Flavell et al., 1987), even when the experimenter tries to make this distinction as clear as possible.

Furthermore, preschool-age children do not seem to operate on the same kinds of general principles or rules that older children use. They can solve problems sometimes or under special conditions, but not consistently, not based on principles. It is precisely a switch to general rules that Piaget thought characterized the transition to the next stage of concrete operations.

CONCRETE OPERATIONAL THOUGHT: FROM 6 TO 12 YEARS

Piaget's View of Concrete Operations

The new skills we see at age 5, 6, or 7 build on all the small changes we have already seen in the preschooler, but from Piaget's perspective there is a great leap forward that occurs when the child "discovers" or "develops" a set of immensely powerful abstract general rules or strategies for examining and interacting with the world. Piaget calls the new set of skills **concrete operations,** with the term **operation** used specifically to refer to powerful *internal* manipulations such as addition, subtraction, multiplication, division, and serial ordering. The child now understands the *rule* that adding to something makes it more and subtracting from it makes it less; she understands that objects can belong to more than one category at once and that categories have logical relationships.

Even more important from Piaget's perspective is that the child now grasps the fundamental rule or operation of *reversibility*. The child understands that a basic property of actions is that they can be undone or reversed—either physically or mentally—and that you will then get back to the original position. The clay can be made back into a ball; the water can be poured back into the shorter, fatter glass. This understanding of the basic reversibility of actions lies behind many of the gains made during this period.

Signs of this shift in "mental gears" can be seen in myriad areas, but let me be more specific by following some of the same lines of development I described in the section on preoperational thought: identities, classification, and logic.

Identities in the Concrete Operations Period.

It is in this period that the child grasps the principle of conservation, by using any one of a number of different operations: reversibility ("If I changed it back it would be the same"), addition or subtraction ("You didn't add any so it has to be the same"), or compensation ("It's bigger around but it's thinner, so it's the same"—the child is paying attention to more than one thing at a time).

However, the child does not go from no principle to full principle in one leap. Instead, she seems to come to understand each of several conservations in a particular sequence over the course of several years. Conservation of number is understood early, at about age 5; but conservation of weight (changing an object's shape does not change its weight) is not understood till about age 8, and conservation of volume (changing an object's shape does not change the amount of space it takes up) is not understood until about age 11 or 12. So although we can talk about the concrete operational child as having "principles" or "rules," these rules are not initially used nearly as abstractly or as broadly as they will be at age 11 or 12.

Classification.

Here the big change is one I have already described: the understanding of the principle of class inclusion. A good way to illustrate this is with the game of 20 questions (which you can try out in the project for this chapter). In one of my favorite older studies, Frederic Mosher and Joan Hornsby (1966) showed 6- to 11-year-old children a set of 42 pictures of animals, people, toys, machines, and the like. The child was to figure out which one of the pictures the experimenter was thinking of by asking questions that could be answered "yes" or "no."

There are several ways to figure out which questions to ask. The child could simply start at one end of a row of pictures and ask, "Is it this one?" about each one in turn until she hit on the right one, or she could point to them in some random order. Mosher and Hornsby called this strategy *hypothesis scanning*. A second way is to classify the pictures mentally into a hierarchy of groups and then ask first about the highest level in the hierarchy—a strategy that requires understanding class inclusion. The child might start, for example, by asking, "Is it a toy?" If the answer is "yes," she might then ask about the subcategories: "Is it a red toy?" Mosher and Hornsby called this second strategy *constraint seeking*.

You can see in Figure 7.5, which shows the main results of this study, that 6-year-olds almost never used a constraint (classification) strategy. They relied essentially on hypothesis scanning (a form of guessing). By age 8, however, the majority of children's questions reflected a constraint strategy, and by age 11, that strategy strongly dominated.

Logic in the Concrete Operations Period. Piaget argued that during these years the child develops the ability to use **inductive logic**. He can go from his own experience to a general principle. For example, he can go from the observation that when you add another toy to a set and then

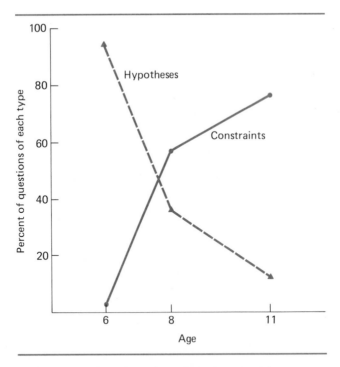

Figure 7.5 When they play 20 questions with pictures, 6-year-olds use nearly all guessing (hypotheses), but 8-year-olds, who are into the period of concrete operations, use a strategy (constraints) that involves organizing the pictures into classes and hierarchies. (*Source:* Mosher & Hornsby, 1966, p. 91.)

count the toys, the set always has one more, to a general principle that adding always "makes it more." In science, we use inductive reasoning a lot. We make systematic observations and then try to figure out why things turned out the way they did.

Elementary-school children are pretty good observational scientists and will enjoy cataloging, counting species of trees or birds, or figuring out the nesting habits of guinea pigs. What they are not yet good at is going from a general principle to some anticipated experience (like going from a theory to a hypothesis), a process that requires **deductive logic.** This is harder than inductive logic because it requires imagining things that you may never have experienced—something the concrete operations child typically does not do. Piaget thought that deductive reasoning did not develop until the period of formal operations in junior high or high school.

Current Work on the Concrete Operations Period

Current research on the concrete operations period, unlike the newer research on the sensorimotor and preoperational periods, has not been focused primarily on the question of whether Piaget underestimated or overestimated the thinking of children of this age or stage. Instead, attention has mostly been on two issues: (1) What is the sequence in which the several concepts develop in these years? and (2) Are children's skills consistent across tasks? There has also been a good deal of research on areas of children's abilities that Piaget touched on only briefly but which now appear to be highly significant, such as memory strategies. I'll save the question of memory strategies to the discussion of the information-processing approach, but let me say at least a few words about sequences and consistency across tasks.

Sequences of Development in the Concrete Operations Period. The best study of sequences I know of was done by Carol Tomlinson-Keasey and her colleagues (1979). They studied a group of 38 children from kindergarten through third grade, testing them with five traditional concrete operations tasks each year: conservation of mass (there's the same *amount* of clay after you squish one into a pancake), conservation of weight, conservation of volume, class inclusion, and hierarchical classification (organizing classes into hierarchies). You can see from Figure 7.6 that the children got better at all five tasks over the three-year period, with two spurts— one between the end of kindergarten and the start of first grade (about the age that Piaget thought that concrete operations really began) and another during second grade. More important, the different tasks were not equally easy. Conservation of mass was easier than conservation of weight, and conservation of volume was the hardest of the three. Class inclusion was also generally harder than conservation of mass. In fact, the researchers

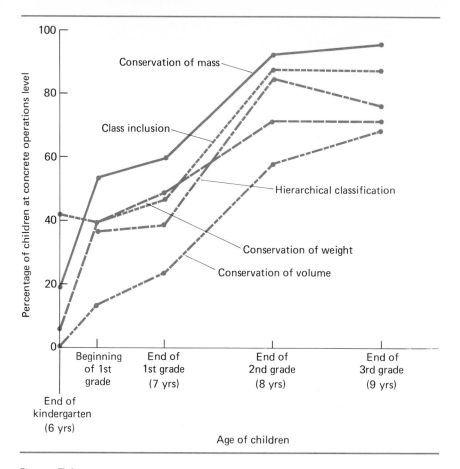

Figure 7.6 These results are from a longitudinal study in which the same children were given a set of concrete operations tasks five different times, beginning in kindergarten and ending in the third grade. As you can see, the percentage of children "solving" each type of problem increased, with several spurts. But the tasks differed in difficulty too. (*Source:* Tomlinson-Keasy et al., 1979, adapted from Table 2, p. 1158.)

found that conservation of mass seemed to be a necessary precursor for the development of class inclusion.

Tomlinson-Keasey also found that a child's skill on these tasks, relative to that of the other children, stayed approximately the same throughout the three years of testing. A 6-year-old who developed conservation of mass early continued to be ahead of other children later on; a late-developing child went through the same sequence about two years later.

There is certainly a good deal of confirmation of Piaget's observations in this study. In particular, it shows that each step in the sequence of cognitive development builds from what has gone before and that the sequence remains the same regardless of the rate of progress the child may show.

Consistency Across Tasks. The more difficult question, though, is whether we can talk about a child generally being "at" concrete operations or "at" formal operations. Do children perform at about the same "level" on a whole series of tasks? The very fact that Tomlinson-Keasey found that the traditional concrete operations tasks developed in a sequence rather than all at once shows that at least in the early years of this stage, children show complex or abstract thinking on some problems and not others. Others have found the same thing (Martorano, 1977; Roberge & Flexner, 1979). Piaget recognized this lack of simultaneity in development of concrete operations (using the phrase **horizontal decalage** to describe it). But acknowledging it does not explain why it occurs.

Overview of the Concrete Operational Child

My own sense about this period is that Piaget is correct about the general character and significance of the shift in children's thinking that takes place between about age 5 and 7. Children do seem to be able to step back a bit from compelling, immediate sensations or experiences and work out the beginnings of general rules, general strategies. We see the ramifications of this change in an enormous number of ways. For example, children of about this age get a lot better, a lot more systematic, at searching for lost toys, and their understanding of classes helps them learn beginning mathematics.

At the same time, these new skills seem to be much more narrowly applied than Piaget's original view would lead us to believe. The child is still tied to his own specific experience to a very marked degree. Five- and six-year-olds may be good at putting blocks in order from large to small if they have spent a lot of time playing with those blocks or with objects like them. But they may not show the same ability to put things into serial order with less-familiar material, such as sets of sticks (Achenbach & Weisz, 1975). Or a child may be better at creating hierarchical classes out of toys he has played with than out of a group of totally new toys. In other words, the 7-year-old *does* show some impressive new cognitive skills, but she does not apply them as consistently or broadly as Piaget's theory proposes.

FORMAL OPERATIONAL THOUGHT: FROM AGE 12 ON

Piaget's View of Formal Operational Thought

The final step of cognitive development proposed by Piaget is taken during adolescence, beginning at about age 12 and continuing into early adulthood. The child's major task in this period, according to Piaget, is to develop a new, still more powerful set of cognitive skills (**formal operations**), organized into a structure that allows her to think about *ideas* as well as about objects. Ideas can be classified and organized, just as objects can. In fact, they can be manipulated much more flexibly.

Piaget does *not* say that this new level of abstraction is achieved all at once one morning on a child's twelfth birthday: concrete operations do not develop suddenly, either. There are steps and substages, with fully consolidated formal operations probably not completed until about age 15 or later. But he did believe that there was a fairly rapid spurt of development over a period of several years, when the major elements of this new level of abstract thinking were acquired. Let me describe some of those major elements.

From the Actual to the Possible. One of the first steps in this process is for the child to extend her reasoning abilities to objects and situations that she has not seen or experienced firsthand or that she cannot see or manipulate directly. Instead of thinking only about real things and actual occurrences, she must start to think about possible occurrences. She can also now begin to think about the "ideal," such as the "ideal parent." (This new ability can sometimes be a source of conflict between parents and children, since few of us are ideal parents!)

An interesting implication of the teenager's new ability to consider unseen possibilities is that kids of this age should be able to consider the *future* much more systematically. In this culture, we certainly expect teenagers to have such skills—to think about what kind of job they might have when they grow up, what kind of further education they should have, and the like. In fact, there is some research showing an increase in the ability to think about future consequences of actions between the ages of 12 and 16 or 17 (e.g., Lewis, 1981).

Systematic Problem Solving. Another important feature of formal operations is the ability to search systematically and methodically for the answer to a problem. To study this, Piaget and his colleague Barbel Inhelder (Inhelder & Piaget, 1958) presented adolescents with complex tasks, mostly drawn from the physical sciences. In one of these tasks, the youngsters are given varying lengths of string and a set of objects of various weights which can be tied to the strings to make a swinging pendulum. They are shown how to start the pendulum by pushing the weight with differing amounts of force and by holding the weight at different heights. The subject must figure out which one or which combination of these four factors (length of string, weight of object, force of push, or height of push) determines the "period" (amount of time for one swing) of the pendulum. (In case you have forgotten your high-school physics, the answer is that only the length of the string affects the period of the pendulum.) If you give this task to a concrete operational child, she will usually try out many different combinations of length and weight and force and height in an inefficient way. She might try a heavy weight on a long string and then a light weight on a short string. Since both string length and weight have changed, there is no way to draw a clear conclusion about either factor.

An adolescent, in contrast, is likely to try a much more organized approach, attempting to vary just one of the four factors at a time. She may try a heavy object with a short string, then with a medium-length string, then with a long one. After that, she might try a light object with the three lengths of string. Of course, not all adolescents (or all adults, for that matter) are quite this methodical in their approach. But there is a very dramatic difference in the overall strategy used by 10-year-olds and 15-year-olds that marks the shift from concrete to formal operations.

Logic. Piaget argued that another facet of this shift is the appearance of deductive logic in the child's repertoire of skills. As I mentioned earlier, the concrete operational child is able to do inductive reasoning, which involves arriving at a conclusion or a rule based on a lot of individual experiences. The more difficult kind of reasoning, deductive reasoning, involves if-then relationships: "If all people are equal, then you and I must

Figure 7.7   Science classes in high school may require students to use deductive logic—to reason from the general to the particular, to work with theories and figure out expected results on the basis of the theories.

be equal." Children as young as 4 or 5 can understand some such relationships, but only if the premises given are factually true. Only at adolescence
are young people able to understand and use the basic *logical* relationship
(Moshman & Franks, 1986; Overton et al., 1987).

A great part of scientific logic is of this deductive type. We begin
with a theory and propose, "If this theory is correct, then I should observe
such and such." In doing this, we are going well beyond our observations.
We are conceiving things that we have never seen that *ought* to be true
or observable. We can think of this process as being part of a general
decentering process that began much earlier in cognitive development.
The preoperational child gradually moves away from his egocentrism and
comes to be able to take the physical perspective of others. During formal
operations, the child takes the next step by freeing himself even from his
reliance upon specific experiences.

Current Work on the Formal Operations Period

Most of the current work on formal operations has centered around three
questions: (1) Is there really a change in the child's thinking at adolescence,
and if so, when does it happen? (2) Why can't we see this change in
every youngster? (3) How general are these new abilities?

Is There Really a Change?   All the recent research tells us that the
answer to this question is clearly "yes." As Edith Neimark says, "an enormous
amount of evidence from an assortment of tasks shows that adolescents
and adults are capable of feats of reasoning not attained under normal
circumstances by [younger] children, and that these abilities develop fairly
rapidly during the ages of about 11 to 15" (1982, p. 493).

A large cross-sectional study by Susan Martorano (1977) is a good
illustration. She tested 20 students (all girls) at each of four grades (sixth,
eighth, tenth, and twelfth) on 10 different tasks that require one or more
of the formal operations skills. Some of her results are in Figure 7.8. You
can see that older students generally did better, with the biggest spurt
between eighth and tenth grades (between ages 13 and 15). This is somewhat
later than Piaget originally proposed, but it is consistent with all the other
recent findings. You can also see that the problems are not equally difficult.
Problems that require the child to consider two or more separate factors
simultaneously are harder than problems that simply require the child to
search for the logical possibilities. For example, the easiest problem, called
"colored tokens," asks the child how many different pairs of colors can be
made using tokens of six different colors. This requires only thinking up
and organizing possible solutions. The two hardest problems require understanding multiple, simultaneous causation. In the "chemicals" problem,
the young person is shown that when a drop of a special liquid (called *g*)
was put into a glass of colorless liquid, the liquid turns yellow. The youngster
is then given four beakers of liquids and a small supply of the *g* liquid

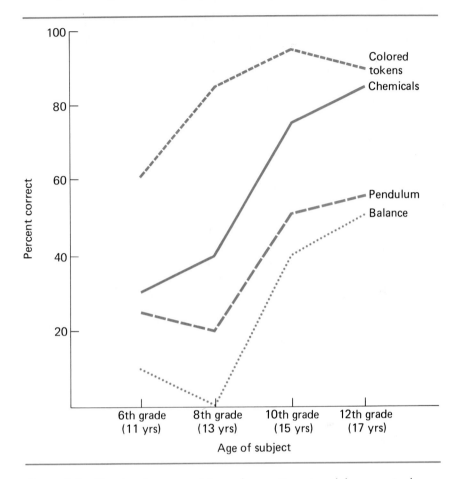

Figure 7.8 The development of formal operations in adolescence is shown by the response of groups of American girls to four different formal operations tasks. As was true for concrete operations, we can see a big spurt in correct solutions during one age period (between 13 and 15, in this case), but the problems differed consistently in difficulty, depending on the number of different formal "operations" the child had to apply at once. (*Source:* Martorano, 1977, p. 670. Copyright by the American Psychological Association.)

and is asked to figure out how to reproduce the effect. The solution requires systematic testing of all possible combinations. In the "balance" problem, the youngster must predict whether or not two varying weights, hung at varying distances on either side of a scale, will balance. To solve this problem using formal operations, the teenager must consider both weight and distance at the same time.

Does Everybody Reach Formal Operations? The answer to this question seems to be "no." In Piaget's original studies, there were signs that, unlike concrete operations, formal operations was not a universal achievement. Those early hints have been repeatedly confirmed in more recent research. Keating (1980) estimates that only about 50 to 60 percent of 18- to 20-year-olds seem to use formal operations at all, let alone consistently. For example, Martorano found that only two of her 20 twelfth-grade subjects used formal operations on all the problems, and none of the younger students did.

Why? There are several possibilities. The first is that the usual methods of measuring formal operations are simply extremely difficult or unclear. When the instructions are made clearer or the subjects are given hints or rules, they can demonstrate some aspects of formal operations (e.g., Danner & Day, 1977).

A second possibility is that most of us have some formal operational ability, but we can only apply it to topics or tasks with which we are familiar. For example, I use formal operations reasoning about psychology because it is an area I know well. But I am a lot less skillful at applying the same kind of reasoning to fixing my car—about which I know next to nothing. Willis Overton and his colleagues (1987) have found considerable support for this possibility in their research. They found that as many as 90 percent of adolescents could solve quite complex logic problems if they were stated using familiar content, while only half could solve an identical logic problem when it was stated in abstract language.

Still a third possibility is that because most of our everyday experiences and tasks do not require formal operations—concrete operations is quite sufficient most of the time—we get into a cognitive "rut," applying our most usual mode of thinking to new problems as well. We can kick our thinking "up a notch" under some circumstances, especially if someone reminds us that it would be useful to do so, but we simply don't rehearse formal operations very much.

How General Are These Abilities? I have already partly answered this one: somewhat, but not perfectly. Some people do seem to use formal operations logic a good deal of the time; others do so rarely or never. In between, there are a lot of adults who use such skills on some problems (particularly familiar ones) but not on others (Neimark, 1982).

None of that sounds much like Piaget's description, of course. In his view, once the new structures are in place they ought to be applied fairly generally. The fact that they are not—at least not for many people—is a troublesome finding for his theory to handle.

OVERVIEW OF THE STAGES OF COGNITIVE DEVELOPMENT

The child comes a long way in only about 15 years. He moves from very rudimentary abilities to represent things to himself with images and words, to classifications, to conservation, to abstract deductive logic. As Piaget sees it, the progress along this chain is continuous but marked off into stages, with each stage characterized by particular kinds of logic. In broad outline, that seems to be true; but there are some distinct problems with Piaget's theory, many of which have been evident in what I have already said. Since these problems are, in part, what has led to the new information-processing approach, let me be explicit about several of the key difficulties.

CRITICISMS OF PIAGET'S THEORY

Of the myriad criticisms that have emerged in the past decades of intensive research and commentary, three broad issues stand out.

The Timing of Developments

The most obvious criticism is that Piaget seems to have been wrong about just how early many cognitive skills develop. In particular, virtually all the achievements of the concrete operations period appear to be present in at least rudimentary or fragmentary form in the preschool years. This might simply mean that Piaget just had the ages wrong—that concrete operations really begins at 3 or 4. But I think by now there is agreement even among modern Piaget enthusiasts that the problem goes far deeper than that. Piaget was really saying that each stage was a coherent structural whole. If that is true, then until a child reaches a particular stage she should be *unable* to use particular forms of logic, even if the problem is presented in simplified form. The fact that younger children can demonstrate parts or beginning phases of complex logic if the problems are made simple calls this whole assumption into serious doubt. Thus it appears that while there are real changes in children's thinking, what happens at age 6 or 7 (or at 13 or 14) is not a radically different *kind* or *form* of thinking, but simply a new *level* of thinking, a new step in a sequence that began much earlier. If all that is true, then the concept of stages is dubious at best.

The Role of Specific Knowledge or Expertise

A similar doubt is raised by a second body of research, to which I have alluded only in passing, that explores the role of specific task knowledge on performance. It will not surprise you that experts in any field are better at remembering things, organizing things, analyzing things in that field than are novices. So, for example, Michelene Chi (1978; Chi et al., 1982) has shown that expert chess players can remember the placement of chess pieces on a board much more quickly and accurately than can novice chess players, *even when the expert chess players are children and the novices are adults.* As Flavell says, "evidence is beginning to suggest . . . that having a great deal of knowledge and experience in an area has all sorts

Figure 7.9 Chi's fascinating research on chess players shows that experts—even experts like these children—are able to remember the placement of pieces with remarkable accuracy. They perform at a much higher level than do chess novices, even adult novices. So it is not age that is critical in this case but expertise.

of positive, beneficial effects on the quality of one's cognitive functioning in that area. . . . In short, the expert looks very, very smart—very, very 'cognitively mature'—when functioning in her area of expertise" (1985, p. 83).

Since young children are novices at almost everything while older children are more expert at many things, perhaps the difference in apparent cognitive strategies or functioning between younger and older children is just the effect of more specific knowledge, more experience, and *not* the result of stagelike changes in fundamental cognitive structures.

Are There Stages?

The most fundamental theoretical issue is whether there are really stages at all. The evidence on both timing and expertise already leads to major doubts about the stage concept. But the most direct test of Piaget's stage concept remains the issue of consistency in performance across tasks that are thought to require the same form of logic, the same stage. If Piaget's stage concept is correct, if there really are internally consistent structures emerging in sequence, then we ought to find that a concrete operational child applies very similar logic to a whole range of problems; we ought to find *horizontal* consistency. But researchers have generally not found such consistency from one task to another. A child may be at one stage on one task and at a different stage on another task (e.g., Uzgiris, 1973; Martorano, 1977; Keating & Clark, 1980; Flavell, 1982a, 1982b).

There are some dissenting voices in this chorus of criticisms of the stage concept. Robbie Case (1985, 1986), for example, has offered his own "neo-Piagetian" theory, which includes stages very like Piaget's. The key difference is that Case does *not* assume that each new stage involves totally new types or forms of thinking; he assumes only that each stage requires more complex *levels* or integrations of the same basic processes. Case is not surprised that young children can do simple versions of some of Piaget's tasks. That is precisely what he would expect and predict. But Case also argues (and has a good deal of supporting data to demonstrate) that at any given time, a child will apply very similar strategies to a diversity of tasks.

Kurt Fischer (1980; Fischer & Pipp, 1984; Fischer & Canfield, 1986), another modern developmental theorist, gets around the problem another way. He proposes a series of "developmental levels," but he sees them as representing the *optimal level,* the upper limit of performance of which the child is then capable under maximally supportive conditions—clear instructions, familiar content, high levels of motivation, and so on. In Fischer's theory, the optimal level rises discontinuously with age in a series of spurts as a result of the emergence of new strategies or the integration of old strategies (Fischer, Pipp, & Bullock, 1984). At any given moment, however, a child's actual performance on different kinds of tasks will vary a great deal, depending on her expertise or the clarity or simplicity of the instructions or other situational factors. Thus Fischer proposes stagelike changes at the underlying level of competence but more variability at the level of performance.

Whether Case's or Fischer's proposals will ultimately provide the framework for a persuasive stage theory I simply can't tell at this point. What is clear now is that Piaget's version of structurally distinct stages of cognitive development does *not* work.

What is also clear is that cognitive development is made up of a large number of apparently universal sequences. That is, in any given area—such as number concepts, concepts of gender, or ideas about appearance and reality—children seem to learn the basic rules or strategies in the same order. To quote John Flavell, "Sequences are the very wire and glue of development. Later cognitive acquisitions build on or are otherwise linked to earlier ones, and in their turn similarly prepare the ground for still later ones" (1982b, p. 18).

Thus, while Piaget appears to have been at least partially off-target in talking about stages, he was very much on-target in talking about sequences. Furthermore, I am convinced that Piaget was right in arguing that the changes in cognitive skill between preschool age and adolescence are more than merely quantitative increases in specific task knowledge and experience—although Piaget himself acknowledged that such experience was a critical ingredient in the developmental process. There seem to be real differences in the way 2-year-olds and 10-year-olds approach problems—not merely differences in experience. But if those differences are not in the basic structure, as Piaget thought, just what might those differences consist of? It is here that the third approach, *information processing* (see Chapter 6), may offer some answers.

INFORMATION PROCESSING IN CHILDREN

The information-processing approach is not really a theory of cognitive development; it is an approach to studying thinking and remembering—a set of questions and some methods of analysis. Theorists who study cognitive power ask *how well a child does intellectual tasks* compared to others; those who study structure ask *what type or structure of logic the child uses* in solving problems and how those structures change with age. Information-processing theorists ask *what the child is doing* intellectually when faced with a task, what intellectual *processes* she brings to bear, and how those processes might change with age.

The information-processing approach has a whole series of theoretical parents and grandparents. The direct line of inheritance is from studies of adult intelligence, particularly computer simulations of adult intelligence. In fact, the basic metaphor underlying the entire information-processing approach is that of the human mind as computer. We can think of the "hardware" of cognition (the "wiring" such as nerves and synapses) and the "software" of cognition (the program that uses the basic hardware). To understand thinking in general, we need to understand how the hardware is constructed (the *capacity* of the system) and just what programs have to be "run" to perform any given task. What inputs (facts or data) are needed, what coding, decoding, remembering, or analyzing are required? To understand cognitive development, we need to discover whether there are any changes with age in the basic processing capacity of the system (the hardware) and/or in the nature of the programs used. Do children develop new types of processing (new programs)? Or do they simply learn to use basic programs on new material?

In studies of children's thinking, there are at least two branches to the information-processing family tree. On one side is a group of researchers and theorists with a somewhat Piagetian flavor, who have given up the notion of stages but are still committed to the notion of qualitatively changing sequences of development (e.g., Siegler, 1981). On the other side are researchers with a strong intellectual-power flavor, who have been looking for those basic information-processing capacities or strategies that may help to explain or underlie differences in IQ. What is it that "brighter" people really do that is different when they are confronted with a problem? These two approaches to the study of information processing are not divorced from one another, but for the moment let me talk about them somewhat separately.

Developmental Approaches to Information Processing

Changes in Processing Capacity. The first place to look for some underlying developmental change is in basic processing capacity. Any computer has physical limits to the number of different operations it can perform at a given time, the number of bits of data it can operate on simultaneously. Some computers have greater capacity than others. Perhaps as the brain and nervous system develop in the early years of life, the number of different "bits" that can be dealt with simultaneously simply increases. George Miller showed years ago (1956) that in active short-term memory, most adults can handle only seven "chunks" of information (plus or minus two). If you look up a number in the phone book, you can remember the seven digits for a short time fairly readily; you can remember a seven-item list for the grocery store. This seems to be the limit of the system. (But each "chunk" may be made up of many bits if each chunk is organized internally.)

One standard way to measure the capacity of short-term memory is to read a subject a string of numbers and ask her to repeat them right back (in fact, such a measure is a common task on an IQ test). You start by reading perhaps four numbers, then give a list of five, then six, and so forth, until the subject no longer can remember them all. When children are given such tests, they can remember fewer numbers than can adults, and young children can remember fewer than can older children, as you can see in Figure 7.10 (Dempster, 1981).

Findings like these *could* mean that there are changes with age in the cognitive hardware—that 2-year-olds are physically wired so that they can handle only two bits or chunks while adults can handle seven. Since we know that the brain does continue to grow and that more and more connective links (synapses) between neurons are formed over the early years, such an interpretation is at least plausible. But children also have less *experience* with numbers. Perhaps their poorer performance on tests of digit span is simply another example of the fact that experts can do

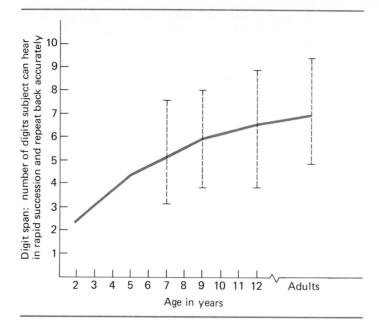

Figure 7.10   One way psychologists have tried to measure the brain's capacity to process information is by studying very basic memory operations such as remembering lists of things for short periods of time. Strings of digits are the most common items used. You can see that the number of digits that can be repeated goes up steadily with age. (*Source:* Dempster, 1981, Figure 1, p. 66.)

things better than novices. Or both explanations could be true. At the moment we do not know how to sort out the options. But whether it is because of experience or because of changes in the underlying physical capacity of the organism, older children clearly have greater functional information-processing capacity than do younger children.

Changes in Processing Strategies.   It is also clear that there are systematic changes in processing strategies with age. Processing strategies are just ways to reduce the load, tricks for organizing information, rules for handling whole collections of experience. The concept of conservation, for example, is a rule that helps to organize information. Once the child has figured out that concept, she doesn't need to keep checking to see if the two balls contain the same amount of clay; she knows that if they were the same to begin with, they will stay the same unless you add or take away. Processing strategies thus help tell us what to ignore, what to pay attention to, and how to organize information or problem solving into helpful chunks. As children get older, it is clear that they use increasingly complex and powerful strategies, much as Piaget described.

Some examples will probably help make this clearer. Let me look first at memory strategies.

Strategies for Remembering.

You're about to go out the door to run some errands. You need to stop at the cleaners; buy some stamps; copy your IRS forms; and buy milk, bread, orange juice, carrots, lettuce, spaghetti, and spaghetti sauce at the grocery store. How do you remember all those things? There are many possible strategies, some of which I have listed (with examples) in Table 7.3. You could rehearse the list; you could organize the route in your mind; you could remember your menu for dinner when you get to the grocery store.

Do children do these things when they try to remember? Until fairly recently, the conventional wisdom was that toddlers and even 5-year-olds rarely used such strategies (e.g., Ornstein et al., 1985). For example, in one early study of the strategy of rehearsal (Keeney, Cannizzo, & Flavell, 1967), children were shown a row of seven cards with pictures on them and were told to try to remember all the pictures in the same order in which they were laid out. Then a "space helmet" was placed over the

Table 7.3
███████

Some Common Information-Processing Strategies Involved in Remembering

- **Rehearsal.** Perhaps the most common strategy, involving either mental or vocal repetition or repetition of movement (as in learning to dance). Rehearsal may occur in children as young as 2 years under some conditions.

- **Clustering or chunking.** Grouping ideas or objects or words into clusters to help in remembering them, such as "all animals," "all the ingredients in the lasagna recipe," or "the chess pieces involved in the move called castling." This is one strategy that clearly benefits from experience with a particular subject or activity, since possible categories are learned or are discovered in the process of exploring or manipulating a set of material. Primitive chunking occurs in 2-year-olds.

- **Elaboration.** Finding shared meaning or a common referent for two or more things that need to be remembered. The helpful mnemonic for recalling the names of the lines on the musical staff ("Every Good Boy Does Fine") is a kind of elaboration, as is associating the name of a person you have just met with some object or another word. This form of memory aid is not used spontaneously by all individuals and is not used skillfully until fairly late in development, if then.

- **Systematic searching.** "Scanning" the memory for the whole domain in which something might be found. Three- and four-year-old children can begin to do this to search for actual objects in the real world, but they are not good at doing this in memory. So search strategies may be learned first in the external world and then applied to mental searches.

Source: Flavell, 1985.

███████

child's head so that she could not see the cards but the experimenter could see if she seemed to be rehearsing the list by muttering under her breath. Children under 5 almost never showed any rehearsal, while 8- to 10-year-old children usually did. Interestingly, when 5-year-olds were taught to rehearse, they were able to do so and as a result improved their memory scores. But when these same 5-year-olds were then given a new problem without being reminded to rehearse, they stopped rehearsing. That is, they could use the strategy if they were reminded, but they did not use it spontaneously.

Recent research by Judy DeLoache and others (e.g., DeLoache, Cassidy, & Brown, 1985; DeLoache, 1986), however, brings us back to a familiar refrain: children as young as 2 and 3 show some signs of rehearsal or other memory-aiding strategies on simple memory tasks, such as the game of hide-and-seek. The child watches the experimenter hide an attractive toy in some obvious place (e.g., behind a couch) and is then told that when a buzzer goes off, she can go and find the toy. While playing with other toys during the four-minute delay interval, 2-year-olds often talked about the toy's hiding place or pointed to or looked at the hiding place— all of which seem clearly to be early forms of mnemonic strategies.

These results tell us that once again we have probably underestimated the preschool child. But they do not tell us that rehearsal is equally well established or as flexibly used throughout the age span. For example, we know that younger children do not rehearse in the same way that older ones do. When learning a list of words, for instance, 8-year-olds typically practice the words one at a time ("cat, cat, cat") while 13-year-olds practice them in groups ("desk, lawn, sky, shirt, cat") (Ornstein, Naus, & Liberty, 1975). Efficient and silent rehearsal does not become common until children are 9 or 10 years of age.

Other strategies that help improve memory involve putting the items to be learned or remembered into some meaningful organization. When you organize your grocery shopping list in your mind so that all the fruits and vegetables are in one group and all the canned foods in another, you are using this principle, which is usually called *clustering* or *chunking*.

In studies of such clustering or organizing strategies, children or adults are often given lists of words to learn which have potential categories built into them. For example, I might ask you to remember a list of words that includes names for furniture, animals, and foods. I let you learn the list any way you wish, but when you then name off the items later, I can check for the kind of organization you used by seeing whether you name the same-category words together.

Children do show this kind of internal organization when they recall things, but as we would expect, younger children do this less consistently and less efficiently than older ones (e.g., Bjorklund & Arce, 1987; Bjorklund & Muir, in press). Younger children use more chunking with familiar material, and they use a greater number of small categories rather than a few larger ones.

Research like this and equivalent studies of other types of memory strategies have led to some interesting conclusions. First, we can see some primitive signs of memory strategies under optimum conditions as early as age 2 or 3 (DeLoache, Cassidy, & Brown, 1985), but with increasing age, children use more and more powerful ways of helping themselves remember things. Second, in the use of each strategy, children shift from a period in which they don't use it at all, to a period in which they will use it if reminded or taught, to one in which they use it spontaneously. Third, they use these strategies more and more skillfully and generalize them to more and more situations.

Rules for Problem Solving.　Another area in which we see essentially the same progression is problem solving. Some of the best-known work in this area has been Robert Siegler's research on the development of *rules* (Siegler, 1976, 1978, 1981). Siegler's approach is a kind of cross between Piagetian theory and information processing. He argues that cognitive development consists of acquiring a set of basic rules, which are then applied to a broader and broader range of problems on the basis of experience. There are no stages, only sequences.

In one test of this approach, Siegler uses a balance scale with a series of pegs on either side of the center. Weights are placed on these pegs and the child is asked to predict which way the balance will fall (after a lever holding it in place has been released). Siegler predicts that four rules will develop, in order. Rule 1 is basically a "preoperational" rule. The child takes into account only one dimension, the number of weights. A child using this rule will predict that the side with more weights will go down, no matter which peg they are placed on. Rule 2 is a transitional rule. The child still judges on the basis of number except when there are the same number of weights on both sides, and in that case he takes distance from the fulcrum into account. Rule 3 is basically a concrete operational rule. The child tries to take both distance and weight into account simultaneously. But when the information is conflicting (such as when there are more weights on one side, but they are closer to the fulcrum) the child simply guesses. Rule 4 is basically a formal operational rule. At this point the child/youth figures out the actual formula (distance × weight for each side). Siegler has found that virtually all children perform on this and similar tasks as if they were following one or another of these rules and that the rules seem to develop in the given order. Further, he found that if children were given practice with the balance scale, making predictions and then checking which way the balance actually falls, many showed rapid shifts "upward" in the sequence of rules.

Thus, as experience accumulates, the older child is able to take more than one dimension into account at once and to do so systematically. In general, very young children behaved as if they didn't have a rule (they guessed or behaved randomly, so far as Siegler could determine); when a rule developed, it was always rule 1 that came first.

Metacognition and Executive Processes. A third area in which information-processing researchers have been active is in studying how children come to know what they know. If I gave you a list of things to remember and then asked you later how you had gone about trying to remember it, you could tell me what you had done. You may even have consciously considered the various alternative strategies and then selected the best one. You could also tell me good ways to study or which kinds of tasks will be hardest and why. These are all examples of **metamemory** or **metacognition**—knowing about remembering and knowing about knowing, respectively. Information-processing theorists sometimes refer to these skills as **executive processes,** since they involve planning and organizing in some central way, just as an executive may do.

These skills are of particular interest because there is some suggestion that it may be precisely such metacognitive or executive skills that emerge with age. Performance on a whole range of tasks will be better if the child can monitor her own performance or recognize when a particular strategy is called for and when it is not. While quite young children do show some such monitoring (e.g., Revelle et al., 1985), it clearly does improve with age and may form the foundation of some of the other age changes I have been describing.

Changes in Processing Strategy: A Summary

On the basis of research like Siegler's, the work on memory, and a wide range of other studies, several reasonable generalizations have emerged about age changes in (development of) information-processing strategies (Flavell, 1985; Sternberg & Powell, 1983):

1. There *may* be an increase in the basic processing capacity of the system.
2. The sheer amount of specific knowledge the child has about any given task increases as the child experiments, explores, studies things in school. This leads to more and more "expert" approaches for remembering and for solving problems.
3. Genuinely new strategies are acquired, probably in some kind of order. In particular, the child seems to develop in middle childhood some "executive" or "metacognitive" abilities—she knows that she knows and can *plan* a strategy for the first time.
4. Existing strategies are applied to more and more different domains and more and more flexibly. If a child learns to rehearse on one kind of memory problem, the older child is more likely to try it on a new memory strategy; the younger child (particularly younger than 5 or 6) is not likely to generalize the strategy to the new task—although once again it is true that some transfer is seen in children as young as 2 when the conditions are carefully constructed (Crisafi & Brown, 1986).
5. A wider range of different strategies can be applied to the same problem, so that if the first doesn't work, a back-up or alternative strategy can

be used. If you can't find your misplaced keys by retracing your steps, you try a back-up, such as looking in your other purse or in the pocket of your jacket or searching each room of the house in turn. Young children do not do this; school-age children and adolescents do.

Thus, some of the changes that Piaget observed and chronicled with such detail and richness seem to be the result simply of increased experience with tasks and problems (a quantitative change, if you will). But there also seems to be a qualitative change in the complexity, generalizability, and flexibility of strategies used by the child.

Individual Differences in Information Processing

While some researchers in the information-processing tradition have been asking about developmental changes or sequences, others have been searching for the "underlying sources of cognitive ability differences" (Keating, List, & Merriman, 1985). IQ tests are intended to measure such underlying ability differences by giving people fairly complex cognitive tasks, each of which may require a whole series of more fundamental information-processing strategies. Perhaps we could come closer to understanding individual differences in intelligence or intellectual performance if we shifted our attention to those more fundamental processes. Generally the strategy has been to look at the relationship between IQ scores (from standard tests of the type I have already described) and measures of information processing. This strategy has yielded a few preliminary connections.

Speed of Information Processing. One of the possible underlying sources of individual differences is simply the speed with which an individual can perform basic information-processing tasks, such as remembering things or recognizing whether two letters or numbers are the same or different. In a whole series of studies, Earl Hunt and his colleagues and Philip Vernon and his associates have found just such a link. Subjects who are able to do basic recognition and memory tasks more quickly also have higher IQ scores on standard tests (e.g., Hunt, Frost, & Lunneborg, 1973; Vernon, 1983; Vernon & Kantor, 1986). Most of this research has been done with adults, but the same link has also been found in a few studies with children (e.g., Keating, List, & Merriman, 1985).

But where would such speed differences come from? Are they built into the system, possibly in the "hardware" rather than the "software?" Maybe. Certainly that possibility is further supported by a second line of research on recognition memory in infants.

Differences in Recognition Memory. **Recognition memory** is simply the ability to recognize that one has seen or experienced something before. When you meet a person after a long period and say to yourself, "I know that person," that is a form of recognition memory. In infants, we saw this same process at work in much of the research on early perception. We know that infants will spend more time looking at or exploring a new object than a familiar one. This fact allows us to measure recognition memory: just how long does it take for an object to become familiar enough to a baby for him to lose interest in it and prefer to look at something new? That is, how long does it take before the baby "recognizes" the familiar object?

It turns out that when we measure recognition memory or preference for novelty in babies as young as a few months of age, their scores are remarkably highly correlated with IQ scores in later childhood. In the 15 or so longitudinal studies of this type, the average correlation between recognition memory and later IQ is about .45 (Fagan, 1984; Bornstein & Sigman, 1986)—surprisingly high in view of the very low correlations between other measures of infant IQ and later IQ (recall Table 6.2.). Fagan argues that this ability to detect similarities and differences (and to do so quickly) is a fundamental information process that is part of what we tap with a standardized IQ test.

Flexibility of Information Processing. Speed and recognition memory, however, are not the only dimensions of information processing that distinguish high- and low-IQ children or adults. Another key dimension seems to be flexibility or generalizability of strategy. Joseph Campione and Ann Brown, for example, found in several studies (e.g., 1984; Campione et al., 1985) that both retarded and normal-IQ children could learn to solve problems like those in (a) through (c) of Figure 7.11, but the retarded children could not transfer this learning to slightly differing problems of the same general type, like (d) in Figure 7.11, while normal-IQ children could. Findings like these suggest that flexibility of use (or, stated another way, the degree of transfer) of any given strategy may be another key dimension of individual differences in intelligence. There is an element of recognition memory involved here as well, since to transfer a problem strategy, you must recognize that a new task is the same in some way.

PUTTING THE THREE APPROACHES TOGETHER

I hope it is clear by now that the information-processing approach offers us some important bridges between the power and structure theories of intelligence in children. It now looks as if there are some basic inborn strategies (such as noting differences and sameness) and that these strategies change over the course of the early years of life. More complex strategies or "rules" emerge and old strategies are used more flexibly. Plain old experience is also part of the process. The more a child plays with blocks, the better she will be at organizing and classifying blocks; the more a person plays chess, the better he will be at seeing and remembering relationships between pieces on the board. So some of the changes that Piaget thought

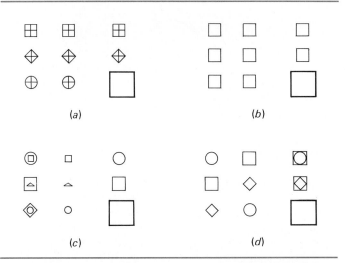

Figure 7.11 Figures in panels (*a*) through (*c*) are problems like those Campione and his colleagues used to train retarded and normal-IQ children. The subject must figure out the "system" in each set and then describe what pattern should go in the empty box in the bottom right-hand corner. Panel (*a*) shows rotation. Panel (*b*) shows addition of element. Panel (*c*) shows subtraction of elements. The figure in panel (*d*) is a problem Campione used during the transfer phase of the test. (The "transfer" phase of such experiments involves testing the subject's ability to apply the rules already learned to some similar but not identical problem.) In this case, the transfer problems were quite difficult because the child had to apply two different rules simultaneously, as in panel (*d*), where the subject had to apply both rotation and addition rules. Retarded children could do the problems in (*a*) through (*c*) as well as normal-IQ children, but they had much more difficulty with (*d*). (*Source:* Campione et al., 1985, Figures 1 and 4.)

of as changes in underlying structure are, instead, specific task learning. But there seems to be some structural change, as well. It is as if the computer were programmed to develop, to add or construct new methods of processing over time as experiences accumulate.

Individual differences in what we normally think of as intelligence can then be conceived of as resulting both from inborn differences in the speed or efficiency of the basic processes (differences in the hardware, perhaps) and from differences in experiences. The child with a slower or less-efficient processing system is going to move through all the various steps and stages more slowly; he will *use* the experience he has less efficiently

PIAGET'S THEORY AND EARLY EDUCATION

Piaget's theory is really not a theory of teaching. He has said only a little (Piaget, 1970) about how teachers confronted daily by classrooms full of children can apply his ideas. But many preschool and elementary-school educators and some developmental psychologists have tried to apply at least some of Piaget's concepts to education (e.g., Appel, 1977; Kamii, 1985; Lawson, 1985; Weikart, 1972). Those applications are of several varieties.

Home Schooling and Other Experimental Education

If you listen to parents or educators who advocate home schooling or who argue for little or no schooling at all, you will often hear Piaget's name used as support for their position. After all, Piaget himself said that the goal of education ought to be *autonomy* (Piaget, 1948/1973)—the rearing of children who were governed by themselves, who knew how to solve problems on their own. And of course, Piaget's own theory of cognitive development places greatest emphasis on the child's own *constructive* role in his own emerging understanding. The typical didactic, find-the-right-answers approach to education found in public schools seems antithetical to this view. So some educators have advocated allowing children the autonomy to teach themselves.

There are some good arguments against the most extreme version of this interpretation of Piagetian theory. We know, for example, that while children who do not go to school at all (either in a school building or in classes at home) do indeed learn many concrete operations forms of reasoning on their own, we also know that unschooled children typically have major gaps in their thinking. In particular, they seem to be less skillful at generalizing from specifics to broader concepts. Such children typically lack abstractions (Sharp, Cole, & Lave, 1979; Rogoff, 1981).

But there is a great deal of support for the argument that the development of children's reasoning is furthered in school environments that foster autonomy. For example, Constance Kamii (1985) finds that teaching techniques that allow and encourage the young child's own discovery of mathematical concepts and reasoning promote such reasoning much more than do the typical math workbook approaches. And when researchers and educators have attempted to teach formal operations reasoning to adolescents, the most successful techniques have been those that emphasized the students' own involvement, own control of the learning process (Lawson, 1985).

In general, then, one impact of Piaget's theory has been to strengthen the hand of those who have advocated or practiced "discovery" learning as opposed to rote or didactic processes.

Sequences and Stages

Another application of Piaget's theory has been based explicitly on the sequence of cognitive stages Piaget describes. Preschool educators may map out the steps involved in such concepts as classification and then try to move the child along that sequence by presenting materials that "lead" the child from where he is "up" to the next step. You can see some elements of this in Sesame Street (which I urge you to watch occasionally, by the way) when they "teach" classification by having children figure out which things go together. You can see it in preschool programs like David Weikart's (1972), in which concepts are taught by first using sensorimotor experience, with more abstract experience added later. The word *boat*, for example, might be introduced by having the children play in a life-sized rowboat (sensorimotor), then with a toy boat that stands for the larger boat, then with pictures of boats, and finally—with much older children—with the written word *boat*.

This same use of the basic sequences can be seen in some mathematics and science programs now used in some elementary and high schools. Marilyn Appel (1977) describes one science program called PASE (Personalized Approach to Science Education). Science projects are arranged in a sequence from preoperational (involving basic classification, for example) through the transition to concrete operations (involving reversibility or conservation tasks, for example) and on upward in complexity. At each level there are many different experiences, and the child chooses which one she wants to work on. A child may work on many projects at one level before moving on to the next group of experiments.

But just as the broader use of Piagetian theory to support self-schooling may misread Piaget, so there are some pitfalls here, too. As Joseph Lawton and Frank Hooper (1978) point out, merely presenting concepts in the "correct" sequence is not sufficient; it is the child's *activity* with materials that is critical. The teacher can help this process by providing things to play with and explore that are at a level of difficulty that will foster further growth in the child. Or the teacher might ask questions that will force the child to rethink old concepts (accommodate). But in Piaget's view, the teacher cannot *force* the child along the sequence. (Nor, in Piaget's view, is there any particular purpose in trying to speed up the process, either. He regarded this desire to push children along faster as a very curious American preoccupation.)

It seems to me that the PASE science program, focused as it is on the child's own activity, avoids this particular misapplication of Piaget's theory, but many other Piaget-based educational systems do not.

A second pitfall lies in the fact that American educators seem to be particularly vulnerable to the trap of paying attention to the "right" answers. We want children to say that the two balls of clay are the same in the conservation experiment, for example. Piaget has always been more interested in *why* a child says something and not in whether the answer is right by some adult standard. Our preoccupation with rightness may lead teachers to listen too little to the child's logic and to focus instead on teaching the child the right words to say. In Piaget's views, the right words don't necessarily mean that the child has achieved the fundamental understanding.

In sum, a number of American educators have seized on the stages Piaget describes and tried to overlay them onto educational practice and onto curricula. Some of this application has been useful and worthwhile, but in many cases I think we have missed the subtleties of Piaget's theory.

or effectively and may never develop as complete a range of strategies as does the initially quicker child.

The information-processing approach may also have some real, practical applications. The studies of recognition memory in infancy, for example, may give us a way to identify retarded children very early in life or to sort out from among low-birth-weight infants those that seem at particular risk for later problems. By identifying the key differences between retarded and nonretarded children (or between brighter and less-bright children), we may also be able to point to specific kinds of training that would be useful for a retarded child or for a child with a specific learning disability. And as educators learn more and more about the sequences in which children acquire such things as number concepts, they can devise better and better materials and teaching strategies. Some of these applications have already begun; Piagetian concepts have been rather widely (if loosely) applied in many schools, as I have described in the box on pages 266–267. But the newer work on information processing offers the hope of much more precise educational interventions (e.g., Case, Sandieson, & Dennis, 1986).

I do not want to wax too rhapsodic about the information-processing approach. It is well to remember that we do not yet have any tests of information-processing ability that could replace the careful use of IQ tests in schools and clinics. Nor are the sequential theories of information-processing development far enough along yet to explain all the differences we see between infants, preschoolers, and older children in performance on various Piagetian tasks. In short, information processing is an important, integrative addition to our understanding of cognitive development, but it does not explain away all the other approaches.

SUMMARY

1. The study of cognitive power does not tell us what we need to know about the shared changes in the *ways* children think about the world around them. Piaget's studies of cognitive structure fill that gap.

2. Piaget assumed that the child was an active agent in his own development, adapting to the environment through the use of the functional invariants of assimilation, accommodation, and equilibration, beginning with primitive schemes at birth and progressing sequentially through several stages.

3. The stages of development Piaget proposed are as follows:
   a. The sensorimotor stage, from birth to 18 months, when the child moves from reflexive to intentional behavior. Current work places the development of internal representation earlier in this period than Piaget thought.
   b. The preoperational stage, from 18 months to 6 years, when the child develops beginning forms of reasoning and classification and shows some primitive ability to see things from others' perspectives. Current work on children in this age range shows earlier signs of complex thought than Piaget had proposed.

    c. Concrete operations, from 6 to 12 years, when the child acquires powerful new mental tools called operations (such as addition, subtraction, multiplication, and serial ordering). Current work on this age period shows that these operations are applied less broadly by children than Piaget thought.

    d. Formal operations, from age 12 and up, when the young person becomes able to manipulate *ideas* as well as objects and can approach problems systematically. Deductive logic appears. Unlike earlier stages, which virtually all children achieve, formal operations are achieved by perhaps only half of adolescents.

4. Piaget's theory, although immensely influential, suffers from significant problems: (1) children develop at least the beginning forms of complex thinking much sooner than Piaget thought; (2) children show much more complex levels of thinking in areas in which they are extremely knowledgeable than in less-familiar areas, making developmental change look more like accumulating experience than structural change; and (3) children do not show consistent levels of performance on tasks that appear to demand the same levels of cognitive skill.

5. Some modern theorists, such as Case and Fischer, have proposed theories that avoid some of these problems, but in general the idea of broad, structurally coherent stages of cognitive development is no longer widely accepted.

6. Piaget's theory has had some effect on educational practices; but the application is more difficult than it appears to be, and the verdict is still not in on the impact that Piagetian educational programs have on cognitive development.

7. The apparent validity of *sequences* of development and the relative failure of the *stage* concept has been one force pushing psychologists toward a broad information-processing approach to cognitive development.

8. Information-processing theorists ask not about structure but about the basic processes that make up any cognitive activity, such as decoding, encoding, remembering, planning, analyzing.

9. Information-processing specialists interested in development have asked what ways the basic processes change with age in children. Some argue that there is an increase with age in basic processing capacity, in the "hardware" of the brain.

10. Others, such as Siegler, focus on changes in strategies or problem solving. In memory, a series of mnemonic strategies such as rehearsal and clustering appear to develop and to be used more and more consistently beginning at age 4 or 5.

11. Metacognitive skills or executive skills (knowing what you know, being able to plan good strategies) appear to develop at about the same time.

12. Other information-processing specialists, such as Campione or Fagan, focus on individual differences in efficiency of basic processes. Higher-IQ individuals, for example, appear to process information more quickly and apply strategies or knowledge more broadly.

▬▬▬▬▬▬ **KEY TERMS**

accommodation That part of the adaptation process by which a person modifies existing schemes (ideas, actions, or strategies) to fit new experiences.

assimilation That part of the adaptation process that involves the taking in of new experiences or information into existing schemes. Experience is not taken in "as is," however, but is modified (or interpreted) somewhat so as to fit the preexisting schemes.

class inclusion The relationship between classes in which a subordinate class is included in a superordinate class, as bananas are part of the class "fruit."

concrete operations The stage of development proposed by Piaget for ages 6 to 12, in which mental operations such as subtraction, reversibility, and multiple classification are acquired.

conservation The concept that objects or a group of objects remains the same in fundamental ways, such as weight or number, even when there are external changes in shape or arrangement. The concept is achieved by children between 5 and 10 years of age.

deductive logic Reasoning from the general to the particular, from a rule to an expected instance, or from a theory to a hypothesis. Characteristic of formal operational thought.

equilibration The third part of the adaptation process, as proposed by Piaget, involving the balance between assimilation and accommodation; the periodic restructuring of schemes into new structures.

executive processes Proposed subset of information processes involving organizing and planning strategies. Similar in meaning to metacognition.

formal operations Piaget's name for the fourth and final major stage of cognitive development, occurring during adolescence, when the child becomes able to manipulate and organize ideas as well as objects.

horizontal decalage Piaget's term for the sequential (rather than simultaneous) application within a particular stage of a given concept or logic to a series of different tasks or materials. For example, the principle of conservation is applied sequentially to number, weight, and volume.

inductive logic Reasoning from the particular to the general, from experience to broad rules. Characteristic of concrete operational thinking.

metacognition General and rather loosely used term describing an individual's knowledge of her own thinking processes. Knowing what you know, and how you go about learning or remembering.

metamemory A subcategory of metacognition; knowledge about one's own memory processes.

operation Term used by Piaget for complex, internal, abstract, reversible schemes, first seen at about age 6.

preoperational stage Piaget's term for the second major stage of cognitive development, from age 2 to 6, during which the child develops basic classification and logic abilities.

recognition memory The identification of the familiar; the speed with which an individual recognizes (remembers) that some object or individual or situation has been seen or experienced before.

scheme Piaget's word for the basic actions, ideas, and strategies to which new experience is assimilated and which are then modified (accommodated) as a result of the experience.

sensorimotor stage Piaget's term for the first major stage of cognitive development, from birth to about 18 months, when the child moves from reflexive to voluntary action.

transductive reasoning Reasoning from the specific to the specific; assuming that when two things happen together, one is the cause of the other.

▬▬▬▬▬▬ **SUGGESTED READING**

Chance, P., & Fischman, J. (1987, May). The magic of childhood. *Psychology Today*, pp. 48–51, 55–58.

A good article describing some of the current research on childhood that shows us that Piaget's view was too simple.

Flavell, J. H. (1985). *Cognitive development* (2nd ed.). Englewood Cliffs, NJ: Prentice-Hall.
This is a first-rate basic text in the field, written by one of the major current figures in cognitive-developmental theory. Flavell has a fairly easy, anecdotal style, even when describing complex theory and research.

Flavell, J. H. (1986, January). Really and truly. *Psychology Today*, pp. 38–44.
A brief, highly readable description of some of Flavell's recent research on the emergence of the child's ability to distinguish between appearance and reality.

Furth, H. (1970). *Piaget for teachers*. Englewood Cliffs, NJ: Prentice-Hall.
Not a new book, but an excellent discussion of the application of Piaget's theory to education, written as a series of letters to teachers.

Piaget, J. (1972). Development and learning. In C. S. Lavatelli & F. Stendler (Eds.), *Readings in child behavior and development* (3rd ed.). New York: Harcourt Brace Jovanovich. (Reprinted from R. Ripple & V. Rockcastle (Eds.),

Piaget rediscovered, Ithaca, NY: Cornell University Press, 1964.)
This relatively brief paper is one of the clearest of Piaget's writings. It presumes that you know something about his terminology, but it is an excellent place to read about his view of the role of maturation and experience in cognitive development.

Siegler, R. S., & Richards, D. D. (1982). The development of intelligence. In R. J. Sternberg (Ed.), *Handbook of human intelligence*. Cambridge, England: Cambridge University Press.
This is not at all an easy paper, but it is one of the best descriptions I can find of the information-processing approach to cognitive development. Happily, it also includes excellent discussions of the Piagetian view and the traditional IQ-measurement approaches.

Trotter, R. J. (1986, July). The mystery of mastery. *Psychology Today*, pp. 32–38.
A popularly written report of some of the fascinating current work on expertise, such as Chi's work on chess experts.

PROJECT: THE GAME OF 20 QUESTIONS

General Instructions

The first step is to locate a child between the ages of 5 and 10. Tell the parents that you want to play some simple games with the child as part of a school project, reassuring them that you are not "testing" the child. Obtain their permission, describing the games and tasks if you are asked to do so.

Arrange a time to be alone with the child if at all possible. Having the mother, father, or siblings there can be extremely distracting, both for the child and for you.

Come prepared with the equipment you will need. Tell the child that you have some games you would like to play. Play with the child for a while to establish some kind of rapport before you begin your experimenting. At the appropriate moment, introduce your "game."

The Task

"I am thinking of something in this room, and your job is to figure out what I am thinking of. To do this, you can ask any question at all that I can answer by saying 'yes' or 'no,' but I can't give you any other answer besides 'yes' or 'no.' You can ask as many questions as you need to, but try to find out in as few questions as you can."

Choose the door to the room as the answer to your first game. (If there is more than one door, select one particular door as correct; if there is no door, use a particular window.) If the child asks questions that cannot be answered "yes" or "no," remind her or him that you can't answer that kind of question and restate the kind of question that can be asked. Allow the child as many questions as needed (more than 20 if necessary). Write down each question verbatim. When the child has reached the correct answer, praise her or him and then say, "Let's try another one. I'll try to make it harder this time. I'm thinking of something in the room again. Remember, you ask me questions that I can answer 'yes' or 'no.' You can ask as many questions as you need, but try to find out in as few questions as possible."

Use your pencil or pen as the correct answer this time. After the child has solved the problem, praise her or him. If the child has not been successful, find something to praise. ("You asked some good questions, but it's a really hard problem, isn't it?") When you are satisfied that the child's motivation is still reasonably high, continue. "Now we're going to play another question-asking game. In this game, I will tell you something that happened, and your job will be to find out how it happened by asking me questions I can answer 'yes' or 'no.' Here's what happened: A man is driving down the road in his car; the car goes off the road and hits a tree. You have to find out how it happened by the way I answer questions you ask me about it. But I can only answer 'yes' or 'no.' The object of the game is to find out the answer in as few questions as possible. Remember, here's what happened: A man is driving down the road in his car; the car goes off the road and hits a tree. Find out what happened."

If the child asks questions that cannot be answered "yes" or "no," remind her or him that you cannot answer that kind of question and that you can only answer "yes" or "no." If the child can't figure out the answer, urge her or him to try until you are persuaded that you are creating frustration, at which point you should quit with lots of positive statements. The answer to the problem is that it had been raining and the car skidded on a curve, went off the road, and hit the tree.

Scoring

Score each question the child asks on each of the three problems as belonging to one of two categories.

1. *Hypothesis.* A hypothesis is essentially a guess that applies to only one alternative. A "yes" answer to a hypothesis solves the problem; a "no" answer eliminates only one possibility. In the first two problems, a hypothesis would be any question that applied to only one alternative, only one object in the room—for example, "Is it your hair?" or "Is it the picture?" In the third problem, a hypothesis would be any question that covers only one alternative: "Did the man get stung in the eye by a bee?" "Did he have a heart attack?" "Was there a big snowbank in the middle of the road that the car ran into and then skidded?"

2. *Constraint.* A constraint question covers at least two possibilities, often many more. A "yes" answer to a constraint question must be followed up. ("Is it a toy?" "Yes." "Is it the truck?") A "no" answer to a constraint question allows the questioner to eliminate a whole class of possibilities. In the first two problems, any of the following would be constraints: "Is it in that

half of the room?" "Is it something big?" "Is it a toy?" "Is it something red?" (assuming there is more than one red thing in the room). In the third problem, any of the following would be constraints: "Was there something wrong with the car?" "Was the weather bad?" "Did something happen to the man?"

Data and Analysis

For your own analysis or for an assignment to be turned in to a course instructor, you should examine at least the following aspects:

1. How many questions did the child ask for each problem?
2. On each problem, how many questions were hypotheses and how many were constraints?
3. Did the child do better (ask more constraints) on the concrete operations problems (the first two) than on the formal operations problem (the story)? Or was the performance the same on both?
4. Is the child's overall performance on this task generally consistent with the findings from Mosher and Hornsby's 1966 study (Figure 7.5)? Does your subject behave in a way that would be expected on the basis of his or her age? If not, what explanation can you offer?

8 The Development of Language in Children

What Is Language, Anyway?
The Early Steps
   Before the First Word: The Prelinguistic Phase
   The First Words
   The First Sentences
The Development of Grammar
   Stage 1 Grammar
   Longer and More Complex Sentences
Learning Two Languages: Bilingual Children
   Later Grammar Development
   Overview of Grammar Development
The Development of Word Meaning
   Which Comes First, the Meaning or the Word?
   Extending the Class
   Form Versus Function: What Does the Child Attend To?
Using Language: Communication and Self-Direction
Explaining Language Development
The Influence of the Environment on Language Development
   Early Theories: Imitation and Reinforcement
   Newer Environmental Theories: Talking to the Child and Other Input
      Theories
The Child's Role in Language Development
   Innateness Theories
   Cognitive-Processing Explanations
A Combined View
Language in the Deaf
Individual Differences in Language Development
   Power Differences
   Differences in Style of Language
An Application of the Basic Knowledge: Learning to Read
   The Basic Steps in Learning to Read
   The Effect of Language Skill on the Steps of Reading
Summary
Key Terms
Suggested Reading
Project: Beginning Two-Word Sentences
Project: Conversation Between Mother and Child

A friend of mine listened one morning at breakfast while her 6-year-old and her 3-year-old had the following conversation about the relative dangers of forgetting to feed the goldfish versus overfeeding the goldfish:

6-year-old: It's worse to forget to feed them.
3-year-old: No, it's badder to feed them too much.
6-year-old: You don't say badder, you say worser.
3-year-old: But it's baddest to give them too much food.
6-year-old: No it's not. It's worsest to forget to feed them.

Young children's language is full of inventive constructions and "mistakes" like *baddest* or *worsest*. It can be a vehicle for the fascinating logic of the preschool-age child, too: "Bees eat bruises because people don't want them," or "The moon has melted! Did the wind blow it away?" Aside from the "poetry," of this early language, perhaps the most astonishing thing about it is how fast it changes. An 8-month-old is making sounds like *kikiki* or *dadada*. By 18 months the child will probably be using 30 or 40 separate words, and by 3 years children construct long and complex sentences, like those of the 3-year-old in the conversation about the goldfish. Parents usually find this whole sequence delightful, charming, probably an occasion for pride. But most of us don't spend a lot of time worrying about just how a child manages this. For psychologists and linguists, though, the child's rapid and skillful acquisition of language has remained an enduring puzzle.

From perhaps age 18 months on, children's language appears to be *complex, creative,* and *rule-governed.* The child conveys complex meanings, he regularly combines words into patterns he has never heard, and he seems to follow certain rules even with the first two-word "sentences." My friend's children were trying to apply the rules for creating superlatives and just happened to hit on an irregular version of that rule. But the fact that they were creating words that followed a logical pattern (even though by adult standards they were "wrong") shows that they were operating with a rule.

How does this remarkable accomplishment come about? Is it built into the organism? Is the child "taught" language in some direct way? Does the child "figure it out" on the basis of what she hears?

In delving into these mysteries, I'll use the same distinction I introduced in Chapters 6 and 7, by looking at structure and at power. The vast majority of research on language development in the past two decades has focused on describing and explaining structural changes in both grammar (which the linguists call **syntax**) and word meaning (called **semantics**). Lately there have also been some attempts to explain differences in the *rate* of language development from one child to the next and differences in individual children's form or use of language—questions which take us into the realm of both power and style differences.

WHAT IS LANGUAGE, ANYWAY?

Let me begin at the beginning. What do we mean by language? Roger Brown has defined language as an arbitrary system of symbols

> which taken together make it possible for a creature with limited powers of discrimination and a limited memory to transmit and understand an infinite variety of messages and to do this in spite of noise and distraction. (Brown, 1965, p. 246)

The critical element in this definition is the phrase *infinite variety of messages.* Language is not just a collection of sounds. Very young babies make several different sounds, but we do not consider that they are using language. They do not appear to use those sounds to *refer* to things or events (that is, they do not use the sounds as symbols), and they do not combine individual sounds into different orders to create varying meaning. So far as we know, for example, it does not matter whether a 6-month-old says "kikiki bababa" or "bababa kikiki."

Some other animals, most notably primates like chimps and possibly other mammals like dolphins, can apparently be taught to use sound or gestural systems in the symbolic and combinatorial way that we define as language. Chimps, for example, can learn to use sign language and may even make up new combinations of signs (e.g., Gardner & Gardner, 1980; Scanlon, Savage-Rumbaugh, & Rumbaugh, 1982). But it takes a long time to teach them, and they have to be given a steady dose of delicious goodies as reinforcers in order to maintain the language. In contrast, as Flavell puts it, "Draconian measures would be needed to *prevent* most children from learning to talk" (1985, p. 248). And as any parent can tell you, once they learn, it is virtually impossible to shut them up!

The developmental process in infants and young children, from prelanguage sounds and gestures to language, follows a common set of steps.

THE EARLY STEPS

Before the First Word: The Prelinguistic Phase

Many of you no doubt think that language development only really starts when a child first uses sounds as a "word"—as a symbol, with some specific referent. But what recent researchers have found is that the sounds and gestures that infants make in the **prelinguistic phase**—before the first-word milestone—are intimately linked to the emergence of those first words. So let's go back to the beginning.

Early Perception of Language. Recall from Chapter 5 that babies are born with (or very soon develop) remarkably good ability to discriminate

Figure 8.1 Chimps like this one have been taught sign language. Linguists who have worked with them agree that the animals can fairly easily learn signs for individual objects or actions. But they do not agree about whether the chimps use these symbols creatively, to make new meanings, as children do from the beginning.

speech sounds. We know that by 3 or 4 months, they pay attention to and can tell the difference between many individual letter sounds, intonation patterns, even syllables or words. Babies this age also have figured out that these speech sounds are matched by the speaker's mouth movements. Thus, from very early—perhaps from birth—the baby is tuned quite acutely to the language she hears around her.

Early Sounds.   This early perceptual skill is not matched right away by much skill in producing sounds. From birth to about 1 month of age, just about the only sound an infant makes is a cry. Infants do have several different cries to signal different kinds of discomfort or problems, and many parents become quite skilled in "reading" these cries to diagnose the baby's particular need at that moment. I also mentioned in Chapter 3 that sick or low-birth-weight babies and those rated as having difficult temperaments are likely to make more unpleasant or grating crying sounds. So the quality of the child's cry may turn out to be a helpful diagnostic tool for physicians or parents.

Starting at about 1 or 2 months, the baby begins to add some laughing and **cooing** vowel sounds to his repertoire, like *uuuuuu.* Sounds like this are usually signals of pleasure in babies. They may show quite a lot of variation in tone, running up and down in volume or pitch. But infants rarely produce consonant sounds much before 5 or 6 months (Bates, O'Connell, and Shore, 1987).

A really big change—quite noticeable by parents as well as by linguists—takes place some time between 6 and 10 months, when the child rather suddenly begins **babbling.** She begins combining consonant and

Figure 8.2   Babbling strikes again! (*Source:* Johnston, 1978, p. 8.)

vowel sounds to produce a kind of syllable, such as *ma* or *dah*. Often these syllables are repeated over and over, so that we hear sounds like *dah dah* (which fathers often quite delightedly, but erroneously, assume means "Daddy").

There is some indication, too, that over the last months of the first year, infants' babbling acquires some of the sound contour (the *intonation pattern*) of the language they are hearing—a process Elizabeth Bates refers to as "learning the tune before the words" (Bates, O'Connell, & Shore, 1987). At the very least, infants do seem to use at least two such "tunes"— a rising intonation at the end of a string of sound, which may signal a desire for a response, and a falling intonation, which seems not to require a response.

Another intriguing facet of the babbling period is that in the early stages, an infant may make sounds that are not matched very well to the sounds in the speech she hears. Children hearing English may use vowel sounds characteristic of German or French; babies hearing Japanese may use an *l* sound that does not occur in Japanese. If you have tried to learn a foreign language that includes sounds not used in English (like the German vowel sounds I am just now struggling with), you know how hard it is to "hear" the sounds correctly. It turns out that babies are particularly good at making such fine discriminations in sounds when they are about 7 or 8 months old. But they rapidly begin to lose this ability. By age 9 or 10 months, the baby's babbling begins to drift more and more toward the sample of sounds that are in the heard language; the nonheard sounds drop out, and the baby becomes *less* able to discriminate among sounds that she is not hearing (e.g., Oller, 1981; Werker & Tees, 1984). For many years, linguists and psychologists thought that babbling was quite unconnected to later language—that it was merely a kind of automatic vocal play. But these more recent findings seem to show that babbling is a significant precursor to language.

Gestures in the First Year.   Another significant precursor may be a kind of "gestural" language that develops at around 9 or 10 months. At this age, we first see babies "demanding" or "asking for" things using gestures or combinations of gestures and sound. A 10-month-old baby who apparently wants you to hand her a favorite toy may stretch and reach for it, opening and closing her hand, and she may accompany the gestures with whining sounds or other heartrending noises. There is no mistaking her meaning. At about the same age, babies will enter into those gestural games much loved by parents, like pat-a-cake, "so big," and "wave bye-bye" (Bates, Camaioni, & Volterra, 1975; Bates et al., 1987).

Interestingly, **receptive language** (the ability to *understand* the meaning of individual words) seems to begin at about this same age and thus occurs before **expressive language** (the ability to communicate verbally). The baby may respond appropriately to her name, to the word "no," or to a sentence like "Look at the doggie." So a whole series of changes seem to come together at 9 or 10 months: the beginning of meaningful

Figure 8.3 Before they can even say their first words, babies successfully use gestures and body language in consistent ways to communicate meaning. This gesture obviously means "give that to me."

gestures, the "drift" of babbling toward the heard-language sounds, imitative gestural games, and the first comprehension of individual words. It is as if the child now understands something about the process of communication and intends to communicate to the adult.

The First Words

Somewhere in the midst of all the babbling, the first words appear. The baby's first word is an event that parents eagerly await, but it's fairly easy to miss. A *word*, as linguists usually define it, is any sound or set of sounds that is used consistently to refer to some thing, action, or quality. But it can be *any* sound. It doesn't have to be a sound that matches words the adults are using. Brenda, a little girl studied by Ronald Scollon (1976), used the sound *nene* as one of her first words. It seemed to mean primarily liquid food, since she used it for milk, juice, and bottle. But she also used it to refer to mother and sleep. (You can see some of Brenda's other early words in the left-hand column of Table 8.1.)

Table 8.1

Brenda's Vocabulary at 14 and 19 Months

14 months	19 months[a]		
aw u (I want, I don't want)	baby	nice	boat
nau (no)	bear	orange	bone
d di (daddy, baby)	bed	pencil	checkers
d yu (down, doll)	big	write	corder
nene, (liquid food)	blue	paper	cut
e (yes)	Brenda	pen	I do
maem (solid food)	cookie	see	met
ada (another, other)	daddy	shoe	Pogo
	eat	sick	Ralph
	at	swim	you too
	(hor)sie	tape	climb
	mama	walk	jump
	mommy	wowow	

[a] Brenda did not actually pronounce all these words the way an adult would; I have given the adult version since that is easier to read.
Source: R. Scollon, *Conversations with a one year old.* Honolulu: The University Press of Hawaii, 1976, pp. 47, 57–58.

Often a child's earliest words are used only in one or two specific situations and in the presence of many cues. The child may say "doggie" or "bow-wow" only to such promptings as "What's that?" or "How does the doggie go?" Later the child may use a word spontaneously and in a wider variety of contexts. Some linguists see this shift as a signal of a basic change in the child's understanding of language—that words are *symbols* for objects or events. There is some suggestive evidence in research by Snyder and Bates (Snyder, Bates, & Bretherton, 1981; Bates, O'Connell, & Shore, 1987), that toddlers who show such broad and apparently symbolic use of words very early also show more rapid development at later stages of language than do those children whose early words are more "context-bound." Whether this is the case or not, we know that virtually all children begin to use individual words in symbolic ways by about 13 months of age.

Adding New Words.   Once the milestone of the first word is reached, toddlers go through a period of slow vocabulary growth. Katherine Nelson (1973) found that it typically took three to four months for a child to add the next 10 words. But past the 10-word point, there was usually a very rapid increase in vocabulary, with a new word added every few days. Even more impressive is the burst in vocabulary growth that occurs at about the 50-word point. At that stage—usually between 16 and 20 months—the toddler's vocabulary may multiply 5- or 10-fold in only a few weeks.

Thus, the average 18-month-old child has a vocabulary of 40 to 50 words; the average 24-month-old knows 300 words. (Amazingly enough, by age 6 the typical child knows *14,000* words [Templin, 1957].) You can get some sense of the early stages of this rapid change from Table 8.1, which shows Brenda's vocabulary at both 14 and 19 months.

Kinds of New Words. The early words in children's vocabularies are most likely to be what Katherine Nelson (1973) calls *general nominals*— names ("nouns") for classes of objects or people, like *ball, car, milk, doggie, he,* or *that.* Over half of the first 50 words of the eight children she studied were of this type, while only 13 percent were action words ("verbs"). Dedre Gentner (1982) has observed the same thing in her study of a little boy named Tad (whose early words are listed in Table 8.2) and in studies of children learning other languages as well (including Japanese, Mandarin Chinese, German, and Turkish).

However, this "noun-before-verb" pattern does not hold for all children. Katherine Nelson (1973) first noticed that some toddlers used what she labeled an **expressive style,** in which the early words seem to be linked not to objects but to social relationships. These children often learn pronouns (*you, me*) early, and they use many more of what Nelson calls *personal-social* words (*no, yes, want, please*). Their early vocabulary may also include

Table 8.2
▬▬▬▬▬

Words Learned by Tad from 11 to 21 Months of Age

Age	Nominals ("nouns")			Predicates ("verbs")	Expressive words	Indeterminate words
11–16 mo.	dog duck daddy mama	teh (teddy bear) dipe (diaper) car owl	keys cheese eye	yuk		toot toot
18–19 mo.	cow cup spoon apple knee ball jeep	truck juice bowl teeth elbow block	kitty bottle towel cheek map bus	hot happy down up	oops boo hi bye uh oh	bath pee pee TV
21 mo.	toe moon bird water	happy sauce bee pole cookie	tree wheel peach	stuck off down out		back (piggyback ride)
Percentage	68			15	8	8

Source: After Gentner, 1982, Table 11.1, p. 306.

▬▬▬▬▬

some multiword strings, like "Love you" or "Do it" or "Go away." (This is in sharp contrast to the children who use what Nelson describes as a **referential style,** in which the early vocabulary is made up predominantly of nominals.)

I'll talk further about such style differences at the end of the chapter, when I deal more generally with individual variations in language. For now I only want to point out that while nounlike terms are the most common early words, they are not the only ones, and some children use them relatively infrequently in the early months.

The First Sentences

After the first word, the next big step is when the child begins to string words into sentences. The first two-word sentences usually appear between 18 and 24 months (in fact, you can see two examples in the list of Brenda's 19-month vocabulary in Table 8.1).

We can see the precursors of this development at an early point. Just as the first spoken words are preceded by apparently meaningful gestures, the first two-word sentences are preceded by combinations of word and gesture that linguists call **holophrases.** When a child says "Cookie!" and at the same time reaches to grab the cookie from your hand, she conveys a whole meaning ("Give me the cookie!") in the intonation and the gesture. Similarly, to use an example Elizabeth Bates suggests (Bates, O'Connell, & Shore, 1987), the infant may point to her father's shoe and say "Daddy," as if to convey "Daddy's shoe." In both cases, while only one word is used, a sentencelike meaning is conveyed.

Still, it is a big step forward for the child to combine two words. For some months after this, the child continues to use single words as well as two-word sentences. Eventually, the one-word utterances drop out almost completely, and the child begins to use three- and four-word sentences and to create more complex combinations of words. This is a fairly steady (and remarkably rapid) process—the description of which takes me into the realm of grammar, or syntax.

THE DEVELOPMENT OF GRAMMAR

In describing the emergence of grammar, most linguists follow the lead of Roger Brown (1973b) and differentiate between several steps or phases.

Stage 1 Grammar

The first step, which Brown called stage 1 grammar, has several distinguishing features: the sentences are *short*—generally two or three words—and they are *simple.* Nouns, verbs, and adjectives are usually included, but virtually all the purely grammatical markers (which linguists call **inflec-**

tions) are missing. At the beginning, for example, children learning English do not normally use the *s* for plurals or put the *ed* ending on verbs to make the past tense, nor do they use the *'s* of the possessive or auxiliary verbs like *am* or *do.* Across languages, there is some indication that the child's early sentences include primarily words that are normally vocally *stressed* in the speech of adults using that language. (If you think about English, you will realize that it is precisely the nouns and verbs and adjectives that you are most likely to stress when you speak, not the grammatical inflections.)

Because only the really critical words are present in these early sentences, Brown (Brown & Bellugi, 1964; Brown, 1973b) describes this as **telegraphic speech.** The child's language sounds rather like what we say when we send a telegram. We keep in all the essential words—usually nouns, verbs, and modifiers—and leave out all the prepositions, auxiliary verbs, and the like.

At this early stage, children's imitation of adults' speech, as well as their spontaneous speech, is telegraphic. If you ask a child of 20 to 24 months to say "I am playing with the dogs," the child is likely to say "Play dog" or "I play dog," thus omitting the auxiliary verb (*am*), the verb ending (*ing*), the preposition (*with*), the article (*the*), and the plural ending (*s*).

Despite the shortness of these early sentences and their apparent grammatical simplicity, it is clear that even at this beginning point children create sentences following rules. Not adult rules, to be sure, but rules nonetheless. They focus on certain types of words and put them together in particular orders.

When evidence of this regularity in children's early sentences began to emerge in the early 1960s, a number of linguists (perhaps most notably Martin Braine, 1963) tried to write a grammar for this "foreign" language spoken by toddlers. Such efforts have now been largely abandoned, for two reasons. First, although all children studied seem to have some kinds of rules for their first sentences, all individual children do not seem to use precisely the same rules (Braine, 1976). Second, it became clear quite quickly that children convey many different *meanings* with exactly the same sentence forms. If we are going to understand this early language, we have to pay attention to semantics as well as to grammar.

For example, young children frequently use a sentence made up of two nouns, such as "Mommy sock" or "sweater chair" (to use some often-quoted examples from Lois Bloom's 1973 analysis). We might conclude from this that a "two-noun" form is a basic grammatical characteristic of children's early language. But we would miss the complexity. For instance, the child in Bloom's study who said "Mommy sock" said it on two different occasions. The first time was when she picked up her mother's sock, and the second was when the mother put the child's own sock on the child's foot. In the first case, "Mommy sock" seems to mean "Mommy's sock" (a possessive relationship). But in the second instance, the child seems to

Table 8.3

Some of the Different Meanings Children Appear to Express in Their Stage 1 Grammar

Meaning	Examples
Agent-action	Sarah eat; Daddy jump
Action-object	Eat cookie; read book
Possessor–possessed object	Mommy sock; Timothy lunch
Action-location	Come here; play outside
Located object–location	Sweater chair; juice table
Attribute–modified object	Big book; red house
Nomination	That cookie; it dog
Recurrence	More juice; other book

Source: Maratsos, 1983.

convey "Mommy is putting a sock on me," which is an *agent* (Mommy) to *object* (sock) relationship.

Some other different meanings that children convey with their earliest sentences are listed in Table 8.3. Not all children express all of these relationships or meanings in their early word combinations, and there does not seem to be a fixed order in which these meanings or constructions are acquired, but all children appear to express at least several of these patterns in their earliest, simplest sentences (Maratsos, 1983).

Despite the variations in forms from one child to the next, it is still true that these earliest sentences have notable common features, heard in children learning any language (Slobin, 1985). These findings certainly tell us that the desire to communicate is immensely powerful. They also suggest the possibility that the biological and cognitive underpinnings of language at this age are universal, so children's early language attempts are bound to have these similarities, no matter what language they speak.

Longer and More Complex Sentences

Most linguists consider that a new phase or stage (Brown's stage 2) begins when the child starts to use any of the grammatical inflections, such as plurals, past tenses, auxiliary verbs, and prepositions. You can get a better feeling for the sound of the change from Table 8.4, which lists some of the sentences of a little boy named Daniel, recorded by David Ingram (1981). The left-hand column lists some of Daniel's sentences at about 21 months of age, when he was still using the simplest forms; the right-hand column lists some of his sentences only two and a half months later

Table 8.4

Examples of Daniel's Stage 1 and Stage 2 Sentences

Stage 1 sentences (age 21 months)	Stage 2 sentences (age 23 months)
A bottle	A little boat
Broke-it	Cat there
Here (the) bottle	Doggies here
Hi daddy	Boat here
Horse doggie	Give you the book
Broke it	It's a boy
It a bottle	Its a robot
Kitty cat	It's cat
Oh a doggie	Little box there
Poor Daddy	No book
Thank you	Oh cars
That hat?	Oh doggie
That monkey	Sit down
Want a bottle	This a bucket
Want bottle	That flowers
What that?	There's a boat there
	Those little boat
	What those?
	What's that?
	What this?
	Where going?
	Where the boat?

Source: Reprinted by permission of the publisher from "Early patterns of grammatical development" by D. Ingram, in R. E. Stark (Ed.), *Language behavior in infancy and early childhood,* Tables 6 and 7, pp. 344–345. Copyright 1981 by Elsevier Science Publishing Co., Inc.

(age 23 to 24 months), when he had just moved into the more complex phase.

I do not want to give you the impression that children move from primitive to very complex sentences all in one leap. They don't. Within any given language community, children seem to add inflections and more complex word orders in fairly predictable sequences. For example, Roger Brown (1973b) found that in English-speaking children, the earliest inflection seems to be *ing* added onto a verb, such as in "I playing" or "Doggie running." Then come prepositions like *on* and *in;* the plural *s* on nouns; irregular past tenses, such as *broke* or *ran;* possessives; articles, such as *a* and *the* in English; the *s* that we add to third-person verbs, as in "He wants"; regular past tenses like *played* and *wanted;* and the various forms of the auxiliary verb, as in "I am not going."

Linguists are still arguing about just why these grammatical parts are added in this order (e.g., Maratsos, 1983). But there does seem to be some link to the amount of information processing required by each particular form. The easiest ones—the ones that require the child to notice the fewest things—are generally added first.

There are also predictable sequences in the child's developing use of questions and negatives. In each case, the child seems to go through periods when he creates types of sentences that he has not heard adults use but that are consistent with the particular set of rules he is using. For example, in the development of questions there is a point at which the child puts a *wh* word (*who, what, when, where, why*) at the front end of a sentence but doesn't yet put the auxiliary verb in the right place. (Why it is resting now?). Similarly, in the development of negatives there is a stage in which the *not* or *n't* or *no* is put in but the auxiliary verb is omitted ("I not crying" or "There no squirrels.").

Another intriguing phenomenon of this second phase of sentence construction underlines the rule-making and rule-following quality of even the earliest sentences: **overregularization,** or overgeneralization. This is what the two little girls were doing in the conversation about the goldfish when they created new "regularized" forms of superlatives (*badder, baddest, worser,* and *worsest*). We can see the same thing in the use of past tenses as well. Children say *wented* or *goed* or *ated.* Stan Kuczaj (1977, 1978) has found that young children initially learn a small number of irregular past tenses and use them correctly for a short time. But then, rather suddenly, the child seems to discover the rule of adding *ed* and overgeneralizes this rule to all verbs. This type of "error" is particularly common among children between ages 3 and 5.

All the changes I have been describing are delightful to listen to. But the changes are important for theorists, too, who are impressed with the fact that the child creates sentences she could not have heard but which make excellent sense within the rules of her own grammar.

Incidentally, all of what I've said so far describes what happens when a child learns a *single* language. But what about children who are exposed to two or more languages from the beginning? How confusing is this for a child? And how can parents ease the process? I've discussed the problems of bilingual children in the box on pages 290–291.

Later Grammar Development

Past these early stages, children's language continues to develop in various ways. Vocabulary continues to be added at an astonishing rate (perhaps 5 to 10 words a day) into elementary school. More complex and difficult sentence forms are also added throughout elementary school, and recurrent overregularization errors are eliminated (Bowerman, 1985). For instance, passive forms, like "The food is eaten by the cat," are not well understood even by 5- and 6-year-olds and are not used much in spontaneous speech until several years later. "Tag questions" also develop quite late in English-speaking children. These are the words we stick onto the end of a declarative sentence to turn it into a question—"You can play the piano, can't you?" or "They are studying math, aren't they?" Getting the right tag onto the sentence is a fairly complex process, and children are simply not skilled at it until age 8 or 9 (Dennis, Sugar, & Whitaker, 1982). Children also learn gradually how to string two sentences or clauses together or to embed one within another, as in "John is chewing gum and so am I" or "The apple that fell off the tree is red."

Obviously, grammar development does not end in first grade. Vocabulary continues to increase, and more complex sentence forms are learned later. But the really giant strides occur between 1 and 5 years of age, as the child moves from single words to complex questions, negatives, and commands.

Overview of Grammar Development

Let me pause for a brief summary of the key points about grammar development before I move on to a discussion of word meaning.

1. The earliest sentences created by children speaking any language have certain features in common, including shortness, simplicity, and the predominant use of nouns, verbs, and modifiers.
2. These earliest sentences also seem to follow some set of rules. The rule system is not the same as for adult language and is not identical from one child to the next, but all children appear to create sentences in a nonrandom manner.
3. Subsequent changes in children's grammar, while not the same in all languages, are predictable and sequential within any one language. The *rate* of development varies, but the basic outline of the sequence seems to be shared, especially the early steps in the sequence.
4. From the earliest two-word sentences, children's language is creative. The child is not just copying sentences she has heard; she is creating new ones according to the rules of her own grammar.

THE DEVELOPMENT OF WORD MEANING

To understand language development, it is not enough to know how children learn to string words together to form sentences. We also have to understand how the words in those sentences come to have meaning. Linguists are still searching for good ways to describe (or explain) children's emerging word meaning. So far, several sets of questions have dominated the research.

Which Comes First, the Meaning or the Word?

The most fundamental question is whether the child learns a word to describe a category or class he has *already* created through his manipulations

LEARNING TWO LANGUAGES: BILINGUAL CHILDREN

A couple of years ago I spent an evening with a group of parents of infants to answer some questions about day care and normal development. In one of the couples, the father was a native speaker of Lithuanian. He wanted to know if he should try to teach his son Lithuanian along with English. This is an unusual combination of languages, but the question is relevant for a great many parents who speak different native languages or who want to preserve a family linguistic heritage. If you want your child to grow up speaking two (or more) languages, how should you go about it? Will it have a detrimental effect?

The answers I usually give to such questions go like this:

First, there is no evidence that children come to any harm when they learn two (or more) languages in early childhood. Their early grammar development may be slightly slowed, but they catch up rapidly later on. Some research even shows that bilingual children have slightly advanced cognitive development compared to monolingual children (Segalowitz, 1981; Hakuta & Diaz, 1985). In some cases, the IQ scores of bilingual children are temporarily depressed while they are in the process of learning both languages, but that effect does not persist.

Second, children appear to learn correct pronunciation more easily than adults do, so if you want your child to speak both family languages fluently, sounding like a native speaker, by all means provide the opportunity early.

There are at least two good ways to go about it. One choice is to speak both languages to the child from the beginning. If you do this, however, the child will have a much easier time distinguishing the two and will show fewer mistakes and confusions between them if the sources of the two languages are clearly distinguished. So if Mom's native language is English and Dad's is Italian, have Mom speak only English to the infant/toddler while Dad speaks only Italian. (The parents will, of course, speak to each other in whatever language they have in common.) If both parents speak both languages to the child or mix them up in their own speech, this is a much more difficult situation for the child and language learning will be delayed (McLaughlin, 1984). It will also work if one language is always spoken at home and the other in a day-care center, with playmates, or in some other outside situation.

If simultaneous exposure to both languages is not feasible, it works just about as well for the child to learn one language first and then the other one. Just how early this second one needs to be learned in order to become equally strong or equally well pronounced is still a matter of dispute among linguists (e.g., McLaughlin, 1984). But we do know that young children can learn to speak two or more languages with native-speaker skill.

Some of you will have seen a parallel here with the problems facing children who come to school speaking other than the dominant cultural language. This has been an issue for many Spanish-speaking children in parts of the United States as well as for other minority groups. Until recently, it was also frequently a difficulty for French-speaking children in Canada. Educators have had to grapple with the task of teaching children a second language at the same time that they are trying to teach them subject matter such as reading and mathematics. Just what is the best way for the schools to do this? Should the child be immediately immersed in the new language, or should there be a period of transition?

These are hard questions to answer, in part because so many different variations have been attempted, with widely varying quality of teaching. Messy as the research is, however, one thread still runs through it: the best system seems to be what is usually called *bilingual* education, in which the child is given at least some of her instruction in basic subject matter in her native language in the first year or two of school, combined with exposure to the second language (Willig, 1985). By second or third grade in most bilingual programs, the children are being taught exclusively in the main school language. Children in programs like this typically do better than those who are simply immersed immediately in the new language in kindergarten or first grade. Interestingly, in her analysis of this research, Ann Willig has found that the ideal arrangement is very much like what works best at home with toddlers: if some subjects are always taught in one language and other subjects in the other language, children learn both most easily. But if each sentence is translated, children do not learn the new language as quickly or as well.

Equally interesting—and surprising, in light of the theories about early childhood being a critical period for language learning—researchers have found some indications that teenagers and older elementary-school children learn a second language more quickly than do 6- to 8-year-olds. Just about the hardest time for a second language to be learned seems to be first-grade age, presumably because the child is simultaneously grappling with all the new subject matter of school.

of the world around him (Nelson, 1982, 1985) or whether the existence of a word forces the child to create new cognitive categories (Clark, 1973). This may seem like a highly abstract argument, but it touches on the fundamental issue of the relationship between language and thought. Does the child learn to represent objects to himself *because* he now has language, or does language simply come along at about this point and make the representations easier?

The answer seems to be that both are true (Greenberg & Kuczaj, 1982; Clark, 1983). In the early stages of language development, children seem to apply words (or even to create words) to describe categories or classes they have already created in actions or images. Brenda's word *nene,* for instance, which seemed to mean liquid food and the pleasure that goes with it, was probably a word to describe an already existing mental category or scheme.

Further support for the cognitive basis of early language is that some grammatical categories, such as prepositions, are not added all at once, but only appear in the child's language over several years. They are added only when the child appears to understand the underlying relationship. So, for example, the word *in* is used before the word *between,* and both appear before *in front of* (Johnston, 1985). Other sequences of word usage seem to follow cognitive understanding as well, such as the use of *wh* questions. All the bits of evidence of this type point to the likelihood that in the early years, concepts *precede* language in many instances.

But it seems equally clear that children's concepts and classification systems are affected by the labels attached to objects, too. As Lev Vygotsky, a notable Russian psychologist, pointed out years ago (1962), there is a point somewhere in the child's second year when she "discovers" that objects have names. If children this age hear a strange word and see an unfamiliar object, they seem to figure out that the two go together. In this way, the words help create new categories.

Extending the Class

Just as knowledge of the child's cognitive skills can help illuminate early language development, so the child's use of words can tell us a great deal about the kinds of concepts he is creating.

Suppose your 2-year-old, on catching sight of the family tabby, says "See kitty." No doubt you will be pleased that the child has applied the right word to the animal. But this sentence alone doesn't tell you much about the word meaning the child has developed. What does the word kitty mean to the child? Does she think it is a name only for that *particular* fuzzy beast? Or does she thinks it applies to all furry creatures, to all things with four legs, to things with pointed ears, or what? One way to figure out what class or category the child has created is to see what *other* creatures or things a child also calls a kitty. That is, how is the class *extended* in the child's language? If the child has created a *kitty* category that is based on furriness, then many dogs and perhaps sheep would also be called "kitty." If a tail is a crucial feature, then a Manx cat might not be called kitty by the child. Or perhaps the child used the word *kitty* only for the family cat. This would imply a very narrow category indeed. The general question for researchers has been whether children tend to use words narrowly or broadly, overextending or underextending them.

Our current information tells us that children *overextend* their early words more often than they *underextend* them, so we're more likely to hear the word *cat* applied to dogs or guinea pigs than we are to hear it used for just one animal or for a very small set of animals or objects (Clark, 1983). Some examples of the overextensions that children create, collected by Eve Clark (1975), are listed in Table 8.5.

All children seem to show overextensions like these. But the particular classes each child creates are unique. There doesn't seem to be any tendency for all children to use the word *cat* to apply to all four-footed animals or to all furry creatures or whatever. Each child overextends his words using his own distinct rules, and those rules change as the child's vocabulary grows.

These overextensions *may* tell us something about the way children think, such as that they create broad classes. But before we jump to sweeping

Table 8.5
▬▬▬

Some Examples of Overextensions in the Language of Young Children

Word	Object or event for which the word was originally used	Other objects or events to which the word was later applied
mooi	Moon	Cakes, round marks on windows, writing on windows and in books, round shapes in books, tooling in leather book covers, round postmarks, letter *O*
buti	Ball	Toy, radish, stone spheres at park entrance
baw	Ball	(By another child) apples, grapes, eggs, squash, bell clapper, anything round
sch	Sound of train	All moving machines
em	Worm	Flies, ants, all small insects, heads of timothy grass
fafer	Sound of trains	Steaming coffeepot, anything that hissed or made a noise
va	White plush dog	Muffler, cat, father's fur coat

Source: Reprinted with permission from Eve V. Clark, "Knowledge, context, and strategy in the acquisition of meaning." In *Georgetown University Round Table 1975: Developmental psycholinguistics: Theory and applications.* Edited by Daniel P. Dato. Copyright 1975 by Georgetown University, Washington, D.C., pp. 83–84.

conclusions, we have to remember that part of the child's problem is that she simply doesn't know very many words. If she wants to talk about something, point out something, or ask for something, she has to use whatever words she has that are fairly close. Overextensions may thus arise from the child's desire to communicate and may not tell us that the child fails to make the discriminations involved. The example Clark uses (1977) is a child who wants to call attention to a horse. She may know that the horse is different from a dog, but she doesn't know the word. So she says "Doggie," and the linguist says "Aha! Another overextension of the class." As the child learns the separate labels that are applied to the different subtypes of fuzzy four-legged creatures, the overextension disappears (Clark, 1987).

Parents may also contribute to a child's overextensions. Carolyn and Cynthia Mervis (1982) found that mothers give things labels that they think match the child's categories rather than using the more precise labels. So they may call leopards and lions "kitty cats" or a toy fire engine a "car." This may well aid communication between the mother and child, but it also may be one contributing factor in the child's overextensions of categories.

Form Versus Function: What Does the Child Attend To?

Another dispute among researchers studying the development of word meaning is whether the child initially creates categories based on what objects *look like* (form) or whether she bases her early classifications mostly on what you can *do with* the object (function).

Eve Clark (1973) originally took the first view, and if you go back and look at the overextensions in Table 8.5, this position makes a lot of sense. Children do seem to base their overextensions on the shape or sounds or textures of objects, all of which are perceptual qualities.

The second view has been proposed by Katherine Nelson (1973, 1982), who has been very much struck by the fact that the child's first words nearly always refer to objects that have particular functions or to objects that the child can play with or move. The young child is more likely to learn the word *ball*, for example, than the word *sofa*, even though both are part of her world on a daily basis. But she *plays with* the ball and only *looks at* or sits on the sofa. Similarly, Nelson points out that words that describe changes in state, like *dry* or *dirty*, are understood and spoken earlier by most children than are words that describe constant qualities, like *rough* or *square*.

Nelson concluded that children's concepts are most often organized around a *functional core*—a set of things that an object does or is. A ball *is* something round that rolls, bounces, and can be thrown. Extensions of this concept may then be based on perceptual qualities, as Clark suggests. New round things may be labeled *balls*, for example. But if the child discovers that the new round thing does not bounce, it will no longer belong in the same category.

As is so often true when two competing theories have been proposed, the evidence tells us that both theories are at least partially correct. Children's early word meanings seem to be based on both form and function, although form is perhaps the more critical (e.g., Corrigan & Schommer, 1984). More generally, there is some indication that what children do is develop a sort of mental *prototype* (a mental picture of the average or standard example of that category) (Greenberg & Kuczaj, 1982) and generalize to other examples on the basis of how close the new instance is to the prototype. Adults do this, too. Think of a bird. Birds come in a very large variety of shapes, sizes, and colors. But probably when you first thought of a bird, a picture of a *particular* bird came to your mind. (If your prototype is anything like mine, you probably thought of something vaguely robinlike.) This is your prototype of a bird—a central example that "defines" the category for you. When you encounter some new creature that *might* be a bird, you compare it mentally to the prototype to see if it fits (Does it have wings? Does it have a beak? Does it have four toes?).

Children seem to do the same thing. Their early prototypes may be based on either form or function, and the prototypes change (accommodate, in Piaget's language) as the child has more experiences and learns new words for related categories. When the child learns the word *horse,* she stops calling horses "dogs" and develops a horse prototype as well as a dog prototype.

The whole process of developing word meanings is clearly complicated, and it seems to vary even more from child to child than does the process of grammar development. Obviously, what linguists are searching for are the rules that govern this process, so that we can understand how and why children use words the way they do. So far, only a few general principles have emerged.

USING LANGUAGE: COMMUNICATION AND SELF-DIRECTION

In the past decade or so, linguists have also turned their attention to a third aspect of children's language—namely, the way children learn to *use* language either to communicate with others (an aspect of language often called **pragmatics**) or to regulate their own behavior. How early do children know what kind of language to use in specific situations? How early do they learn the rules of conversation, such as that you are supposed to take turns?

From this large body of research, two general points are important. First, children seem to learn the pragmatics of language at a remarkably early age. For example, D. R. Rutter and Kevin Durkin (1987) have recently found that children as young as 18 months show adultlike gaze patterns when they are interacting with a parent; they look at the person who is talking, look away at the beginning of their own speaking turn, and then look at the listener again when they are signaling that they are about to stop talking. (Watch yourself and your partner in your next conversation to see these gaze patterns in action.)

Furthermore, children as young as 2 years adapt the form of their language to the situation they are in or the person they are talking to. Such a child may say "Gimme" to another toddler as he grabs the other child's glass but might say "More milk" to an adult (Becker, 1982). Among older children, language is even more clearly adapted to the listener: 4-year-olds use simpler language when they talk to 2-year-olds than when they talk to adults (e.g., Tomasello & Mannle, 1985); first-graders explain things more fully to a stranger than to a friend (Sonnenschein, 1986) and are more polite to adults and strangers than to peers, and both of these trends are still clearer among fourth-graders.

Partly, of course, all of this tells us something about the child's diminishing egocentrism. Changing one's language to adapt to another's need demonstrates the ability to comprehend that the other person has different needs or a different viewpoint. But this research also tells us that from the beginning, the child's language is meant to *communicate* and that the child will adapt the language form in order to achieve better communication.

The second general point about language use is that children learn to use it to help control or monitor their own behavior. Such "private speech," which may consist of more fragmentary sentences, muttering, or instructions to the self, is detectable in the earliest use of words and sentences. Many years ago, Ruth Weir (1962) listened by tape recorder as her 2-year-old son Anthony talked to himself in his crib, saying things like "What color; what color blanket; what color mop; what color glass," as if he was trying out sentence forms. And when 2- or 3-year-olds play by themselves, they give themselves instructions, stop themselves with words, or describe what they are doing: "No, not there," "I put that there," or "Put it" (Furrow, 1984).

In older children, this self-regulatory use of language is still apparent, particularly when they are working on hard problems (such as the muttering Flavell heard children doing when they were trying to remember things, discussed in Chapter 7). Interestingly, this use of language seems to peak at about age 5 to 7 and then largely disappears by age 9 or 10. In higher-IQ children, this shift occurs earlier (Berk, 1986). As Vygotsky originally suggested, it is as if the child, at about 5 or 6, discovers that language can be used to help thinking, particularly complex thinking. Initially, this language is audible, but later it goes underground and becomes silent, although it may be audible even among adults if they are given particularly difficult problems to solve. (You might want to think for a minute about your own use of language to guide your own behavior. When are you most likely to mutter to yourself?)

The study of the child's use of language shows that we won't fully understand children's language development until we understand the development of both cognitive and social skills. This reminds us once again that the child is not divided up into tidy packages labeled "physical development" or "social development" or "language development." Each child is a coherent, integrated system.

EXPLAINING LANGUAGE DEVELOPMENT

If merely describing language development is hard—and it is—explaining it has proved still harder. This may surprise you, since most of us simply take for granted that children just "learn" to talk by listening to the language they hear. It doesn't seem very magical or amazing until you think about it a bit. And then the more you think about it, the more amazing and mysterious it becomes. Of course, such mystery has not kept the theorists silent, so we have several explanations to choose from. The most helpful way to organize the theories is to divide them into two groups: those that emphasize aspects of the environment as critical and those that look at processes inside the child.

THE INFLUENCE OF THE ENVIRONMENT ON LANGUAGE DEVELOPMENT

Early Theories: Imitation and Reinforcement

The earliest attempts to explain language development were primarily based on learning-theory approaches and on the commonsense idea that learning a language was a fairly straightforward process of imitation or reinforcement.

Imitation. Imitation obviously has to play *some* part, since the child does learn the language he is hearing and doesn't invent his own. Children do imitate sentences they hear; they do repeat the name of some new object when they hear it (Leonard, et al., 1983); they do learn to speak with the accent of those they are listening to. There is even some evidence from research by Elizabeth Bates (Bates et al., 1982) that those babies who show the most imitation of actions and gestures in the first year of life are also the ones who later learn language more quickly. Thus, the *tendency* to imitate may be an important ingredient in the language-learning process.

Still, if you think about all the facts I've given you, you can see that imitation just won't work as a sole explanation of language development. In particular, remember that children create types of sentences and forms of words that they have never heard. When a child overregularizes the past tense and invents words like *goed* or *beated* or invents wonderful questions like "Why it can't turn off?," she is not imitating what she hears. Furthermore, when a child does imitate an adult's sentences directly, she reduces them to a form that is like her own sentences.

Reinforcement.   A more formal theory of language development based on learning theory was proposed by B. F. Skinner (1957). He argued that children are directly *taught* language by their parents or others around them. The adults, he thought, *shape* the child's first sounds into words and then the words into sentences by selectively reinforcing those that are understandable or "correct." If your child says "Coo" while reaching for a cookie and you say "No, say *cookie*" and withhold the cookie until she says something closer, you are shaping the child's language.

This extreme version of a reinforcement theory of language has been largely discredited because of a number of key flaws. First, parents don't, in fact, explicitly correct children's grammar very much or respond with any kind of criticism when the child creates a nongrammatical sentence. Instead, parents are remarkably forgiving of all sorts of peculiar constructions and meaning, responding instead to the "truth value" of the child's sentences (Brown & Hanlon, 1970; Hirsh-Pasek, Treiman, & Schneiderman, 1984). Second, some explicit correction, when it does occur, may actually *slow down* language development rather than speeding it up. Katherine Nelson observed this in her study of early vocabulary growth. Children whose mothers engaged in systematic correction of poor pronunciation and rewarded good pronunciation had smaller vocabularies than did children whose mothers corrected less.

Third, children's language gets better even when the "incorrect" forms have been repeatedly reinforced (Gleitman & Wanner, 1984), as Dale points out in this example:

> My son Jonathan at age twenty-six months requested the repetition of some favored activity by saying " 'Gain," with a characteristic rising intonation; at age thirty-one months he said "Do that again, Dad." The latter sentence is far more complex linguistically but no more effective. (Dale, 1976, p. 141)

Fourth, Skinner's theory simply cannot account for the apparent creative and rule-governed aspects of children's early language. All in all, the whole process just doesn't sound like shaping.

Newer Environmental Theories: Talking to the Child and Other Input Theories

Even though neither direct imitation nor shaping seem to account for the development of language, it still seems plausible that the language the child is hearing has *some* effect.

At the simplest possible level, we know that children who hear a lot of language develop vocabulary a little faster in the early years than do those who are talked to less (e.g., Engel, Nechlin, & Arkin, 1975). But it may not be sheer quantity that is critical here; rather, it seems that those infants whose parents use language *responsively*—who talk to the infant when the baby makes some noise or in response to some other behavior of the child—later are slightly faster in language development (e.g., Clarke-Stewart, 1973; Olson, Bayles, & Bates, 1986). We know that at the very least, some *minimally sufficient* amount of exposure to language is necessary for children to develop language at all. Beyond that minimal level, variations in quantity or responsiveness of the parents' language make some difference, but the effect is not very large—an interesting fact in itself.

Motherese.   Beyond sheer quantity, another facet of early talk to children that may be important in language learning is the *simplicity* of the language children typically hear. Virtually all adults speak in much simpler sentences to children than they do with one another, but since this distinctively simpler language is most often heard from mothers to their youngsters, it has acquired the name **motherese** (Snow & Ferguson, 1977; Schachter & Strage, 1982.) Motherese has several key features:

1. It is spoken in a higher-pitched voice and at a slower pace than is speech to adults, with clear pauses at the ends of sentences (Jacobson et al., 1983).
2. The sentences are short and nearly always grammatical (unlike speech to adults, which includes many more long sentences and is frequently ungrammatical).
3. The sentences are grammatically simple, with relatively few modifiers and few clauses. Mothers of 2-year-olds are more likely to say "Mrs. Smith was at the store today" than "I saw your preschool teacher, Mrs. Smith, when I went to the grocery store today."
4. It is highly repetitive. The adult tends to use the same sentences or minor variations of the same sentences over and over when talking to a young child (e.g., "Where is the ball? Can you see the ball? Where is the ball? There is the ball!"). The adult also repeats the child's sentences frequently—perhaps 10 percent of the time. Usually these are not perfect repetitions, but "expansions" or "recastings" of the child's sentence which turn the child's sentence into a more complete grammatical form. (For example, if the child said "Mommy coat," the mother might say "Yes, that's mommy's coat.")
5. The vocabulary is concrete, nearly always referring to objects or people that are immediately present. The vocabulary is also limited; adults choose words they think the child will understand. In particular, when choosing nouns, adults are likely to pick the label for a category of intermediate generality rather than either a specific term or a superordinate. For example, they will use the word *dog* rather than either *collie* or *animal* (Blewitt, 1983).

⌐MULTIMEDIA LEARNING CENTRE ⌐
DEESIDE COLLEGE
∟ ⌐

6. As the child's sentences become longer and more complex, the adults' language moves ahead slowly in length and complexity, always a notch or two ahead of the child (Phillips, 1973; Stern et al., 1983).

Presumably, parents talk this way to their young children not because they have figured out that this is the right way to teach language but, much more simply, because in this way they are most likely to be understood by their children and most likely to keep their children's interest. But even though it isn't intended to be helpful for grammar development, motherese might nonetheless help to explain language development.

We know, for example, that infants, given a choice between motherese and less high-pitched or faster speech, prefer to listen to motherese (Fernald, 1985; Werker, 1987). So there seems to be something about the sound or shape of such talk that attracts the child, with the result that the child's attention is repeatedly focused on the language input. The very simplicity of the adults' speech may also permit the child to pick out repeating grammatical patterns. Erika Hoff-Ginsberg (1986, 1987), for example, has found that parents who use a lot of repetitions or partial repetitions or who use a lot of *wh* questions have children whose grammar develops more rapidly. Hoff-Ginsberg's findings suggest further that the child derives somewhat different benefits from these two kinds of input. Repetitions seem to benefit the child by emphasizing the structure of the language itself; questions seem to help mostly because they keep the child talking with the adult.

More-Specific Feedback. A related possibility is that as part of motherese, parents provide various forms of specific feedback to the child about the adequacy of her constructions. The expansions and recastings I mentioned in item 4 above are one such form of feedback; the child's sentence is repeated back in a grammatically more complete form, thus modeling a more complex grammar. Several researchers, most notably Keith Nelson and his colleagues (e.g., Nelson, 1977), have been able to show that such expansions or recastings have beneficial effects. He worked with $2\frac{1}{2}$-year-old children who were not yet spontaneously producing forms such as negative *wh* sentences (e.g., "Why doesn't it work?") or future tenses of verbs. He then gave the children five 1-hour training sessions over two months. In these sessions, the adult recast either the child's questions or his verb forms—thereby giving the child a consistent model for one type of more complex form. What Nelson found was that the children whose questions were expanded showed more rapid growth in their spontaneous use of questions, and those whose verbs were recast showed improvement in that area. A study by Hirsh-Pasek and her colleagues (1984) applies this to real-life encounters. They found that mothers more often corrected or recast their 2-year-old children's sentences if they were "ill-formed" rather than "well-formed." Hirsh-Pasek did not find the same pattern for 3-, 4-, or 5-year olds in conversations with mothers, and even among 2-year-olds, many well-formed sentences were corrected subtly. Still, these findings and those of Nelson and others make it plausible that such expansions or corrections are useful for a child's language development.

Other forms of correction may also have an impact. For example, if a child says something to an adult and the adult simply does not understand or misunderstands, the child is receiving feedback about the adequacy of her language. Similarly, if the adult asks for clarification, that tells the child something. Thus, while it may be true that parents do not often explicitly correct children's grammar or intentionally withhold treats until the child says something "correctly," they do provide negative feedback in other forms, which may help the child to "tune" the form of her language.

These newer versions of environmental theories are a great deal more subtle and undoubtedly more accurate than the earlier, simpler versions. But here, too, there are problems. For example, while it is true that children who hear more "recastings" learn grammar sooner, children who rarely hear such forms nonetheless acquire a complex grammar, albeit more slowly. Thus, while motherese or language feedback may make a child's task simpler, it does not seem to be the *cause* of the child's language learning. Furthermore, as Melissa Bowerman points out, "listener misunderstandings, requests for clarification, repetitions, and recasts . . . follow well-formed utterances as well as those that are ungrammatical. . . . If a child's first impulse on hearing such responses is to question the adequacy of her grammar, she would continually be trying to revise perfectly acceptable rules" (1987, p. 457).

THE CHILD'S ROLE IN LANGUAGE DEVELOPMENT

If such environmental input can't fully explain language development, then we have to turn to the other actor in this drama, the child. Maybe it is what the child *does* with the language he hears that is the critical ingredient. There are two kinds of theories that approach the problem from this end: innateness theories and cognitive theories.

Innateness Theories

At the extreme end of the continuum of internal or child-related explanations of language development are theorists who take a nativist position very similar to the nativist position in perceptual development. Think back to what I said in Chapter 1 about maturation: whenever we see a clear sequence of development that is shared by children in widely differing environments (even in deaf children—a group I have discussed in the box on page 302), it looks very much as if some physiological maturation may lie behind it. Early language development seems to meet both tests (sequences and consistency across cultures), so perhaps it is "built in" in some fashion.

Noam Chomsky (1965, 1975) has been the theorist most strongly associated with this position. He argues that language is not learned—

LANGUAGE IN THE DEAF

Linguists have been interested in the language of deaf children for both practical and theoretical reasons. Can we use any of the information about basic language development to help the deaf child? And can the deaf child help us to understand the process of language development better? In particular, studies of the deaf have been used to address the question of a critical period in language development. Many deaf children do not learn any language during their early years. Does this interfere with their ability to learn language later? Does language *have* to be learned during the first few years for it to be acquired readily?

Let me tackle the practical and theoretical questions by beginning with a summary of what we know at this point about language in the deaf child.

1. The vast majority of deaf children (about 90 percent) are born to *hearing* parents and thus grow up in a world dominated by spoken language.
2. Most deaf children have major deficits in both spoken and written language. They have difficulty speaking; most do not lip-read well; and most read at only the most basic level. Hilde Schlesinger and Katheryn Meadow (1972), for example, found that the teenage deaf children in their study read at about the fourth-grade level.
3. Among the deaf, those with deaf parents usually do as well as or *better* than those with hearing parents on measures of written and spoken language (Liber, 1978).

It is this last fact that is the most surprising and which raises key practical and theoretical questions. Why would children raised by deaf parents have a better prognosis? Schlesinger and Meadow argue that the major reason is that these children are learning a language—in this case, sign language—at the normal time. Deaf parents use sign language with each other and with their children, so the children learn that language. And in their early use of signs, deaf children seem to go through the same stages as those we hear in the spoken language of hearing children. There is a kind of simple two-word grammar of signs, for example, and the inflections are added later, just as with spoken language.

This basic finding provides some support for the existence of a critical period in language development. Children who learn to sign are able to learn spoken and written language later fairly well. But deaf children who are not taught (or not allowed) to use signs when they are young, and thus do not learn a language at the normal time, have more difficulty later.

From the viewpoint of a deaf child's parent, the message seems to be fairly clear: a combination of sign language and spoken language works well for the child and for the relationship between the child and the parent. Not only is the child exposed to a language at the normal time, but the child and parent can communicate with each other—something that is very difficult for the hearing parent who does not sign with a deaf child.

Not everyone who works with the deaf agrees with this conclusion. There are still those who argue for the oral method rather than the "total communication" method I am advocating here, particularly for elementary-school-age children. But I find the evidence in favor of early signing persuasive.

rather, it unfolds or emerges as part of the maturational process. Just as the maturation of physical skills such as walking requires a basic supportive environment, so the maturation of language requires that the child hear language being spoken. The built-in mechanism, which David McNeill (1970) called the **language acquisition device,** is not programmed especially for English or Hindi or Arabic. It is programmed for language in some more general sense—just as a computer program is designed to "read" certain kinds of input and analyze that input in specific ways. The particular language the child hears is passed through this system, and the child acquires the appropriate set of rules for the language she hears and speaks.

A more recent and influential variant of this view has been proposed by Dan Slobin (1973, 1985), who assumes that every child possesses a basic *language-making capacity* made up of a set of fundamental information-processing strategies, which he calls *operating principles.* The essential argument should not be new to you. Just as the newborn infant seems to come programmed with "rules to look by," Slobin argues, infants and children come programmed with "rules to listen by." In support of this contention is all the evidence I described in Chapter 5 (and reviewed earlier in this chapter) showing that very young infants already focus on individual sounds and syllables in the stream of sounds they hear and that they pay attention to sound rhythm. Slobin also proposes that babies are "preprogrammed" to pay attention to the beginnings and endings of strings of sounds, and to stressed sounds. Together, these operating principles would help to explain some of the features of children's early grammars.

More complex operating principles involve the child's keeping track of certain repetitions or regularities in the language she hears. For example, children note the repetition of strings of words (*thank-you-very-much*).German children must note which article (masculine, feminine, or neuter—*der, die,* or *das*) goes with each naming word.

There are some powerful attractions in this approach. It fits with all the evidence emerging from studies of early perceptual skills, and it introduces the child's own activity into the explanatory process. Most important, it can account for the strong similarities in children's early language development both between languages and within any given language. But this great strength of the theory is also its potential weakness. Both Chomsky's and Slobin's approaches *require* that language development be highly similar from one language community to the next. And while there are some striking similarities, researchers studying a wider variety of languages have begun to find some significant variations as well (Bates, et al., 1984; Akiyama, 1984; Maratsos, 1983).

In addition, by describing an essentially automatic or built-in process, Slobin seems to be ignoring the child's own emerging cognitive skills. Other theorists (perhaps most notably Melissa Bowerman) who have come at the problem from the cognitive end agree that the child does indeed *construct* language and may well start with basic operating principles, but they argue that the process is less automatic and is more tied to the broader sweep of cognitive development than Slobin's analysis suggests. In this view, we might think of the child as a "little linguist," applying her emerging cognitive understandings to the problem of language, searching for regularities and patterns.

Cognitive-Processing Explanations

I pointed out earlier that, at least in the early stages, children seem to learn words for categories or relationships they have already constructed through their own actions or play. As Bowerman puts it:

> Children possess powerful cognitive skills that enable them to structure and interpret their experiences on a nonlinguistic basis, that is, to develop notions of agency, spatial location, causality, possession, and so on. When language starts to come in, it does not introduce new meanings to the child. Rather, it is used to express only those meanings the child has already formulated independently of language. (Bowerman, 1985, p. 372)

As further illustration of this link, a number of observers have noted relationships between the patterns of children's play and their language. Symbolic play (like pretending to eat from an empty spoon, which I described in the box on pages 234–235) and imitation of sounds and gestures both appear at about the same time as the child's first words. In children whose language is significantly delayed, both symbolic play and imitation are generally delayed, too (Snyder, 1978; Bates, O'Connell, & Shore, 1987; Ungerer & Sigman, 1984). And about when two-word sentences appear, children also begin to combine several gestures into a sequence in their pretend play, such as pouring imaginary liquid, drinking, then wiping the mouth. Those children who are the first to show this sequencing in their play are also the first to use two- or three-word sentences in their speech (Bates, O'Connell, & Shore, 1987; Shore, 1986).

The child's cognitive process is also more directly involved in analyzing the language that she hears. Children not only use rules in their early language—they seem to *search* for rules. As Flavell puts it, children "act as if they are constantly forming and testing hypotheses about the lawful and systematic properties of their language. They learn by rote when they must, but learn by rule when they can" (1985, p. 256). This is certainly clear in the overregularizations I talked about earlier (*wented* and *goed*, *footses*). Since children seem to show the same rule-searching behavior in areas other than language, it is hard to see how this can be a process unique to language learning. If the child is programmed to look for rules, then the programming covers all of cognitive development and not just language.

The differences between Slobin's operating-principles approach and a more cognitive approach are more a matter of emphasis than of fundamental disagreement. The key assumption is that the child *analyzes* the language he hears and constructs his own language based on that analysis. The disagreement is over whether the process of analysis is governed by built-in rules or principles or whether it results from the child's more general construction of the world around him.

A COMBINED VIEW

Each of the theories I have described has at least some merit; no one of them really does the whole job. Perhaps if we combined them in some way, we could do better. Stan Kuczaj (1982) has offered one such combination that I find helpful.

He argues that language development is influenced by three things. First, there are innate "organizing predispositions," such as perhaps Slobin's organizing principles. A second, critical influence is the *input*, that is, the set of language experiences actually encountered by the child. In the most extreme cases, we know that a child who hears *no* language or only very limited language will not develop in the same way as does a child who encounters a rich array of sounds and sentences. Possibly, such language input has to occur in the early years for it to be effective (a critical-period hypothesis about language first proposed by Lenneberg, 1967). Deaf children offer one test of this hypothesis, as I have explored in the box on page 302. A second group of children linguists have studied for clues about the importance of language input are those who have been severely deprived of human contact in their early years. One of these children, Genie (Curtiss, 1977; Pines, 1981), really only began to learn language when she was 12, and her language has never progressed much beyond the simplest two-word sentences, despite valiant attempts to teach her. Of course, Genie was severly traumatized, too, and probably malnourished as well, so we can't be sure of the causality. But it looks as if some input in the early years of life is a vital ingredient.

Furthermore, the specific form of the input seems to make a difference; some forms are more informative, more helpful to the child than others are, with repetitions, recastings, and expansions high on the list of helpful forms.

Kuczaj argues that the third crucial element in language development is what the child *does* with the input. The child begins with the built-in strategies (rules), receives input (hears people talking), processes that sound according to his initial strategies, and then changes the strategies or rules to fit the new information. The result is a series of rules for understanding and creating language. Undoubtedly, this rule-making process is not unique to language. To some degree, very young children seem to develop broader strategies that are *reflected* in language. The strong similarities we see among children in their early language constructions come about both because all children share the same initial processing rules and because most children are exposed to very similar input from the people around them.

In a sense, all Kuczaj has done is to add pieces of three different theories. This seems to me to be a step in the right direction, but it is still way too simple. If we know anything about development, it is that separate influences rarely just *add.* They nearly always combine and interact in important ways. What we need to understand now are the ways in which the child's rules, her own processing of experience, and the quality of her experience interact to produce language. Linguists and psychologists who have studied language have made progress. We know a lot more now about how *not* to explain language. But we have not yet cracked the code. The fact that children learn complex and varied use of their native tongue within a few years remains both miraculous and largely mysterious.

INDIVIDUAL DIFFERENCES IN LANGUAGE DEVELOPMENT

All along, I have been talking about the fact that there are wide variations in the speed with which children acquire language skill. I have also mentioned in passing that there may be style differences as well. Let me explore both of these forms of individual variation more fully.

Power Differences

Anyone who has been around children knows that there are big differences in the timing of their language development. As just one illustration, look at the differing rates for the three children Roger Brown studied (Eve, Adam, and Sarah, shown in Figure 8.4). The figure shows the **mean length of utterance (MLU),** which is the number of "meaningful units" per sentence for each child. Individual words are meaningful units, but so are the various grammatical markers, such as the *s* for plurals or the *ed* for past tense. So the sentence "Sarah eat" has two meaningful units, while the sentence "I beated him" has four. I have drawn a line at roughly the point in the general rise of the MLU at which the child switches from simple sentences to more complex ones. You can see that Eve made this transition at about 21 months, while Adam and Sarah passed over this point about a year later. The possible explanations of such differences should be familiar by now.

Genetic Explanations. One fairly obvious possibility is that the rate of language development may be something you inherit—in the same way that intelligence may be influenced by heredity. Certainly if we assume that part of language is built into the brain, it makes sense to think that some children may inherit a more efficient built-in system than others.

Twin studies and adoption studies designed to test this possibility

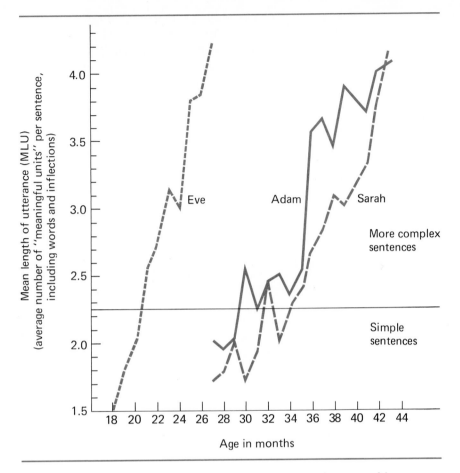

Figure 8.4 Children go through the various steps and stages of language development at markedly different rates, as you can see clearly here. Eve reached the stage of more complex sentences (noted by the horizontal line across the graph) at about 21 months, while Adam and Sarah were much slower. This does *not* mean, by the way, that Eve has a higher IQ or is "brighter" in some way. Within this range of language development, there is essentially no correlation with IQ. (*Source:* R. Brown, 1973, *A First Language,* Cambridge, MA: Harvard University Press, p. 55. Reprinted by permission.)

have yielded the typical mixture of findings. For example, in their extensive study of adopted children, Plomin and DeFries and their colleagues (Hardy-Brown, Plomin, & DeFries, 1981; Plomin & DeFries, 1985b) have found that the children's language skill at age 2 was about equally well predicted by the IQs or language skills of either the natural or the adoptive parents. They also found that among the adoptive families, those parents who talked the most and provided the most toys had children whose language was more advanced. In twin studies, the common finding is that vocabulary size, but *not* grammatical complexity, is more similar in identical than in fraternal twins (e.g., Mather & Black, 1984).

All of this points to the conclusion that there are some aspects of language development, such as speed of learning new words and understanding other people's language, that are strongly related to the child's overall cognitive abilities. Since cognitive abilities have a significant genetic influence, so do these language abilities. Other aspects of language, such as pronunciation and possibly the rate of grammar development, may be equally influenced by variations in the richness of the child's linguistic environment.

Environmental Explanations.   I have already talked about some environmental influences. Parents who talk more and who respond contingently to the child's language seem to have children who develop language sooner. The fact that this same set of relationships is found in families of *adoptive* children is impressive, since we can be fairly sure that what we are seeing here is not just genetic influence in disguise.

Overall, as with IQ, it seems obvious that both the particular genes the child inherits and the environment in which the child grows up contribute to the rate of language development she will show. I should emphasize once again, however, that although children do differ widely in the timing of their language development, virtually all children progress adquately through the sequence of steps I have been describing. Nearly all children learn to communicate reasonably well; most do so with great skill, regardless of their early rate of progress. One moral for parents is that you should not panic if your child is still using fairly primitive sentences at $2\frac{1}{2}$ or even 3. Instead of worrying, you should listen with pleasure to your child's emerging language—to the poetry of it, the wonderfully funny mistakes, the amazingly rapid changes. It is a fascinating process.

Differences in Style of Language

In talking about the child's earliest words, I pointed out that there seem to be two distinct "types" of early vocabulary, which Katherine Nelson originally called referential and expressive styles. Later researchers have found further signs of such a difference in grammar and articulation. I have summarized some of the differences in Table 8.6. Elizabeth Bates and her colleagues (1987) argue that the difference may run fairly deep. Referential-style children are, in some sense, more cognitively oriented children. They are drawn to objects, spend more of their time in solitary play with objects, and interact with other people more often around objects, too. They learn a lot of object names and adjectives very early, and they also seem to understand complex adult language early. There are some hints that such children are more likely to be firstborn or girls, but that is not consistently found.

Expressive-style toddlers, on the other hand, are oriented more toward people, toward social interactions. Their early words and sentences include a lot of "strings" of words that are involved in common interactions with

Table 8.6
▬▬▬▬

Some Differences Between Expressive and Referential Children in Early Language

	Expressive	Referential
Early words	Relatively fewer nouns; more pronouns; personal-social words.	Predominantly nominals (names for things).
Early sentences	Many social routines used in their entirety (e.g., "I want it").	Few social routines.
	Many rote strings (formulas) inserted into sentences (e.g., "What do you want?").	Few rote strings; more novel combinations.
	May contain inflections.	Rarely contain inflections.
Later words	Few adjectives; slower vocabulary growth.	Many adjectives; focus on object labeling or description.
Articulation	Less-clear speech.	Clearer speech.

Source: After Nelson, 1981; Bates, O'Connell, & Shore, 1987.

adults, which often makes such children's early language sound more advanced than that of a referential child. There are some hints that such children are generally more social.

Just how these differences come about is still being hotly debated. It could be that such children are simply matching the quality of the language they are hearing; it could be that such differences reflect underlying temperamental variations or differences in cognitive style. Whatever the source, the existence of such large differences in the form or style of early language raises questions about the assumption that the early stages of language development are the same for all children. Instead, what we find is that children may go about learning language in rather different ways.

AN APPLICATION OF THE BASIC KNOWLEDGE: LEARNING TO READ

In Chapter 5, I talked briefly about some of the *perceptual* aspects of learning to read. It seems useful to say a further word here about some of the *linguistic* aspects.

The Basic Steps in Learning to Read

Research by Eleanor Gibson and Harry Levin (1975), among others, suggests that children go through three basic steps in learning to read. We can see

Figure 8.5 When children are first learning to read, they often "read" words that would make sense in the sentence but have no connection to the letters on the page. In this way the child is using her knowledge about the structure of language to help make guesses in reading.

these steps most clearly by watching what children do when they try to read and come upon a word they don't know. The first (earliest) strategy seems to be to try to make the written sentence make oral sense. Children using this strategy substitute words that may be totally unlike the one on the page but that make sensible, meaningful sentences. Children at this stage aren't really reading all of what is on the page.

In the next step, however, the child has figured out that what she reads out loud has to have *some* connection to the letters on the page. At this stage, when she comes to a word she doesn't know, she is likely to stop short. She may stop reading or just leave out that word. Finally, in the last step, instead of staying silent, the child will begin to try to decode the word—to figure out what it must be on the basis of the letters in it. Thus, the kind of mistakes the child makes will depend on what she's paying attention to, whether it is the sense of the sentence, the letters on the page, or both.

The Effect of Language Skill on the Steps of Reading

Recent research suggests that this learning process goes much faster and more smoothly in children whose *awareness* of the form and structure of language (sometimes called *metalinguistic knowledge*) is high. Children who are more aware of what words or what grammatical class of words can go in specific places in sentences are at an advantage not only in the first step of reading but also at later stages. If you come to a word you don't know, it is a great help to have some idea of the *type* of word that could go there, or even some good guesses about which specific words might be likely. Then it is possible to accept or reject those guesses on the basis of the actual letters on the page. In one recent study, for example, Dale Willows and Ellen Ryan (1986) found that children with higher levels of "grammatical sensitivity" were consistently better readers in first, second, and third grade. This is not just a matter of knowing lots of words—although that helps, too. It is more a matter of being aware of or knowing the ways in which sentences are put together.

When the child gets to the point of decoding individual words, another form of language awareness also seems to be critical—namely, awareness of the fact that words are made up of individual sounds. Suppose you say to a child, as Maclean, Bryant, and Bradley (1987) did, "Tell a word which starts the same as *tap*." To do this, the child has to understand that the word has a starting sound (*t*) plus other sounds and then must be able to match the starting sound. You can get at this same skill in other ways, too, such as by asking children to recognize or produce rhyming words or to say the first sound in a syllable. There is now abundant evidence that children who are more skilled at such tasks at age 3 or 4 or 5 later learn to read much more easily (Maclean, Bryant, & Bradley, 1987; Vellutino & Scanlon, 1987). Overall, then, the child's knowledge of language—of grammar, meaning, and sound—has a profound effect on early reading. And as I'll discuss in Chapter 14, the lack of such skills may be a major reason for significant reading disabilities.

▬▬▬ SUMMARY

1. From the earliest use of two-word sentences, children's language is complex, creative, and rule-governed.

2. Language can be defined as an arbitrary system of symbols that permits us to express and to understand an infinite variety of messages.

3. Many of the developments during the prelinguistic phase (before the first word) are significant precursors to language. The child discriminates language sounds, begins to make babbling sounds, and uses gestures in communicative ways.

4. At about 1 year of age, the earliest words appear. The child begins to use sounds with consistent referents. Some of these early words are combined with gestures to convey whole sentences of meaning.

5. By 16 to 20 months, most children have a vocabulary of 50 or more words; by age 2, the vocabulary may include 300 words. The first two-word sentences normally appear between 18 and 24 months.

6. The earliest sentences are short and grammatically simple: they lack

the various grammatical inflections. Many different meanings, such as location, possession, or agent-object relationships, can nonetheless be conveyed by the child.

7. Within a year or so of beginning to speak, the child starts to add the many grammatical inflections—the auxiliary verbs, prepositions, superlatives, past tenses, and so on. In English, these additional grammatical elements are added in a particular order. Other languages also have order, but a different sequence from that of English.

8. In later years, children slowly add other elements, such as passive forms and tag questions, and they correct earlier "errors."

9. The development of word meanings (semantic development) follows a less-predictable course. Children appear to have concepts or categories before they have words for them. When children begin to use words, they also "overextend" their usage.

10. Children's early word meanings seem to be based both on what they can do with objects (function) and on the perceptual properties of the objects (form). There are also hints that children form "prototypes" as the central meaning of words, just as adults do.

11. Children appear to have two uses for language: to communicate and to direct their own activity. Communication is the dominant use, and children become increasingly skillful in adapting their language to the needs of the listener.

12. Several theories have been offered to explain language development. Two early environmental explanations, based on imitation or reinforcement, have been largely set aside. More recently, emphasis has been placed on the helpful quality of the simpler form of parent-to-child language called motherese and on the role of expansions and recastings of children's sentences.

13. Other contending theories today focus more on the role of the child, either positing a set of built-in "operating principles" or emphasizing the child as a little linguist who analyzes the regularities of language.

14. Combining many of these elements, we may see language development to be a joint result of the built-in organizing principles, the nature or quality of the input, and the child's processing of that input.

15. Children differ in the rates at which they develop both vocabulary and grammar. There is some support for a genetic explanation of such differences, but environmental explanations also seem valid.

16. Despite these variations in rate of early development, most children learn to speak skillfully by about age 5 or 6.

17. In the early years of language development, two styles of language can be distinguished: referential (focusing on objects and their description) and expressive (focusing on words and forms that describe or further social relationships).

18. Research on language can also help us to understand the development of reading skill. Some metalinguistic awareness of the grammar, semantics, and segmented sounds of language seems to be critical for reading.

▬▬▬ KEY TERMS

babbling The often-repetitive vocalizing of consonant-vowel combinations by an infant, typically beginning at about 6 months of age.

cooing An early stage during the prelinguistic period, from about 1 to 4 months of age, when the infant repeats vowel sounds, particularly the *uuu* sound.

expressive language The child's ability to communicate in words.

expressive style One of two styles of early language proposed by Katherine Nelson. Expressive style is characterized by low use of nounlike terms and high use of personal-social words and phrases.

holophrases The expression of a whole idea by a combination of word and gesture. Characteristic of the child's language from about 12 to 18 months.

inflections The grammatical markers, such as plurals, possessives, and past tenses.

language acquisition device A hypothesized brain structure that may be "programmed" to make language learning possible.

mean length of utterance (MLU) The average number of meaningful units in a sentence. Each basic word is one meaningful unit, as is each inflection, such as the *s* for a plural or the *ed* for a past tense.

motherese The particular pattern of speech by adults to young children. The sentences are shorter, simpler, more repetitive, and higher-pitched.

overregularization The tendency on the part of children to make the language regular, such as by using past tenses like *beated* or *goed.*

pragmatics The rules for the use of language in communicative interaction—rules for taking turns, the style of speech appropriate for different listeners, and the equivalent.

prelinguistic phase The period before the child speaks her first word.

receptive language The child's ability to understand (receive) language, as contrasted to his ability to express language.

referential style One of two styles of early language proposed by Katherine Nelson. Referential style is characterized by emphasis on objects and their naming and description.

semantics The rules for conveying meaning in language.

syntax The rules for forming sentences; also called grammar.

telegraphic speech A characteristic of children's early sentences, in which everything but the crucial words is omitted, as if for a telegram.

▬▬▬ SUGGESTED READING

Anisfeld, M. (1984). *Language development from birth to three.* Hillsdale, NJ: Erlbaum.
An introductory text covering both language and cognition in the early years. Much more detailed than I have had space for in this chapter, and reasonably up to date. A good place to go next if you are interested in this area.

Berk, L. E. (1986, May). Private speech: Learning out loud. *Psychology Today,* pp. 34–39, 42.
A discussion of some recent work on the ways in which children use language to help themselves when they are doing hard tasks.

Brown, R. (1973). Development of the first language in the human species. *American Psychologist, 28,* 97–106.
This is now out of date, but I recommend it primarily because Roger Brown is one of the clearest writers around, and he is one of the major figures in the early research on grammar development.

Hakuta, K. (1986). *Mirror of language: The debate on bilingualism.* New York: Basic Books.
An elegant and readable discussion of many of the issues of bilingualism described in the box on pages 290–291.

Pines, M. (1981, September). The civilizing of Genie. *Psychology Today,* pp. 28–34.
Genie was a girl raised under conditions of extreme deprivation. She had almost no language when she was found at the age of 12. Maya Pines describes the attempts by linguists to teach Genie language—attempts that raised important theoretical and practical issues about language development.

Schachter, F. F., & Strage, A. A. (1982). Adults'

talk and children's language development. In
S. G. Moore & C. R. Cooper (Eds.), *The young
child. Reviews of research* (Vol. 3). Washington, D.C.: National Association for the Education of Young Children.
This whole book is full of really good chapters
on current issues about children, all intended
for students or educated laymen. Schachter

and Strage's chapter discusses what we know
about motherese.
Terrace, H. S. (1979, November). How Nim
Chimpsky changed my mind. *Psychology Today*, pp. 65–76.
This paper sparked a renewed controversy
about whether chimps really create complex
sentences or not. Very interesting reading.

PROJECT: BEGINNING TWO-WORD SENTENCES

Some of you have been around young children a lot and already have some
sense for the delightful quality of their early language. But you'll get a much
better "feel" for it if you do some listening. I would particularly like you to
locate a child who is still in the earliest stages of sentence formation or just
beginning to add a few inflections. This is most likely to be a child of 20 to
24 months, but a child between 24 and 30 months may do fine, too. The
one essential ingredient is that the child be speaking at least some two-word
sentences. If you are unsure, ask the parents; they can nearly always tell
you whether the child has reached this stage or not.

Arrange to spend enough time with the child at his or her home, in a
day-care center, or in any other convenient setting so that you can collect a
list of 50 different *spontaneous* utterances, including both one-word utterances
and two- or more-word sentences. (By *spontaneous* I mean those that the
child speaks without prompting; try to avoid getting into the situation in which
the mother or some other adult actively tries to elicit language from the child,
although it is certainly okay to collect a sample from a time when the child
is playing with an adult or doing some activity with a parent or older sibling.
The most fruitful time is likely to be when the child is playing with someone,
and it is okay to ask the mother to play with the child—but it's not okay to
play the sort of game in which the object is to get the child to talk.) Write
down the child's sentences in order, and stop when you have 50. Whenever
you can, make notes about the context in which each sentence occurred so
that you can judge the meaning more fully.

When you have your list of 50 utterances, take a crack at describing
the child's language in any terms used in this chapter. For example, is the
child using any grammatical inflections? Which ones? Does the pattern conform
to what I have described? What about questions or negatives? And what
about the different meanings expressed? How long is the child's average sentence? Here are some specific rules to follow in calculating the mean length
of utterance:

1. Do not count sounds like *uh, um,* or *oh,* but do count *no, yeah,* and *hi.*
2. Count as one word any compound words, such as *birthday, choo-choo,
   night-night,* or *pocketbook.*
3. Count as one word any irregular past tenses, such as *got, did, want,* and

saw. But count as two any regular past tense, such as *played,* or any erroneous extension of the past tense, such as *wented.*

4. Count as one all diminutives, such as *doggie* or *mommy.*
5. Count as one all combinations like *gonna, wanna,* or *hafta.*
6. Count as one each auxiliary, such as *is, have, will can,* and *must,* and count as one each inflection, such as the *s* for a plural or a possessive, the *s* for the third person singular verb form, and the *ing* on a verb.

Compare the MLU you obtain with those shown for Adam, Eve, and Sarah in Figure 8.4.

   If you are completing this project for a class assignment, turn in your record of the child's sentences along with a page or two of comment.

PROJECT: CONVERSATION BETWEEN PARENT AND CHILD

This time I would like you to focus on the social environment—what is said *to* the child as well as the child's response. Again find a child in the second year of life—though it's okay to go up to about $3\frac{1}{2}$. (It can be the same child you listened to in the last project, but you should collect the two sets of observations separately.)

   Arrange to spend some time with the child while a parent is around. If you are working in a nursery school or day-care center or have access to such a setting, it is all right to study a child and a teacher. But you'll have to get a teacher alone with the child for a period of time. As with the last project, the interaction should be as spontaneous as possible. It is okay if the adult and child play together, but it should not be a "repeat after me" game or a naming game.

   Record the conversation between the parent or teacher and the child, making sure that you have the sentences of the two people in the right order. Continue to record the conversation until you have at least 25 sentences for each. You may use a tape recorder if you wish, but you'll find it helpful to write down the sentences as they occur as well.

   When you have collected the sentences, see if you can detect any signs of motherese in the adult's language. Did the adult adapt her or his language to that of the child? Did she or he repeat the child's utterances with minor modifications? Was there any obvious reinforcement or shaping going on? Did the adult attempt to correct the child's speech, and if so, what was the effect?

   If you are completing this project for a class assignment, turn in your record of the conversation along with a page or two of analysis and comment.

THE SOCIAL CHILD

9 Personality Development: Alternative Views

What Do We Mean by Personality?
The Major Alternative Views of Personality
A Biological Approach: Temperament
   The Evidence
Temperament and Behavior Problems
   Strengths, Weaknesses, and Implications of Biological Theories
Learning Approaches to Personality
   Radical Behaviorists and Personality
   Social-Learning Theorists and Personality
   Strengths, Weaknesses, and Implications of Learning Theories
Psychoanalytic Theories
Freud's Theory
   The Psychosexual Stages
Erikson's Theory
   The Psychosocial Stages
   Some Evidence on Psychoanalytic Theory
Being Raised Without a Father: The Effects of Divorce
   Strengths, Weaknesses, and Implications of Psychoanalytic Theories
A Tentative Synthesis
Summary
Key Terms
Suggested Reading

If you could be a fly on the wall of a kindergarten classroom on the first day of school, you would be treated to a wonderful example of the differences in children's ways of coping with stress and novelty. Probably at least one child would cling to his mother, perhaps weeping and begging her not to leave him alone. Another child would say goodbye to Mom, walk right into the room without a backward look, and begin talking to other children immediately. You might see another child standing quietly in the back of the room and still another child busily exploring the whole room right away, looking at the blocks and storybooks, trying out several different chairs and desks for size.

If you came back to the same classroom six months later, when the situation was no longer scary and new, some of these differences would be less obvious, but the children's styles of approaching their world and the nature of their relationships with other people are likely to be recognizable. The shy child who waited at the back of the room is likely to have one or two pals in the class but not to be the center of the crowd. The child who could hardly bear to let Mom leave may be sitting right up near the teacher; the gregarious, talkative child is probably the one who decides what game they will all play at recess.

All these different patterns of behavior are facets of what we call personality.

WHAT DO WE MEAN BY PERSONALITY?

The term *personality* is one of the slipperiest in all of psychology—maybe even worse than the term *intelligence*. In fact, the two terms have a good deal in common. Both are concepts designed to help us describe or explain *enduring individual differences* in behavior. The concept of intelligence was invented to describe enduring individual differences in intellectual ability or competence. **Personality** describes a broader range of individual characteristics, mostly having to do with the typical ways each of us interacts with the people and the world around us. Whether we are gregarious or shy, whether we plunge into new things or hold back, whether we are independent or dependent, whether we are confident or uncertain—all these characteristics (and many more) are usually thought of as elements of personality.

Underlying the concept of personality is the assumption that these tend to be *persisting* aspects of the individual—that a shy child is likely to become a shy adult or that a confident 5-year-old will still have some element of confidence 40 years later. Obviously, this assumption matches our own experience with ourselves as well as with the people we know. We see in other people a *coherence,* to use Alan Sroufe's term (1979), and a continuity of behavior patterns. We sense the same coherence and continuity in our own behavior as we age. I am not the same as I was at age 5 or 10, but there are ways in which my behavior, my attitudes, my beliefs about myself, my style of responding are similar.

Figure 9.1   By kindergarten age (if not considerably sooner), children already have highly recognizable and individual patterns of interacting with one another and with the world around them. Where do these differences in "personality" come from?

Unlike the concept of intelligence, however, the concept of personality is not reduced to numbers like an IQ score. Children do not have an *amount* of personality; they have a *kind* or *type* of personality, a style or pattern. The dimension of personality that is most analogous to intellectual power is *healthiness*. Some children seem to have developed patterns of interacting with the people and world around them that are adaptive, positive, and supportive of the child's own needs. Other children behave in ways that irritate others or that interfere with loving or supportive contacts with other people. As was true for the study of intelligence, which was originally spurred by an interest in children who did *not* function well in school, a great deal of the interest in personality development in children arose from a desire to understand how some children came to have "unhealthy" or "nonadaptive" patterns of interaction with others.

One of my tasks in the next few chapters is to examine what we know about the origins of those unique and consistent patterns of individual behavior that we call personality. What have various theorists said about how those differences might come about?

But it is a mistake to cast all the discussion of children's relationships with others in the language of individual differences. As with cognitive development, it is also important to look at *shared* developmental patterns— at changes in the "structure" of the child's relationships. For example, you can probably think of some adult you know who is highly dependent on others. We'd call that an aspect of his or her personality. But *all* of us were clinging and dependent when we were infants and toddlers. So there seem to be both individual *enduring characteristics* and some *developmental patterns* shared by all children.

It is not always possible to disentangle the individual and developmental approaches when we talk about personality and social development (just as questions of "power" and "structure" get tangled in descriptions of cognitive development). But let me begin this chapter by discussing the origins of individual differences in personality. How do children come to have distinctive and enduring patterns of interacting with the world and the people in it? Do they inherit these patterns? Are they "taught" their different styles of interacting? Do the patterns result from the child's interactions with the significant people in her life?

Unfortunately, there is no agreed-on basic description of personality differences in children. Instead, what we have are several distinctive theories of personality development, each of which casts the question differently and each of which has led to quite separate bodies of research. In this case it makes sense to talk about the theories first, so that you can get some sense of the range of questions that fall under the general label of "personality." Then, with the theoretical alternatives as background, I can explore what we know about the basic *developmental* patterns in children's self-concepts and social relationships in Chapters 10 and 11.

THE MAJOR ALTERNATIVE VIEWS OF PERSONALITY

Three kinds of descriptions or explanations of individual differences in personality have existed side by side for some time: (1) biological explanations, based primarily on the assumption that differences are inherited; (2) learning explanations, based either on fairly strict application of the principles of classical and instrumental conditioning I discussed in Chapter 1 or on broader principles of social learning; and (3) psychoanalytic explanations, based on the assumption that personality arises from an interaction between inborn impulses and the response of the parents to the child.

A BIOLOGICAL APPROACH: TEMPERAMENT

The concept of temperament has become one of the "hottest" concepts in developmental psychology in recent years, and it certainly represents the dominant biological approach to personality today (e.g., Plomin & Dunn,

1986). I have talked about this concept in Chapters 1 and 3, so it is not new to you. As it is currently used, the term *temperament* refers to one facet of personality—the individual's "emotional reactivity or behavioral style in interacting with the environment" (Carey, 1981). The term thus describes *how* the child reacts rather than what he can do or why.

Theories of temperament differ in some important respects, but there are common themes or assumptions, which I can state as a series of propositions—a pattern I will follow with each of the three theoretical approaches. I can identify three such assumptions in the biological approach.

Proposition 1: Each individual is born with characteristic patterns of responding to the environment and to other people. Alexander Thomas and Stella Chess have emphasized such qualities as activity rate, rhythmicity, adaptability to new experiences, intensity of response, general mood, and persistence as being basic properties of temperament in infants and young children. Combinations of these properties create the several distinctive temperaments—easy, difficult, and slow to warm up—that I described in Chapter 3.

An alternative formulation of basic temperament, which I mentioned briefly in Chapter 1, has been offered by Arnold Buss and Robert Plomin (1984, 1986), who propose the three main dimensions of temperament listed in Table 9.1. Obviously, there is not yet agreement on just what aspects of behavior we should label with the term *temperament*. There is agreement among temperament theorists, though, on the assumption that these temperament qualities are present at birth and are inherited.

Proposition 2: Temperamental characteristics persist through childhood and into adulthood. No theorist is proposing that temperamental characteristics remain unchanged by experience. The individual's

Table 9.1
▬▬▬▬▬

Three Dimensions of Temperament Proposed by Buss and Plomin

- **Emotionality.** The tendency to become upset or distressed easily and intensely; high levels of arousal. Highly emotional children are hard to soothe.
- **Activity.** The amount of any behavior a person shows—amount of movement, speed of talking, amount of energy put into activities, restlessness.
- **Sociability.** The seeking of and being especially gratified by rewards from social interaction. Preferring to be with others; sharing activities; responsiveness to others, seeking responsiveness *from* others.

Source: Buss & Plomin, 1984.

eventual pattern of behavior (phenotype) is a product of both the original genetic blueprint (genotype) and the subsequent experience. Temperament thus does not inevitably determine personality. Rather, it creates a kind of bias in the system toward particular patterns. Given such a bias, there should be at least *some* stability of temperament over time.

Proposition 3: Temperamental characteristics affect the way any individual responds to people and things and, conversely, affect the way others respond to him. Highly sociable children seek out contact with others; children low on the activity dimension are more likely to choose sedentary activities like puzzles or board games than baseball. At the same time, the sociable child, who may smile more than the detached child, elicits different responses from others. Her parents may smile, pick her up, and talk to her more, simply because she has reinforced their behavior by her positive temperament. The temperamentally difficult child may elicit higher rates of criticism or punishment or receive less praise.

Thomas and Chess and their colleagues have taken this proposition a step further by proposing that the impact of a child's temperament on her development and on her eventual personality will depend on the *goodness of fit* between the child's particular qualities and the demands of the environment. That is, regardless of the specific temperamental characteristics a child may have, that child will develop as a healthy, well-functioning individual if her temperament matches (fits with) the demands of the environment, including the parents' expectations.

The Evidence

All three of these propositions have been at least partially supported by the findings of recent research.

Inheritance of Temperament. The strongest evidence for the genetic basis of temperament is that identical twins are quite a lot more alike in their temperament than are fraternal twins. You can see one particularly clear set of results in Table 9.2, which is based on the work of Buss and Plomin (1984). In these studies, correlations between temperament ratings of identical twins are consistently high, while correlations between temperament scores of fraternal twins are essentially zero. On the other hand, correlation between the temperament scores of adopted children and their birth parents are not a whole lot higher than correlations with adoptive parents' temperament (Scarr & Kidd, 1983), a finding which weakens the genetic argument. Still, the evidence points to at least some genetic component in our usual measures of temperament.

Consistency of Temperament over Time. The accumulating findings on the consistency of temperament over age are beginning to look a lot like the findings on IQ consistency. There is some short-term consistency in infancy. In particular, difficultness, sociability, and activity level all seem to be at least moderately stable during the first year of life. Cranky newborns

Table 9.2

Similarity of Identical and Fraternal Twins on Temperament Dimensions

	Twin correlations	
Temperament scale	Identical	Fraternal
Emotionality	.63	.12
Activity	.62	−.23
Sociability	.53	−.03

Source: After Buss & Plomin, 1984, Table 9.2, p. 122.

tend to be cranky at 9 or 12 months; babies who smile more are friendlier as toddlers (e.g., Rothbart, 1986). Similarly, among children 2 or 3 or older, and even between childhood and adulthood, there is a reasonable amount of consistency, as I listed in Table 3.5. Further evidence from the New York Longitudinal Study (the sample originally selected by Thomas and Chess) shows that in the elementary-school years, correlations between temperament scores obtained four years apart averaged about .42 (Hegvik, McDevitt, & Carey, 1981), while the correlation between a rating made in early adolescence and another in early adulthood was a robust .62 (Korn, 1984).

But like the pattern in IQ scores, there is little consistency between measures of *infant* temperament and measures in the preschool years or later. It could be that quite different aspects of behavior are being measured in infancy and in later years. Emotionality ratings in infancy, for example, are heavily influenced by how much a baby cries. In older children and adults, crying is not so much a part of the rating. It is also possible, of course, that whatever inborn temperamental differences we see in infancy are shaped and changed by the parents' (and others') responses to the child. The consistency we see later, then, results both from whatever inborn differences there may be and from the consistency of the environment.

Temperament/Environment Interactions. The simplest thing I can say about the research on temperament/environment interactions is that the findings are complex. Buss and Plomin (1984) have proposed that in general, children in the middle range on temperament dimensions typically adapt *to* their environment, while those children whose temperament is extreme—like very difficult children—force their environment to adapt to them. So, for example, temperamentally difficult children are punished more (Rutter, 1978b) than are more adaptable children (a pattern that may help to contribute to the higher rates of significant emotional problems in such children, which I have explored in the box on page 326). But

TEMPERAMENT AND BEHAVIOR PROBLEMS

One consistent research finding is that children with difficult temperaments—who are on the extreme ends of the distribution of temperament scores—are much more likely to show various kinds of emotional disturbances or *behavior problems*. Included in the category of behavior problems (which I'll be talking about in more detail in Chapter 14, when I discuss abnormal development) are such patterns as overaggressiveness, anxiety, depression, and hyperactivity.

The typical finding is that children who are rated as having aspects of difficult temperament—nonadaptive, irregular rhythm or pattern; withdrawal; high intensity; or negativity of mood—are perhaps twice as likely to show one or another of these behavior problems as are children with less-difficult temperaments (e.g., Korn, 1984; Chess & Thomas, 1984; Guerin, DiBello, & Nordquist, 1987). Chess and Thomas have even found that ratings of temperament of children when they were 3 years old were predictive of poor or good adjustment in adulthood.

Such findings may sound like a simple restatement of consistency of temperament. Hyperactivity or aggressiveness or other behavior problems in 5- or 7-year-olds may be further manifestations of the basic temperament. But it is not so simple. The majority of children who are rated as showing difficult temperament in infancy or the preschool years do *not* develop behavior problems at later ages. They are *more likely* to exhibit such problems, but the relationship is not at all inevitable.

As usual, there is a complex interactive process at work. The key seems to be whether the infant's or child's "difficultness" is acceptable to the parents or can be managed by the family in some effective way. So, for example, a child with a difficult temperament who is less liked by his mother is far more likely to develop behavior problems than is a child with a difficult temperament whose mother likes him more. Difficult temperament also seems to increase the risk of behavior problems if there are any other stresses in the family system (such as divorce) or other deficits in the child. For instance, the great majority of retarded children with difficult temperaments also show behavior problems (Chess & Korn, 1980). Difficult temperament does not *cause* later behavior problems; rather, it creates a *vulnerability* in the child. Such children seem to be less able to deal with major life stresses. But in a supportive, accepting, low-stress environment, many such youngsters move through childhood without displaying any significant behavior problems.

The lesson for parents is not always an easy one to carry out. If you are under severe stress, that is precisely the moment when it is hard to provide a maximally supportive, accepting environment for your child. But if you have a child with a more difficult temperament, it may help to keep in mind that at points of life change for the child, such as when you move or when the child starts a new school, this particular child is going to need more attention, more help, more support than will a temperamentally less volatile child.

even this statement is too simple. The parents' own child-rearing skills, the stress they experience, and the amount of social or emotional support they have all affect their ability to deal with an irritable or difficult child (Crockenberg, 1986). Mavis Hetherington (1987), for example, reports that children with difficult temperaments show more problem behavior in response to divorce if the mother is *also* depressed and has inadequate social support. Those difficult children whose divorcing mothers were not depressed did not show heightened levels of problems. Thus, the child's temperament clearly seems to have an impact, but the effect is not simple or straightforward.

Strengths, Weaknesses, and Implications of Biological Theories

There are two great strengths in this approach to the origins of personality. The first is that it forces us to consider the role of heredity—an important theoretical antidote to the dominance of environmental explanations over the past decades.

The second strength is the emphasis in this theory on the interactions (or transactions) between the child's temperament and the responses of the people around her. This is not a purely biological approach; it is an interactionist approach, very much in keeping with much of the current theorizing about development.

On the other side of the ledger, I see three weaknesses. First, neither a common definition nor a common method of measuring temperament have been agreed on by researchers in this area. So the concept is still fuzzy. Second, we just don't have enough information yet, particularly about the impact of children's temperament on the responses of the parents. The "goodness of fit" model proposed by Thomas and Chess is appealing, but it is probably too simple. And third, there is a sort of "bandwagon" effect in the latest work on temperament. The idea of inherited temperamental differences has become the latest favored explanation for virtually everything infants do or do not do. Temperamental differences do seem to exist, but they do not explain everything.

LEARNING APPROACHES TO PERSONALITY

The emphasis shifts rather dramatically when we look at learning approaches. Instead of looking at what the child brings to the equation, learning theorists have looked primarily at the reinforcement patterns in the environment as the primary cause of differences in children's patterns of behaviors. Albert Bandura, one of the major figures in this theoretical tradition, puts the basic proposition flatly:

> Except for elementary reflexes, people are not equipped with inborn repertoires of behavior. They must learn them. (Bandura, 1977, p. 16)

Bandura is not rejecting biology. He goes on to say that biological factors like hormones or inherited propensities (such as temperament, presumably) can affect behavior. But he and others following this approach clearly come down hard on the side of the environment as the major "cause" of the behavior we observe.

These are not new ideas for you. You have already read about the basic concepts in Chapter 1. The question here is how to apply learning theory specifically to such "personality" characteristics as dependency, nurturance, aggressiveness, activity level, or gregariousness.

In this case, it is not so simple to provide a set of agreed-upon basic propositions. As you will remember from Chapter 1, there are two distinct schools of thought within the learning camp: the radical behaviorists and the much more numerous social-learning theorists. Since the two groups make some different assumptions about personality and its origins, let me subdivide.

Radical Behaviorists and Personality

Two basic propositions underlie the application of strict learning principles to personality development.

Proposition 1: Behavior is strengthened by reinforcement. If this rule applies to all behavior, then it should apply to attachment, shyness, sharing, and competitiveness, too. Children who are reinforced for clinging to their parents, for example, should cling more than children who are not reinforced for it. Similarly, a nursery-school teacher who pays attention to children only when they get rowdy or aggressive should find that the children get steadily more rowdy and aggressive over the course of weeks or months.

Proposition 2: Behavior that is reinforced on a "partial schedule" should be even stronger and more resistant to extinction than behavior that is consistently reinforced. I talked about this phenomenon in Chapter 1 and have already given you some examples of the application of the principles of partial reinforcement (see the box on page 18). Parents are nearly always inconsistent in their rewards to their children, so most children are on partial schedules of some kind. Given the strong persistence of behavior rewarded in this way, we should look for what is being reinforced by the parents on a partial schedule if we want to understand how children develop those distinctive and stable patterns of behavior that we call personality.

Some Evidence and Applications. An *immense* collection of studies supports these basic propositions. For example, when experimenters have systematically rewarded some children for hitting an inflated rubber clown on the nose and then watched the children in a play situation, the children who were rewarded hit, scratched, and kicked more than did children who hadn't been rewarded for punching the clown (Walters & Brown, 1963). And partial reinforcement in the form of inconsistent behavior from parents also has the expected effect. For example, Sears, Maccoby, and Levin (1957/ 1977) found that parents who usually allow their children to be quite aggressive (who are thus *permissive* toward it) but occasionally react by punishing quite severely have more aggressive children than do parents who are nonpermissive and nonpunitive.

Both of these principles have been used successfully in therapeutic interventions with families of out-of-control children, such as those who throw frequent tantrums or are overly aggressive or belligerently defiant. Gerald Patterson's work is a particularly lovely example (1975, 1980, 1986) of such **behavior therapy.** He has spent years trying to understand the origins of such aversive patterns of behavior in children, analyzing in detail the reinforcement patterns that occur in the families. For example, imagine a child playing in his very messy room. His mother comes and tells the child to clean up the room. The child whines or yells at her that he doesn't want to do it or won't do it. The mother gives in and leaves the room, and the child stops whining or shouting.

Patterson analyzes this exchange as a pair of negatively reinforced events. The mother's giving in is negatively reinforced by the ending of the child's whining or yelling. This makes it more likely that she will give in the next time. She has *learned* to back down in order to get the child to shut up. The child has been negatively reinforced for yelling or whining, since the unpleasant event for him (being told to clean his room) stopped as soon as he whined. So he has learned to whine or yell. Imagine such exchanges occurring over and over, and you begin to understand how a family can create a *system* in which an imperious, demanding, noncompliant child rules the roost.

Patterson's thinking has moved beyond the simple propositions I have outlined here. Like the current temperament theorists, he emphasizes that what happens in a given family for a particular child is a joint product of the child's own temperament or response tendencies, the parents' discipline skills, the parents' personalities, and the social context of the parents' lives. A mother who has other sources of positive reinforcement—from her husband or her work or from friends—may respond quite differently to the coercive child than a mother who has fewer resources. But Patterson is still assuming that basic learning principles can both describe and explain the ways in which the child's behavior patterns (her personality) are formed or changed.

Social-Learning Theorists and Personality

Social-learning theorists like Bandura do not reject either of the propositions I have just listed. But they add two more that fundamentally change the nature of the theory.

Proposition 3: Children learn new behaviors largely through modeling.   Bandura has argued that the full range of social behaviors, from competitiveness to nurturance, is learned through **modeling**—by watching others perform those actions. Thus, the child who sees her parents making a donation to the local Cancer Society volunteer or taking a casserole next door to the woman who has just been widowed will learn generosity and thoughtful behavior. The child who sees her parents hitting each other when they are angry will most likely learn violent ways of solving problems.

Children learn from TV, too, and from their playmates, their teachers, and their brothers and sisters. A boy growing up in an environment where he observes playmates and older boys hanging around street corners, shoplifting, or stealing hubcaps is going to learn all those behaviors. His continuous exposure to such antisocial models makes it that much harder for his parents to reinforce more constructive behavior.

As I mentioned in Chapter 1, Bandura has taken the concept of modeling a large step further in his most recent thinking, pointing out that what an individual learns from watching someone else will depend on what she pays attention to and what she is able to remember (both *cognitive* processes), on what she is physically able to copy, and on what she is motivated to imitate. Although Bandura has not placed much emphasis himself on the potential developmental ramifications of these ideas, it seems clear that all these factors are likely to change with age. Thus, what a child models will change with age as well.

Proposition 4: What children learn from reinforcement and from modeling is not just overt behavior but also ideas, expectations, internal standards, and self-concepts.   The child learns standards for her own behavior and expectancies about what she can and cannot do (which Bandura calls *self-efficacy*) from specific reinforcements and from modeling. Once those standards and those expectancies or beliefs are established, they affect the child's behavior in consistent and enduring ways. It is these beliefs and expectancies that form the core of what may be called personality and that are reflected in behavior.

Some Evidence and Applications.   The impact of observational learning has been demonstrated in literally hundreds of studies (e.g., Bandura, 1973, 1977). One interesting—and very practical—sidelight to the process of modeling has been the repeated finding that when there is a conflict between what a model does and what he or she says, it is the *behavior* that is likely to be imitated. In one study, Joan Grusec and her co-workers (1978) found that telling children to be generous did little good, but showing them generosity led them to be generous. So the old adage "Do what I say and not what I do" doesn't seem to work.

In his explorations of the concept of self-efficacy, Bandura has also shown that changing someone's belief about her ability to do something has a greater impact on her behavior than merely reinforcing her for perform-

Figure 9.2 These children clearly show aggressive behavior and postures learned through observation, probably from television. The fact that a "victim" is not actually killed does not mean that the children have not learned the full set of responses.

ing that behavior (Bandura, 1982). He has been able to use this principle in therapeutic situations—for example, in working with people with phobias, like fear of snakes.

Strengths, Weaknesses, and Implications of Learning Theories

Several implications of this theoretical approach are worth emphasizing. First of all, unlike temperament theorists, who expect at least a certain amount of consistency of behavior in different situations, learning theorists can handle either consistency or inconsistency in children's behavior. If a child is friendly and smiling both at home and at school, this can be explained by saying that the child is being reinforced for that behavior in both settings or that the child has learned that such behavior is successful, not by assuming that the child has a gregarious temperament. But it is equally possible to explain how a child can be the soul of helpfulness at school but refuse to mind his mother at home or do whatever his father asks but disobey his mother. In cases like this, learning theorists merely go searching for the differing patterns of reinforcement in the different settings or for the different expectancies the child may have acquired.

A related implication is that this view of behavior is a very hopeful

Figure 9.3 This child, the soul of helpfulness at nursery school, may be the despair of his mother's life at home. Learning theories of personality development can handle this kind of inconsistency across situations better than most other theories simply by arguing that the reinforcement contingencies may be quite different in the two settings.

one. Children's behavior can change if the reinforcement system or their beliefs about themselves change, so "problem behavior" can be modified, as Patterson has done with families of aggressive children.

The great strength of this view of social behavior is that it gives an accurate picture of the way in which many behaviors are learned. It is perfectly clear that children do learn through modeling; and it is equally clear that children (and adults) will continue to perform behaviors that "pay off" for them.

The addition of the cognitive elements to Bandura's theory adds further strength, since it offers a beginning integration of learning models and cognitive-developmental approaches. If we were to apply Piaget's language to Bandura's theory, we could talk about the acquisition of a "self-scheme"— a concept of one's own capacities, qualities, standards, and experiences. New experiences are then assimilated to that scheme. You will recall from Chapter 7 that one of the characteristics of the process of assimilation as Piaget proposed it is that new experiences and information are modified as they are taken in. In the same way, Bandura is saying that once the child's self-concept is established, it affects what behaviors she chooses to perform, how she reacts to new experience, whether she persists or gives up on some new task, and the like. If a child believes he is unpopular, for example, then the occasional times when someone chooses to sit next to him at lunch in the cafeteria or he gets invited to a birthday party are chalked up to other factors (there was no place else to sit or all the kids in the class got invited), and the underlying scheme isn't modified (accommodated) very much.

Thus, the self-concept, once well formed, serves as a central mediating process, leading to stable differences in behavior. It *can* be modified (accommodated) if the child accumulates enough experience or evidence that doesn't fit with the existing scheme. If the "unpopular" child noticed that classmates chose to sit next to him at lunch even when other seats were available, eventually he might have to change the "unpopular" part of his self-concept. But since the child (like the adult) will choose activities or situations that fit his self-concept (e.g., sitting in the corner where no one is likely to see him or never giving birthday parties) he will be partially protected from such "nonconfirming" experiences.

To be sure, Bandura and Piaget would not agree on how this self-concept or self-scheme develops. Piaget emphasizes internal processes, while Bandura emphasizes reinforcement as a causal factor. But they agree on the impact that such a scheme will have once it has developed.

At the same time, learning theories have significant weaknesses, particularly in the more radical versions. First, from the perspective of many psychologists, too much emphasis is still placed on what happens *to* the child and not enough on what the child is doing with the information she has. Bandura's theory is much less vulnerable to this charge, but most learning theories of personality are highly mechanistic and are focused on external events. Second, they are not really *developmental* theories. They can say how a child might acquire a particular behavior pattern or belief, but they do not take into account the underlying developmental changes that are occurring. Given Bandura's emphasis on the cognitive aspects of the modeling process, a genuinely developmental social-learning theory could be proposed. But no such theory exists now, so far as I know. Still, all the theories in this group offer useful descriptions of one source of influence on the child's developing pattern of behavior.

PSYCHOANALYTIC THEORIES

The third theoretical approach is psychoanalytic theory. Like some temperament theorists and like social-learning theorists of Bandura's stripe, psychoanalytic theorists emphasize the importance of the interaction between inborn or internal qualities and environmental pressures. But the psychoanalytic theorists come at it from a different angle.

There is a whole family of psychoanalytic theories, beginning with Freud and continuing with Carl Jung (1916, 1939), Alfred Adler (1948), Erik Erikson (1950/1963, 1964, 1974), and many others.

The Greek word *psyche* refers to the soul, spirit, or mind. So *psychoanalysis* means the analysis of the mind or spirit. All the theorists who share this general tradition have been interested in explaining human behavior by understanding the underlying processes of the mind and the personality. And nearly all psychoanalytic theorists have begun by studying and analyzing adults or children who are disturbed in some way. Many believed they could come to understand the normal processes by analyzing how it had gone wrong.

Of all the theorists in this large group, Freud and Erikson have dealt most thoroughly with the *developmental* questions about the origin of personality in infancy and childhood. Since the two theories differ in important ways, I want to describe them to you separately.

FREUD'S THEORY

I can summarize Freud's basic ideas in five propositions.

Proposition 1: All behavior is energized by fundamental instinctual drives. Freud thought there were three such instinctual drives or motivating forces—sexual drives, which he called *libido; life-preserving* drives, including instincts such as hunger and pain; and *aggressive drives.* Of the three, he thought the most interesting—and perhaps most important—were the sexual drives.

Proposition 2: Throughout life, the child (and later the adult) is focused on gratification of these basic instincts. The specific *form* of gratification sought and the strategies used to obtain it change with age, as we'll see later; but the inner push to obtain gratification remains.

Proposition 3: Over the course of childhood, each of us develops three basic structures of personality that aid in gratifying the instincts. These three structures Freud called the id, the ego, and the superego, and he suggested that they developed in that order. The **id** is the basic storehouse of raw, uninhibited instinctual energy. Freud thought that this was all that was present in the infant. The baby tries to gratify his needs very directly. He has no ability to delay. He wants what he wants when he wants it.

This basic instinctual push for gratification remains a part of the personality; but because gratification can frequently be achieved more successfully by planning, talking, delaying, and other "cognitive" techniques than by demands for instant satisfaction (and because the child must deal with threats from outside, such as the threat of punishment from Mom or Dad), the child gradually transfers energy from the id to the ego. In Freud's terms, the **ego** is the planning, organizing, thinking part of the personality. The child is still trying to get what she wants, but now she is trying to gratify her desire and avoid punishment by using more reality-based strategies.

Finally, there is the **superego,** which is roughly the same as what we call the **conscience.** This is the part of the personality that "monitors" the rest, that decides what is right and wrong, that channels the basic energy into forms of gratification that are acceptable to parents and to society.

These three parts of the personality are, in some sense, at war with one another. The id says, "I want it now!" The ego says, "You can have it later" or "Take it easy, we'll get there eventually if we do it this way." The superego says, "You can't have it that way. That way's wrong. Find another way."

Proposition 4: When conflicts arise between the different parts of the personality, the result is anxiety. You all know the feeling of anxiety, so I don't need to try to define it for you. Many times the ego can handle the anxiety directly. If I send in a paper to a professional journal and have it rejected, I feel anxious. But I know what I'm anxious about and may be able to handle it realistically.

But sometimes (often, in fact) the anxiety is too much to be handled this way, so we resort to **defense mechanisms**—automatic, unconscious strategies for reducing anxiety. For example, I can *repress* the feelings when my paper is rejected and insist that I really don't mind at all. Or I can *project:* "The people who reviewed my paper are really stupid! They don't know what they're doing." In this way, I ascribe to the other people the qualities I fear may be true of me (stupidity, in this case).

The key things to realize about defense mechanisms as Freud conceived them is that they are *unconscious,* they involve *self-deception,* and they are quite *normal.* They can be taken to extremes, in which case they become neurotic. But Freud believed that defending yourself against anxiety is a normal process.

Proposition 5: In the course of development, the child goes through a series of distinct psychosexual stages. Two things develop in stages. First, the ego and the superego are not present in the infant and must be developed. And second, the goals of gratification change. At each stage, the sexual energy is focused on ("invested in," as Freud says) a single part of the body, which he called an *erogenous zone,* such as the mouth, the anus, and the genitals. The infant first focuses on stimulation in the mouth because that is the part of the body that is most sensitive. Later, when her neurological development progresses, other parts of her anatomy become sensitive and her focus of sexual energy changes.

There is a strong maturational element in this part of Freud's theory. He thought that the transitions from one psychosexual stage to the next were determined largely by the changes in body sensitivity.

The Psychosexual Stages

Freud proposed five stages of development, called **psychosexual stages.** I've summarized the stages very briefly in Table 9.3, but I need to describe them in more detail as well.

The Oral Stage: Birth to 1 Year. Freud emphasized that the oral region—the mouth, tongue, and lips—is the first center of pleasure for the baby. His earliest attachment is to the one who provides pleasure in the mouth, usually his mother. For normal development the infant requires not too much and not too little oral stimulation. If the needed amount of stimulation is not available, the child may *fixate* on this form of gratification and continue to seek oral pleasures in later life. (Some of the characteristics of adults who are supposedly "stuck" at the oral stage are listed in Table 9.3.)

The Anal Stage: 1 to 3 Years. As the baby matures and the trunk comes under more voluntary control, the anal region becomes more and more sensitive. At about the same time, the baby's parents begin to place great emphasis on toilet training and show pleasure when she manages to perform in the right place at the right time. These two forces together help to shift the major center of sexual energy from the oral to the anal erogenous zone.

The key to the child's successful completion of this stage is whether the parents allow the child sufficient anal exploration and pleasure. If toilet training becomes a major battleground, then some fixation of energy at

Table 9.3

Freud's Stages of Psychosexual Development

Stage	Age	Erogenous	Major developmental task (potential source of conflict)	Some adult characteristics of children who have been "fixated" at this stage
Oral	0–1	Mouth, lips, tongue	Weaning	Oral behavior, such as smoking and overeating; passivity and gullibility.
Anal	2–3	Anus	Toilet training	Orderliness, parsimoniousness, obstinacy, or the opposite (extreme untidiness, for example).
Phallic	4–5	Genitals	Oedipus complex; identification with parent of same sex	Vanity, recklessness, and the opposite.
Latency	6–12	No specific area; sexual energy quiescent	Development of ego-defense mechanisms	None: fixation does not normally occur at this stage.
Genital	13–18 and adulthood	Genitals	Mature sexual intimacy	Adults who have successfully integrated earlier stages should emerge from this stage with a more sincere interest in others, realistic enjoyments, mature sexuality.

this stage may occur—with the possible adult consequences of excessive orderliness, stinginess, or the opposite.

The Phallic Stage: 3 to 5 Years. At about 3 or 4 years of age, the genitals increase in sensitivity, ushering in a new stage. (One sign of this new sensitivity, incidentally, is that children of both sexes quite naturally begin to masturbate at about this age.)

According to Freud, the most important event that occurs during the phallic stage is the so-called *Oedipus conflict.* He described the sequence of events more fully (and more believably!) for boys, so let me trace that pattern for you.

The theory suggests that first the boy somehow becomes "intuitively aware of his mother as a sex object" (Rappoport, 1972, p. 74). Precisely how this occurs is not completely spelled out, but the important point is that the boy at about age 4 begins to have a sort of sexual attachment to his mother and to regard his father as a sexual rival. His father sleeps

Figure 9.4 Most children are toilet trained at about age 2, which is during Freud's anal stage. For many parents and children, toilet training becomes a battleground, with the child enjoying both the anal sensations and the control he can exert over himself (and his parents!). The parents, meanwhile, are doing their darndest to exert control over the child.

with his mother, holds her and kisses her, and generally has access to her body in a way that the boy does not. The boy also sees his father as a powerful and threatening figure who has the ultimate power—the power to castrate. The boy is caught between desire for his mother and fear of his father's power.

Most of these feelings and the resultant conflict are unconscious. (The boy does not have overt sexual feelings and does not behave in a sexual way toward his mother.) But unconscious or not, the result of this conflict is anxiety. How can the little boy handle this anxiety? In Freud's view, the boy responds with a defensive process called **identification:** the boy "incorporates" his image of his father and attempts to match his own behavior to that image. By trying to make himself as like his father as possible, the boy not only reduces the chance of an attack from the father—he also takes on some of the father's power as well. Furthermore, it is the "inner father," with his values and moral judgments, that serves as the core of the child's superego or conscience.

A parallel process is supposed to occur in girls. The girl sees her mother as a rival for her father's sexual attentions and also fears her mother (though less than the boy fears his father, since the girl may assume she has already been castrated.) In this case, too, identification with the mother is thought to be the solution to the girl's anxiety.

The Latency Stage: 5 to 12 Years.   Freud thought that after the phallic stage there is a sort of resting period before the next major change in the child's sexual development. The child has presumably arrived at some preliminary resolution of the Oedipus conflict, so there is a kind of calm after the storm. During these years, the child's peer interactions are almost exclusively with members of the same sex. The identification with the same-sex parent at the end of the phallic stage is followed by a long period during which the identification and interaction extends to others of the same sex.

The Genital Stage: 12 to 18 and Older.   The further changes in hormones and the genital organs that take place during puberty reawaken the sexual energy of the child. During this period a more mature form of sexual attachment occurs. From the beginning of this period, the child's sexual objects are people of the opposite sex. Freud placed some emphasis on the fact that not everyone works though this period to a point of mature heterosexual love. Some have not successfully completed the Oedipal period, so they may have confused identifications that affect their ability to cope with rearoused sexual energies in adolescence. Some have not had a satisfactory oral period and thus do not have a foundation of basic love relationships. This too will interfere with full resolution of the conflicts of puberty.

What we see as the child's personality, then, is a complex result of all these processes, depending on the particular stages at which the child may have become fixated, on the particular form of the child's identification with the parents, and on the defense mechanisms that the child adopts.

Many of these same themes—inborn drives, critical elements of early parent-child interaction, stages of development, and "fixation"—are part of Erikson's theory as well.

ERIKSON'S THEORY

Erik Erikson belongs firmly in the psychoanalytic tradition, but he has focused his attention on the ego—the conscious self—rather than on the unconscious drives or instincts. He has always been much more interested in the cultural and social demands made on the child than in the sexual drives. So Erikson's stages are referred to as **psychosocial stages,** whereas

Freud's are called **psychosexual stages.** Most broadly, Erikson has been interested in how the child (and later the adult) develops her *sense of identity.* In Erikson's view, this process takes a full lifetime. As usual, let me break down the theoretical concepts into a series of basic propositions.

Proposition 1: Over the life span, each individual goes through a series of distinct developmental periods (stages), with a specific developmental task at each stage. (See Table 9.4.) The central task of each period is the development of a particular "ego quality," such as trust, autonomy, or intimacy.

Proposition 2: The developmental periods are defined partly by maturation and partly by the society in which the person grows. In our culture, a stage may begin at age 6 because that is when the child goes off to school. In a culture in which schooling was delayed, the timing

Table 9.4
▬▬▬▬▬

The Eight Stages of Development Proposed by Erik Erikson

Approximate age	Ego quality to be developed	Some tasks and activities of the stage
0–1	Basic trust versus basic mistrust	Trust in mother or central caregiver and in one's own ability to make things happen. A key element in an early secure attachment.
2–3	Autonomy versus shame, doubt	Walking, grasping, and other physical skills lead to free choice; toilet training occurs; child learns control but may develop shame if not handled properly.
4–5	Initiative versus guilt	Organize activities around some goal; become more assertive and aggressive. Oedipus-like conflict with parent of same sex may lead to guilt.
6–12	Industry versus inferiority	Absorb all the basic culture skills and norms, including school skills and tool use.
13–18	Identity versus role confusion	Adapt sense of self to physical changes of puberty, make occupational choice, achieve adultlike sexual identity, and search for new values.
19–25	Intimacy versus isolation	Form one or more intimate relationships that go beyond adolescent love; marry and form family groups.
26–40	Generativity versus stagnation	Bear and rear children, focus on occupational achievement or creativity, and train the next generation.
41+	Ego integrity versus despair	Integrate earlier stages and come to terms with basic identity. Accept self.

of the developmental task might change as well. In this view, Erikson obviously differs from Freud, for whom maturation was the critical element in moving the child from one stage to the next.

Proposition 3: The child's (or adult's) success in completing the task at each stage is heavily dependent on the interactions that take place between the child and her parents or the child and her teacher(s). This is a heavily *interactive* theory, just as Freud's is. The child is a key partner in the exchange, but the responses of the people around her shape her development as well.

Proposition 4: Any developmental task that is not successfully completed leaves a residue that interferes with later tasks. Actually, Erikson thinks that no task is every fully completed; there are always bits and pieces left over. But the number and size of those bits and pieces may be critical for later health. A child who has not formed a trusting first relationship, for example, will have greater difficulty completing every later task; a teenager who does not complete the task of developing her sexual or occupational identity will have a harder time later on entering into a fully intimate relationship at age 20 or 25. In this proposition, Erikson is obviously very like Freud, who also thought that truly "mature" or "healthy" adult functioning required the successful sequential resolution of all the different stages or tasks.

The Psychosocial Stages

Basic Trust Versus Basic Mistrust: Birth to 1 Year. The first task (or "crisis," as Erikson sometimes says) occurs during the first year of life (Freud's oral period). At issue is the child's development of a sense of basic trust in the predictability of the world and in his ability to affect the events around him. Erikson believes that the behavior of the major caregiver (usually the mother) is critical to the child's successful or unsuccessful resolution of this crisis. Children who emerge from the first year with a firm sense of trust are those with parents who are loving and who respond predictably and reliably. A child who has developed a sense of trust will go on to other relationships carrying this sense with him. While the development of trust is critical, Erikson does emphasize that the child should also develop some *healthy* sense of mistrust as well—to learn to discriminate between dangerous situations and safe ones, for example (Evans, 1969). Thus there is some risk in being totally trusting. Still, the greater risk is for the child who fails to develop a core sense of trust in those around him. Such a child will carry the sense of mistrust into later relationships.

Autonomy Versus Shame and Doubt: Years 2 and 3. Erikson sees the child's greater mobility at this age as forming the basis for the sense of independence or autonomy. But if the child's efforts at independence are not carefully guided by the parents and she experiences repeated failures or ridicule, then the results of all the new opportunities for exploration may be excessive shame and doubt instead of a basic sense of self-control and self-worth.

Initiative Versus Guilt: Years 4 and 5. This phase (Freud's phallic stage) is again ushered in by new skills or abilities in the child. The 4-year-old is able to plan a bit, to take initiative in reaching particular goals. The child tries out these new cognitive skills, tries to conquer the world around him. He may try to go out into the street on his own; he may take a toy apart, then find he can't put it back together and throw it—parts and all—at his mother. It is a time of vigor of action and of behaviors that parents may see as aggressive. The risk is that the child may go too far in his forcefulness or that the parents may restrict and punish too much—either of which can create an imbalance, producing too much guilt.

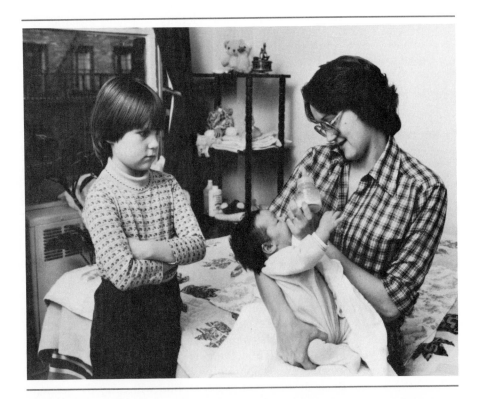

Figure 9.5   If looks could kill! This boy, clearly jealous of his infant sibling, may be harboring all sorts of angry and aggressive thoughts. A younger child would probably simply act out those feelings and thoughts; a child of this age has the feelings, but also feels guilty about them.

Industry (Competence) Versus Inferiority: Years 6 to 12.　The beginning of schooling is a major force in ushering in this stage (so if schooling began at a different age, Erikson would assume this stage would occur at a different time, too). The child is now faced with the need to win approval through specific competence—through learning to read and do sums and other specific skills. The task of this period is thus simply to develop the repertoire of abilities society demands of the child. The flip side is that the child may be unable to develop the expected skills and will develop instead a basic sense of inferiority. (Of course, the opposite problem can occur, too; if too much emphasis is placed on achievement, the child becomes a "workaholic.")

Identity Versus Role Confusion: Years 13 to 18.　The task occurring during puberty (Freud's genital stage) is a major one, in which the adolescent reexamines her identity and the roles she must occupy. Erikson suggests that two identities are involved—a sexual identity and an occupational identity. The adolescent should emerge from this period with a reintegrated sense of self, of what she wants to do and be, and of her appropriate sexual role. The risk is that confusion can arise from the profusion of roles opening to the child at this age.

Adult Stages.　As you can see in Table 9.4, Erikson proposed three further stages in adulthood (and he is thus one of the few theorists to offer a truly life-span theory). These stages are intimacy versus isolation, generativity versus stagnation, and ego integrity versus despair. Successful adult development thus requires the establishment of a truly intimate relationship; some form of "generativity" (bearing and rearing children, creative accomplishments, serving as mentor to younger colleagues, or the like); and a final reflective integration, resulting in acceptance of who one is and what one has done. (I find the idea of such continued opportunities for growth in adulthood to be an extremely comforting thought, by the way.)

Some Evidence on Psychoanalytic Theory

There are no direct tests of the propositions of either Freudian or Eriksonian theory, mostly because both theories are so general that specific tests are very difficult. But the influence of psychoanalytic theories can nonetheless be seen in a great many issues that are being studied intensively today. For example, what is the impact on a child of being reared without a father? Given current divorce rates, there are obviously pressing social reasons for wanting to know what the effect might be. But there are important theoretical questions at issue, too, some of which I have explored in the box on pages 344–345.

　　Current work on the security or insecurity of children's early attachments also has its roots in part in psychoanalytic theory. Specifically, both

BEING RAISED WITHOUT A FATHER: THE EFFECTS OF DIVORCE

It is estimated that approximately one-third of all children now alive in the United States will experience their parents' divorce before they are 18 (Glick, 1979). An equally startling statistic: in 1984, one of every five families in the United States with children under 18 was headed by a single parent (Norton & Glick, 1986), and in about 85 percent of those families only the mother was present.

What is the effect on the child of growing up without a father present full time? Freud thought that the impact could be substantial, even devastating. In particular, he thought that the damage would be greatest if the father was missing during the Oedipal period (approximately age 3 to 5), when identification was taking place, and that it would be greatest for a boy. A girl still has her mother to identify with, so at least her sex-role identification is appropriate. But the boy lacking a father may never go through the identification process properly and may end up with a very confused sex-role orientation and perhaps a weaker superego.

From the social-learning point of view, too, divorce or father absence should have an effect, since it may profoundly alter the specific reinforcement patterns in the family, as well as change the child's expectancies. In confirmation of this, Mavis Hetherington and her colleagues (Hetherington, 1979; Hetherington, Cox, & Cox, 1978) have found that mothers become less affectionate and more inconsistent in their discipline in the first few years after a divorce. We might expect that, as a result, the children would become less obedient, less eas-

ily managed. Social-learning theorists also point to the lack of a male role model for the boy; this should affect the development of sex-role behaviors, particularly if the loss of the father occurs early.

The results of studies of children in divorced families support some, but not all, of these depressing expectations.

First of all, virtually all children show at least short-term distress or disruption following a parental separation. In the first two years or so after a divorce, children typically become more defiant, more negative, and often more depressed, angry, or aggressive. On average, their school performance goes down for at least a while, and they may be ill more often. (In fact, children show some of these symptoms before the separation, too, during the period when the parents may be experiencing maximum levels of discord [Block, Block, & Gjerde, 1986]). As virtually all the research shows, this is a profoundly *disruptive* process for children, no matter what their age (e.g., Wallerstein & Kelly, 1980; Guidubaldi et al., 1986; Hetherington, 1984). The effect lasts, too, at least for some children. Wallerstein and Kelly (1980), in the only really long-term longitudinal study so far, have found that five years after the divorce, about a third of the children they studied showed significant disturbance, including depression.

Second, the effects do seem to be greater for boys, particularly in the short term, just as both Freud and the social-learning theorists would expect (e.g., Hetherington, 1984; Tschann et al., 1987). Boys whose parents have divorced show more distress, more negative and noncompliant behavior, and more school problems than do girls from equivalent families.

Whether younger children are more severely affected is less clear. Children's *symptoms* differ, depending on their age when the parents split up. Wallerstein and Kelly, in their detailed study of 60 divorcing families (1980), found that 3- to 5-year olds showed more severe immediate symptoms, including fearfulness and "regression" to infantile behavior, than did older children. Older children showed more sadness or anger. Over the long term, though, there was no indication that 3- to 5-year olds had a more difficult time adjusting to the change. In fact, Wallerstein has found some indication that 10 years after the divorce, the very young children—those 2 to 6 years old when the divorce occurred—showed fewer residual signs of sadness or distress than did those who had been 9 or 10 or older when their parents separated (Wallerstein, 1984). The whole question of the relationship between the child's age at the time of the separation and the degree, severity, or persistence of the effect is simply not answered yet. We may even find that the impact varies for girls and boys of different ages. Some research hints, for example, that girls may be especially adversely affected if they are in adolescence when their parents divorce. At the least, there seems to be no indication that there is something *uniquely* difficult for a child about having a parental separation during the Oedipal period.

So much for bad news. The good news is that we are now beginning to understand some of the factors in families and in children that can soften or shorten these effects. On the basis of all the research, it looks as if the *smallest* or *shortest* effects occur for children in the following circumstances:

1. Their families are economically secure after the divorce.
2. Their parents had low levels of open conflict before the divorce and have maintained civility afterward. (It is not the conflict between the parents that seems to matter but the degree of conflict that the child actually sees or hears.)
3. Their parents can agree on child rearing and discipline after the divorce.
4. They see the noncustodial parent (usually the father) regularly and have a positive relationship with him.
5. Their lives are changed or disrupted the least in other ways. So a child who can stay in the same house or the same school seems to be better off than one who must adjust to multiple changes at once.
6. The custodial parent (usually the mother) has a relatively stable life, with adequate emotional support from friends and family.

These are not easy conditions to meet for many families. And because that is true, many children—particularly boys—do show persisting emotional effects from their parents' divorce. The list of mitigating conditions also points out again that we cannot understand the effects of any family experience without understanding the whole system—the network of relationships, the individual personalities, and the emotional and social setting of the family.

Erikson and Freud argue that the quality of the child's first relationship with the central caregiver will shape her relationships with other children and with other adults at later ages. I'll be talking a great deal more about early attachments in Chapter 11, but for now I want to point out that this particular aspect of psychoanalytic theory has received a good deal of support from recent studies, particularly the work of Alan Sroufe and his colleagues (e.g., Sroufe, 1983; Erickson, Sroufe, & Egeland, 1985). In a large number of studies, children have first been rated at about age 1 on the security of their attachments to their mothers. Later, at age 3 or 4 or 5 years, the same children are observed in preschool settings or when meeting a strange adult. The consistent finding from studies like this is that securely attached infants are later more capable, more friendly, more open to new relationships, more skillful with peers.

Some typical findings from a study by Erickson, Sroufe, and Egeland (1985) are in Figure 9.6. They observed a group of 4- to 5-year-old children in various preschools and rated each child on a series of seven-point scales describing such things as "agency" (how confidently and assertively the child approaches tasks and activities), dependency on the teacher, and social skills with other children. They then compared these ratings for securely and insecurely attached children. As you can see in the figure, those children who had been securely attached at 1 year were significantly more confident and skillful and less dependent at age 4 or 5.

None of these researchers have yet observed their subjects much past early elementary school, so we don't yet know how lasting these differences may be. But this research suggests that the relationship formed during this first stage of psychosexual development may create what Sroufe calls a prototype for later relationships.

Strengths, Weaknesses, and Implications of Psychoanalytic Theories

Psychoanalytic theories like Freud's or Erikson's have several great attractions. First of all, they are *sequential* theories, and there is now increasing evidence (as I've described in earlier chapters) that sequences are built into many of the child's developing skills. Second, they focus our attention on the importance of the child's relationship with the caregivers. More important, both of these theories suggest that the child's needs or "tasks" change with age, so the parents must constantly adapt to the changing child. One of the implications of this is that we should not think of "good parenting" as if it were a global quality. Some of us may be very good at meeting the needs of an infant but quite awful at dealing with teenagers' identity struggles; others of us may have the opposite pattern. The child's eventual personality and her overall emotional health thus depend on the interaction or transaction that develops in the particular family. This is an extremely attractive element of these theories, since more and more of the research within developmental psychology is moving us toward exactly

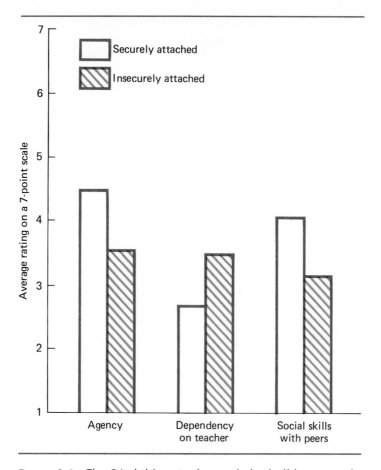

Figure 9.6 The 96 children in this study had all been rated for the security or insecurity of their attachments when they were 1 year old. Three to four years later, they were observed while playing in preschool and rated for several aspects of their interaction. (The rating of "agency" describes how confidently and assertively the child approaches tasks and classroom activities.) As you can see, the children who had earlier been rated as insecurely attached were less confident (lower-agency), more dependent on the teacher, and less skillful in interacting with other children. Thus, some effects of an early lack of trust appear to last at least to age 4 or 5. (*Source:* Erickson, Sroufe, & Egeland, 1985, Table 1, p. 154.)

this conception of the process (as I have already pointed out in talking about both temperament theory and social-learning theory).

A third strength is that psychoanalytic theory has offered several useful new concepts, such as defense mechanisms and identification. The concept of identification, in particular, has been widely adopted in one form or another. For example, Bandura's concept of modeling may be thought of as a variation of the identification concept.

These strengths have led in recent years to a resurgence of the influence of psychoanalytic approaches, particularly Erikson's theory. In addition to his impact on researchers studying early attachment, Erikson has had a marked influence on the growing literature on adult development, since he offers one of the few frameworks for describing adult change.

The great weakness of all the psychoanalytic approaches is fuzziness. As Jack Block puts it:

> For all the richness, insight, and seriousness of psychoanalytic theory regarding the understanding of personality functioning, it has also been imprecise, overly facile with supposed explanations, and seemingly inaccessible scientifically. (Block, 1987, p. 2)

How does one tell whether a particular child is in the Oedipal period? By what means does one determine whether a child has "successfully" resolved such a crisis? Identification may be an intriguing theoretical notion, but how are we to measure it? How do we measure ego strength or accurately detect the presence of specific defense mechanisms? Without more-precise definitions, we cannot test the theory or disprove it in any way. The general concepts of psychoanalytic theory have been fruitfully applied to our understanding of development in some areas—usually those in which other theorists or researchers have offered more precise definitions or methods for measuring some Freudian or Eriksonian construct, such as security of attachment. Psychoanalytic theory may thus sometimes offer a provocative framework for our thinking, but most observers find that it is not a sufficiently precise theory of development.

A TENTATIVE SYNTHESIS

I have given you three different views of the origins of those unique, individual patterns of behavior we call personality. Each view can be at least partially supported with research evidence, so it seems impossible to choose one of the three as the "correct" view. But can we combine them in any sensible way? Some argue that theories as different as these cannot ever be combined (Reese & Overton, 1970; Overton & Reese, 1973) because they make such different assumptions about the child's role in the whole process. I agree in part. I do not think we can simply add up the different sources of influence and say that personality is merely the sum of inborn temperament, reinforcement patterns, interactions with parents, and some kind of self-scheme.

But more complex combinations may be fruitful. I have suggested one in Figure 9.7. I propose that the child's inborn temperament is a beginning point—an initial bias in the system. Thus there is a *direct* relationship

A model of personality development

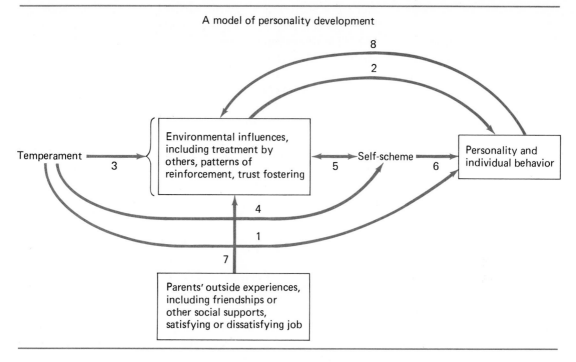

Figure 9.7 Here is my own proposal for a complex interactive model describing (or explaining) the formation of individual personality. The effects of inborn temperament and environmental influences do not merely add. Both influence each other and help to create the child's unique self-scheme, which in turn affects the child's experiences. And all of this occurs within the context of the family, which is itself influenced by the parents' own life experiences. What we think of as personality is a complex product of all these forces. (See text for discussion of numbered arrows.)

between that inborn temperament and the eventual personality or behavior we see in a child (arrow 1).

I suggest a second direct effect (arrow 2) between the child's environment and his or her eventual behavior. Whether the parents respond reliably and contingently to the infant will affect the child's trust, which will show up in a range of behaviors later; whether the parents reinforce bratty behavior or friendly behavior will influence the child's future as well.

But most of what happens is much more complicated than that. The child's temperament influences the way she is treated (arrow 3), and both her basic temperament and the family environment affect the child's self-scheme—her expectations for others and herself, her beliefs about her own abilities (arrows 4 and 5). This self-scheme or self-concept, in turn, helps to shape the behavior we see, the "personality" of the child (arrow 6).

Furthermore, this system does not exist in a vacuum. In Chapter 13 I'll be talking a good deal more about the family and the cultural context in which development occurs. For now let me add just one more element to the model, namely, the degree of support or help the parents may have from others in their environment (arrow 7). Such support may affect the quality of the parents' relationship with the child.

Finally, we must consider the *transactional* elements of the system (arrow 8). Once the child forms her unique pattern of behaviors and attitudes (personality), it affects the environment she will encounter, the experiences she will choose, and the responses of the people around her, which in turn affect her behavior (Scarr & McCartney, 1983).

The complexity of such a system is nicely illustrated in a study by Susan Crockenberg (1981). Crockenberg studied a group of 40 mothers and their infants over the first year of the children's lives. The child's irritability (an aspect of temperament) was measured when the baby was 5 to 10 days old, and the security of the child's attachment to the mother was measured when the child was 12 months old. We might expect that irritable babies would be more likely to be insecurely attached, merely because they are more difficult to care for. In fact, Crockenberg found a small effect of this kind (see Table 9.5). But Crockenberg didn't stop there. She also measured the level of the mother's social support—the degree to which she had family and friends whom she perceived as being sufficiently helpful, assisting her in dealing with the strains of a new child or other life changes she might be experiencing. The results of the study show that insecure attachment in the child was likely only when the mother had *both* an irritable infant *and* perceived low levels of support. If the baby was irritable but the mother had good support, the child's attachment developed securely. Only when two difficult conditions occurred together was there a poor outcome for the child.

Table 9.5

Influence of Child's Temperament and Mother's Social Support on Child's Secure or Insecure Attachment.

Child's irritability	Mother's support	Children with secure attachment	Children with insecure attachment
High	Low	2	9
High	High	12	1
Low	Low	7	2
Low	High	13	2

Source: From Crockenberg, 1981, Table 5, p. 862. © The Society for Research in Child Development, Inc.

Thus the outcome for a child depends not on the sum of individual influences, but on complex interactions among them.

▬▬▬▬▬ SUMMARY

1. The word *personality* refers to a person's unique, individual, relatively enduring pattern of relating to others and responding to the world. *Personality* is a more inclusive term than *temperament;* the latter refers primarily to inborn style of response to the environment.

2. The origins of personality differences have been described in three distinct theoretical frameworks: temperament theories (a primarily biological approach), learning theories, and psychoanalytic theories.

3. Temperament theory proposes that each child is born with innately determined patterns or styles of reacting to people and objects. These patterns shape the child's interactions with the world and affect others' responses to the child as well.

4. Some research supports the idea that there is a genetic contribution to temperamental differences and points to moderate stability of temperamental qualities.

5. Traditional learning theorists emphasize the role of basic learning processes, such as reinforcement patterns, in shaping individual behaviors, including patterns of interaction with others. Behavior may vary from situation to situation.

6. Social-learning theories emphasize, in addition, the role of observational learning and of the child's learned expectancies, standards, and self-efficacy in creating more enduring patterns of response.

7. Freud's psychoanalytic approach emphasizes a maturationally based developmental sequence of psychosexual stages. In each stage, a particular erogenous zone is dominant. Of particular importance is the phallic stage, beginning at about age 4, when the Oedipal crisis is met and mastered through the process of identification.

8. Erikson emphasizes psycho*social* stages, each one shaped in part by age-graded social demands and by the child's physical and intellectual skills. Each of the major stages has a central task or "crisis," which relates to some aspect of the development of identity.

9. Recent research (on such topics as the effect of a child's early attachment on his peer relationships and approach to new experiences) has provided support for some aspects of the psychoanalytic view.

10. Elements of all three theories of personality development can be combined into an interactionist view. Temperament may serve as the base from which personality grows, by affecting behavior directly and by affecting the way others respond to the child. Both the child's termperament and responses from other people affect her self-concept or self-scheme, which then helps to create stability in her unique pattern of behavior.

behavior therapy A therapeutic intervention based on principles of reinforcement.

conscience Roughly equivalent to the term *superego*. In Freudian theory, the part of the personality that monitors one's behavior, judging it to be acceptable or unacceptable.

defense mechanisms In Freudian theory, strategies of the ego, for coping with anxiety (denial, repression, identification, projection, and many others).

ego In Freudian theory, that portion of the personality that organizes, plans, and keeps the person in touch with reality. Language and thought are both ego functions.

id In Freudian theory, the first, primitive portion of the personality; the storehouse of basic energy, continually pushing for immediate gratification.

identification The process of taking into oneself (incorporating) the qualities and ideas of another person, which Freud thought was the result of the Oedipus complex at age 3 to 5. The child attempts to become like the parent of the same sex.

modeling A term used by Bandura and others to describe observational learning.

Oedipus conflict The pattern of events that Freud believed occurred between age 3 and 5, when the child, fearing possible reprisal from the parent of the same sex for "sexual" desire for the parent of the opposite sex, identifies with the parent of the same sex.

personality The collection of individual, relatively enduring patterns of reacting to and interacting with others that distinguishes each child or adult.

psychosexual stages The stages of personality development suggested by Freud, including the oral, anal, phallic, latency, and genital stages.

psychosocial stages The stages of personality development suggested by Erikson, including trust, autonomy, initiative, industry, identity, intimacy, generativity, and ego integrity.

superego In Freudian theory, the "conscience" part of personality, which develops as a result of the identification process. The superego contains the parental and societal values and attitudes incorporated by the child.

■■■■■■■■ **SUGGESTED READING**

Asher, J. (1987, April). Born to be shy? *Psychology Today,* pp. 56–64.
An easy-to-read, up-to-date discussion of some of the current information on shyness as an inborn temperament or personality trait. Asher presents evidence from studies of both monkeys and children suggesting that while some temperamental differences may be inborn, the environment can change them.

Bandura, A. (1977). *Social learning theory.* Englewood Cliffs, NJ: Prentice-Hall.
Not easy reading, but a good, complete statement of Bandura's theory—at least as it was formulated in 1977.

Erikson, E. H. (1980). *Identity and the life cycle.* New York: Norton. (Original work published 1959)
The middle section of this book, "Growth and Crises of the Healthy Personality," is the best description I have found of the psychosocial stages of development.

Patterson, G. R. (1975). *Families. Applications of social learning to family life.* Champaign, IL: Research Press.
As a general rule, I don't lean much toward behavior modification approaches, but this is a wonderful book—clear, easy to understand, and very helpful, particularly if you are struggling with a child whose behavior stymies you.

Sroufe, L. A. (1979). The coherence of individual development: Early care, attachment, and subsequent developmental issues. *American Psychologist, 34,* 834–841.
A readable brief paper that reflects much of what I see as the new direction of thinking about personality development.

10 The Concept of Self in Children

The Concept of Self: Developmental Patterns
   The First Step: The Existential Self
   The Next Step: The Categorical Self
   Identity in Adolescence
   Summary of Developmental Changes in Self-concept
Individual Differences in the Self-concept
   Differences in Self-esteem
   Differences in Identity Achievement
   The Origins of Self-esteem and Identity
The Self-concept: A Summing Up
The Development of Gender and Sex-Role Concepts
   Some Definitions
   Developmental Patterns
Theories of the Development of Sex-Role Concepts and Sex-Role Behavior
   Social-Learning Explanations
   Psychoanalytic Explanations
   Cognitive-Developmental Explanations
   A New Alternative: Gender Schemas
Sex Stereotyping on TV and in Books
Individual Differences in Sex Typing and Stereotypes
   Cross-Sex Children
   Androgyny
Some Real-Life Applications: Occupational Choices, Occupational
     Behavior, and Family Roles
   Occupational Choices
   Occupational Behavior
   Family Roles
Summary
Key Terms
Suggested Reading
Project: Sex Roles on TV

In the state where I now live, one of the hot political issues has been the idea of "comparable worth" as a basis for determining pay levels for government workers. Those who oppose it say (among other things) that women have not been forced out of the higher-paying types of jobs. Rather, they say, women *choose* to be secretaries or nurses or file clerks. As long as there is free choice involved, the argument goes, there is no government responsibility to equalize pay. The counterargument is that no one's choice of occupation is "free." We are all influenced by our images or concepts of ourselves and by the idea each of us has about the appropriate or suitable jobs for our own gender. A woman can choose to become a carpenter or a truck driver, but to do so flies in the face of the sex stereotypes in our culture and may thus conflict with the woman's own concept of herself.

I give you this example not to get embroiled in political argument but to show you that the subject we are about to explore has important practical relevance for each of us. The self-concept each of us develops, as I pointed out in Chapter 9, serves as a sort of filter for experience, shaping our choices, affecting our responses to others. Our ideas about our own sex role are a powerful part of that self-concept. In this chapter I want to explore the origins of these concepts in childhood.

In the previous chapter I talked about various theories of how children come to have different personalities (including different self-concepts). Here I want to focus primarily on the developmental process that is common to all children. When does a young child first realize that he is separate from others? Can we identify steps or sequences in the content or organization of children's self-concepts? Is the development of the self-concept linked to the broader sequences of cognitive development I described in Chapter 7? And where does the child's concept of himself or herself as a boy or a girl fit into the developmental picture?

THE CONCEPT OF SELF: DEVELOPMENTAL PATTERNS

The First Step: The Existential Self

Both Piaget and Freud emphasized that in the first months of life the infant does not distinguish between himself and other people. Freud talks about the **symbiotic relationship** between the mother and the infant, in which the two are joined together as if they are one. For the infant, the first step in developing a self-concept thus must be to develop some primitive sense of a separate self. Michael Lewis and Jeanne Brooks-Gunn (1979; Lewis, 1981) call this first step the development of the **existential self.**

Lewis and Brooks-Gunn argue that the basic underpinnings of this sense of separateness are the contingent interactions the baby has with the people around him. When he cries, someone picks him up; when he drops his rattle, someone returns it to him; when his mother smiles, he smiles back. By this process the baby slowly begins to grasp the basic difference between self and other. I have already pointed out the importance of contingent responsiveness for the development of both language and cognitive skills in the infant and young child. Now we see that this same pattern may also be critical for the development of the concept of the separate self as well.

It is not easy to figure out just when infants begin to understand that they are separate from others. The beginning steps seem to come at around 9 to 12 months, and a separate self is pretty clearly established by about 15 to 18 months of age.

One of the cleverest techniques used to explore early self-awareness involves the use of a mirror. First the baby is placed in front of a mirror, just to see how she behaves. Most infants of about 9 to 12 months will look at their own images, make faces, or try to interact with the baby in the mirror in some way. After allowing this free exploration for a time,

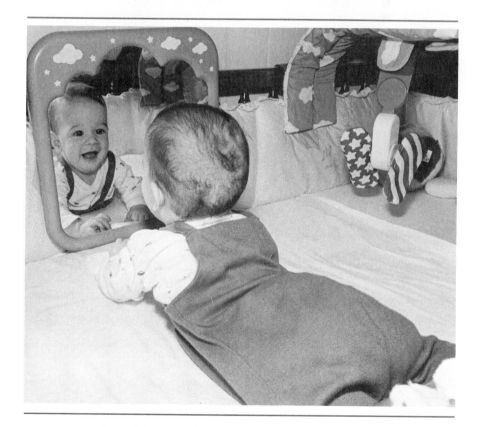

Figure 10.1   One of the signs that a child has understood his own separateness is that he recognizes himself in a mirror. Research by Michael Lewis and others shows that a child of 18 or 20 months normally can do this.

the experimenter, while pretending to wipe the baby's face with a cloth, puts a spot of rouge on the baby's nose and then again lets the baby look in the mirror. The crucial test of self-recognition, and thus of awareness of the self, is whether the baby reaches for the spot on her *own* nose (not the nose on the face in the mirror).

The results from one of Lewis's studies using this procedure are shown in Figure 10.2. As you can see, none of the 9- to 12-month-old children in this study touched their noses, but by 21 months, three-quarters of the children showed that level of self-recognition. The figure also shows the rate at which children refer to themselves by name when they are shown a picture of themselves. You can see that this development occurs at almost exactly the same time as self-recognition in a mirror. In another study, Lewis and Brooks-Gunn (1979) also found that 15- to 18-month-old children smiled and looked more at pictures or videotapes of themselves than at pictures or videotapes of other children.

These findings certainly suggest that the ability to recognize the self and distinguish the self from others is present by at least the middle of the second year of life, but probably there are precursors at earlier ages. Susan Harter (1983) suggests the five steps listed in Table 10.1. Infants seem to "know" themselves as agents in the world (that they can make things happen) before they see themselves as an object with features and characteristics. But by 18 months or so, they not only see themselves as

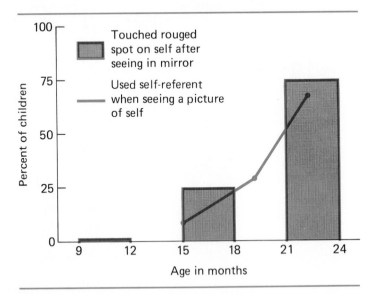

Figure 10.2 Another sign of self-awareness is the child's use of her own name when she sees a picture of herself. These results from a study by Michael Lewis show that self-naming emerges at almost exactly the same time that we see mirror recognition. (*Source:* Lewis & Brooks, 1978, pp. 214–215.)

Table 10.1

Some Steps in the Infant's Emerging Sense of the Existential Self

Age	Step
The self as subject, as an active, independent causal agent	
5–8 months	Interested in mirror image, but shows no indication that she sees herself as a causal agent.
9–12 months	Understands the relationship between his own movement and the movement in the mirror (e.g., he may wave at the mirror). Seems clear that the infant sees himself as an active agent in space, able to cause things to happen by his own movement.
12–15 months	Can use a mirror to locate people or objects in space; she reaches for the object, not the mirrored version of it. Grasps the fact that other people cause their movements just as she causes hers.
The self as an object of one's knowledge	
15–18 months	In mirror studies, this is the age at which the child reaches for the rouge spot on his own nose. Also will point to himself. If shown pictures, can distinguish between self and others; thus has some kind of schema of his own face.
18–24 months	Infant can state her own name; may give her name to the figure in the mirror. Can distinguish between a picture of herself and one of another girl her age.

Source: Harter, 1983, p. 283.

---

separate, they have some sense of their own appearance. When you think about it, that is quite an accomplishment in less than two years.

The Next Step: The Categorical Self

Once the infant has clearly understood that she is separate and distinct from others, the process of defining the self begins. Lewis and Brooks-Gunn refer to this as the **categorical self** because the definition takes the form of placing oneself in a whole range of categories. Other researchers refer to this more simply as the **self-concept.** In the beginning, the child focuses particularly on age, size, and gender, noting ways in which people differ (old/young, big/small, boy/girl) and places himself somewhere along each dimension or in one category. In the early stages, young children seem to place themselves at one end or the other of each dimension. They think of themselves as either big or small, old or young. The terms are absolute rather than relative (Harter, 1983).

By about age 5 to 7, a child can give you quite a full description of

Figure 10.3 Preschool-age children, like this boy, frequently insist on doing things for themselves. This may reflect aspects of autonomy (in Erikson's sense), but it may also reflect the child's emerging sense of self—an extension of the self to "things I can do." By trying out the boundaries of his skills, the child is defining himself.

himself on a whole range of dimensions, including size, age, and gender. These early self-concepts, though, are highly concrete. Just as the 4- to 5-year-old pays attention to the outside appearance of objects rather than to their enduring, inner qualities, so he also describes himself with reference to his visible characteristics—what he looks like, what he plays with, where he lives, what he is good at or bad at doing.

School Age.   This pattern begins to change, gradually, but noticeably, in the elementary-school years—as we would expect, given all that we know about the underlying changes in cognitive development that are occurring between ages 6 and 12. For one thing, children's self-descriptions at this age begin to be significantly more comparative; for example, they see themselves not just as "smart" or "dumb" but as "smarter than most other kids" or "not as good at baseball as my friends" (Ruble, 1987). The self-concept also becomes more complex, more elaborated, focused less and less on external characteristics and more and more on internal qualities (Harter, 1983, 1985). The child assumes that her own (and other people's) characteristics are relatively stable. This shift is illustrated particularly nicely in a study by Montemayor and Eisen (1977) of self-concepts in 9- to 18-year-olds.

These researchers asked each child to give 20 answers to the question "Who am I?" They found that the younger children in this study were still using mostly surface qualities to describe themselves, as in the description by this 9-year-old:

> My name is Bruce C. I have brown eyes. I have brown hair. I have brown eyebrows. I am nine years old. I LOVE! Sports. I have seven people in my family. I have great! eye site. I have lots! of friends. I live on 1923 Pinecrest Dr. I am going on 10 in September. I'm a boy. I have a uncle that is almost 7 feet tall. My school is Pinecrest. My teacher is Mrs. V. I play Hockey! I'm almost the smartest boy in the class. I LOVE! food. I love fresh air. I LOVE school. (Montemayor & Eisen, 1977, pp. 317–318)

In contrast, look at the self-description of this 11 year-old-sixth-grader:

> My name is A. I'm a human being. I'm a girl. I'm a truthful person. I'm not very pretty. I do so-so in my studies. I'm a very good cellist. I'm a very good pianist. I'm a little bit tall for my age. I like several boys. I like several girls. I'm old-fashioned. I play tennis. I am a *very* good swimmer. I try to be helpful. I'm always ready to be friends with anybody. Mostly I'm good, but I lose my temper. I'm not well-liked by some girls and boys. I don't know if I'm liked by boys or not. (Montemayor & Eisen, 1977, pp. 317–318)

This girl, like the other youngsters of this age in the study by Montemayor and Eisen, not only describes her external qualities; she also emphasizes her beliefs, the quality of her relationships, and her general personality traits. Thus, as the child moves through the concrete operations period, her self-definition becomes more complex, less tied to external features, more focused on feelings, on ideas.

Adolescence.   This trend toward greater abstraction in the self-definition continues during adolescence. Compare the answers of this 17-year-old to the "Who am I?" question with the ones you just read:

I am a human being. I am a girl, I am an individual. I don't know who I am. I am a Pisces. I am a moody person. I am an indecisive person. I am an ambitious person. I am a very curious person. I am not an individual. I am a loner. I am an American (God help me). I am a Democrat. I am a liberal person. I am a radical. I am a conservative. I am a pseudoliberal. I am an atheist. I am not a classifiable person (i.e. I don't want to be). (Montemayor & Eisen, p. 318)

Obviously, this girl's self-concept is even less tied to her physical characteristics or her abilities than is that of the 11-year-old. She is describing abstract traits or ideology.

You can see the shift I'm describing graphically in Figure 10.4, which

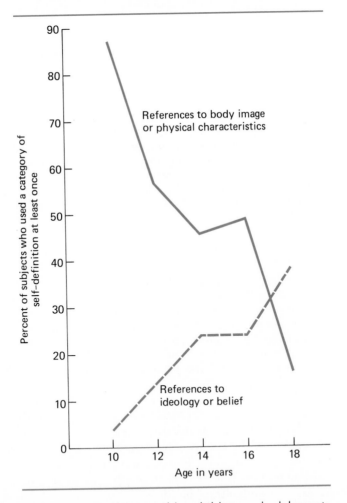

Figure 10.4 As they get older, children and adolescents define themselves less and less by what they look like and more and more by what they believe or feel. (*Source:* Montemayor & Eisen, 1977, from Table 1, p. 316.)

is based on the answers of all 262 subjects in the study by Montemayor and Eisen. Each of the subjects' answers to the "Who am I?" question was placed in one or more specific categories, such as references to physical properties ("I am tall," "I have blue eyes") or references to ideology ("I am a Democrat," "I believe in God"). As you can see, older teenagers define themselves less by their physical properties and more by ideology.

Identity in Adolescence

This increasing preoccupation with ideology may reflect the central task of adolescence, as Erikson described it: *identity versus role confusion.* The teenager's old definition of himself is called into question, in part because of the changes of puberty but also because of changing expectations by his family and society. He is expected to be more independent, more responsible for himself. And he is expected to look to the future, to plan, to decide what or who he *will* be as well as what or who he is.

The changes in the self-concept that occur at adolescence thus reflect not just greater cognitive abstractness but also a search for a new understanding of the self. It is precisely this search that is referred to as the *identity crisis.* In particular, the adolescent must develop an *occupational identity* (what will she *do* as an adult?), an *ideological identity* (what does she believe in?), and a *sexual identity* (what pattern of sexual behavior is acceptable, and what sex role is desired?)

Nearly all the current work on formation of these elements of adolescent identity have been based on James Marcia's descriptions of *identity statuses* (1966, 1980). Following Erikson's basic formulation, Marcia argues that there are two key parts to any adolescent identity formation: a *crisis* and a *commitment.* By a *crisis* Marcia means a period of decision making when old values, old choices are reexamined. This may occur as a sort of upheaval—the classic notion of a crisis—or it may occur gradually. The outcome of the reevaluation is a commitment to some specific role, some particular ideology.

If you put these two elements together, as in Figure 10.5, you can see that four different identity statuses are possible:

- **Identity achievement.** The young person has been through a crisis and has reached a commitment.
- **Moratorium.** A crisis is in progress, but the young person has not yet made a commitment.
- **Foreclosure.** The young person has made a commitment without having gone through a crisis. The person has not reassessed old positions; instead, he or she has simply accepted a parentally defined commitment.
- **Identity diffusion.** The young person is not in the midst of a crisis (although there may have been one in the past) and has not made a commitment. Diffusion may represent either an early stage in the process (before a crisis) or a failure to reach a commitment after a crisis.

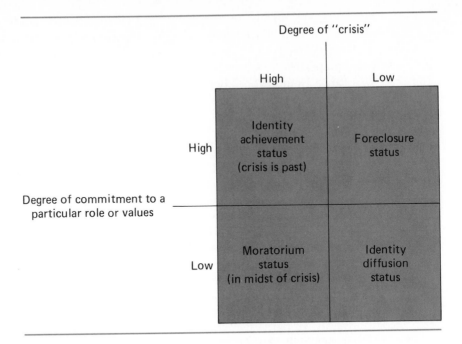

Figure 10.5   The four identity statuses proposed by Marcia (based on Erikson's theory). To fully achieve identity, the young person must both examine his or her values or goals and reach a firm commitment. (*Source:* Marcia, 1980.)

Whether every young person goes through some kind of identity crisis I don't know, since there have been no longitudinal studies covering all the relevant years. But there have been a number of cross-sectional studies, eight of which Alan Waterman (1985) has combined into a single analysis. You can see the pattern of results for vocational identity in Figure 10.6.

Several things about these results are interesting. First, notice that identity achievement occurs most typically not in high school but at college age. Second, note that the moratorium status is relatively uncommon except in the early years of college. So if most young people go through an identity crisis, that crisis is fairly late and does not last terribly long. Third, it is interesting that about a third of young people at every age are in the foreclosure status, which may indicate that many young people simply do not go through a crisis at all but follow well-defined grooves.

Collectively, these findings suggest that the identity crisis occurs somewhat later than Erikson originally proposed. But this conclusion requires one qualification: probably this dilemma is resolved earlier among young people who go to work immediately after high school than among those who go to college. Attending college is in some sense a postponement of full adult status. The years in college are a period in which students are actively encouraged to question, doubt, and try out alternatives. Those who go directly into the working world do not have that luxury. In one of the

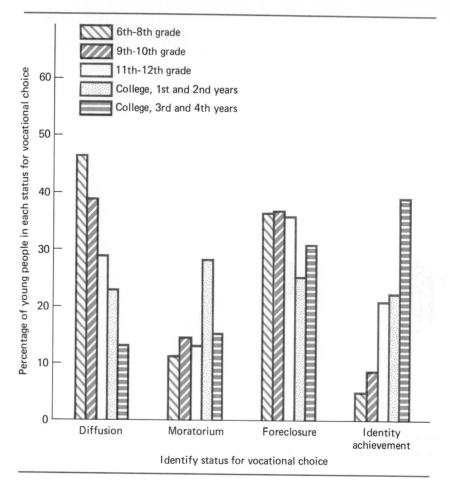

Figure 10.6 These data come from eight different cross-sectional studies comparing the identity statuses of young people of different ages. As you can see, diffusion and foreclosure are the most common statuses among the younger teenagers, while identity achievement is the most common status among the college juniors and seniors. (*Source:* Waterman, 1985. From Table 2, p. 18.)

few studies of non-college-attending youth, Gordon Munro and Gerald Adams (1977) found that 45 percent of those who were already working could be described as in the identity achievement status, which is higher than the levels shown in Figure 10.6 for college students.

Summary of Developmental Changes in Self-concept

Let me sum all this up for you. The young child develops first a primitive sense of her own separateness. This is followed quickly by beginning definitions of herself in terms of her physical properties (age, size, gender) and what she does. Over the periods of concrete and formal operations (from age 6 through adolescence), the content of the child's self-concept becomes more abstract, less and less tied to outward physical qualities, more based on presumably enduring inner qualities. During late adolescence, the whole self-concept also appears to undergo a kind of reorganization, and a new future-oriented sexual, occupational, and ideological identity is created.

INDIVIDUAL DIFFERENCES IN THE SELF-CONCEPT

So far, I have talked about the self-concept as if there were no values attached to the categories by which we define ourselves. But that's clearly not the case. Recall from Chapter 9 that Bandura's theory of personality development emphasized the emergence of strong internal standards and self-evaluations. You can see such evaluations in the "Who am I?" answers I have already quoted. The 9-year-old clearly makes a lot of positive statements about himself, while the two older subjects offer more mixed evaluations. This evaluative, positive/negative dimension of the self-concept is usually referred to as **self-esteem.** It is that part of the self-concept in which we judge our own competence in comparison to some internalized standard or expectation (Harter, 1985; Rosenberg, 1985). Thus, children who have high self-esteem see themselves as meeting their own standards. They are satisfied with themselves. Those with low self-esteem see a discrepancy between what they would like to be (or think they *ought* to be) and what they are, and they are not satisfied.

You will find it encouraging to know that self-esteem generally rises during late elementary school and through adolescence: young people usually think of themselves more positively at 18 or 20 than they did at 12 or 14 (O'Malley & Bachman, 1983; Rosenberg, 1985). But within this general developmental trend there appear to be some persisting individual differences.

Differences in Self-esteem

What does it mean for a child to have high or low self-esteem? Table 10.2 lists some of the other characteristics of high-self-esteem children. It certainly appears that evaluating yourself positively is a good thing. It is associated with many other qualities that most of us see as valuable (such as doing well in school, having more friends, or being less depressed). At the same time, let me enter one note of caution about what I've listed in the table. If you read women's magazines or other popular press, you may have concluded that a child's or adult's self-esteem is the most central element in mental or emotional health. But the research on children's self-esteem is (with one or two notable exceptions) inconsistent and messy. Any conclusions must be tentative. One of the difficulties may be that we

Table 10.2

▨▨▨▨▨▨▨

Characteristics of Children with High Self-esteem Compared to Those of Children with Low Self-esteem

- They get somewhat better grades in school and on achievement tests.
- They see themselves as responsible for their own success or failure.
- They have more friends.
- They see their relationship with their parents more positively.
- As adolescents, they are more likely to have achieved "identity status" (LaVoie, 1976).
- They are less likely to be depressed (Rosenberg, 1985).

▨▨▨▨▨▨▨

have assumed that children (and adults) operate with *global* evaluations of themselves, which we can describe as overall self-esteem. But in fact, our self-judgments may be much more specific than that. Most of us know that we are good at some things and bad at others, and children make these discriminations, too. Clearly, these self-evaluations affect our behavior and our feelings. But adding them up into a single score and calling it "self-esteem" may be less useful than looking at the individual judgments.

Differences in Identity Achievement

Research on differences in identity achievement is much newer, and here, too, the conclusions are only tentative. The findings so far suggest that compared to those who are in the diffusion or foreclosure statuses, teenagers and young adults in the identity achievement or moratorium statuses are more independent and autonomous, get better grades in college, are more likely to reason at the level of formal operations, are more successful in establishing satisfying intimate relationships as young adults, and have higher self-esteem (Marcia, 1980). LaVoie's results (1976) on identity status and self-esteem, shown in Figure 10.7, are typical. LaVoie also included a measure of the degree of trust versus mistrust (Erikson's first stage, as you'll recall) and found that those teenagers with a clearer identity also described themselves as having more "basic trust." Such a link between the successful resolution of the earlier and later dilemmas is certainly consistent with Erikson's theory, although LaVoie's study does not tell us whether this is a *causal* connection or not.

The Origins of Self-esteem and Identity

Where do these differences in self-esteem or in identity achievement come from? From either a social-learning or psychoanalytic point of view, the

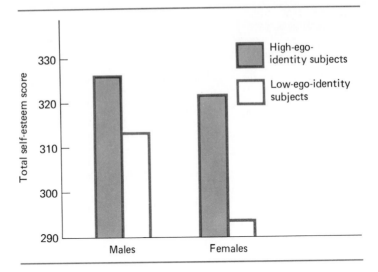

Figure 10.7 Those young people who have achieved a clearer ego-identity (those who are closer to an achieved identity, in Marcia's system) are also likely to have higher self-esteem. Just what is cause and what is effect here is not entirely clear, but this linkage has been found by several investigators. (*Source:* LaVoie, 1976. From Table II, p. 378.)

logical place to look is in the child's family. And when we look there, we find an intriguing pattern.

Diana Baumrind (1972) has proposed that we can analyze child-rearing patterns along several key dimensions: (1) the degree of warmth and nurturance the parents express toward their children, (2) the extent to which the parents expect the child to be mature and independent, (3) the clarity of rules and the consistency with which those rules are applied, and (4) the amount of communication between parent and child and the extent to which the child's opinion is sought and listened to. From her observations of families of preschool children, she derived three patterns or styles of child rearing. The **permissive parental style** is high in nurturance but low in maturity demands, control, and communication; the **authoritarian parental style** is high in maturity demands and control but low in nurturance and communication; the **authoritative parental style** is high in all four qualities.

I am oversimplifying a bit to state it this way, but as a general rule it is the authoritative style that is associated with higher self-esteem in young children and with earlier or more complete identity achievement in adolescence. The key combination seems to be firm but reasoned control, positive encouragement of independence, and a warm and loving atmosphere. Stanley Coopersmith (1967) found this in his large study of self-esteem in elementary-school-age children. Campbell and his colleagues

(1984) have found essentially the same pattern in their study of identity development among first-year college students. Rosenberg (1985) has also found that adolescents with higher self-esteem have the sense that they *matter* to their parents.

Aside from the general style of discipline and the warmth of the family, another way parents seem to affect the child's self-esteem is simply by labeling the child to herself. A child who is repeatedly told that she is "pretty" or "smart" or "a good athlete" is likely to have higher self-esteem than a child who is told that she is "dumb" or "clumsy" or a "late bloomer"— a process that fits with what Bandura has suggested about the origins of children's self-standards and sense of self-efficacy. (I even know of one mother and father who call their son "jerk" or "the jerk.") Similarly, parents' more general beliefs about their child's competence seem to be conveyed as well, perhaps in many subtle ways. Deborah Phillips (1987), for example, has found that among academically bright children, those who underestimate their own abilities are much more likely to think that their parents don't see them as especially bright than do children who see their own skills more accurately.

▬▬▬▬▬ ## THE SELF-CONCEPT: A SUMMING UP

There are obviously many questions still to be answered. But I want to emphasize once again that a child's self-concept appears to be a highly significant mediating concept. As Diane Ruble puts it:

> Children, in part, socialize themselves . . . they are motivated to construct rules or theories about themselves and their social environments and . . . such constructions influence their behavior and, in turn, how others respond to them (Ruble, 1987, p. 244).

Once such a "theory" of the self is well established, especially if she sees her own qualities as internal and enduring, the child systematically chooses experiences and environments that are consistent with her beliefs. The child who believes she can't play baseball behaves differently from the child who believes that she can. She is likely to avoid baseballs, bats, playing fields, and other children who play baseball. If forced to play, she may make self-deprecating remarks, like "You know I can't play," or she may play self-defeating games, like refusing to watch the ball when she swings at it or not running after the ball in right field because she knows she couldn't catch it even if she did get there on time. (If you think all this sounds autobiographical, you're right! Those of you who were bad at baseball, as I believed I was, know that the poorest players are *always* put in right field.)

A child who believes that she can't do long division will behave quite differently in the classroom from the child whose self-concept includes the idea "I am good at math" (or, even more potently, "I am better at math than other kids.") She may not try to work long-division problems on the theory that if you don't try, you can't fail. Or she may try much harder, paying the price in anxiety about failure.

The point is that these beliefs are pervasive, they develop early, and they are not easily changed. We need to know a good deal more about the origins of the child's self-definitions if we are to understand how to modify the inaccurate elements.

THE DEVELOPMENT OF GENDER AND SEX-ROLE CONCEPTS

So far in the discussion, I have mostly left out one element of the child's self-concept: the gender concept and the accompanying concept of sex roles. How does a child come to understand that he or she is a boy or a girl, and when and how do children learn what behaviors are "appropriate" for each gender? I have saved this set of questions for a separate discussion partly because this has been an area of hot debate and extensive research for the past decade (so there is a lot to say) and partly because this set of questions has such central personal relevance for so many of us. Women's roles and men's roles are changing rapidly in our society. But our stereotypes about men and women and our own inner sense of what it means to be male or female have not always kept pace. If we are to understand ourselves (and rear our children with less confusion, perhaps), we need to know more about the ways in which children learn about gender and about sex roles.

Some Definitions

Before I can delve into these questions, though, I need to define some terms for you. These words and phrases often get used fuzzily and interchangeably, which only confuses things. I will use these terms and phrases this way:

The **gender concept** is the idea that one is a boy or a girl and that gender is constant over time.

Sex roles are the set of behaviors, attitudes, rights, duties, and obligations that are part of the role of being a boy or a girl, a male or a female, in any given society. All roles have such collections of duties, rights, and expected behaviors. Teachers are supposed to behave in certain ways, as are employees or mothers or baseball managers. These are all roles. Sex roles are somewhat broader than most other roles in our culture, but they are nonetheless roles. A **sex-role concept** in the set of ideas any one of us has about the specific content of a sex role—what males and females do and are "supposed to" do.

Sex-role stereotyping is a process of overextending the sex roles or applying them too rigidly. Any stereotype involves assigning people to rigidly defined categories without taking into account the individual qualities. When we say "Men are unemotional," we are displaying a stereotype. The male sex role may include "unemotional" as one of its qualities (for example, men are not "supposed to" cry), but clearly, many men show their emotions easily. Stereotypes thus go beyond statements of what is "supposed to be" to inaccurately broad statements about "what is."

Sex typing and **sex-role behavior** refer to the extent to which a child's behavior (or an adult's) matches the cultural expectation for her or his sex role. A girl may know quite well that she is a girl and may be able to describe the sex roles accurately, but she may still behave in a tomboyish way. We would say that her behavior is less *sex-typed* than is the behavior of a girl who adopts more traditional play patterns.

If we are going to understand the development of the child's concept of gender, we have to understand all these elements. How does the child come to know what gender she is? How and when does she develop ideas about sex roles or about sex-role stereotyping? And how well do children match their behavior to the sex roles or the stereotypes?

Developmental Patterns

The Development of the Gender Concept. How soon does a child figure out that she is a girl or he is a boy? It depends on what we mean by "figure out." There seem to be three steps. The first is **gender identity,** which is simply a child's ability to label his or her own sex correctly and to identify other people as men or women, boys or girls. Children seem to notice some of the external features that differentiate male from female quite early—as early as 15 to 18 months. And by age 2, if you show them a set of pictures of a same-sex child and several opposite-sex children and say "Which one is you?", most children can correctly pick out the same-sex picture (Thompson, 1975). By $2\frac{1}{2}$ or 3, most children can correctly label and identify the sex of others as well (can point out "Which one is a girl?" or "Which one is a boy?" in a set of pictures). Children seem to be using hair length and clothing as the primary cues for these early discriminations.

Accurate labeling, though, does not signify complete understanding. Like the various concepts I talked about in Chapter 7 (such as concepts of identity, or number, or conservation), which show increasing subtlety and complexity over the preschool and early school years, the gender concept undergoes further refinements. The second step is **gender stability,** the understanding that you stay the same gender throughout life. Researchers have measured this by asking children such questions as "When you were a little baby, were you a little girl or a little boy?" or "When you grow up, will you be a mommy or a daddy?" Ronald Slaby and Karin Frey (1975) found that most children understand the stability aspect of gender by about age 4.

Finally, there is the development of true **gender constancy,** which is the recognition that someone stays the same gender even though he or she may appear to change (by wearing different clothes or having hair a different length). For example, girls don't change into boys by cutting their hair very short or by wearing boys' clothes. It may seem odd that a child who understands that he or she will stay the same gender throughout life (gender stability) can nonetheless be confused about the effect of changes in dress or appearance on gender. But numerous studies show this sequence, even in children growing up in other cultures, such as Kenya, Nepal, Belize, and Samoa (Munroe, Shimmin, & Munroe, 1984).

The underlying logic of this sequence may be a bit clearer if I draw a parallel between gender constancy and the concept of conservation, which I described in Chapter 7. Conservation of mass or number or weight involves recognition that an object remains the same in some fundamental way even though it changes externally in some fashion. Gender constancy is thus a kind of "conservation of gender," and it is not typically understood until about 5 or 6, when the other conservations are first grasped. Dale Marcus and Willis Overton (1978) studied this link in a study in which kindergarten and first- and second-grade children were tested for both conservation of quantity and gender constancy. The results, which are shown in Table 10.3, clearly show that children typically understand either both or neither.

In sum, children as young as 2 or $2\frac{1}{2}$ know their own sex and that of people around them, but they do not have a fully developed concept of gender until they are 5 or 6.

Table 10.3
░░░░░░░░░░░░░░░

Relationship Between Gender Constancy and Conservation of Quantity in Young Children

Pattern of constancy and conservation	Child's grade in school		
	Kindergarten	First	Second
Child has neither gender constancy nor conservation of quantity.	17	4	1
Child has conservation but not gender constancy.	3	4	4
Child has both.	4	14	18

Source: After Marcus & Overton, 1978, Table 3, p. 440. © The Society for Research in Child Development, Inc.

The Development of Sex-Role Concepts and Stereotypes.　Obviously, figuring out your gender and understanding that it stays constant is only part of the story. Learning what *goes with* or *ought to go* with being a boy or a girl is also a vital part of the child's task.

Researchers have studied this in two ways—by asking children what boys and girls like to do and what they are like (which is an inquiry about stereotypes) and by asking children if it is *okay* for boys to play with dolls or for girls to climb trees or to do equivalent "cross-sex" things (an inquiry about roles).

In our society, adults have clear sex-role stereotypes. We think of men as competent, skillful, assertive, aggressive, and able to get things done. We think of women as warm and expressive, tactful, quiet, gentle, aware of others' feelings, and lacking in competence, independence, and logic (Broverman et al., 1972; T. L. Ruble, 1983). Such stereotypes may be weaker or more blurred now than they were even a few decades ago, but they are nonetheless present. Furthermore, sex-role stereotypes are already partially in place by age 5 or 6 and are quite firmly held by age 7 or 8. For example, Deborah Best and John Williams and their colleagues (Best et al., 1977; Williams, Bennett, & Best, 1975) found that fourth- and fifth-graders in the United States, England, and Ireland see women as weak, emotional, soft-hearted, sentimental, sophisticated, and affectionate. They see men as strong, robust, aggressive/assertive, cruel, coarse, ambitious, and dominant. Kindergartners in these studies showed some of these themes, but not as strongly. Interestingly, adolescents' stereotypes seem to be somewhat more flexible (Emmerich & Shepard, 1982; Huston-Stein & Higgens-Trenk, 1978).

This pattern of increasing and then declining sex-role stereotyping (ideas about what men and women *are* like) is matched by changes in children's ideas about what boys and girls *ought to be* like. This trend emerges particularly clearly in a study by William Damon. He told a story to children aged 4 through 9. In this story, a little boy named George likes to play with dolls. His parents tell him that only little girls play with dolls; little boys shouldn't. They buy him some other toys, but still George prefers dolls. The children were then asked a batch of questions about this (Damon, 1977, p. 242):

> Why do people tell George not to play with dolls?
> Are they right?
> Is there a rule that boys shouldn't play with dolls?
> What should George do?
> Does George have a right to play with dolls?

Four-year-olds in this study thought it was okay for George to play with dolls. There was no rule against it and he should do it if he wanted to. Six-year-olds, in contrast, thought it was *wrong* for George to play with dolls. By about age 9, children had differentiated between what boys and girls usually do and what is "wrong." One boy said, for example, that breaking windows was wrong and bad but that playing with dolls was not bad in the same way: "Breaking windows you're not supposed to do. And if you play with dolls, well you can, but boys usually don't."

What seems to be happening here is that the 5- or 6-year-old, having figured out that she is permanently a girl or he is a boy, is searching for a *rule* about how boys and girls behave (Martin & Halverson, 1981). The child picks up information from watching adults, from watching TV, from listening to the labels that are attached to different activities (e.g., "Boys don't cry"). Initially, children treat these as absolute, moral rules. Later they understand that these are social conventions, at which point sex-role concepts become more flexible and stereotyping declines somewhat (although it does not in any sense disappear; sex stereotyping is very strong among adults).

One of the interesting sidelights in the research on stereotyping is that the male stereotype and sex-role concept seems to develop a bit earlier and to be stronger than the female stereotype or sex-role concept. More children agree on what men are or should be than on what women are or should be. This might happen because children have seen women in more different roles (mother and teacher, for example) than they have seen men in. Or it could mean that the female role in our society is more flexible than the male role. At any rate, it is clear that the qualities attributed to the male are more highly *valued* than are the female traits (Broverman et al., 1970). It is "good" to be independent, assertive, logical, and strong; it is less good to be warm, quiet, tactful, and gentle. Perhaps girls recognize early that the male role is seen more positively and aspire to some of the valued male qualities. That would lead to a female role perceived more broadly. Whatever the reason, it is an interesting finding—one with considerable relevance for understanding adult male and female sex roles and stereotyping.

The Development of Sex-Role Behavior. The final element in the equation is the actual behavior children show with their own sex and with the opposite sex.

We have several pieces of information. First of all, if you observe children while they play in a room stocked with a wide range of attractive toys, you'll see that children as young as 2 or 3 show sex stereotyping in their toy choices. Little girls play with dolls or at various housekeeping games, including sewing, stringing beads, or cooking. Boys play with guns, toy trucks, fire engines, and carpentry tools (Fagot, 1974; O'Brien & Huston, 1985).

Second, children begin to choose same-sex playmates very early—as young as $2\frac{1}{2}$ or 3—and they are much more sociable with playmates of the same sex at these ages (Jacklin & Maccoby, 1978). This preference is not nearly as strong as it becomes at school age—when peer relationships are almost exclusively same-sex. But there is already a tilt in this direction among toddlers, as you can see in Figure 10.8 in the results of a study of play groups in preschool activities by La Freniere, Strayer, and Gauthier (1984). By age 3, about 60 percent of the spontaneous play groups were same-sex groupings.

The other intriguing pattern is that children in early elementary school seem to begin to pay more attention to the behavior of same-sex than opposite-sex adults or playmates and to play more with new toys that are labeled as being appropriate for their own sex (e.g., Ruble, Balaban, & Cooper, 1981; Bradbard et al., 1986). Thus, although quite young children

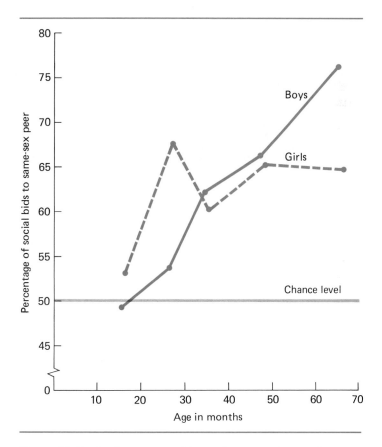

Figure 10.8 La Freniere and his colleagues observed groups of preschool children playing with their peers and noted how often they played with same-sex or opposite-sex playmates. As you can see, children as young as $2\frac{1}{2}$ years (30 months) already showed a noticeable preference for same-sex playmates. (*Source:* La Freniere, Strayer, & Gauthier, 1984, Figure 1, p. 1961. © The Society for Research in Child Development, Inc.)

are aware of and are apparently influenced by gender in both toy and play-mate choice, gender seems to become a still more potent force in guiding behavior and attitudes at around age 5 or 6.

THEORIES OF THE DEVELOPMENT OF SEX-ROLE CONCEPTS AND SEX-ROLE BEHAVIOR

How can we explain the development of sex-role concepts and sex-role behavior? As you might expect, theorists of virtually every persuasion have tried their hand.

Social-Learning Explanations

The major proponent for a social-learning explanation of the development of sex-role behavior has been Walter Mischel (1966, 1970). He has argued that children learn their sex roles by being reinforced directly, both for doing sex-appropriate things and for imitating same-sex models (particularly the same-sex parent). Mischel assumes that parents pay more attention to children when they imitate the "right"-sexed person. In this way, the child learns the appropriate sex role. More recent extensions of social-learning theories focus also on the child's development of expectancies about what behaviors are appropriate for a given sex by observing which sex performs them. According to this view, the more clearly any given behavior is stereotyped for one sex, the more likely the child of that sex would be to imitate that behavior (e.g., Perry & Bussey, 1979).

There is a fair amount of support for this position. We know, for example, that parents buy different kinds of toys for boys and girls, beginning in infancy, and use different kinds of toys when they play with boys and girls (Huston, 1983). Parents also reinforce different kinds of behaviors in their sons and daughters. Boys are rewarded more for independent activities, for active and manipulative play. Girls are rewarded more for dependent behavior and feminine sex-typed play. All in all, both boys and girls are rewarded for behaviors that are sex-typed for their sex. Interestingly, such differential treatment of sons and daughters is more common among fathers than mothers, and fathers are particularly likely to be concerned with the appropriate sex-role behavior of their sons (Siegal, 1987).

Parents also punish their children for sex-inappropriate behavior. Once again, this is generally more true of fathers than of mothers, and more for sons than for daughters. Fathers are apparently uncomfortable with "girlish" behavior in their sons, and they are much more likely to show disapproval of such behavior in their sons than they are to disapprove of "tomboyish" behavior in their daughters. (This may be one reason that the male stereotype develops earlier and is stronger than the female stereotype.)

All these different types of treatment may combine to convey quite different messages about appropriate sex-role behavior to boys and girls. Jeanne Block (1983) has offered a particularly intriguing analysis of these subtle messages about sex differences. She suggests that there are at least three basic differences: (1) Boys are taught (through toy choice, through the type of play they are encouraged in by the parents) a greater sense of mastery or competence, a sense that they can have an impact on the world around them. Girls develop less of a sense of self-efficacy. (2) Boys are given more opportunities to "experiment with nature" and are generally encouraged to be more exploratory and independent than are girls. (3) The two sexes are taught different ways of handling discrepant or disconfirming experiences. Block suggests that girls are taught to assimilate—to work to make new information fit into the old system. Boys, in contrast, are socialized to accommodate—to change the way they think or do something. If this is true, it would help to make boys bolder, more creative, better able to see old things in new ways. In the same vein, other researchers have pointed out that girls are more often trained to ask for help while boys are trained to try to work things out for themselves and that girls are generally seen as more fragile and vulnerable than boys and thus in need of protection. (I noted in earlier chapters that by many yardsticks girls are actually much *less* vulnerable than are boys. However, it is not the fact that matters here but what parents and children believe.)

Collectively, these findings (and speculations) provide a good deal of support for a social-learning theory of sex-role development. Parents do provide different environments for their boys and girls and are differentially tolerant of appropriately or inappropriately sex-typed behavior. But, helpful as it is, this approach still can't account for all the facts I've given you. First of all, there is less differential reinforcement than you'd expect, and there is probably not enough to account for the very early and robust discrimination children seem to make on the basis of gender. After all, 2-year-olds are already showing a preference for same-sex playmates.

A second difficulty is that there is little evidence that children imitate same-sex adults or children more than opposite-sex adults or children until they are 5 or 6 years old. In other words, we don't see differential imitation until *after* the child has already developed a strong set of ideas about sex roles. Thus, children do not seem to be learning their sex roles by imitating or being rewarded for imitating same-sex adults.

What we see instead is that children are differentially *sensitive* to reinforcements from same-sex children and adults. Beverly Fagot (1985), for example, has found that nursery-school teachers typically reward *both* boys and girls for more stereotypically *female* or neutral behavior (e.g., cooperativeness, lower levels of activity, quieter play), but boys nonetheless persist in showing stereotypic male behavior. In this study the boys' behavior changed only if other boys showed disapproval or approval. So the boys were more sensitive to reinforcements from other boys; girls were responsive to the teacher's reinforcements and to those from other girls.

Psychoanalytic Explanations

Freud saw the process of identification as a major vehicle for the child's acquisition of sex-role concepts and behavior. As you'll remember from Chapter 9, identification is the result of the Oedipus conflict, at about age 4 or 5. The child takes in (incorporates) all the qualities of the same-sex parent as a way of lessening his or her anxiety. If Freud is correct, then we should see children begin to imitate the same-sex parent and other same-sex adults pretty consistently, beginning at age 4 or so. But as I just mentioned, that's not what we see. Most children do not show such differential imitation until later. Freud's view also doesn't help us explain why children would show sex-typed toy choices or playmate choices as early as 2 or 3, before the Oedipal crisis has occurred. All in all, this theory has not been very helpful in explaining this particular developmental pattern.

Cognitive-Developmental Explanations

Lawrence Kohlberg (1966; Kohlberg & Ullian, 1974) offered a third alternative, grounded in Piagetian theory. Kohlberg argued that we have to look at the cognitive part of the child's understanding of gender. Until the child has fully grasped the constancy of gender, we shouldn't see very much sex-typed behavior, and we certainly shouldn't see much imitation of same-sex models. Once the child has understood the gender concept, however, and realizes that he is a boy or she is a girl forever, then (in order to maintain cognitive consistency) it becomes highly important to learn how to behave in a way that fits the category one belongs to. Thus Kohlberg predicts that we should see systematic same-sex imitation only *after* the child has shown full gender constancy.

In fact, that's what the research generally shows. Diane Ruble's study is a good example (Ruble, Balaban, & Cooper, 1981). She showed 4- to 6-year-old children a cartoon with a "commercial" in the middle. The commercial showed either two girls playing with a toy or two boys playing with the same toy. After seeing the cartoon, each child was encouraged to play with any of the toys in the room, which included the toy he or she had seen in the commercial.

As you can see in Figure 10.9, children who had already achieved full gender constancy were much more influenced by the gender of the models in the commercial than were children at earlier levels of development of the gender concept. Other researchers have found that children who understand gender constancy are more likely to watch same-sex adult models (Slaby & Frey, 1975). This result is not found in every study, but it is common enough to provide some support for this aspect of Kohlberg's theory.

Despite such support for this key prediction, however, Kohlberg's approach still has weaknesses, the most glaring of which is the fact that children show clear signs of sex-typed behavior many years before they

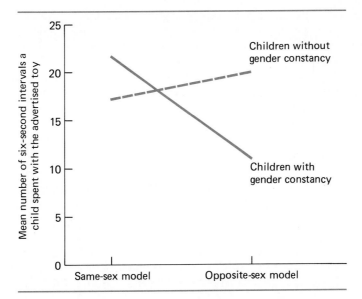

Figure 10.9   Results from Ruble's study show that children who had already achieved gender constancy were much more likely to imitate the same-sex model in a commercial than the opposite-sex model. This suggests that once children figure out that gender is permanent, they spend a lot of time trying to determine just what they are supposed to do in order to be a boy or a girl—figuring out the "rule." (*Source:* After Ruble, Balaban, & Cooper, 1981, Figure 1, p. 670. © The Society for Research in Child Development, Inc.)

have fully grasped gender constancy. Two- and three-year-olds show sex-appropriate toy and playmate choice at a point when they barely can label their own and others' genders accurately. Obviously, something else, such as parental reinforcement for certain toy choices, is at work in the early years.

A New Alternative: Gender Schemas

A more recent alternative, which sidesteps many of these difficulties, is an essentially cognitive approach offered by a number of theorists (e.g., Ruble, 1987; Martin & Halverson, 1981, 1983). Like the self-concept, the child's understanding of gender can be thought of as a "schema" or "self-theory." As Carol Martin and Charles Halverson put it:

> The basic idea [is] that stereotypes are "schemas," or naive theories that are relevant to the self, and function to organize and structure experience

by telling the perceiver the kinds of information to look for in the environment and how to interpret such information. Martin & Halverson, 1983,
p. 563)

The gender and sex-role rule or schema develops gradually over the first
six to eight years of life and affects the child's attention, memory, and
behavior.

After figuring out their own gender, 2- and 3-year-olds begin with a
basic "rule" that organizes objects and people into two big groups: "own
sex" and "other sex." Some of the information for forming this first rule
comes from comments by parents or from specific reinforcements; some
comes from observation. When the child later understands the permanence
of gender (at about 5 or 6), information about gender-appropriate behavior
becomes still more salient to the child, and she develops a more elaborated
rule or schema of "what people who are like me do" (perhaps incorporating
some of the subtle messages Block describes). Initially, the child of this
age treats this "rule" the same way she treats other rules—as absolutes.
Later, the child's knowledge of the "gender rule" continues to develop,
but her application of it becomes more flexible. (She knows that most boys
don't play with dolls but that they *can* do so if they like, for example).

Martin and Halverson emphasize that such rule learning is absolutely
normal, and so is the rigid stereotyping that we see in elementary-school
children's ideas about sex roles. Many of us, committed to the philosophical
goal of equality for women, have taken the rigidity of children's early sex
stereotypes as evidence that we have made little progress toward equality
("Mommy, you can't be a psychology doctor, you have to be a psychology
nurse"). But I think that Martin and Halverson are quite correct; children
are searching for order, for rules that help to make sense of their experiences.
And a rule about "what men do" and "what women do" is a helpful schema
for children. Like they do with grammatical rules, children first apply this
new rule too rigidly and then later learn the exceptions. But the rule-learning
process seems to be a natural one.

Obviously, the particular rule about sex roles that a child will develop
depends on the kinds of models he encounters and the reinforcement
pattern he experiences. In our culture, a key source of this rule-generating
information is TV and children's books—a subject I have explored in the
box on pages 380–381.

INDIVIDUAL DIFFERENCES IN SEX TYPING AND STEREOTYPES

The developmental patterns I have been describing seem to be true for
virtually all children, but children do differ quite a lot in the rigidity of
the rule they develop and in the sex typing of their behavior.

As a group, boys usually have stronger (more rigid and more traditional) sex-role stereotypes. Among both boys and girls, however, children whose mothers work outside the home have *less* stereotypic views—more flexible rules (e.g., Powell & Steelman, 1982). This makes perfectly good sense if you think about the origin of the child's sex-role schema. Presumably, the child is learning "what women do" partly from observing her mother; if her mother is doing the same sort of work as her father, her schema is bound to include this greater equality.

Cross-Sex Children

Children with cross-sex preferences—girls who would rather be boys and boys who would rather be girls—also seem to have less distinctly different sex-role stereotypes (Nash, 1975; Kuhn, Nash, & Brucken, 1978). Such cross-sex children are particularly interesting. How does a child come to prefer to be the other sex or to choose cross-sex playmates or toys?

One possibility is that these children are directly trained that way. They may have been specifically reinforced for aspects of the opposite sex's role. Some girls are given trucks and carpentry tools and are taught football by their fathers (or mothers). They may come to wish to be boys. In fact, there are far more girls who say they would like to be boys than there are boys who say they would rather be girls, which makes sense from a social-learning point of view. Tomboy behavior is more accepted and reinforced than is "girlish" behavior in a boy.

On the other side, though, is evidence from a recent study by Carl Roberts and his colleagues (Roberts et al., 1987) of a group of boys who showed strong preference for female sex-typed toys, behavior, and playmates from their earliest years of life. When Roberts compared these boys to a group of boys with more typical masculine sex-role behaviors, he found little evidence that the more feminine boys had been specifically reinforced for these behaviors, nor were their fathers providing models for such behavior. What Roberts found instead was that compared to the masculine boys, the feminine boys were more feminine in appearance from early babyhood, they were more often ill or hospitalized early in life, and they had relatively less contact with both their mothers and fathers on a daily basis. This pattern of findings does not fit nicely with a simple social-learning explanation.

Alternatively, there might be some biological differences. Roberts's finding that the behaviorally more feminine boys looked more feminine from infancy is at least consistent with such a possibility, as is their finding that in adulthood, three-quarters of the more feminine boys were homosexual or bisexual in orientation. Further evidence for some biological influence on cross-sex behavior comes from studies of girls who have experienced heightened levels of androgen prenatally. (Recall from Chapter 4 that androgen is largely a "male" hormone.) These "androgenized" girls, in comparison to their normal sisters, are later found to be more interested in rough-and-tumble play, more often prefer to play with boys, show less interest

SEX STEREOTYPING ON TV AND IN BOOKS

If children are searching for information about what men and women do, as part of the creation of their sex-role "rules" or "schemas," then TV and children's books may have a major impact on them. Certainly children watch a lot of TV—3 to 6 hours per day, by recent estimates (Murray, 1980). In fact, many children spend more time watching TV than they do in school or playing or talking with their parents. So the portrayals of men and women, boys and girls, in TV programs are bound to be a very important source of data for the child's emerging sex-role concept.

What researchers have found when they have counted specific behaviors by men and women on TV is that the sexes are portrayed in highly stereotypic ways (Huston, 1983). Many more male characters are shown (even in commercials selling women's products), and the men are more active, aggressive, and independent. The men solve problems. The only behaviors that women show more often than men on TV are deference and passivity. Females generally play the "handmaiden" roles— they hand the male character his coat, type

his reports, and listen to his troubles.

A continuous exposure to these stereotyped males and females does seem to have at least a small effect on child's vision of men and women and their roles. Terry Frueh and Paul McGhee (1975) found that elementary-school children who watched more than 25 hours of TV a week had more traditional sex-role concepts than did children who watched less than 10 hours a week. The effect is not large, but it has been found by a number of different researchers. Even more persuasive is an experiment by Emily Davidson (Davidson, Yasuna, & Tower, 1979), who found that 5- and 6-year-old children who were shown highly sex-stereotyped cartoons gave more stereotyped answers to questions about the qualities of men and women than did children who had seen cartoons depicting men and women in more equal roles.

At a more subtle level, in several studies Aletha Huston and her colleagues (e.g., Huston et al., 1984) have found that toy commercials aimed at boys and those aimed at girls are simply designed differently. Boys' commercials are fast, sharp, and

---

in dolls or babies, and have fewer fantasies about being mothers—although they did expect to marry and were interested in dating (Meyer-Bahlberg, Ehrhardt, & Feldman, 1986).

Findings like these suggest that actual sex typing of behavior is affected by prenatal hormones. At the same time, it is also clear that a child's basic gender identity—the gender she thinks of herself as being—is essentially determined by the label she is given (and the treatment she receives) from her parents. Children born with ambiguous genitals, for example, will grow up to think of themselves as being whichever gender they were reared as, even if that gender does not match the genotype (Money, 1975).

Clearly, the gender a child *thinks* he or she is affects the gender *schema* he or she develops. The environment is extremely potent. But at the risk of being unpopular, I want to say that I think we would do well

loud—lots of quick cuts, activity, loud music. Girls' commercials are gradual, soft, and fuzzy—camera fades and dissolves, softer background music. Children as young as first grade notice these differences, too. They can watch a commercial of some nonstereotyped toy and tell you whether the *style* of the commercial is suited to a boys' or girls' toy.

Children's textbooks and storybooks show similar stereotyping. In one analysis, Terry Saario, Carol Jacklin, and Carol Tittle (1973) found that there were very few major female characters in children's books; those there were tended to be weaker, less able to solve problems on their own, and more dependent on male characters. The boys and men in the children's books are shown as strong, dominant, and problem-solving. In one reading book, for example (O'Donnell, 1966), a little girl is shown having fallen off her roller skates. The caption said, " 'She cannot skate,' said Mark. 'I can help her. I want to help her. Look at her, Mother. Just look at her. She is just a girl. She gives up.' "

Fortunately, blatant examples like this have disappeared from children's reading books, partly as a result of the efforts of parent groups. But many books still contain subtle messages about sex roles and sex-role stereotypes.

Clearly, TV and children's books have an impact on children's ideas about men and women (just as those same sources influence their aggressive behavior.) Current research points to the fact that children of 5 to 8 quite naturally construct rigid rules or schemas about male and female roles as a normal part of their search for regularity in the world around them. But sex-role portrayals on TV seem to foster even more stereotyped (and thus inaccurate) sex-role concepts in children, and they reinforce such stereotyped concepts well into elementary-school and high-school ages. If we showed men and women in more equal roles on TV, we might make it more difficult for the 5- or 6-year-old to develop a simple sex-role schema, but we would be reflecting reality far more. Of course, you could turn off the TV set.

to keep an open mind about the possible biological origins of some sex-role behaviors. The evidence is not all in yet.

Androgyny

A very different approach to the study of cross-sex sex typing has emerged in the past decade in the study of **androgyny.** Until perhaps the early 1970s, psychologists had thought of "masculinity" and "femininity" as opposite ends of a single continuum. A person could be one or the other but couldn't be both. Since then, Sandra Bem (1974), Janet Spence and Robert Helmreich (1978), and others have argued that it is possible for a person to express *both* masculine and feminine qualities—to be both compassionate and independent, both gentle and assertive. In the language I have been using in this chapter, this would mean that a child or adult's self-concept could include elements of both male and female sex roles.

In this new way of looking at sex roles, masculinity and femininity are conceived of as two separate dimensions. Any person can be high or low on either one or on both. The terms used to describe the four possible "types" created by this two-dimensional conception are shown in Figure 10.10. The two traditional sex roles are the masculine and the feminine combinations. But two new types become evident when we think about sex roles in this way: androgynous individuals describe themselves as having both masculine and feminine traits, and undifferentiated individuals describe themselves as lacking both. (These undifferentiated people sound to me a lot like those with a "diffuse" identity in Marcia's system.)

Notice that this categorization system says nothing about the accuracy of the child's or the adult's role or schema about sex roles. What it tells us about is the degree of match between the traditional sex roles and how a person thinks of herself or himself.

I cannot find any research on androgyny in young children (perhaps because androgyny ought to be quite uncommon at early ages, when children are creating their rigid rules about sex roles). But there is a growing body of research on androgyny in adolescents, and the results are tantalizing.

First of all, about 25 to 35 percent of high-school students can be

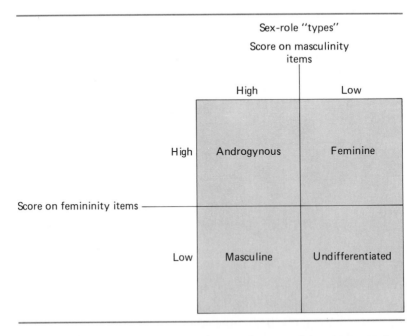

Figure 10.10 The current view of masculinity and femininity is that each of us may express some amount of *both* kinds of qualities, which produces the four possible combinations of sex-role "types" shown here.

described as androgynous (Spence & Helmreich, 1978; Lamke, 1982a). More girls seem to show this pattern than do boys, and there are more girls in the "masculine" category than there are boys in the "feminine" group.

Second, for *both* boys and girls, either a masculine or an androgynous sex-role self-concept is associated with higher self-esteem (Lamke, 1982a, 1982b). A boy can achieve high self-esteem and success with his peers by adopting a traditional masculine sex role. For girls, though, adoption of a traditional feminine sex role (without some balancing "male" characteristics) seems to carry a risk of lower self-esteem and even poorer relationships with peers (Massad, 1981).

Thus, although the creation of rigid rules or schemas for sex roles is a normal—even essential—process in young children, a blurring of those rules may be an important process in adolescence, particularly for girls, for whom a more androgynous self-concept is associated with positive outcomes.

SOME REAL-LIFE APPLICATIONS: OCCUPATIONAL CHOICES, OCCUPATIONAL BEHAVIOR, AND FAMILY ROLES

I began this chapter by talking about the question of whether occupational choices are really "free," given sex roles, sex-role stereotypes, and self-concepts in males and females. So let me return to that question, as well as to several other real-life applications of the research and concepts I have been talking about in this chapter.

Occupational Choices

Most of the research on the impact of sex roles and sex-role stereotypes on occupational choices has focused on girls and women—on why women choose to work or not and at what kind of job. But the same principles are presumably at work for boys and men, too.

In addition to the myriad other factors that affect an individual's job choice (social class, race, opportunity, education, specific ability, and so on), sex roles and self-concept have an impact in a whole series of ways.

Male Jobs and Female Jobs. Our definitions of sex roles, which are passed on to children very early, include designations of "male jobs" and "female jobs." As early as age 6 or 7, children can correctly classify jobs in this way, and their fantasies about their own future jobs are already affected (Eccles & Hoffman, 1984). Gottfredson (1981) has even suggested that at this early age, children simply eliminate from further consideration those occupations that they see as inappropriate for their gender. Such early sorting of prospective jobs into "acceptable" or "unacceptable" categories can be changed by later experience, but the early perceptions may be more powerful and more lasting than many of us may realize.

Sex Roles and Sex Typing.   Both the extent to which young people perceive themselves as feminine, masculine, or androgynous and the specific ideas a young person may have about appropriate male and female roles affect job choices. Girls who hold more traditional sex-role self-concepts, for example, are more likely to choose the occupation of wife and mother than are girls whose sex-role concept is more egalitarian. And if she works outside the home, the more traditional woman is more likely to choose a traditionally feminine occupation. In contrast, girls whose sex-role self-concepts fall into the masculine or androgynous categories are the ones who are most likely to choose unconventional or traditionally male jobs (Eccles & Hoffman, 1984; Fitzgerald & Betz, 1983).

Self-concept, Self-esteem, and Self-efficacy.   I mentioned earlier that girls who view themselves as more masculine or more androgynous are also likely to have higher self-esteem. Given that, you won't be surprised that there is separate evidence that, in women, higher self-esteem and greater self-confidence are associated with the choice of more nontraditional careers and with stronger job orientations.

Furthermore, specific beliefs about one's ability to do particular jobs (self-efficacy, in Bandura's language) affect job choices too. Since in general, boys and young men have a stronger sense of self-efficacy about a wider range of jobs than do girls and young women (Greenhaus & Parasuraman, 1986), boys and men are more comfortable choosing a wider variety of occupations. I talked about one example of this in Chapter 6: parents' ideas about their daughters' and sons' mathematical ability. Among girls and boys with equally high math ability (as measured on a standardized test), girls are more likely to think that their performance results from effort rather than basic ability, while boys are more likely to assume that underlying ability makes the difference. Perhaps as one consequence, girls less often choose mathematics-related occupations.

Specific Family Influences.   Beyond the specific (and subtle) ways in which families help to shape girls' or boys' self-concepts and sex typing, three other family characteristics have been found to be linked to higher rates of nonconventional ("masculine") occupations in women.

First, girls whose mothers work—particularly if the mother likes her job—are more likely to have more "masculine" self-concepts and to select more nonconventional occupations. Second, girls without brothers are more likely to be strongly career-oriented and to go for higher-status jobs. And third, girls whose fathers take a more active interest in their rearing and have warm and supportive relationships with their daughters are more likely to have high self-esteem and to be more successful in their jobs.

Hening and Jardim (1976), in a particularly fascinating study of a group of highly successful women executives, found that none had had brothers and nearly all had been treated "like a son" by their fathers. In these families, then, the subtle, implicit messages about what girls "could" or "should" do were quite different than in more traditional families.

The individual young person's occupational choice is obviously made with all these complex elements as part of the equation. Thus, the choice is not "free" in a psychological sense.

Occupational Behavior

The impact of sex roles and sex-role stereotypes on adult work life does not stop at the point of job choice. Day-to-day behavior on the job is also affected, as are the expectations and judgments of co-workers or supervisors. Such effects are particularly nicely illustrated in a recent study of women executives by Ann Morrison, Randall White, and Ellen Van Velsor (1987). They compared women who had made it into the top ranks of business executives with those who had been "derailed" short of the top. Their results point to the enduring potency of our cultural sex-role definitions and stereotypes.

The successful executive women were those whose behavior fit into a narrow band of androgyny, as shown in Figure 10.11. These women described themselves and were described by others as willing to take risks

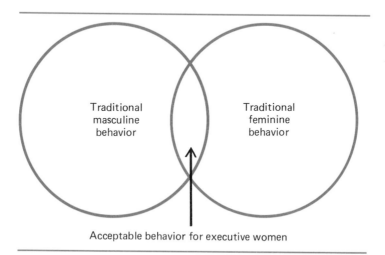

Figure 10.11 Research by Ann Morrison and her colleagues suggests that to be successful in business, a woman's behavior must fit into a very narrowly defined range. Because the job of business executive generally falls within the definition of a male sex role, the task for a man is much less difficult. (*Source:* After Morrison, White, & Van Velsor, 1987, p. 21.)

and as tough, ambitious, and willing to take responsibility—all qualities that are part of the masculine stereotype. But they were also described as willing to follow others' advice and as "feminine" in certain key respects: demure, not *too* tough, not "macho." Being perceived as *too* tough was often a key reason for a career derailment.

Thus, although the majority of women now work and the majority of adults subscribe to the philosophical ideal of equal opportunity, the sex roles and sex-role stereotypes acquired in childhood continue to have powerful limiting effects on those opportunities.

Family Roles

Similar limitations can be seen in the division of labor within the family. In his book *Working Wives/Working Husbands,* Joseph Pleck (1985) points out that in families in which both spouses work, women still do the majority of the housework and child care. The cause of this appears to be not the actual work schedules of husband and wife but rather our sex-role expectations for men and women. The relatively more rigid male role emphasizes a whole series of skills and qualities that are most often expressed in the world of work and usually excludes the more nurturing skills and behaviors involved in family roles. *Both* spouses perceive men's roles this way, so even though women say they would like their husbands to be more involved in family work, they too are imbued with the cultural sex-role definitions. Just as the woman executive who is perceived as "too tough" loses standing and respect, so may the man who is perceived as "too soft."

My point in all these examples is not that sex roles or sex-role concepts are bad. Rather, I want to emphasize that our ideas about sex roles develop early in life, are deeply held, and are difficult (but not impossible) to change. As a result, they affect a great many aspects of adult life in powerful ways.

SUMMARY

1. The child's emerging self-concept has several elements, including the awareness of a separate self (sometimes called the existential self) and the definition of the self in comparison to others (the categorical self).

2. In infancy, the child develops a sense of a separate self by about 15 to 18 months, as indicated by self-recognition.

3. In early childhood, the child begins to place herself in basic categories such as age, size, and gender. These early self-definitions appear to be based primarily on physical attributes and things the child can do.

4. At school age, the self-concept continues to include many actions but also includes likes and dislikes. In adolescence, beliefs and more general personality characteristics become part of the self-concept.

5. At adolescence, there is also a reevaluation of the self, a process Erikson talks of as the "identity crisis." Most adolescents move from a diffuse

sense of future occupational or ideological identity through a period of reevaluation (moratorium) to a commitment to a new self-definition.

6. Self-concepts also include an evaluation dimension (Am I as good as I can be? Am I the sort of person I want to be?), often referred to as self-esteem. Children with high self-esteem (positive self-concepts) appear to do somewhat better in school, see themselves in control of their own destiny, have more friends, get along better with their families, and are less often depressed.

7. There are individual differences in the speed or completeness of the identity reevaluation at adolescence.

8. Children with higher self-esteem and those who achieve a clear identity earlier or more completely are more likely to have parents who use an authoritative style of child rearing: high levels of nurturance, clear rules, encouragement of independence, and good communication.

9. Gender identity is part of the self-concept. Children generally acquire gender identity (labeling themselves and others correctly) by about age 2 or 3; they develop gender stability (knowing you stay the same gender throughout life) by about 4, gender constancy (you don't change gender by changing appearance) by about 5 or 6.

10. Gender constancy is developed at about the same time that most children acquire other "conservation" concepts, such as conservation of number or mass.

11. Children's ideas about what males and females do and what they *ought* to do are clearly established and maximally stereotyped in early elementary school. Older children are aware of the social conventions but do not treat them as incontrovertible rules.

12. Sex-typed behavior also appears at age 2 or 3, when children show sex-typed toy preferences and begin to choose same-sex playmates.

13. Theorists of several different traditions have attempted to explain these patterns. Mischel emphasizes the role of reinforcement and modeling and argues that children are reinforced for imitating same-sex models. Parents do appear to treat boys and girls in systematically different ways, including punishing boys for girlish behavior.

14. Freud's explanation of sex-role differences rests on the concept of identification, by which the child comes to imitate the same-sex parent and thus acquires appropriate sex-typed behavior.

15. Kohlberg proposes a cognitive-developmental model: children begin to imitate same-sex models only after they have achieved gender constancy. There is some evidence to support this, but the theory does not explain sex-typed behavior at age 2 or 3.

16. Current theorists have proposed a "schema" or "rule" model: children begin to acquire a rule about what boys do and what girls do as soon as they figure out the difference. After the development of gender constancy, however, the issue becomes more salient.

17. One important source of information for children's development of a sex-role rule is the portrayal of men and women on TV and in children's books. These portrayals are highly stereotyped.

18. More girls than boys show cross-sex preferences in toy choices and behavior. Both environmental and biological elements may play a part in such cross-sex choices.

19. Young people also differ in the extent to which they see themselves as having feminine and/or masculine qualities or traits. Those who describe themselves as having both kinds of qualities are called androgynous.

20. Girls who see themselves as more masculine or as androgynous—those who have less-stereotypic views of female and male roles—are more likely to choose nontraditional occupations in adulthood.

21. Sex-role concepts and stereotypes also affect job behavior as well as family-role distributions, defining the range of behavior seen as acceptable for men and women.

▬▬▬▬▬ **KEY TERMS**

androgyny A self-concept including, and behavior expressing, high levels of both masculine and feminine qualities.

authoritarian parental style Pattern of parental behavior described by Baumrind, among others, including high levels of directiveness and low levels of affection and warmth.

authoritative parental style Pattern described by Baumrind, including high control and high warmth.

categorical self The definition of the self by comparing the self to others in one or more categories, such as age, gender, size, or skill.

existential self Term used by Lewis and Brooks-Gunn to refer to the most basic part of the self-concept, the sense of being separate and distinct from others.

foreclosure One of four identity statuses proposed by Marcia, whereby a young person makes an ideological or occupational commitment without having gone through a reevaluation.

gender concept The understanding of one's own gender, including the permanence and constancy of gender.

gender constancy The final step in developing a gender concept, in which the child understands that gender doesn't change even when such external things as clothing or hair length change.

gender identity The first step in gender concept development, in which the child labels herself correctly and categorizes others correctly as male or female.

gender stability The second step in gender concept development, in which the child understands that a person's gender continues to be stable throughout the lifetime.

identity achievement One of four identity statuses proposed by Marcia, in which the young person has successfully resolved an identity crisis and made a new commitment.

identity diffusion One of four identity statuses proposed by Marcia, in which the young person is not currently reevaluating ideas and has not made a firm personal commitment.

moratorium One of four identity statuses proposed by Marcia, in which the young person is making an ongoing reexamination but has not made a new commitment as yet.

permissive parental style Pattern described by Baumrind, among others, which includes high warmth and low levels of control.

self-concept The broad idea of "who I am," including the existential self, the categorical self, and a level of self-esteem.

self-esteem The positive or negative evaluation of the self.

sex-role behavior The performance of behavior that matches the culturally defined sex role, such as choosing "sex-appropriate" toys or playing with same-sex children.

sex-role concept The set of ideas of what males and females do and are "supposed to" do.

sex-role stereotyping The overextension or too-rigid definition of sex roles or sex-role behavior.

sex roles The set of behaviors, attitudes, rights, duties, and obligations that are part of the role of being male or female in any given society.

symbiotic relationship In Freudian theory, the mutually interdependent relationship between the mother and infant during the earliest months of life. Freud believed the infant was not aware of being separate from the mother at this stage.

▬▬▬ ## SUGGESTED READING

Fagot, B. I., & Kronsberg, S. J. (1982). Sex differences: Biological and social factors influencing the behavior of young boys and girls. In S. G. Moore & C. R. Cooper (Eds.), *The young child: Reviews of research* (Vol. 3). Washington, D.C.: National Association for the Education of Young Children.
A very readable paper that touches on many of the issues I have raised. It also includes mention of the role of school and teachers in shaping sex-role concepts and sex-role behavior.

Hennig, M., & Jardim, A. (1976). *The managerial woman.* Garden City, NY: Doubleday (Anchor Books).
This book is not primarily about children or childhood; it is about women in executive roles. But it describes the early childhood and adolescence of a group of highly successful women. I found it fascinating.

Kimmel, M. S. (1987, July). Real man redux. *Psychology Today*, pp. 48–52.
This brief paper describes the thinking and research of Joseph Pleck, one of the key figures in current thinking about the adult male's sex role.

Maccoby, E. E. (1980). *Social development. Psychological growth and the parent-child relationship.* New York: Harcourt Brace Jovanovich.
An excellent basic text that includes two chapters that touch on the material I have covered here.

▬▬▬

PROJECT: SEX ROLES ON TV

You may want to combine this project with the one at the end of Chapter 13, which involves watching for aggressive episodes on TV. Recording both aggression or violence and sex-role behaviors will give you a very good sense of the portrayals of "real life" given on TV.

For this project, you can select any one of several patterns of watching—I want you to get some practice designing your own project.

- Option 1. Watch at least five hours of TV, spread over several time periods, and record the number of male and female characters and whether each is a central character or a minor character.
- Option 2. Watch four to six hours of TV, selecting several different types of programs, and note the activities of each male and female character in the following categories: aggression, nurturance, problem solving, conformity, and physically exertive behavior.
- Option 3. Watch and analyze the commercials on at least 10 programs, making sure that the programs cover the full range of types, from sports to soap operas. You might count the number of male and female participants in the commercials and the nature of their activity in each case, using some of the same categories listed in option 2.

Whichever one of these projects you choose, you must define your terms carefully and record your data in a manner that makes it understandable. In writing up your report, be sure to state clearly what you did and what you think your results may mean.

Alternatively (if your instructor prefers), you might write up your report using the standard scientific format. Include the following: an *introductory* section, in which you describe some of the background literature and your hypotheses; a *procedure* section, in which you must include details of the programs you observed, how you selected them, what specific behaviors you recorded, how you defined your behavioral categories, and any other points that a reader would need to understand what you actually did; a *results* section, in which you report your findings, using graphs or tables as needed; and a *discussion* section, in which you compare your results to those of other researchers (as cited in this book or elsewhere) and you discuss and, if possible, explain any puzzling or unexpected findings. You may also want to suggest additional projects that might help clarify unresolved points in your own findings.

MULTIMEDIA LEARNING CENTRE
DEESIDE COLLEGE

11 The Development of Social Relationships

Attachment and Attachment Behavior: Definitions
The Attachment Process: Parent to Child
 The First Step: The Initial Bond
 The Second Step: The Meshing of Attachment Behaviors
When Mutuality Fails: Child Abuse and Other Consequences of Failure
  of Attachment
 Attachments by Fathers
The Attachment Process: Child to Parent
 Phase 1: Initial Preattachment
 Phase 2: Attachment in the Making
 Phase 3: Clear-cut Attachment
 Phase 4: Multiple Attachments
 Attachments to Parents in Preschool and Elementary-School Children
 Parent-Child Relationships at Adolescence
Attachments to Fathers and Mothers
Individual Differences in the Quality of Attachments
 Secure and Insecure Attachments
 Is the Security of Attachment Stable Over Time?
 How Is a Secure Attachment Formed?
 Temperament and Security of Attachment
 Long-term Effects of Secure/Insecure Attachment
Beyond the First Attachment: Children's Relationships with Other
  Children
Positive Social Interactions Among Children: Developmental Patterns
 Peer Interactions in Infancy and Early Childhood
Rearing Helpful and Altruistic Children
 Positive Social Interactions at School Age
 Positive Social Interactions at Adolescence
Individual Differences in Positive Interactions: Popularity
Negative Social Interactions Among Children
 Aggression
 Competition and Dominance
Sex Differences in Social Interactions
Summary
Key Terms
Suggested Reading
Project: Observation of Children's Play Groups

Several years ago, at a social gathering, I watched two young friends, Mark and Marcie, with their 4-month-old son, Alexander. With very little effort, Alexander managed to attract everyone's attention. He looked around him, occasionally gave brief smiles, kicked his feet, shook a rattle, and cried once in a while. Those simple behaviors were enough to have all the adults in the room hovering over him, trying their best to entice a smile. I was not immune to his charms. I trotted out all my playing-with-baby tricks, raising my eyebrows, smiling broadly, calling his name, tickling him a bit on the cheek or on his feet, making clucking noises. My reward was one very small smile and a brief period of attention from Alexander.

But Mark and Marcie, after four months of practice, were a whole lot better than any of the rest of us at soothing, flirting with, and eliciting responses from young Alexander. Either Mom or Dad could get him to smile within just a few seconds; when he cried, either one of them could soothe him quite easily, after the rest of us had failed in the attempt.

My most immediate reaction to this scene was simple pleasure at seeing loving and attentive parents with their infant. But the psychologist in me was watching too, and I was struck by some other elements in the interaction. First of all, even at 4 months, Alexander is really quite skillful in social exchanges. He can't do very many things, but what he does do is very successful in getting attention and care. The second thing is that Alexander and his parents have developed a sort of "dance" that they do much more skillfully with each other than he does with other folks. They have *adapted* to each other.

This brief scene focuses our attention on an aspect of development I have largely neglected so far, namely, the child's relationships with others. The self-concept is a critical element in the child's eventual "personality," but the self-concept and the style and pattern of the child's behavior emerge from and are displayed in social exchanges with others. If we are to have the barest grasp of the nature of the child's development, we have to describe and understand the ways in which the child's *social* behavior develops and changes. How does the first relationship with the parents change over time? What is the effect on a child of a supportive and well-adapted relationship with the parents, compared to a maladjusted one? How and when does the child begin to be interested in other children? What about friendships in childhood and adolescence? These are all vital questions I will be exploring in this chapter.

ATTACHMENT AND ATTACHMENT BEHAVIOR: DEFINITIONS

One of the key concepts in the study of social relationships is that of **attachment,** a term used particularly in the theoretical work of John Bowlby (1969, 1973, 1980) and Mary Ainsworth (1972, 1982; Ainsworth et al.,

Figure 11.1   By the time babies are 2 or 3 or 4 months old, most fathers and mothers have become skillful and confident in their interactions and are securely attached to the baby.

1978). As Bowlby has described it, an attachment is an important emotional link, an "affectional bond," between two people. The child or adult who is attached to another person uses her (or him) as a "safe base" from which to explore the world, as a source of comfort when distressed or stressed, and for encouragement.

We know when an attachment exists by observing **attachment behaviors,** just as we infer the child's cognitive competence by looking at the way she solves problems. Attachment behaviors are all those behaviors that allow a child or adult to achieve and maintain proximity to someone else to whom he or she is attached. These could include smiling, making eye contact, calling out to the other person across a room, touching, clinging, crying. (Alexander showed many of these behaviors, didn't he?)

It is important to make clear that there is no one-to-one correspondence between the number of different attachment behaviors a child (or adult) shows on any one occasion and the strength of the underlying attachment. A child with a strong, secure attachment to a parent may play happily in the same room with the parent, glancing at the parent or initiating a brief contact only occasionally. On another occasion, the same child may show high levels of attachment beahaviors. It is the *pattern* of these behaviors, not the frequency, that tells us something about the strength or quality of the attachment.

One of the useful features of the concept of attachment is that we can apply it equally to the parents' attachment to the child and the child's attachment to the parents. Let me begin by looking at how parents form their bond to the baby.

THE ATTACHMENT PROCESS: PARENT TO CHILD

There seem to be two steps or two parts to the development of a parent's attachment to an infant. An initial bond may be formed in the first hours after birth, especially if the parent has an opportunity for early contact with the baby. The really critical element for the parent's attachment, though, is the opportunity to engage in mutual attachment behaviors with the baby.

The First Step: The Initial Bond

If you read the popular press at all, I am sure you have come across articles proclaiming the absolute importance of immediate contact between mother and newborn. This belief—which became a dominant theme in the past decade—has been based primarily on the work of two pediatricians, Marshall Klaus and John Kennell (1976), who bucked formerly dominant medical practices and assumptions by hypothesizing that the first few hours after an infant's birth was a "critical period" for the mother's development of an attachment to her baby. Mothers who were denied early contact, Klaus and Kennell thought, were likely to form weaker attachments and thus to be at higher risk for a range of disorders of parenting.

Klaus and Kennell's theory and their supporting research did help lead to real changes in hospital practices, with mothers and fathers encouraged to hold their newborns immediately after delivery. For many reasons, this seems like a very good change—among other things, parents report that they find this first "acquaintance" time to be a joyful occasion (as I pointed out in Chapter 3). But recent research makes it seem more doubtful that such early contact is critical for the parent's formation of a stable long-term attachment to the child (e.g., Lamb and Hwang, 1982; Goldberg, 1983). Let me review some of the evidence.

Short-term Effects. Mothers who have handled their newborns within the first few hours often do show more tender fondling and more gazing at the baby in the first few days than mothers who did not have an opportunity to hold their newborn until later (e.g., Campbell & Taylor, 1980; de Chateau, 1980).

Not every researcher has found this kind of effect, and some have found it only for mothers with their firstborns (e.g., de Chateau, 1980), but I am reasonably well satisfied that there is at least a small short-term effect of early contact, perhaps especially for those mothers who are least experienced with infants or who have the least support from spouse or families.

It seems more and more doubtful, however, that this small short-term effect is based on some hormonal "readiness" of the mother (as Klaus and Kennell suggested). It seems more likely that it is the infant's greater alertness in the first hours after birth that is the key. For example, newborns are able to make eye contact in the first few hours, but they do not easily do so again for some days. Whatever the explanation, the effect is not nearly so large as Klaus and Kennell first proposed (or as the popular press would have you believe).

Long-term Effects.   The conclusions are still more tentative when we look at studies of longer-term effects of the amount or timing of early contact. Several studies, including Klaus and Kennell's own early work (e.g., Kennell et al., 1974), show a persisting effect. But many others do not. In general, when researchers have measured highly specific maternal behaviors, such as the amount of tender touching or smiling toward the child, they have rarely found lasting effects. An exception to this generalization, however, is the fairly common finding that mothers with extra or early contact breast-feed their infants for more months than do mothers with routine contact at birth (de Chateau, 1987).

Lasting effects are more often found when researchers have used broader measures of the mother's attitude toward her infant, her confidence in child rearing, or her attachment (Sostek, Scanlon, & Abramson, 1982). Such broader measures might include the number of months the mother chooses to stay home with her child before going back to work or global measures of the adequacy of her care. On measures such as these, for *some* mothers we can still detect the impact of early contact versus no early contact as long as a year or two after the child's birth.

One study I find especially convincing in this regard is by Susan O'Connor and her colleagues (1980). They studied a large group of poverty-level mothers who were given contact through a "rooming-in" arrangement in a Nashville, Tennessee, hospital. Other mothers from similar backgrounds were randomly assigned to a more traditional care arrangement in the same hospital, and these two groups were then tracked through the first 18 months of the children's lives. O'Connor's interest has been in a global measure of the mother's behavior that she calls "adequacy of parenting." Inadequate parenting was indicated if the child was physically abused or neglected, if the child was repeatedly hospitalized, or if the parents relinquished custody of the child.

As you can see in Table 11.1, very few mothers in either the rooming-in or regular care groups showed inadequate parenting, but the rate was higher for the group that had had less contact with the infant in the early days. These findings raise the possibility that early contact may help *prevent* later parenting problems among mothers who may be at especially high risk for abuse. For the majority of mothers, however, early or extended

Table 11.1

"Parenting Inadequacy" and Abuse

	Rooming-in group (143 cases)	Regular hospital care group (158 cases)
Number of mothers who showed *any* kind of parenting inadequacy in first 18 months (including either or both of those listed below)	2	10
Number referred to Children's Protective Service for suspicion of abuse	1	5
Number of children hospitalized for illness or for "failure to thrive"	1	8

Source: O'Connor et al., 1980, pp. 356–357.

contact does not seem to be an essential ingredient in the long-term attachment process.

The Second Step: The Meshing of Attachment Behaviors

Much more critical for the establishment of the parents' attachment to the child is the opportunity to interact with the child over the early months of life. Over those early weeks, the parents and child develop a natural interlocking pattern of attachment behaviors. The baby signals her needs by crying or smiling; she responds to being held by snuggling or being soothed; she looks at the parents when they look at her. The parents, in their turn, enter into this two-person "dance" by picking the baby up, by waiting for and responding to her signals of hunger or other needs, by smiling at her when she smiles, by gazing into her eyes. It was this smooth "dance" that I could see between Mark and Marcie and 4-month-old Alexander.

One of the most intriguing things about this process is that we all seem to know how to do this particular dance. In the presence of a young infant, most adults will automatically shift into a "baby-play act," which includes smiling, raised eyebrows, very wide-open eyes, and a quiet, high-pitched voice (see Figure 11.2). The baby runs through her half of the dance pretty automatically, too. But while we can perform all these attachment *behaviors* with many infants, we do not become *attached to* every baby we coo at in the grocery store. I can run through my baby routine with Alexander, but I am not attached to him.

For the adult, the critical ingredient for the formation of a genuine

Sensorimotor play

Early pretend play

Sociodramatic play

*Games
with
rules*

Figure 11.2 Virtually every adult, when interacting with a young baby, shows this "mock surprise" expression, including the raised eyebrows, wrinkled forehead, and open mouth or wide smile. This combination of features is, in fact, quite likely to elicit a smile from a young baby. (Check yourself next time you are holding or interacting with an infant and see if your expression isn't very like this.)

attachment seems to be the opportunity to develop real mutuality—to practice the dance until the partners follow one another's lead smoothly and with pleasure. This takes time and many rehearsals, and some parents (and infants) become more skillful at it than others, as you can see in Figure 11.3. In general, the smoother and more predictable the process becomes, the more satisfying it seems to be to the parents and the stronger their attachment to the infant becomes.

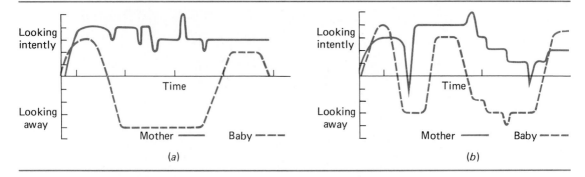

Figure 11.3   Berry Brazelton and his colleagues videotaped mothers interacting with their infants and then went back and rated the intentness of looking or looking away for each second of interaction by each member of the pair. (*a*) This mother-infant pair illustrates a lack of synchrony. When the infant looks away, instead of waiting for the infant to reengage the mother trots out her bag of attention-getting tricks: she talks, touches the child, makes faces, nods her head—all to little avail. The baby looks at her again only after she stops talking. (*b*) This pair are definitely "dancing" together. (*Source:* Brazelton, Koslowski, & Main, 1974, pp. 62, 64.)

This second step appears to be *far* more important than the initial bond at birth in establishing a strong attachment by the parents to the child. But this second process, too, can fail. I've explored some of the possible reasons for such a failure in the box on pages 400–401.

Attachments by Fathers

I have used the word *parents* in the discussion so far, but most of the research I have talked about has involved studies of mothers. Still, many of the same principles seem to hold for fathers as well.

In Chapter 3 I talked about the impact of the father's presence during delivery and pointed out that there is no very strong or convincing evidence that early contact between father and newborn is an essential ingredient in fostering the father's attachment to the child.

Interestingly, whether fathers have been present at delivery or not, their initial attachment behaviors directed toward the newborn are virtually identical to mothers' reactions. Ross Parke has observed fathers and mothers with their newborns in several studies (e.g., Parke & Tinsley, 1981), and he finds that when fathers are actually holding their infants, they touch, talk to, and cuddle their babies as much as and in the same ways that mothers do. It certainly appears, then, that fathers' initial attachment to the infant is as strong as is mothers'.

Past the early weeks of life, however, we see signs of a kind of "specialization" of parents' behaviors with their infants and toddlers. The "mother role" seems to involve not only routine caregiving but also more talking and smiling and more quiet interactions. The "father role" involves more playfulness. Fathers do more physical roughhousing with their children (see Figure 11.4), and they are more likely to play games of some kind (Parke & Tinsley, 1987). This does not mean that fathers are less attached; it does mean that the attachment behaviors they show toward the infant typically differ somewhat from those shown by mothers.

But where do such "parenting roles" come from? There are at least a couple of possibilities. One is that the person who is doing the major physical caregiving is quite logically going to end up doing less playing. Since mothers do more caregiving (even in families in which both parents work), the "mother" and "father" roles may really be "caregiver" and "non-caregiver" roles. Another possibility (consistent with what I said in Chapter 10) is that these patterns may be part of the sex-role definitions for men and women in our culture. If the sex roles change, we might see changes in parenting behaviors too. Of course, a third possibility is that these are "natural" or built-in differences in the ways males and females approach infants.

One way to decide between these several alternatives is to see just how modifiable these different patterns are. What happens, for example, in families in which the father is the major caregiver or in which both parents work and share caregiving?

There are now a few studies exploring these questions, and the findings are simply not clear. In one study of 8-month-old infants in Sweden —

Figure 11.4   At least in American and other Western cultures, the role of father with a young baby seems to involve a lot more play, including roughhousing or physical actions like these. Obviously, the baby is enjoying it immensely!

MULTIMEDIA LEARNING CENTRE
DEESIDE COLLEGE

WHEN MUTUALITY FAILS: CHILD ABUSE AND OTHER CONSEQUENCES OF FAILURE OF ATTACHMENT

The two-part system for fostering strong attachment by the parent for the infant is normally robust and effective. Most parents *do* become attached to their babies. But attachment is a process requiring two partners, both of whom have the necessary signals and skills and the energy to enter into the dance. When either partner lacks the skills, the result can be a failure of attachment or a weaker attachment by the parent to the child. Child abuse or neglect is one possible consequence of such a failure.

When the Infant Lacks Skills

For the system to work, the baby has to possess a sufficient repertoire of attachment behaviors to entice and hold the parent's attention and interaction. If some behaviors are missing, real problems can ensue. For example, Selma Fraiberg (1974, 1975) has studied a group of blind babies, who smile less than sighted infants and do not show mutual gaze. Most parents of blind infants, after several months of this, begin to think that their infant is rejecting them, or they conclude that the baby is depressed. These parents feel less attached to their blind infants than to their sighted infants.

Similar problems can arise with premature infants, who may be separated from their parents for the first weeks or months (which *may* interfere with the first bond) and then are likely to be quite unresponsive for the first weeks after they are home from the hospital. Most mothers of premature infants work extra hard in those first months to stimulate their infants. In fact, such mothers show *higher* rates of involvement with and stimulation of their babies in the early months than do mothers of full-term babies (Field, 1977; Barnard, Bee, & Hammond, 1984a). But eventually the mothers withdraw somewhat from the interaction since the babies so seldom respond with real mutuality.

Obviously, not all blind infants, premature infants, or others who are different in some way end up being physically abused. Many parents manage to surmount these problems. But the rate of abuse is higher among prematures than full-term infants and higher among babies who are sick a lot in the first few months (e.g., Sherrod et al., 1984).

When the Parent Lacks Skill

The other partner in the dance is obviously the parent, and failure of attachment can just as well come from the parent's end of the system. A parent might lack attachment skill because she or he did not form a secure attachment with her or his own parents and did not learn the needed behaviors in later relationships (Sroufe & Fleeson, 1986). In fact, many abusing parents were apparently abused *themselves* as children, which makes this argument seem plausible. Or the parent could lack skill because she or he approaches the child-care task from an essentially *egocentric* stance. For exam-

400

ple, Carolyn Newberger and Susan Cook (1983) have found that abusing parents are more likely to describe the task of parenting in terms of their *own* needs that may be met. They may thus be less sensitive or less responsive to the child's signals.

Depression in a parent can also alter the interactive balance. Tiffany Field (1984), for example, has found that infants respond very differently to a mother who is depressed, or even to a mother who has been told to "look depressed," than they do to a mother with a normally animated facial expression. Infants confronted with a depressed-looking expression are more disorganized and more distressed, which in turn may affect the quality of the interaction with the parent.

Whether any of these conditions will result in abuse seems to depend on a variety of things, including such complicating conditions as alcoholism in one parent (Famularo et al., 1986) or the presence of other stresses on the family. Single parents, parents with many children, parents with small living spaces or uncertain incomes, or parents who lack friends or other sources of emotional support are much more likely to abuse their children than are parents with lower levels of stress (Garbarino & Sherman, 1980; Sack, Mason, & Higgins, 1985).

When both the child and the parent lack skills or are under significant stress, the likelihood that there will be a failure of attachment, and possibly neglect or abuse of the child, is greatly increased.

What Can Be Done?

Fortunately, it's possible to intervene to help the unattached parent become more attached. Fraiberg (1974) found that she could help the parents of blind babies to "read" the child's hand and body movements instead of waiting for smiles or eye contact. After such training, the parents of the blind babies found their attachment to the infant was strengthened. Rose Bromwich (1976; Bromwich et al., 1981) has used a similar procedure with parents of children with other physical handicaps. She begins by finding some activity that the child and parent can do together that brings pleasure to both. When that level of basic mutual pleasure has been achieved, she then tries to help the parent become more attentive to the child's individual signals. Through this process, the parent's attachment to the child can be enhanced.

When actual abuse has already occurred, more extensive intervention may be needed. Henry Kempe and his colleagues in Denver (Kempe & Kempe, 1978), for example, report that they have had an 80 percent success rate with abusing families, using a combination of a crisis hotline to help deal with life stresses (among other things) and personal counseling to help the parents deal with their own early relationships and develop the skills needed to relate to their child. This is not a simple or a quick process, but it can and does succeed.

where paternal leave after the birth of a child is a well-established social policy—Michael Lamb and his colleagues (1982) found that even in families in which the father had been the major caregiver for from one to three of the three preceding months, mothers still talked to and held the infants more, showed more affection, and gave more physical care than did fathers. But in a study in the United States, Tiffany Field (1978) found that although primary-caregiving fathers played more with their infants than did mothers, they otherwise showed the more typical "mothering" pattern of interaction with their 4-month-olds. In still a third study, in Australia, G. Russell (1982) found no differences in play or caregiving behavior between mothers and fathers who shared caregiving.

Probably these findings allow us to reject the hypothesis that distinctively different father and mother roles are somehow instinctive. But we are left with more questions than answers.

THE ATTACHMENT PROCESS: CHILD TO PARENT

For parents, the process of attachment formation seems to begin with the development of an initial emotional bond and then extends to more and more skillful attachment behaviors. For the infant, the process seems to begin with attachment behaviors and then progresses to the full attachment somewhat later. On the basis of their research, Mary Ainsworth and her colleagues (1978) suggest that the emergence of a genuine attachment in an infant occurs in several steps.

Phase 1: Initial Preattachment

During the first three to four months of life, the baby displays a wonderful range of attachment behaviors that Ainsworth describes as "proximity-promoting"—they bring people closer. As I pointed out in Chapter 3, the infant can cry, make eye contact, smile, and respond to caregiving efforts by being soothed. Yet babies of this age seem to show no consistent preference for any one caregiver over another. They seem to direct their attachment behaviors at almost any caregiver, so we cannot say that they are attached to any one person yet.

Phase 2: Attachment in the Making

Some time around 3 months, the baby begins to dispense her attachment behaviors more discriminatingly. At this stage, babies (like Alexander) smile more at the people who regularly take care of them, and they may not smile readily at a stranger. Yet despite the change, this is not yet a full-blown attachment to a *single* figure; there are still a number of people who are favored with the child's proximity-promoting behaviors.

Phase 3: Clear-cut Attachment

Two important changes take place at about 6 to 7 months of age. First and most important, the child typically now directs her attachment behaviors primarily toward *one* person. We can say for the first time that the child is genuinely *attached* to someone. Second, the dominant mode of her attachment behavior changes: she shifts from using mostly "come here" (proximity-promoting) signals to what Ainsworth calls "proximity seeking" (which we might think of as "go there" behaviors). Because the 6- to 7-month-old begins to be able to move about the world more freely by creeping and crawling, she can move *toward* the caregiver as well as enticing the caregiver to come to her. We also see a child of this age using the "most important person" as a safe base from which to explore the world around her—one of the key signals that an attachment exists.

Just why the first obvious attachment does not appear until this age is not clear. You may remember from Chapter 5 that the newborn baby can make discriminations between voices (and already seems to prefer his mother's voice) and that by 3 months of age, he can tell the difference between faces solely on the basis of visual clues. Yet infants do not show clear attachments at these early stages. One possible explanation—still speculative—relates to the emergence of the concept of object permanence, which does not normally appear until about age 6 or 7 months. It may be that a full-blown attachment does not develop until the infant understands that Mom continues to exist when not in sight and that she remains the same from different views.

I should note that not all infants have a *single* attachment figure, even at this early point. Some show strong attachment to both parents or to a parent and another caregiver, such as a baby-sitter or a grandparent. But even these babies, when under stress, may show a preference for one of their favored persons over the others.

Two related patterns of behavior also emerge once the child has developed a clear attachment: social referencing and separation protest.

Social Referencing. By about 10 months, the infant not only uses the mother (or other attachment figure) as a safe base—he also uses this preferred person for clues about new situations. When infants of this age are confronted with a stranger or a new toy, for example, they will first look at their caregiver's face, to check for her or his expression. Since infants of this age can "read" emotional expressions (as I mentioned briefly in Chapter 5), they are able to tell in this way whether this new situation or object is supposed to be fearful or delightful or neutral. Psychologists call this process *social referencing*. Babies seem mostly to use their key attachment figures in this way, although they may also use other familiar adults as references. Strangers, though, do not seem to fill this role for babies (e.g., Klinnert et al., 1986; Zarbatany & Lamb, 1985). There is a practical lesson to be learned here for parents whose children are in the stage of wariness toward strangers: your child is more likely to accept the stranger if he sees you talking to and smiling at the stranger first.

Separation Protest and Fear of Strangers.   In many (but not all) children, one of the striking signs of the strong single attachment is that the child may both protest at separation from the preferred person and show fear of strangers. Both are rare before 5 or 6 months, rise in frequency until about 12 to 16 months, and then decline. Virtually identical peak times for these behaviors have been observed in children from a number of different cultures and in both home-reared and day-care-reared children in the United States, all of which makes it look as if there are some basic cognitive or other age-related developmental timetables underlying this pattern (Kagan, Kearsley, and Zelazo, 1978).

But while the timing may be widely shared, the intensity of the fearful reaction varies widely from one child to another. Nearly all children are more likely to be fearful in stressful situations (as in Figure 11.5), but some children are only a little wary of strangers; others show more striking withdrawal, such as crying, clinging to the parent, or other signs of fear (Batter & Davidson, 1979). As psychologists have tried to figure out where such individual differences in fearfulness might come from, a few clues have emerged (Thompson & Lamb, 1982):

- Children whose mothers rate them as being generally more fearful—not just of strangers but of other new things—are likely to show more fear of strangers, as are infants rated as "fussy" (Berberian & Snyder, 1982). Thus, the child's basic temperament may be part of the picture.
- Children whose families have recently gone through some major change, such as the birth of a new sibling, a move, or a parent changing jobs, show more fear of strangers than do children whose families have been more stable.
- There is *no* consistent relationship between the child's fear of strangers and the number of different caregivers he has had. You might expect a child who has been cared for by more different people to have less fear of new people. But that is not what researchers have found.

Phase 4: Multiple Attachments

As I mentioned earlier, some infants form several strong attachments from the beginning. But the majority first form one single intense attachment and then rather rapidly expand their attachments to include older siblings, regular baby-sitters, grandparents, or other regularly seen adults. These attachments appear to have the same qualities as the attachments to the principal caregiver; the child will use any of her preferred people as a safe base for exploration, smiles more at them, and will turn to any of them for comfort in distress.

Figure 11.5　In more predictable everyday circumstances, this youngster probably shows relatively little clinging to Mom or the nursery school teacher, but under stress, as when hurt or frightened, more immature forms of attachment behaviors reappear. (Of course, the same is often true for adults, too, if you think about it.)

Attachments to Parents in Preschool and Elementary-School Children

During the preschool years, the overall level of the child's proximity seeking declines. A 12-month-old child stays pretty close to the safe base most of the time, remaining within sight of the mother or other caregiver. But by 2 or 3, children seem to be comfortable being on their own more, playing in the next room or a bit further from Mom or Dad. This is made easier by the fact that the child can now talk well enough to stay in contact from a distance. A child of 2 can even use a photograph of his mother in a strange situation as a "safe base" for exploration (Passman & Longeway, 1982).

This reduction in proximity seeking does not mean that the child is less *attached to* the caregiver. Rather, it says that the attachment behaviors change and become less visible. We can still see clear attachment behaviors in 2-, 3-, or 4-year-olds who are frightened, tired, or under stress (as in Figure 11.5). But in normal circumstances they move more freely from the safe base of their preferred persons.

At elementary-school age, attachment behaviors toward parents become still less visible (the child may, for example, come to the parent for a hug less often), while involvement with peers—a set of relationships I'll talk more about shortly—becomes a much more dominant theme in the child's social world.

Parent-Child Relationships at Adolescence

Most of you can remember quite clearly the changes in your own relationships with your parents when you hit adolescence, so the research findings are not going to surprise you much. At first there is typically an increase in conflict. Laurence Steinberg (1981, 1987a) and John Hill and his colleagues (Hill et al., 1985) have found that the hormonal and physical changes of puberty trigger behavioral changes that in turn lead to increases in family conflict. The teenager interrupts more, questions more, disagrees more. This conflict seems to peak fairly early in the pubertal change and then declines. At the same time, the separation between parents and the adolescent is also increased by the parents' granting the youngster more and more room to make independent choices or to participate in family decision making. This "distancing" (to use Steinberg's term) seems to be a normal— even an essential—part of the adolescent development process.

Another very clear trend is that the child spends an increasing amount of time with peers. Yet the temporarily heightened conflict, the distancing from the parents, and the increased involvement with the peer group do not seem to signify that the young person's underlying emotional attachment to the parent has disappeared or even greatly weakened. This apparently paradoxical state of affairs is nicely illustrated in a study by Fumiyo Hunter and James Youniss (1982).

Hunter and Youniss had groups of fourth-, seventh-, and tenth-graders and college students respond to eight different statements about their relationships with mother, father, and best same-sex friend—for example, "My mother (father, best friend) gives me what I need" or "I like to talk to my mother (father, best friend) about my problems." For each statement subjects used a four-point scale where 1 meant "not very often" and 4 meant "almost always." Figure 11.6 shows the average score for those statements that dealt with the intimacy of the relationship (e.g., "We talk about problems" or "The other person knows how I feel") and for those statements that concerned the nurturance of the relationship ("The other person gives me what I need" or "The other person helps me to solve my problems"). As you can see, during adolescence (the seventh- and tenth-graders), intimacy

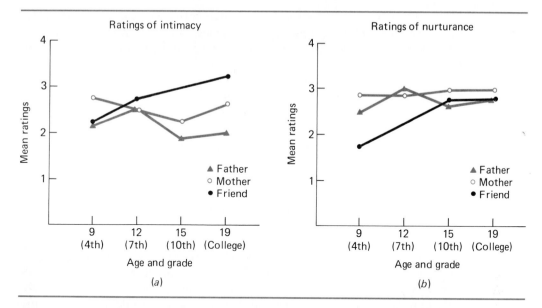

Figure 11.6 Relationships with friends become increasingly intimate during the adolescent years; friends tell each other more about themselves, resolve disagreements, share activities. But young people continue to see their parents as a major source of nurturance throughout these same years, suggesting that the attachment to the parents remains strong, even while peer attachments strengthen too. (*Source:* F. T. Hunter & J. Youniss (1982). Changes in functions of three relations during adolescence. *Developmental Psychology,* 1982, 18, Figures 2 and 3, pp. 809, 810. Copyright 1982 by the American Psychological Association. Reprinted by permission of the publisher and author.)

with the mother and father goes down while intimacy with the friend goes up. But young people across this age range see their parents as consistently high sources of nurturance.

Furthermore, the quality of the teenager's attachment to the parent seems to be more closely related to his sense of well-being or happiness than is the quality of his attachment to his peers (Greenberg, Siegel, & Leitch, 1983). So this central relationship with the parent continues to be highly significant in adolescence, even while the teenager is becoming more autonomous.

ATTACHMENTS TO FATHERS AND MOTHERS

I pointed out earlier that both fathers and mothers become attached to their infants, although their behavior with infants differs somewhat. But what about the child's half of this attachment? Are infants and children equally attached to their fathers and mothers?

In general, yes. From the age of 7 to 8 months, when strong attachments are first seen, infants prefer both the father and the mother to a stranger. And when both the father and the mother are available, an infant will smile at or approach either or both, *except* when he is frightened or under stress. When that happens, especially between 8 and 24 months, the child typically turns to the mother rather than the father (Lamb, 1981).

As you might expect, the strength of the child's attachment to the father at this early age seems to be related to the amount of time he has spent with the child. Gail Ross and her colleagues (1975) found they could predict a baby's attachment to the father by knowing how many diapers Dad changed in a typical week. The more diapers, the stronger the attachment! But greatly increased time with the father does not seem to be the only element, since Michael Lamb and his colleagues (1983) have found that infants whose father was the major caregiver for at least a month in the first year of the child's life (with an average of about three months) were nonetheless more strongly attached to their mothers than their fathers. Thus fathers who invest more time becoming attuned to the infant's signals are likely to have infants who are more strongly attached to them. But for the father to be consistently *preferred* over the mother would probably require essentially full-time paternal care. As this option becomes more common in our society, it will be possible to study such father-child pairs to see if a preference for the father develops.

INDIVIDUAL DIFFERENCES IN THE QUALITY OF ATTACHMENTS

Virtually all babies seem to go through the sequence I've described, from preattachment to attachment. But the *quality* of the attachment they form to their parents differs. In the language that has become popular in recent writings about attachment, each infant has a different **internal working model** of his or her relationships with parents and key others. This concept, originally suggested by John Bowlby (1969), introduces a distinctly cognitive flavor to the discussion, not unlike the concepts of the "self-scheme" and the "sex-role scheme" I talked about in Chapters 9 and 10. This internal working model of attachment relationships includes such information as whether people usually respond when the infant calls for help, whether affection and attention are reliably available, and the like.

Like a self-scheme, such a working model of attachment can change with experience, but Bowlby argues (1980) that it is not in a state of constant flux. Once developed, it serves to shape and explain experience and will affect memory and attention. We notice and remember experiences that fit our model, and we miss or forget experiences that don't match. More important, the model also affects the child's behavior; the child essentially attempts to recreate, in each new relationship, the pattern with which she is familiar.

According to this view, the first attachment relationship is an important ingredient in forming the internal working model. It is not a permanent template; changes can and do occur as the child is faced with different forms of subsequent relationships. But as Alan Sroufe puts it, "development is hierarchical; it is not a blackboard to be erased and written upon again. Even when children change rather markedly, the shadows of the earlier adaptation remain" (1983, pp. 73–74).

Secure and Insecure Attachments

The most widely accepted way of describing variations in the first attachment relationship (and the accompanying internal working model) has been proposed by Mary Ainsworth (Ainsworth & Wittig, 1969; Ainsworth et al., 1978), who distinguishes between **secure attachment** and two types of **insecure attachment.** Ainsworth's method of measuring the security of attachment, called the strange situation, has also been widely used.

The **strange situation** consists of a series of episodes in a laboratory setting. The child is first with the mother, then with the mother and a stranger, then alone with the stranger, then left completely alone for a few minutes. Next the child is reunited with the mother, then left alone again, and finally reunited first with the stranger and then with the mother. Ainsworth suggested that children's reactions to this situation could be classified into three groups: *securely attached, insecure/avoidant* (or *detached*), and *insecure/ambivalent* (also sometimes called *insecure/resistant*). Mary Main (Main & Solomon, 1985) has recently suggested a fourth group, which she calls *insecure/disorganized/disoriented.* I have listed some of the characteristics of the different types in Table 11.2.

In studies of stable middle-class families, secure attachment has been observed in 50 percent to 70 percent of children; in samples drawn from poverty-level families, families with a history of abuse, or families in which the mother is diagnosed as seriously depressed, the probability of a secure attachment is lower, ranging from perhaps 20 percent to as high as 70 percent in different studies (Spieker & Booth, 1988). Among the several types of insecure attachment, the avoidant pattern is the most common, observed in as many as 25 percent of children in stable families.

There is an obvious parallel between Ainsworth's distinction between secure and insecure attachment and Erikson's distinction between trust and mistrust. Erikson sees the first attachment as the model for later relationships, a view consistent with the current thinking about the emergence of internal working models of attachment relationships. Because the present work on the security of attachments has so many theoretical and practical ramifications, I need to take some time to explore some of the issues and implications.

Table 11.2

Behavior of Securely Attached and Insecurely Attached Infants in Ainsworth's Strange Situation at 12 Months of Age

- *Securely attached.*　Child shows low to moderate levels of proximity seeking to mother; does not avoid or resist contact if mother initiates it. When reunited with mother after absence, child greets her positively and can be soothed if upset. Clearly prefers mother to stranger.
- *Insecurely attached; detached/avoidant.*　Child avoids contact with mother, especially at reunion after an absence. Does not resist mother's efforts to make contact, but does not seek much contact. Treats stranger and mother about the same throughout.
- *Insecurely attached: resistant/ambivalent.*　Greatly upset when separated from mother, but mother cannot successfully comfort child when she comes back. Child both seeks and avoids contact, at different times. May show anger toward mother at reunion, and resists both comfort from and contact with stranger.
- *Insecurely attached: disorganized/disoriented.*　Dazed behavior, confusion, or apprehension. Child may show strong avoidance following strong proximity seeking; may show simultaneously conflicting patterns, such as moving toward mother but keeping gaze averted; may express emotion in a way that seems unrelated to the people present.

Sources: Ainsworth et al., 1978; Main & Solomon, 1985; Sroufe & Waters, 1977.

Is the Security of Attachment Stable Over Time?

One of the key questions is whether the security of attachment is stable over time. Does a child who is securely attached to her mother at 12 months still show the same secure attachment at 24 or 36 months? Is it still present at school age? This is a particularly important question for those researchers and therapists who are concerned about the possible permanence of effects of early abuse or neglect or other sources of insecure attachment. Can children recover from such early treatment? And is an initially securely attached child permanently buffered from the effects of difficult circumstances later in life?

As you might imagine, this is not easy to answer. The strange situation is a suitable measure of attachment security for only a brief period (between 12 and perhaps 20 months). At later ages, other measures must be devised, and there is always the question of whether such new measures are really tapping the same underlying quality or process. With this important caveat in mind, however, I can offer some preliminary answers.

When the child's family environment or life circumstances are reasonably consistent, the security or insecurity of attachment does remain stable.

For example, Everett Waters (1978) found that only 2 out of the 50 infants he studied changed in their category of attachment security from 12 to 18 months. And in a stable middle-class sample, Mary Main and her colleagues (Main, Kaplan, & Cassidy, 1985) found strong correlations between ratings of security of attachment at 18 months and at 6 years. But when the child's circumstances change in some major way—such as when she starts going to day care or nursery school, Grandma comes to live with the family, the family moves, or the parents divorce—the security of the child's attachment may change as well, either from secure to insecure or the reverse (e.g., Thompson, Lamb, & Estes, 1982, 1983). In poverty-level families, in which instability of circumstances is more common, changes in attachment security are also common (Vaughn et al., 1979).

Findings like this are quite consistent with the notion of attachment as an internal working model. Although the first relationship may provide the data for the first working model, the model can and will change if the child is forced to adapt to new circumstances or if the people caring for the child change markedly in their pattern of response. An insecure/avoidant child attending a preschool with highly caring teachers who consistently respond in a loving and accepting way may (slowly) change his working model. A securely attached child whose parents divorce and whose mother becomes erratic in her responsiveness (a typical response to divorce by parents) may become ambivalent in her attachment as her working model changes. Thus, a child may "recover" from an initially insecure attachment or lose a secure one. Nonetheless, consistency and not change in security of attachment is the most common pattern.

How Is a Secure Attachment Formed?

The common denominators in the backgrounds of securely attached babies seem to be *contingent responsiveness* from the parents to the infant (Sroufe & Fleeson, 1986) and acceptance of the infant by the parents (e.g., Benn, 1986). The parents match their behaviors to the child's or follow the child's rhythm (as in Figure 11.3). The parents of secure babies also seem to be more likely to be emotionally expressive toward their babies—smiling more, using their voices in more expressive ways, touching the infant more (e.g., Egeland & Farber, 1984).

In contrast, mothers of babies rated as insecure/avoidant are likely to be "psychologically unavailable" to their infants (to use Alan Sroufe's phrase). These mothers often show signs of significant depression and may report that they did not like physical contact with their infant in the infant's early months of life (e.g., Radke-Yarrow et al., 1985). These mothers reject or avoid their infants as much as the babies avoid them. The third group of infants, those rated as insecure/ambivalent, are likely to have mothers who are inconsistent in their responses to the infant, who reject the infant's bids for contact some of the time and respond positively at other times.

The fourth group, those recently described as insecure/disorganized/disoriented, have not been so well studied, but early signs are that this internal working model is common among children who are maltreated (Main, Kaplan, & Cassidy, 1985).

One of the hotly debated questions among developmental psychologists at the moment is whether infants in day care are at greater risk for insecure attachment. Early research showed no such increased risk, but Jay Belsky, among others, has recently reopened the debate on the basis of a number of current studies that show that children who enter alternate care some time in the first year of life may be somewhat more likely to show avoidant attachment (Belsky, 1987; Belsky & Rovine, 1988). I'll be coming back to this issue in Chapter 13, when I talk more generally about day care, but I wanted to alert you here to the fact that there is still dispute about this important question.

Temperament and Security of Attachment

The findings I have reported so far are consistent with the general theoretical notion that the child's attachment model evolves out of his interactions with his mother (or other major caregivers). But another explanation is possible. If you look again at the description of the insecurely attached child—especially the resistant/ambivalent type—you may find that it sounds a lot like the description Thomas and Chess give of temperamentally difficult children (see Chapter 3). In fact, Chess and Thomas have themselves noted this similarity (1982), and they argue that the strange situation is really only tapping temperamental differences.

I am not persuaded by this argument, for several reasons. First, as Sroufe points out (1985), the fact that a child's attachment classification can change in response to environmental changes would be hard to account for if we were only measuring inborn temperament. Similarly, if it is only temperament, how can we explain the fact that a child can be securely attached to one person and insecurely attached to another at the same time (something that a number of researchers have observed)?

Still, there are links between temperament and security of attachment. One possibility, suggested by Jay Belsky and Michael Rovine (1987), is that the child's temperament may affect the *form* of insecure or secure attachment she develops (e.g., whether an avoidant or a resistant type of insecure attachment). A second possibility is that children who are temperamentally difficult in the first months of life may be somewhat more *likely* to become insecurely attached (Goldsmith, Bradshaw, & Riesser-Danner, 1986). Such a pattern is clearly not inevitable. Many difficult children develop secure attachments. But the chance of an insecure one may be increased, perhaps because some parents find it harder to respond contingently and lovingly to a more difficult infant, or perhaps because children of this temperament are simply likely to create a different kind of internal working model of their relationships.

Long-term Effects of Secure/Insecure Attachment

One of the reasons I have spent so much time talking about secure and insecure attachment is that this classification has proved to be extremely helpful in predicting a remarkably wide range of other differences between children, as toddlers and even as elementary-school-age children. I talked about some of those differences in Chapter 9 (recall Figure 9.6). In Table 11.3 I have expanded the list. As you can see, those children rated as

Table 11.3

Some Differences Between Securely and Insecurely Attached Children

- *Sociability with peers.*   Up through age 5 or 6 (the latest ages studied), securely attached children show consistently higher rates of social behaviors and greater popularity with peers.
- *Self-esteem.*   Securely attached children have higher self-esteem at age 4 to 5.
- *Flexibility and resourcefulness.*   Securely attached children rate higher in these aspects of "ego resiliency" at age 4 and 5.
- *Dependency.*   Insecurely attached children show more clinging attention seeking from a teacher as well as "negative attention seeking" (getting attention by being "bad") in preschool years.
- *Tantrums and aggressive behavior.*   Insecurely attached children show more of this behavior.
- *Compliance and good deportment.*   Securely attached children are easier to manage in the classroom.
- *Empathy.*   Secure children show more empathy toward other children and toward adults. They also do not show pleasure on seeing others' distress, which is fairly common among avoidant children.
- *Behavior problems.*   At age 6, behavior problems are more common among boys who were insecurely attached as infants; no such pattern has been found for girls.
- *Self-recognition.*   At age 2, insecurely attached children show earlier and more complete self-recognition (in a mirror test), suggesting that individuation and attachment may be somewhat reciprocal processes at this age.
- *Sociability with a strange adult.*   As preschoolers, securely attached children show faster and smoother interaction with a strange adult.
- *Problem solving.*   Securely attached toddlers show longer attention span in free play. They are more confident in attempting solutions to tasks involving tool use, and they use the mother more effectively as a source of assistance.
- *Symbolic play.*   At age 18 to 30 months, secure children show more mature and complex play.

Sources: Easterbrooks & Goldberg, 1987; Lewis et al., 1984; Lewis, Brooks-Gunn, & Jaskir, 1985; Londerville & Main, 1981; Lutkenhaus, Grossmann, & Grossmann, 1985; Matas, Arend, & Sroufe, 1978; Pastor, 1981; Slade, 1987; Sroufe, 1983.

securely attached to their mothers have also been found to be more sociable, more positive (and less negative) in their behavior toward others, and more emotionally "mature" in their approach to school and other nonhome settings. How long such differences may be detectable we still do not know, since groups of children studied so far have not yet been followed much past first grade. But it does appear at the moment that the internal working model of relationships that a child creates from the data of his early relationships with his parents is carried forward and affects a wide variety of interactions later on.

BEYOND THE FIRST ATTACHMENT: CHILDREN'S RELATIONSHIPS WITH OTHER CHILDREN

So far I have talked almost exclusively about the child's relationship with her father and mother, with only occasional references to other adults (such as day-care workers or grandparents) and even more fleeting mention of same-age friends. But beginning in the preschool years, other children play an increasingly central role in the child's social world.

Most of the work on children's social interactions with one another has focused on the two ends of a positive-negative continuum. On the positive end, researchers have looked at children's friendships, at popularity, at helpfulness or generosity among peers. On the negative end, psychologists have looked at aggression among peers and at dominance in play groups. Although such a division misses some of the subtleties of children's peer interactions, for both convenience and clarity I will divide my own discussion in a similar way.

POSITIVE SOCIAL INTERACTIONS AMONG CHILDREN: DEVELOPMENTAL PATTERNS

Peer Interactions In Infancy and Early Childhood

Children first begin to show some positive interest in other infants as early as 6 months of age. If you place two babies on the floor facing each other, they will look at each other, touch, pull each other's hair, imitate each other's actions, and smile at one another (e.g., Hay, Nash, & Pedersen, 1983). By 10 months these behaviors are even more evident. Children this age apparently still prefer to play with objects, but they will play with each other if no toys are available. By 14 to 18 months, we begin to see two or more children playing together with toys—sometimes cooperating together, sometimes simply playing side by side with different toys. These changes occur earlier in toddlers who have had a lot of contact with other youngsters, such as those in day care or preschool, suggesting that to some extent children *learn* how to play with one another (e.g., Harper & Huie, 1985).

Figure 11.7 Children begin to show a definite interest in playing with one another as young as 1 year, but their play becomes increasingly complex and coordinated through the preschool years—as in this picture.

While 1- and 2-year-old children show real social interactions with one another, it is not clear whether children this age have consistent friendships. Carollee Howes (1983, 1987) has observed that children as young as 14 to 24 months old in day-care settings showed consistent preferences for one or more playmates over a full-year period. Using a somewhat stricter definition of friendship, Robert Hinde and his co-workers (1985) have found that in a group of 3½-year-olds, only about 20 percent showed signs of a stable friendship; by age 4, half of these same children regularly played more often with one child than with others. Boys and girls were equally likely to show such strong associations.

Whether we should consider these early playmate preferences to be *attachments* or not is also still open to debate. We know that 4- and 5-year-old children show more positive and less negative behavior toward their friends than toward nonfriends and that they try to respond to their friends' needs. It is also clear that many of these early friendships are reciprocal. Probably children of this age can and do use their friends as a "safe base" for exploring strange or somewhat scary objects or environments. At the same time, the early friendships seem to be less stable and to be more based on proximity and shared play interests than is true of friendships in older children (Berndt, 1981). No doubt for some children these early friendships are a form of attachment; for others they are more transitory or less-intense relationships.

Children as young as 2 or 3 also show another type of positive social behavior: **altruism.** They will offer to help another child who is hurt, offer a toy, or try to comfort another (Zahn-Waxler & Radke-Yarrow, 1982; Marcus, 1986). As I pointed out in Chapter 7, children this young have only a beginning understanding of the fact that others feel differently from themselves, but they obviously understand enough about the emotions of others to respond in supportive and sympathetic ways when they see other children or adults hurt or sad.

It turns out, though, that children vary a lot in the amount of such altruistic behavior they show at this early age. For those of you interested in knowing more about how helpful children come to be that way, I've explored some of the research in the box on pages 418–419.

Positive Social Interactions at School Age

Individual friendships play a much larger role in the social patterns of elementary-school-age children. In one study, John Reisman and Susan Shorr (1978) found that second-graders named about four friends each; by seventh grade this had increased to about seven friends each.

Many of these friendships are remarkably stable. Thomas Berndt, who has studied children's friendships extensively, finds that between half and three-quarters of close friendships in the elementary-school years persist as long as a full school year; many last much longer (e.g., Berndt & Hoyle, 1985; Berndt, Hawkins, & Hoyle, 1986). Within this age range, stability of friendships does not seem to vary predictably by age or by sex. Stable relationships are about as likely in first-graders as they are in eighth-graders. Boys tend to gather in larger groups, while girls are more likely to spend time with a single chum. Most observers see the girls' friendships as more intimate, more based on personal disclosure than is true for boys.

Children treat these friends quite differently than they treat strangers. They are more *polite* to strangers or nonfriends. With chums they are more open, more intimate with one another, which means not only that they exchange supportive comments but also that they are more critical toward one another than toward strangers.

These individual friendships are highly sex-segregated. John Gottman (1986) reports that perhaps 35 percent of friendships in preschool children in the United States are cross-sex friendships, but by age 7 or 8, cross-sex friendships are virtually nonexistent. Similar sex segregation is clear in children's play groups in elementary schools, and "boundary violations" are highly ritualized, as I am sure you can all remember from your own childhood. For example, Barrie Thorne (1986), who has spent years on playgrounds watching children's play groups and games, describes wonderful boy-girl games. They sometimes begin with poking or with taunts like

"You can't catch me, nyah nyah." Then comes the chase, accompanied by the girls' screams. There are "invasions," too, usually by the boys of the girls' games or the girls' space. Up to about fourth or fifth grade, it is taken as an insult to say that a boy likes some girl or that a girl likes some boy. By fifth grade that pattern begins to change, although there is still a great deal of teasing about any kind of boy-girl contact.

Positive Social Interactions at Adolescence

Although I am sure you remember your elementary-school years as a time when friendships with your school chums were important, it is the period of adolescence that most of us think of as being dominated by peer relationships. It is also part of our cultural stereotype of adolescents that they are overly influenced by peers.

To a considerable extent these recollections and stereotypes are based on fact. Adolescents report that they spend more time talking to peers than doing any other thing (Csikszentmihalyi, Larson, & Prescott, 1977), and this "peer time" may be an essential mechanism for making the transition from dependent child to independent adult. As Erikson (1968), among others, has pointed out, relationships with peers (unlike those with parents) are interactions among equals, so they allow the young person to practice many of the aspects of relationships that will be critical in a later marriage or on the job or with adult friends (Berndt, 1982).

Berndt's research shows that the influence of the peer group on a teenager's ideas, habits, and behaviors is very high at all ages but may peak between about age 12 and 14 (1979)—particularly for antisocial activities, like soaping windows on Halloween. That is, 13- and 14-year-olds may be most vulnerable to peer pressure to take part in such activities.

Lest you think that all 13- and 14-year-olds run amok with their peers, I should point out two things. First, teenagers report that peer pressure is more likely to be *against* misconduct than toward it (Brown, Clasen, & Eicher, 1986); and second, susceptibility to negative peer pressure is less common among young people who are close to their parents (Steinberg & Silverberg, 1986). Thus, while peer influence is particularly strong in these adolescent years, there are also important mitigating factors.

Over the same years, the structure of the peer group changes, too (Czikszentmihalyi & Larson, 1984; Dunphy, 1963). Dunphy's 1963 study of the several steps or stages in the shape and function of the peer group during adolescence is particularly fascinating. He observed the formation, dissolution, and interaction of groups of teenagers in a high school in Sydney, Australia, between 1958 and 1960. Two types of groups were visible. The first type Dunphy called a **clique.** They were made up of four to six young people who appeared to be strongly attached to one another. Cliques had strong cohesiveness and high levels of intimate sharing. In the early years of adolescence, these cliques are almost entirely same-sex groups—left over from the preadolescent pattern. Gradually, however, several cliques

REARING HELPFUL AND ALTRUISTIC CHILDREN

I have said that children as young as 2 or 3 will show helpful, generous, and kind behavior toward one another at least occasionally. This is quite true, but some children show much more altruism and kindness than others. Since most of us would like our children to behave in this way toward us, toward their brothers and sisters, and toward other children, it's worthwhile to take a look at what we know about the kinds of family environments that seem to foster this type of positive social interaction.

Several things parents can do seem to make a difference.

Creating a Loving and Warm Family Climate

It shouldn't surprise you to know that first of all, parents who behave in loving, nurturing, and supportive ways toward their children have children who are more helpful, more empathetic, and more thoughtful of others (Zahn-Waxler, Radke-Yarrow, & King, 1979). Undoubtedly, this is partly the effect of modeling. But it may also reflect the effect of a more secure attachment of the child to the parent or even the effect of a good mood. Studies with adults show that we are more likely to help someone in distress if we are in a good mood, and this may be true for children as well.

Explaining Why and Giving Rules

A second significant element in the equation is to be clear to children about what your rules and standards are. The combination of clear rules and loving support is what Baumrind calls "authoritative" parental style. It certainly seems to be a pattern that fosters several "good" things in children, such as high self-esteem and popularity. It reappears in studies of altruism in children as well. This shows up particularly clearly in research by Carolyn Zahn-Waxler and her colleagues (Zahn-Waxler, Radke-Yarrow, & King, 1979; Zahn-Waxler & Radke-Yarrow, 1982).

They asked a group of 16 mothers of young children to keep daily diaries of every incident in which someone around the child showed distress, fear, pain, sorrow, or fatigue. For example, John's mother described an incident in which her 2-year-old son was visited by a friend, Jerry:

Today Jerry was kind of cranky; he just started completely bawling and he couldn't stop. John kept coming over and handing Jerry toys, trying to cheer him up, so to speak. He'd say things like "Here, Jerry," and I said to John: "Jerry's sad; he doesn't feel good; he had a shot today." John would look at me with his eyebrows kind of wrinkled together like he really understood that Jerry was crying because he was unhappy, not that he was just being a crybaby. He went over and rubbed Jerry's arm and said "Nice Jerry" and continued to give him toys. (Zahn-Waxler et al., 1979, pp. 321–322)

Zahn-Waxler found that mothers who both explained the consequences of the child's actions ("If you hit Susan, it will hurt her") *and* who stated the rules clearly, explicitly, and with emotion ("You mustn't hit people!") had children who were much more likely to react to others with helpfulness or sympathy. Research with older children, too, shows that stating the *reason* for generosity or helpfulness—particularly if the reason focuses on the feelings of other people—increases the likelihood that a child will behave in a kind or helpful manner (Grusec & Arnason, 1982).

Many of us, as parents, spend a lot of time telling children what *not* to do. The research on altruism in children points to the importance of telling children *why* they should not do things, especially in terms of the potential impact on other people. Equally important is stating *positive* rules or guidelines—for example, "It's always good to be helpful to other people" or "We should share what we have with people who don't have so much."

Having Children Do Helpful Things

A third thing that fosters helpfulness is giving children a chance to do really helpful things—around the house or in school (Staub, 1979). Children can help cook (a nurturing activity), take care of pets, make toys to give to hospitalized or poor children, assist in making a casserole to take to the recently widowed neighbor, teach younger siblings how to play games (or even how to "share"), and the like.

Obviously, not all children do such things spontaneously. They have to be asked, sometimes coerced. If the coercion is too strong, the effect changes: the child may now attribute his "good" behavior to the coercion ("Mother made me do it") rather than to some inner trait of his own ("I am a helpful person"). When that happens, the coerced altruistic actions do not seem to foster future altruism (Grusec & Dix, 1986). So it matters how the "doing of helpful things" is managed.

Modeling Thoughtful and Generous Behavior

The fourth key—perhaps the most significant—is to demonstrate to your children exactly the generous, thoughtful, and helpful behavior you would like them to show. If there is a conflict between what you say and what you do, children will imitate your actions (Grusec & Arnason, 1982). So stating the rules or guidelines clearly will do little good if your own behavior does not match what you say.

The importance of demonstrating altruism is very clear in a study by Gil Clary and Jude Miller (1986) of adult volunteers in a telephone crisis-counseling agency. Obviously, all these volunteers were showing a significant level of altruistic behavior simply by offering any of their time. But Clary and Miller found that those volunteers who stuck with it, compared to those who dropped out before completing their agreed-upon six months of effort, described their parents as more loving and warm. These "sustained altruists" also said that their parents had preached the importance of generosity and helpfulness and had lived up to their own preaching, more than was true for the parents of the volunteers who dropped out. This research and similar studies point to the conclusion that young people from families like this are more likely to develop "autonomous" altruism—kindness or thoughtfulness or generosity that comes from a genuine concern, an internal value, rather than from a desire to be liked or approved. So if such autonomous altruism is your goal for your children, you will need to look at your own behavior first.

combine into a larger set called a **crowd.** Finally, the crowd breaks down again into heterosexual cliques and finally into loose associations of couples (see Figure 11.8). The period of the fully developed crowd occurred at about age 13 to 15—the very years when we see the greatest conformity to peer pressure.

According to Dunphy, the crowd performs the highly important function of serving as a vehicle for the shift from unisexual to heterosexual social relationships. The 13- or 14-year-old can begin to try out her new heterosexual skills in the somewhat protected environment of the crowd; only after some confidence is developed do we see the beginnings of committed heterosexual pair relationships.

While these changes in peer groups are taking place, young people continue to have important individual friendships as well. These friendships continue to be quite stable, as they were in earlier years. These friendships also become increasingly intimate over the adolescent years (Berndt, 1982). Adolescents share their inner feelings and secrets with their friends more

Figure 11.8 Dunphy's observations of Australian teenagers led him to suggest that there were two "phases" in teenagers' group formation: cliques, which are closely knit groups of six or eight friends, and, later, crowds, which may be looser-knit associations of cliques. Which do you think is shown here? Does Dunphy's description fit with your own memory of the groups you were involved with in high school?

than do elementary-school-age children, and they are more knowledgeable about their friends' feelings as well. This trend continues throughout the teen years, with intimate sharing reaching a peak in the early twenties (just as Erikson suggested).

I think it is important to understand the *function* of friendships and peer group relationships for adolescents. Parents are often horrified at the conformity they see and at their reduced influence on their children. But the teenager is struggling to make a slow transition from the protected life of the family to the independent life of adulthood. Peer culture in adolescence is a *vehicle* for that transition.

INDIVIDUAL DIFFERENCES IN POSITIVE INTERACTIONS: POPULARITY

Superimposed on these developmental shifts are significant differences in children's competence in social interactions and in their popularity with others. I have already mentioned the findings from several studies showing that children who are securely attached to their parents are also more skillful in playing with and relating to their peers in the early years. Some such link may also continue in later years as well. We have learned most of what we know about individual differences in social competence in the elementary-school years, however, by coming at the question from the other end—by identifying children who are popular and asking what other characteristics they may have.

To simplify the discussion, I have summarized the main findings in Table 11.4. Some of the items on this list are obviously things that a child can't control, such as physical size or attractiveness. These characteristics do make some difference, but the crucial element in popularity is not how the child looks—it is how he or she *behaves*. Popular children are liked because they behave in positive, supporting, nonpunitive, and nonaggressive ways toward most other children (Asher, 1983). Of course, once a child has become popular it is far easier for him or her to be friendly, positive, and supportive of others, so a feedback loop is involved here. But we also know that when you put groups of previously unacquainted children together in play groups or work groups and chart the emergence of popularity, you find that those children who are most consistently positive and supportive from the beginning are those who end up being chosen as leaders or as friends (e.g., Dodge, 1983), while those who consistently participate in conflicts are more often rejected (Shantz, 1986).

Interestingly, rejection by one's peers in elementary school is one of the very few aspects of childhood functioning that consistently predicts behavior problems or emotional disturbances in adolescence and adulthood (Hartup, 1984). This might mean that problems with peers is merely the most visible reflection of a general maladjustment that later manifests as delinquency or emotional disturbance. It could also mean that a failure to

Table 11.4
▬▬▬▬▬▬▬▬▬

Some Characteristics of Popular and Rejected Children in Elementary School

Popular children are more likely to be:
- Friendly toward others, less punitive, more reinforcing, more supportive.
- Outgoing and gregarious.
- Physically attractive.
- Physically larger or taller or more mature.
- The youngest child in the family.
- Good at specific task skills, such as sports or games.
- More successful in school.

Rejected children are more likely to be:
- Physically unattractive.
- Physically or emotionally immature.
- Aggressive or disruptive.
- Less friendly, more likely to be critical than supportive.

Sources: Asher, Oden, & Gottman, 1977; Hartup, 1984; Masters & Furman, 1981; Shantz, 1986.

▬▬▬▬▬▬▬▬

develop friendships itself causes problems that later become more general. Or it could signify a seriously warped internal working model of relationships. Whatever the source of the problem, you will be glad to know that it is possible, within limits, to increase a child's acceptance by his peers by teaching him the social skills that seem to be required for friendship, including listening, smiling, and supportiveness (e.g., Bierman, 1986).

What kinds of families do popular children come from? I've already mentioned two elements: families that foster secure attachment have children who show greater skill with peers in the preschool period, and families that foster high self-esteem also have more-popular children. Other research suggests several other similarities in families of popular children (Asher, Renshaw, & Hymel, 1982): (1) they discourage aggression and antisocial behavior in their children; (2) they try not to frustrate the child and use little punishment; (3) they like their child and tell her so; (4) they make sure their child has plenty of opportunity to play with other children (play groups, picking up and delivering playmates, participation in children's groups like Scouts, and so on); and (5) they provide toys and materials that foster pair or group interaction, such as dress-up materials or puppets. For a boy to be popular with his peers, a strong father figure, one who is warm and positive toward the son, also seems to be important.

If you think back to what I said in Chapter 10, this combination of parental treatment sounds a lot like the pattern Baumrind calls authoritative child rearing. Thus the origins of high self-esteem and the origins of popularity may have something in common.

NEGATIVE SOCIAL INTERACTIONS AMONG CHILDREN

If you have watched children together, you know that all is not sweetness and light in the land of the young. Children do show affectionate and helpful behaviors toward one another, but they also tease, fight, yell, criticize, and argue over objects and territory. Researchers who have studied this "negative" side of children's interactions have looked mostly at aggressive behavior.

Aggression

Developmental Patterns. Every child shows at least some **aggression,** which we can define as behavior with the apparent intent to injure some other person or object (Feshbach, 1970). The basic built-in "signal" for aggression in most instances seems to be frustration. Some early theorists (e.g., Dollard et al., 1939) argued that aggression *always* followed a frustration and that all aggressions were preceded by frustration. This extreme version of the "frustration-aggression hypothesis" turns out to be wrong, but it does seem to be true that the human child is born with a fairly strong natural tendency to behave aggressively after being frustrated.

Over the early years of life, the frequency and form of aggression change, as I've summarized in Table 11.5. When 2- or 3-year-old children are upset or frustrated, they are more likely to use physical aggression. As their verbal skills improve, however, there is a shift toward greater use of verbal aggression, such as taunting or name-calling.

Individual Differences in Aggressiveness. If you went to a school playground or a day-care center and watched for a while, it wouldn't be hard to pick out some children who are consistently more aggressive than others. They get into more fights, yell more at other children, and generally make a nuisance of themselves. Other children play together for long stretches without getting into disputes. What is even more striking is the fact that such differences tend to persist. Leonard Eron, in a 22-year longitudinal study, has found that aggressiveness toward peers at age 8 was related to various forms of aggressiveness at age 30, including "criminal behavior, number of moving traffic violations, convictions for driving while intoxicated, aggressiveness toward spouses, and how severely the subjects punished their own children" (1987, p. 439). Where do such differences come from?

If you think back to the theories I discussed in Chapter 9, you should be able to figure out the major kinds of explanations that have been offered.

Table 11.5

A Summary of Developmental Changes in the Form and Frequency of Aggression in Children

	2- to 4-year-olds	4- to 8-year-olds
Frequency of physical aggression	At its peak from 2 to 4.	Declines over the period from 4 to 8.
Frequency of verbal aggression	Relatively rare at 2; increases as the child's verbal skill improves.	A larger percentage of aggression in this period is verbal rather than physical.
Form of aggression	Primarily "instrumental aggression," which is aimed at obtaining or damaging an object rather than directly hurting someone else.	More "hostile aggression" at these ages, aimed at hurting another person or another person's feelings.
Occasion for aggression	Most often occurs after conflicts with parents.	Most often occurs after conflicts with peers.

Source: Goodenough, 1931; Hartup, 1974.

One possibility, of course, is that such behavior is caused partly by temperamental differences. Another alternative is that aggressiveness results from a failure of the process of identification and thus a lack of full development of the superego. Eron and his colleagues have found, for example, that aggressiveness is less common in adolescence and adulthood in those who, as children, seemed more clearly identified with parents and who reported more guilt after doing something wrong.

Still another possibility is that aggression is learned more directly, through modeling and from differential reinforcement patterns, as I discussed in Chapter 9 when talking about Gerald Patterson's work with highly aggressive or out-of-control children.

Yet another possibility is that the aggressive child has developed a quite different internal working model of relationships. Thus, whether a child behaves aggressively may depend a good deal on how she interprets other people's behavior—in particular, whether she assumes or "reads in" hostile intent in ambiguous situations. Kenneth Dodge and Cynthia Frame (1982) have found precisely this: given an ambiguous event, such as being hit in the back with a kickball, typically aggressive boys are much more likely to assume that the ball was thrown on purpose, and they retaliate. Of course, such retaliation is likely to bring them hostility in return, so their expectation that other people are hostile to them is further confirmed.

Like the child's working model of attachment, such expectancies may have their roots in the child's earliest family interactions, with siblings as well as with parents. Consistent with this possibility is the repeated finding that parents who are rejecting toward the child have more aggressive children. Often, of course, rejection is combined with high rates of physical punishment of the child, which further reinforces the child's working model. It is not surprising that children growing up in such families show higher rates of aggression themselves.

Competition and Dominance

A related, but quite separable, aspect of "negative" encounters between children is **competition** or **dominance.** Whenever there are too few toys for the number of children, there is not enough time with the teacher to go around, or there is some other scarcity of desired objects, there will be competition. Sometimes competition results in outright aggression. More often, though, competition results in the development of a clear **dominance hierarchy,** more popularly known as a "pecking order." Some children seem to be more successful than others at asserting their rights to desired objects, by threats, by simply taking the object away, by glaring at the other child, or the equivalent.

Clear dominance hierarchies are seen in play groups of children as young as 2 to 5 years old (e.g., Strayer, 1980). That is, among 10 or 15 children who play together regularly, it is possible to predict who will "win" in any given competition over some desired object or space. Children high in the dominance hierarchy win out over nearly all other children; children at the bottom of the pecking order lose to everyone.

Research on dominance in young children has revealed some extremely interesting patterns. Among 2- to 5-year-olds, a child's place in the group dominance system is *not* related to popularity or to positive interactions to or from the child. But among elementary-school-age children, the dominance and popularity/friendship systems may be linked. When Strayer (1980) observed 5- and 6-year-olds in play groups, he found that the dominant children were also the most popular. So among children this age, popularity may reflect both positive actions and perceived dominance.

Overall, the picture that emerges is that past the age of 4 or 5, *socially competent* children are those who are at the middle to higher end of the dominance hierarchy; who are positive, helpful and supportive of others; and who refrain from overt acts of physical aggression.

SEX DIFFERENCES IN SOCIAL INTERACTIONS

So far I have steered clear of any discussion of sex differences in social interactions. But since this is an area in which the sex-role stereotypes are very strong, I need to face the question as squarely as I can. Take a look at Table 11.6. In the table I've listed both the stereotype (the basic cultural expectation) and the actually observed sex differences, so you can see how well they match.

Table 11.6

Sex-Role Stereotypes and Observed Sex Differences in Social Behavior

Behavior and stereotype	Observed difference
Aggression/dominance/competitiveness. Boys expected to show more of all three.	Boys are quite consistently found to show more rough-and-tumble play in the early years and more aggression and competitiveness at virtually all ages.
Risk taking. Boys expected to show more.	Boys are willing to try new and daring or faintly dangerous things, such as riding an elephant at the zoo.
Dependency. Girls expected to show more.	No consistent sex difference has been found in such behaviors as clinging, proximity seeking, or attention seeking in young children.
Nurturance/helping/generosity. Girls expected to show more of all three.	Mixed results. Most studies show no sex difference, but when a difference is found, girls are usually slightly more generous or slightly more likely to help or nurture.
Interest in others/sociability. Girls thought to show more.	Mixed results. Boys seem to be more peer-oriented in preschool. In elementary school, boys have more friends and play in larger groups; girls have fewer but stronger friendships. In adolescence, no difference in number of friends, but girls' friendships are more intimate.
Compliance. Girls expected to show more.	Preschool girls comply more with adult requests. Among older children there is no consistent finding expect that those who exhibit very high levels of noncompliance are more often boys.
Crying. Girls expected to show more.	No difference.

Sources: Berndt, 1982; Ginsburg & Miller, 1982; Hyde, 1984; Maccoby & Jacklin, 1974, 1980; Minton, Kagan, & Levine, 1971; Patterson, 1980; Shigetomi, Hartmann, & Gelfand, 1981.

In many areas the match is not good. Girls don't seem to be more dependent or consistently more nurturant or more socially oriented. The *patterns* of social behavior boys and girls show do differ somewhat: boys play in larger groups and appear to have less-intimate individual friendships. But there are no differences in involvement with others. The one area in which the stereotype seems to be most accurate is in a cluster of related behaviors: aggression, assertiveness, and dominance. As expected, boys show more of all three.

Where might such differences come from? Eleanor Maccoby and Carol Jacklin (1974), who summarized all the studies done up to 1974, concluded that there is an important biological basis for the aggression differences.

> Let us outline the reasons why biological sex differences appear to be involved in aggression: (1) Males are more aggressive than females in all human societies for which evidence is available. (2) The sex differences are found early in life, at a time when there is no evidence that differential socialization pressures have been brought to bear by adults to "shape" aggression differently for the two sexes. (3) Similar sex differences are found in man and subhuman primates. (4) Aggression is related to levels of sex hormones, and can be changed by experimental administration of these hormones. (Maccoby & Jacklin, 1974, pp. 242–243)

Other psychologists (including Maccoby and Jacklin in more recent writings) have emphasized that there are important social influences, at least in our culture, which also may foster higher levels of aggression in boys (Brooks-Gunn & Matthews, 1979; Tieger, 1980). For example, in research with Margaret Snow, Maccoby and Jacklin have found that with children as young as age 1, fathers punish or prohibit behavior in their sons more than in their daughters (Snow, Jacklin, & Maccoby, 1983).

It seems clear that both biological and environmental influences play a role. There probably are hormonal or other biological factors creating higher rates of aggressiveness in boys to begin with. But as I pointed out in Chapter 10, there is also pressure from parents (particularly fathers) for 4- and 5-year-old boys to adopt more "boyish" behaviors and attitudes, which includes playing physical games and being assertive with others. The manner in which parents respond to the child's aggression also helps to shape it, which shows clearly that aggression is not entirely determined by biology.

Despite this difference in aggressiveness, the striking thing about sex differences in social behavior is how few are found consistently. Boys and girls are much more like each other than they are different in the quality and content of their encounters with each other.

SUMMARY

1. Relationships with adults and peers are of central significance in the development of all children. Of particular importance is the development of an internal working model of close relationships, based initially on the first attachments to parents.

2. An important distinction is between *attachment behavior* and underlying *attachment*. The latter is the basic bond between two people. The former is the manner in which that bond is expressed in actual behavior.

3. The parents' attachment to the infant may develop in two phases: (1) an initial strong bond may be formed in the first hours of the child's

life, and (2) a growing attachment may result from the repetition of mutually reinforcing and interlocking attachment behaviors.

4. The short-term strength of the initial bond appears to be somewhat increased if the parents have immediate contact with the newborn, but the long-term effect of this early contact seems to be small and is seen only in some subgroups of parents.

5. Fathers as well as mothers form strong attachments to their infants. After the early weeks of life, however, fathers show a more playful interactive pattern with their children than do mothers.

6. At first, the infant shows attachment behaviors toward nearly anyone but shows no preferential attachment.

7. By 5 to 6 months, most infants have formed at least one strong attachment, usually to the major caregiver (most often the mother).

8. In toddlers and preschoolers, the basic attachment remains but the form of attachment behaviors changes. The child becomes less clinging except when under stress, when the earlier forms reappear.

9. In adolescence, too, the basic attachment to the parents appears to remain strong, although the young person now spends considerably more time with peers than with parents and parent-child conflict becomes more common.

10. Children typically develop strong attachments to both father and mother. Children 12 to 24 months old typically prefer the mother over the father in stressful situations.

11. Children differ in the security of their first attachments. The secure infant uses the parent as a safe base for exploration and can be readily consoled by the parent.

12. The security of the initial attachment is reasonably stable and is fostered by contingent responsiveness and acceptance by the parent. Insecure attachment is somewhat more likely in temperamentally difficult children.

13. Securely attached children appear to be more socially skillful, more curious and persistent in approaching new tasks, and more mature.

14. Children's relationships with other youngsters become more and more central to their social development from age 1 or 2. Toddlers are aware of other children and will play with them; by age 2 or 3 children show specific social approaches to others.

15. By age 4 or 5, children have formed individual friendships and show preferential positive behavior toward friends. Friendship becomes more common and more stable in the elementary-school years.

16. The peer group is particularly significant in adolescence, when it may serve as a "bridge" between the role of dependent child and that of independent adult. Teenagers are maximally influenced by peer pressure at around age 14, a time when large groups of teens ("crowds") may associate regularly. Individual friendships also are significant in adolescence.

17. Young children also show such negative social patterns as aggressiveness and dominance. Physical aggression peaks at age 3 or 4 and is

replaced more and more by verbal aggression among older children. Children who are reinforced for aggressiveness show more aggression with their peers; rejected children and those who are permitted to be aggressive and are then punished for it show heightened aggression.

18. Dominance patterns are visible in groups of toddlers as well as older children.

19. Popularity among peers, in elementary school or later, is associated with greater intelligence, greater dominance, and greater attractiveness. But it is most strongly associated with the amount of positive and supportive social behavior shown by a child.

20. The most consistent sex differences in social behavior is that boys are more aggressive than girls. In other areas the similarities are more striking than the differences.

■■■■■ KEY TERMS

aggression Usually defined as intentional physical or verbal behaviors directed toward a person or an object with the intent to inflict damage on that person or object.

altruism Giving or sharing objects, time, or goods with others, with no obvious self-gain.

attachment The positive affective bond felt by one person for another, such as the child for the parent or the parent for the child.

attachment behaviors The collection of (probably) automatic behaviors of one person toward another that bring about or maintain proximity and caregiving, such as the smile of the young infant; behaviors that reflect an attachment.

clique A group of four to six friends with strong attachment bonds and high levels of group solidarity and loyalty.

competition Interaction between two or more persons in which each person attempts to gain control over some scarce resource, such as toys, attention from a preferred person, or "success."

crowd A larger and looser group of friends than a clique, with perhaps 20 members; normally made up of several cliques joined together.

dominance The ability of one person consistently to "win" competitive encounters with other individuals.

dominance hierarchy A set of dominance relationships in a group, describing the rank order of "winners" and "losers" in competitive encounters.

insecure attachment Includes both ambivalent and avoidant patterns of attachment in children. The child does not use the parent as a safe base and is not readily consoled by the parent if upset.

internal working model A child's cognitive construction of social relationships. The earliest relationships may form the template for an internal model of the workings of relationships, such as expectations of support or affection, trustworthiness, and so on.

secure attachment Demonstrated by the child's ability to use the parent as a safe base and to be consoled after separation, when fearful, or when otherwise stressed.

strange situation A series of episodes used by Mary Ainsworth and others in studies of attachment. The child is observed when with the mother, with a stranger, left alone, and reunited with stranger and mother.

■■■■■ SUGGESTED READING

Asher, S. R., Renshaw, P. D., & Hymel, S. (1982). Peer relations and the development of social skills. In S. G. Moore & C. R. Cooper (Eds.), *The young child: Reviews of research* (Vol 3). Washington, D.C.: National Association for the Education of Young Children.
A very nice discussion of social skills in children and of some of the attempts that have

been made to increase such skills in socially isolated children.

Greif, G. L. (1985). *Single fathers.* Lexington, MA: Lexington Books.
If you are interested in fatherhood, and particularly in what happens when a father raises children on his own, you may find this book of interest. It is based on a (nonrandom) sample of over 1000 men who responded to a questionnaire in a magazine for single parents. The focus is not specifically on attachment, but the book discusses fathers' relationships with their children as well as many other aspects of single fatherhood.

Lickona, T. (1983). *Raising good children.* Toronto: Bantam Books.
One of the very best "how-to" books for parents I have ever seen, with excellent concrete advice as well as theory. The emphasis is on many of the issues I raised in the box on pages 418–419.

Maccoby, E. E. (1980). *Social development: Psychological growth and the parent-child relationship.* New York: Harcourt Brace Jovanovich.
A fine text that includes chapters on attachment, on aggression, and on sex differences in social behavior.

Oden, S. (1982). Peer relationship development in childhood. In L. G. Katz (Ed.), *Current topics in early childhood education* (Vol. 4). Norwood, NJ: Ablex.
Another good current review of information on children's peer relationships and friendships, with a focus on the early years of life.

Rubin, Z. (1980). *Children's friendships.* Cambridge, MA: Harvard University Press.
Zick Rubin writes wonderfully; this book is both delightful and informative.

Steinberg, L. D. (1987, September). Bound to bicker. *Psychology Today*, pp. 36–39.
In this brief article, Steinberg discusses his work on the impact of puberty on the relationships between parents and adolescents.

PROJECT: OBSERVATION OF CHILDREN'S PLAY GROUPS

Let me give you a tougher assignment than many of the earlier projects. This will really stretch your skills as an observer and researcher. Arrange to spend several hours in a day-care center or preschool that includes groups of children of about age 2 to 4. Be sure to do the observation during a time that includes some "free play." (If all you observe is snack time, nap, and organized play, you will not get a chance to observe the things I want you to look for.)

Watch for about 15 minutes without writing anything down, making an effort to identify (to yourself) 10 different children, about half of whom should be boys and half girls. Label them in some way that you can use as shorthand, and be sure to indicate whether each is a boy or a girl.

Now begin your real observations. At the beginning of each three-minute period, note down which other child or children each of your 10 focal children is playing with at that moment. Note for each child: (1) how many other children there are in the play group, (2) the genders of all children in the play group, (3) the specific identity of any child in the group you can identify, and (4) the activity the children are engaged in (e.g., doll play, blocks, swings).

Continue this procedure for each three-minute period for at least an hour. Inevitably you will have some periods in which one or more of the focal children are not in sight (they may be in the bathroom or elsewhere), and perhaps there will be some three-minute periods in which all children are playing together in some activity organized by the teachers. For the former case, merely omit that child from the record for that interval. For the latter (full-group activity), omit that three-minute period from your record entirely.

I recommend that you make up a data sheet (it might look something like the one below) to be used for each three-minute period. So each time you start a fresh set of observations, you should note it on a separate sheet.

When you are done, you should have 20 data sheets, with up to 20 notations for each of your focal children. For each child, (1) compute the average number of children in the groups that child played in; and (2) determine the percentage of periods in which that child played in same-sex groups, with only opposite-sex playmates, and in mixed-sex groups.

Then compute the same scores summed across all of your focal children (average number of children in play groups and percentages of time in same-sex, opposite-sex, and mixed-sex groups). Also see if you can find any pairs of children who seemed to play together frequently. Were these "friends" usually same-sex pairs?

How do your observations match the patterns of early peer associations I have described in the text? Are there consistent pairings of "friends"? Did you see some children who were consistently solitary in their activity, while others were in larger groups? Do children this age mostly choose same-sex playmates? How large are the groups typically formed? What kinds of activities were these groups engaged in?

What difficulties did you have in completing the assignment? Was it difficult to determine who was "in" a particular group? This is a difficult kind of observation to do, so don't be discouraged if you found it confusing. You may end up with more respect for the attention to detail required for researchers to do this kind of study well.

Three-Minute Observation Period No. _____

Focal child	No. of children in play group	Gender of playmates	Identities of playmates	Activity
1 (boy)				
2 (boy)				
3 (boy)				
4 (boy)				
5 (boy)				
6 (girl)				
7 (girl)				
8 (girl)				
9 (girl)				
10 (girl)				

12 Thinking About Relationships: The Development of Social Cognition

Some General Principles and Issues
   The Cognitive Side of Social Cognition
   The Social Side of Social Cognition
Thinking About Other People: Feelings, Qualities, Relationships
   The Development of Empathy
   Describing Other People
   Thinking About Relationships
Thinking About What People *Ought* to Do
   Piaget's Early Ideas About Moral Judgments
   Kohlberg's Stages of Moral Development
   Eisenberg's Model of Prosocial Reasoning
   Gilligan's Ethic of Caring
Social Cognition and Behavior
Moral Education and Moral Development
Social Cognition and General Cognitive Development
Summary
Key Terms
Suggested Reading
Project: Understanding of Friendship

Think for a minute about the conversations you have with your friends. Haven't you said things like "I thought you knew that I admire you" or "I thought Jack was my friend, but now it turns out I can't really trust him" or "I've been trying to figure Jane out. Sometimes she's shy and sometimes she's the life of the party. What do you think is behind that?" or "You can see through my cover; but lots of people believe that I'm really the confident person I look like on the outside"?

All these statements reflect some aspect of what psychologists have come to call **social cognition**—thinking about people, what they do and should do, how they feel. If you are anything like I am (and I assume you are), then you, too, spend a great deal of time and energy analyzing other people—trying to understand them, trying to predict what your friends, partner, or co-workers will do. In our everyday life, in fact, knowledge about people and relationships is probably more important than many of the kinds of knowledge or thinking I talked about in Chapters 6 and 7 (although such knowledge makes up a part of what Sternberg calls *contextual intelligence,* as you may recall from Chapter 6). Where does such knowledge come from? How do children learn about people, about relationships, about right and wrong?

These questions are not new to you. I have touched on many facets of social cognition as I have gone along. The infant's emerging ability to recognize individuals and to use facial expressions and other body cues for social referencing is one kind of social cognition, as is the older child's process of learning that other people have different perspectives or different views from his own (the loss of egocentrism, in Piaget's language). One could also argue that the proposed internal working model of attachment is a kind oif social cognition—it is a sort of theory about relationships, based on the child's own early interactions. Finally, *self*-knowledge is also an aspect of social cognition. As I pointed out in Chapters 9 and 10, the child creates a concept or schema of himself—a process that has both cognitive and social aspects. What I need to do now is to pull these various threads together and describe some of the more general ideas about social cognition that have been emerging in the past few years. In the process, I hope to be able to build a few bridges between the otherwise quite separate discussions of thinking and social relationships.

SOME GENERAL PRINCIPLES AND ISSUES

As you might imagine, researchers and theorists have come to the questions and research on social cognition from two different directions—from studies of cognition and from studies of social interaction. So let me begin by looking at the subject from each of those perspectives.

The Cognitive Side of Social Cognition

One way to think about social cognition is simply to conceive of it as the application of general cognitive processes or skills to a different topic, in this case, people or relationships. In Chapter 7 I talked about all the ways in which children's thinking changes from infancy through adolescence. We can assume that at any given age, a child applies these fundamental *ways* of thinking to her relationships as well as to objects. In this view, the child's understanding of self and other, of social relationships, simply *reflects* her level of cognitive development. Robert Selman (1980), for example, has proposed that a child's developing social ideas depend on systematic developmental shifts in her perspective-taking skills.

This way of looking at social cognition has a powerful intuitive appeal. After all, as John Flavell points out (1985), it is the same head doing the thinking when a child works on a conservation problem and when she tries to understand people. Furthermore, as you will see very clearly when we go through the evidence, many of the same principles that seem to apply to general cognitive development hold here as well:

- *Outer to inner characteristics.*   Younger children pay attention to the surface of things, to what they look like; older children look for principles, for causes.
- *Observation to inference.*   Young children initially base their conclusions only on what they can see or feel; later they make inferences about what ought to be or what might be.
- *Definite to qualified.*   Young children's rules are very definite and fixed (such as sex-role rules); by adolescence, at the latest, rules have been qualified.
- *Observer's view to general view.*   Children also become less "egocentric" with time—less tied to their own individual viewpoint, more able to construct a model of some experience or some process that is true for everyone.

All these dimensions of change describe children's emerging social cognition, just as they describe the development of thinking about objects. But to reduce social cognition merely to such general principles is to ignore some critical differences.

The Social Side of Social Cognition

The most obvious difference is that people, as objects of thought, are simply not the same as rocks or beakers of water or balls of clay. Among many other things, people behave *intentionally,* and they can reveal or conceal information about themselves. In fact, learning to "read" the cues that people give is one of the key social-cognitive skills, as is grasping and taking into account the possibility that people can conceal the truth or give misleading cues. Furthermore, unlike relationships with objects, relationships with people are mutual and reciprocal. Other people talk back, respond to your distress, offer things, get angry.

Children also have to learn about special rules that apply to social interactions, such as politeness rules or rules about when you can and cannot speak, and about power or dominance (such as the "pecking orders"

Figure 12.1 When you look at this person's smile, what do you see? Is the smile genuine? That is, does it signify that the person is really pleased or happy? Or is this a "social smile" that involves a pretense of pleasure? One of the difficult things that children have to learn about social interactions is that people sometimes mask their real feelings or intentions.

I talked about in Chapter 11). Schank and Abelson (1977) have used the word *script* to describe these special social rules, which I think conveys the basic idea nicely. Children presumably learn these scripts from their own experience, developing strong expectations about how people will behave and in what order in particular settings. Furthermore, these scripts probably change with age not just because children's cognitive skills change but also because the rules (scripts) themselves change as children move from one social setting to another. One obvious example, as Higgins and Parsons have pointed out (1983), is the set of changes when children start school. The script associated with the role of "student" is quite different from the one connected with the role of "little kid." Classrooms are more tightly organized, expectations for obedience are higher, and there are more drills and routines to be learned than was probably true at home or even in nursery school. These changes are bound to affect the child's pattern of thinking.

Most of the research on children's emerging social understanding puts the cognitive horse before the social relationship cart, implying that it is the "understanding" part of the system that is paramount. I will inevitably foster this impression further in this chapter, since most of what I will describe will be research on the cognitive side. But it is important to keep the social side in mind as well. I will try to balance the scales as I go along.

THINKING ABOUT OTHER PEOPLE: FEELINGS, QUALITIES, RELATIONSHIPS

The child's first task in social interactions is to learn to "read" people—to understand what other people may be feeling or thinking or what they may be like. One way to study this is to look at **empathy**—the child's ability to match his own feelings with that of another person. More generally, we can study children's descriptions of other people to see what kinds of features they pay attention to.

The Development of Empathy

Empathy has many different definitions. Often it is used to refer to a situation in which a person responds to someone else's emotion by feeling the *same* emotion himself. Or it may be used more generally, as when a person feels a *similar* or congruent emotion (sometimes also called *sympathy*). Martin Hoffman, who has written the largest body of work on the development of empathy (e.g., 1982, 1984), defines it as "a vicarious affective response that does not match another's affective state but is more appropriate to someone else's situation than to one's own" (1984, p. 285).

Hoffman sees four broad steps in the emergence of empathy in childhood and adolescence, which I've summarized in Table 12.1. Stage 1, global empathy, seems to be a kind of automatic matching of emotion, perhaps arising out of the infant's lack of clear distinction between herself and others. But in stage 2, as early as age 1, we do see some more specific awareness of other people's emotions, although the response is still egocentric. Hoffman gives an example: a 13-month-old who saw an adult looking distressed looked sad himself and then offered the adult his own favorite doll. (I suspect that this kind of egocentrism is not totally absent in adulthood, either—for example, when we buy someone else the gift that we ourselves would like.)

Very soon, though, as the child's ability to take another's role begins to develop (at age 2 or 3), toddlers begin to show less-egocentric responses. Children's empathetic responses become more and more subtle over the preschool and elementary-school years as they become better readers of others' emotions. By middle childhood, many children can even empathize with several contradictory emotions at once, such as when they see another child make a mistake and fall during a game. The observing child may see and empathize with both the hurt and the sense of shame or embarrassment. She may even be aware that the victim might prefer *not* to be helped. In adolescence a still more abstract level emerges, when the child in stage

Table 12.1

Hoffman's Stages in the Development of Empathy

- **Stage 1: Global empathy.**   Observed during the first year. If the infant is around someone expressing a strong emotion, he may match that emotion—for example, beginning to cry when he hears another infant crying.
- **Stage 2: Egocentric empathy.**   Beginning at about 12 to 18 months, when the child has a fairly clear sense of her separate self, she responds to another's distress with some distress of her own. She may attempt to "cure" the other person's problem by offering what she herself would find most comforting. She may, for example, show sadness when she sees another child hurt and go to get her *own* mother to help.
- **Stage 3: Empathy for another's feelings.**   Beginning as young as 2 or 3 and continuing through elementary school, children note others' feelings, partially match those feelings, and respond to others' distress in nonegocentric ways. Over these years, children distinguish a wider and wider (and more subtle) range of emotions.
- **Stage 4: Empathy for another's general plight.**   In late childhood or in adolescence, some children develop a more generalized notion of others' feelings and respond not just to the immediate situation but to the other individual's general situation or plight. So if a young person at this level knows that another's person's sadness is chronic or the person's general situation is particularly tragic, he may become more distressed than he would if the problem were more transient.

Source: Hoffman, 1982.

4 moves beyond the immediate situation and empathizes with another person's general plight.

Notice that these changes reflect several of the general principles I outlined earlier (and parallel the changes Piaget described, too)—particularly a shift from observation to inference. With increasing age, the child's empathic response is guided less and less by just the immediate, observed emotions and much more by his inferences or deductions about the other person's feelings. But this is not a swift process. Research in England by Paul Harris and his associates (Harris, Olthof, & Terwogt, 1981), for example, shows that it isn't really until adolescence that young people are fully aware that other people may hide their emotions or act differently from the way they feel "inside."

Describing Other People

We can see the same kind of shift in studies of children's descriptions of others, as well as a clear change from a focus on external characteristics to internal ones. There seem to be at least three steps. Up to perhaps age 6 to 8, when children are asked to describe others they focus almost exclusively on external features—what the person looks like, where he lives,

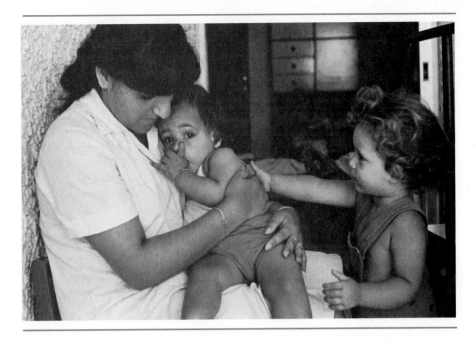

Figure 12.2 Quite young children—as young as 2 or 3—show this kind of empathic response to other people's distress or delight. As they get older, children empathize with still more subtle emotions, or even with contradictory emotions.

what he does. This description by a boy 7 years and 10 months old, taken from a very nice study in England, is typical:

> He is very tall. He has dark brown hair, he goes to our school. I don't think he has any brothers or sisters. He is in our class. Today he has a dark orange jumper [a sweater] and grey trousers and brown shoes. (Livesley & Bromley, 1973, p. 213)

When young children do use internal or evaluative terms to describe people, they are likely to use quite global terms, such as *nice* or *mean* or *good* or *bad*. Furthermore, young children do not seem to see these qualities as lasting or general traits of the individual, applicable in all situations or over time (Rholes & Ruble, 1984). In other words, the young child has not yet developed a concept we might think of as "conservation of personality."

Between about age 7 or 8 and adolescence, however, we see the emergence of precisely such a notion of enduring personality in others. The child begins to focus more on the inner traits or qualities of another person and to assume that those traits will be visible in many situations. You can see the shift in this (widely quoted) description by a child nearly 10 years old:

> He smells very much and is very nasty. He has no sense of humour and is very dull. He is always fighting and he is cruel. He does silly things and is very stupid. He has brown hair and cruel eyes. He is sulky and 11 years old and has lots of sisters. I think he is the most horrible boy in the class. He has a croaky voice and always chews his pencil and picks his teeth and I think he is disgusting. (Livesley & Bromley, 1973, p. 217)

This description still includes many external, physical features, but it goes beyond such concrete surface qualities to the level of personality traits (such as lack of humor or cruelty).

In adolescence there is another shift. Now young people's descriptions contain more comparisons of one trait with another or one person with another, more recognition of inconsistencies and exceptions, more shadings of gray (Shantz, 1983), as in this description by a 15-year-old:

> Andy is very modest. He is even shyer than I am when near strangers and yet is very talkative with people he knows and likes. He always seems good tempered and I have never seen him in a bad temper. He tends to degrade other people's achievements, and yet never praises his own. He does not seem to voice his opinions to anyone. He easily gets nervous. (Livesley & Bromley, 1973, p. 221)

I can show you some of these changes less anecdotally with some findings from two studies by Carl Barenboim (1977, 1981). He asked children ranging in age from 6 to 16 to describe three people. Any descriptions that involved comparing a child's behaviors or physical features with another child or with a norm he called *behavioral comparisons* (e.g., "Billy runs a lot faster than Jason" or "She draws the best in our whole class"). Statements that involved some internal personality construct he called *psychological constructs* (e.g., "Sarah is so kind" or "He's a real stubborn idiot!"). Any that included qualifiers, explanations, exceptions, or mentions of changes in character he called *organizing relationships* (e.g., "He's only shy around people he doesn't know" or "Usually she's nice to me, but sometimes she can be quite mean"). Figure 12.3 shows the combined findings from the two studies. You can see that behavioral comparisons peaked at around age 8 or 9, psychological statements peaked at about age 14, and organizing relationships did not appear until age 10 and were still increasing at age 16.

I am sure that many of you have noticed that this series of changes strongly resembles the pattern of development of children's self-descriptions I discussed in Chapter 10 (see Figure 10.4). This illustrates once again that the emergence of the self-concept is an aspect of social cognition and that the same underlying cognitive shifts seem to be involved in both understanding of others and understanding of the self.

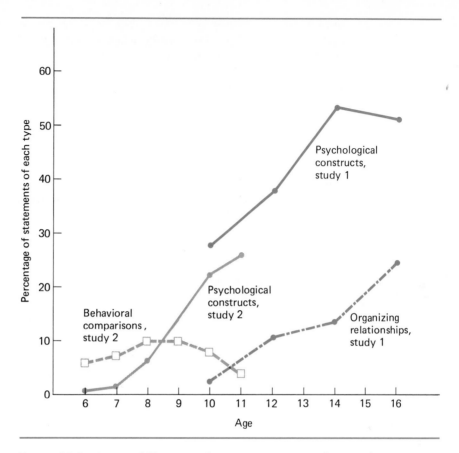

Figure 12.3 In two different studies spanning somewhat overlapping age groups, Carl Barenboim asked children to describe others. You can see that references to psychological constructs rise steadily during the elementary-school years and in early adolescence and seem to peak at about age 14. References to organizing relationships (including exceptions, qualifications, explanations of others' actions, and the like) were uncommon as late as age 10 or 12 but became quite common by early high-school age. (*Sources:* Barenboim, 1977, Table 1, p. 1471; Barenboim, 1981, Figure 1, p. 134.)

Thinking About Relationships

When we shift from the child's understanding of individuals (self or other) to the study of children's understanding of relationships, I can sing many of the same songs again. Some studies have focused on children's understanding of authority relationships, others on their relationships with parents and with peer groups, but the richest vein of research focuses on children's understanding of friendships, so let me take that as illustration.

Remember from Chapter 11 that we can see the first signs of friendships in children as early as age 2 or 3. These earliest relationships seem to be understood mostly in terms of physical characteristics. If you ask a young child how people make friends, the answer is usually that they "play together" or spend time physically near each other (Selman, 1980; Damon, 1977, 1983). Friendship is understood to involve sharing toys or giving of goods to one another.

Selman's research and extensive studies by Thomas Berndt (1983, 1986) show that in elementary school this early view of friendship gives way to one in which the key concept seems to be *reciprocal trust.* Friends are now people who help and trust one another. Since this is also the age at which children's understanding of others becomes less external, more psychological, we shouldn't be surprised that friends are also seen as special people, with particular desired qualities other than mere proximity. In particular, generosity and helpfulness become part of the definition of friendship for many children.

At adolescence Berndt finds a further change, as friends come to be seen as people who *understand* one another, who share their innermost thoughts or feelings. Friendships are also seen as more exclusive, more long-term. Friends should comfort one another, be with one another, forgive one another. Friendships at this stage are often intense relationships, with many hours spent on the phone or talking in person, sharing every detail, every thought, every activity (Damon, 1983).

Damon suggests that still another change takes place for some young people in late adolescence or early adulthood; it is parallel to the shift to more qualified statements Barenboim found in his studies of children's descriptions of others. At this point young people understand that even very close friendships cannot fill every need. They also see that friendships are not static: they change, grow, or dissolve as each member of the pair changes. A really good friendship, then, is one that *adapts* to these changes. So at this age, young people say things about friendship like "Trust is the ability to let go as well as to hang on" (Selman, 1980, p. 141).

Let me again make these generalizations concrete with some actual research findings, this time from the work of Brian Bigelow and John La Gaipa (1975). They asked children to write an essay about what they expected from their best friends that was different from what they expected from other acquaintances. The answers were scored along many dimensions, three of which I have shown in Figure 12.5. You can see that references to demographic similarity (e.g., "We live in the same neighborhood") peaked in the fourth grade, while mentions of loyalty and commitment peaked in the seventh grade. References to intimacy potential (e.g., "I can tell her things about myself I can't tell anyone else") did not appear at all until after the sixth grade and then increased further through the eighth grade.

In an intriguing series of interviews, Robert Selman (1980) has also studied friendships by asking children and adolescents how they settle disagreements or arguments with friends. Table 12.2 lists some of the answers children of various ages gave. You'll notice that among the younger

Figure 12.4 The youngsters in the lower picture are likely to have been friends for longer than the pair above; as I pointed out in Chapter 11, friendships become more stable between preschool and elementary school. But the older pair is also likely to have quite different *expectations* about what their friend should be for them. They *understand* friendship differently.

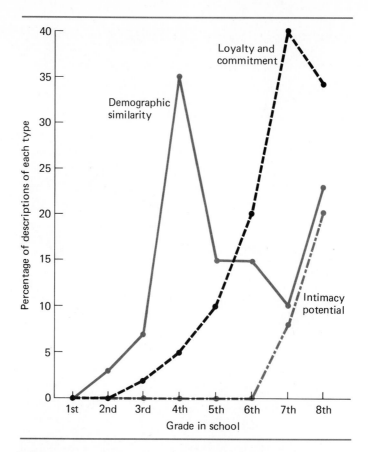

Figure 12.5 Some of the changes in children's ideas about friendship are clear from these findings from a study by Bigelow and La Gaipa. The children in this study were asked to write an essay about their best friend, describing what they expected of their friend that they didn't expect from nonfriends. You can see that younger children were more likely to mention demographic similarity (simple proximity or other external similarity); by late elementary school, though, loyalty became a key quality, with intimacy becoming important as well in early adolescence. (*Source:* Bigelow & La Gaipa, 1975, from Table 1, p. 858.)

children, it is enough that the "guy who started it" apologizes. This strategy seems to be based on an assumption that each fight has one cause, one person who starts it. Among older children and adolescents, however, there is some recognition that both parties are involved and that saying you're sorry may not be enough. Some deeper resolution may be required. Finally, still later, adolescents and adults recognize that some conflicts will fade without anything further being done or that a conflict may reflect problems

Table 12.2

Comments by Children of Various Ages About How to Solve Disagreements or Arguments Between Friends

- "Go away from her and come back later when you're not fighting." (Age 5)
- "Punch her out." (Age 5)
- "Around our way the guy who started it just says he's sorry." (Age 8)
- "Well if you say something and don't really mean it, then you have to mean it when you take it back." (Age 8½)
- "Sometimes you got to get away for a while. Calm down a bit so you won't be so angry. Then get back and try to talk it out." (Age 14)
- "If you just settle up after a fight that is no good. You gotta really feel that you'd be happy the way things went if you were in your friend's shoes. You can just settle up with someone who is not a friend, but that's not what friendship is really about." (Age 15½)
- "Well, you could talk it out, but it usually fades itself out. It usually takes care of itself. You don't have to explain everything. You do certain things and each of you knows what it means. But if not, then talk it out." (Age 16)

Source: Selman, 1980, pp. 107–113.

that each individual brings to the relationship rather than something between the friends themselves.

You may find, as I do, that these patterns provide some food for thought about your own friendships, your own ways of resolving conflicts. Can you recognize your own thinking in these comments? The assumptions underlying these definitions, which we might also think of as internal working models of friendship, affect adult relationships as well as childhood or teenage relationships.

THINKING ABOUT WHAT PEOPLE *OUGHT* TO DO

So far I have been talking about children's understanding of individual people and relationships. But social understanding also requires the child to think about or explain other people's *actions*. The facet of this that has most intrigued developmental psychologists is the child's judgment of the morality of actions. How does a child decide what is good or bad, right or wrong, in other people's behavior and in her own behavior? When you serve on a jury, you are asked to make a judgment of this kind. In everyday life, too, you make such judgments—when you decide whether to give the store clerk back the excess change she handed you, when you consider whether it is right or wrong to withhold part of your income tax as an antiwar protest, when you decide whether to take advantage of a friend's offer of an "advance look" at a course exam.

The two theorists whose ideas on the development of moral reasoning have been most influential are Piaget (1932) and Lawrence Kohlberg (1964, 1976, 1980, 1981; Colby et al., 1983). Piaget described early steps in moral reasoning in preschool and elementary-school-age children. Kohlberg's work grew out of Piaget's early studies and extended the stages of moral reasoning upward into adolescence and adulthood.

Piaget's Early Ideas About Moral Judgments

Piaget described several stages in children's reasoning about right and wrong. He described the child up to about age 3 or 4 as *premoral.* Children of this age do not yet understand rules, so they do not make judgments about rule violations. The first stage of actual moral reasoning, according to Piaget, is **heteronomous morality** (also sometimes called **moral realism).** It is characteristic of preschool children (about age 3 to 6 or so). Children of this age are "moral absolutists." They think rules are absolute, fixed, and unchangeable. This is true for rules parents give and for the rules of games as well. The children also believe that if they break a rule, punishment (from parents, teachers, or even God) will inevitably follow (this is called a belief in *immanent justice.*) A third element of heteronomous morality is that children of this age generally judge the goodness or badness of other people's actions largely on the basis of the consequences rather than the intent. By this reasoning, a child who breaks five glasses accidentally is seen as worse than a child who throws one down and breaks it intentionally.

Piaget saw a change at about 6 or 7. He called the second stage **autonomous morality** or the **morality of reciprocity.** Children of this age accept social rules but see them as more arbitrary, more changeable. Rules of a game, for example, can be changed if the children playing the game agree on the change. The belief in immanent justice fades, too; rule violations are no longer thought to result in inevitable punishment. Most strikingly, the intent of the person performing some action is now taken into account in judging the morality of the action.

There is some support for this element of Piaget's theory (e.g., Ferguson & Rule, 1980, 1982). Children under about age 6 or 7 seem to be influenced more by outcomes than by intentions, although children as young as 3 or 4 are aware of intention or motive and will take it into account if it is made clear and salient (e.g., Nelson, 1980). Among children older than 9 or 10, however, judgments are much more consistently based on intention. So, for example, if children hear a story about a child who purposely pushes another child off the monkey bars at school, older children (9- and 10-year-olds) think this is naughty even if the pusher only means to cause *a little* damage (thus ill will is *always* bad) while younger children think that intending only a small hurt is not so bad as intending a big hurt (Ferguson & Rule, 1982).

Kohlberg's Stages of Moral Development

Kohlberg's description of moral development overlaps Piaget's but extends into adolescence and adulthood. Since virtually all the recent research on moral development has been based on Kohlberg's stages, I need to describe them and the procedures he used to measure them in some detail.

In order to explore a child's or young person's reasoning about difficult moral issues, such as the value of human life or the reasons for doing "right" things, Kohlberg devised a series of dilemmas. One of the most famous is the dilemma of Heinz:

> In Europe, a woman was near death from a special kind of cancer. There was one drug that the doctors thought might save her. It was a form of radium that a druggist in the same town had recently discovered. The drug was expensive to make, but the druggist was charging ten times what the drug cost him to make. He paid $200 for the radium and charged $2000 for a small dose of the drug. The sick woman's husband, Heinz, went to everyone he knew to borrow the money, but he could only get together about $1000 which is half of what it cost. He told the druggist that his wife was dying, and asked him to sell it cheaper or let him pay later. But the druggist said, "No, I discovered the drug and I'm going to make money from it." So Heinz got desperate and broke into the man's store to steal the drug for his wife. (Kohlberg & Elfenbein, 1975, p. 621)

After hearing this story, the child or young person is asked a series of questions such as the following: Should Heinz have stolen the drug? What if Heinz didn't love his wife? Would that change anything? What if the person dying was a stranger? Should Heinz steal the drug anyway?

Some critics (e.g., Baumrind, 1978) have claimed that these dilemmas are too artificial, that they cannot tell us about children's or teenagers' reasoning about everyday problems. But Kohlberg and his colleagues have found very similar results when they used more real-life dilemmas (e.g., Higgins, Power, & Kohlberg, 1984). So pervasive and robust processes seem to be tapped here, even by these artificial dilemmas. Kohlberg is interested not in the actual choice the child makes when answering the dilemma but in the *kind* of reasoning she uses in grappling with the problem.

On the basis of answers to dilemmas like this one, Kohlberg concluded that there are three main levels of moral reasoning, with two substages within each level. I've summarized the stages in Table 12.3, but I need to expand on them here, too.

At level 1, **preconventional morality,** the child's (or teenager's or even adult's) judgments are based on sources of authority who are close by and physically superior to himself—usually the parents. Just as his descriptions of others are largely external at this same stage, so the standards the child uses to judge rightness or wrongness are external rather than internal. He bases his judgment on what others will do as a result of his behavior rather than on some internal model or belief system of his own.

Table 12.3

Kohlberg's Stages of Moral Development

Level 1: Preconventional morality
- *Stage 1: Punishment and obedience orientation.* The child decides what is wrong on the basis of what is punished. Obedience is valued for its own sake, but the child obeys because adults have superior power.
- *Stage 2: Individualism, instrumental purpose, and exchange.* The child follows rules when it is in his immediate interest. What is good is what brings pleasant results. Right is also what is fair, what is an equal exchange, a deal, an agreement.

Level 2: Conventional morality
- *Stage 3: Mutual interpersonal expectations, relationships, and interpersonal conformity.* The family or small group to which the child belongs becomes important. Moral actions are those that live up to others' expectations. "Being good" becomes important for its own sake, and the child generally values trust, loyalty, respect, gratitude, and keeping mutual relationships.
- *Stage 4: Social system and conscience (law and order).* A shift in focus from the young person's family and close groups to the larger society. Good is fulfilling duties one has agreed to. Laws are to be upheld except in extreme cases. Contributing to society is also seen as good.

Level 3: Principled or postconventional morality
- *Stage 5: Social contract or utility and individual rights.* Acting so as to achieve the "greatest good for the greatest number." The child is aware that there are different views and values, that values are relative. Laws and rules should be upheld in order to preserve the social order, but they can be changed. Still, there are some basic nonrelative values, such as the importance of each person's life and liberty, that should be upheld no matter what.
- *Stage 6: Universal ethical principles.* The young person develops and follows self-chosen ethical principles in determining what is right. Since laws usually conform to those principles, laws should be obeyed; but when there is a difference between law and conscience, conscience dominates. At this stage, the ethical principles followed are part of an articulated, integrated, carefully thought-out and consistently followed system of values and principles.

Sources: After Kohlberg, 1976, and Lickona, 1978.

In stage 1 of this level—the *punishment and obedience orientation*—the child relies on the physical consequences of some action to decide if it is right or wrong. If he is punished, the behavior was wrong; if he is not punished, it was right. He is obedient to adults because they are bigger and stronger.

In stage 2—*individualism, instrumental purpose, and exchange*—the child begins to do things that are rewarded and to avoid things that are punished. (For this reason, stage 2 is sometimes called a position of "naive hedonism.") If it feels good or brings pleasant results, it is good. There is the beginning of some concern for other people during this phase, but only if that concern can be expressed as something that benefits the child himself as well. He can enter into agreements like "If you help me, I'll help you," but even this is based on the idea of rewards and punishments.

At level 2, **conventional morality,** there is a shift from judgments based on external consequences and personal gain to judgments based on rules or norms of a group to which the child belongs, whether that group is the family, the peer group, a church, or the nation. What the chosen reference group defines as right or good *is* right or good in the child's view, and she internalizes these norms to a considerable extent.

Stage 3 (the first stage of level 2) is the stage of *mutual interpersonal expectations, relationships, and interpersonal conformity* (sometimes also called the *good boy/nice girl* stage). Children at this stage believe that good behavior is what pleases other people. They value trust, loyalty, respect, gratitude, and maintenance of mutual relationships. Kohlberg interviewed Andy, a boy at stage 3, who said:

> I try to do things for my parents, they've always done things for you. I try to do everything my mother says, I try to please her. Like she wants me to be a doctor and I want to, too, and she's helping me get up there. (Kohlberg, 1964, p. 401)

Another mark of stage 3 is that the child begins to make judgments based on intentions as well as on outward behavior. If someone "means well" or "didn't mean to do it," her wrongdoing is seen as less serious than if she did it "on purpose."

Stage 4 (the second stage of level 2) shows the child turning to larger social groups for her norms. Kohlberg labeled this the stage of *social system and conscience.* (It is also sometimes called the *law and order* orientation.) Young people in this stage focus on doing their duty, respecting authority, and following rules and laws. The emphasis is less on what is pleasing to particular people (as in stage 3) and more on adhering to a complex set of regulations. However, the regulations themselves are not questioned.

The transition to level 3, **principled morality** (also called *postconventional morality*), is marked by several changes, the most important of which is a shift in the source of authority. Children and young people in stages 3 or 4 (in level 2—conventional morality) see the source of authority as outside themselves; young people at level 3 (principled morality) see themselves as the authority or part of the authority. They think of society as "we" rather than "they." And they see laws as something that can be changed.

In stage 5 at this level—called the *social contract* orientation by Kohlberg—rules, laws, and regulations are all seen as important ways of ensuring fairness. But people operating at stage 5 also see times when the rules, laws, and regulations need to be ignored or changed. Our American system of government is based on moral reasoning of this kind, since we have provisions for changing laws, and for allowing personal protests against a given law (for example, the civil rights protests of the 1960s, the Vietnam War protests of the 1960s and 1970s, and the more recent protests against apartheid in South Africa).

In his original writing about moral development, Kohlberg also included stage 6, the *universal ethical principles* orientation. People who reason in this way assume personal responsibility for their own actions, and their moral position is based upon fundamental and universal principles, such as the sacredness of human life. Kohlberg now concedes that stage 6, if it exists at all, is extremely rare (Kohlberg, 1978). It seems likely that such universal ethical principles guide the moral reasoning of only a few very unusual individuals—perhaps those who devote their lives to humanitarian causes, such as Martin Luther King, Mother Theresa, or Mohandas Gandhi.

So far, so good. The description is fairly straightforward. But Kohlberg has not been satisfied merely to describe a sequence. He has argued that this sequence is both universal and hierarchically organized. That is, each stage follows and grows from the preceding one. Individuals should not move "down" the sequence but only "upward" along the stages, if they move at all. Kohlberg has *not* argued that all individuals eventually progress through all six stages or even that each stage is tied to specific ages. But he has insisted that the order is invariant and universal. Let me take a critical look at these claims.

Age and Moral Reasoning.

Kohlberg's own findings, confirmed by many other researchers (reviewed by Rest, 1983), show that preconventional reasoning (stages 1 and 2) is dominant in elementary school, and stage 2 reasoning is still evident among many early adolescents. Conventional reasoning (stages 3 and 4) emerges as important in middle adolescence and remains the most common form of moral reasoning in adulthood. Postconventional (principled) reasoning is relatively rare, even in adulthood. You can see all these patterns in Figure 12.6, based on the findings from Kohlberg's longitudinal study of 58 boys who have now been studied over a 20-year period (Colby et al., 1983).

Universality.

Although psychologists have not given moral dilemmas to children from every culture in the world, there have been enough studies to be fairly persuasive, including research in Taiwan, Turkey, Mexico, Kenya, India, the Bahamas, and Israel. In every case, the older children studied had higher levels of moral judgment than the younger children and used forms of judgment that were parallel to those found in American children (e.g., Rest, 1983; Snarey, Reimer, & Kohlberg, 1985; Nisan & Kohlberg, 1982). There are some suggestions, however, that the rate of moral development through the stages may vary from culture to culture. In a Turkish sample, for example, stage 3 was the typical "end point" of the progression; stage 4 reasoning was extremely rare. In contrast, stage 4 reasoning was

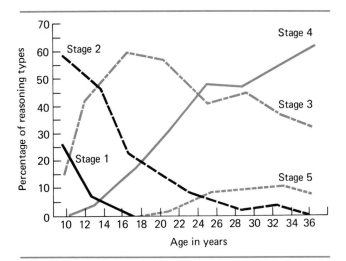

Figure 12.6 These findings are from a long-term longitudinal study of a group of boys by Colby and Kohlberg. The subjects were asked about Kohlberg's moral dilemmas every few years. You can see that as they got older, the stage or level of their answers changed, with conventional reasoning appearing fairly strongly at high-school age. Postconventional or principled reasoning, though, was not very common at any age. (*Source:* Colby et al., 1983, Figure 1, p. 46. © The Society for Research in Child Development, Inc.)

much more common among young adults in both Israel and the United States (Snarey, Reimer, & Kohlberg, 1985).

Sequence of Stages. The evidence seems fairly strong that the stages described by Kohlberg do develop in the order he gives. In Kohlberg's own major longitudinal studies of teenagers and young adults in the United States, in Israel, and in Turkey (Colby et al., 1983; Nisan & Kohlberg, 1982; Snarey, Reimer, & Kohlberg, 1985), not all of the subjects show any change in level of reasoning, but when change does occur, it occurs in the order Kohlberg describes. Subjects do not skip stages, and only about 5 to 7 percent of the time is there any indication of regression (movement down the sequence rather than up it.) Such a percentage is about what you would expect to find, given the fact that the measurements of stage reasoning are not perfectly reliable. Other longitudinal studies, using more standardized measurements rather than Kohlberg's typical interview, also show changes that follow Kohlberg's proposed sequence. Furthermore, there is evidence that subjects can understand moral arguments at their own level or lower or at a stage one step higher than their own but do not understand arguments two or more steps above their own (Walker, de Vries, & Bichard, 1984), which is precisely what we would expect if the stages were organized hierarchically. On the whole, I agree with James Rest (1983) when he says that the evidence is "fairly compelling" that moral judgment changes over time in the sequence Kohlberg describes.

Moral Development: A Critique. Kohlberg's theory about the development of moral reasoning has been one of the most provocative theories in all of developmental psychology. Over 1000 studies have explored or tested aspects of the theory, and several competing theories have been proposed. The remarkable thing is how well Kohlberg's theory has stood the test of this barrage of research and commentary. There does appear to be a clear set of stages in the development of moral reasoning, and these stages seem to be universal.

Still, the theory has not emerged unscathed. In particular, a number of critics have argued that Kohlberg's view of moral reasoning is simply too limited. Kohlberg focused on the development of ideas of justice and fairness; but what about moral reasoning about doing good or reasoning based on some ethic other than justice, such as the "ethic of caring" that Carol Gilligan describes? Let me take a quick look at two such alternative views.

Eisenberg's Model of Prosocial Reasoning

Most of the moral dilemmas Kohlberg posed for his subjects deal with wrongdoing—with stealing, punishment, disobeying laws. Few tell us anything about the kinds of reasoning children use in justifying *good* behavior— what psychologists call **prosocial behavior.** I mentioned in Chapter 11 that we can see altruistic behavior in children as young as 2 and 3; but how do children explain and justify such behavior?

Nancy Eisenberg and her colleagues (e.g., Eisenberg, 1986) have explored such questions by proposing dilemmas to children in which self-interest is set against the possibility of helping some other person. One story, for example, involves a child walking to a friend's birthday party. On the way, he comes upon another child who has fallen and hurt himself. If the birthday-bound child stops to help, he will probably miss the cake and ice cream. What should he do?

On the basis of children's answers to dilemmas like this, Eisenberg proposed a series of five levels of prosocial reasoning, which I've listed in Table 12.4. (I know you are overloaded with lists of stages, but hang in there!) Some sample data from Eisenberg's longitudinal study of a small group of preschoolers are given in Figure 12.7. You can see that hedonistic reasoning—reasoning in which the individual's own needs are put first— declines through the elementary-school years, while reasoning that acknowledges the need of the other goes up. In early adolescence, arguments at

Table 12.4

Eisenberg's Levels of Prosocial Reasoning

- *Level 1: Hedonistic, self-focused orientation.* Characteristic particularly of preschoolers and younger elementary-school children. The child is concerned with self-oriented consequences rather than moral considerations (e.g., "I'd help because she'd help me the next time," "I won't help because I'd miss the party").

- *Level 2: Needs-oriented orientation.* Seen in some preschoolers and most elementary-school children. The child expresses concern for the other person's needs rather directly, even if the other's needs conflict with his own. There is no clear evidence here of sympathy, of reflectiveness about the other's role, or of internalized values (e.g., "He's hurt," "He'd feel better if I helped").

- *Level 3: Approval and interpersonal orientation and/or stereotyped orientation.* Characteristic of some elementary-school and some high-school students. The child does good things because others will like him if he does, because it is expected of him, or because there is a social rule (e.g., "They'd like him if he helped," "It's nice to help").

- *Level 4a: Self-reflective empathic orientation.* Not generally seen until high-school age. The young person shows evidence of some sympathetic response (e.g., "I'd feel sorry for him") or explicit role taking (e.g., "I'm trying to put myself in her shoes").

- *Level 4b: Transitional level.* Seen in some high-school students and some adults. Justifications for helping or doing good are based on internalized norms, duties, or responsibilities, but these ideas are not yet strongly stated (e.g., "I'd feel good if I helped").

- *Level 5: Strongly internalized stage.* Justifications for helping are stated in terms of clear values, such as maintaining self-respect or belief in the dignity or rights of individuals (e.g., "I'd feel a responsibility to help because of my values," "If everyone helped, society would be a lot better"). Never observed in elementary-school children and only rarely seen in high-school students.

Source: After Eisenberg, 1986, pp. 136, 137, 144.

level 3—the approval and interpersonal orientation, which is highly similar to Kohlberg's stage 3—become more evident.

　　There are obviously strong parallels between the levels of prosocial reasoning Eisenberg has described and the levels and stages Kohlberg proposed. Children seem to move from a self-centered orientation ("What feels good to me is right") to a stance in which social approval guides reasoning about both justice and doing good. What is right is what other people define as right; you should do good things because others will approve of you if you do. Much later, some young people seem to develop internalized, individualized norms to guide both kinds of reasoning.

　　Despite these obvious parallels, though, researchers have typically found that children's reasoning about prosocial dilemmas such as Eisenberg's is only moderately correlated with their reasoning about Kohlberg's

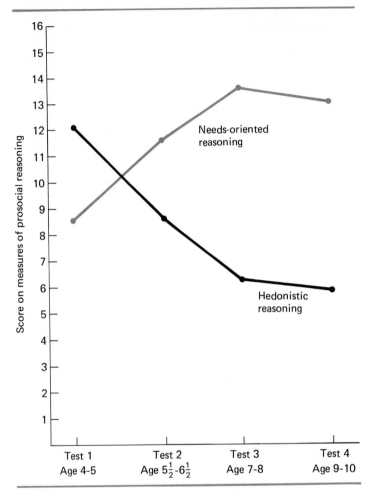

Figure 12.7   Over 5 years, Eisenberg repeatedly asked a group of children what a person should do when confronted with each of a series of dilemmas about doing good (such as helping someone who is hurt). The answers changed steadily with age. The minimum score on these measures is 4 and the maximum is 16. You can see that hedonistic reasoning (in which self-interest is placed first) drops to nearly minimum levels by age 7 or 8, while needs-oriented reasoning (such as "He needs help") rises to high levels at the same age. (*Source:* Eisenberg, 1986, Table 7.7, p. 143.)

justice or fairness dilemmas. The sequences of steps may be similar, but as was true of so many aspects of cognitive development I talked about in Chapter 7, children seem to move through these sequences at somewhat different speeds. Eisenberg has found that in young children, at least, prosocial reasoning is a bit ahead of their Kohlbergian reasoning.

Eisenberg's research, as well as the work of others in the same vein, helps to broaden Kohlberg's original conception without changing the fundamental arguments. In contrast, Carol Gilligan has questioned some of the basic tenets of Kohlberg's model.

Gilligan's Ethic of Caring

Gilligan (1982a, 1982b), in her influential book *In a Different Voice: Psychological Theory and Women's Development,* suggests that Kohlberg's strong emphasis on justice and fairness as the basis for moral reasoning, and his omission of reasoning based on caring for others, arise from the fact that he has studied mostly males. Gilligan argues that boys and girls are socialized quite differently and as a result end up basing their moral judgments on different criteria. For boys, an ethic of justice and fairness seems to be central, but for girls, an ethic of caring and responsibility seems to form the basis of moral judgments and behavior.

Take, for example, the answers of two bright 11-year-olds, Jake and Amy, to the Heinz dilemma. Jake says:

> For one thing, a human life is worth more than money, and if the druggist only makes $1000, he is still going to live, but if Heinz doesn't steal the drug, his wife is going to die. [*Why is life worth more than money?*] Because the druggist can get a thousand dollars later from rich people with cancer, but Heinz can't get his wife again. [*Why not?*] Because people are all different, and so you couldn't get Heinz's wife again. (Gilligan, 1982a, p. 203)

Jake's responses are scored as conventional, a mixture of stages 3 and 4, but he is clearly bringing some early formal operations logic to bear on this problem. In fact, Jake specifically compares the dilemma to a math problem and searches for the logical solution. He is grappling with the relationship between individual rights and society's rights and working out logical solutions.

Amy understand the question differently. As Gilligan points out, Amy focuses not on the question of whether Heinz *should* steal the drug but on whether he should *steal* the drug. For her, the problem is to find a solution that recognizes and protects the network of relationships. In answer to the question about whether Heinz should steal the drug, she says:

> Well, I don't think so. I think there might be other ways besides stealing it, like if he could borrow the money or make a loan or something, but he really shouldn't steal the drug, but his wife shouldn't die either. [If he stole the drug, she explains] he might save his wife then, but if he did, he might have to go to jail, and then his wife might get sicker again, and he couldn't get more of the drug, and it might not be good. So, they should really just talk it out and find some other way to make the money. (Gilligan, 1982a, p. 204)

Amy assumes that if the druggist really understood that Heinz's wife will die, he will be willing to help in some way. As Gilligan says, "seeing a world comprised of relationships rather than of people standing alone, a world that coheres through human connection rather than through systems of rules, she finds the puzzle in the dilemma to lie in the failure of the druggist to respond to the wife" (1982a, p. 205).

Because responses like Amy's are often scored at a lower stage than answers like Jake's, Gilligan initially asserted that Kohlberg's analysis routinely underestimated the level of moral reasoning of girls, assigning them lower scores because they searched for different kinds of solutions. That assertion has not been supported by the evidence. Studies using Kohlberg's interview and his revised scoring system do not typically find any sex differences at all in level of moral reasoning (e.g., Walker, 1984, 1986, 1987). Girls can and do use fairness or justice reasoning when the problem calls for it and boys equally often use reasoning based on relationships or caring, and this is true whether one uses hypothetical dilemmas or real-life dilemmas. Furthermore, both boys' and girls' reasoning moves through the stages that Kohlberg described (e.g., Snarey, Reimer, & Kohlberg, 1985). Whether girls are more likely to use an ethic of caring or responsibility in other settings we simply don't yet know. Gilligan's own research does not offer clear evidence, and other research has not yet accumulated.

Despite this lack of support for Gilligan's central claim, I am still struck by the potential parallels between Gilligan's observations about girls' solutions to moral dilemmas and all the findings I described in Chapter 11 that show girls' actual friendships to be more intimate and lasting than are boys'. Intimate relationships thus may be more central to girls' development than they are to boys', a conclusion entirely in keeping with Gilligan's arguments.

SOCIAL COGNITION AND BEHAVIOR

So far in this chapter I have sidestepped what I am sure many of you think is the most critical question: Is children's or adolescent's *thinking* about people, about relationships, about morality, related at all to what those children actually *do* with people or in moral situations? The short (and no doubt unsatisfying) answer is "yes and no." It is simply not possible to predict *precisely* what a child will do in a real-life situation from knowing the form or level of his reasoning. But there are some important links between thinking and behavior.

Interpersonal Understanding and Behavior.   Are more empathetic children more likely to be helpful to others? There are some weak indications among preadolescent children that such a link exists. When researchers have measured children's empathy by actually watching them interact with one another, they normally find that the most empathetic children are also the ones most likely to help others. But when empathy is measured by having children respond to hypothetical stories, no such link emerges (Eisenberg & Miller, 1987). Among adolescents, however, an empathy–kind behavior link is found much more consistently, even using hypothetical stories.

For example, Martin Ford (1982) studied teenagers' empathy and their "social competence." Ford asked ninth- and twelfth-graders about six hypothetical situations that would demand real social skill, like the following:

> One of your school's best teachers has tragically died in an accident. The students in your grade have gotten together and decided to do something for the teacher's family. The class decides that someone should make a personal visit to the teacher's family. This person would bring flowers and try to tell the family how sorry the students were to lose such a good teacher and a good friend. Who in your grade do you think would be a good person to make the visit to the teacher's family? (Ford, 1982, p. 339)

These situations are hypothetical, but by having students rate *each other,* Ford could see which teenagers were perceived by their classmates as being particularly skillful or thoughtful in demanding social situations. What he found was that adolescents who were chosen by their peers as being the best in such situations also tested as having more empathy and role-taking ability.

Friendship Understanding and Friendship Behavior.

Similar connections appear between thinking about relationships and the quality of actual relationships. As a general rule, children with more mature reasoning about friendships are less likely to be aggressive with their peers and more likely to show sharing or other helpful behavior toward their friends in real-life interactions.

For example, Lawrence Kurdek and Donna Krile (1982) found that among children in the third through the eighth grades, those with higher scores on a measure of understanding of individuals and friendships were more likely to be involved in mutual friendships than were children with lower scores. Selman and Berndt have both reported similar findings. Selman (1980) compared children's scores on a measure of social reasoning with teachers' ratings of the children's social strengths and weaknesses. He found that children with more mature reasoning were more likely to be described by their teachers as showing higher levels of helpful or other prosocial behaviors.

An intriguing exception to this pattern, however, is the finding that in friendships between boys, competition and not sharing or helpfulness is often the dominant pattern. Berndt, for example, finds that in settings in which children can achieve success either by cooperating or competing, pairs of boys compete *more* if they are friends than if they are not, while this is not true for girls. And the boys' level of competition or cooperation is unrelated to their overall level of reasoning about friendship or about the justification for helpfulness (Berndt, 1983).

Thus, while it is true that in general there is a correlation between more mature forms of social reasoning and having the social skills necessary to make friends, it is also true that such mature reasoning does *not* invariably increase the level of helpfulness or cooperation in actual friendship pairs.

Moral Judgment and Behavior.

Kohlberg's theory has sometimes been criticized on the grounds that children's or adults' moral behavior does not always match their reasoning. But Kohlberg never said that there should be a one-to-one correspondence between the two. Reasoning at stage 4 (conventional reasoning) does not mean that you will never cheat or that you will always be kind to your mother. But the form of reasoning a young person typically applies to moral problems should have at least *some* connection with real-life choices. Furthermore, Kohlberg argued that the higher the level of reasoning a young person shows, the stronger the link to behavior ought to become. Thus, young people reasoning at stage 4 or stage 5 should be more likely to follow their own rules or reasoning than should children reasoning at lower levels.

For example, Kohlberg and Candee (1984) studied students involved in the Free Speech movement at Berkeley in the late 1960s (a precursor to the Vietnam War protests). They interviewed and tested the moral judgment levels of a group that had participated at a sit-in in the administration building and of a group randomly chosen from the campus population. Of those students who thought it was morally right to sit in, nearly three-quarters of those reasoning at stages 4 or 5 actually did sit in, compared to only about a quarter of those reasoning at stage 3. Thus, the higher the stage of reasoning, the more consistent the behavior was with the reasoning.

In other studies, Kohlberg and others investigated whether there is a link between stage of moral reasoning and the probability of making some "moral choice," such as not cheating. For example, Kohlberg (1975) found that only 15 percent of students reasoning at the principled level (stage 5) cheated when they were given an opportunity, while 55 percent of conventional-level and 70 percent of preconventional students cheated.

A study of much younger children by Nancy Eisenberg-Berg and Michael Hand (1979) shows a similar link. The preschool children in this study who answered Eisenberg's prosocial moral dilemmas with hedonistic reasoning were much less likely to share toys with other children in their nursery school than were youngsters who considered the needs of others in their moral reasoning.

Several psychologists who have reviewed the very rich literature in this area (e.g., Blasi, 1980; Rest, 1983) have concluded that, in general, delinquents have lower levels of moral reasoning than do nondelinquents and that moral reasoning can be linked to various political attitudes or actions, such as civil rights protests and approval of or opposition to capital punishment.

Despite this abundance of evidence for a link between moral reasoning and behavior, though, no one has found the correspondence to be perfect. After all, in Kohlberg's studies, 15 percent of the principled moral reasoners did cheat, and a quarter of stage 4 and stage 5 reasoners who thought it morally right to sit in did not do so. As Kohlberg says, "one can reason in terms of principles and not live up to those principles" (1975, p. 672).

What else besides level of reasoning might matter? We don't have all the answers to that question yet, but some influences are clear. First, simple habits are involved—what Randy Gerson and William Damon (1978) called *habitual* moral reactions. Each of us faces small moral issues every day that we have learned to handle in a completely automatic way. Sometimes these automatic choices may be at a lower level of reasoning than we would use if we sat down and thought about it. (For example, I may make the same donation to a particular charity every year, automatically, without stopping to consider whether I could now afford more or whether that charity is really the place where my money could best be used.)

Second, in any given situation, even though you might think it morally right to take some action, you may not see that action as morally *necessary* or obligatory. I might be able to make a good argument for the moral acceptability of a sit-in protest but still not see it as my *own* duty or responsibility to participate.

Third, there are often competing motives or ethics at work as well, such as the pressure of a peer group or motives for self-protection or self-reward. Gerson and Damon found this very clearly in a study in which they asked groups of four children to divide up 10 candy bars. The candy was a reward for work the children had done on a project, and some of the group members had worked harder than others. When asked separately about how the candy bars ought to be divided, children usually argued for various kinds of fair arrangements, such as a model in which the child who worked the hardest should get the most. But when faced with the actual distribution of the candy bars, some children gave themselves the most; others went along with a group consensus and divided the candy equally. We might expect that in early adolescence, when the impact of the peer group is particularly strong, this group effect on moral actions would be especially strong, too. So youngsters this age may be most susceptible to group decisions to go joyriding or to sneak beer into a party or to soap the teachers' car windows on Halloween (Berndt, 1979).

Still, even at adolescence not every child is equally vulnerable to this type of group pressure. There are some hints, for example, that young people who are reasoning at Kohlberg's stage 5 (postconventional reasoning) are less likely to be swayed by group pressure or pressure from authority than are youngsters reasoning at less-mature levels (Kohlberg, 1969). Rest also points out that young people who are generally rated as higher in "ego strength" (having perseverance, willpower, the ability to plan and

MORAL EDUCATION AND MORAL DEVELOPMENT

A lot of what I have been saying in this chapter may seem pretty abstract to you. In fact, though, both Kohlberg himself and many educators have seen the possibility of some direct educational applications in Kohlberg's theory. Most specifically, the question is whether children or young people can be taught higher stages of moral reasoning and whether that will affect their behavior in school.

We know from early research by Elliot Turiel (1966) that at least under some conditions, exposing young people to moral arguments one step above their own level of reasoning can lead to an increase in their level of moral judgment. Also, young people who attend college continue to show increases in moral stage scores, while those who quit school after high school typically show no further increase (Rest & Thoma, 1985). Since arguments about moral and philosophical issues in class and over coffee (or a few beers) into the wee small hours of the morning are one of the hallmarks of the college experience for many young people, perhaps it is the discussion—the exposure to other people's ideas, other people's logic—that makes a difference.

If that's true, what would happen if high-school students were given systematic opportunities to explore moral dilemmas?

Would that change them, too? Apparently it can.

One educational application has involved the creation of special discussion classes in which Kohlberg's moral dilemmas (or similar dilemmas) are presented and argued. In the process, the teacher attempts to model higher levels of reasoning. Other programs are broader-based, involving not just discussion but also cross-age teaching (to encourage nurturance and caring), empathy training, cooperation games, volunteer service work, and the like. When Andre Schaefli and his colleagues (Schaefli, Rest, & Thoma, 1985) summarized the dozens of studies on the effectiveness of programs of this kind, they found that on the average, the programs succeed in shifting young people's moral reasoning upward about half a stage. The largest effects are generally found in programs focusing exclusively on discussions of moral dilemmas, but broader-based programs work, too. Courses lasting longer than 3 or 4 weeks seem to work better than very short programs, and the effects are generally larger with older students—college students and even postcollege-age adults. Among high-school students, there is some impact, but it is not as large.

An even broader-based educational organize) are less likely to cheat, regardless of their level of moral reasoning.

Thus, moral *behavior* results from a complex of influences, of which the level of moral reasoning is only one element. Our knowledge about these links is improving, but we badly need to know more, both about group pressure and about all the other factors that lead each of us to behave in ways that are less thoughtful, considerate, or fair than we "know how" to do.

Kohlberg's own fascination with this set of questions and with the question of how one raises a person's level of moral reasoning led him

application has been the development of the so-called "just environment," in which an entire school is designed as a laboratory for moral education. Kohlberg and his colleagues (Higgins, Power, & Kohlberg, 1984; Power & Reimer, 1978) have studied two such experimental schools in the Boston area. Each was set up as a "school within a school" in which a group of perhaps 60 students formed a separate community. All rules were established in weekly communitywide meetings. In these meetings, the basic rule was one person, one vote, with students and teachers on an equal footing in both establishing and enforcing the rules. Thus, students become *responsible* for the rules and for one another.

Under these conditions, not only did the students' level of Kohlbergian moral reasoning shift upward, so did their reasoning about responsibility and caring. The link between moral reasoning and moral behavior was strengthened as well. Stealing and other petty crime virtually disappeared, for example, after the students had repeatedly discussed the problem and arrived at a just solution. Such an effect makes sense when you think about the factors I listed earlier that seem to affect moral behavior. In these schools, two elements were added that would tend to support more moral behavior:

a sense of personal responsibility and a group norm of higher moral reasoning and caring.

Among teenagers, the emotional impact of group pressure may be especially significant, in addition to whatever effect there may be from exposure to more mature arguments. If you are arguing your position about some moral dilemma but find yourself in the minority, the "social disequilibrium" you feel may help to make you more open to other arguments and thus to change your view. In experimental schools like those studied by Kohlberg, this added emotional impact is certainly part of the process (Haan, 1985).

Classes in moral education have not proved to be the "quick fix" that many educators hoped for. The gains in moral reasoning are not huge, and they may not be reflected in increases in moral behavior in the school unless there is an effort to alter the overall moral atmosphere of the entire school. But these programs do show that there are provocative and helpful applications of at least some of the abstract developmental theories.

and his colleagues to a series of fascinating attempts to apply the theory to schooling. I've explored some of this research in the box above.

SOCIAL COGNITION AND GENERAL COGNITIVE DEVELOPMENT

Before I leave this subject, I need to consider whether these sequences of development of social cognition I have just discussed are somehow linked to the general sequences of cognitive development I described in Chapter 7. Earlier in this chapter I suggested several key dimensions that seem to characterize both sets of changes, such as a shift in focus from outer to inner characteristics. But I need now to look at those possible connections more systematically.

Researchers have generally found weak positive relationships between cognitive power (IQ) and social reasoning. That is, higher-IQ children typically show social reasoning at a slightly higher level than that of lower-IQ children of the same age (correlations are in the range of .20 to .40 [Shantz, 1983]).

Surprisingly, there have been relatively few attempts to look at cognitive *structure* and social-cognitive reasoning, so we don't yet know what all the connections might be. The most concrete proposal has come from Kohlberg, who hypothesized that the child first moves to a new level of logical thought, then applies this new kind of logic to relationships as well as objects, and only then applies this thinking to moral problems. More specifically, Kohlberg argued that at least some formal operations and at least some mutual perspective taking in relationships are necessary (but not sufficient) for the emergence of conventional moral reasoning. Full formal operations and still more abstract social understanding may be required for postconventional reasoning.

The research examining such a sequential development is scant, but it supports Kohlberg's hypothesis. Lawrence Walker (1980) found that of a group of fourth- to seventh-graders he tested on all three dimensions (concrete and formal operations, social understanding, and moral reasoning), half to two-thirds were reasoning at the same level across the different domains, which makes the whole process look unexpectedly "stagelike." But when a child was ahead in one progression, the sequence was always that the child developed logical thinking first, then more advanced social understanding, and then the parallel moral judgments.

What this research seems to tells us is that there is *some* coherence in a child's or young person's thinking or reasoning about quite different problems. Children who have not yet understood principles of conservation are not likely to understand that another person's behavior may not match her feelings. But once conservation is understood, the child rapidly extends this principle to people and to relationships. Similarly, a young person still using concrete operations is unlikely to use postconventional moral reasoning. But the coherence is not automatic. The basic cognitive understanding makes advances in social and moral reasoning *possible* but does not guarantee them. Experience in relationships and with moral dilemmas is necessary, too.

The moral of this (if you will excuse the pun) is that just because a young person or adult shows signs of formal operations, it does *not* necessarily mean that she will show sensitive, empathetic, and forgiving attitudes toward friends or family. You may find it helpful to bear this in mind in your own relationships.

SUMMARY

1. The study of social understanding, and the field of *social cognition* in general, has provided researchers with an important new link between cognitive development and social relationships.

2. Many of the principles of developmental change that apply to cognitive development in general also seem to apply to changes in social cognition: a shift in focus from outer to inner characteristics, from observation to inference, from definite to qualified judgment, and from a particular to a general view.

3. Social cognition differs from other aspects of cognition in that the child must learn that people behave with intention, that they can mask their feelings, and that they follow special socially defined scripts or rules.

4. Learning to "read" people is a key skill in social cognition. A part of this is the development of empathy—being able to match or approximate the emotion of another. Children as young as 12 months show some egocentric empathy, with more complete empathy visible by age 2 or 3.

5. A child's descriptions of others shift in a way that parallels the changes in her self-descriptions. She shifts from a focus on external features to a focus on personality traits and then, at adolescence, to more qualified comparative descriptions.

6. Children's thinking about their relationships, such as friendships, shows strongly parallel shifts. Their early definitions of friends as people who share physical space or activities give way to descriptions emphasizing trust and then, at adolescence, to descriptions emphasizing intimacy.

7. Piaget and Kohlberg studied the similar progression in children's reasoning about what people ought to do, which is usually called moral reasoning.

8. Kohlberg proposed three levels of moral reasoning, divided into six stages. The child moves from preconventional morality (dominated by punishment and "what feels good") to conventional morality (dominated by group norms or laws) to postconventional or principled morality (dominated by social contracts and basic ethical principles).

9. Findings from cross-sectional and longitudinal research show that these stages occur in subjects from all countries studied, that the stages occur in the order listed, and that in the United States and many other countries most young adults are at stage 4 ("law and order").

10. Alternative models of moral reasoning include Eisenberg's stages of prosocial reasoning (reasoning about why to do something good) and Gilligan's theory that sex differences in reasoning are based on an ethic of justice or fairness versus an ethic of caring or relationship.

11. A child's level of social cognition is at least somewhat predictive of her social behavior. More empathic teenagers show somewhat higher levels of social skill; children with higher levels of reasoning about friendships have more, and more intimate, friendships; higher-level

moral reasoning is associated with higher likelihood of "moral" behavior or resistance to temptation.

12. Other factors that may influence moral behavior include group pressure, whether the individual sees a moral action as necessary or obligatory, and the presence of other motivations (such as self-interest).

13. Social-cognitive development is somewhat related to broader sequences of cognitive development. In particular, conventional levels of moral reasoning seem to require (as a necessary but not sufficient condition) at least beginning formal operations, as well as fairly advanced reasoning about social relationships.

14. The stages of moral reasoning have formed the basis of many programs of "moral education" in schools, designed to raise students' levels of moral reasoning through exposure to discussion of moral dilemmas. Such programs appear to be at least partially successful.

■■■■■■■ KEY TERMS

autonomous morality Piaget's second proposed stage of moral reasoning, which develops some time after age 7 and is characterized by judgment of intent and emphasis on reciprocity.

conventional morality The second level of moral reasoning proposed by Kohlberg, in which the person's judgments are dominated by considerations of group values and laws.

empathy An emotional response to another's feelings or situation that approximates or matches the other's emotions.

heteronomous morality Piaget's first proposed stage of moral reasoning, characterized by moral absolutism and belief in immanent justice. Judgments are based on consequences rather than intent.

morality of reciprocity Another term for autonomous morality.

moral realism Another term for heteronomous morality.

preconventional morality The first level of moral reasoning proposed by Kohlberg, in which the child's judgments are dominated by consideration of what will be punished and what "feels good."

principled morality The third level of moral reasoning proposed by Kohlberg, in which considerations of justice, individual rights, and contracts dominate.

prosocial behavior Behavior that is the opposite of "antisocial," including helping, kindness, sharing, generosity.

social cognition A relatively new area of research and theory focused on the child's *understanding* of social relationships.

■■■■■■■ SUGGESTED READING

Damon, W. (1977). *The social world of the child.* San Francisco: Jossey-Bass.
Not new, but a very readable book discussing many of the developmental themes I have been talking about in this chapter.

Flavell, J. H. (1985). *Cognitive development* (2nd ed.). Englewood Cliffs, NJ: Prentice-Hall.
I have recommended this excellent text before. In this case, you may want to look at the very good chapter on social cognition.

Rubin, K. H., & Everett, B. (1982). Social perspective-taking in young children. In S. G. Moore & C. R. Cooper (Eds.), *The young child: Reviews of research* (Vol. 3). Washington, DC: National Association for the Education of Young Children.
A very helpful integrated discussion of all aspects of perspective taking (social and physical), and of the implications of the research and theory for education.

PROJECT: UNDERSTANDING OF FRIENDSHIP

For this project you will need to locate a child between the ages of about 6 and 12. Arrange with the parents to spend some time with the child, explaining that you want to talk to the child for a school project and that this is not a "test" of any kind. Try to find a time and a place to be alone with your subject; it will not work as well if siblings or parents are present.

Say to the child something like, "I'd like to talk to you about friends. Let me tell you a story about some children who were friends." Then read the following story:

Kathy and Becky have been best friends since they were 5 years old. They went to the same kindergarten and have been in the same class ever since. Every Saturday they would try to do something special together, go to the park or the store, or play something special at home. They always had a good time with each other.

One day a new girl, Jeanette, moved into their neighborhood and soon introduced herself to Kathy and Becky. Right away Jeanette and Kathy seemed to hit it off very well. They talked about where Jeanette was from and the things she could be doing in her new town. Becky, on the other hand, didn't seem to like Jeanette very well. She thought Jeanette was a showoff, but was also jealous of all the attention Kathy was giving Jeanette.

When Jeanette left the other two alone, Becky told Kathy how she felt about Jeanette. "What did you think of her, Kathy? I thought she was kind of pushy, butting in on us like that."

"Come on, Becky. She's new in town and just trying to make friends. The least we can do is be nice to her."

"Yeah, but that doesn't mean we have to be friends with her," replied Becky. "Anyway, what would you like to do this Saturday? You know those old puppets of mine, I thought we could fix them up and make our own puppet show."

"Sure, Becky, that sounds great," said Kathy. "I'll be over after lunch. I better go home now. See you tomorrow."

Later that evening Jeanette called Kathy and surprised her with an invitation to the circus, the last show before it left town. The only problem was that the circus happened to be at the same time that Kathy had promised to go to Becky's. Kathy didn't know what to do, go to the circus and leave her best friend alone, or stick with her best friend and miss a good time. (Selman, 1980, p. 321–322)

After reading the child the story, you need to ask some open-ended questions and then probe the child's understanding of friendship.

Open-ended Questions

1. What do you think the problem is in this story?
2. What do you think Kathy will do—choose to be with her old friend, Becky, or go with the new girl, Jeanette? Why? Which do you think is more important: to be with an old friend or to make new friends? Why?

3. Do you have a best friend? What kind of friendship do you have with that person? What makes that person your best friend?

On the basis of the child's answers, you may then want or need to probe as follows (you probably will not need to ask *all* these questions; be selective, depending on your subject's comments).

Probes

1. What kind of friendship do you think Kathy and Becky have? Do you think it is a good or close friendship? What is a really good, close friendship? Does it take something special to have a very good friendship? What kinds of things do friends know about each other?
2. What does being friends for a long time, like Kathy and Becky, do for a friendship?
3. What makes close, good friendships last?
4. What kinds of things can good friends talk about that other friends sometimes can't? What kinds of problems can they talk over?
5. What makes two friends feel really close to each other?
6. What's the difference between the kind of friendship Becky and Kathy have and Kathy and Jeanette's friendship? Are there different kinds of friendship? What's the difference between "regular" and "best" friendship?
7. Is it better when close friends are like each other or different from each other? Why? In what ways should good friends be the same? In what ways should they be different?
8. Which is better to have (be with)—one close friend or a group of regular friends? Why? (Selman, 1980, p. 321–323)

Scoring

Transcribe your subject's answers as close to verbatim as you can (tape the conversation if that will help). Compare the child's answers to the levels of social understanding described in this chapter. At what level does the child appear to be reasoning?

THE WHOLE CHILD

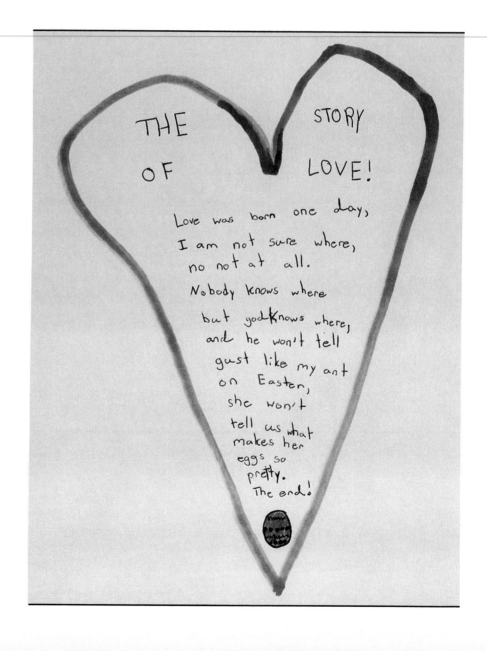

THE   STORY

OF   LOVE!

Love was born one day,
I am not sure where,
no not at all.
Nobody knows where
but god knows where,
and he won't tell
gust like my ant
on Easter,
she won't
tell us what
makes her
eggs so
pretty.
The end!

13 The Ecology of Development: The Impact of Families, Schools, and Culture

The Influence of the Family
  The Emotional Tone of the Family
  Methods of Control
To Spank or Not to Spank
  Communication Patterns
  Cognitive Enrichment
  Patterns of Child Rearing
Things That Can Affect Family Functioning
  The Child's Characteristics
  The Structure of the Family
  The Family Environment: Poverty and Wealth
  Short-term Family Stress
  Parents' Work Roles
  Social Support for Parents
Professional Advice and Support for Parents
Beyond the Family: The Direct Influence of Other Institutions on Children
  Day Care
  Schooling
  Television
A Final Point: Systems and Interpretations
Summary
Key Terms
Television Aggression

Thirty years ago, most child development texts and books of advice to parents emphasized the role of the parents in "molding" the child, as if the child were some sort of shapeless block of clay (Hartup, 1978). The parents' task was thought to be to *socialize* the child, to shape the child's behavior so that it fit well into the expectations and rules of society.

In the first 12 chapters of this book I have repeatedly emphasized a quite different view—namely, that many dimensions of development appear to have their own internal timetables, their own inevitability. Given basic environmental support, virtually all children learn to walk and talk; they figure out they are separate people; and they develop more and more complex ways of analyzing and understanding the objects and the people around them. Some of these sequences seem to be maturational, dictated by basic genetic instructions. Some seem to come from the child's own encounters with and manipulation of the environment. And for many purposes, a remarkably wide range of environments seem to be "good enough" to provide the child with the "food" for her development (just as many different diets are "good enough" to sustain physical growth).

Such an emphasis on *intrinsic* developmental processes comes about partly because that is what the current research is telling us and partly as an antidote to the older "clay-molding" view of development. But I would certainly be a fool if I tried to persuade you that the child's family and the child's culture have no impact on the form, rate, or content of a child's developmental pattern.

As we have gone along, I have talked about ways in which the parents' behavior makes a difference—in attachment, language, cognitive development, self-concept, and the like. But now I need to explore the role of parents much more systematically. I also need to talk about the impact on the child of other social institutions that may affect her directly, such as day care, schooling, and TV. Finally, and perhaps most interesting, I need to consider some of the social institutions and events that may influence children *indirectly,* through their impact on parents—such as the parents' jobs and their networks of social relationships. To gain some understanding of the potential impact of such influences, we need to move our focus outward from the child in a series of steps—to the family, to the school, to the culture—and see how all these elements affect the child's development.

The field of developmental psychology is indebted to Urie Bronfenbrenner (1979, 1986) both for the phrase *ecology of development* and for insisting that we extend our gaze past the dyad of mother and child, past the family, and into the intricate network of cultural and personal relationships that forms the *system* or *ecological niche* in which the child grows. Understanding how such interlocking and interpenetrating forces may influence or even shape the trajectory of a given child's development is an immensely complex task—one I can only begin to explore here. But let us plunge into the complexities and see how far we can go.

THE INFLUENCE OF THE FAMILY

With rare exceptions, children grow up in families (even if the "family" consists of only one adult and one child). It is no simple thing to describe the ways families behave. Over the course of just the first few years of a child's life, the child and the parents have literally millions of conversations or encounters—feeding, changing diapers, dressing, undressing, providing names for objects, answering questions, rescuing the child from danger, and so on and on. In the midst of this richness and diversity, psychologists have identified several major dimensions on which families differ that seem to be significant for the child: the emotional tone of the family, the manner in which control is exercised, the quality and amount of communication, and the quality and quantity of cognitive enrichment provided.

The Emotional Tone of the Family

The first key element for the child seems to be the relative **warmth versus hostility** of the home. *Warmth* is difficult to define and measure, but intuitively and theoretically it is clear that it is highly important for the child. A warm parent cares about the child, expresses affection, frequently or regularly puts the child's needs first, shows enthusiasm for the child's activities, and responds sensitively and empathically to the child's feelings (Maccoby, 1980b). On the other end of the continuum are parents who overtly reject their children—saying and expressing with their behavior that they do not love or want the child. Such differences have an effect. Psychologists have found that children in warm and loving families

- Are more securely attached in the first two years of life.
- Have higher self-esteem.
- Are more empathetic, more altruistic, more responsive to others' hurts or distress.
- Have higher measured IQs in preschool and elementary school.

I suspect that the role of warmth in fostering a secure attachment of the child to the parent is one of the key elements in this picture. You already know from Chapters 10 and 11 that securely attached children are more skillful with their peers, more exploratory, more sure of themselves. At the same time, as Maccoby (1980b) points out, warmth also makes children generally more responsive to guidance, so the parents' affection and warmth increase the potency of the things that parents say to their children and the efficiency of their discipline.

Methods of Control

It is the nature of children that they will often do things their parents do not want them to do, ask for things they cannot have, or refuse to obey

Figure 13.1 I am sure it is obvious to all of you that loving a child is a critical ingredient in the child's optimum development. But sometimes it helps to restate the obvious.

their parents' requests or demands. From early days, parents are inevitably faced with the task of controlling the child's behavior. It is this dimension of parental behavior that people usually mean when they talk about *discipline*. It will help, though, to break this dimension apart into several elements.

Clarity and Consistency of Rules. One element of control is simply making it clear to the child what the rules are and what the consequences of disobeying (or obeying) them are, and then enforcing them consistently. Some parents are very clear and consistent; others waffle or are fuzzy about what they expect or will tolerate. Studies of families show clearly that parents who are clear and consistent have children who are more obedient (which is wonderful reinforcement for the parents). But such clarity does not produce little robots. Children from families with consistent rules are also more competent and sure of themselves (Baumrind, 1967, 1971, 1973) and less aggressive (Patterson, 1980).

Level of Expectations.   A related element is the level of expectations the parents have for the child's behavior. Is the child expected to show relatively more mature behavior, or does the parent feel it is important not to expect too much too soon?

Studies of such variations show that, within limits, higher expectations seem to be associated with better outcomes. Children whose parents make high demands on them, expecting them to help around the house or to show relatively mature behavior for their age, have higher self-esteem, show more generosity and altruism toward others, and show lower levels of aggression. Obviously, this can be carried much too far. It is totally unrealistic and counterproductive to expect a 2-year-old to set the table every night or to tie his own shoes. But when parents expect the child to be as independent and helpful as possible for his age, that does seem to foster a sense of competence in the child that carries over into other situations.

Restrictiveness.   Another element of parental control is the degree of **restrictiveness** imposed. This is not the same thing as clear or consistent rule setting. A parent can be relatively low in restrictiveness and still have clear rules. For example, you might have a rule that your 10-year-old can stop off at another child's house after school to play without arranging it ahead of time but that she must call you to tell you where she is. That would be a clear rule but relatively low restrictiveness. On the other hand, a parent who insists on keeping a child within eyesight at all times, or who puts a toddler in a playpen for most of the day rather than risk having her pull the drawers open or touch the stereo, would be considered restrictive.

Restrictive parents also frequently use a distinctive form of language with their children—namely, *imperative* sentences, such as "Stop that" or "Come here" or "Do what I tell you." They are less likely to explain the rules to the children but instead use their own power to control the child.

The other end of the continuum is usually called *permissive parenting,* which frequently also includes relatively few rules and few imperatives. Sometimes permissive parenting styles emerge from a sense of helplessness about controlling the child at all: the parent has given up. Often, though, permissiveness emerges from a specific philosophy of child rearing that emphasizes the child's need for freedom and opportunity to explore.

Evidence on the impact of restrictiveness and permissiveness is mixed. Highly restrictive parents are likely to have quite obedient, unaggressive children. But such children are also likely to be somewhat timid and may have difficulty establishing close relationships with peers. Results from some of my own longitudinal studies (Barnard, Bee, & Hammond, 1984b) suggest that restrictiveness is also associated with lower IQ, particularly in middle-class children, possibly because of the lowered opportunity to explore freely.

Low restrictiveness (permissiveness), on the other hand, is also not a wholly positive strategy. Children with highly permissive parents—who

TO SPANK OR NOT TO SPANK

The short, emphatic answer to the question "Should I spank my child?" is *"No!"* I am well aware that this is easier to say than to do (and I admit to having applied a hand to my own children's rear ends on one or two occasions, even knowing that it would do little good and some potential damage). But the information we have about the effects of physical punishment, including spanking, seems to me to be so clear that I can give a firm answer to the question.

In order to make the point clear, I need to distinguish between the short-term effects of spanking and the longer-term effects. In the short term, spanking a child usually *does* get the child to stop the particular behavior you didn't like, and it seems to have a *temporary* effect of reducing the chance that the child will repeat the bad behavior. Since that's what you wanted, it may seem like a good strategy. But even in the short term there are some negative side effects. The child may have stopped writing on the walls or throwing water at you or swearing (or whatever behavior you had forbidden), but after a spanking he is undoubtedly crying, which is unpleasant. Crying is also a behavior which spanking

does not decrease (it is virtually impossible to get children to stop crying by spanking them!). So you have exchanged one unpleasantness for another, and the second unpleasantness (crying) can't be dealt with by using the same form of punishment.

Another short-term side effect is that because the child stopped doing something unpleasant when you spanked him, *you* were reinforced for spanking. So the more effective the spanking is in reducing the child's unwanted behavior, the more you are being "trained" to use spanking again. A cycle is thus built up.

Whatever apparent benefits come in the short run from spanking disappear when we take a longer look. Three long-term effects are particularly significant:

1. The child observes you using physical force or violence as a method of solving problems or getting people to do what you want. You thus serve as a model for a behavior you do *not* want your child to use with others. Telling the child that it's okay for parents to behave this way, but not for children, is likely to have little effect, since children will do what

may exert far too little control—are likely to show only moderate independence and to be relatively thoughtless of others. On this dimension, as on many others, the "ideal" appears to lie somewhere in the middle.

In general, it seems that children respond very positively when parents set clear rules and enforce them consistently, make realistic demands, have high but realistic expectations, and are only moderately restrictive.

Punishment. I have saved for the last the one thing most of us probably think of when we think about "controlling" the child—namely, punishment. When a child does something you don't want (like writing on the wall or hitting her brother) or fails to do something you do want (like cleaning his room), most parents respond with some kind of punishment, such as withholding privileges or treats, assigning extra chores, sending a child to

you do and not what you say when there is a conflict between the two messages.

2. By repeatedly pairing your presence with the unpleasant or painful event of spanking, you are undermining your own positive value for your child. Over time, this means that you are less able to use *any* kind of reinforcement effectively. Eventually, even your praise or affection will be less powerful in influencing your child's behavior. That is a very high price to pay.

3. There is frequently a strong underlying emotional message going with spanking—anger, rejection, irritation, dislike of the child. Even very young children "read" this emotional message quite clearly. Spanking thus helps to create a family climate of rejection instead of warmth, with all the consequences I have described in the main part of this chapter.

I am *not* saying that you should never punish a child. I *am* saying that *physical punishment*, such as spanking, is rarely (if ever) a good way to go about it. Children whose parents use high rates of physical punishment are frequently highly aggressive (Bandura, 1973) or less compliant with adults (Power & Chapieski, 1986). More important, their relationships with peers are frequently less good than are those of children whose parents use other forms of control.

But what other forms of control will work? If you have been brought up in a family in which spanking was the standard method, you may simply not know other ways. If you find yourself in this position, a parenting class might be of help. What you would learn in any such class is that the key is to intervene *early* in problem sequences, to do so consistently, and to use the mildest possible form of punishment that will stop the behavior—taking away a favored toy, separating two children, sending the child to her room or to a special place for a "time-out" period, withholding an anticipated privilege. Spanking typically happens when you have let things get well beyond this early stage and you are at your wit's end. The best way to avoid it is to not let yourself get to that point.

her room, "grounding," verbal scolding, or spanking. The most controversial of these is spanking. Because of the importance of the question, I have explored the pros and cons of such physical punishment in the box above. But I want to make two other points about punishment strategies in general.

First, as Gerald Patterson says, "punishment 'works.' If you use it properly it will produce rapid changes in the behavior of other people" (1975, p. 19). The operative word here, though, is *properly*. The most effective punishments—those that produce long-term changes in the child's behavior without unwanted or negative side effects—are those used *early* in some sequence of misbehavior, with the lowest level of emotion possible and at the mildest level of punishment possible (Patterson, 1975; Johnston, 1972). Taking a desired toy away when the child *first* uses it to hit the

Figure 13.2 Spanking is probably the most common form of discipline used by parents, but it has many negative side effects.

furniture (or a sibling) or consistently withholding small privileges when a child misbehaves will "work," especially if the parent is also warm, clear about the rules, and consistent. It is far less effective if the parent waits until the screams have reached a piercing level or until the fourth time a teenager has gone off without saying where she's gone—and *then* weigh in with yelling and strong punishments.

Second, to a considerable degree parents get back what they give out in the way of punishment. As I pointed out in Chapter 9, children learn by observation as well as by doing, so they learn the adults' ways of coping with stress and their forms of punishment. Yelling at children to stop doing something, for example, may bring a *brief* change in their behavior (which thus reinforces the parent for yelling, by the way). But it also increases the chances that children will yell back on other occasions.

Communication Patterns

Two things about communication within the family seem to make a difference for the child: the amount and richness of language spoken *to* the child and the amount of conversation and suggestions *from* the child that the parent encourages. Listening is important as well as talking.

When I say "listening," I have in mind more than merely saying "unhunh" periodically while the child talks. I also mean conveying to the child the sense that what she has to say is *worth* listening to, that she has ideas, that her ideas are important and should be considered in family decisions. Most broadly, I am describing a pattern of high levels of *communication* between parent and child.

There is much less research on the quality of communication within families than on some of the other dimensions I have been describing, so we are a long way from understanding all the ramifications. In general, children from families with open communication are seen as more emotionally or socially mature (Bell & Bell, 1982; Baumrind, 1971, 1973), although there are some hints from earlier research (e.g., Baldwin, 1948, 1949) that children from highly "democratic" families are also more bossy and aggressive.

More recent work has pointed to the importance of open communication not just for the child but also for the functioning of the family as a unit. For example, in a study of a national sample of families with adolescents, Howard Barnes and David Olson (1985) measured communication by asking the parents and teenagers to agree or disagree with statements like "It is easy for me to express all my true feelings to my [mother/father/ child]." As you can see in Figure 13.3, they found that when parents and children reported good, open communication, they also described their families as more adaptable in the face of stress or change and said they were more satisfied with their families than did members of families with poorer communication.

Cognitive Enrichment

The final dimension of family interaction patterns I want to emphasize is again a reprise from earlier chapters. As you'll recall from Chapter 6, both the richness and variety of the *inanimate environment* (toys, objects, varied experiences) and the contingent responsiveness and variety of the *animate environment* (people) have an impact on the child (Wachs & Gruen, 1982). This can be seen most clearly in cognitive development and language, but I am sure that the richness of the environment affects other areas of the child's functioning as well.

Patterns of Child Rearing

Variations in any one of these four dimensions or facets of the family environment—emotional tone, control, communication, and cognitive enrichment—do seem to make a difference in the rate or quality of a child's development and in the style of interaction with others that she may develop. But in the real world these four dimensions don't occur in isolation; they combine into intricate patterns, or styles. Given the infinite complexity of human behavior and of family interaction, the number of different individual styles

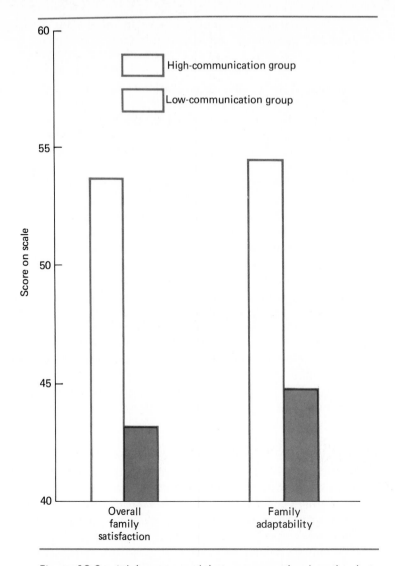

Figure 13.3 Adolescents and their parents who describe their interactions as involving good, open communication also describe themselves as more satisfied with their overall family life and see their families as more adaptable than do adolescents and parents whose communication is not as good or as open. (Source: Barnes & Olson, 1985, Table 3, page 445.)

is probably infinite, too. But some combinations are more common than others, and it helps our understanding to look for some basic types.

Eleanor Maccoby and John Martin (1983) have proposed a particularly helpful set of types, based heavily on the work of Diana Baumrind, whose

	Accepting; responsive; child-centered	Rejecting; unresponsive; parent-centered
Demanding; controlling	Authoritative-reciprocal; high in bidirectional communication	Authoritarian; power-assertive
Undemanding; low in control attempts	Indulgent; permissive	Neglecting; ignoring; indifferent; uninvolved

Figure 13.4 Different combinations of parental behaviors or attitudes toward children can be classified into types. This particular typology, suggested by Maccoby and Martin, focuses on two dimensions of difference: demanding or controlling versus undemanding or noncontrolling, and accepting-responsive versus rejecting-unresponsive. Note that three of the four types that emerge from this classification are highly similar to the types Baumrind suggests. (*Source:* Adapted from E. E. Maccoby & J. A. Martin (1983). Socialization in the context of the family: Parent-child interaction. In E. M. Hetherington (Ed.), *Handbook of Child Psychology,* Figure 2, p. 39. New York: Wiley, 1983.)

research and thinking I described briefly in Chapter 10 (page 366). You can see in Figure 13.4 that Maccoby and Martin have focused on two particular dimensions: the degree of demand or control, on the one hand, and the amount of acceptance/rejection or responsiveness on the other. The intersection of these two dimensions creates four parental types. Three of these types correspond fairly closely to Baumrind's authoritarian, authoritative, and permissive parental styles. The fourth, the neglecting or uninvolved type, was not identified by Baumrind in her early work but certainly does occur and seems important to study.

The Authoritarian Type. Children growing up in authoritarian families—with high levels of demand and control but relatively low levels of warmth or responsiveness—typically are less skilled with peers than are children from other types of families, and they have lower self-esteem. Some of these children appear subdued, others may show high aggressiveness or other indications of being out of control. Which of these two outcomes occurs may depend in part on how skillfully the parents use the various disciplinary techniques. Gerald Patterson, whose work I mentioned in Chapter 9, finds that the "out-of-control" child is most likely to come from a family in which the parents are authoritarian by inclination but lack the skills to enforce the limits or rules they set. In a recent large study, Sandy

Dornbusch and his co-workers (1987) have also found that teenagers from authoritarian families get poorer grades in school than do teenagers from authoritative families.

The Permissive Type.

Children growing up with indulgent or permissive parents show some negative outcomes, too. Dornbusch finds that they do slightly less well in school in adolescence, and they are likely to be more aggressive—particularly if the parents are specifically permissive toward aggressiveness—and to be somewhat immature in their behavior with peers and in school. They are less likely to take responsibility and are less independent.

The Authoritative Type.

The most consistently positive outcomes have been associated with the authoritative pattern, in which the parents are high in both control and warmth, setting clear limits but also responding to the child's individual needs. Children reared in such families typically show higher self-esteem, are more independent, try new things, and may show more altruistic behavior as well. They are self-confident and achievement-oriented in school and get better grades.

The Neglecting Type.

In contrast, the most consistently negative outcomes are associated with the fourth pattern, the neglecting or uninvolved type. You may remember from Chapter 11, in the discussion of secure and insecure attachments, that one of the family characteristics often found in children rated as insecure/avoidant is the psychological unavailability of the mother. The mother may be depressed, or she may be overwhelmed by other problems in her life and may not have made any deep emotional connection with the child. Whatever the reason, these children continue to show disturbances in their relationships with peers and with adults in preschool and later. In less-extreme cases, when the parent may be primarily focused on her or his own needs rather than the child's, the effects are also detectable, even 10 or 15 years later. Such children are more likely to show impulsive or antisocial behavior at adolescence and to be much less achievement-oriented in school (Block, 1971; Pulkkinen, 1982).

Several conclusions from this research are important. First, it seems clear that children *are* affected by the family climate or style. Although we do not have the sorts of longitudinal data needed to be sure, I suspect that these effects persist well into adulthood. Second, many of us are accustomed to thinking about family styles as if permissive and authoritarian patterns were the only options. But Baumrind's work and Maccoby and Martin's analysis show clearly that one can be *both* affectionate and firm and that children respond to this combination in very positive ways.

Third, and most important, even these types do not begin to convey the richness or the complexity of family interactions. Families are *systems* of relationships, each influencing the others. So, for example, the impact on a child of having a restrictive mother will differ depending on whether the father is also restrictive (Hinde & Stevenson-Hinde, 1987). The quality of the parents' own marital relationship will also affect the child, both directly and indirectly (Goldberg & Easterbrooks, 1984). To convey still more of this complexity, let me add a few more pieces to the system.

THINGS THAT CAN AFFECT FAMILY FUNCTIONING

Parents do not operate in a vacuum. Each of us brings to the job of raising a child certain long-standing patterns and personality traits, but in addition to this, our actual behavior with our children and in our family is influenced by a whole host of other things, including the child's characteristics, the structure of the family, the economic condition of the family, our jobs, our network of friendships or supportive relationships, and the stresses we face.

The Child's Characteristics

One of the first things to understand is that the influences in the parent-child system flow both ways. Children influence their parents as well as the other way around. I already talked about one such influence in Chapter 9, namely, the child's temperament. Children with difficult temperaments seem to elicit more punishment and may also affect a parent's mood.

Whether a child is firstborn or later-born also makes a difference. In Table 13.1 I've summarized some of what we know about the ways parents treat their firstborns compared to the way they treat later-born children. Some of the differences are undoubtedly the result of simple lack of experience with a first child: parents are more anxious and press a little harder to do everything right. But part of the explanation also lies in the fact

Table 13.1
▬▬▬

How Parents Treat Their Firstborn Children Compared to Later-born Children

Firstborns receive:
- More achievement pressure (they are expected to achieve at higher levels).
- More complex language and more total language, especially in infancy.
- More intrusive and restrictive child rearing.
- More anxiety from parents ("Am I doing this right?").
- More child-centered environment: family activities center around the individual child more than with later-borns.
- More coercive discipline (more punishment of all kinds). Less-skilled parenting.

that the family configuration is different. The task of parenting is not the same when there are two children as when there is only one. There is less time for highly individualized play or story reading or one-on-one interactions, and the children spend more time playing with each other.

Still another factor that affects the way parents behave is the child's age. This may seem so obvious that it is hardly worth stating, but I think the point is vital. As the child develops, very different demands are made on the parents. As any parent can tell you, caring for an infant is a different task than caring for a 2-year-old or a 12-year-old. The areas in which control will need to be exercised change; the degree of push for independence changes; and the child's intellectual and language abilities grow—she can "talk back" more effectively and argue her side more cogently.

We should not fall into the trap of thinking that parents have a consistent or permanent style or pattern of child rearing that is the same for all children in a family or the same for each child over time. There are threads of consistency that run through the variations, I am sure. But each parent-child system is an evolving one, to which both parties contribute.

The Structure of the Family

Just as having more than one child changes the family structure in ways that affect everyone, other variations in structure, such as the changes brought about by separation or divorce, also alter the system. You all know, I am sure, that divorce rates are extremely high, but I suspect that most of you have not grasped the full implications of that fact for the family structures children grow up in today.

Sandra Hofferth (1985) has generated some particularly startling estimates, based on a longitudinal study of over 5000 families who have been followed since 1968. She projects that only 30 percent of white children born in 1980 will still be living with their two natural parents by age 17. For black children, the figure is only 6 percent. Other estimates, based on cross-sectional comparisons, are somewhat more optimistic (e.g., Bumpass, 1984; Norton & Glick, 1986). But it would appear that at least 60 percent and possibly as many as 70 or 80 percent of today's children are likely to spend at least *some* time in a single-parent household, and perhaps 35 percent will spend at least a part of their childhood living with a stepparent.

Figure 13.5 shows the other types of family structures Hofferth predicts for the children born in 1980, so you can see the very large variety. Even this, though, does not convey the enormous variety of family combinations. Shep Kellam, for example, found 86 different family structures in a large sample of children from a poor black Chicago neighborhood in 1966 (Kellam, Ensminger, & Turner, 1977). Further complexities are added by the fact that families change from one structure to another, sometimes repeatedly. Divorced mothers, for example, may have live-in relationships with one or more men before a remarriage, or they may live for a while with their own parents. All in all, it is clear that the *majority* of children today experi-

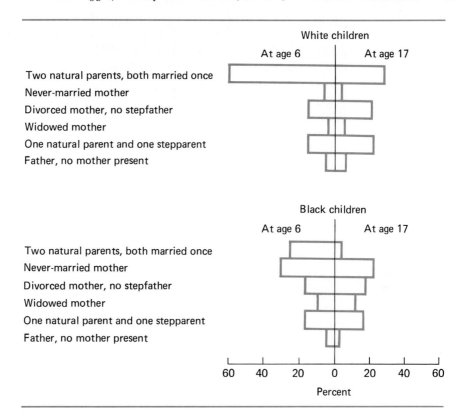

Figure 13.5 These figures represent Sandra Hofferth's estimates of the percentage of all children born in 1980 who will be in each of several family types or structures at age 6 and at age 17. The patterns are quite different for black and for white children, as you can see. Note that Hofferth estimates that approximately one-quarter of all children will spend at least part of their childhood with a stepparent and that only about the same number will spend all of childhood with both natural parents. At least one change in family structure is therefore now the norm for children in the United States. (*Source:* Hofferth, 1985, Tables 1 and 2, pp. 99–100, 102–103.)

ence at least two different family structures, and often many more than that, in the course of their growing up.

Research on the effects of such structures on family interaction patterns and on children has not kept pace with the rate of change in families. In particular, we know relatively little about the many varieties of stepparent families. But let me make a few points.

First, any change in the family structure is accompanied by dislocation and stress. Whenever a person is added to or subtracted from the family unit, the system has to adjust. This seems particularly troublesome in the case of divorce or separation, when an adult is subtracted from the family. I described some of the effects of divorce on children in Chapter 9, in the box on pages 344–345, so you already know that there is typically disruption of the child, reflected in poorer school performance and higher rates of problem behavior in the first few years following the separation. The same sort of disruption occurs in the parents' behavior, too. The adults may show wide mood swings or experience problems at work or have poor health (Hetherington & Camara, 1984). Their interactions with their children change, too; parents make lower maturity demands, are less consistent about rules, show less warmth, and communicate less. In most cases, it is not fair to describe the pattern as neglectful, but divorced parents become distinctly less authoritative.

Interestingly, it appears that many of these negative effects for both the adult and the children are mitigated when the mother has another adult in the home—her own mother, a friend, a live-in boyfriend (Dornbusch et al., 1985; Kellam, Ensminger, & Turner, 1977)—which suggests that a two-adult system in a family may simply be more stable or easier to manage. However—and this is an important however—there are various hints that this buffering effect of a second adult in the home does *not* extend to stepparent family structures (mother/stepfather or father/stepmother). Dornbusch finds, for example, that stepparent families show higher levels of authoritarian and lower levels of authoritative child-rearing styles (Dornbusch et al., 1987), and the children get lower school grades and have higher rates of delinquency than do children who live with both natural parents. (Having been a stepparent, I can assure you it is not easy!)

These are only preliminary findings. It is too early for sweeping generalizations about the effects of step families or other family structures on children's development. We do know, though, that the family structure affects the pattern of interactions within the family and thus has both direct and indirect effects on the child's development.

The Family Environment: Poverty and Wealth

A very different category of influences on the family is the total economic and social environment in which the family exists—the "ecological niche" or **social class** of the family. Most often, the focus of research has been on the contrast between families living in poverty and those in middle-class or more affluent circumstances.

I have talked about some of the characteristics and effects of poverty in several earlier chapters, so you know that whether a family lives in a poverty environment or in a working-class or middle-class environment is related to the child's development in a whole host of ways. Let me pull these several threads together for you here and add a few bits of new information along the way.

• Women in poverty circumstances have less access to prenatal and other health care. They are thus at higher risk for problems during pregnancy, and their children are more likely to be born with some sort of disability. Family diets also tend to be worse, for the children as well as for the mother. One group of researchers a decade ago (Read & Felson, 1976) estimated that 20 to 30 percent of children under age 6 in the United States have too few calories on a daily basis, and most of these are from poor families.

- Women at the lower end of the economic spectrum are more likely to work than are middle-class mothers (although this is changing). Their children are thus more likely to be in day care, from earlier ages, and to have less well equipped or poorer-quality care.

- Poor families are larger (Broman, Nichols, & Kennedy, 1975), with children more closely spaced. They live in smaller and less-adequate housing as well. Thus, the total environment experienced by the family and by the child because of poverty is very different from what is experienced by a child in a more affluent family.

Possibly because of this combination of circumstances, mothers and fathers living in poverty treat their children quite differently than better-off parents treat theirs. They talk to their children less, provide fewer age-appropriate toys, spend less time with them in intellectually stimulating activities, are stricter and more physical in their discipline, and explain things less often and less fully (Farran, Haskins, & Gallagher, 1980). In the category system shown in Figure 13.4, these parents are more likely to be authoritarian or neglecting than authoritative (e.g., Dornbusch et al., 1987).

Some of this pattern of parental behavior is undoubtedly a response to the extraordinary stresses of the poverty environment. Some of the pattern may also be simple imitation of the way these same parents were brought up in their own childhood; and some may be a product of ignorance of children's needs. Poor parents with relatively more education, for example, typically talk to their children more and provide more intellectual stimulation than do equally poor parents with lower levels of education. But whatever the cause, children reared in poverty experience not only different physical conditions but quite different interactions with their parents.

Not surprisingly, such children turn out differently, as I have pointed out repeatedly in earlier chapters. Children from poverty environments have higher rates of birth defects and early disabilities; they recover less well from early problems; they are more often ill and malnourished throughout their childhood years. Typically, they also have lower IQs and move more slowly through the sequences of cognitive development described by Piaget. They do less well in school and are less likely to go on to college. Such children, in turn, are more likely to be poor as adults, thus continuing the cycle through another generation.

The effects of family poverty on children are thus both direct, such as in poorer diet, and indirect, such as through changes in the way parents treat the child. The combined effects are very large indeed.

Short-term Family Stress

The types of influences on family life I have described so far—characteristics of the child, family structure, and income level—are all fairly long-term and relatively difficult to change. But most families also experience shorter-term upheavals or stresses. Moving to another city, changing jobs, having your own parent die—all of these are major life changes, major sources of stress. They affect each family member directly and may alter the way children and parents interact.

In general, it looks as if most major life changes or stresses experienced by families have a temporary disorganizing effect on family interactions, similar to what I have described following a divorce. For example, studies of families in which the father lost his job during the Great Depression of the 1930s (Elder, 1974, 1981, 1984) show that the family pattern was often severely disrupted. The fathers often became depressed or irritable and more critical and authoritarian toward their children. The effect was much greater, by the way, on a temperamentally difficult child than on less-irritating children, and it was much more negative when the children were quite young when the father lost his job. Once again, this illustrates that the outcome can only be understood by looking at the entire system.

Long-term consequences of such life changes or stresses on the child seem to be greatest or most negative when the family is repeatedly stressed—for example, when there is instability or constant change, such as when a child is moved frequently from one day-care arrangement to the next, or when a mother moves in and out of the work force repeatedly or changes jobs often. Particularly good support for this generalization comes from Emmy Werner's longitudinal study of all the children born on the Hawaiian island of Kauai in 1955 (Werner & Smith, 1982). She found that families with the highest cumulative levels of stressful life events over the child's first 18 years of life had children who exhibited more behavior problems and did less well in school. This was not merely the result of poverty, either, since the same pattern was found among middle-class families with high levels of stress or life change.

Parents' Work Roles

Still another facet of adult life that has an impact on the family, and thus on the child, is the parents' jobs. Studies of mothers' and fathers' work/family connections have been quite different: with mothers, the basic question has been whether it makes any difference for the child if she works at all; with fathers, the emphasis has been on the effect, if any, on family functioning of the father's satisfaction with his work or of the type of work that he does.

Mothers' Employment.　　There are hundreds of studies comparing the children of working and nonworking mothers. The cumulative findings are now fairly clear: for children past infancy, maternal employment has

Figure 13.6 Over half of all women with preschool-age children are now employed, like this Mom on the way out the door to take her child to the day-care center. The figure is far higher for women with older children. For daughters, the effects of the mother's employment seems to be essentially positive; for sons, there are hints of some small negative effects.

a generally positive effect for girls but sometimes is associated with negative effects for boys (I'll be coming back to the research on employment during the child's infancy when I talk about day-care later in the chapter). Girls whose mothers work are more independent, have more positive views of the female role, and admire their mothers more than do girls whose mothers do not work. Boys whose mothers work also have more positive views of the female role, but in contrast to the findings for girls, boys whose mothers work are sometimes found to have lower academic achievement than do boys whose mothers stay home (Bronfenbrenner & Crouter, 1982; Duckett, Raffaelli, & Richards, 1987).

Most researchers in this area assume, as I do, that it is not employment per se that produces these effects, but rather that the mother's work creates changes both in the mother herself (her self-esteem or her morale, for example) and in the family's interaction patterns. But just what the specific links may be is still a matter of considerable debate. We do know that the mother's attitude toward her work or nonwork makes a difference. The most negative outcomes for children are typically found for two subgroups: mothers who would prefer to work but are staying at home and mothers who dislike their jobs or are unwilling workers (Hoffman, 1984; DeMeis, Hock, & McBride, 1986; Lerner & Galambos, 1986). We also know that women who work have more decision-making power within the family (Blumstein & Schwartz, 1983), and they may also have higher self-esteem, particularly if they are satisfied with their work. Such power or self-esteem may spill over particularly into the woman's interaction with her children, perhaps especially with a daughter. Bronfenbrenner finds, for example (Bronfenbrenner, Alvarez, and Henderson, 1984), that working mothers give more positive descriptions of their young daughters than do nonworking mothers, which may help to account for the more positive outcomes for girls whose mothers are employed. But these connections are still tentative.

Fathers' Employment.   Older research on the impact of fathers' work on family life focused on unemployment—a set of findings I have already described. It is only very recently that psychologists have begun to look for more subtle kinds of connections between family interactions and the father's work satisfaction, his particular job demands, or work values. So I can only give you fragments.

One fragment is the finding by Melvin Kohn (1980; Kohn & Schooler, 1983) from his longitudinal studies that nonroutine jobs that require self-direction and autonomy tend to increase a worker's intellectual flexibility, while routine, more highly supervised jobs lead to decreases in intellectual flexibility. Furthermore, Kohn has found that men in the more routine jobs are likely to place greater emphasis on obedience from their children. Other researchers have found that some specific jobs seem to have a predictably negative spillover into family life. Both police work and military positions, for example, are linked with higher rates of abuse or family violence or disruption (Hoffman, 1984). And men with particularly demanding jobs may have less time to spend with their families, which will again alter the interaction patterns.

These few bits illustrate, I hope, that the kinds of questions psychologists are now asking about parents' employment have become much more subtle. But these questions are also much tougher to answer than the simpler ones we started with. What is clear is that a child's development *is* affected by such aspects of the parents' lives as outside stress or work patterns.

Social Support for Parents

Do you remember those old movie Westerns in which the brave settlers were surrounded by hostile forces and the cavalry came to the rescue at the last moment? Well, this section might be subtitled "The Cavalry Returns!" Just when you are probably thinking that *everything* makes the task of raising children in a consistent and loving fashion nearly impossible, I will come to the rescue by telling you about the beneficial or helpful effects of a class of events that has come to be called **social support.**

The general point is fairly easy to state: Parents who are giving each other adequate emotional and physical support and who have friends and family members from whom they also receive information, assistance, and affection are able to respond to their children more warmly, more consistently, and with better control (Cochran & Brassard, 1979; Crockenberg, 1983; Crnic et al., 1983).

The effect of social support on parents is particularly evident when they are experiencing stress of some kind, such as poverty, teenage childbirth, a handicapped or temperamentally difficult infant, divorce, or even just fatigue. You may recall the discussion in Chapter 9 of a study by Susan Crockenberg (1981) that illustrates the point nicely. She found that temperamentally irritable infants were very likely to end up with an insecure attachment to their mothers when the mother *lacked* adequate social support. When the mother felt that she had enough support, similarly irritable children became securely attached. Lois Wandersman and Donald Unger (1983) have given us another link in the chain. They have shown that teenage mothers who have temperamentally difficult infants are more able to provide affectionate and stimulating environments if they have good support from the father and from family members than if the support is inadequate. A new mother who lacks good social and emotional support is also more likely to suffer from postpartum depression—again, particularly if she has a temperamentally difficult infant (Cutrona & Troutman, 1986).

Hetherington and her co-workers report a similar effect in their study of divorced parents. Those who had help and emotional support from friends or family members were much more able to maintain a stable and affectionate environment for their children than were those who grappled with their problems in isolation.

There are other sources of information and support besides families and friends (some of which I have discussed in the box on page 490). And of course, not all "help" from families or friends feels like support (I'm sure you have all been given unwanted advice from your parents or in-laws or friends). The key is not the objective amount of contact or advice received but the parents' *satisfaction* with the level and quality of the support he or she is experiencing. The moral seems to be that at those times of greatest difficulty or stress—when a new child is born, when a child presents special difficulties, when the family moves or experiences major changes— parents most need the emotional and physical support of others. But if you wait until that difficult moment to look around and see who is there to help, you may not find what you need. Social networks must be developed and nurtured over time. But they certainly seem to pay dividends for parents, and thus for children.

PROFESSIONAL ADVICE AND SUPPORT FOR PARENTS

Assistance, advice, and emotional support from families and friends seem to be critical ingredients in good family functioning. But professionals and institutions can play a helpful role as well. I admit that we don't know very much about the ways in which families use professional help or about the best way for such help to be offered. But there are at least some models that have been tried and that seem to work.

One of the most striking examples is the impact of the Parent Child Development Centers (PCDCs), which were created in the early 1970s as part of the War on Poverty. The centers were designed to support the optimum development of children in poverty environments by providing information and support to mothers. The centers offered classes for mothers (primarily mothers of preschool children) on child development and child rearing, home management, nutrition, how to use the social system to get help, and the like. There were some direct services for children as well, such as child care, but the main focus was on helping the parents to become more knowledgeable and skillful with their children, reinforcing strengths and responding to individual needs.

Apparently it worked. Not only did parents use these centers, they learned from them. Mothers who participated in these centers praised their children more, used more complex language with them, encouraged more conversation with them and used more reasoning and less physical punishment than did mothers in equivalent neighborhoods that did not have PCDCs (Andrews et al., 1982). In other words, mothers who had access to supportive and informative help from professionals shifted their child-rearing styles quite markedly. And their children responded. Children of mothers who participated in the centers had higher IQs at age 3 and 4 than did children whose mothers had not been involved (Andrews et al., 1982).

There are similar programs in some cities, such as Earladeen Badger's program for teenage mothers in Cincinnati (Badger, 1981), but in most towns and cities a parent must dig into local resources with some diligence to find good assistance and advice. Let me suggest some places to look:

- *Community colleges.* Classes in parenting are frequently offered at community colleges, often in combination with cooperative day-care or preschool programs.
- *Health services.* The local public health department may also offer parenting classes or may be able to direct parents to such classes (as might a pediatrician). Public health departments can also provide nutrition information as well as facts on eligibility for special nutritional supplements for mothers and children.
- *Parents Anonymous (PA).* Parents who are having serious difficulties managing their children might contact the local chapter of PA. This group can provide immense emotional support as well as practical information and guidance.

We do not know whether these professional or organized forms of support are as helpful to parents as are more informal personal networks. But we do know that such programs can make a significant difference for individual parents or families. So if you find yourself lacking enough help from your family and friends, it is worth your while to seek out the resources in your own community.

BEYOND THE FAMILY: THE DIRECT INFLUENCE OF OTHER INSTITUTIONS ON CHILDREN

One of the curious things in the field of developmental psychology has been our blithe assumption that the family is the key to the child's development. We have spent a great many hours observing mother-infant and mother-child interactions (and more recently, father-child interactions). The ecological approach I have been describing in the past few pages expands our horizons a good deal, by looking at the internal and external influences on the family's functioning. But the fact is that children past the age of 5 or 6 spend as much or more of their awake time in school as they do at home. With the enormously rapid rise in mothers' employment, infants and preschoolers are also spending more of their days outside the family. And when children *are* at home, they spend an extraordinary amount of time sitting in front of a television set rather than interacting with live people. If we are to understand children's development, we must obviously understand the ways in which these other institutions or forces influence the child.

Day Care

By 1986, 55 percent of all women with children 6 years old and below were in the work force; those children have to be taken care of by someone. For families, this poses an immense practical problem. For researchers (and for society), it poses an equally important set of questions: What is the impact of such away-from-home care on the child's emotional, social, and mental development? Is such care detrimental to children? What are the qualities of good day care?

In attempting to answer such questions, researchers and theorists have been through several phases. Early commentaries, relying heavily on psychoanalytic theories, emphasized the potentially damaging effect on a child of being separated from his mother. (In fact, President Nixon vetoed a bill in 1971 that would have provided for some government funding of day care, on the grounds that such care would be damaging to the child and would threaten the stability of the nuclear family.) As the next phase of research accumulated in the 1970s, however, the gloomy predictions were largely forgotten. Many developmental psychologists concluded (as I did in earlier editions of this book) that the research simply showed no replicable negative effects. The third phase of this research odyssey began in the 1980s, as a number of studies were published that pointed to possible negative effects on children's emotional development. At the moment, the best I can do is to give you a sense of our current evidence. You should bear in mind, though, that this story is not over.

The Effects of Day Care on Intellectual Development. Under some circumstances, day-care experiences appear to enhance children's intellectual development. You may recall from Chapter 6 (e.g., Figure 6.11) that children from poverty environments who attend highly enriched day-care centers have shown significant and lasting gains in IQ. Even less-intensive programs like Head Start have been found to have long-term effects on children's school performance (e.g., Weikart, 1983; Miller & Bizzell, 1984). It seems clear that for "high-risk" infants and children (those from families in which lower IQ scores are typical), good day care can offer very real benefits. More ordinary, run-of-the-mill neighborhood day-care centers may also have a beneficial effect, although the effect is smaller (e.g., Clarke-Stewart, 1984).

In contrast, children from middle-class families rarely show any positive intellectual effect from being in day care. But neither do they show any deficit. In sum, as Bettye Caldwell puts it, "there is no need to fear cognitive declines in young children who participate in quality child-care programs" (1986, p. 19), and in some conditions there are cognitive increases.

The Effects of Day Care on Children's Attachments.

The arguments about the possible effects of day care on children's attachments with their caregivers have been much more heated, and it is primarily in this area that recent research may call for some significant rethinking of our conclusions. Can an infant or toddler develop a secure attachment to her mother or father if she is repeatedly separated from them? We know that infants routinely develop secure attachments to their fathers even though the father typically goes away every day to work, so it is clear that such regular separations do not *preclude* secure attachment. But does separation from both parents on a daily basis affect the security of the child's attachment? Does it matter how old the infant is when day care begins?

Let me begin to try to answer this by narrowing the range of uncertainty. There is now little dispute about the conclusion that children who first enter day care at 18 months or 2 years or later show no consistent loss of security of attachment to their parents. The uncertainty revolves around the effect of day care begun in the first year of life or shortly thereafter.

The concern arises because of the results of four or five recent studies showing that infants who enter full-time day care in the first year of life have higher levels of insecure attachment than those who are reared entirely at home or those whose mothers work only part-time (e.g., Belsky, 1987; Belsky & Rovine, 1988; Barglow, Vaughn, & Molitor, 1987; Vaughn, Gove, & Egeland, 1980). When Jay Belsky and Michael Rovine (1988) combined the findings of these several studies (involving a total of nearly 500 infants from both poor and middle-class families), they found that 57 percent of infants whose mothers worked more than 20 hours per week were securely attached, compared to 75 percent of infants whose mothers did not work or worked less than 20 hours per week. Furthermore, when infants in full-time day care showed insecure attachment in these studies, it was more likely to be of the avoidant than the resistant variety.

In the United States today, it is the exception rather than the rule for a child to spend all of his growing-up years in a family with his own natural mother and father. Most children will spend at least part of childhood being reared by a mother alone, by a father alone, or even taking care of himself for a big part of each day. These changes in family structure, along with the much more complex forms of families that also exist (with stepparents, grandparents, and other caregivers), obviously have a major impact on the child, but we do not yet understand all of the effects.

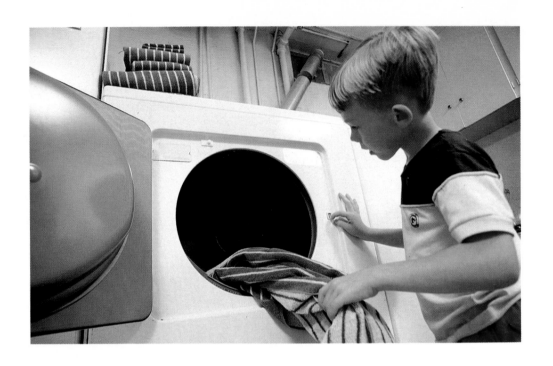

Certainly these findings raise some red flags. But we do not yet understand what is going on here. Let me give you some other, less consistent, bits of evidence:

• Not all researchers find the pattern that Belsky and Rovine have described. In a number of studies, there are simply no differences in the rate or type of security of attachment between infants reared at home and those in day care (e.g., Chase-Lansdale & Owen, 1987; Jaeger, Weinraub, & Hoffman, 1987).

• When researchers have observed the actual reunions of infants with their mothers at day-care centers, they found that those infants who had been in day care the *longest* showed the *least* resistance or avoidance of their mothers at reunion (e.g., Blanchard and Main, 1979). This raises the possibility that the higher rate of resistant attachment observed by Belsky and others comes about because many of the infants in these studies had not been in day care for very long. Thus, the effect *may* "wear off."

• It is clear from Belsky's own summary figures that over half the infants in full-time day care show secure attachment. Rita Benn (1986) has found that among a group of infant boys she observed in full-time day care, those whose mothers showed the highest levels of acceptance and sensitivity to their sons *and* those whose mothers returned to work significantly *earlier* were most likely to be securely attached to their mothers at 18 months of age.

• Brian Vaughn has found that the security or insecurity of attachment in infants in day care does not predict later social or emotional problems nearly so well as is true in home-reared infants (Vaughn, Deane, & Waters, 1985). Thus, the meaning of an insecure attachment may be different for day-care and home-reared children.

There are several different interpretations of all this information. One possibility is that there may be a real and important increased risk of insecure attachment among infants placed in full-time care in the first year of life. (Belsky describes this as a "window of vulnerability.") More speculatively, such increased risk may be particularly acute if the child enters day care during the time when she is forming her strongest first attachment (age 6 to 12 months). Peter Barglow and his colleagues (Barglow, Vaughn, & Molitor, 1987) suggest that the infant may interpret the repeated and lengthy absences of the mother as rejection, an interpretation which would negatively affect the infant's internal working model of attachment.

A less-alarmed reading is that some infants may initially respond to day-care placement with some withdrawal or avoidance of the mother but that this effect may wear off, especially if the mother (and father) can maintain responsive and supportive interactions with the infant when they are together. Any conclusion about which of these readings is correct will have to await further research.

Effects of Day Care on Children's Relationships with Peers.
Another hint of potential problems comes from studies on the effect of

day care on children's social relationships with peers and teachers. Some (but not all) of these studies indicate that day-care children may later be more aggressive, more argumentative, and less compliant with both other children and teachers (e.g., Haskins, 1985; McKinney & Edgerton, 1983). Other researchers have sometimes found that children who have had day-care experience are later more apathetic or less attentive in school or with other youngsters (e.g., Schwartz, 1983).

The fact that both heightened aggressiveness and passivity have been found in different studies of day-care children suggests that it may not be day care per se that is the causal factor here but rather the social environment of particular day-care settings. Just as some families foster heightened aggression in their children, so some day-care centers may also encourage or support such behavior. For example, one program that seems to have inadvertently raised levels of aggression in day-care children was the one created by Ramey and Haskins for children from low-income families (the same program described in Chapter 6 in the discussion of intellectually enriching programs). When the program was later altered to place greater emphasis on the development of positive social skills, the heightened aggressiveness disappeared (Finkelstein, 1982).

Thus, it is simply not clear whether day care itself has consistent negative (or positive) effects on children's social skills or personality or self-concept. The specific qualities of particular day-care environments appear to be much more critical for the child's development than the simple fact of day-care attendance.

Still, all these red flags deserve (and are receiving) much more research attention. If there are potential short-term or long-term negative effects of early day care, we need to understand them and how to avoid them.

The Quality of Care. How are we to judge the quality of care? Day-care settings differ on a large number of dimensions, among them the following: *where* the care takes place, by *whom* with *how many* other children, for *how long*, and with *what* specific forms of stimulation.

The *where* of day care is anything but homogeneous. It can range from day-care centers (in which large numbers of children are cared for together in somewhat schoollike settings) to family day care (in which infants or children are cared for in small groups in someone else's home) to home care by someone other than the parent (such as a full-time babysitter or a grandparent). The majority of children in day care in the United States are in family day care and not center care (Long, Peters, & Garduque, 1985), in part because there are fewer spaces in centers, but mostly because many parents prefer the more homelike atmosphere in family day care.

But which is better for the child? It won't surprise you that there is no simple answer to this. Many family day-care providers are untrained and unlicensed; some provide essentially custodial care, with little cognitive enrichment. Children in settings like that do not thrive intellectually. On the other hand, well-trained family day-care providers do create emotional

Figure 13.7 Ten or fifteen years ago, it would have been fairly unusual to see children this young in day care; now it is commonplace, although the majority of infants and toddlers whose parents work are cared for in family day-care homes rather than in day-care centers like this one. Recently new questions have been raised about the potentially negative effects of such care for children's attachments.

and social conditions more like home care than is true for center care, so on some measures of the child's social development, family day-care children look better (Long, Peters, & Garduque, 1985; Clarke-Stewart, 1987).

The crucial issue, of course, is what is actually happening in the center or the family day-care setting. In Table 13.2 I have summarized some of the characteristics of day-care centers and family day care that seem to have an impact. You can see that the list bears a strong resemblance to the descriptions of optimum family care I have given in earlier chapters, which again should not surprise you. Still, this table might serve as a starting point if or when you find yourself facing this choice for your own children.

Schooling

The quality of later schooling also has an effect. For decades, real estate agents have touted "good" school districts as a reason for settling in one town or in one part of a town rather than another. But it is only recently that psychologists have begun to look systematically at the qualities of schools that might matter for children's development.

Table 13.2
▬▬▬▬▬▬

Some Characteristics of Day-Care Settings That Affect Outcomes for Children

- *Teacher/child ratio.*   In general, the lower the better, although one national study shows that within the range of 5:1 to 10:1 it doesn't matter much. Ratios of 15:1 and higher are much less good.
- *Number of children per group.*   Regardless of how many adults there are with each group of children, the smaller the number of children cared for together—whether in one room in a day-care center or in a home—the better for the child. Thus a group of 30 children cared for by 5 adults is less good than three smaller groups of 10 children cared for by 1 adult each.
- *Amount of personal contact with caregiver.*   In general, the more time the child spends in one-to-one interaction with an adult, the better. In a day-care home or center, the amount of personal contact with an adult is an important feature.
- *Richness of verbal stimulation.*   Regardless of the variety of toys available, the complexity and variety of the language used with the child will stimulate faster language and cognitive development.
- *Space, cleanliness, and colorfulness.*   The overall physical organization of the space seems to make a difference. Children show more creative play and exploration in colorful, clean environments that are well adapted to child play. Lots of expensive toys are not critical, but there should be activities that children will find engaging, and there should be enough space for the children to move around freely.
- *Caregiver's knowledge of child development.*   Children's development is better in centers or homes in which the caregivers have specific training in human development.
- *Marital status of caregiver.*   Family day-care providers who are single (and thus responsible for all the care of the home as well as the children) spend more time in housekeeping and thus less time with the children than do married caregivers.

Sources: Anderson et al., 1981; Clarke-Stewart, 1987; Hunt, 1986; Long, Peters, Garduque, 1985; Ruopp & Travers, 1982; Smith & Spence, 1981.

The studies of school effects have been done primarily in England and the United States. Essentially, the strategy has been to search for unusually "effective" or "successful" schools, those in which the pupils consistently do better than you would predict from knowing the kinds of families or neighborhoods the pupils come from. By "better," I mean such things as higher scores on standardized tests, higher attendance rates, lower rates of disruptive classroom behavior or delinquency, a higher percentage of pupils who go on to college, or higher self-esteem in the pupils. If there are schools that consistently produce such good outcomes, then the next step is to ask how they are different in organization or functioning from schools in similar neighborhoods that have less-impressive track records.

Table 13.3

Characteristics of Unusually Effective Schools

- *Qualities of pupils.*   A *mixture* of backgrounds or abilities seems to be best, although the key appears to be to have a large enough concentration of pupils who come to school with good academic skills. Too great a concentration of children with poor skills makes it more difficult for the rest of the things on this list to occur.

- *Goals of the school.*   A strong emphasis on academic excellence, with high standards and high expectations, characterizes effective schools. These goals are clearly stated by the administration and shared by the staff.

- *Organization of classrooms.*   Classes are focused on specific academic learning. Daily activities are structured, with a high percentage of time spent in actual group instruction (as opposed to planning and organizing for instruction or in behavior management). High expectations of performance are conveyed to pupils.

- *Homework.*   Homework is assigned regularly, graded quickly. Effective schools assign markedly more homework than do less-effective schools.

- *Discipline.*   Most discipline is handled within the classroom, with relatively little fallback to "sending the child to the principal" or the like. But in really effective schools, not much class time is actually spent in discipline, because these teachers have very good control of the class. They intervene early in potentially difficult situations rather than imposing heavy discipline after the fact.

- *Praise.*   High doses of praise for good performance, for meeting expectations, are given to pupils. These are structured but warm schools.

- *Teacher experience.*   Teacher *education* is not related to effectiveness of schools, but teacher *experience* is, presumably because it takes time to learn effective class management and instruction strategies. It probably also takes specific guidance and training from experienced administrators or master teachers to help in this learning.

- *Building surroundings.*   Age or general appearance of the school building is not critical, but maintenance in good order, cleanliness, and attractiveness do appear to matter.

- *School leadership.*   Clear values, shared and regularly stated by school administrators, are a major key. The academic emphasis of the school must be apparent in all school activities, in allocation of funds, in priorities of time use.

- *Responsibilities for children.*   In effective schools, children are more likely to be given real responsibilities—in individual classrooms and in the school as a whole.

Source: Rutter, 1983.

Apparently, such effective schools really do exist (Rutter, 1983; Good & Weinstein, 1986). More important, some achieve good results consistently, year after year, so the effect is apparently not just chance variation. What are these successful schools like?

I've summarized the key characteristics of effective schools, compared to average or less-effective schools, in Table 13.3. You may be struck (as I was when I read this literature) by the similarities between the qualities

Figure 13.8 Each school has its own "climate," its own ethos. Recent research shows that the dozens of small ways in which teachers, staff, and students express the school goals and values all affect children in important ways. An authoritative school (high in control and in acceptance and responsiveness) not only increases students' academic achievement—it also affects their motivation, their attendance, and their behavior.

of effective schools and the qualities of effective parents that emerge from the discussion of parenting you just read. Effective schools sound to me a lot like *authoritative* schools rather than either permissive or authoritarian schools. These schools set clear goals and rules and have good control, good communication, and high nurturance.

Another key is that it is the school *as a whole*—the ethos or climate of the school, if you will—that seems to matter. Individual teachers are important, but the overall effect seems to be greater than the sum of individual teachers. The school climate is made up of the shared goals of the administration and staff, dedication to effective teaching, and the concrete assistance provided for such teaching. It is reflected in respect for pupils, for parents, for the building.

One moral to be drawn from this research appears to be that campaigns to improve schools by changing primarily *what* is taught, such as "back to basics" programs, may be focusing on only part of the problem. Another key seems to be *how* teaching is done and the overall climate of the school.

Television

Time spent watching television ranks right up there with school, sleeping, and play as central activities in children's days. Estimates vary, but it appears that preschoolers watch TV two to four hours per day (Anderson et al., 1986). Most researchers find that the peak amount of viewing is among children in early elementary school, with a decline in adolescence. To be sure, some of the time the child may be playing with toys or talking to Mom while the set is on. Daniel Anderson and his colleagues (1986) find this is especially true of preschool children, who actually watch the TV less than half of the time they are in the room while the set is on. Still, over the years of childhood, kids spend a *lot* of hours watching the tube.

Just what are children seeing during all of those hours? Obviously, a great many things. Some of it is specifically educational, such as "Sesame Street" or "Mister Rogers' Neighborhood." Much more of the programming, though, is "entertainment" in the form of cartoons, situation comedies, adventure programs, and the like. Most of the research (and public attention) has focused on the content of such entertainment programs, particularly the sex-role stereotypes they convey (recall Chapter 10) and the violence they portray.

Violence on TV. The inescapable fact is that TV is full of violence. For the past 15 years, George Gerbner and his colleagues have been systematically measuring the violence shown in TV programs, which they define as the "overt expression of physical force against others or self, or the compelling of action against one's will on pain of being hurt or killed" (Gerbner, 1972, p. 31). You can see the scores on their "violence index" for the period up to 1979 in Figure 13.9. More recently, Nancy Signorielli (1986) estimates that in 1985, situation comedies averaged about two incidents of violence per hour, action/adventure programs eight per hour. The rate is much higher in children's cartoons.

I want to emphasize several points about the violence children (and adults) see on TV: (1) The numbers of violent episodes I have just listed involve *physical* aggression. If verbal aggression were counted, too, the rate of aggression on TV would be many times higher. (2) The "good guys" are just as likely to be violent as the "bad guys." (3) Violence on most TV programs is rewarded; people who are violent get what they want. In fact, violence is usually portrayed as a successful way of solving problems. (4)

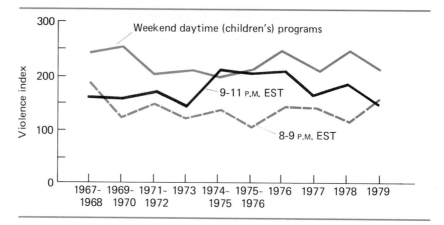

Figure 13.9 Despite major sets of Congressional hearings, and despite the findings of research, violence in children's programs and on prime-time TV is still remarkably high. The "violence index" shown here translates into about 17 episodes of violence per hour for children's weekend programs (mostly cartoons) and about 6 per hour for prime-time programs. Gerbner has not repeated these same analyses in recent years, but other evidence suggests that similar rates are still typical. (*Source:* G. Gerbner, L. Gross, M. Morgan & N. Signorielli. The "mainstreaming" of America: Violence profile No. 11. *Journal of Communication,* 1980, *30,* p. 13. Copyright 1980 by the Annenberg School of Communications.)

The consequences of violence—pain, blood, damage—are seldom shown, so the child is protected from seeing the painful and negative consequences of aggression and thus receives an unrealistic portrayal of those consequences.

The Effects of TV Violence on Children's Behavior. Just what effect does it have on a child to watch such high rates of violence? There is a *vast* amount of research and commentary on this question, not all of it of high quality. Demonstrating a *causal* connection between watching violent TV and behaving violently is extremely difficult. Children who already behave aggressively may *choose* to watch more TV, and more violent TV. And families in which TV is watched a great deal may also be more likely to use patterns of discipline that will foster aggressiveness in the child. For example, Leonard Eron (1987), in his 22-year longitudinal study of aggressiveness from age 8 to 30 (which I mentioned in Chapter 11), has found that those youngsters who watched the most violent TV programs when they were 8 were more violent at age 30 than were those who watched less-violent TV as children. Among other things, Eron found that the heavy viewers of violent TV at age 8 were more likely to be convicted of violent crimes in adulthood. This is suggestive and impressive evidence, but it does not prove a causal connection.

Some of these difficulties can be counteracted by carefully designed experiments in which children are randomly assigned to groups that are either exposed or not exposed to specific violent TV programs under controlled conditions. Typically (but not invariably), such studies show some short-term effects of the exposure to violent TV. But such experiments are, by definition, artificial. It is hard to generalize from experimental results to the real world. Because of these methodological difficulties (not unlike the problem of demonstrating a causal connection between smoking and lung cancer), some debate is still going on about the impact of TV violence on children (e.g., Friedrich-Cofer & Huston, 1986; Freedman, 1986). But as in the example of smoking and lung cancer, I think that the weight of evidence in favor of a link between violent TV and aggressive behavior is very heavy indeed. Let me summarize what I think are the basic points that emerge from this body of research.

First, children *do* learn specific aggressive actions from watching them—on TV or in real life. So children are learning about guns, knives, karate, and aggressive actions from watching TV.

Second, children who watch violent TV *are* more aggressive with their playmates than are children who watch less-violent TV (Murray, 1980). The most persuasive single piece of evidence I know of on this point is a study of a group of isolated Canadian towns by Tannis MacBeth Williams and her colleagues (Williams, 1986). One of these towns, which they call Notel, had no television reception at all at the beginning of the study. A nearby town, called Unitel by the researchers, received a single channel, while a third town, Multitel, received four channels, three of them commercial stations. A year later, Notel was receiving one channel and Unitel was receiving two. The researchers were able to observe children in all three towns in natural playground settings both one year before and one year after TV had come to Notel. In addition, they obtained both teacher and peer ratings of children's aggressiveness before and after the advent of TV. The observations of children's aggression on the playgrounds are summarized in Figure 13.10. It is clear that the levels of both physical and verbal aggression rose after Notel children began watching TV. The pattern held for both boys and girls. Furthermore, within each town the researchers found a correlation between the amount of time a child watched TV and the amount of aggression he or she showed.

The third basic point is that effects of seeing violence on TV seem to be cumulative. The more violent programs a child sees, the more aggressive he or she seems to become (Steuer, Applefield, & Smith, 1971).

Fourth, children (and adults) who watch a lot of violent TV have different attitudes about aggression. They are more likely to think that aggression is a good way to solve problems; they are likely to be more fearful and less trusting (Gerbner et al., 1981; Dominick & Greenberg, 1972); and they seem to be desensitized to the emotional impact of aggression when they do see it.

Obviously, the best way to control all these effects is to turn off the

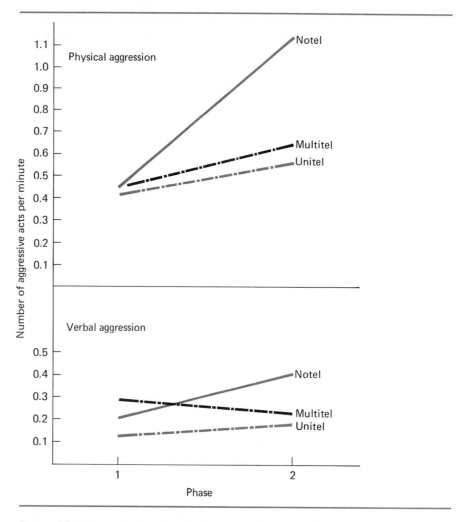

Figure 13.10 In this longitudinal study, phase 1 is the time before television came to Notel; phase 2 is one year after television came to Notel. The crucial finding is that levels of both physical and verbal aggression rose in Notel after the children began watching TV. It is also interesting, though, that in Notel, children's level of aggression before TV was about the same as what the researchers observed in neighboring towns with TV. Clearly, TV violence is not the only causal agent at work here. (*Source:* Williams, 1986, Figure 7.1, p. 320.)

violent programs on TV or (heaven forbid!) to turn off the TV altogether. Short of such a drastic step (which adults find more painful than children, by the way), there are some ways to soften the impact of the violence the children see. One way is simply to make clear your own disapproval of violence or aggression. Children from families that show such disapproval are affected less by viewing violent TV. Another possibility is to watch TV with your children and comment on some of the action, perhaps pointing out some of the consequences of violence—although this strategy suffers from the problem that children are more likely to copy what they see than what they hear. Pointing out the *unreality* of TV programs may also be useful ("It's only pretend. People aren't really like that"). Leonard Eron's work (1982) shows clearly that children who believe that TV is like real life or actually presents real life are more likely to be highly aggressive. Another thing you can do is talk to your child about the effects of watching all that violent TV. When Eron (1982) had some children write paragraphs and make speeches about the harmful effects of TV violence, he found that the aggression scores of these children declined over a four-month period, no matter how much violent TV they watched.

Nonviolent Television. I do not want to leave you with the impression that all TV is bad stuff. It is not. The important point, really, is that TV is an educational medium. Children are learning from what they watch. If they watch violent TV, they learn violence and behave more aggressively. But if they watch programs that emphasize sharing, kindness, and helpfulness, such as "Mister Rogers' Neighborhood," "Sesame Street," or even "Lassie," they show more kind and helpful behavior (Murray, 1980). If you choose to have a television set (and nearly everyone does), then I would urge you to think hard about what your children are watching and whether you want to limit or control it in some way. It seems to me that if you go to the trouble of worrying about good discipline and about good schools, it is just as important to worry about (and attempt to control) what your children learn from TV.

A FINAL POINT: SYSTEMS AND INTERPRETATIONS

If you read this chapter one section at a time, it is easy to see how each individual factor has an effect on the child's short-term and long-term development. It seems obvious that the family's discipline pattern matters, just as it seems obvious that school experience and TV are bound to exert some influence. It is a bit more of a leap to think of the parents' jobs or their social support network as important for the child, but the basic point makes sense.

What *is* difficult (for me as well as for you) is to get your mind around the idea that all these different elements interact with one another in the life of any individual child. It is not enough just to add up the different influences. It simply doesn't work that way. Nor is it enough even to search for the interactions among sets of experiences at any given moment. The really tough fact to deal with is that the experiences themselves are not the critical factor—the child's (or the adult's) *interpretation* of those experiences is what really matters. As Jerome Kagan says, "the effects of most experiences are not fixed but depend upon the child's interpretation. And the interpretation will vary with the child's cognitive maturity, expectations, beliefs, and momentary feeling state" (1984, p. 240). Since the expectations and beliefs a child or adult has—about herself, about her relationships— each have a history, that history is "read into" each new encounter. In other words, the parents and the child develop internal working models of their relationships and of the family functioning as a whole. Such models or expectancies, once formed, then have an impact on further interactions. What this means for psychologists trying to understand the effects of families and of wider experiences on children is that it will not be enough simply to observe behaviors; we must also try to measure the way in which the child and each family member *perceive* or *understand* their relationships and experiences. A tall order.

▬▬▬▬ ## SUMMARY

1. Children develop within families, and families exist within larger cultural influences. This complex of forces has a significant impact on the child's development.

2. Within the family, several dimensions of parental behavior toward children seem to be particularly significant, including the emotional tone of the family, the method of maintaining control, the patterns of communication, and the degree of cognitive enrichment provided.

3. Families that provide high levels of warmth and affection, compared to those that are more cold or rejecting, have children with more secure attachments and better peer relationships.

4. Families that set clear rules and standards, set relatively high levels of expectation or maturity demands for the child, and enforce their rules and expectations consistently appear to have children with the greatest self-esteem and the greatest competence across a broad range of situations.

5. Children who are talked to frequently, in complex sentences, and who are listened to in turn not only develop language more rapidly—they also have more positive and less-conflicted relationships with their parents.

6. Parents who provide a rich array of inanimate stimulation (including toys and opportunities for new experiences) along with responsive and contingent animate stimulation have children who show the most rapid cognitive development.

7. These elements of parental behavior can be combined into several styles of child rearing. Maccoby and Martin suggest four styles, based on high and low positions on dimensions of acceptance/rejection and degree of responsiveness (authoritarian, authoritative, permissive, and neglecting). These are similar to Baumrind's parental styles, discussed in Chapter 10 (*authoritative*—high in warmth, control, communication, and maturity demands; *authoritarian*—high in control and maturity demands but low in warmth and communication; and *permissive*—

high in warmth and communication but low in control and maturity demands). The authoritative style appears to be the most generally effective for producing confident, competent, independent, and affectionate children.

8. Parents are, in turn, influenced by a series of factors, including the child's own temperament and developmental level.

9. The structure of the family, such as the presence or absence of both parents or the presence of other adults, also affects family functioning. The majority of children born today will spend at least a portion of their childhood in one-parent families. Changes in family structure are associated with significant stress and typically with a reduction in authoritative child-rearing patterns.

10. The overall level of poverty or affluence of the family also affects the family interaction, by affecting health and health care, diet, discipline patterns, and levels of stress and support.

11. Short-term stresses or life changes also affect the ways parents interact with their children. For example, immediately following divorce (or other major upheavals), parents show lower levels of control, lower maturity demands, less warmth, and poorer communication with their children.

12. The parents' work situation also affects family functioning. Girls whose mothers work typically show more positive outcomes; for boys the effects are more mixed. The quality of the father's job may also affect his values and his flexibility in family functioning.

13. The effects of poverty and of changes in family structure or other short-term stresses are mitigated by the presence of adequate social support for the parent or parents. Supporting each other is important, but having other sources of emotional and material support from family and friends is also critical.

14. Children are also influenced directly by other institutions, such as day care, schools, and television.

15. Day care is associated with improved intellectual functioning for some poverty-level children. Possible negative effects highlighted by recent research include higher rates of avoidant attachment and perhaps heightened aggressiveness or apathy, depending on the specific quality of the care received and the quality of the child's interaction with the parents at home.

16. "Effective" schools have many of the same qualities as authoritative parents: they have clear and shared goals, including an emphasis on academic achievement; they have high levels of control without invoking heavy punishment; they are warm; and they have excellent communication, both among staff and between staff and students.

17. Children spend almost as much time watching television as they do in school. They learn significant new behaviors or skills from TV, particularly adult roles. They also learn and display higher rates of violent or aggressive behavior. The effect appears to be cumulative and to touch children's attitudes about aggression as well as their behavior.

████████ KEY TERMS

restrictiveness A particular pattern of parental control involving limitation of the child's movements or options, such as by the use of playpens or harnesses with a young child or strict rules about play areas or free choices with an older child.

social class Broad categories in economic and social positions within society. Four groups are most often described: upper class, middle class, working class, and lower class (also called poverty level). The designation for an individual family is based on the occupations and education of the adults in the household.

social support The emotional, material, and informational assistance available to any one individual from family and friends in times of need.

warmth versus hostility The key dimension of emotional tone used to describe family interactions.

████████ SUGGESTED READING

Bronfenbrenner, U. (1979). *The ecology of human development.* Cambridge, MA: Harvard University Press.
This book is sometimes tough sledding, but it is worth the effort. Bronfenbrenner has gone further than anyone in describing the many forces that affect the child's development and how those forces may connect to one another.

Maccoby, E. E. (1980). *Social development. Psychological growth and the parent-child relationship.* New York: Harcourt Brace Jovanovich.
Chapter 10, on child-rearing practices, is particularly clear and useful as an expansion on what I have said in this chapter. (In fact, you will easily detect Maccoby's influence on my own thinking.)

Meredith, D. (1986, February). The nine-to-five dilemma. *Psychology Today,* pp. 36–44.
A nice current paper on day care: the difficulties of finding good options and the results of research on the various types of care.

Meyerhoff, M. K., & White, B. L. (1986, September). Parenting. Making the grade as parents. *Psychology Today,* pp. 38–45.
A very readable article with a nice checklist of things to do and things not to do in rearing children.

Patterson, G. R. (1975). *Families. Applications of social learning to family life.* Champaign, IL: Research Press.
Once again I suggest this book, particularly for those among you who are already parents and who may feel the need for very concrete guidance on how to establish clear and consistent control with your children.

████████

PROJECT: TELEVISION AGGRESSION

As I suggested earlier, you may want to combine this project with the one at the end of Chapter 10, which involved observing sex-role presentations on TV. If so, you or your instructor may wish to modify the following instructions somewhat. But if you are doing this project by itself, proceed as follows.

Using the definition of violence offered by George Gerbner ("overt expression of physical force against others or self, or the compelling of action against one's will on pain of being hurt or killed"), select a minimum of four half-hour television programs normally watched by children and count the number of aggressive or violent episodes in each. Extend Gerbner's definition somewhat, however, to count verbal aggression as well as physical aggression.

You may select any four (or more) programs, but I would strongly recommend that you distribute them in the following way:

1. At least one "educational" television program, such as "Sesame Street" or "Mister Rogers' Neighborhood."
2. At least one Saturday morning cartoon. I haven't watched these in a while, so I can't point you to particularly grisly examples. Select at random.
3. At least one early evening adult program that is watched by young children: a family comedy, a Western, a crime film, or one of each.

For each program that you watch, record the number of violent episodes, counting the instances of verbal and physical violence separately.

In thinking or writing about the details of your observations, consider the following questions:

1. How much variation is there in the number of violent episodes in the programs that you watched?
2. Are some programs more verbally aggressive, some more physically aggressive?
3. Do the numbers of violent episodes per program correspond to the numbers found by Gerbner?
4. What about the consequences of aggression? Are those characters who act violently rewarded or punished? How often do reward and punishment occur?
5. What behaviors other than aggression might a child have learned from watching the programs you viewed? (This question is particularly relevant for "Sesame Street" or "Mister Rogers' Neighborhood," but it applies to more traditional entertainment programs as well.)
6. In view of the material in this chapter and your own observations for this project, what rules or limits (if any) would you place on TV viewing for your own child? Why?

14 Atypical Development

Frequency of Problems
Mentally Atypical Development
   The Mentally Retarded
   Children with Learning Disabilities
   The Gifted Child
Emotionally Atypical Development
   Attention-Deficit Hyperactivity Disorder
   Conduct Disorders
   Depression and Anxiety
   The Role of Short-term Stress in Behavior Problems
Vulnerable and Invulnerable Children
   Severe Emotional Disturbances
Physically Atypical Development
   The Deaf and Hearing-Impaired
   The Blind Child
Basic Attachments Between Blind Babies and Their Mothers
   Other Physical Problems
Sex Differences in Atypical Development
The Impact of an Atypical Child on the Family
Interventions and Treatments
   Treatment for the Child, Training for the Parents
   Interventions in the Public Schools: Mainstreaming Versus Special
     Classes
   Residential Treatment
A Final Point
Summary
Key Terms
Suggested Reading

Nine-year-old Archie seemed "different from other children even when he started school." Often he was "disoriented" or "distractible." Although he scored in the normal range on an IQ test, he had great difficulty learning to read. Even after several years of special tutoring, he could read only by sounding out the words each time; he didn't recognize even familiar words by sight (Cole & Traupmann, 1981).

Tommy, who is 4 years old, seems to be bright but is fearful and inhibited. He is both imperious and anxiously compliant with the other children. His nursery-school teacher is worried about him (Solnit & Provence, 1979).

Vicki is 11. "She absolutely loves to roller-skate, and like any other 11-year-old, she squeals with delight when she's careening down the sidewalk. . . . But Vicki doesn't speak . . . sucks her thumb . . . and has a great deal of trouble making eye contact with others" (*San Francisco Chronicle*, August 21, 1979).

When Jeffrey was 4, he couldn't walk or talk and spent most of his time in a crib. His parents fed him pureed baby food through a bottle. After six years with a loving foster family, at age 10 Jeffrey is now in a special class in a regular elementary school and is learning to print and read.

Each of these children is atypical in some way. In each, the developmental processes I have been describing in the past 13 chapters didn't quite work in the normal way. Archie has some kind of learning disability. Tommy shows some mild or moderate form of emotional disturbance, often called a behavior problem. Vicki has a much more serious type of disorder, usually called autism. Jeffrey is a Down's syndrome child and is mentally retarded.

I have touched on some subgroups of atypically developing children, such as deaf children and those with serious eating disorders, in earlier chapters. But in this chapter, I want to try to give you some sense of the range of problems that can occur, the causes of the problems, and the sorts of treatments that are used. The topic is enormous, so I will of necessity be giving you breadth rather than depth. Still, I can alert you to some of the difficult issues and questions still facing us in understanding the reasons for atypical development and in designing successful treatments.

Before exploring this long litany of problems, it is important to emphasize one critical fact: children whose development is atypical in some respect are much more *like* normally developing children in other respects than they are unlike them. Blind and deaf and retarded children all form attachments in much the same way that physically and mentally normal children do; children with conduct disorders go through the same sequences of cognitive development that more adjusted children show. So the fact that a child is different in one way should not blind us to the fact that he is probably quite typical in many other ways.

FREQUENCY OF PROBLEMS

How common are the various types of atypical development? Given the critical practical relevance of this question, you'd think that psychologists and epidemiologists would long ago have come to some agreement. But we haven't, partly because of persisting disagreements about definitions, but, more important, because the line between typical and atypical is very much a matter of degree. *Most* children show at least some kinds of "problem behavior" at one time or another. For example, parents report that among

Table 14.1

▬▬▬▬▬▬▬

Estimated Incidence of Various Types of Atypical Development in the United States

Type of problem	Percentage of children age 0–18 affected
Problems with language or cognition	
IQ below 70 (mental retardation)	3.0
Speech and language problems, including delayed language, articulation problems, and stuttering	3.5
Serious learning disability (estimate varies depending on definition used)	2–8
Problems in relating to others or to society	
Attention deficit disorder	2.0
Conduct disorders (e.g., antisocial behavior, high levels of aggression)	4 to 8
Arrested by police	3.0
Anxiety and fear	2.5
Mild depression or "the blues"	
Elementary-school age	10.0
Adolescents	30–40
Depression at serious or severe level	
Elementary-school age	0.15
Adolescence (low estimate)	1.5
Autism and other severe disorders	1.0
Physical problems	
Significant hearing impairment	0.5
All other problems, including blindness, cerebral palsy, epilepsy	0.2

Sources: Achenbach, 1982; Farnham-Diggory, 1986; Gallagher, 1985; Graham, 1979; Hobbs, 1975; Rutter & Garmezy, 1983.

7-year-olds, 10 to 20 percent still wet their beds at least occasionally, 30 percent have nightmares, 20 percent bite their fingernails, 10 percent suck their thumbs, and 10 percent swear enough for it to be considered a problem. Another 30 percent or so have temper tantrums (Achenbach & Edelbrock, 1981). Problems like these are so common, in fact, that many of them—especially if they last only a short time—should be considered part of "normal" development.

Usually we label a child's development atypical or deviant only if a problem persists over a long period of time or if the child's behavior is at the extreme end of the continuum. More extreme or persisting problems are less common. Table 14.1 (page 511) gives some recent guesses about their frequency. I've taken these estimates from several different sources, and there is considerable overlap in the categories. For example, many children with serious learning disabilities also show an attention deficit disorder or conduct disorders. Still, even if we allow for some overlap, the numbers are astonishing. Something like 15 to 20 percent of all the children in the United States show at least one form of atypical development. At least one in six, and probably as many as one in five, will require some form of special help in school or in a child guidance clinic or the equivalent. When you think of these figures in terms of the demands this places on the school system and on other social agencies, the prospect is staggering.

For society as a whole, and for the several helping professions in particular, at least three tasks are involved in coping with these large numbers of children in need. First, we have to understand the nature and origins of the problems we are facing. Second, we need to develop effective intervention programs. And third, we need to consider the possibility of prevention. Can any of these disorders be avoided if we provide proper prenatal care to mothers or special programs for children and families in early infancy? Most of what I'll say in this chapter speaks to the first of these tasks (description and understanding), but I will talk a bit about possible treatments and prevention.

MENTALLY ATYPICAL DEVELOPMENT

The Mentally Retarded

Of all the problems listed in Table 14.1, probably mental retardation has been studied most thoroughly. Not too many decades ago, when mental ability was thought of as a fixed trait, mental subnormality was considered a kind of incurable disease. Labels like "idiot" or "feeble-minded" were used. But this older view has changed a great deal. Not only have the old negative labels been changed, but the basic assumptions about the nature of retardation have changed, too.

Mental retardation is now (correctly, I think) viewed as a *symptom* rather than as a disease. And like any symptom, it can change. A child's life circumstances or her health may change, and her IQ score may go up or down at the same time. Remember from Chapter 6 that *many* children's IQ test scores vary as much as 30 or 40 points over the childhood years. Of course, many children with low IQ scores will continue to function at a low level throughout life. But it is important for educators and parents to understand that a single low IQ score need not invariably mean that the child will function at that level forever. For many children, improvement is possible.

The Assessment of Retardation.   A child is normally designated as **mentally retarded** if he tests below an IQ of 70 *and* has significant problems in **adaptive behavior**—such as an inability to dress or eat alone or a problem getting along with others or adjusting to the demands of a regular school classroom. As Thomas Achenbach says, "children doing well in school are unlikely to be considered retarded no matter what their IQ scores" (1982, p. 214).

Labels.   Low IQ scores are customarily divided up into several ranges, with different labels attached to each, as you can see in Table 14.2. I've given both the labels used by psychologists and those that may be more common in the school system. (There are no school system labels for children with IQs below about 35, since schools very rarely deal with children functioning at this level.)

The farther down the IQ scale you go, the fewer children there are. Seventy or eighty percent of all children with IQs below 70 are in the "mildly retarded" range; only about two percent of the low IQ-youngsters (perhaps 3500 children in the United States) are profoundly retarded.

Cognitive Functioning in Retarded Children.   In recent years there has been a great deal of fascinating research on thinking and information processing in retarded children, much of it by Joseph Campione and

Table 14.2

IQ Scores and Labels for Children Classified as Retarded

Approximate IQ score range	Label used by psychologists	Label used in schools
68–83	Borderline retarded	(No special label)
52–67	Mildly retarded	Educable mentally retarded (EMR)
36–51	Moderately retarded	Trainable mentally retarded
19–35	Severely retarded	(No special label)
Below 19	Profoundly retarded	(No special label)

Ann Brown (Campione, Brown, & Ferrara, 1982). As you may recall from Chapter 7, this research has been a significant ingredient in the emerging information-processing approach to studying cognitive development in children.

Campione and Brown find that retarded children

1. Think and react more slowly.
2. Require much more complete and repeated instruction to learn new information or a new strategy compared to normal-IQ children (who may discover a strategy for themselves or profit from incomplete instruction).
3. Do not generalize or transfer something they have learned in one situation to a new problem or task. They thus appear to lack those "executive" functions that enable older or higher-IQ children (or adults) to compare a new problem to familiar ones or to scan through a repertoire of strategies until they find one that works.

On simple tasks, retarded children learn in ways and at rates that are similar to younger normal-IQ children. The more significant deficit lies in higher-order processing. These children *can* learn, but they do so more slowly and they require far more exhaustive and task-specific instruction.

What are the causes of low IQ scores or inefficient information processing? Conventionally, the causes are divided into two broad categories: *physical causes* and *cultural-familial causes* (also called *sociocultural causes.*)

Physical Causes of Retardation.   About 25 percent of mental retardation (including nearly all the cases of profound and severe retardation) has an identifiable physical origin, including brain damage and several kinds of inherited disorders.

Chromosomal anomalies, such as Down's syndrome and the fragile-X syndrome, are typically (but not invariably) accompanied by mild or moderate retardation. As Scarr and Kidd (1983) put it, "having too much or too little chromatin [genetic material] will affect intelligence, always for the worse" (p. 380). A child may also inherit a specific disease or **inborn error of metabolism** that can cause retardation if not treated. The best-known such inherited metabolic disorder is phenylketonuria (PKU), which was discussed in Chapter 2.

Still a third physical cause of retardation is **brain damage.** You'll recall from Chapter 2 that several prenatal influences may have such effects, including disease (e.g., cytomegalovirus), malnutrition, and alcoholism. Brain damage may also occur during delivery or because of some accident after birth (e.g., an auto accident or falling out of a tree house onto one's head).

Before you get discouraged at this long list of rather awful things that can cause retardation, you should remember that a great many of

Figure 14.1 Programs like the Special Olympics, in which Mark was participating when these pictures were taken, have helped to enrich the lives of children with Down's syndrome and other retarded children.

the things I've mentioned here are preventable. Some genetic disorders can be diagnosed in utero using amniocentesis; others, like PKU, can be treated effectively if diagnosed early; and many maternal diseases can be prevented by immunization. Good *preventive* health care, then, helps to reduce the number of children with physically caused mental retardation.

Cultural-Familial Causes of Retardation.

The remaining 75 percent of retarded children show no signs of any brain damage or other physical disorder. In almost all cases, such children come from families in which the parents have low IQs or where there is serious family disorganization, mental illness in the parents, or emotional or cognitive deprivation in the home. Often both genetic and environmental influences operate simultaneously.

As I pointed out in Chapter 6, psychologists are still arguing about the extent to which heredity influences a child's measured IQ. But nearly all agree that there is at least *some* effect. So it is reasonable to assume that many children who score below 70 on an IQ test start out life with several strikes against them.

But genetic endowment is clearly not the only ingredient in this soup. When children from families like the ones I have just described are placed from early infancy in special enrichment programs, their IQs can be significantly increased, as I described in Chapter 6. We also know that many children with some physical disorder at birth, such as low birth weight or cytomegalovirus, turn out to have normal IQs when they are reared in enriched or supportive environments (Haskins, 1986).

Research like this shows us the power of the environment in causing (or preventing) retardation in some children. It also seems to point the way to a solution. But before you leap to the conclusion that we should immediately begin intervention programs like this for all children who are likely to function at a retarded level, I have to caution you.

First, we know amazingly little about the specific kinds of experiences that a child has to have in order to develop cognitive skills at the normal rate. I can give you a *general* prescription: enough toys and materials for exploration, warm and responsive (and talkative) adults, and (within limits) a nonrestrictive and nonpunitive environment. But it is another matter to turn this general statement into specific programs for children.

Second, enrichment programs such as Ramey's (described in Figure 6.11) may not work nearly so well for children with chromosomal anomalies or brain damage as it does for children with a heightened cultural-familial risk for retardation. This is not to say that we should ignore environmental enrichment or specific early training for children with physically caused retardation. Greater breadth of experience will enrich their lives and may improve their functioning. But even massive early interventions are not likely to make most brain-damaged or genetically anomalous children intellectually normal, although they may foster a level of functioning closer to the child's intellectual limits and permit him or her to function much more independently (Spitz, 1986).

Third, interventions of the type Ramey and others have used are *expensive*. Obviously, if we knew more precisely just what kinds of experiences a particular child needs for optimal growth, we could "aim" our programs more narrowly and they would probably cost far less. In the meantime, we use a sort of "shotgun" approach, doing everything we think might help; and that costs money. In the long run, I think that such an investment would pay off handsomely, both for the child's happiness and for society. The cost to society over the lifetime of an individual child would be far less if he grows up to be a well-functioning, capable adult than if he emerges as a borderline retardate requiring public assistance. But even if we were sure that early interventions could have large and persisting effects (and as yet we are not), it is not at all clear to me that as a society we are prepared to pay the very high initial cost of intervening. It is even less clear to me that we have agreed that we have some shared responsibility to do so.

Children with Learning Disabilities

Some children with normal IQs and essentially good adaptive functioning nonetheless have difficulty learning to read or write or do arithmetic. There are a lot of labels for children with this kind of problem. The ones you are likely to encounter in a school include *learning disability* (LD) and **specific learning disability (SLD).** In theory, the SLD label is applied only if the child's problem is confined to a fairly narrow range of tasks, but in fact, the SLD label is used more broadly than that. Another broadly used label is **dyslexia.** This term, too, is used inaccurately to refer to almost any kind of problem with reading, writing, or arithmetic.

The most common form of learning disorder is difficulty learning to read. Many children with this problem also have difficulty with spelling, as you can see from Figure 14.2. As I indicated in Table 14.1, somewhere between 2 and 8 percent of children have *serious* problems of this kind. Another 14 to 15 percent have more moderate difficulty. Common as reading difficulty is, we are still a long way from understanding it fully or treating it effectively.

Problems of Definition.   One of the difficulties, as you will have guessed from the wide range of estimates of incidence, is that there is still major disagreement among researchers and clinicians about just how to define and identify learning disabilities. The definition problem has been seriously confounded by the fact that school districts receive federal funds to pay for special education for children identified as learning-disabled but do *not* receive such funds for education of children labeled as "slow learners." Thus, there is a strong financial incentive to call almost any kind of delayed or slow learning a learning disability.

Furthermore, even setting aside this political consideration, the designation of a learning disability is basically a *residual* diagnosis. It is the label we apply to a child who does *not* learn some school task, who is generally *not* retarded, and who does *not* show emotional disturbance or a hearing or vision problem. Thus, we can say what learning disability is *not;* what we cannot say is what it *is*.

The identification problem is complicated still further by the fact that

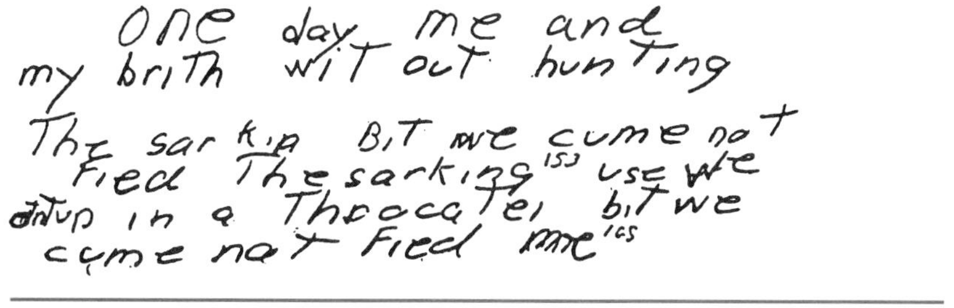

Figure 14.2 This is part of a story written by 13-year-old Luke, who has a significant persisting learning disability. It translates as follows: "One day me and my brother went out hunting the Sark. But we could not find the Sark. So we went up in a helicopter but we could not find him." There are also little numbers next to some of the words. Luke was supposed to write a 200-word story, so he is keeping track. You can imagine that a child with this degree of difficulty would have serious problems with almost any form of employment. (*Source:* Farnham-Diggory, 1978, p. 61.)

among children identified as LD, the specific form of the problem varies widely. Some display difficulties only in reading, some have trouble with reading and spelling, and others have more difficulty with arithmetic. Given such variability, we shouldn't be surprised that the search for causes has been fraught with difficulties. As Sylvia Farnham-Diggory says, "we are trying to find out what's wrong with children whom we won't be able to accurately identify until after we know what's wrong with them" (1986, p. 153).

Possible Causes. The most common explanation of specific learning disability has been that the child suffers from some kind of "minimal brain damage." Such children rarely exhibit any outward signs of brain damage, but perhaps there is some lesser damage, undetected by normal neurological tests, which nonetheless shows itself when the child is faced with a complex task like learning to read.

This hypothesis avoids the stigma of mental retardation and makes it clear that no one is at fault for the child's problem. But you should understand that this is a *hypothesis* and not a fact. Most children with specific learning disabilities do *not* show any signs of brain damage on any standard tests.

A weaker version of this hypothesis is that such children suffer not from brain *damage* but from brain *dysfunction*—that is, that their brains simply do not work in quite the same way as do normal children's. One theory is that the right and left hemispheres of LD children's brains do not participate in various kinds of cognitive processing in the usual way. Another theory is that parts of the LD child's brain may simply mature more slowly, thus giving a kind of unevenness of skill (Brumback & Staton, 1983). But the evidence for both of these theories is weak, at best (Obrzut, Hynd, & Boliek, 1986).

Another possibility, as you may recall from the discussion of reading in Chapter 8, is that reading disability reflects a more general problem with language. There is now abundant evidence that children with reading problems are likely to have one or both of two kinds of language problems: (1) a relative lack of awareness of the individual sounds in words, and (2) a relative lack of knowledge of the semantic and grammatical structure of language (e.g., Vellutino & Scanlon, 1987; Bohannon, Warren-Leubecker, & Hepler, 1984). Furthermore, researchers have shown that if poor readers are trained in hearing individual sounds, their reading skills improve. Of course, findings like these do not tell us why a child might have such language deficits in the first place; they only tell us that this is a common attribute of children with learning disabilities.

I want to emphasize that this confusion and disagreement about how to identify and explain learning disability persists despite thousands of research studies and a great deal of theorizing by thoughtful and capable people. Not surprisingly, the uncertainty at the theoretical level is reflected in confusion at the practical level. Children are labeled "learning-disabled" and assigned to special classes, but whether a child will be helped by a particular type of intervention program will depend on whether that specific program is any good and whether it happens to match his or her type of disability. Remediation does seem to be possible, but it is *not* simple, and a program that works well for one child may not work at all for another. Of course, this is not good news for parents whose child may be having difficulty with some aspect of schooling; their only recourse is trial and error and eternal vigilance. But it reflects the disordered state of our knowledge.

The Gifted Child

The problem for parents of children at the other end of the intellectual continuum, the gifted, is almost as tough. Finding good programs for such children is a continuing dilemma. Let me give you an extreme example—a child named Michael, described by Halbert Robinson:

> When Michael was 2 years and 3 months old, the family visited our laboratory. At that time, they described a youngster who had begun speaking at age 5 months and by 6 months had exhibited a vocabulary of more than 50 words. He started to read English when he was 13 months old. In our laboratory he spoke five languages and could read in three of them. He understood addition, subtraction, multiplication, division, and square root, and he was fascinated by a broad range of scientific constructs. He loved to make puns, frequently bilingual ones. (Robinson, 1981, p. 63)

Michael's IQ on the Stanford-Binet was in excess of 180 at age 2; two years later, at $4\frac{1}{2}$, he performed on the test like a 12-year-old and was listed as having an IQ beyond 220.

Definitions. We can certainly all agree that Michael is astonishingly gifted. The term *gifted*, though, is used in almost as many ways as the phrase *learning-disabled* (Sternberg & Davidson, 1986). **Giftedness** includes exceptional specific talents, such as musical or artistic skills or specific mathematical or spatial ability, as well as very high IQ. This broadening of the definition of giftedness has gained support in recent years, so that now I think there is agreement that giftedness is not a single thing; there are many kinds of exceptional ability, each of which may reflect unusual speed or efficiency with one or another type of cognitive function. Within school systems, however, by far the most common definition of giftedness is based on IQ test scores. Robinson suggests that it may be useful to divide high-IQ children into two sets: the "garden-variety gifted," with high IQs (perhaps 130 to 150) but without extraordinary ability in any one area, and the "highly gifted" (like Michael) with extremely high IQ scores and/or remarkable skill in one or more areas. These two groups of children may have quite different experiences, at home and in school.

Characteristics of Gifted Children.   Whereas retarded children show slower and less-efficient information processing, the gifted show extremely rapid and flexible strategies. They learn quickly and transfer that learning broadly (Sternberg & Davidson, 1985). Furthermore, they seem to have unusually good *metacognitive* skills: they know what they know (and do not know) and make good use of cognitive plans (Jackson & Butterfield, 1986).

Whether such advanced intellectual abilities transfer to *social* situations is not so well established. Many parents are concerned about placing their gifted child in a higher grade in school, for example, because of fears that the child will not be able to cope socially; others have assumed that rapid development in one area should be linked to rapid development in all areas.

One famous and remarkable early study of gifted children, by Lewis Terman, pointed to the latter conclusion. Terman selected about 1500 high-IQ children from California schools in the 1920s. These children—now adults in their sixties, seventies, and even eighties—have been followed regularly throughout their lives (Terman, 1925; Terman & Oden, 1947, 1959; Sears & Barbee, 1977; Sears, 1977). Terman found that the gifted children he studied were better-off than their less-gifted classmates in many ways besides school performance. They were healthier; they were interested in many things, such as hobbies and games; and they were successful in later life. Both the boys and the girls in this study went on to complete many more years of education than was typical of children of their era, and they had successful careers as adults.

More recent research has painted a somewhat less uniformly rosy picture, but the weight of the evidence supports the assumption that the gifted are at least as well-off socially as are less-bright children. Their self-esteem is as high (or higher), and they are not more likely to show depression or other disturbances. Some do see themselves as less popular, but this is not always found (e.g., Brody & Benbow, 1986). Furthermore, such positive social development seems to be just as likely for gifted children who have been accelerated through school as for those who have been in "enrichment" programs (Janos & Robinson, 1985; Robinson & Janos, 1986).

Such optimism about the social robustness of gifted children may have to be tempered somewhat, however, in the case of the "highly gifted" subgroup, such as those with IQs above 180. These children are *so* different from their peers that they are likely to be seen as strange or disturbing. And these highly gifted children show higher rates of emotional problems than do nongifted children (Janos & Robinson, 1985).

Families of Gifted Children.   Children with very high IQs are far more likely to come from middle-class or otherwise advantaged families than from working-class or poor families (Terman found this, and so have more recent researchers [Freeman, 1981; Robinson, 1981]). Doubtless there is some genetic influence at work here: very bright parents are not only more likely to have very bright children—they are also likely to be well educated and financially well-off. But the environmental enrichment provided to the child is also an important ingredient in gifted performance. Joan Freeman (1981) suggests that what we call giftedness is most often a product of "good genes" *and* a stimulating environment. Even if "good genes" are equally distributed across social class groups, environmental enrichment is not, so a bright child in a middle-class family is more likely to receive that extra boost of stimulation that turns "bright" into "gifted." But there is little evidence from the research on the families of gifted children to show that these mothers and fathers are "pushing" their children. In fact, the parents nearly always express surprise at their children's remarkable achievements (Robinson, 1981).

EMOTIONALLY ATYPICAL DEVELOPMENT

Problems in relating to others and in the child's emotional state can range from relatively minor (and basically normal) brief depressions or fears to broader or more lasting patterns of disturbed behavior (usually called **behavior problems**) such as hyperactivity or excessive aggression, to still more severe problems that affect all the child's encounters and make normal relationships virtually impossible.

Before I go further, I need to say a word or two about labels and classifications of such problems. There are almost as many ways of classifying emotionally atypical development as there are psychologists, but most government and clinical agencies now use the classification system provided by the American Psychiatric Association's *Diagnostic and Statistical Manual of Mental Disorders* (**DSM-III-R**). I've listed the broad categories of disorders from DSM-III-R in Table 14.3, and I will roughly follow this category system in this section of the chapter. But since many of the labels and terms that parents hear from teachers or other professionals do not match the DSM-III-R designations, I will try to give you the everyday words as well.

Attention-Deficit Hyperactivity Disorder

The first listing in Table 14.3, **attention-deficit hyperactivity disorder,** is the label used in DSM-III-R for a behavior pattern more commonly called simply **hyperactivity.** Children diagnosed as having this disorder are typically restless, impulsive, distractible, and overactive, with a short attention span. They have difficulty concentrating on any one activity or any one task for very long. They may have a hard time staying seated for long, don't listen well, and are "on the go" all the time. Parents and teachers frequently describe them as "off the wall."

The diagnosis of hyperactivity has become a favorite one in the United States—something of a catchall to describe children who may be aggressive, who act up to receive attention, or who are simply more energetic than a

Table 14.3

Major Diagnostic Categories of Emotional Disorders in Children and Adolescents

- *Attention-deficit hyperactivity disorder.*   Hyperactivity; problems of attention without hyperactivity.
- *Conduct disorders.*   "Undersocialization" in children who may or may not also show aggression. Excessive aggressiveness and juvenile delinquency are typically classified in this group.
- *Anxiety disorders.*   Serious separation anxiety and any other form of excessive anxiety.
- *Eating disorders.*   Anorexia nervosa, bulimia, and other patterns of atypical eating.
- *Pervasive developmental disorders.*   Infantile autism, childhood-onset pervasive developmental disorder, and all learning disabilities.

Sources: After the American Psychiatric Association, 1987.

particular parent or teacher can tolerate. But when these broad definitions are eliminated, there is still a core group of perhaps 1 to 3 percent of children who show consistently high levels of restlessness and difficulty with concentrating (Trites & Laprade, 1983).

Children who are diagnosed as hyperactive typically have low school achievement, even in adolescence (when the behavioral signs of hyperactivity have waned somewhat). Many children diagnosed as hyperactive in childhood "recover" from this problem and lead relatively normal adult lives, but as a group, these youngsters are likely to show greater impulsive behavior, perhaps more drug use, and perhaps poorer social skills as adults (Hechtman & Weiss, 1983). Poor outcomes are especially likely for children who are *both* hyperactive and aggressive.

Attempts to figure out the origins of hyperactivity and to design effective treatment have been extensive. I am sorry to say, though, that the results are inconclusive (Achenbach, 1982). Hyperactivity appears *not* to be the result of any general brain damage, since most brain-damaged children are not hyperactive and most hyperactive children (like learning-disabled children) show no overt signs of brain damage. There *may* be other neurological or physical causes, however, such as neurotransmitter deficiencies, habitually low levels of arousal (which the child overcomes with high levels of activity), or even food sensitivities or allergies. No one of these possibilities has been strongly supported by research, however. In particular, the hypothesis that sensitivities to artificial food dyes might be the cause—a proposal strongly advanced by Dr. Ben Feingold (1975)—has *not* been supported by controlled experiments (Harley et al., 1978).

Results of treatment studies are equally mixed. By far the most common treatment for hyperactive children is medication with a *stimulant* drug, most often Ritalin. Such medication does reduce hyperactive behavior and improve concentration in the short run, but it does not affect the hyperactive child's typically poor academic performance over the long run, nor does it improve the social relationships of hyperactive children with their classmates. In addition, not all children respond well to the drug treatment, and there may be undesirable physical side effects, such as insomnia, weight loss, or increased heart rate or blood pressure (Achenbach, 1982; Quay & Werry, 1979). Behavior modification programs in classrooms, aimed at reinforcing more controlled and attentive behaviors, have also been moderately successful, but the child's behavior change does not typically generalize to other settings (Achenbach, 1982). Thus the underlying problem remains. No doubt children who show this behavior will continue to be given medication, if only because it makes them much easier to live with. In the meantime, the long-term task for researchers is to uncover the causes of hyperactivity so that more effective treatments can be found.

Conduct Disorders

This second group of problems in Table 14.3 includes primarily *antisocial* behavior of one kind or another, particularly excessive aggressiveness and juvenile delinquency. Children described as aggressive are argumentative, bullying, disobedient, irritable, threatening, and loud. They may throw temper tantrums or physically or verbally attack others (Achenbach & Edelbrock, 1982). Those labeled as delinquent show all these patterns, but in addition, the definition of delinquency usually involves some deliberate violation of the law.

Many antisocial or delinquent behaviors—such as fighting, threatening others, cheating, lying, or stealing—are just as common in 4- and 5-yearolds as they are in adolescence (Achenbach & Edelbrock, 1981). In adolescence, however, these behaviors often become more serious, more lethal, more consistent a pattern. At every age, more boys show this pattern than girls.

Among younger children, aggressive conduct disorders are linked to a number of family conditions, including poverty and high levels of family stress or life change. Such antisocial behavior is also more common among children with significant learning problems or with hyperactivity—though what is cause and what is effect in such a linkage is simply not clear.

Many children who show such behaviors in preschool or elementary school do not become delinquent in adolescence. But conduct disorders do tend to persist. (For example, recall that in Chapter 11, I mentioned a long-term longitudinal study by Leonard Eron [1987], who found that highly aggressive boys are more likely to show a variety of antisocial or damaging aggressive behaviors as adults.) Those who do continue such behaviors are most often those who showed the earliest and most varied forms of troublemaking (Kelso & Stewart, 1985).

Among those who become delinquent, psychologists have found two distinct subgroups: (1) *socialized-subcultural delinquents,* who hang around with bad companions, stay out late, have a strong allegiance to their peer group or gang, and may commit various crimes as part of their peer activities; and (2) *unsocialized psychopathic delinquents,* who are more often loners and who seem to lack conscience or guilt. These are young people who appear to enjoy conflict and who appear to have little trust in anyone.

These two groups of delinquents seem to come from different backgrounds, although there are some common elements. Socialized delinquents most often come from poor families living in poor neighborhoods. In the families themselves, there is erratic discipline and little affection, and the parents themselves are often criminals (Achenbach, 1982; Moore, Pauker, & Moore, 1984). In the same kinds of poor neighborhoods, families whose children do *not* become delinquent are distinguished most by a single ingredient: high levels of maternal love. Young people whose mothers are loving and affectionate toward them are simply far less likely to show delinquency (Glueck & Glueck, 1972; McCord, McCord, & Zola, 1959), regardless of poverty conditions.

Psychopathic delinquency, in contrast, is characterized by high rates of a variety of different types of criminal acts, often beginning quite early in childhood. Unlike the socialized delinquent pattern, psychopathic delinquency can be found about equally in teenagers from every social class level. Furthermore, while socialized delinquency occurs more frequently in broken homes, this is not true of psychopathic delinquency. The best predictors of this pattern are early and high rates of delinquent behavior and a pattern of equivalent antisocial or criminal behavior by the child's father (Achenbach, 1982).

Depression and Anxiety

A third pattern of disturbed behavior that frequently results in a child's being seen by a psychologist or mental health clinic is some combination of depression, fearfulness, or anxiety. Such feelings are quite common in young children, but they become much more prominent in adolescence. Both Thomas Achenbach and Michael Rutter, in separate large studies, have found that approximately 10 percent of preadolescent children are described by parents or teachers as appearing miserable, unhappy, sad, or depressed (Achenbach & Edelbrock, 1981; Rutter, Tizard, & Whitmore, 1970/1981). Rutter finds, though, that this rises to perhaps 40 percent among teenagers. When teenagers themselves are asked about their state of mind, perhaps a fifth describe moderate to severe levels of depression (Siegel & Griffin, 1984; Gibbs, 1985). Interestingly, among preadolescents, males are slightly more likely to be described as unhappy or depressed; among teenagers (as among adults), females more often report high or chronic levels of depression (e.g., Baron & Perron, 1986; Petersen, Ebata, & Sarigiani, 1987).

Teenagers and preadolescents who describe themselves as depressed do not invariably display all the symptoms of a full-blown clinical depression as seen in adulthood (which includes loss of appetite, sleep disturbances, feelings of worthlessness, loss of energy, loss of pleasure in daily activities, and a lack of ability to think or concentrate). However, depressed youngsters do show significant hormonal and other endocrine changes during their depressed episodes, so we know that depression in children is a real and potentially serious clinical state, not just a "normal" or transitory unhappiness (Puig-Antich, 1983).

There is not a great deal of information about the backgrounds of children who show marked sadness or depression. But it appears that such children tend to have parents who are similarly withdrawn and anxious. Usually at least one of the parents shows a consistently disturbed pattern. There are also hints from several studies that the second and third years of life may be a sensitive period for the development of disturbances of this type. Children reared by depressed mothers look quite normal during the first year, even showing secure attachment at 12 months. But by 18 months, their attachments become insecure and they manifest more depressionlike symptoms than do children reared by nondepressed mothers (e.g., Gaensbauer et al., 1984; Zahn-Waxler et al., 1984). Since the children in these early longitudinal studies have not yet been followed past preschool age, we do not know whether such initial manifestations of problems will be associated with later risk of depression. But these findings do begin to link some of the intriguing work on early attachments I talked about in Chapter 11 to the search for causes of behavior problems in childhood and adolescence.

The Role of Short-term Stress in Behavior Problems

In talking about some of the possible causes of the disturbances I have been describing, I have emphasized mostly patterns of family interactions. But we know that many children who show significant behavior disturbance come from families who look reasonably supportive and loving; other children growing up in what look like nonoptimal families show no disturbance at all. One additional important factor seems to be the presence of significant stress.

James Anthony (1970) suggests that in any child, a behavior problem emerges only when there is some accumulation of risks or stresses above the threshold that the child can handle. When the level of stress goes down, the child's symptoms often disappear, without any special intervention.

I have already talked about the fact that children experiencing a *major* upheaval, such as their parents' divorce, show increased behavior problems—disobedience, depression, or anxiety (Wallerstein & Kelly, 1980; Hetherington, Cox, & Cox, 1978). But an *accumulation* of stresses seems to be even worse. Michael Rutter (Rutter et al., 1975), for example, has found that in families in which there was only one stress at a time (such as marital discord, overcrowding, psychiatric disorder in one or both parents, or the death of a family member), the children were no more likely to have behavior problems than were children from families with no stresses. But any *two* stresses occurring together enormously increased the possibility that the child would show serious symptoms.

The concept of stress also raises the very interesting issue of differences in children's vulnerability. Why do some children show symptoms in the face of only a few stresses, while others can handle a much greater load? I've discussed this issue in the box on the facing page.

Severe Emotional Disturbances

Probably the majority of children show some form of behavior problem at one time or another. A far smaller number—perhaps one in every 1000 children (Achenbach, 1982)—show really severe disturbances. In DSM-III-R these are called **pervasive developmental disorders.** Such children show disturbance in virtually every aspect of their functioning—in their relationships, their thinking, even their language.

Clinicians who work with such severely disturbed children agree that there are several types of problems, but there is not yet perfect agreement on the labels that should be applied to the subgroups or even the characteristics of some of them. Three types seem most common: autism, childhood-onset pervasive developmental disorder (described in DSH-III-R as "pervasive developmental disorder not otherwise specified"), and childhood schizophrenia. I've listed some of the defining characteristics of each disorder in Table 14.4, but the really critical difference is in *when* the problem emerges. Autistic children show significant peculiarities or disorders from earliest infancy; schizophrenia, on the other hand, normally appears much later (most often in adolescence) and thus represents a *loss* of function. Severe disturbances that begin after infancy but before adolescence are nowadays put into the diagnostic grab bag of childhood-onset pervasive developmental disorder. Let me say just a few further words about the two best-defined of these syndromes, autism and childhood schizophrenia.

Autism. Children suffering from **autism** are generally unresponsive to the people around them, do not cuddle or respond to affection as do normal infants, do not make eye contact in a normal way, and show significant retardation of language. Some do not develop language at all. Others develop vocabularies and may even use two-word sentences, but they may develop their own words for common objects and do not adapt their language to the person they are talking to—that is, their language *pragmatics* are abnormal (Landry et al., 1987). Autistic children also typically show resistance to new events or to any changes in their environment, and they often display ritualistic or repetitive behavior (twirling, finger movements, or the like). Most generally, they do not show any reciprocity in their social

VULNERABLE AND INVULNERABLE CHILDREN

Throughout the book, when I've talked about the impact of the environment on a child, I've generally talked as though the effect were equal for all children. But that is clearly not the case. Some children raised in the most punitive, rejecting, unstimulating homes turn out to be successful and distinguished adults; some children face far fewer difficulties but develop chronic emotional problems, delinquency, or other life problems. Why?

As I pointed out in Chapter 1, psychologists have only recently begun to ask about "invulnerable" children, so we have few answers. But there are bits and pieces I can pass on to you.

First, males seem to be more vulnerable to stresses than females are—a point I'll be coming back to later in the chapter. Second, the child's temperament seems to make a difference. The "difficult" child is much more likely to show emotional problems during the preschool period than is the "easy" child. This could reflect an inborn vulnerability of the difficult child or an inborn invulnerability of the easy child. Or it could reflect differences in the patterns of interaction that develop between the child and the parents. The difficult child is more likely to be criticized by her parents, for example (Rutter, 1978a). So the developing transactions between a parent and child may simply aggravate an already existing tendency in the difficult child to react strongly to stress or to change.

Most important, the *in*vulnerable child—the child who seems later to be able to cope with life's stresses without lapsing into serious behavior problems—seems to have one important thing going for him. He nearly always has at least one good, strong, secure relationship with a parent or with another adult (Rutter, 1971, 1978c). The existence of this early secure attachment seems to "buffer" the child against the later slings and arrows of normal life.

I mentioned in earlier chapters that children with secure attachments have more successful peer relationships and better approaches to solving problems during the preschool years. Now we have another piece to the puzzle: children with secure early attachments seem better able to cope with such life stresses as their parents' divorce or a death in the family.

Let me be careful here not to make the mistake of placing too much emphasis on the first attachment. Important as it seems to be, a child *can* recover from a highly stressed early relationship if the family situation improves. Note, however, that "improvement" in the family situation almost by definition means that the child now has some one person—a stepparent, a grandparent, an older sibling—with whom he can form a strong, supportive relationship. The fundamental point seems to be that for a child to be able to handle temporary stresses without showing serious behavior problems, he must have *some* close attachment. But it need not be the *first* attachment of infancy.

Table 14.4

Some Symptoms of Autism, Childhood-Onset Pervasive Developmental Disorder, and Childhood Schizophrenia

- *Autism.*   Onset before 30 months of age. Pervasive lack of responsiveness to other people; gross deficits in language development, including excessive echolalia or other peculiar speech patterns. Resistance to change in the environment or schedule. Peculiar attachments to animate or inanimate objects.
- *Childhood-onset pervasive developmental disorder.*   Onset after 30 months and before 12 years. Sustained impairment in social relations, which might include inappropriate clinging, lack of appropriate emotional expression, or asocial behavior. Any three of the following: sudden bursts of anxiety; extreme mood swings or inappropriate emotions; resistance to change in the environment; oddities in motor movement or posturing; abnormalities of speech, particularly intonation (such as monotone voice); hypersensitivity to sensory stimuli; self-mutilation.
- *Childhood schizophrenia.*   Deterioration from previous level of adequate or near-adequate functioning. Delusions, hallucinations, or disturbances in the form of thought. Disturbance in social relationships. Any of several specific symptoms, depending on the subtype of schizophrenia involved.

Sources: After the American Psychiatric Association, 1987; Achenbach, 1982.

interactions. In the language I used in Chapter 11, these children simply do not enter into the "dance" of interaction. All of these symptoms are typically present from the earliest months of life.

We are still a long way from understanding this pattern of deviance, but all the evidence I have read points to one clear conclusion: children are *born* with this disorder. It is not caused by poor parenting. Understandably, parents rearing an autistic child may *become* less responsive or less affectionate with the child, but there is simply no indication that parents are causing this problem by inadequate or unloving child rearing.

Instead, as Michael Rutter has argued persuasively, it seems most likely that these children are born with some basic physiologically linked cognitive deficit (Rutter & Garmezy, 1983). We know, for example, that perhaps as many as 10 percent of autistic children have fragile-X syndrome (a chromosomal anomaly, discussed in Chapter 2). They are frequently retarded and very often have epileptic seizures, beginning in adolescence. Other evidence suggestive of a significant cognitive deficit is the fact that the best single predictor of long-term adjustment is whether the autistic child has developed useful speech by age 5. Autistic children who do not achieve useful speech are likely to remain highly deviant throughout life (Rutter, 1978b).

Childhood Schizophrenia.   **Schizophrenia** is a far more loosely defined category. Some clinicians use this label to cover adolescent-onset

Figure 14.3   This autistic child, who makes little eye contact and shows few signs of friendliness or involvement with others, is being treated in an operant conditioning program. Every time he shows one of the desired behaviors, he is quickly reinforced with some food he likes. Such programs have been moderately successful in improving the social behavior of autistic children.

disturbances that include hallucinations or delusions; others use it to cover virtually all severe emotional disturbances in children that develop after infancy. Because of this confusion about definitions, the research results are hard to add up. Different investigators may be studying very different types of children, even though they are all called schizophrenic.

Nonetheless, some reasonable conclusions are possible. First, unlike autism, in the case of schizophrenia (and childhood-onset pervasive developmental disorders), family interaction patterns are implicated as partial causes. We know, for example, that children reared by parents with schizophrenia or other severe emotional disorders are likely to develop one or another form of deviant behavior, including schizophrenia (Sameroff, Seifer, & Zax, 1983). A hereditary influence is part of this; adopted children whose birth parents were schizophrenic *also* have heightened rates of schizophrenia (Rosenthal et al., 1971).

Arnold Sameroff (Sameroff, Seifer, & Zax, 1983) argues that a transactional process is set up: a child with some form of genetic or constitutional vulnerability is born into a family with disturbed or inadequate parents. In the process of mutual adaptation, in some families both the child and the parent develop symptoms or deviancies. Schizophrenia in the child is thus seen as an *adaptation* by the child to the family, given the inborn capacities or tendencies of the child. Not every child of schizophrenic parents will end up disturbed; similarly, reasonably effective parents may have a seriously disturbed child if the adaptation pattern goes awry.

PHYSICALLY ATYPICAL DEVELOPMENT

If you look back to Table 14.1, you'll see that children with major physical problems, such as blindness, deafness, or significant motor dysfunction, are relatively rare, especially in comparison to the frequency of other types of problems. Yet although the numbers may be small, the degree of difficulty encountered for the physically atypical child may be very great indeed. Most of the children I'll be talking about here require special schooling or special facilities in school; many require continued assistance throughout life. Still, with improved instruction, intervention, and mechanical assistance, many children with significant physical handicaps are leading full and satisfying lives.

The Deaf and Hearing-Impaired

Most children with hearing loss can function adequately with the assistance of a hearing aid. In fact, many physicians are now fitting **hearing-impaired** children with hearing aids during infancy rather than waiting until preschool age. The situation is quite different, though, for the profoundly deaf—the child whose hearing loss is so severe that even with assistance his comprehension of sound, especially language, is significantly reduced. I raised some of the issues connected with the early rearing of deaf children in Chapter 8, in the box on page 302, and you may want to go back and reread it. The basic point is that if the emphasis is placed exclusively on *oral* language, the deaf child has much more difficulty developing either speech or reading than if she is taught sign language, lipreading, and oral language at the same time (e.g., Greenberg, Calderon, & Kusche, 1984; Moores, 1985). Some such children can function in a normal school environment, but even with good early training, most deaf children require special schooling.

The Blind Child

If I had asked you, before you read this chapter, to tell me which would be worse, to have been blind or deaf from birth, most of you would have said it would be far worse to be blind. Yet from the point of view of the child's ability to function in most normal settings, including school, blindness is a smaller handicap. The blind child can learn to read (with braille), can talk with others, can listen to a teacher, and so on. Because of this greater academic potential, and because of the enormous role of language in forming and maintaining social relationships, more options are open to the blind adult than to most deaf adults.

BASIC ATTACHMENTS BETWEEN BLIND BABIES AND THEIR MOTHERS

In Chapter 11, I mentioned Selma Fraiberg's work with blind infants as part of the discussion of the parent's attachment to the child. Because Fraiberg's work is so fascinating, I want to expand on that brief discussion here.

Fraiberg (1974, 1975, 1977) found that blind babies begin to smile at about the same age as sighted babies (about 4 weeks) but that they smile less often. And at about 2 months, when the sighted baby begins to smile regularly at the sight of the parent's face, the blind baby's smiles become less and less frequent. The blind infant's smile is also less intense, more fleeting.

The other thing blind babies don't do is enter into mutual gaze. They don't look right at their parents, and everything we know about parents' responses to their babies underlines the importance of mutual gaze for the parents' feeling of attachment to the baby. When the blind baby does not look, the parents often report feeling "rejected."

Generally, the facial expressions of the blind infant are muted and sober. Many observers, including parents, conclude that the baby is depressed or indifferent.

Fraiberg found that most of the mothers of the blind babies in her studies gradually withdrew from their infants. They provided the needed physical care, but they stopped playing with their babies and gave up trying to elicit smiles or other social interactions. They often said they didn't "love" this baby.

Fortunately, it's possible to solve this particular problem. Fraiberg found that these mothers could be helped to form a strong bond with their infants if they could be shown how to "read" the babies' other signals. The blind child's face may be sober and relatively expressionless, but her hands and body move a lot and express a great deal. When the child *stops* moving when you come into the room, this means she is listening to your footsteps. Or she may move her hands when she hears your voice, rather than smiling as a sighted child would do.

When parents of blind children learn to respond to these alternative "attachment behaviors" in their babies, then the mutuality of the relationship can be reestablished. And when this happens, and the parents are able to provide more varied stimulation, blind children develop more normal behavior in other ways. In particular, they don't show the "blindisms" so often observed in blind youngsters, such as rocking, sucking, head banging, and other repetitive actions.

Still, there are obviously important limitations for the blind, and important potential pitfalls. One of these lies in the earliest relationship with the parent, which I've discussed in the box above. Later relationships may be impaired for the same reasons.

What does seem to be critical, for both the deaf and the blind, is early intervention with the family as well as with the child. In Sameroff's terms, the transactional process between parent and child needs attention. The child can't be "cured," but many of the potential emotional and intellectual problems can be lessened if there is early treatment.

Figure 14.4   These deaf children are being taught sign language. Research on the deaf shows that children have the best academic and linguistic prognosis when they are simultaneously taught to sign, to lipread, and to speak.

Other Physical Problems

Among the most heart-wrenching youngsters are those with multiple handicaps or with physical disabilities so severe that they are unable to communicate, move, or play. Some severely afflicted cerebral-palsied youngsters, for example, are unable to move without assistance, cannot speak comprehensibly, and may be retarded as well. They require full-time care for their entire lives. Still, they *can* learn and love. Among the health care professionals dealing with severely or multiply handicapped children, the move today is toward very early intervention. The family is ordinarily involved from the beginning, not only learning how to care for and stimulate the child but also getting help in developing their own attachments to the child.

Children with chronic diseases such as muscular dystrophy or cystic fibrosis also have significant physical problems. In every instance, early diagnosis and treatment are critical—not because the disease can be eliminated, but because such early intervention may prolong the child's life or the period of comfort.

SEX DIFFERENCES IN ATYPICAL DEVELOPMENT

One of the most fascinating facts about atypical development is that virtually all disorders are more common in boys than in girls. I've put some of the comparisons in Table 14.5.

Table 14.5

Sex Differences in the Incidence of Atypical Development

Type of problem	Approximate ratio of males to females
Academic problems (including learning disabilities)	3:2
Physical handicaps	
Visual problems	1:1
Hearing problems	5:4
Speech defects	3:2
Emotional problems	
Attention deficit disorder (hyperactivity)	3:1
Conduct disorders (including delinquency)	5:1
Anxiety and depression in preadolescence	1:1
Anxiety and depression in adolescence	1:2
Severe emotional problems (autism and other)	3:1
Estimated number of all children with all diagnoses seen in psychiatric clinics	2:1

Sources: Achenbach, 1982; Anthony, 1980; Eme, 1979; *Profiles of Children*, 1970; Rutter & Garmezy, 1983.

How are we to explain differences like this? One possibility is that the female, as I mentioned in the box on page 527, is somehow naturally "buffered" against environmental stresses. Girls are less likely to inherit any recessive disease that is carried on the X chromosome. Perhaps the second X chromosome provides some general kind of added protection that the boy does not have. On the other side of the argument, the fact that girls show higher rates of depression at adolescence is evidence against any general "buffering" hypothesis.

Hormonal differences may also play a role, such as in the higher levels of aggression in boys (see the discussion of aggression in Chapter 11). Sex differences in other areas might result from greater demands being placed on boys, thus creating greater stress for them to deal with.

Whatever the explanation—and none of the existing explanations seem satisfactory to me—it is nonetheless extremely interesting that girls do seem to be less vulnerable.

THE IMPACT OF AN ATYPICAL CHILD ON THE FAMILY

Throughout this chapter I have touched on the impact of a child's problem on the family. In some instances, of course, deficiencies or inadequacies in the family are part of the *cause* of the child's atypical development.

But whether the cause lies (partly or wholly) in the family or not, once a child does show some form of deviant development, the family is inevitably affected, often adversely. Even parents of gifted children face remarkably complex problems as they try to keep up with their child's rapid development. (Imagine being Michael's parents, for example.) Most of what I want to focus on here, though, is what happens in a family with a mentally or physically handicapped child.

Grief. When parents first realize that their child is not normal—whether that realization comes at birth or much later—the natural reaction is a form of grief, almost as if the child had died. (In fact, of course, the fantasy "perfect child" did die or was never born. The parents grieve for the child that never will be.) As with other forms of grief, the parents experience denial, depression, and anger. Many parents also feel some guilt (e.g., "If only I hadn't been drinking while I was pregnant").

In some cases, this process may result in an emotional rejection of the infant. And some atypical infants' difficulty in joining or total inability to enter into mutually adaptive interactions further aggravates the situation (for example, see the discussion of blind infants in the box on page 531). Such rejection seems to be particularly common when the marital relationship is conflicted or when the family lacks adequate social support (Howard, 1978).

Adaptation by the Family. Once the initial shock and grief are dealt with (to the extent that they can be), the family must work toward an ongoing adaptive system with the atypical child. There are often massive financial burdens; there are problems of finding appropriate schooling; there are endless daily adjustments to the child's special needs.

Many parents pay a very great price for this adaptation. Parents of retarded or atypical children are more likely to be chronically depressed, to have lower self-esteem, and to have lower feelings of personal competence (Howard, 1978). Where the marital relationship was poor before the birth of the child, the presence of the handicapped child in the family system seems to increase the likelihood of further discord. However, there is no consistent indication that having an atypical child results in an average increase in marital disharmony or risk of divorce (Howard, 1978; Longo & Bond, 1984).

The fact that many (even most) parents manage to adapt effectively to the presence of an atypical child is testimony to the devotion and immense effort expended. But there is no evading the fact that rearing such a child is very hard work and that it strains the family system in ways that rearing a normal child does not.

INTERVENTIONS AND TREATMENTS

One of the keys to effective adaptation for many parents of atypical children is the availability of support outside the family. If special treatment, intervention programs, parent groups, or even institutions to care for the child are available, they make the parents' task simpler. Let me touch on just a few of the options.

Treatment for the Child, Training for the Parents

Probably the most common intervention is some kind of individual therapy or training for the child. Special classes in schools, physical therapy for children with physical handicaps, and braille training for the blind are all examples.

In recent years, many intervention programs—particularly those for preschool children or infants—have included parents as well, either by having them participate with the child in the special program or by training them to deliver the service to the child at home (Wiegerink et al., 1980; Hanson, 1981). Parents of children with behavior problems may be helped to examine the pattern of their discipline with their children; parents of physically handicapped children may be taught how to stimulate and play with their children; parents of children with learning problems may be taught specific games or projects to undertake at home.

For example, Marci Hanson (1981) has described a special stimulation program for Down's syndrome infants that began when the infants were a few months old. The parents were taught special stimulation procedures and then implemented them with their own infants at home. Staff members visited the families regularly (weekly or biweekly), and together the parent and staff member planned the program for the next period. Children who received this treatment showed less decline in developmental rate than is typical of untreated Down's infants (although their development was still slower than normal).

Most experts conclude that such special programs are particularly effective if they begin early (before age 3) and if they include both direct service to the child and involvement and training of the parent (e.g., Harvard Education Letter, 1986; see White, 1985–1986, for an alternative view). But such programs are not a panacea, either. Among other things, I suspect that some parents are much less ready, willing, or able than others to undertake major home-based training programs with their handicapped child. Interventions that focus on the parents may thus be useful or effective with only some families. Still, the shift toward inclusion of parents in intervention plans seems to me to be a very good change.

Interventions in the Public Schools: Mainstreaming Versus Special Classes

Despite newer intervention programs for infants and toddlers, a large portion of the task of responding to the needs of atypical children falls on the public school system. The Federal Education for All Handicapped Children Act (Public Law 94-142), passed in 1975, requires that each state have

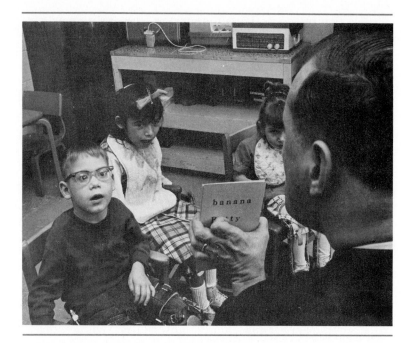

Figure 14.5 This is a good example of a special class for retarded children within a public school. Such classes typically have only a few children so that there can be a great deal of individual instruction. With mainstreaming now the dominant theme in education for the handicapped, these special classes have become less common, but they still exist—either full-time or for half days— for those children with severe handicaps or significant retardation.

programs for all school-age and preschool handicapped children. Further, it requires that wherever possible, the handicapped child be mainstreamed— a word that many of you may have heard bandied about (Schroeder, Schroeder, & Landesman, 1987).

Mainstreaming does *not* mean that every atypical child must be taught full-time in a regular classroom. It *does* mean that children must be placed in what Public Law 94-142 calls the "least restrictive environment" consistent with their disability. This has meant that many children who were previously taught in special segregated classes are now spending part or all of their school hours in a regular classroom. In most instances, educable mentally retarded children are being assigned full-time to regular classes; children with physical handicaps such as blindness and those with learning problems are spending part of each day in a regular classroom and part with a special education teacher or in a special classroom.

The alternative to mainstreaming is some sort of special class (see Figure 14.4)—a system that dominated school treatment of the atypical child until recently.

It would be splendid if I could tell you which of these two alternatives is best for atypical children, but I cannot—at least, not with any confidence. There is a great scarcity of the kind of research we need to settle this question—research in which children have been assigned randomly to either regular or special classes. The evidence we do have shows no big advantage to regular classroom placement. Borderline retarded children (those with IQs of 80 or so) seem to do somewhat better academically in regular classrooms (Budoff & Gottlieb, 1976), but retarded children with lower IQs may do better in special classes. This may only be true, though, if the special classes are clearly organized, with maximum expectations for the children's development.

Handicapped children do not do better socially in regular classrooms. There was some hope in the beginning that exposure to handicapped children would reduce some of the prejudice against them on the part of "able-bodied" children, but there is little evidence that this has happened (Vandell et al., 1982).

As Edward Zigler has cogently pointed out, whether mainstreaming will ultimately be found to benefit children will depend very heavily on whether regular classroom teachers are adequately trained and given adequate support: "Without adequate support personnel to assist regular-class teachers with the education of handicapped (particularly EMR) students, mainstreaming is doomed to fail" (Zigler & Muenchow, 1979, p. 994).

What Public Law 94-142 *has* done is to put a significant legal tool in the hands of parents. They are now in a far better position to insist on information and on treatment for their children than they were. But the new law has not magically solved the problem of educating atypical children.

Residential Treatment

A third type of treatment, recommended primarily for those children with such severe handicaps that they cannot readily be cared for at home, is some form of institutional or residential care. With the increasing emphasis on parental involvement in the treatment of atypical children, the number of children in institutional care has declined. Still, some children can't be handled at home or in the school, so there is a need for residential facilities. The most common are institutions for profoundly retarded children and adults. Many children in such institutions also have physical handicaps.

Children with severe emotional problems, such as some autistic or schizophrenic children, are also cared for in institutions. In most cases, the expressed aim of the care is to provide therapy of some kind for the child so that he can be returned to his family. Regrettably, the success of these efforts for the severely disturbed child is not outstanding. Many excellent programs have succeeded in modifying children's behavior sufficiently so that they can live at home, but the beneficial changes often don't last outside the supportive environment of the residential community (Quay, 1979).

Similarly, institutional treatment for delinquents has not been impressively successful. Jails and traditional reform schools have the worst records of preventing further delinquency. Seventy or eighty percent of young men who spend time in such institutions are rearrested within a few years of release. Some small experimental group homes that emphasize work training, group therapy, or learning-theory-based behavior modification have had more success, with rearrest rates of perhaps 40 percent. Clearly, there is a very great need for more information about forms of intervention that will work for all types of handicapped or disturbed youngsters.

A FINAL POINT

I want to end this chapter as I began it, by stating strongly that the development of the atypical child is really much more like typical development than unlike it. When dealing with an atypical child, we can easily be overwhelmed by the sense of differentness. But the sameness is there, underneath.

SUMMARY

1. Approximately 15 to 20 percent of all children in the United States will need some form of special assistance because of atypical development at some time in childhood or adolescence.
2. The most common problems are reading difficulties and short-term behavior problems.
3. Children with mental retardation, normally defined as IQ below 70 combined with significant problems of adaptation, represent approximately 3 percent of the population. They show slower development and more immature or less-efficient forms of information-processing strategies.
4. The two basic categories of causes of mental retardation are physical problems, such as genetic anomalies or brain damage, and cultural-familial problems. Children with cultural-familial retardation ordinarily come from families in which the parents have low IQs and provide little cognitive stimulation.
5. Interventions with children affected by cultural-familial retardation have been successful in raising some children's IQ to the normal range, which demonstrates the important role of the environment in some forms of retardation.
6. Children with serious specific learning disabilities make up 2 to 8 percent of the school population. Such problems *may* be caused by undetected minimal brain damage, uneven or slow brain development, or other kinds of physical dysfunction. Or they may reflect broader language or cognitive deficits.
7. Gifted children have very high IQs or are unusually creative or excel

in a special skill. Their information processing is unusually flexible and generalized. They appear to be generally well adjusted socially, except for the small group of unusually highly gifted children.

8. Moderate forms of emotional disturbance include attention deficit disorder (commonly called hyperactivity), behavior problems such as aggressiveness or delinquency, and anxiety or depression.

9. Hyperactivity affects perhaps 2 percent of children, more often boys. There may be some physiological origin, but that has not been conclusively demonstrated.

10. Excess aggressiveness or delinquency is generally more common among children from poverty-level families, particularly those with erratic discipline or lack of love. A subset of delinquents, however—"unsocialized" or "psychopathic" delinquents—come from all social classes. These are marked by the early onset and broad range of their delinquent activities.

11. Sadness or mild depression is observed sometimes in early childhood but much more often in adolescence. Moderate or severe depression affects 1 to 2 percent of teenagers.

12. All three of these types of behavior problems appear to be more common in children experiencing multiple stresses.

13. Serious emotional problems, including autism and childhood schizophrenia, are much scarcer. Autism develops in the early months of life and includes problems in relating to others and with language. Schizophrenia develops later and includes immature or bizarre behavior and delusions or hallucinations.

14. The best prognosis for the deaf child occurs when identification is made early, hearing aids are used where possible, and the child is taught signing and lipreading from the earliest years of life. Special schooling is usually required.

15. Blind children, in contrast, can often function in regular school classrooms, but they may have difficulty with personal relationships because of lack of typical attachment behaviors.

16. Boys show almost all forms of atypical development more often than girls do. This may reflect genetic differences, hormone differences, or differences in cultural expectations.

17. Families with atypical children experience chronically heightened stress and demands for adaptation. This is frequently accompanied by depression or other disturbance in the parents.

18. Interventions with atypical children increasingly involve the parent as well as the child.

19. Mainstreaming of atypical children into regular school classrooms, wherever possible, is now legally mandated. The verdict is still out on the effects of that practice.

▬▬▬▬ KEY TERMS

adaptative behavior An aspect of a child's functioning often considered in diagnosing mental retardation. Can the child adapt to the tasks of everyday life?

attention-deficit hyperactivity disorder The technical term for what is more often called simply hyperactivity. It is characterized by short attention span, distractibility, and heightened levels of physical activity.

autism A severe form of emotional/language disorder, appearing in infancy.

behavior problem The general phrase used to describe mild or moderate forms of emotional difficulty, including aggressiveness, shyness, anxiety, and hyperactivity.

brain damage Some injury to the brain, either during prenatal development or later, that results in its improper functioning.

childhood-onset pervasive developmental disorder Term used in DSM-III-R to describe a pattern of severe emotional disturbance that begins after infancy (and is thus not autism) but does not include the delusions common in schizophrenia.

DSM-III-R The *Diagnostic and Statistical Manual of Mental Disorders* of the American Psychiatric Association, listing the currently agreed-upon categories of emotional disturbance.

dyslexia A form of specific learning disability in which the individual has difficulty with reading.

giftedness Normally defined in terms of very high IQ (above 140 or 150), but may also be defined in terms of exceptional creativity or remarkable skill in one or more specific areas, such as mathematics or memory.

hearing-impaired The phrase currently used (in place of *hard-of-hearing*) to describe children or adults with significant hearing loss.

hyperactivity The brief common term for attention-deficit hyperactivity disorder.

inborn error of metabolism An inherited disorder (such as PKU) resulting in an inability to perform a particular metabolic function. Some such disorders are associated with retardation if not treated.

mainstreaming The placement of atypical children in regular school classrooms whenever possible.

mental retardation A pattern of functioning that includes low IQ, poor adaptive behavior, and poor information-processing skills.

pervasive developmental disorders Serious emotional disturbances such as autism and schizophrenia.

schizophrenia A severe form of emotional disturbance seen in adults and in some adolescents. The term *childhood schizophrenia* is also sometimes used to describe children with childhood-onset pervasive developmental disorder.

specific learning disability (SLD) A disorder in understanding or processing language or symbols.

▬▬▬▬ SUGGESTED READING

Edgerton, R. B. (1979). *Mental retardation.* Cambridge, MA: Harvard University Press.
This is an excellent, brief, readable introduction to the whole topic.

Farnham-Diggory, S. (1978). *Learning disabilities.* Cambridge, MA: Harvard University Press.
Another excellent brief introductory discussion from the same series as the Edgerton book.

Goleman, D. (1980, February). 1,528 little geniuses and how they grew. *Psychology Today, 13,* pp. 28–43.
A brief and fascinating description of some of the findings from the latest interviews with the gifted individuals first studied by Terman in the 1930s.

Granger, L., & Granger, B. (1986). *The magic feather: The truth about "special education."* New York: Dutton.
The Grangers' son was diagnosed by his school as being retarded—a diagnosis that turned out to be totally wrong. The book describes their experiences with the special education system, detailing many of the flaws in that system.

Meisels, S. J., & Anastasiow, N. J. (1982). The risks of prediction: Relationships between etiology, handicapping conditions, and developmental outcomes. In S. G. Moore & C. R.

Cooper (Eds.), *The young child: Reviews of research* (Vol. 3). Washington, DC: National Association for the Education of Young Children.

An excellent discussion of several different theories of the causes or origins of atypical development.

Rutter, M. (1975). *Helping troubled children.* New York: Plenum.

This is not a new book, but I like Michael Rutter's style so much that I recommend it anyway. This book should give you a good introduction to the full range of emotional problems in children and their treatment.

Turkington, C. (1987, September). Special talents. *Psychology Today,* pp. 42–46.

A very upbeat article about Down's syndrome children, emphasizing their potential when they are given good intervention.

15 Putting It All Together: The Developing Child

Ages and Stages
  Two Key Concepts
  From Birth to 18 Months
  The Preschool Years: From 18 Months to 6 Years
  The Elementary-School Years: From 6 to 12
  Adolescence: From 12 to 20
Returning to Some Basic Questions
  What Are the Major Influences on Development?
  Does Timing Matter?
  What Is the Nature of Developmental Change?
Individual Differences
  Sex Differences in Development
  Vulnerability and Resilience
A Final Point: The Joy of Development
Summary
Suggested Reading

I remember the sense of unfairness I had in a world history class in high school when, after I had carefully learned all the rulers of England and those of France in order, I was asked to say who had been king of France at the same time that Henry VIII ruled England. I hadn't the foggiest idea; we had never studied it that way.

You may have something of the same feeling about the developing child. For example, you know a good deal about the sequence of development of language and about the sequential changes in cognitive functioning and in attachments, but you probably have not hooked these different developmental sequences to one another very well. If I asked you now what else was happening at the same time that the child first uses two-word sentences, you would probably have a difficult time answering. So what I want to do in this brief chapter is to put the child back together a bit by looking at the things that are happening at the same time.

I also want to take another look at many of the key questions I raised in Chapter 1 in light of all the information you have read since then: What are the major influences on development? Does the timing of experience matter? What is the nature of developmental change? Are there stages or sequences? And how best can we understand individual differences in development?

AGES AND STAGES

Two Key Concepts

Several concepts will be helpful in looking at simultaneous developments at each of several ages or stages.

Transitions and Consolidations. The process of development appears to be made up of a series of alternating periods of rapid growth (accompanied by disruption or disequilibrium) and periods of relative calm or consolidation. Change is obviously going on all the time, from conception throughout childhood (and adulthood, too). But there are particular times when the changes pile up or when one central change affects the whole system. This might be a major physiological development, like puberty, or a change from one status or role to another, like the shift from preschooler to schoolchild. These role or status changes are frequently accompanied by the development of major cognitive or language skills, too. These "pileups" of change often seem to result in the child's coming "unglued" for a while. The old patterns of relationships, of thinking, of talking don't work very well any more, and it takes a while to work out new patterns.

Erikson frequently uses the work *dilemma* to label these periods. Klaus Riegel (1975) once suggested the phrase *developmental leaps*, which conveys nicely the sense of excitement and blossoming opportunity that often accompanies these pivotal periods. I'm going to use the more pedestrian term *transition* to describe the times of change or upheaval and the term *consolidation* to describe the in-between times when change is more gradual.

Development As a System.

Another basic principle, which I emphasized particularly in Chapter 13, is that development is a system. There are two possible meanings to such a phrase, both of which I think are useful.

First, the different aspects of any one child—his cognitive development, social development, and physical development—all interact to produce an individual pattern that varies from one child to the next and from one time period to the next. One aspect of change may be relatively dominant at a particular time, but the entire system operates as a complex whole. Thus, the child's early attachment may affect his congitive development by altering the way he approaches new situations; later on, the hormonal changes of puberty may affect parent-child relations, but the quality of that change may be also affected by the history of attachments in that specific family.

Second, as I emphasized in Chapter 13, the child develops within a family system, and the family in turn exists within a larger cultural system. These factors impinge on the child, interacting with her emerging skills and with her internal working models of relationships or of the self. Remember that in a *system,* all parts affect one another, so the child influences the family, too. As the child develops, she makes different kinds of demands on the parents, and these changing demands interact with the parents' particular qualities and with the demands of the other roles they must fill.

Difficult as it is, I think it is essential to try to keep all these forces in mind if we are to understand the complex tapestry of influences that shape a child's development (Ramey & MacPhee, 1986). With these thoughts in mind, let me look at several age periods.

From Birth to 18 Months

Figure 15.1 shows the various changes during the first 18 months of life. The rows roughly correspond to the chapters of this book; what we need to do now is read up and down the columns. You will see in the figure that I have subdivided this period into three sections: the first from birth to about age 2 months, the second from 2 to 8 months, and the final one from 8 to 18 months.

From Birth to 2 Months.

The overriding impression one gets of the newborn infant is that despite her remarkable skills and capacities, she is very much on "automatic pilot." There seem to be built-in "rules" or "schemas" that govern the way the infant listens, looks around her, explores the world, and relates to others.

One of the really remarkable things about these rules, as I pointed

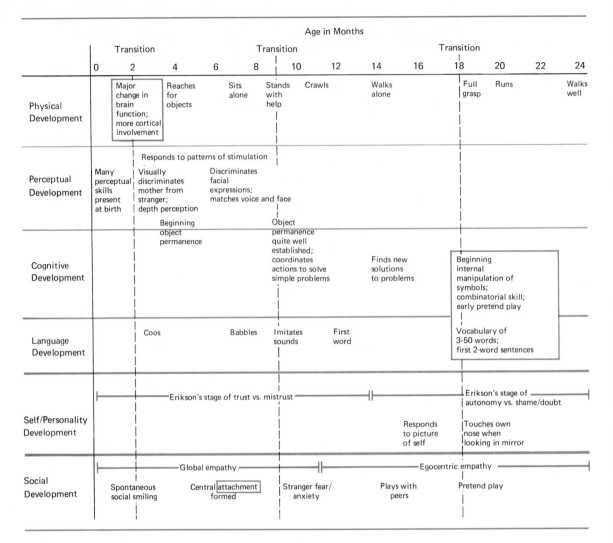

Figure 15.1 This brief summary chart shows some of the simultaneous developments during infancy as well as some of the possible transitions or subperiods. For each transition point, I have highlighted the one development or set of developments that seems to me to be pivotal.

out in Chapters 3 and 5, is how well they are designed to lead both the child and the caregivers into the "dance" of interaction and attachment. Think of an infant being breast-fed: The baby has the needed rooting, sucking, and swallowing reflexes to take in the milk. The mother's face is at just about the optimum distance from the baby's eyes for the infant's best focusing. The mother's facial features, particularly her eyes and mouth, make up just the sort of visual stimulus that the baby is most likely to look at. The baby is particularly sensitive to the range of sounds of the

Figure 15.2   The physical transition at 2 months helps to make the baby much more responsive, much more social, as you can see in this infant's smile. Because the parents are getting more skillful at care and at responding to the child's cues, the interaction between baby and parents becomes more pleasant, more relaxed, more deeply engaging.

human voice, particularly the higher-pitched, lilting voice most mothers use. And during breast-feeding the release of a hormone called *cortisol* in the mother has the effect of relaxing her and making her more alert to the baby's signals. Both the adult and the infant are thus primed to interact with one another.

From 2 to 8 Months.   Some time around 6 to 8 weeks, however, there are several changes in the system. Perhaps because of early explorations, and perhaps because of simple physical maturation, the infant's active and perceptual examinations of the world seem to switch into a different gear, one controlled much more by the cortex and less by the primitive portions of the brain. The child now looks at objects differently, begins to discriminate one face from another, smiles more, sleeps through the night, and generally becomes a more responsive creature.

Because of these changes in the baby, and also because it takes most mothers six to eight weeks to recover physically from the delivery (and for the mother and father jointly to begin to adjust to the immense change in their routine), there are big changes in mother-infant interaction patterns at this time as well. The need for routine caretaking continues, of course (ah, the joys of diapers!), but the child stays awake for longer periods and smiles and makes eye contact more. Exchanges between parent and child are more playful and smoother-paced.

Once this transition has occurred, there is a brief period of consolidation—though of course, change continues. There are gradual neurological changes, with the motor and perceptual areas of the cortex continuing to develop. The child's perceptual skills change rapidly as well; the baby begins to be able to combine information from several senses, and makes finer discriminations of sound and other cues. The child is also exploring the world in an active way, which seems essential for the development of the object concept and other cognitive skills.

From 8 to 18 Months. Somewhere around 8 or 10 months, two changes bring about a disequilibrium: (1) the child forms a strong central attachment (perhaps accompanied by fear of strangers), and (2) she begins to move around independently (albeit very slowly and haltingly at first). The combination of these two changes—one social/cognitive and one motor—requires a new adaptation by both the child and the parents.

These readjustments in the last part of the first year of life are followed by another consolidation period, which may last until 18 or 20 months of age. At that point the child's language and cognitive development appear to take another major leap forward—a set of changes I'll describe shortly.

So far, all I have done is to talk about simultaneous developments in various subperiods. That's helpful for grasping the totality of development, but it doesn't help much with understanding the system of interactions— the causal connections between the various changes. So let me speculate a bit about some possible causal limits.

The change at 2 months seems simplest to understand. The key causal event seems to be a physiological change in the brain. At a later age, beginning object permanence may be linked to the child's first attachment. An attachment probably requires not only that the child be able to discriminate between one face or body and another (which the baby can do from auditory cues from the earliest days of life but can consistently do visually only at 3 or 4 months), but also that the child have at least some beginning grasp of object permanence. That is, the child must begin to realize that Mom is a permanent person and continues to exist even when out of sight. Thus, the *social* development of attachment no doubt has important *cognitive* underpinnings.

But the reverse may also occur. That is, the child's attachment may affect cognitive development. There is a growing body of evidence, for example, showing that securely attached toddlers explore more freely, persist longer in their play, and develop the object concept more rapidly (e.g., Bates et al., 1982). Such a connection might exist because the securely attached child is simply more comfortable exploring the world around him from the safe base of his secure person. He thus has a richer and more varied set of experiences, which may stimulate more rapid cognitive development. A second possible explanation of this same correlation is that the sort of parent-child interaction that fosters a secure attachment may *also* be optimal for fostering language and cognitive skill. In particular, *contingent responsiveness* from the parent seems to be a positive ingredient not only in the emergence of a secure attachment but also in more rapid cognitive growth.

The currently popular theoretical notion that the infant constructs an internal working model of attachment relationships points to still another possible connection between cognitive and emotional/social development during these years. The observed long-term consequences of secure or insecure attachments may occur not because the behavior of the parents toward the child was somehow printed permanently on the child's forehead, but because the child has *understood* the parent's behavior in a particular way. That understanding may persist, even when the behavior changes.

The Preschool Years: From 18 Months to 6 Years

The Transition. The most striking thing about the transition at 18 to 24 months is that the child begins to use symbols in language and in thinking. As Flavell points out, this is not at all a trivial change:

> I think a good case could be made for Piaget's claim that infants have cognitive systems that are fundamentally different in some ways from those of older humans, including very young children. In particular, a cognitive system that uses symbols just seems on that account to be radically, drastically, qualitatively different from one that does not and cannot. So great is the difference that the transformation of one system into the other during the first 2 years of life still seems nothing short of miraculous to me, no matter how much we learn about it. (Flavell, 1985, p. 82)

This fundamental shift is reflected in many different aspects of the child's life. We see it in language, in the child's approach to cognitive tasks, and in play, where the child pretends, having an object *stand for* something else.

I pointed out briefly in Chapter 8 that at this same age, the child also shows a rapid and broad emergence of *combinatorial skills* (Brownell, 1986; Seibert, Hogan, & Mundy, 1986). At about 18 to 20 months, the child first strings two words together into a sentence. At about the same time, children's pretend play first shows strings of *two* pretend actions, just as their play with other children similarly first shows strings of turn taking. Interestingly, when researchers have studied mentally retarded children as well as intellectually normal children over this transition, they find that it is *mental age* and not chronological age that is the critical

	Transition 2	3	4	5	6
Physical Development	Runs easily; climbs stairs one step at a time	Rides trike; uses scissors; draws	Climbs stairs one foot per step; kicks and throws large ball	Hops and skips; some ball games with more skill	Jumps rope; skips
Cognitive Development	Symbols; 2- and 3-step play sequences	Classification mostly by function	Beginning systematic classification by shape or size or color		Conservation of number and quantity
			Beginning ability to take others' physical perspective	No spontaneous use of rehearsal in memory tasks	
		Transductive reasoning			
Language Development	2-word sentences	3- and 4-word sentences with grammatical markers		Continued improvement of inflections, past tense, plurals, passive sentences, and tag questions.	
Self/Personality Development	Self-definition based on comparisons of size, age, gender; gender identity		Gender stability	Categorical self based on physical properties or skills Gender constancy	
	⊢Erikson's stage of autonomy vs——shame/doubt		⊢Erikson's stage of initiative vs. guilt————————		
Social Development	⊢Attachments to parents shown less frequently, mostly under stress ————————————				
	⊢Empathy for another's feelings ————————				
	Multi-step turn-taking sequences in play with peers	Some altruism; same-sex peer choice	Beginning signs of individual friendships	Sociodramatic play	Roles in play

Age in Years

Figure 15.3 A brief summary of parallel developments during the preschool years. The major transition that I see is right at the beginning, when the child first masters the use of symbols and is able to combine strings of actions or concepts together.

predictor of these changes (Seibert, Hogan, & Mundy, 1986). It is when the child reaches the mental age of about 20 months that all these combinatorial skills emerge in rapid order—a pattern which suggests the possibility that there may be some basic physiological change at work here, affecting the child's cognitive development, which in turn affects language and social interactions.

The Consolidation. Following this transition, there is a long period of consolidation, which I've summarized in Figure 15.3. The major breakthroughs of language and cognition usher in whole collections of new skills and opportunities, but it takes the child three to four years to master the new skills completely.

These new skills make the child more independent, as does his growing mobility. An 18-month-old walks well; a 2-year-old can run. As any parent can tell you, children in this period vigorously push the limits of this new-found independence.

Collectively, these new skills also influence the form of the child's attachment behavior. When language is rudimentary and the child's locomotion is poor, then clinging, touching and holding, or crying are just about the only stress-related attachment behaviors available to the child. But as language becomes more skillful, he becomes able to stay in touch with adults and peers in new ways—even symbolically, by thinking about his mother or father. The attachment may be no less strong, but it can be maintained at greater physical distance.

But advances in cognition, language, and motor skill are not the only factors that affect the pattern of development in the preschool years. The cognitive changes are, in turn, affected by the child's play, particularly play with peers.

A 2- or 3-year-old, left alone, will play with toys and may show some pretend play. But when children play together, they expand each other's experience with objects, suggesting new ways of pretending to one another. This play with objects seems to be a key part of the child's growing cognitive skill, so time spent in play with other youngsters is much more than social. Conflict and disagreement are also key parts of children's play, affecting the child's emerging social skills and stimulating cognitive development as well (Bearison, Magzamen, & Filardo, 1986). When two children disagree about how to explain something or insist on their own different views, such experience enhances the awareness that there *are* other perspectives, other ways of thinking or playing.

Of course, play with other children is also a part of the child's developing concept of sex roles. Noticing whether other children are boys or girls, and what toys boys and girls play with, is a step in the long chain of sex-role learning.

The sense one gets of this period is that the child is making a slow but immensely important shift from dependent baby to independent child. This shift is made possible by physical change, by language, by many and varied play encounters with other children, by new abilities to control impulses. At the same time (and from some of the same causes), the child's thinking is *decentering*, becoming less egocentric and less tied to the outside appearances of things. Pretend play is probably a key ingredient in these changes.

All these changes, of course, alter the family system in profound ways. On the plus side is the fact that the child now uses and understands language, which helps enormously in parent-child communication. At the same time, the 2-year-old has figured out that he is a distinct person and different from Mom; he is trying out his limits. But all these newfound skills and this new independence are not accompanied by impulse control. Two-year-olds are pretty good at doing; they are lousy at *not* doing. They see something, so they go after it; when they want something, they want it *now!* If frustrated, they wail, or scream, or shout (isn't language wonderful?). A large part of the conflict parents experience with children at this age comes about because the parent *must* limit the child, not only for the child's own survival but to help teach the child impulse control (Escalona, 1981).

Once this transition has been weathered, the years from 3 to 6 are often relatively smooth within the family, although the arrival of a new baby or the child's transition to day care or preschool may be occasions for additional family adjustments.

The Elementary-School Years: From 6 to 12

The Transition. For most children, the next major transition occurs somewhere between 5 and 7 (White, 1965; Kegan, 1985). One of the most noticeable aspects of this transition is the much-discussed cognitive shift from preoperational to concrete operational thinking (to use Piaget's labels). As I pointed out in Chapter 7, it is not so clear that what is going on here is a rapid, pervasive, structural change to a whole new way of thinking. Children don't make this shift all at once in every area of their thinking or relationships. But there is agreement, I think, that important changes take place at about this age in the types of information-processing strategies children use, the abstractness of the concepts they grasp.

Most children start school at this age, too. Schooling is begun at about age 5 to 7 in virtually every culture, perhaps reflecting some recognition that children of that age are cognitively and socially "ready" for the demands of formal schooling.

Like the earlier transitions, this one is often marked by increases in problem behavior, difficulties adjusting to school, or other symptoms. But it is also frequently a time of excitement, even joy, for children.

The Consolidation. Figure 15.5 shows the parallel lines of development during the elementary-school years. Freud called this the latency period, as if it were a period of waiting, with nothing very important happening. In one sense he was right; it appears to be a relatively calm period. But there is a great deal of change nonetheless.

The cognitive changes are pervasive. One facet is that the child looks beyond the surface of things to search for underlying rules. We see this in the development of conservation principles, in gender constancy, and in children's relationships with one another. Another facet is the child's growing ability to take others' perspectives. She understands that others think and feel differently than she does. This is reflected in her peer interactions as well as her thinking. It is in elementary school that we see the beginnings of reciprocal friendships, for example.

Just what role does physical change play in this collection of developments? Clearly, there *are* physical changes going on. Girls, in particular,

Figure 15.4 Children in this age period insist on trying out new things, such as tying their own shoes. This is a fine thing, except when the parent is in a hurry or when it means getting everyone up a half hour earlier in the morning to give young Tom time to experiment.

	Age in years						
	6	7	8	9	10	11	12
Physical Development	Jumps rope; draws figures like squares	Begins to ride two-wheeled bike	Rides bike well	Beginning puberty for some girls; first stage of breast development	Early menarche	Early genital development in boys	Growth spurt in girls
Cognitive Development	Gender constancy; class inclusion; conservation of mass and number; rehearsal and other memory strategies; beginning metacognition		Inductive logic; conservation of weight		Multiple strategies for solving problems (e.g., searching for lost objects)	Conservation of space/volume	
Social Cognition	Kohlberg's stage 1	Kohlberg's stage 2 (naive hedonism) ——————————————————————— Kohlberg's stage 3 (good boy/nice girl) —————→ Friendship thought to be based on reciprocal trust			Descriptions of others begin to emphasize inner traits or qualities		
Self/Personality Development	Strong sex-role stereotyping; imitation of same-sex models Erikson's stage of industry vs. inferiority ————————————————————————————————————			Self-definition begins to include more inner qualities, more complex qualities			
Social Relationships	Same-sex play groups	Enduring friendships appear regularly ——————————————————————————————————→					

Figure 15.5   A summary of parallel changes during the elementary-school years. The keys to the transition at age 5 or 6 seem to be both the many cognitive changes and the beginning of school (which brings with it new social demands as well as new intellectual challenges).

are going through the first steps of puberty during elementary school. But we simply don't know whether the rate of physical development in these years is connected in any way to the rate of the child's progress through the sequence of cognitive or social understandings. There has been no research that I know of that hooks the first row in Figure 15.5 with any of the other rows, except that bigger, more coordinated, early-developing children are more likely to be popular with peers. Obviously, this is an area in which we need far more knowledge.

Adolescence: From 12 to 20

The Transition.   In some ways, the early years of adolescence have a lot in common with the early years of toddlerhood. Toddlers (the now-familiar 2-year-olds) are famous for their negativism and for their constant

Figure 15.6 One of the consequences of the child's new gender constancy in early elementary school is a *strong* preference for playmates of the same sex. Most social institutions, like Boy Scouts or Girl Scouts, are organized by sex for this age range, presumably in response to children's strong preferences.

push for more independence. At the same time, they are struggling to learn a vast array of new skills. Teenagers show many of these same qualities, albeit at much more abstract levels. Many of them go through a period of negativism, particularly with parents, right at the beginning of the pubertal changes. And many of the conflicts with parents center around issues of independence—teenagers want to come and go when they please, listen to the music they prefer at maximum volume, and wear the clothing and hair styles that are currently "in."

While this push for independence is going on, adolescents are also facing a whole new set of demands and skills to be learned—new social skills, new levels of cognitive complexity found in formal operations tasks. Perhaps because of these many changes, both physical and social, we also see a very large increase in the rate of depression in adolescence (recall Chapter 14). In fact, Roberta Simmons and her colleagues (Simmons, Burgeson, & Carlton-Ford, 1987) have found that those adolescents who have the greatest number of changes at the beginning of puberty—changing to junior high school, moving to a new town or new house, perhaps a parental separation or divorce—also show the greatest loss in self-esteem and the biggest drop in grade point average. Adolescents who can cope with these

	Age in Years							
	12	13	14	15	16	17	18	19
Physical Development	Major pubertal change begins for boys Girls' height spurt	Average age of menarche		Boys' maximum height spurt				
Cognitive Development	Beginning formal operations: systematic analysis "Early basic" formal operations: deductive logic					Consolidated formal operations (for a few)		
Social Cognition	Kohlberg's stage 3 continues ⟶ 		Descriptions of others and of self begin to include exceptions, comparisons, special conditions; deeper personality traits; empathy with another's general plight			Kohlberg's stage 4 ("law and order") for a minority ⟶	Kohlberg's stage 5 (rare) ⟶	
Self/Personality Development	Incidence of depression rises Erikson's stage of identity vs. role diffusion ⟶	Understanding of self, as above					Clear identity developed for perhaps half	
Social Relationships	Cliques Stable and intimate friendships continue and become more intimate ⟶ Parent-child conflict peaks at beginning of puberty		Crowds Maximum impact of peer group	Pairs				

Figure 15.7 A brief summary of parallel developments during adolescence. The transition at age 12 or so seems to be most centrally triggered by puberty and by the change in roles that puberty brings. Major cognitive and social-cognitive changes, are also prominent, however, and they are not clearly linked to the physiological changes of puberty.

changes one at a time—for example, remaining in the same school through eighth grade rather than moving on to a junior high school—show fewer symptoms of stress.

Still, although the effects of this transition are certainly broad and easy to see (as in Figure 15.7), it is difficult to pin down the causes and connections among the several different manifestations of change. I have already talked about some of the possible connections. It seems likely that the changes in the child's thinking from concrete operations to at least beginning formal operations help to cause other developments. One of the characteristics of formal operations thinking is the ability to imagine possibilities that you have never experienced and to manipulate ideas in your head. These new skills seem to help foster the broad questioning of old ways, old values, old patterns which is part of adolescence for many teenagers. In support of such a link, recall the research I mentioned in Chapter 12 that shows that beginning formal operations thinking seems to be a necessary precursor to the emergence of more advanced forms of social cognition and moral judgment.

Other researchers have also found some links between early formal reasoning and the process of identity formation (Leadbeater & Dionne, 1981; Rowe & Marcia, 1980). Using Marcia's identity status categories, these investigators have shown that teenagers and young adults who have achieved a clear identity are also much more likely to be reasoning at formal operations than are those who are still in the diffusion or moratorium statuses. Thus, formal operations thinking may *enable* the young person to rethink many aspects of his life, but it does not guarantee that he will do so.

The most speculative links at present are those between the physical changes of puberty and the social, cognitive, and personal changes at adolescence. One possibility, of course, is that there is a direct causal connection between hormonal and other physical changes and the emergence of new cognitive skills or social behaviors. As J. M. Tanner says:

> There is clearly no reason to suppose that the link between maturation of [brain] structure and appearance of [cognitive] function suddenly ceases at age 6 or 10 or 13. On the contrary, there is every reason to believe that the higher intellectual abilities also appear only when maturation of certain structures is complete. (Tanner, 1970, p. 123)

There is not much research exploring such possible linkages, but some recent bits of evidence are consistent with such a view. Steinberg's research, which I talked about in Chapter 11, shows one such link. He has found that the rise in parent-teenager conflict at adolescence seems to be predicted not by age but by pubertal status. Another fragment is the finding (mentioned in Chapter 6) that girls who go through puberty later seem to show better spatial ability than do those who go through puberty earlier. Still a third piece of the puzzle is that specific hormones seem to be linked to mood and aggressiveness. Elizabeth Susman and Editha Nottelman and their co-workers (Susman et al., 1987; Nottelmann et al., 1987) have found that in boys (but not in girls), higher levels of adrenal androgen are associated with both more sad feelings and more delinquent and rebellious behavior.

Indirect effects of physical change are probably also substantial at this age. When the child's body grows and becomes more like that of an adult, the parents begin to treat the child differently and the child begins to see himself as a soon-to-be-adult. Both of these changes may help to trigger some of the searching self-examinations that are part of this period of life.

For the family, these combined changes require some major adapta-

Figure 15.8 In the United States, at least, one of the major family adjustments that has to be made when children reach adolescence centers around the use of the family car. How much should a 16-year-old be trusted? What rules should be in force? This mark of independence is similar to what happens at age 6 or 7 when the child is allowed to go off on her bicycle.

tions. The teenager is demanding new levels of authority and power while simultaneously asking for nurturance and guidance. The presence of a sexually charged pubescent young person in the house may also reawaken unresolved adolescent issues in the parents, just when they are themselves facing a sense of physical decline in their forties or fifties. Then, too, teenagers stay up late, which severely restricts private time for parents. Perhaps it is not surprising that many parents (particularly fathers) report that marital satisfaction is at its lowest ebb during their children's adolescence (Rollins & Galligan, 1978). Despite these strains, though, it is impressive that most families manage to move through this adjustment time rather well, and a new equilibrium is formed in the late teen years.

The Consolidation.   Beyond the first year or two of puberty, there is a long period of consolidation, with more gradual change occurring throughout the high-school years. This is not an entirely smooth process, of course; you will remember from Chapter 10 that a clear identity is often not achieved until college age, if then. The formation of emotionally intimate sexual or presexual partnerships is also a relatively late development during the teenage years. So, as with all of the other periods that I have labeled consolidations, change is continuous. But once the major disequilibrium of puberty is weathered, the period of adolescence is not nearly as full of storm and stress as popular literature might have us believe.

━━━━ RETURNING TO SOME BASIC QUESTIONS

With this brief overview in mind, let me now go back to the key questions I raised in Chapter 1 and see if the answers can be made any clearer.

What Are the Major Influences on Development?

The short answer is easy: Every aspect of development is influenced by internal forces (such as specific heredity, physical intactness at birth, illness, and maturationally governed biological changes), by environment, and by the interaction of the two. But you could have said that before you read this book. What I hope is clear after reading your way through 14 chapters is that the relative weight of these different influences varies as a function of the aspect of development we are talking about and with the child's age. It may help to think of different facets of development as being along a continuum, with those most internally determined on one end and those most externally determined on the other.

Physical development defines one end of this continuum, since it is very strongly shaped by internal forces. Maturational timetables are extremely powerful and robust, particularly during infancy and adolescence. But even here there is a minimum necessary environment for normal development, and specific environmental factors, such as poor diet, can have an impact, too.

Next along the continuum is probably language (although some experts will argue with this conclusion, given that language development may depend upon prior cognitive attainments). Language seems to emerge with only minimal environmental support—though at the very least, the child must hear language spoken (or see it signed). Specific features of the environment seem to matter a bit more than is true for physical development. The amount parents talk to the child affects vocabulary growth, for example, and parents who respond contingently to their children's vocalizations seem to be able to speed up the process.

Cognitive development falls somewhere in the middle of the continuum. Clearly, there are powerful internal forces at work. As John Flavell puts it:

> There is an impetus to childhood cognitive growth that is not ultimately explainable by this environmental push or that experiential shove. (Flavell, 1985, p. 283)

We don't yet know whether the impressive regularity of the sequences of cognitive development arises from built-in processes like assimilation and accommodation, from physiological changes in information-processing capacity, or from some combination of the two. But it is clear that this engine is moving along a shared track. We do know that the specific qualities of the environment affect both cognitive power and structure. Children show faster cognitive development and higher eventual IQ scores when they have access to varied and age-appropriate toys and their parents respond to their overtures and encourage exploration and achievement.

Social and emotional development lie at the other end of the continuum, where the impact of the environment seems to be the greatest. I do not want to imply here that inborn or physical changes are unimportant. Temperament may well be inborn, and attachment behaviors may be instinctive; both of these factors certainly shape the child's earliest encounters with others. But the balance of nature/nurture seems to lean more toward nurture in this area. In particular, the security of the child's attachment and the quality of her relationships with people outside the family seem to be powerfully affected by the specific quality of the interactions within the family. The overall stress or support in the family also make a difference in the emergence of various behavior disorders as well as on the child's everyday encounters with significant others.

Even this fairly complex analysis, however, only begins to scratch the surface. For one thing, many of the statements I have just made need to be modified in terms of *when* a particular environmental event takes place.

Does Timing Matter?

Over the years, a great many psychologists have assumed that environmental experiences in the first few months or years are especially critical, especially important in shaping the trajectory of development for all of the child's life. A. D. B. Clarke (1968; Clarke & Clarke, 1976) poses the question with an analogy: When we construct a house, does the shape of the foundation determine the final structure completely, does it partially influence the final structure, or could many different final structures be built on the original foundation? What if there are flaws or weaknesses in the original foundation? Are these flaws permanent, or can they be corrected later, after the house is completed?

There are data on both sides. Several respected theorists, including Sandra Scarr (Scarr-Salapatek, 1976) and Robert McCall (1981), have proposed that cognitive development in the first 12 to 18 months of life is highly *canalized* (a term first suggested by Waddington, 1957). That is, the path or sequence of early development is very powerful (a narrow canal), and nearly all basic child-rearing environments provide enough support for it to proceed normally. Furthermore, infants seem to have excellent "self-righting" tendencies: if the child is deflected from the underlying pathway because of some inadequacy of the environment or some accidental occurrence, the power of the underlying developmental system is such that he can often recover later. (For example, Winick [Winick, Meyer, & Harris, 1975] found that Korean orphans who had been severely malnourished and often emotionally neglected in the first 3 years of life nonetheless recovered to normal intellectual levels after they were adopted into middle-class families in the United States.) These theorists argue that beyond infancy canalization seems to be much weaker. Optimum development at later ages seems to demand much more specific input, so that only a narrower range of environments provide sufficient support.

On the other side of the argument are the obvious cases in which an early experience has been highly formative. Some prenatal influences are permanent; some effects of early cognitive impoverishment, malnutrition, or abuse may also be long-lasting. In the Winick study, for example, those Korean orphans who had had the most severe malnutrition in the early years showed less-complete recovery than did those whose malnutrition had been more moderate.

My own resolution of this dispute is (paradoxically) to agree with both positions. Yes, development is highly canalized in the early months. But if a child's particular environment *does* fall outside the range of supportive environments, the effects can be strongly negative and long-lasting. The earlier such a deviation occurs, the more pervasive the effects seem to be. Thus, infancy may be less *frequently* pivotal in the pattern of the child's development than more minor deviations in toddlerhood or the preschool years. But when the deviations in infancy are extreme enough to deflect the infant from the normal developmental path—such as in the case of severe abuse or malnutrition—the effect is substantial.

A second, very different way to think about timing of experience is in terms of the development of internal working models. Beginning perhaps at 12 or 18 months of age, the child seems to develop such cognitive understandings of various experiences. These models are not immutable; they can be and are altered by subsequent experience. But they form a bias in the system. And since at least some of these models are formed early and carried forward, the early experience that shapes them may play a more significant role in the child's pattern of development than does later experience.

Still a third way to think about timing is to emphasize the importance of specific psychological tasks at different ages. Erikson's theory, for example, emphasizes each of a series of psychological dilemmas. Any experience that affects the way a child resolves a particular task will be formative at that time; the same experience may have much less effect at an earlier or later time. Alan Sroufe and Michael Rutter (1984) have offered a broader list of age-graded tasks, given in Table 15.1. In this way of looking at things, the child is seen as *focusing* on different aspects of the environment at different times. Thus, during the period from 1 to $2\frac{1}{2}$, when the child is focused on mastery of the object world, the quality and range of his experi-

Table 15.1

▬▬▬▬▬▬▬

Tasks or Issues in Each of Several Age Periods, as Proposed by Sroufe and Rutter

Age in years	Issues or tasks
0–1	Biological regulation; harmonious dyadic interaction; formation of an effective attachment relationship.
1–2$\frac{1}{2}$	Exploration, experimentation, and mastery of the object world (caregiver as secure base); individuation and autonomy; responding to external control of impulses.
3–5	Flexible self-control; self-reliance; initiative; identification and gender concept; establishing effective peer contacts (empathy).
6–12	Social understanding (equity, fairness); gender constancy; same-sex friendships; sense of "industry" (competence); school adjustment.
13 +	Formal operations (flexible perspective taking, "as-if" thinking); loyal same-sex friendships; beginning heterosexual relationships; emancipation; identity.

Source: Sroufe & Rutter, 1984.

▬▬▬▬▬▬▬

ences with inanimate objects may be of special importance—a hypothesis which matches the facts I gave you in Chapter 6 about the impact of the early environment on children's IQs and cognitive development.

All in all, I do not think that any specific age is critical for all aspects of development; I do think that for any aspect of development, some ages are more central than others, and that during those times, patterns are set which affect later experience. As Alan Sroufe says, "Development is hierarchical; it is not a blackboard to be erased and written upon again. Even when children change rather markedly, the shadows of the earlier adaptation remain" (1983, p. 73–74).

What Is the Nature of Developmental Change?

My bias has no doubt been apparent all through the book, so you can predict my conclusion that developmental change is more qualitative than quantitative. Certainly, the child acquires more neurons, more vocabulary words, more information-processing strategies. But these are used in different ways by older children than by younger ones. Furthermore, it seems clear that these qualitative changes occur in sequences. Such sequences are apparent in physical development, in cognitive development, in social and moral development.

Stages. Whether it is meaningful to speak of stages, however, is still an open question. Some examples of hierarchically organized stages have certainly been found, Kohlberg's stages of moral reasoning being the most obvious example. But as I mentioned in Chapter 7, the evidence for broad changes in structure is not so impressive. That is, a child's new understanding or a new information-processing strategy is not initially applied broadly to new instances or related problems. Each new skill, each new understanding, seems to be acquired in a fairly narrow area first and only later generalized more fully. In fact, one of the things that differentiates the gifted or higher-IQ child from the lower-IQ or retarded child is how quickly and broadly the child generalizes some new concept or strategy to new instances.

Despite this nonstagelike type of change, it is still true that if you compare the patterns of relationships, thinking, or problem solving of two children of widely differing ages—say a 5-year-old and an 11-year-old— they will differ in almost every respect. So we see orderliness in the sequences and some linkages between them, but there probably are no major stages quite like those Piaget proposed.

Continuities.　In the midst of all this change, all these sequences, all the new forms of relating and thinking, there is also continuity. Each child carries forward some core of individuality, too. The notion of temperament certainly implies such a core, as does the concept of an internal working model. Alan Sroufe once again offers a elegant way of thinking about this central core. Continuity in development, he says, "takes the form of coherence across transformations" (1983, p. 51). Thus, the specific behavior that we see in the child may change; the clinging toddler may not become a clinging 9-year-old. But the underlying attachment model or the temperament that led to the clinging will still be at least partially present, manifest in new ways. In particular, it has become increasingly clear that some *mal*adaptations persist over time, as seen in the consistency of high levels of aggression or tantrum behavior (which I talked about in Chapters 11 and 14) and in the persistence of some of the maladaptive social interactions that flow from insecure attachments. Our task as psychologists is to understand both coherence or consistency and the underlying patterns of development or transformation.

INDIVIDUAL DIFFERENCES

The whole issue of individual continuities emphasizes the fact that development is individual as well as collective. I have talked about individual differences in virtually every chapter, so you know that children exhibit both inborn differences (such as temperament and physical intactness or vulnerabilities) and emergent or environmentally produced differences. Most of the patterns of individual variation we see are the product of the interaction between inborn tendencies and the conditions of the child's rearing. Attachment security, for example, is affected by the child's temperament as well as by the specific pattern of her early interactions with her parents; behavior problems such as excess aggressiveness may be the product of interactions between inborn temperament, male hormones, and family relationships.

All this is familiar stuff by now. But there are two dimensions of individual differences I want to explore further: sex differences and vulnerability or resilience.

Sex Differences in Development

Although I have talked about sex differences in nearly every chapter, it may be helpful to you to see all the findings pulled together into the summary in Table 15.2.

At the risk of repeating myself, I want to make a couple of points about these data. First, even where the differences are very clear, such as with aggressiveness, the actual magnitude of the difference is normally quite small, and the two distributions (male and female) overlap almost completely. That is, *within* each sex there is almost a full range of performance or behavior on each of the dimensions listed in the table. It is only when we look at average scores for the two sexes that we see a difference. There are a few exceptions to this statement, perhaps most notably the markedly higher rate of abnormality and deviance among boys, but as a general rule the actual impact of gender on behavior is suprisingly small.

Second, both biological and environmental causes seem to be at work in producing the differences we do see. The difference in aggressiveness seems to have biological roots, but parental treatment may well magnify the biological difference. Similarly, differences in early language skill may be partly biological (emerging from differing maturational rates). I know that it is not particularly popular today to look for any kind of biological causes of sex differences. But the evidence at the moment compels me to accept the plausibility of at least some biological differences interacting with environmental shaping.

A third point is not apparent in Table 15.2, but it is nonetheless critical. Psychologists are beginning to discover that apparently similar experiences may have quite different effects on boys and girls. For instance, I mentioned that a link between specific hormones and mood or behavior had been found for teenage boys but not for girls. Another illustration comes from the work of Simpson and Stevenson-Hinde (1985), who found that shyness was associated with *negative* family interactions in boys but with *positive* family interactions in girls. As Michael Rutter puts it, "it is not only that parents may treat boys and girls somewhat differently, which they do . . . but also that the patterns of effects differ between the sexes" (1987, p. 1262). This conclusion has now led nearly all researchers to analyze their results separately for boys and girls, but we are a long way from understanding the pattern that is emerging.

Vulnerability and Resilience

Another dimension of individual differences may have as broad an effect on children's development as gender (and it may help to tie together many

Table 15.2

Summary of Sex Differences in Development in Childhood and Adolescence

Physical development

- *Rate of maturation.* Girls are on a faster developmental timetable; this is particularly apparent prenatally and at adolescence.
- *Quality of maturation.* Girls' physical growth is more regular and predictable, with fewer uneven spurts.
- *Strength and speed.* Little difference until puberty, when boys become both stronger and faster, developing a larger percentage of muscle and a smaller percentage of fat.
- *Heart and circulation.* At puberty boys develop larger heart and lungs and a greater capacity for carrying oxygen in the blood.

Perceptual development

- *Perceptual acuity.* No sex differences.
- *Discrimination.* No sex differences in ability to make discriminations.
- *Perceptual style.* Boys are more likely to be field-independent, girls to be field-dependent.

Cognitive development

- *Cognitive structure.* No sex differences until adolescence, when boys show a somewhat higher incidence of formal operations thinking.
- *IQ.* No sex difference in total IQ.
- *Verbal skills.* Girls are slightly faster in some aspects of early language; girls have better articulation and fewer reading problems; at adolescence, girls are better at verbal reasoning.
- *Mathematical skills.* Before adolescence, girls are slightly better at arithmetic computation; at adolescence, boys show slightly but consistently better scores at tasks requiring mathematical reasoning.
- *Spatial ability.* Boys are better at almost any task requiring spatial visualization. This becomes a larger and more consistent difference at adolescence.

Social development

- *Aggression /dominance.* Boys are more aggressive and more dominant on virtually all measures, beginning in toddlerhood and continuing through adolescence.
- *Competitiveness.* Boys are more competitive, although this difference does not appear as early as the aggression difference.
- *Nurturance.* No clear sex difference.
- *Sociability.* Girls typically have fewer but closer friendships; this is seen beginning in elementary school and continues through adolescence (and in adulthood).
- *Compliance.* Girls appear to be somewhat more compliant to adult requests in early childhood.
- *Identity.* No clear differences.

Other

- *Vulnerability.* Boys are more likely to show virtually all forms of physical, emotional, and cognitive vulnerability to stress, as well as higher levels of deviant development.

of the points I have been making in this summary chapter): the child's general level of vulnerability or resilience. One useful way to define this dimension is in terms of the *range of environments which will be sufficiently supportive for optimal development.* A vulnerable infant is one with a narrow range of potentially supportive environments. For such a child, only the most stimulating, the most responsive, the most adaptive environment will do. When the child's environment falls outside that range, the probability of a poor outcome is greatly increased. A resilient child, in contrast, is one for whom any of a very wide range of environments will support optimum development. Of course, a given child may be relatively more vulnerable or more resilient in some areas of development than others. So a child might be vulnerable intellectually but quite resilient emotionally or personally. But the general concept is nonetheless helpful. It is similar to Horowitz's model, which I presented in Chapter 1 (go back and look again at Figure 1.2).

Some kinds of vulnerabilities are inborn. Any child who comes into the world with abnormalities, prenatal trauma or stress, preterm birth, malnutrition, or whatever is more vulnerable in this sense; such children thrive only in highly supportive environments. You've encountered this pattern again and again through the chapters of this book.

- Low-birth-weight infants typically have normal IQs if they are reared in middle-class homes, but have a high risk of serious retardation if they are reared in poverty (Werner, 1986).
- Prenatally malnourished infants or those with other complications during pregnancy or delivery look normal if they attend highly stimulating special preschools, but they have significantly lower IQs if reared at home by mothers with low education (Zeskind & Ramey, 1981; Breitmayer & Ramey, 1986).
- Temperamentally irritable babies are more likely to become insecurely attached if their mothers have insufficient emotional and social support (Crockenberg, 1981).
- Children born with cytomegalovirus are much more likely to have learning problems in school if they are reared in poverty-level environments than if they are reared in middle-class families (Hanshaw et al., 1976).

Similarly, I think that some attributes that contribute to greater resilience may also be inborn. Emmy Werner, in her 20-year longitudinal study of all the infants born on the Hawaiian island of Kauai in 1955 (Werner, 1986), has found that among children reared in poverty environments, those who turned out well (whom she calls resilient), compared to those who turned out badly, were more likely to have been perceived as "easy" or "good-natured" as babies and were more often firstborn. Thus, an easy temperament may be one inborn characteristic that significantly increases the child's resilience. Other protective factors (to use Norman Garmezy's phrase) may include a secure attachment, a relatively high tolerance for frustration, and an ability to recover rapidly from disturbances.

Figure 15.9 I have used this photo at the end of every edition of this book because it speaks to me so eloquently of the quality of joy, of discovery, that is so much a part of development.

So far that's fairly straightforward. But let me propose a more speculative variation on this concept. I think that vulnerability in this sense does not remain constant throughout life. A more general proposition, which I suggest as a working hypothesis, is that each time the environment falls outside the range of acceptably supporting environments *for that child* (that is, each time there is a mismatch between the child's needs and what is available), the child becomes *more vulnerable,* while during each period in which the child's needs are met, the child becomes more resilient. For example, I would predict that a temperamentally difficult child whose family environment is nonetheless sufficient to foster a secure attachment will become more resilient, more able to handle the next set of tasks, while a temperamentally easy child who nonetheless develops an insecure attachment will become more vulnerable to later stress or environmental insufficiency.

Furthermore, which qualities of the environment are critical for a child's optimum development no doubt change as the child passes from one age to another. Responsive and warm interactions with parents seem particularly central in the period from perhaps 6 months to 18 months; richness of cognitive stimulation seems particularly central between perhaps 1 year and 4 years; opportunity for practicing social skills with peers may be especially central at a later age. Thus, as the tasks (such as those listed in Table 15.1) change with age, the optimum environment will change also. Among other things, this means that the same family may be very good with a child of one age and not so good with a child of another age.

Most generally, this model leads to the conclusion that even the most vulnerable child can show improvement if her environment improves markedly. Because some congenitally vulnerable children do not encounter sufficiently supportive environments, their vulnerability will continue to increase. In this way, early problems will often persist. But at the same time, improvement is possible, even likely. *Most* children manage to survive and thrive despite stresses and vulnerabilities. As Emmy Werner puts it, "we could not help being deeply impressed by the resilience of most children and youth and their capacity for positive change and personal growth" (1986, p. 5).

A FINAL POINT: THE JOY OF DEVELOPMENT

On a similarly optimistic note, I want to end both this chapter and the book by reminding you of something I said at the very beginning. In the midst of all the crises and transitions and vulnerabilities, there is a special *joyous* quality to development. When a child masters a new skill, she is not just pleased—she is delighted, and she will repeat that new skill at length, quite obviously getting vast satisfaction from it. A 5-year-old I know learned to draw stars and drew them on everything in sight, including paper, walls, clothes, and napkins. It was so much *fun* to draw stars! A 10-year-old who learns to do cartwheels will practice endlessly and will delightedly display this new talent to anyone who will watch.

The same joyous quality can be part of the family's development as well. Confronting and moving successfully through one of the periodic (and inevitable) upheavals in family life can be immensely pleasing. Watching your child progress, liking your child, enjoying walking or talking together are all deeply satisfying parts of rearing children. When parents cry at their son's or daughter's high-school graduation or wedding, it is not merely sentiment. It is an expression of that sense of love, pride, and wonderment that you have gotten this far.

SUMMARY

1. The child's development may be thought of as a series of alternating periods of transition and consolidation. The transitions occur when there are individual major changes or pileups of smaller changes.

2. Within infancy, there appear to be at least two transition periods, one at about 2 months and the other at 8 to 10 months.

3. The several threads of development in infancy are not independent of one another. For example, changes in the brain at 2 months affect the child's discrimination ability, which helps make recognition of the mother possible, which helps makes specific attachment possible.

4. The transition at 18 months is marked by the remarkable emergence of symbolic activity, evidenced in language, in thinking, in play. A general combinatorial ability (stringing several concepts or actions together) also appears at about this time.

5. These cognitive accomplishments combine with major new motor skills to allow the child significantly greater independence, which in turn fosters further cognitive growth. Play with peers also seems critically important for both social and cognitive development.

6. The transition at age 5 to 7 is marked both by the beginning emergence of still more powerful cognitive skills and by the beginning of school. A general "decentering" is manifested in children's relationships with their peers as well as in their thinking.

7. The transition at adolescence is triggered primarily by the physical changes of puberty, but it is accompanied by still further cognitive changes, major alterations in patterns of peer interaction, increases in family disruption, and increases in depression.

8. A shift toward formal operations at adolescence may be one contributor to a rise in self-questioning; pubertal changes may have both direct and indirect effects on the other developments of this period.

9. The various facets of development can be arrayed along a continuum from those most governed by internal influences to those most governed by external influences, in the following order: physical development, language, cognition, and social/personality development.

10. The timing of experience also makes some difference, although this issue is still being debated. Development in the first year may be particularly highly canalized, but marked environmental insufficiencies at this age may be especially harmful.

11. Each age period can also be thought of as having a set of central tasks; experiences that are especially important for the successful completion of those tasks will thus be critical for that age.

12. Development seems clearly to be made up of a large number of widely shared (if not universal) sequences. But whether there are broad, structurally different stages is less clear.

13. Individual differences result not only from varying heredity and differing prenatal experience but also from differing training and experience after birth. Sex differences, however, are less substantial than popular ideas might lead us to think, although boys and girls may nonetheless respond quite differently to similar experiences.

14. A dimension of vulnerability/resilience is another way to think about individual differences. The dimension may be defined in terms of the range of environments which will support optimal development for a particular child. A large range implies resilience; a narrow range defines vulnerability.

15. Vulnerability may be increased or decreased over time, depending on the adequacy or inadequacy of environments at each of a series of points in development. Children may thus recover from, or surmount, even very poor starts.

16. For both the child and the parent, development is full of joy as well as travail.

SUGGESTED READING

Many of the books I have suggested in earlier chapters are relevant here as well. But let me also suggest several books that give the flavor of particular ages.

Adelson, J. (Ed.). (1980). *Handbook of adolescent psychology.* New York: Wiley-Interscience.
Like Collins's book listed below, this is a collection of papers covering virtually every facet of adolescence. Most of these papers were written in the late 1970s, but this is still the broadest and most detailed single source I know of on adolescence.

Brazelton, T. B. (1974). *Toddlers and parents.* New York: Dell.
This is the companion book to the infancy book I recommended in Chapter 3. It covers children through about age 3, with lots of specific examples and very sensitive advice.

Collins, W. A. (Ed.). (1984). *Development during middle childhood: The years from six to twelve.* Washington, DC: National Academy Press.
This collection of papers touches on all facets of school-age children: biology, cognition, self-understanding, family and peer relationships, school, and atypical development. An excellent source of information about this often-neglected age period.

White, B. L. (1975). *The first three years of life.* Englewood Cliffs, NJ: Prentice-Hall.
A highly readable book, full of descriptions of the development of children in the early years, along with specific advice to parents about such things as choosing toys and coping with 2-year-olds. I do not agree with all of what White says, but there is a great deal of useful information in this book.

Glossary

accommodation   That part of the adaptation process by which a person modifies existing schemes (ideas, actions, or strategies) to fit new experiences.

achievement test   A test, usually given in schools, designed to assess a child's learning of specific material, such as spelling or arithmetic computation.

acuity   sharpness of perceptual ability—how well or clearly one can see or hear or use other senses.

adaptive behavior   An aspect of a child's functioning often considered in diagnosing mental retardation; can the child adapt to the tasks of everyday life?

aggression   Usually defined as intentional physical or verbal behaviors directed toward a person or an object with the intent to inflict damage on that person or object.

altruism   Giving or sharing objects, time, or goods with others, with no obvious self-gain.

amniocentesis   A medical test for genetic abnormalities in the embryo or fetus that may be done at about 16 weeks' gestation.

androgyny   A self-concept including, and behavior expressing, high levels of both masculine and feminine qualities.

anoxia   A shortage of oxygen. Prolonged anoxia can result in brain damage. This is one of the potential risks at birth.

Apgar score   An assessment of a newborn's condition. Scores of 0, 1, or 2 are summed for five criteria at one and five minutes after birth.

assimilation   That part of the adaptation process that involves the taking in of new experiences or information into existing schemes. Experience is not taken in "as is," however, but is modified (or interpreted) somewhat so as to fit the preexisting schemes.

attachment   The positive affective bond felt by one person for another, such as the child for the parent or the parent for the child.

attachment behaviors   The collection of (probably) automatic behaviors of one person toward another that bring about or maintain proximity and caregiving, such as the smile of the young infant; behaviors that reflect an attachment.

attention-deficit hyperactivity disorder   The technical term for what is more often simply called hyperactivity. It is characterized by short attention span, distractibility, and heightened levels of physical activity.

authoritarian parental style   Pattern of parental behavior described by Baumrind, among others, including high levels of directiveness and low levels of affection and warmth.

authoritative parental style   Pattern of parental behavior described by Baumrind, including high control and high warmth.

autism   A severe form of emotional/language disorder, appearing in infancy.

autonomous morality   Piaget's second proposed stage of moral reasoning, which develops sometime after age 7 and is characterized by judgment of intent and emphasis on reciprocity.

autosomes   The 22 pairs of chromosomes in which both members of the pair are the same size and carry parallel information.

babbling   The often-repetitive vocalizing of consonant-vowel combinations by an infant, typically beginning at about 6 months of age.

Bayley Scales of Infant Development   The best-known and most widely used test of infant intelligence.

behavior problem   The general phrase used to describe mild or moderate forms of emotional difficulty, including aggressiveness, shyness, anxiety, and hyperactivity.

behavior therapy   A therapeutic intervention based on principles of reinforcement.

blastocyst   The name used for the small mass

of cells that implants itself into the wall of the uterus about two weeks after conception.

brain damage Some injury to the brain, either during prenatal development or later, that results in its improper functioning.

categorical self The definition of the self by comparing the self to others in one or more categories, such as age, gender, size, or skill.

cephalocaudal From the head downward. Describes one pattern of physical development in infancy.

cesarean section Delivery of the child through an incision in the mother's abdomen.

childhood-onset pervasive developmental disorder Term used in DSM-III to describe a pattern of severe emotional disturbance that begins after infancy (and is thus not autism) but does not include the delusions common in schizophrenia.

chromosome The structure in each cell in the body that contains genetic information. Each chromosome is made up of many genes.

classical conditioning One of three major types of learning. An automatic, unconditioned response such as an emotional feeling or a reflex comes to be triggered by a new cue, called the conditioned stimulus (CS), after the CS has been paired several times with the original unconditioned stimulus.

class inclusion The relationship between classes in which a subordinate class is included in a superordinate class, as bananas are part of the class "fruit."

clique A group of four to six friends with strong attachment bonds and high levels of group solidarity and loyalty.

cohort A group of persons of approximately the same age who have shared similar major life experiences, such as cultural training, economic conditions, or type of education.

color constancy The ability to see the color of an object as remaining the same despite changes in illumination or shadow. One of the basic perceptual constancies that make up object constancy.

competence The behavior of a person as it would be under ideal or perfect circumstances. It is not possible to measure competence directly.

competition Interaction between two or more persons in which each person attmepts to gain control over some scarce resource, such as toys, attention from a preferred person, or "success."

componential intelligence One of three

types of intelligence in Sternberg's triarchic theory of intelligence. This is the type of intelligence typically measured on IQ tests: analytic thinking, remembering facts, organizing information.

conceptual tempo A dimension of individual differences in perceptual/conceptual style, suggested by Kagar. It describes the general pace at which objects (or people) are examined or explored.

concrete operations The stage of development proposed by Piaget for ages 6 to 12, in which mental operations such as subtraction, reversibility, and multiple classification are acquired.

conditioned stimulus In classical conditioning, the stimulus that, after being paired a number of times with an unconditioned stimulus, comes to trigger the unconditioned response.

confluence model Zajonc's term for his explanation of family-size and ordinal position effects on IQ. Assumes that a child's IQ is partially determined by the average intellectual level of the family members with whom the child has contact.

conscience Roughly equivalent to the superego. In Freudian theory, the part of the personality that monitors one's behavior, judging it to be acceptable or unacceptable.

conservation The concept that objects remain the same in fundamental ways, such as weight or number, even when there are external changes in shape or arrangement. The concept is achieved by children between 5 and 10 years of age.

contextual intelligence One of three types of intelligence in Sternberg's triarchic theory of intelligence. Often called "street smarts," this type of intelligence includes skills in adapting to an environment and in adapting an environment to one's own needs.

control group The group of subjects in an experiment that do *not* receive any special treatment.

conventional morality The second level of moral reasoning proposed by Kohlberg, in which the person's judgments are dominated by considerations of group values and laws.

cooing An early stage during the prelinguistic period, from about 1 to 4 months of age, when the infant repeats vowel sounds, particularly the *uuu* sound.

correlation A statistic used to describe the degree or strength of a relationship between two variables. It can range from +1.00 to −1.00. The closer it is to 1.00, the stronger the relationship being described.

cortex The convoluted gray portion of the brain which governs most complex thought, language, and memory, among other functions.

critical period A period of time during development when the organism is especially responsive to and learns from a specific type of stimulation. The same stimulation at other points in development has little or no effect.

crossing over The process that occurs during meiosis in which genetic material may be exchanged between the members of a chromosome pair.

cross-sectional study A study in which different groups of individuals of different ages are all studied at the same time.

crowd A larger and looser group of friends than a clique, with perhaps 20 members; normally made up of several cliques joined together.

cumulative deficit Any difference between groups in IQ (or achievement test) scores that becomes larger over time.

deductive logic Reasoning from the general to the particular, from a rule to an expected instance, or from a theory to a hypothesis. Characteristic of formal operational thought.

defense mechanisms In Freudian theory, strategies of the ego for coping with anxiety (denial, repression, identification, projection, and many others).

deoxyribonucleic acid (DNA) The chemical of which chromosomes are composed.

depth perception The ability to judge the distance of an object from the body on the basis of a number of cues.

dilation The first stage of childbirth, when the cervix opens sufficiently to allow the infant's head to pass into the birth canal.

dominance The ability of one person consistently to "win" competitive encounters with other individuals.

dominance hierarchy A set of dominance relationships in a group, describing the rank order of "winners" and "losers" in competitive encounters.

Down's syndrome A genetic anomaly in which every cell contains three copies of 21 chromosomes rather than two. Children born with this genetic pattern are usually mentally retarded and have characteristic physical features.

DSM-III The third edition of the *Diagnostic and Statistical Manual of Mental Disorders* of the American Psychiatric Association, listing the currently agreed-upon categories of emotional disturbance.

dyslexia A form of specific learning disability in which the individual has difficulty with reading.

ectomorphic Body type defined by bone length. An ectomorphic individual is tall and slender, usually with stooped shoulders.

effacement The flattening of the cervix, which, along with dilation, allows the delivery of the infant.

ego In Freudian theory, that portion of the personality that organizes, plans, and keeps the person in touch with reality. Language and thought are both ego functions.

embryo The name given to the organism during the period of prenatal development from about two to eight weeks after conception, beginning with implantation of the blastocyst into the uterine wall.

empathy An emotional response to another's feelings or situation that approximates or matches the other's emotions.

empiricism The opposite of nativism. The theoretical point of view that all perceptual skill arises from experience.

endocrine glands Glands (including the adrenals, the thyroid, the pituitary, the testes, and the ovaries) that secrete hormones governing overall physical growth and sexual maturing.

endomorphic Body type defined by amount of body fat. An endomorphic individual is soft and round in shape.

equilibration The third part of the adaptation process, as proposed by Piaget, involving the balance between assimilation and accommodation; the periodic restructuring of schemas into new structures.

erogenous zones Portions of the body that in Freudian theory are thought to be sequentially the seat of heightened sexual awareness: the mouth, the anus, and the genitals.

estrogen The female sex hormones secreted by the ovaries.

executive processes Proposed subset of information processes involving organizing and planning strategies. Similar in meaning to metacognition.

existential self Term used by Lewis and Brooks-Gunn to refer to the most basic part of the self-concept, the sense of being separate and distinct from others.

experiential intelligence   One of three types of intelligence described by Sternberg in his triarchic theory of intelligence. Includes creativity, insight, seeing new relationships among experiences.

experiment   A research strategy in which the experimenter assigns subjects randomly to groups and controls or manipulates a key variable of interest.

experimental group   The group (or groups) of subjects in an experiment who are given some special treatment intended to produce a specific consequence.

expressive language   The child's ability to communicate in words.

expressive style   One of two styles of early language proposed by Katherine Nelson. Expressive style is characterized by low use of nounlike terms and high use of personal-social words and phrases.

fallopian tube   The tube down which the ovum travels to the uterus and in which conception usually occurs.

fetal alcohol syndrome (FAS)   A pattern of physical abnormalities, including mental retardation and minor physical anomalies, found often in children born to alcoholic mothers.

fetus   The name given to the developing organism from about eight weeks after conception until birth.

field dependence   One end of a dimension of individual difference in perceptual style, proposed by Witkin. Field-dependent individuals are heavily influenced by the context in which objects appear.

field independence   The other end of the field-dependence dimension. Field-independent individuals can ignore the context or distracting cues around objects.

fontanels   The "soft spots" present in the skull at birth. These disappear when the several bones of the skull grow together.

foreclosure   One of four identity statuses proposed by Marcia, whereby a young person makes an ideological or occupational commitment without having gone through a reevaluation.

formal operations   Piaget's name for the fourth and final major stage of cognitive development, occurring during adolescence, when the child becomes able to manipulate and organize ideas as well as objects.

gender concept   The understanding of one's own gender, including the permanence and constancy of gender.

gender constancy   The final step in developing a gender concept, in which the child understands that gender doesn't change even when such external things as clothing or hair length change.

gender identity   The first step in gender concept development, in which the child labels herself correctly and categorizes others correctly as male or female.

gender stability   The second step in gender concept development, in which the child understands that a person's gender continues to be stable throughout the lifetime.

gene   A uniquely coded segment of DNA in a chromosome that affects one or more specific body processes or developments.

genotype   The unique pattern of characteristics and developmental sequences mapped in the genes of an individual. Will be modified by individual experience into the phenotype.

germ cells   Sperm and ova. These cells, unlike all other cells of the body, contain only 23 chromosomes rather than 23 pairs.

giftedness   Normally defined in terms of very high IQ (above 140 or 150), but may also be defined in terms of exceptional creativity or remarkable skill in one or more specific areas, such as mathematics or memory.

gonadotropic hormones   Hormones produced in the pituitary gland which stimulate the sex organs to develop.

habituation   An automatic decrease in the intensity of a response to a repeated stimulus, which enables the child or adult to ignore the familiar and focus attention on the novel.

hearing-impaired   The phrase currently used (in place of *hard-of-hearing*) to describe children or adults with significant hearing loss.

heredity versus environment   A classic "argument" within psychology, in which two major sources of potential influence on behavior are contrasted.

heteronomous morality   Piaget's first proposed stage of moral reasoning, characterized by moral absolutism and belief in imminent justice. Judgments are based on consequences rather than intent.

holophrases   The expression of a whole idea by a combination of words and gestures. Characteristics of the child's language from about 12 to 18 months.

horizontal decalage   Piaget's term for the sequential (rather than simultaneous) application within a particular stage of a given concept or logic to a series of different tasks or materials. For example, the principle of conservation is applied sequentially to number, weight, and volume.

hyperactivity The brief common term for attention-deficit hyperactivity disorder.

id In Freudian theory, the first, primitive portion of the personality; the storehouse of basic energy, continually pushing for immediate gratification.

identification The process of taking into oneself (incorporating) the qualities and ideas of another person, which Freud thought was the result of the Oedipal crisis at age 3 to 5. The child attempts to become like the parent of the same sex.

identity achievement One of four identity statuses proposed by Marcia, in which the young person has successfully resolved an identity crisis and made a new commitment.

identity diffusion One of four identity statuses proposed by Marcia, in which the young person is not currently reevaluating ideas and has not made a firm personal commitment.

impulsivity One end of the continuum of conceptual tempo described by Kagan. Impulsive individuals examine objects or arrays quickly, making rapid scans, and they may make more errors if fine discriminations are required.

inborn error of metabolism An inherited disorder (such as PKU) resulting in an inability to perform a particular metabolic function. Some such disorders are associated with retardation if not treated.

inductive logic Reasoning from the particular to the general, from experience to broad rules. Characteristic of concrete operational thinking.

inflections The grammatical markers, such as plurals, possessives, and past tenses.

information processing A way of looking at cognition and cognitive development that emphasizes fundamental processes: memory strategies, problem-solving strategies, planning, and basic functions such as noticing differences and similarities.

insecure attachment Includes both ambivalent and avoidant patterns of attachment behavior in children. The child does not use the parent as a safe base and is not readily consoled by the parent if upset.

intellectual power That aspect of intellectual skill that has to do with how well or how quickly a child can perform cognitive tasks.

A dimension of individual difference in intellectual skill.

intelligence quotient See IQ.

internal working model A child's cognitive construction of social relationships. The earliest relationships may form the template for an internal model of the workings of relationships, such as expectations of support or affection, trustworthiness, and so on.

interviews A broad category of research strategy in which people are asked about themselves, their behavior, and their feelings.

intrinsic reinforcements Those inner sources of pleasure, pride, or satisfaction that serve to strengthen the likelihood of whatever behavior triggered the feeling.

IQ Intelligence quotient. Originally defined in terms of a child's mental age and chronological age. IQ is now computed by comparing a child's performance with that of other children of the same chronological age.

language acquisition device A hypothesized brain structure that may be "programmed" to make language learning possible.

Leboyer method A "gentle" birth method proposed by Frederick Leboyer, which includes dimmed lights and quiet, slow-paced birth.

libido The term used by Freud to describe the pool of sexual energy in each individual.

longitudinal study A study in which the same subjects are observed or assessed repeatedly over a period of months or years.

low birth weight The phrase now used (in place of the word *premature*) to describe infants whose weight is below the optimum range at birth. Includes infants born too early (preterm, or short-gestation, infants) and those who are small for date.

mainstreaming The placement of atypical children in regular school classrooms whenever possible.

maturation The sequential unfolding of physical characteristics, governed by instructions contained in the genetic code and shared by all members of the species.

mean length of utterance (MLU) The average number of meaningful units in a sentence. Each basic word is one meaningful unit, as is each inflection (such as the *s* for a plural or the *ed* for a past tense).

medulla A section of the brain in the lower part of the skull. It develops earlier than the cortex and regulates basic functions such as suckling, breathing, heart rate, and muscle tone.

meiosis The process of cell division that produces germ cells, in which only one member of each chromosome pair is passed on to the new cell.

menarche Onset of menstruation in girls.

mental age A way to describe the level of mental tasks a child can perform. A child who can perform tasks normally done by 8-year-olds but not tasks done by 9-year-olds has a mental age of 8.

mental retardation A pattern of functioning that includes low IQ, poor adaptive behavior, and poor information-processing skills.

mesomorphic Body type characterized by amount of muscle mass. A mesomorphic person is square-chested, broad-shouldered, and muscular.

metacognition General and rather loosely used term describing an individual's knowledge of her own thinking processes. Knowing what you know, and how you go about learning or remembering.

metamemory A subcategory of metacognition; knowledge about one's own memory processes.

midbrain A section of the brain below the cortex. It develops earlier than the cortex and regulates attention, sleeping, waking, and other "automatic" functions.

mitosis The process of cell division for all cells other than germ cells, in which both new cells contain 23 pairs of chromosomes.

modeling A term used by Bandura and others to describe observational learning.

morality of reciprocity Another term for autonomous morality.

moral realism Another term for heteronomous morality.

moratorium One of four identity statuses proposed by Marcia, in which the young person is making an ongoing reexamination but has not made a new commitment as yet.

motherese The particular pattern of speech by adults to young children. The sentences are shorter, simpler, more repetitive, and higher-pitched.

motor development Growth and change in ability to perform physical activities, such as walking, running, riding a bike.

myelin The material composing the sheaths around most of the nerves of the body. Myelin sheaths are not completely developed at birth.

myelinization The process by which myelin sheaths are formed around nerve fibers.

nativism The opposite of empiricism. The view that perceptual skills are inborn and do not require experience to develop.

nature/nurture controversy A common description of the classic argument between the advocates of internal and external influences on development.

negative reinforcement The strengthening of a behavior by the removal or cessation of an unpleasant stimulus.

object concept A general term including the concepts of object permanance and object identity.

object constancy The general phrase describing the ability to see objects as remaining the same despite changes in retinal image.

object identity Part of the object concept. The recognition that objects remain the same from one encounter to the next.

object permanence Part of the object concept. The recognition that an object continues to exist even when it is temporarily out of sight.

observational learning Learning of motor skills, attitudes, or other behaviors through observing someone else perform them.

Oedipal crisis The pattern of events that Freud believed occurred between age 3 and 5, when the child, fearing possible reprisal from the parent of the same sex for "sexual" desire for the parent of the opposite sex, identifies with the parent of the same sex.

operant conditioning A learning process in which the probability of a person performing some particular behavior is affected by positive or negative reinforcements.

operation Term used by Piaget for complex, abstract, reversible internal schemes, first seen at about age 6.

ossification The process of hardening by which soft tissue becomes bone.

overregularization The tendency on the part of children to make the language regular, as by using constructions like *beated* or *goed* for the past tense.

ovum The germ cell produced by a woman, which, if fertilized by a sperm from a man, forms the basis for the developing organism.

partial reinforcement Reinforcement of behavior on some schedule less frequent than every occasion.

perception The process of obtaining information about the world through stimulation.

perceptual constancies A set of skills, including shape, size, and color constancy, that permits us to recognize that an object stays the same even when it appears to change.

perceptual learning An increase in the ability to extract information (via the senses) from the environment as a result of practice or experience.

performance The behavior shown by a person under actual circumstances. Even when we are interested in competence, all we can ever measure is performance.

permissive parental style Pattern described by Baumrind, among others, which includes high warmth and low levels of control.

personality The collection of relatively enduring individual patterns of reacting to and interacting with others that distinguishes each child or adult.

pervasive developmental disorders Serious emotional disturbances such as autism and schizophrenia.

phenotype The expression of a particular set of genetic information in a specific environment; the observable result of the joint operation of genetic and environmental influences.

pituitary gland One of the endocrine glands. It plays a central role in controlling the rate of physical maturation and sexual maturing.

placenta An organ that develops during gestation between the fetus and the wall of the uterus. The placenta filters nutrients from the mother's blood, acting as liver, lungs, and kidneys for the fetus.

positive reinforcement Strengthening of a behavior by the presentation of some pleasurable or positive stimulus.

pragmatics The rules for the use of language in communicative interaction—rules for taking turns, the style of speech appropriate for different listeners, and the equivalent.

preconventional morality The first level of moral reasoning proposed by Kohlberg, in which the child's judgments are dominated by consideration of what will be punished and what "feels good."

prelinguistic phase The period before the child speaks her first word.

preoperational stage Piaget's term for the second major stage of cognitive development, from age 2 to 6, during which the child develops basic classification and logical abilities.

preterm infant Descriptive phrase now widely used to label infants born before 37 weeks' gestational age.

primary sex characteristics Sexual characteristics related directly to reproduction, including the uterus and testes.

principled morality The third level of moral reasoning proposed by Kohlberg, in which considerations of justice, individual rights, and contracts dominate.

prosocial behavior Behavior that is the opposite of "antisocial," including helping, kindness, sharing, generosity.

proximodistal From the center outward. With cephalocaudal, describes the pattern of physical changes in infancy.

psychosexual stages The stages of personality development suggested by Freud, including the oral, anal, phallic, latency, and genital stages.

psychosocial stages The stages of personality development suggested by Erikson, including trust, autonomy, initiative, industry, identity, intimacy, generativity, and ego integrity.

puberty The collection of hormonal and physical changes at adolescence that brings about sexual maturity.

punishment Unpleasant consequences administered after some undesired behavior by a child or adult with the intent of extinguishing the behavior.

questionnaire A pencil-and-paper assessment of one or more variables, using standardized questions.

rapid eye movement (REM) One of the characteristics of sleep during dreaming. REM occurs during the sleep of newborns, too.

receptive language The child's ability to understand (receive) language, as contrasted to his ability to express language.

recognition memory The identification of the familiar; the speed with which an individual recognizes (remembers) that some object or individual or situation has been seen or experienced before.

referential style One of two styles of early language proposed by Katherine Nelson. Referential style is characterized by emphasisis on objects and their naming and description.

reflection One end of the "tempo" dimension of perceptual style. Reflective individuals examine objects or arrays very carefully and slowly. They normally perform better than impulsive individuals when fine discriminations are required.

reflexes Automatic body reactions to specific stimulation, such as the knee jerk or the Moro reflex. Many reflexes remain in the adult, but the newborn also has some additional low-level or rudimentary reflexes that disappear as the brain cortex develops fully.

restrictiveness A particular pattern of parental control involving limitation of the child's movements or options, such as by the use of playpens or harnesses with a young child or by strict rules about play areas or free choices with an older child.

rubella A form of measles that, if contracted during the first three months of pregnancy, may have severe effects on the developing baby.

scheme Piaget's word for the basic actions, ideas, and strategies by which new experience is assimilated and which are then modified (accommodated) as a result of the new experience.

schizophrenia A severe form of emotional disturbance seen in adults and in some adolescents. The term *childhood schizophrenia* is also sometimes used to describe children with childhood-onset pervasive developmental disorder.

secondary sex characteristics Sexual characteristics not directly involved in reproduction, including breast and body hair development and changes in body size and proportions.

secure attachment The child's ability to use the parent as a safe base and to be consoled after separation, when fearful, or when otherwise stressed.

self-concept The broad idea of "who I am," including the existential self, the categorical self, and a level of self-esteem.

self-esteem The positive or negative evaluation of the self.

semantics The rules for conveying meaning in language.

sensitive period Similar to a critical period, except broader and less specific. A time in development when a particular type of stimulation is particularly important or effective.

sensorimotor stage Piaget's term for the first major stage of cognitive development, from birth to about 18 months, when the child moves from reflexive to voluntary action.

sex chromosomes The X and Y chromosomes that determine the sex of a child. In humans, XX is the female pattern, XY the male pattern.

sex-role behavior The performance or behavior that matches the culturally defined sex role, such as choosing "sex-appropriate" toys or playing with same-sex children.

sex-role concept The understanding of what males and females do and are "supposed to do."

sex-role stereotyping The overextension or too-rigid definition of sex roles or sex-role behavior.

shape constancy The ability to see an object's shape as remaining the same despite changes in the shape of the retinal image. A basic perceptual constancy.

size constancy The ability to see an object's size as remaining the same despite changes in size of the retinal image. A key element in this constancy is the ability to judge depth.

small-for-date infant An infant who weighs less than is normal for the number of weeks of gestation completed.

social class Broad categories in economic and social positions within society. Four groups are most often described: upper class, middle class, working class, and lower class (also called poverty level). The designation for an individual family is based on the occupations and education of the adults in the household.

social cognition A relatively new area of research and theory focused on the child's *understanding* of social relationships.

social support The emotional, material, and informational assistance available to any one individual from family and friends in times of need.

specific learning disability (SLD) A disorder in understanding or processing language or symbols.

Stanford-Binet The best-known American intelligence test, written by Louis Terman and his associates, and based upon the first tests by Binet and Simon.

states of consciousness Five main sleep/wake states have been identified in infants, from deep sleep to active awake states.

strange situation A series of episodes used by Mary Ainsworth and others in studies of attachment. The child is observed when with the mother, with a stranger, left alone, and reunited with stranger and mother.

structure That aspect of intellectual skill that changes with age and is shared by all children. Focus is on *how* the child arrives at a particular answer rather than on the correctness of the answer.

superego In Freudian theory, the "conscience" part of personality, which develops as a result of the identification process. The superego contains the parental and societal values and attitudes incorporated by the child.

symbiotic relationship In Freudian theory, the mutually interdependent relationship between the mother and infant during the earliest months of life. Freud believed the infant was not aware of being separate from the mother at this stage.

syntax The rules for forming sentences; also called grammar.

telegraphic speech A characteristic of children's early sentences, in which everything but the crucial words is omitted, as if for a telegram.

temperament An individual's unique collection of typical responses or styles of response to experiences. Temperament may be genetic in origin and is somewhat stable over time.

teratogen Any outside agent (such as a disease or a chemical) that significantly increases the risk of deviations or abnormalities in prenatal development.

transductive reasoning Reasoning from the specific to the specific; assuming that when two things happen together, one is the cause of the other.

triarchic theory of intelligence A theory proposed by Sternberg, proposing the existence of three types of intelligence: the compo-

nential, the contextual, and the experiential.

unconditioned response In classical conditioning, the basic unlearned response that is triggered by the unconditioned stimulus.

unconditioned stimulus In classical conditioning, the cue or signal that automatically triggers (without learning) the unconditioned response.

uterus The female organ in which the blastocyst implants itself and within which the embryo/fetus develops. (Popularly referred to as the *womb*.)

very low-birth-weight infants Infants who weigh 1500 g ($1\frac{1}{3}$ pounds) or less at birth.

vicarious reinforcement The strengthening of some behavior through observing someone else being reinforced for that behavior. Thus children who observe others being praised for some behavior may be more likely to perform that behavior themselves.

warmth versus hostility The key dimension of emotional tone used to describe family interactions.

WISC-R The Wechsler Intelligence Scale for Children, Revised. Another well-known American IQ test that includes both verbal and performance (nonverbal) subtests.

References

Abel, E. L. (1984). *Fetal alcohol syndrome and fetal alcohol effects.* New York: Plenum.

Achenbach, T. M. (1978). *Research in developmental psychology: Concepts, strategies, methods.* New York: Free Press.

Achenbach, T. M. (1982). *Developmental psychopathology* (2nd ed.). New York: Wiley.

Achenbach, T. M., & Edelbrock, C. S. (1981). Behavioral problems and competencies reported by parents of normal and disturbed children aged 4 through 16. *Monographs of the Society for Research in Child Development, 46* (1, Whole No. 188).

Achenbach, T. M., & Edelbrock, C. S. (1982). *Manual for the child behavior checklist and child behavior profile.* Burlington: University of Vermont, Child Psychiatry.

Achenbach, T. M., & Weisz, J. R. (1975). A longitudinal study of developmental synchrony between conceptual identity, seriation, and transitivity of color, number, and length. *Child Development, 46,* 840–848.

Acredolo, L. P., & Hake, J. L. (1982). Infant perception. In B. B. Wolman (Ed.), *Handbook of developmental psychology.* Englewood Cliffs, NJ: Prentice-Hall.

Adelson, J. (Ed.). (1980). *Handbook of adolescent psychology.* New York: Wiley-Interscience.

Adler, A. (1948). *Studies in analytical psychology.* New York: Norton.

Ainsworth, M. D. S. (1972). Attachment and dependency: A comparison. In J. L. Gewirtz (Ed.), *Attachment and dependency.* Washington, DC: V. H. Winston.

Ainsworth, M. D. S. (1982). Attachment: Retrospect and prospect. In C. M. Parkes & J. Stevenson-Hinde (Eds.), *The place of attachment in human behavior.* New York: Basic Books.

Ainsworth, M. D. S., Bell, S. M., & Stayton, D. J. (1972). Individual differences in strange situation behavior of one-year-olds. In H. R. Schaffer (Ed.), *The origins of human social relations.* London: Academic Press.

Ainsworth, M. D. S., Blehar, M., Waters, E., & Wall, S. (1978). *Patterns of attachment.* Hillsdale, NJ: Erlbaum.

Ainsworth, M. D. S., & Wittig, B. A. (1969). Attachment and exploratory behavior of one-year-olds in a strange situation. In B. M. Foss (Ed.), *Determinants of infant behavior* (Vol. 4). London: Methuen.

Akiyama, M. M. (1984). Are language-acquisition strategies universal? *Developmental Psychology, 20,* 219–228.

Allen, H. L. (1983). Fathers in the delivery rooms—survey results of anesthesia departments. *Anesthesiology, 50,* 152.

Allik, J., & Valsiner, J. (1980). Visual development in ontogenesis: Some reevaluations. In H. W. Reese & L. P. Lipsitt (Eds.), *Advances in child development and behavior.* New York: Academic Press.

American Psychiatric Association. (1980). *Diagnostic and statistical manual of mental disorders* (3rd ed.). Washington, DC: American Psychiatric Association.

Anderson, D. R., Lorch, E. P., Field, D. E., Collins, P. A., & Nathan, J. G. (1986). Television viewing at home: Age trends in visual attention and time with TV. *Child Development, 57,* 1024–1033.

Anderson, C. W., Nagle, R. J., Roberts, W. A., & Smith, J. W. (1981). Attachment to substitute caregivers as a function of center quality and caregiver involvement. *Child Development, 47*(6, Whole No. 198).

Andrews, S. R., Blumenthal, J. B., Johnson, D. L., Kahn, A. J., Ferguson, C. J., Lasater, T. M., Malone, P. E., & Wallace, D. B. (1982). The skills of mothering: A study of parent-child development centers. *Monographs of the Society for Research in Child Development, 47*(6, Whole No. 198).

Anisfeld, M. (1984). *Language development from birth to three.* Hillsdale, NJ: Erlbaum.

Antell, S. E. G., & Caron, A. J. (1985). Neonatal perception of spatial relationships. *Infant Behavior and Development, 8,* 15–23.

Anthony, E. J. (1970). The behavior disorders of childhood. In P. H. Mussen (Ed.), *Carmichael's manual of child psychology* (Vol. 2, 3rd ed.). New York: Wiley.

Apgar, V. A. (1953). A proposal for a new method of evaluation of the newborn infant. *Anesthesia and Analgesia 32,* 260–267.

Appel, M. H. (1977). The application of Piagetian learning theory to a science curriculum project. In M. H. Appel & L. S. Goldberg (Eds.), *Topics in cognitive development* (Vol. 1). New York: Plenum.

Archer, J. (1981). Sex differences in maturation. In K. J. Connolly & H. F. R. Prechtl (Eds.), *Maturation and development: Biological and psychological perspectives.* Clinics in Developmental Medicine No. 77/78. London: Heinemann.

Asher J. (1987, April). Born to be shy? *Psychology Today,* pp. 56–64.

Asher, S. R. (1983). Social competence and peer status: Recent advances and future directions. *Child Development, 54,* 1427–1434.

Asher, S. R., Oden, S. L., & Gottman, J. M. (1977). Children's friendships in school settings. In L. G. Katz (Ed.), *Current topics in early childhood education* (Vol. 1). Norwood, NJ: Ablex.

Asher, S., Renshaw, P. D., & Hymel, S. (1982). Peer relations and the development of social skills. In S. G. Moore & C. R. Cooper (Eds.), *The young child. Reviews of research* (Vol. 3). Washington, DC: National Association for the education of Young Children.

Badger, E. (1981). Effects of parent education program on teenage mothers and their offspring. In K. G. Scott, T. Field, & E. Robertson (Eds.), *Teenage parents and their offspring.* New York: Grune & Stratton.

Baer, D. M. (1970). An age-irrelevant concept of development. *Merrill-Palmer Quarterly, 16,* 238–245.

Baldwin, A. L. (1948). Socialization and the parent-child relationship. *Child Development, 19,* 127–136.

Baldwin, A. L. (1949). The effect of home environment on nursery school behavior. *Child Development, 20,* 49–62.

Bandura, A. (1973). *Aggression: A social learning analysis.* Englewood Cliffs, NJ: Prentice-Hall.

Bandura. A. (1977). *Social learning theory.* Englewood Cliffs, NJ: Prentice-Hall.

Bandura, A. (1982). The self and mechanisms of agency. In J. Suls (Ed.), *Psychological perspectives on the self* (Vol. 1). Hillsdale, NJ: Erlbaum.

Barenboim, C. (1977). Developmental changes in the interpersonal cognitive system from middle childhood to adolescence. *Child Development, 48,* 1467–1474.

Barenboim, C. (1981). The development of person perception in childhood and adolescence: From behavioral comparisons to psychological constructs to psychological comparisons. *Child Development, 52,* 129–144.

Barglow, P., Vaughn, B. E., & Molitor, N. (1987). Effects of maternal absence due to employment on the quality of infant-mother attachment in a low-risk sample. *Child Development, 58,* 945–954.

Barnard, K. E., & Bee, H. L. (1983). The impact of temporally patterned stimulation on the development of preterm infants. *Child Development, 54,* 1156–1167.

Barnard, K. E., Bee, H. L., & Hammond, M. A. (1984a). Developmental changes in maternal interactions with term and preterm infants. *Infant Behavior and Development, 7,* 101–113.

Barnard, K. E., Bee, H. L., & Hammond, M. A. (1984b). Home environment and mental development in a healthy, low risk sample: The Seattle study. In A. W. Gottfried (Ed.), *Home environment and early mental development.* New York: Academic Press.

Barnard, K. E., & Eyres, S. J. (1979). *Child health assessment. Part 2: The first year of life* (DHEW Publication No. HRA 79-25). Washington, DC: U.S. Government Printing Office.

Barnes, H. L., & Olson, D. H. (1985). Parent-adolescent communication and the circumplex model. *Child Development, 56,* 438–447.

Baron, P., & Perron, L. M. (1986). Sex differences in the Beck depression inventory scores of adolescents. *Journal of Youth and Adolescence, 15,* 165–171.

Barrett, D. E., Radke-Yarrow, M., & Klein, R. E. (1982). Chronic malnutrition and child behavior: Effects of early caloric supplementation on social and emotional functioning at school age. *Developmental Psychology, 18,* 541–556.

Baruffi, G. (1982). Review of the safety of maternity care in different birth locations. In Committee on Assessing Alternative Birth Settings, *Research issues in the assessment of birth settings,* National Research Council, Commission on Life Sciences. Washington, DC: National Academy Press.

Bates, E., Bretherton, I., Beeghly-Smith, M., &

McNew, S. (1982). Social bases of language development: A reassessment. In H. W. Reese & L. P. Lipsitt (Eds.), *Advances in child development and behavior* (Vol. 16). New York: Academic Press.

Bates, E., Camaioni, L., & Volterra, V. (1975). The acquisition of performatives prior to speech. *Merrill-Palmer Quarterly, 21,* 205–226.

Bates, E., MacWhinney, B., Caselli, C., Devescovi, A., Natale, F., & Venza, V. (1984). A cross-linguistic study of the development of sentence interpretation strategies. *Child Development, 55,* 341–354.

Bates, E., O'Connell, B., & Shore, C. (1987). Language and communication in infancy. In J. D. Osofsky (Ed.), *Handbook of infant development* (2nd ed). New York: Wiley.

Batter, B. S., & Davidson, C. V. (1979). Wariness of strangers: Reality or artifact? *Journal of Child Psychology and Psychiatry, 20,* 93–109.

Baumrind, D. (1967). Child care practices anteceding three patterns of preschool behavior. *Genetic Psychology Monographs, 75,* 43–88.

Baumrind, D. (1971). Current patterns of parental authority. *Developmental Psychology Monograph, 4* (1, Part 2).

Baumrind, D. (1972). Socialization and instrumental competence in young children. In W. W. Hartup (Ed.), *The young child. Reviews of research* (Vol. 2). Washington, DC: National Association for the Education of Young Children.

Baumrind, D. (1973). The development of instrumental competence through socialization. In A. D. Pick (Ed.), *Minnesota symposia on child psychology* (Vol. 7). Minneapolis: University of Minnesota Press.

Baumrind, D. (1978). A dialectical materialist's perspective on knowing social reality. In W. Damon (Ed.), *Moral development.* San Francisco: Jossey-Bass.

Bayley, N. (1965). Comparisons of mental and motor test scores for ages 1–15 months by sex, birth order, race, geographical location, and education of parents. *Child Development, 36,* 379–411.

Bayley, N. (1969). *Bayley Scales of Infant Development.* New York: Psychological Corporation.

Bearison, D. J., Magzamen, S., & Filardo, E. K. (1986). Socio-cognitive conflict and cognitive growth in young children. *Merrill-Palmer Quarterly, 32,* 51–72.

Becker, J. A. (1982). Children's strategic use of requests to mark and manipulate social status. In S. A. Kuczaj, II (Ed.), *Language development: Vol. 2. Language, thought, and culture.* Hillsdale, NJ: Erlbaum.

Bee, H. L., Barnard, K. E., Eyres, S. J., Gray, C. A., Hammond, M. A., Spietz, A. L., Snyder, C., & Clark, B. (1982). Prediction of IQ and language skill from perinatal status, child performance, family characteristics, and mother-infant interaction. *Child Development, 53,* 1135–1156.

Bell, L. G., & D. C. (1982). Family climate and the role of the female adolescent: Determinants of adolescent functioning. *Family Relations, 31,* 519–527.

Bellinger, D. (1987, April). *Social class differences in the effects of in utero exposure to lead.* Paper presented at the biennial meetings of the Society for Research in Child Development, Baltimore.

Belsky, J. (1987, April). *Science, social policy and day care: A personal odyssey.* Paper presented at the biennial meetings of the Society for Research in Child Development, Baltimore.

Belsky, J., & Rovine, M. (1987). Temperament and attachment security in the strange situation: An empirical rapprochement. *Child Development, 58,* 787–795.

Belsky, J., & Rovine, M. (1988). Nonmaternal care in the first year of life and the security of infant-parent attachment. *Child Development, 59,* 157–167.

Belsky, J., Spanier, G. B., & Rovine, M. (1983). Stability and change in marriage across the transition to parenthood. *Journal of Marriage and the Family, 45,* 196–205.

Bem, S. L. (1974). The measurement of psychological androgyny. *Journal of Consulting and Clinical Psychology, 42,* 155–162.

Benn, R. K. (1986). Factors promoting secure attachment relationships between employed mothers and their sons. *Child Development, 57,* 1224–1231.

Berberian, K. E., & Snyder, S. S. (1982). The relationship of temperament and stranger reaction for younger and older infants. *Merrill-Palmer Quarterly, 28,* 79–94.

Berg, J. M. (1974). Aetiological aspects of mental subnormality. In A. M. Clarke & A. D. B. Clarke (Eds.), *Mental deficiency: The changing outlook.* New York: Free Press.

Berk, L. E. (1986, May). Private speech: Learning out loud. *Psychology Today,* pp. 34–39, 42.

Berndt, T. J. (1979). Developmental changes

in conformity to peers and parents. *Developmental Psychology, 15,* 608–616.

Berndt, T. J. (1981). Age changes and changes over time in prosocial intentions and behavior between friends. *Developmental Psychology, 17,* 408–416.

Berndt, T. J. (1982). The features and effects of friendship in early adolescence. *Child Development, 53,* 1447–1460.

Berndt, T. J. (1983). Social cognition, social behavior, and children's friendships. In E. T. Higgins, D. N. Ruble, & W. W. Hartup (Eds.), *Social cognition and social development. A sociocultural perspective.* Cambridge, England: Cambridge University Press.

Berndt, T. J. (1986). Children's comments about their friendships. In M. Perlmutter (Ed.), Cognitive perspectives on children's social and behavioral development. *Minnesota symposia on child psychology* (Vol. 18). Hillsdale, NJ: Erlbaum.

Berndt, T. J., Hawkins, J. A., & Hoyle, S. G. (1986). Changes in friendship during a school year: Effects on children's and adolescents' impressions of friendship and sharing with friends. *Child Development, 57,* 1284–1297.

Berndt, T. J., & Hoyle, S. G. (1985). Stability and change in childhood and adolescent friendships. *Developmental Psychology, 21,* 1007–1015.

Best, D. L., Williams, J. E., Cloud, J. M., Davis, S. W., Robertson, L. S., Edwards, J. R., Giles, H., & Fowles, J. (1977). Development of sex-trait stereotypes among young children in the United States, England, and Ireland. *Child Development, 48,* 1375–1384.

Bierman, K. L. (1986). Process of change during social skills training with preadolescents and its relation to treatment outcome. *Child Development, 57,* 230–240.

Bigelow, B. J., & La Gaipa, J. J. (1975). Children's written descriptions of friendships: A multidimensional analysis. *Developmental Psychology, 11,* 857–858.

Binet, A., & Simon, T. (1905). Methodes nouvelles pour le diagnostic du niveau intellectual des anormaux [New methods for diagnosing the intellectual level of the abnormal]. *L'Année Psychologique, 11,* 191–244.

Bissell, J. S. (1973). Planned variation in Head Start and Follow Through. In J. C. Stanley (Ed.), *Compensatory education for children, ages 2 to 8.* Baltimore: Johns Hopkins University Press.

Bjorklund, D. F., & Arce, S. (1987, April). *Acquiring a mnemonic: Age and category knowledge effects.* Paper presented at the meeting of the Society for Research in Child Development, Baltimore.

Bjorklund, D. F., & Muir, J. E. (in press). Remembering on their own: Children's development of free recall memory. In R. Vasta (Ed.), *Annals of child development* (Vol 5). Greenwich, CT: JAI Press.

Blanchard, M., & Main, M. (1979). Avoidance of the attachment figure and social-emotional adjustment in day-care infants. *Developmental Psychology, 15,* 445–446.

Blasi, A. (1980). Bridging moral cognition and moral action: A critical review of the literature. *Psychological Bulletin, 88,* 593–637.

Blewitt, P. (1983). *Dog* versus *collie:* Vocabulary in speech to young children. *Developmental Psychology, 19,* 602–609.

Block, J. (1971). *Lives through time.* Berkeley, CA: Bancroft.

Block, J. (1987, April). *Longitudinal antecedents of ego-control and ego-resiliency in late adolescence.* Paper presented at the biennial meeting of the Society for Research in Child Development, Baltimore.

Block, J. H. (1983). Differential premises arising from differential socialization of the sexes: Some conjectures. *Child Development, 54,* 1335–1354.

Block, J. H., Block, J., & Gjerde, P. F. (1986). The personality of children prior to divorce: A prospective study. *Child Development, 57,* 827–840.

Bloom, L. (1973). *One word at a time.* The Hague: Mouton.

Blumstein, P., & Schwartz, P. (1983). *American couples.* New York: Morrow.

Bohannon, J. N. III, Warren-Leubecker, A., & Hepler, N. (1984). Word order awareness and early reading. *Child Development, 55,* 1541–1548.

Bornstein, M. H. (1984). Perceptual development. In M. H. Bornstein & M. E. Lamb (Eds.), *Developmental psychology: An advanced textbook.* Hillsdale, NJ: Erlbaum.

Bornstein, M. H., Kessen, W., & Weiskopf, S. (1976). Color vision and hue categorization in young human infants. *Journal of Experimental Psychology: Human Perception and Performance, 2,* 115–129.

Bornstein, M. H., & Sigman, M. D. (1986). Continuity in mental development from infancy. *Child Development, 57,* 251–274.

Bornstein, M. H., & Teller, D. Y. (1982). Color

vision. In P. Salapatek & L. B. Cohen (Eds.), *Handbook of infant perception*. New York: Academic Press.

Boukydis, C. F. Z., & Burgess, R. L. (1982). Adult physiological response to infant cries: Effects of temperament, parental status, and gender. *Child Development, 53,* 1291–1298.

Bower, T. G. R. (1966). The visual world of infants. *Scientific American, 215,* 80–92.

Bower, T. G. R. (1975). Infant perception of the third dimension and object concept development. In L. B. Cohen & P. Salapatek (Eds.), *Infant perception: From sensation to cognition.* New York: Academic Press.

Bower, T. G. R. (1977a). *The perceptual world of the child.* Cambridge, MA: Harvard University Press.

Bower, T. G. R. (1977b). Blind babies see with their ears. *New Scientist, 73,* 256–257.

Bower, T. G. R. (1978). Visual development in the blind child. In A. MacFarlane (Ed.), *Clinics in developmental medicine on vision.* London: Spastics International Medical Publication.

Bowerman, M. (1985). Beyond communicative adequacy: From piecemeal knowledge to an integrated system in the child's acquisition of language. In K. E. Nelson (Ed.), *Children's language* (Vol. 5). Hillsdale, NJ: Erlbaum.

Bowerman, M. (1987). Commentary: Mechanisms of language acquisition. In B. MacWhinney (Ed.), *Mechanisms of language acquisition.* Hillsdale, NJ: Erlbaum.

Bowlby, J. (1969). *Attachment and loss: Vol. 1. Attachment.* New York: Basic Books.

Bowlby, J. (1973). *Attachment and loss: Vol. 2. Separation, anxiety, and anger.* New York: Basic Books.

Bowlby, J. (1980). *Attachment and loss: Vol. 3. Loss, sadness, and depression.* New York: Basic Books.

Brackbill, Y. (1979). Obstetrical medication and infant behavior. In J. D. Osofsky (Ed.), *Handbook of infant development.* New York: Wiley.

Brackbill, Y., & Nevill, D. D. (1981). Parental expectations of achievement as affected by children's height. *Merrill-Palmer Quarterly, 27,* 429–441.

Brackbill, Y, Rice, J., & Young, D. (1984). *Birth trap: The legal low-down on high-tech obstetrics.* St. Louis: Mosby.

Bradbard, M. R., Martin, C. L., Endsley, R. C., & Halverson, C. F. (1986). Influence of sex stereotypes on children's exploration and memory: A competence versus performance distinction. *Developmental Psychology, 22,* 481–486.

Bradley, R. J., & Caldwell, B. M. (1976). The relation of infants' home environment to mental test performance at fifty-four months: A follow-up study. *Child Development, 47,* 1172–1174.

Bradley, R. H., & Caldwell, B. M. (1984). 174 children: A study of the relationship between home environment and cognitive development during the first 5 years. In A. W. Gottfried (Ed.), *Home environment and early cognitive development: Longitudinal research.* New York: Academic Press.

Braine, M. D. S. (1963). The ontogeny of English phrase structure: The first phase. *Language, 39,* 1–13.

Braine, M. D. S. (1976). Children's first word combinations. *Monographs of the Society for Research in Child Development, 41* (Whole No. 164).

Brazelton, T. B. (1974). *Toddlers and parents.* New York: Dell.

Brazelton, T. B. (1983). *Infants and mothers. Differences in development.* (rev. ed.). New York: Delta/Seymour Lawrence.

Brazelton, T. B., Koslowski, B., & Main, M. (1974). The origins of reciprocity: The early mother-infant interaction. In M. Lewis and L. A. Rosenblum (Eds.), *The effect of the infant on its caregiver.* New York: Wiley.

Breitmayer, B. J., & Ramey, C. T. (1986). Biological nonoptimality and quality of postnatal environment as codeterminants of intellectual development. *Child Development, 57,* 1151–1165.

Brody, E. B., & Brody, N. (1976). *Intelligence: Nature, determinants and consequences.* New York: Academic Press.

Brody, L. E., & Benbow, C. P. (1986). Social and emotional adjustment of adolescents extremely talented in verbal or mathematical reasoning. *Journal of Youth and Adolescence, 15,* 1–18.

Broman, S. H., Nichols, P. L., & Kennedy, W. A. (1975). *Preschool IQ: Prenatal and early developmental correlates.* Hillsdale, NJ: Erlbaum.

Bromwich, R. M. (1976). Focus on maternal behavior in infant intervention. *American Journal of Orthopsychiatry, 46,* 439–446.

Bromwich, R. M., Khoka, E., Burge, D., Baxter, E., Kass, W., & Fust, S. (1981). A parent behavior progression. In B. Weissbound & J. Musick (Eds.), *Infants: Their social environ-*

ments. Washington, DC: National Association for the Education of Young Children.

Bronfenbrenner, U. (1975). Nature with nurture: A reinterpretation of the evidence. In A. Montague (Ed.), *Race and IQ.* New York: Oxford University Press.

Bronfenbrenner, U. (1977). Toward an experimental ecology of human development. *American Psychologist, 32,* 513–531.

Bronfenbrenner, U. (1979). *The ecology of human development.* Cambridge, MA: Harvard University Press.

Bronfenbrenner, U. (1983). The context of development and the development of context. In R. M. Lerner (Ed.), *Developmental psychology: Historical and philosophical perspectives.* Hillsdale, NJ: Erlbaum.

Bronfenbrenner, U. (1986). Ecology of the family as a context for human development: Research perspectives. *Developmental Psychology, 22,* 723–742.

Bronfenbrenner, U., Alvarez, W. F., & Henderson, C. R., Jr. (1984). Working and watching: Maternal employment status and parents' perceptions of their three-year-old children. *Child Development, 55,* 1362–1378.

Bronfenbrenner, U., & Crouter, A. C. (1982). Work and family through time and space. In S. B. Kamerman & C. D. Hayes (Eds.), *Families that work: Children in a changing world.* Washington, DC: National Academy Press.

Bronfenbrenner, U., & Crouter, A. C. (1983). The evolution of environmental models in developmental research. In W. Kessen (Ed.), *Handbook of child psychology: History, theory, and methods (Vol. 1).* New York: Wiley. (P. H. Mussen, General Editor)

Bronson, G. W. (1974). The postnatal growth of visual capacity. *Child Development, 45,* 873–890.

Brooks-Gunn, J. (1987). Pubertal processes and girls' psychological adaptation. In R. M. Lerner & T. T. Foch (Eds.), *Biological-psychosocial interactions in early adolescence.* Hillsdale, NJ: Erlbaum.

Brooks-Gunn, J., & Matthews, W. S. (1979). *He and she: How children develop their sex-role identity.* Englewood Cliffs, NJ: Prentice-Hall.

Brooks-Gunn, J., & Warren, M. P. (1985). The effects of delayed menarche in different contexts: Dance and nondance students. *Journal of Youth and Adolescence, 13,* 285–300.

Broverman, I. K., Broverman, D., Clarkson, F. E., Rosenkrantz, P. S., & Vogel, S. R. (1970). Sex-role stereotypes and clinical judgments

of mental health. *Journal of Consulting and Clinical Psychology, 34,* 1–7.

Broverman, I. K., Vogel, S. R., Broverman, D. M., Clarkson, F. E., & Rosenkrantz, P. S. (1972). Sex-role stereotypes: A current appraisal. *Journal of Social Issues, 28*(2), 59–79.

Brown, A. L., & Campione, J. C. (1984). Three faces of transfer: Implications for early competence, individual differences, and instruction. In M. E. Lamb, A. L. Brown, & B. Rogoff (Eds.), *Advances in developmental psychology* (Vol. 3). Hillsdale, NJ: Erlbaum.

Brown, B. B., Clasen, D. R., & Eicher, S. A. (1986). Perceptions of peer pressure, peer conformity dispositions, and self-reported behavior among adolescents. *Developmental Psychology, 22,* 521–530.

Brown, J. (1983). *Nutrition for your pregnancy: The University of Minnesota guide.* Minneapolis: University of Minnesota Press.

Brown, K. W., & Gottfried, A. W. (1986). Crossmodal transfer of shape in early infancy: Is there reliable evidence? In L. P. Lipsitt & C. Rovee-Collier (Eds.), *Advances in infancy research* (Vol. 4). Norwood, NJ: Ablex.

Brown, R. (1965). *Social psychology.* New York: Free Press.

Brown, R. (1973a). Development of the first language in the human species. *American Psychologist, 28,* 97–106.

Brown, R. (1973b). *A first language: The early stages.* Cambridge, MA: Harvard University Press.

Brown, R., & Bellugi, U. (1964). Three processes in the acquisition of syntax. *Harvard Educational Review, 334,* 133–151.

Brown, R., & Hanlon, C. (1970). Derivational complexity and order of acquisition. In J. R. Hayes (Ed.), *Cognition and the development of language.* New York: Wiley.

Brownell, C. A. (1986). Convergent developments: Cognitive-developmental correlates of growth in infant/toddler peer skills. *Child Development, 57,* 275–286.

Brumback, R. A., & Staton, R. D. (1983). Learning disability in childhood depression. *American Journal of Orthopsychiatry, 53,* 269–281.

Budoff, M., & Gottlieb, J. (1976). Special-class EMR children mainstreamed: A study of an aptitude (learning potential) treatment interaction. *American Journal of Mental Deficiency, 81,* 1–11.

Buehler, J. W., Kaunitz, A. M., Hogue, C. J. R., Hughes, J. M., Smith, J. C., & Rochat, R. W. (1986). Maternal mortality in women aged 35 years or older: United States. *Journal of the American Medical Association, 255,* 53–57.

Bullock, M., & Gelman, R. (1979). Preschool children's assumptions about cause and effect: Temporal ordering. *Child Development, 50,* 89–96.

Bumpass, L. (1984). Children and marital disruption: A replication and update. *Demography, 41,* 71–82.

Buss, A. H., & Plomin, R. (1984). *Temperament: Early developing personality traits.* Hillsdale, NJ: Erlbaum.

Buss, A. H., & Plomin, R. (1986). The EAS approach to temperament. In R. Plomin & J. Dunn (Eds.), *The Study of temperament: Changes, continuities and challenges.* Hillsdale, NJ: Erlbaum.

Butterfield, E. C., Siladi, D., & Belmont, J. M. (1980). Validating theories of intelligence. In H. W. Reese & L. P. Lipsitt (Eds.), *Advances in child development and behavior* (Vol. 15). New York: Academic Press.

Caldwell, B. M. (1986). Day care and early environmental adequacy. In W. Fowler (Ed.), *Early experience and the development of competence. New Directions For Child Development, 32,* 11–30.

Caldwell, B. M., & Bradley, R. H. (1978). *Manual for the home observation of the environment.* Unpublished manuscript. University of Arkansas, Little Rock.

Campbell, E., Adams, G. R., & Dobson, W. R. (1984). Familial correlates of identity formation in late adolescence: A study of the predictive utility of connectedness and individuality in family relations. *Journal of Youth and Adolescence, 13,* 509–525.

Campbell, S. B. G., & Taylor, P. M. (1980). Bonding and attachment: Theoretical issues. In P. M. Taylor (Ed.). Parent-infant relationships. New York: Grune & Stratton.

Campione, J. C., & Brown, A. L. (1984). Learning ability and transfer propensity as sources of individual differences in intelligence. In P. H. Brooks, C. McCauley, & R. Sperber (Eds.), *Learning and cognition in the mentally retarded.* Hillsdale, NJ: Erlbaum.

Campione, J. C., Brown, A. L., & Ferrara, R. A. (1982). Mental retardation and intelligence. In J. R. Sternberg (Ed.), *Handbook of human intelligence.* Cambridge, England: Cambridge University Press.

Campione, J. C., Brown, A. L., Ferrara, R. A., Jones, R. S., & Steinberg, E. (1985). Break-downs in flexible use of information: Intelligence-related differences in transfer following equivalent learning performance. *Intelligence, 9,* 297–315.

Campos, J. J., Langer, A., & Krowitz, A. (1970). Cardiac responses on the visual cliff in prelocomotor human infants. *Science, 170,* 196–197.

Carey, W. B. (1981). The importance of temperament-environment interaction for child health and development. In M. Lewis & L. A. Rosenblum (Eds.), *The uncommon child.* New York: Plenum.

Caron, A. J., & Caron, R. F. (1981). Processing of relational information as an index of infant risk. In S. Friedman & M. Sigman (Eds.), *Preterm birth and psychological development.* New York: Academic Press.

Case, R. (1985). *Intellectual development. Birth to adulthood.* Orlando, FL: Academic Press.

Case, R. (1986). The new stage theories in intellectual development: Why we need them; What they assert. In M. Perlmutter (Ed.), *Perspectives on intellectual development. The Minnesota symposia on child psychology* (Vol. 19). Hillsdale, NJ: Erlbaum.

Case, R., Sandieson, R., & Dennis, S. (1986). Two cognitive-developmental approaches to the design of remedial instruction. *Cognitive Development, 1,* 293–333.

Casey, M. B. (1986). Individual differences in selective attention among prereaders: A key to mirror-image confusions. *Developmental Psychology, 22,* 58–66.

Cernoch, J. M., & Porter, R. H. (1985). Recognition of maternal axillary odors by infants. *Child Development, 56,* 1593–1598.

Chance, P., & Fischman, J. (1987, May). The magic of childhood. *Psychology Today,* pp. 48–51, 55–58.

Chase, W. P. (1937). Color vision in infants. *Journal of Experimental Psychology, 20,* 203–222.

Chase-Lansdale, L., & Owen, M. T. (1987). Maternal employment in a family context: Effects on infant-mother and infant-father attachments. *Child Development, 58,* 1505–1512.

Chess, S., & Korn, S. J. (1980). Temperament and behavior disorder in mentally retarded children. *Journal of Special Education, 23,* 122–130.

Chess, S., & Thomas, A. (1982). Infant bonding: Mystique and reality. *American Journal of Orthopsychiatry, 52,* 213–222.

Chess, S., & Thomas, A. (1984). *Origins and*

evolution of behavior disorders: Infancy to early adult life. New York: Brunner/Mazel.

Chi, M. T. (1978). Knowledge structure and memory development. In R. S. Siegler (Ed.), *Children's thinking: What develops?* Hillsdale, NJ: Erlbaum.

Chi, M. T., Glaser, R., & Rees, E. (1982). Expertise in problem solving. In R. J. Sternberg (Ed.), *Advances in the psychology of human intelligence* (Vol. 1). Hillsdale, NJ: Erlbaum.

Chipman, S. F., Brush, L. R., & Wilson, D. M. (Eds.). (1985). *Women and mathematics: Balancing the equation.* Hillsdale, NJ: Erlbaum.

Chomsky, N. (1965). *Aspects of a theory of syntax.* Cambridge, MA: M.I.T. Press.

Chomsky, N. (1975). *Reflections on language.* New York: Pantheon Books.

Chumlea, W. C. (1982). Physical growth in adolescence. In B. B. Wolman (Ed.), *Handbook of developmental psychology.* Englewood Cliffs, NJ: Prentice-Hall.

Clark, E. V. (1973). What's in a word? On the child's acquisition of semantics in his first language. In E. Moore (Ed.), *Cognitive development and the acquisition of language.* New York: Academic Press.

Clark, E. V. (1975). Knowledge, context, and strategy in the acquisition of meaning. In D. P. Date (Ed.), *Georgetown University round table on language and linguistics.* Washington, DC: Georgetown University Press.

Clark E. V. (1977). Strategies and the mapping problem in first language acquisition. In J. Macnamara (Ed.). *Language learning and thought.* New York: Academic Press, 1977.

Clark, E. V. (1983). Meanings and concepts. In J. H. Flavell & E. M. Markman (Eds.), *Handbook of child psychology: Cognitive development* (Vol. 3). New York: Wiley. (P. H. Mussen, General Editor)

Clark, E. V. (1987). The principle of contrast: A constraint on language acquisiton. In B. MacWhinney (Ed.), *Mechanisms of language acquisition.* Hillsdale, NJ: Erlbaum.

Clarke, A. D. B. (1968). Learning and human development—the 42nd Maudsley lecture. *British Journal of Psychiatry, 114,* 161–177.

Clarke, A. M., & Clarke, A. D. B. (1976). *Early experience: Myth and evidence.* New York: Free Press.

Clarke-Stewart, A. (1973). Interactions between mothers and their young children: Characteristics and consequences. *Monographs of the Society for Research in Child Development, 38* (Whole No. 153).

Clarke-Stewart, A. (1984). Day care: A new context for research and development. In M. Perlmutter (Ed.), *Minnesota symposia on child psychology* (Vol. 17). Hillsdale, NJ: Erlbaum.

Clarke-Stewart, A. (1987). The social ecology of early childhood. In N. Eisenberg (Ed.), *Contemporary topics in developmental psychology.* New York: Wiley-Interscience.

Clary, E. G., & Miller, J. (1986). Socialization and situational influences on sustained altruism. *Child Development, 57,* 1358–1369.

Clifton, R. K., Morrongiello, B. A., Kulig, J. W., & Dowd, J. M. (1981). Newborns' orientation toward sound: Possible implications for cortical development. *Child Development, 52,* 833–838.

Coates, S. (1972). *Preschool Embedded Figures Test.* Palo Alto, CA: Consulting Psychologists Press.

Cochran, M. M., & Brassard, J. A. (1979). Child development and personal social networks. *Child Development, 50,* 601–616.

Colby, A., Kohlberg, L., Gibbs, J., & Lieberman, M. (1983). A longitudinal study of moral judgment. *Monographs of the Society for Research in Child Development, 48* (1–2, Whole No. 200).

Cole, M., & Traupmann, K. (1981). Comparative cognitive research: Learning from a learning disabled child. In W. A. Collins (Ed.), *Aspects of the development of competence: The Minnesota symposia on child psychology* (Vol. 14). Hillsdale, NJ: Erlbaum.

Collins, W. A. (Ed.). (1984). *Development during middle childhood: The years from six to twelve.* Washington, DC: National Academy Press.

Colombo, J. (1982). The critical period concept: Research, methodology, and theoretical issues. *Psychological Bulletin, 91,* 260–275.

Committee on Assessing Alternative Birth Settings (1982). *Research issues in the assessment of birth settings,* National Research Council, Commission on Life Sciences. Washington, DC: National Academy Press.

Connolly, J. A., & Doyle, A. (1984). Relation of social fantasy play to social competence in preschoolers. *Developmental Psychology, 20,* 797–806.

Cook, M., & Birch, R. (1984). Infant perception of the shapes of tilted plane forms. *Infant Behavior and Development, 7,* 389–402.

Coopersmith, S. (1967). *The antecedents of self-esteem*. San Francisco: Freeman.

Corrigan, R., & Schommer, M. (1984). Form versus function revisited: The role of social input and memory factors. *Child Development, 55*, 1721–1726.

Crisafi, M. A., & Brown, A. L. (1986). Analogical transfer in very young children: Combining two separately learned solutions to reach a goal. *Child Development, 57*, 953–968.

Crnic, K. A., Greenberg, M. T., Ragozin, A. S., Robinson, N. M., & Basham, R. B. (1983). Effects of stress and social support on mothers and premature and full-term infants. *Child Development, 54*, 209–217.

Crockenberg, S. B. (1981). Infant irritability, mother responsiveness, and social support influences on the security of infant-mother attachment. *Child Development, 52*, 857–865.

Crockenberg, S. B. (1983, April). Social support and the maternal behavior of adolescent mothers. Paper presented at the biennial meetings of the Society for Research in Child Development, Detroit.

Crockenberg, S. B. (1986). Are temperamental differences in babies associated with predictable differences in care-giving? *New Directions for Child Development, 31*, 53–74.

Crook, C. (1987). Taste and olfaction. In P. Salapatek & L. Cohen (Eds.), *Handbook of infant perception: Vol. 1. From sensation to perception*. Orlando, FL: Academic Press.

Csikszentmihalyi, M., & Larson, R. (1984). *Being adolescent: Conflict and growth in the teenage years*. New York: Basic Books.

Csikszentmihalyi, M., Larson, R., & Prescott, S. (1977). The ecology of adolescent activity and experience. *Journal of Youth and Adolescence, 6*, 281–294.

Cutrona, C. E., & Troutman, B. R. (1986). Social support, infant temperament, and parenting self-efficacy: A mediational model of postpartum depression. *Child Development, 57*, 1507–1518.

Curtiss, S. (1977). *Genie. A psychological study of a modern day "wild child."* New York: Academic Press.

Dale, P. S. (1976). *Language development: Structure and function* (2nd ed.). New York: Holt, Rinehart and Winston.

Damon, W. (1977). *The social world of the child*. San Francisco: Jossey-Bass.

Damon, W. (1983). The nature of social-cognitive change in the developing child. In W. F. Overton (Ed.)., *The relationship between social and cognitive development*. Hillsdale, NJ: Erlbaum.

Danner, F. W., & Day, M. C. (1977). Eliciting formal operations. *Child Development, 48*, 1600–1606.

Danner, F. W., & Lonky, E. (1981). A cognitive-developmental approach to the effects of rewards on intrinsic motivation. *Child Development, 50*, 597–600.

Darling, C. A., Kallen, D. J., & Van Dusen, J. E. (1984). Sex in transition, 1970–1980. *Journal of Youth and Adolescence, 13*, 385–399.

Davidson, E. S., Yasuna, A., & Tower, A. (1979). The effect of television cartoons on sex-role stereotyping in young girls. *Child Development, 50*, 597–600.

DeCasper, A., & Fifer, W. (1980). Of human bonding: Newborns prefer their mothers' voices. *Science, 208*, 1174–1176.

DeCasper, A. J., & Sigafoos, A. D. (1983). The intrauterine heartbeat: A potent reinforcer for newborns. *Infant Behavior and Development, 6*, 19–25.

DeCasper, A. J., & Spence, M. J. (1986). Prenatal maternal speech influences newborns' perception of speech sounds. *Infant Behavior and Development, 9*, 133–150.

de Chateau, P. (1980). Effects of hospital practices on synchrony in the development of the infant-parent relationship. In P. M. Taylor (Ed.), *Parent-infant relationships*. New York: Grune & Stratton.

de Chateau, P. (1987). Parent-infant socialization in several Western European countries. In J. D. Osofsky (Ed.), *Handbook of infant development* (2nd ed.). New York: Wiley.

DeLoache, J. S. (1986). Memory in very young children: Exploitation of cues to the location of a hidden object. *Cognitive Development, 1*, 123–138.

DeLoache, J. S., Cassidy, D. J., & Brown, A. L., (1985). Precursors of mnemonic strategies in very young children's memory. *Child Development, 56*, 125–137.

DeMeis, D. K., Hock, E., & McBride, S. L. (1986). The balance of employment and motherhood: Longitudinal study of mothers' feelings about separation from their first-born infants. *Developmental Psychology, 22*, 627–632.

Dempster, F. N. (1981). Memory span: Sources of individual and developmental differences. *Psychological Bulletin, 89*, 63–100.

Dennis, M., Sugar, J., & Whitaker, H. A. (1982).

The acquisition of tag questions. *Child Development, 53,* 1254–1257.

Dennis, W. (1960). Causes of retardation among institutional children: Iran. *Journal of Genetic Psychology, 96,* 47–59.

de Regt, R. H., Minkoff, H. L., Feldman, J., & Schwarz, R. H. (1986). Relation of private or clinic care to the cesarean birth rate. *New England Journal of Medicine, 315,* 619–624.

The Diagram Group. (1977). *Child's body.* New York: Paddington.

Dickerson, J. W. T. (1981). Nutrition, brain growth and development. In K. J. Connolly & H. F. R. Prechtl (Eds.), *Maturation and development: Biological and psychological perspectives.* Clinics in Developmental Medicine No. 77/78. London: Heinemann.

Dietrich, K. N., Krafft, K. M., Bornschein, R. L., Hammond, P. B., Berger, O., Succop, P. A., & Bier, M. (1987). Low-level fetal lead exposure effect on neurobehavioral development in early infancy. *Pediatrics, 80,* 721–730.

DiVitto, B., & Goldberg, S. (1979). The effects of newborn medical status on early parent-infant interaction. In T. Field, A. Sostek, S. Goldberg, & H. H. Shuman (Eds.), *Infants born at risk.* New York: Spectrum.

Dobson, V., & Teller, D. Y. (1978). Visual acuity in human infants: A review and comparison of behavioral and electrophysiological studies. *Vision Research, 18,* 1469–1483.

Dodge, K. A. (1983). Behavioral antecedents of peer social status. *Child Development, 54,* 1386–1399.

Dodge, K. A., & Frame, C. L. (1982). Social cognitive biases and deficits in aggressive boys. *Child Development, 53,* 620–635.

Dollard, J., Doob, L. W., Miller, N. E., Mowrer, O. H., & Sears, R. R. (1939). *Frustration and aggression.* New Haven, CT: Yale University Press.

Dominick, J. R., & Greenberg, B. S. (1972). Attitudes toward violence: The interaction of television exposure, family attitudes, and social class. In G. A. Comstock & E. A. Rubenstein (Eds.), *Television and social behavior* (Vol. 3). Washington, DC: U.S. Government Printing Office.

Dornbusch, S. M., Carlsmith, J. M., Bushwall, S. J., Ritter, P. L., Leiderman, H., Hastdorf, A. H., & Gross, R. T. (1985). Single parents, extended households, and the control of adolescents. *Child Development, 56,* 326–341.

Dornbusch, S. M., Gross, R. T., Duncan, P. D., & Ritter, P. L. (1987a). Stanford studies of adolescence using the National Health Examination Survey. In R. M. Lerner & T. T. Foch (Eds.), *Biological-psychosocial interactions in early adolescence.* Hillsdale, NJ: Erlbaum.

Dornbusch, S. M., Ritter, P. L., Liederman, P. H., Roberts, D. F., & Fraleigh, M. J. (1987b). The relation of parenting style to adolescent school performance. *Child Development, 58,* 1244–1257.

Dreyer, P. H. (1982). Sexuality during adolescence. In B. B. Wolman (Ed.). *Handbook of developmental psychology.* Englewood Cliffs, NJ: Prentice-Hall.

Duckett, E. D., Raffaelli, M., & Richards, M. H. (1987, April). *The relationship of maternal employment to young adolescents' daily activities and emotional well-being.* Paper presented at the biennial meetings of the Society for Research in Child Development, Baltimore.

Duke, P. M., Carlsmith, J. M., Jennings, D., Martin, J. A., Dornbusch, S. M., Gross, R. T., & Siegel-Gorelick, B. (1982). Educational correlates of early and late sexual maturation in adolescence. *Journal of Pediatrics, 100,* 633–637.

Dumaret, A. (1985). IQ, scholastic performance and behaviour of sibs raised in contrasting environments. *Journal of Child Psychology and Psychiatry, 26,* 553–580.

Dunn, H. G., McBurney, A. K., Ingram, S., & Hunter, C. M. (1977). Maternal cigarette smoking during pregnancy and the child's subsequent development: II. Neurological and intellectual maturation to the age of 6½ years. *Canadian Journal of Public Health, 68,* 43–50.

Dunphy, D. C. (1963). The social structure of urban adolescent peer groups. *Sociometry, 26,* 230–246.

Dunst, C. J., Brooks, P. H., & Doxsey, P. A. (1982). Characteristics of hiding places and the transition to stage IV performance in object permanence tasks. *Developmental Psychology, 18,* 671–681.

Easterbrooks, M. A., & Goldberg, W. A. (1987, April). *Consequences of early family attachment patterns for later social-personality development.* Paper presented at the biennial meetings of the Society for Research in Child Development, Baltimore.

Eaton, W. O., & Enns, L. R. (1986). Sex differences in human motor activity level. *Psychological Bulletin, 100,* 19–28.

Eccles, J. S., & Hoffman, L. W. (1984). Sex

roles, socialization, and occupational behavior. In H. W. Stevenson & A. E. Siegel (Eds.), *Child development research and social policy* (Vol. 1). Chicago: University of Chicago Press.

Edgerton, R. B. (1979). *Mental retardation.* Cambridge, MA: Harvard University Press.

Egeland, B., & Farber, E. A. (1984). Infant-mother attachment: Factors related to its development and changes over time. *Child Development, 55,* 753–771.

Eichorn, D. H., Hunt, J. V., & Honzik, M. P. (1981). Experience, personality, and IQ: Adolescence to middle age. In D. H. Eichorn, J. A. Clausen, N. Haan, M. P. Honzik, & P. H. Mussen (Eds.), *Present and past in middle life.* New York: Academic Press.

Eisenberg, N. (1986). *Altruistic emotion, cognition, and behavior.* Hillsdale, NJ: Erlbaum.

Eisenberg, N., & Miller, P. A. (1987). The relation of empathy to prosocial and related behaviors. *Psychological Bulletin, 101,* 91–119.

Eisenberg-Berg, N., & Hand, M. (1979). The relationship of preschoolers' reasoning about prosocial moral conflicts to prosocial behavior. *Child Development, 50,* 356–363.

Elardo, R., Bradley, R., & Caldwell, B. (1975). The relation of infants' home environments to mental test performance from six to thirty-six months: A longitudinal analysis. *Child Development, 46,* 71–76.

Elder, G. H., Jr. (1974). *Children of the Great Depression.* Chicago: University of Chicago Press.

Elder, G. H., Jr. (1981). Scarcity and prosperity in postwar childbearing: Explorations from a life course perspective. *Journal of Family History, 5,* 410–431.

Elder, G. H., Jr. (1984). Families, kin, and the life course: A sociological perspective. In R. D. Parke (Ed.), *The family.* Chicago: University of Chicago Press.

Eme, R. F. (1979). Sex differences in childhood psychopathology: A review. *Psychological Bulletin, 86,* 374–395.

Emmerich, W., & Shepard, K. (1982). Development of sex-differentiated preferences during later childhood and adolescence. *Child Development, 18,* 406–417.

Engel, M., Nechlin, H., & Arkin, A. M. (1975). Aspects of mothering: Correlates of the cognitive development of black male infants in the second year of life. In A. Davids (Ed.), *Child personality and psychopathology: Current topics* (Vol. 2). New York: Wiley.

Entwisle, D. R., & Doering, S. G. (1981). *The first birth.* Baltimore: Johns Hopkins University Press.

Erickson, M. F., Sroufe, L. A., & Egeland, B. (1985). The relationship between quality of attachment and behavior problems in preschool in a high-risk sample. In I. Bretherton & E. Waters (Eds.), Growing points of attachment theory and research. *Monographs of the Society for Research in Child Development, 50* (Whole No. 209).

Erikson, E. H. (1963). *Childhood and society.* New York: Norton. (Original work published 1950)

Erikson, E. H. (1964). *Insight and responsibility.* New York: Norton.

Erikson, E. H. (1968). *Identity: Youth and crisis.* New York: Norton.

Erikson, E. H. (1974). *Dimensions of a new identity: The 1973 Jefferson lectures in the humanities.* New York: Norton.

Erikson, E. H. (1980). *Identity and the life cycle.* New York: Norton. (Original work published 1959)

Eron, L. D. (1982). Parent-child interaction, television violence, and aggression of children. *American Psychologist, 37,* 197–211.

Eron, L. D. (1987). The development of aggressive behavior from the perspective of a developing behaviorism. *American Psychologist, 42,* 435–442.

Eron, L. D., Huesmann, L. R., Brice, P., Fischer, P., & Mermelstein, R. (1983). Age trends in the development of aggression, sex-typing, and related television habits. *Developmental Psychology, 19,* 71–77.

Escalona, K. S. (1981). The reciprocal role of social and emotional developmental advances and cognitive development during the second and third years of life. In E. K. Shapiro & E. Weber (Eds.), *Cognitive and affective growth: Developmental interaction.* Hillsdale, NJ: Erlbaum.

Evans, R. I. (1969). *Dialogue with Erik Erikson.* New York: Dutton.

Fagan, J. F. (1984). The intelligent infant: Theoretical implications. *Intelligence, 8,* 1–9.

Fagot, B. I. (1974). Sex differences in toddlers' behavior and parental reaction. *Developmental Psychology, 10,* 544–558.

Fagot, B. I. (1985). Beyond the reinforcement principle: Another step toward understanding sex role development. *Developmental Psychology, 21,* 1097–1104.

Fagot, B. I., & Kronsberg, S. J. (1982). Sex differences: Biological and social factors influencing the behavior of young boys and girls. In S. G. Moore & C. R. Cooper (Eds.), *The young child. Reviews of research* (Vol. 3). Washington, DC: National Association for the Education of Young Children.

Famularo, R. Stone, K., Barnum, R., & Wharton, R. (1986). Alcoholism and severe child maltreatment. *American Journal of Orthopsychiatry, 56,* 481–485.

Fantz, R. L. (1956). A method for studying early visual development. *Perceptual and Motor Skills, 6,* 13–15.

Farber, S. L. (1981). *Identical twins reared apart: A reanalysis.* New York: Basic Books.

Farnham-Diggory, S. (1978). *Learning disabilities.* Cambridge, MA: Harvard University Press.

Farnham-Diggory, S. (1986). Time, now, for a little serious complexity. In S. J. Ceci (Ed.), *Handbook of cognitive, social, and neuropsychological aspects of learning disability* (Vol. 1). Hillsdale, NJ: Erlbaum.

Farran, D. C., Haskins, R., & Gallagher, J. J. (1980). Poverty and mental retardation: A search for explanations. In J. J. Gallagher (Ed.), *Ecology of exceptional children.* San Francisco: Jossey-Bass.

Faust, M. S. (1983). Alternative constructions of adolescent growth. In J. Brooks-Gunn & A. C. Petersen (Eds.), *Girls at puberty. Biological and psychosocial perspectives.* New York: Plenum.

Feingold, B. F. (1975). *Why your child is hyperactive.* New York: Random House.

Ferguson, T. J., & Rule, B. G. (1980). Effects of interential set, consequence severity, and basis for responsibility on children's evaluation of aggressive acts. *Developmental Psychology, 16,* 141–146.

Ferguson, T. J., & Rule, B. G. (1982). Influence of inferencial set, outcome intent, and outcome severity on children's moral judgments. *Developmental Psychology, 18,* 843–851.

Fernald, A. (1985). Four-month-old infants prefer to listen to motherese. *Infant Behavior and Development, 8,* 181–195.

Feshbach, S. (1970). Aggression. In P. H. Mussen (Ed.), *Carmichael's manual of child psychology* (Vol. 2, 3rd ed.). New York: Wiley.

Field, T. M. (1977). Effects of early separation, interactive deficits, and experimental manipulations on infant-mother face-to-face interaction. *Child Development, 48,* 763–771.

Field, T. M. (1978). Interaction behaviors of primary versus secondary caretaker fathers. *Developmental Psychology, 14,* 183–185.

Field, T. M. (1982). Social perception and responsivity in early infancy. In T. M. Field, A. Huston, H. C. Quay, L. Troll, & G. E. Finley (Eds.), *Review of human development.* New York: Wiley.

Field, T. M. (1984). Early interactions between infants and their postpartum depressed mothers. *Infant Behavior and Development, 7,* 517–522.

Field, T. M., Cohen, D., Garcia, R., & Greenberg, R. (1984). Mother-stranger face discrimination by the newborn. *Infant Behavior and Development, 7,* 19–25.

Field, T. M. De Stefano, L., & Koewler, J. H., III. (1982). Fantasy play of toddlers and preschoolers. *Developmental Psychology, 18,* 503–508.

Finkelstein, N. W. (1982). Aggression: Is it stimulated by day care? *Young Children, 37,* 3–9.

Fischer, K. W. (1980). A theory of cognitive development: The control and construction of hierarchies of skills. *Psychological Review, 87,* 477–531.

Fischer, K. W., & Canfield, R. L. (1986). The ambiguity of stage and structure in behavior: Person and environment in the development of psychological structures. In I. Levin (Ed.), *Stage and structure: Reopening the debate.* Norwood, NJ: Ablex.

Fischer, K. W., & Pipp, S. L. (1984). Processes of cognitive development: Optimal level and skill acquisition. In R. J. Sternberg (Ed.), *Mechanisms of cognitive development.* New York: Freeman.

Fischer, K. W., Pipp, S. L., & Bullock, D. (1984). Detecting developmental discontinuities. In R. N. Emde & R. J. Harmon (Eds.), *Continuities and discontinuities in development.* New York: Plenum.

Fitzgerald, L. F., & Betz, N. E. (1983). Issues in the vocational psychology of women. In W. B. Walsh & S. H. Osipow (Eds.), *Handbook of vocational psychology* (Vol. 1). Hillsdale, NJ: Erlbaum.

Flavell, J. H. (1982a). On cognitive development. *Child Development, 53,* 1–10.

Flavell, J. H. (1982b). Structures, stages, and sequences in cognitive development. In W. A. Collins (Ed.), *The concept of development: The Minnesota symposia on child psychology* (Vol. 15). Hillsdale, NJ: Erlbaum.

Flavell, J. H. (1985). *Cognitive development* (2nd ed.). Englewood Cliffs, NJ: Prentice-Hall.

Flavell, J. H. (1986a). The development of children's knowledge about the appearance-reality distinction. *American Psychologist, 41,* 418–425.

Flavell, J. H. (1986b, January), Really and truly. *Psychology Today,* pp. 38–44.

Flavell, J. H. Everett, B. A., Croft, K., & Flavell, E. R. (1981). Young children's knowledge about visual perception: Further evidence for the Level 1–Level 2 distinction. *Developmental Psychology, 17,* 99–103.

Flavell, J. H., Green, F. L., Wahl, K. E., & Flavell, E. R. (1987). The effects of question clarification and memory aids on young children's performance on appearance-reality tasks. *Cognitive Development, 2,* 127–144.

Fogelman, K. (1980). Smoking in pregnancy and subsequent development of the child. *Child Care, Health and Development, 6,* 233–249.

Forbes, G. B. (1972). Growth of the lean body mass in man. *Growth, 36,* 325–338.

Ford, M. E. (1982). Social cognition and social competence in adolescence. *Developmental Psychology, 18,* 323–340.

Fraiberg, S. (1974). Blind infants and their mothers: An examination of the sign system. In M. Lewis & L. A. Rosenblum (Eds.), *The effect of the infant on its caregiver.* New York: Wiley.

Fraiberg, S. (1975). The development of human attachments in infants blind from birth. *Merrill-Palmer Quarterly, 21,* 315–334.

Fraiberg, S. (1977). *Insights from the blind.* New York: New American Library (Meridian Books).

Freedman, J. L. (1986). Television violence and aggression: A rejoinder. *Psychological Bulletin, 100,* 372–378.

Freeman, J. (1981). The intellectually gifted. *New directions for exceptional children, 7,* 75–86.

Freud, S. (1905). Three contributions to the theory of sex. *The basic writings of Sigmund Freud* (A. A. Brill, Trans.). New York: Random House (Modern Library).

Freud, S. (1965). *A general introduction of psychoanalysis* (J. Riviere, Trans.). New York: Washington Square Press. (Original work published 1920)

Friedman, S. L., Zahn-Waxler, C., & Radke-Yarrow, M. (1982). Perceptions of cries of full-term and preterm infants. *Infant Behavior and Development, 5,* 161–173.

Friedrich-Cofer, L., & Huston, A. C. (1986). Television violence and aggression: The debate continues. *Psychological Bulletin, 100,* 364–371.

Frueh, T., & McGhee, P. E. (1975). Traditional sex role development and amount of time spent watching television. *Developmental Psychology, 11,* 109.

Furrow, D. (1984). Social and private speech at two years. *Child Development, 55,* 355–362.

Furth, H. (1970). *Piaget for teachers.* Englewood Cliffs, NJ: Prentice-Hall.

Gaensbauer, T. J., Harmon, R. J., Cytryn, L., & McNew, D. H. (1984). Social and affective development in infants with a manic-depressive parent. *American Journal of Psychiatry, 141,* 223–229.

Gallagher, J. J. (1985). The prevalence of mental retardation: Cross-cultural considerations from Sweden and the United States. *Intelligence, 9,* 97–108.

Gallagher, J. J., & Ramey, C. T. (1987). *The malleability of children.* Baltimore: Paul H. Brookes.

Ganchrow, J. R., Steiner, J. E., & Daher, M. (1983). Neonatal facial expressions in response to different qualities and intensities of gustatory stimuli. *Infant Behavior and Development, 6,* 189–200.

Garbarino, J., & Sherman, D. (1980). High-risk neighborhoods and high-risk families: The human ecology of child maltreatment. *Child Development, 51,* 188–198.

Garber, H., & Heber, R. (1982). Modification of predicted cognitive development in high-risk children through early intervention. In D. K. Detterman & R. J. Sternberg (Eds.), *How and how much can intelligence be increased.* Norwood, NJ: Ablex.

Gardner, B. T., & Gardner, R. A. (1980). Two comparative psychologists look at language acquisition. In K. Nelson (Ed.), *Children's language* (Vol. 2). New York: Gardner Press.

Gardner, H. (1983). *Frames of mind: The theory of multiple intelligence.* New York: Basic Books.

Garn, S. M. (1980). Continuities and change in maturational timing. In O. G. Brim, Jr., & J. Kagan (Eds.), *Constancy and change in human development.* Cambridge, MA: Harvard University Press.

Gelman, R. (1972). Logical capacity of very

young children: Number invariance rules. *Child Development, 43,* 75–90.

Gelman, R. & Baillargeon, R. (1983). A review of some Piagetian concepts. In J. H. Flavell, & E. M. Markman (Eds.), *Handbook of child psychology: Cognitive development* (Vol. 3). New York: Wiley. (P. H. Mussen, General Editor)

Gentner, D. (1982). Why nouns are learned before verbs: Linguistic relativity versus natural partitioning. In S. A. Kuczaj, II (Ed.), *Language development: Vol. 2. Language, thought, and culture.* Hillsdale, NJ: Erlbaum.

Gerbner, G. (1972). Violence in television drama: Trends and symbolic functions. In G. A. Comstock & E. A. Rubenstein (Eds.), *Television and social behavior* (Vol. 1). Washington, DC: U.S. Government Printing Office.

Gerbner, G., Gross, L., Morgan, M., & Signorielli, N. (1980). The "mainstreaming" of America: Violence profile No. 11. *Journal of Communications, 30,* 10–29.

Gerson, R. P., & Damon, W. (1978). Moral understanding and children's conduct. In W. Damon (Ed.), *Moral development.* San Francisco: Jossey-Bass.

Gesell, A. (1925). *The mental growth of the preschool child.* New York: Macmillan.

Gewirtz, J. L., & Boyd, E. F. (1977). Does maternal responding imply reduced infant crying? A critique of the 1972 Bell and Ainsworth report. *Child Development, 48,* 1200–1207.

Gibbs, J. T. (1985). Psychosocial factors associated with depression in urban adolescent females: Implications for assessment. *Journal of Youth and Adolescence, 14,* 47–60.

Gibson, E. J. (1969). *Principles of perceptual learning and development.* New York: Prentice-Hall.

Gibson, E. J., & Levin, H. (1975). *The psychology of reading.* Cambridge, MA: M.I.T. Press.

Gibson, E. J., & Spelke, E. S. (1983). The development of perception. In J. H. Flavell & E. M. Markman (Eds.), *Handbook of child psychology: Cognitive development* (Vol. 3). New York: Wiley. (P. H. Mussen, General Editor)

Gibson, E. J., & Walk, R. D. (1960). The "visual cliff." *Scientific American, 202,* 64–71.

Giele, J. Z. (1982). Women's work and family roles. In J. Z. Giele (Ed.), *Women in the middle years.* New York: Wiley.

Gilligan, C. (1982a). New maps of development: New visions of maturity. *American Journal of Orthopsychiatry, 52,* 199–212.

Gilligan, C. (1982b). *In a different voice: Psycho-*

logical theory and women's development. Cambridge, MA: Harvard University Press.

Ginsburg, H. J., & Miller, S. M. (1982). Sex differences in children's risk-taking behavior. *Child Development, 53,* 426–428.

Ginsburg, H., & Opper, S. (1969). *Piaget's theory of intellectual development.* Englewood Cliffs, NJ: Prentice-Hall.

Gleicher, N. (1984). Cesarean section rates in the United States. *Journal of the American Medical Association, 252,* 3273–3276.

Gleitman, L. R., & Wanner, E. (1984). Current issues in language learning. In M. H. Bornstein & M. E. Lamb (Eds.), *Developmental psychology: An advanced textbook.* Hillsdale, NJ: Erlbaum.

Glick, P. (1979). Children of divorced parents in demographic perspective. *Journal of Social Issues, 35,* 170–182.

Glueck, S., & Glueck, E. (1972). *Identification of pre-delinquents: Validation studies and some suggested uses of Glueck table.* New York: Interconintental Medical Book Corp.

Goldberg, S. (1983). Parent-infant bonding: Another look. *Child Development, 54,* 1355–1382.

Goldberg, W. A., & Easterbrooks, M. A. (1984). Role of marital quality in toddler development. *Developmental Psychology, 20,* 504–514.

Golden, M., & Birns, B. (1983). Social class and infant intelligence. In M. Lewis (Ed.), *Origins of intelligence. Infancy and early childhood* (2nd ed.). New York: Plenum.

Goldman-Rakic, P. S. (1987). Development of cortical circuitry and cognitive function. *Child Development, 58,* 601–622.

Goldsmith, H. H., Bradshaw, D. L., & Riesser-Danner, L. A. (1986). Temperament as a potential developmental influence on attachment. *New Directions for Child Development, 31,* 5–34.

Goleman, D. (1980, February). 1,528 little geniuses and how they grew. *Psychology Today, 13,* 28–43.

Good, T. L., & Weinstein, R. S. (1986). Schools make a difference. Evidence, criticisms, and new directions. *American Psychologist, 41,* 1090–1097.

Goodenough, F. L. (1931). *Anger in young children.* Minneapolis: University of Minnesota Press.

Goodsitt, J. V., Morse, P. A., Ver Hoeve, J. N., & Cowan, N. (1984). Infant speech recognition in multisyballic contexts. *Child Development, 55,* 903–910.

Gottfredson, L. (1981). Circumscription and

compromise: A developmental theory of occupational aspirations. *Journal of Counseling Psychology Monograph, 28,* 545–579.

Gottman, J. M. (1986). The world of coordinated play: Same- and cross-sex friendship in young children. In J. M. Gottman & J. G. Parker (Eds.), *Conversations of friends. Speculations on affective development.* Cambridge, England: Cambridge University Press.

Graham, P. (1979). Epidemiological studies. In H. C. Quay & J. S. Werry (Eds.), *Psychopathological disorders of childhood* (2nd ed.). New York: Wiley.

Granger, L., & Granger, B. (1986). *The magic feather. The truth about "special education."* New York: Dutton.

Gratch, G. (1979). The development of thought and language in infancy. In J. D. Osofsky (Ed.), *Handbook of infant development.* New York: Wiley.

Greenberg, J., & Kuczaj, S. A., II. (1982). Towards a theory of substantive word-meaning acquisition. In S. A. Kuczaj, II (Ed.), *Language development: Vol. 1. Syntax and semantics.* Hillsdale, NJ: Erlbaum.

Greenberg, M., & Morris, N. (1974). Engrossment: The newborn's impact upon the father. *American Journal of Orthopsychiatry, 44,* 520–531.

Greenberg, M. T., Calderon, R., & Kusche, C. (1984). Early intervention using simultaneous communication with deaf infants: The effect on communication development. *Child Development, 55,* 607–616.

Greenberg, M. T., Siegel, J. M. & Leitch, C. J. (1983). The nature and importance of attachment relationships to parents and peers during adolescence. *Journal of Youth and Adolescence, 12,* 373–386.

Greenhaus, J. H., & Parasuraman, S. (1986). Vocational and organizational behavior, 1985: A review. *Journal of Vocational Behavior, 29,* 115–176.

Greif, G. L. (1985). *Single fathers.* Lexington, MA: Lexington Books.

Grinker, J. A. (1981). Behavioral and metabolic factors in childhood obesity. In M. Lewis & L. A. Rosenblum (Eds.), *The uncommon child.* New York: Plenum.

Grover, J. W. (1984). Leboyer and obstetric practice. *New York State Journal of Medicine, 84,* 158–159.

Grusec, J. E., & Arnason, L. (1982). Consideration for others: Approaches to enhancing altruism. In S. G. Moore & C. G. Cooper (Eds.),

The young child. Reviews of research (Vol. 3). Washington, DC: National Association for the Education of Young Children.

Grusec, J. E., & Dix, T. (1986). The socialization of prosocial behavior: Theory and reality. In C. Zahn-Waxler, E. M. Cummings, & R. Iannotti (Eds.), *Altruism and aggression. Biological and social origins.* Cambridge, England: Cambridge University Press.

Grusec, J. E., Saas-Kortsaak, P., & Simutis, Z. M. (1978). The role of example and moral exhortation in the training of altruism. *Child Development, 49,* 920–923.

Guerin, D., DiBello, P., & Nordquist, G. (1987, April). *Infant termperament and behavior problems in early childhood: A longitudinal analysis.* Paper presented at the biennial meetings of the Society for Research in Child Development, Baltimore.

Guidubaldi, J., Cleminshaw, H. K., Perry, J. D., Natasi, B. K., & Lichtel, J. (1986). The role of selected family environment factors in children's post-divorce adjustment. *Family Relations, 35,* 141–151.

Guralnick, M. J., & Paul-Brown, D. (1984). Communicative adjustments during behavior-request episodes among children at different developmental levels. *Child Development, 55,* 911–919.

Gzesh, S. M., & Surber, C. F. (1985). Visual perspective-taking skills in children. *Child Development, 56,* 1204–1213.

Haan, N. (1985). Processes of moral development: Cognitive or social disequilibrium? *Developmental Psychology, 21,* 996–1006.

Haith, M. M. (1980). *Rules that babies look by.* Hillsdale, NJ: Erlbaum.

Haith, M. M., Bergman, T., & Moore, M. J. (1977). Eye contact and face scanning in early infancy. *Science, 198,* 853–855.

Hakuta, K. (1986). *Mirror on language: The debate on bilingualism.* New York: Basic Books.

Hakuta, K., & Diaz, R. M. (1985). The relationship between degree of bilingualism and cognitive ability: A critical discussion and some new longitudinal data. In K. E. Nelson (Ed.), *Children's language* (Vol. 5). Hillsdale, NJ: Erlbaum.

Halpern, D. F. (1986). *Sex differences in cognitive abilities.* Hillsdale, NJ: Erlbaum.

Hanshaw, J. B. (1981). Cytomegalovirus infections. *Pediatrics in Review, 2,* 245–251.

Hanshaw, J. B., Scheiner, A. P., Moxley, A. W., Gaev, L., Abel, V., & Scheiner, B. (1976).

School failure and deafness after "silent" congenital cytomegalovirus infection. *New England Journal of Medicine, 295,* 468–470.

Hanson, M. J. (1981). Down's syndrome children: Characteristics and intervention research. In M. Lewis & L. A. Rosenblum (Eds.), *The uncommon child.* New York: Plenum.

Hardy-Brown, K., Plomin, R., & DeFries, J. C. (1981). Genetic and environmental influences on the rate of communicative development in the first year of life. *Developmental Psychology, 17,* 704–717.

Harley, J. P., Ray, R. S., Tomasi, L., Eichman, P. L., Matthews, C. G., Chun, R., Cleeland, C. S., & Straisman, E. (1978). Hyperkinesis and food additives: Testing the Feingold hypothesis. *Pediatrics, 61,* 818–828.

Harper, L. V., & Huie, K. S. (1985). The effects prior group experience, age, and familiarity on the quality and organization of preschoolers' social relationships. *Child Development, 56,* 704–717.

Harris, P. L., Olthof, T., & Terwogt, M. M. (1981). Children's knowledge of emotion. *Journal of Child Psychology and Psychiatry, 22,* 247–261.

Harter, S. (1983). Developmental perspectives on the self-system. In E. M. Hetherington (Ed.), *Handbook of child psychology: Socialization, personality, and sound development* (Vol. 4). New York: Wiley. (P. H. Mussen, General Editor)

Harter, S. (1985). Competence as a dimension of self-evaluation: Toward a comprehensive model of self-worth. In R. L. Leahy (Ed.), *The development of the self.* Orlando, FL: Academic Press.

Hartup, W. W. (1974). Aggression in childhood: Developmental perspectives. *American Psychologist, 29,* 336–341.

Hartup, W. W. (1978). Perspectives on child and family interaction: Past, present, and future. In R. M. Lerner & G. B. Spanier (Eds.), *Child influences on marital and family interaction.* New York: Academic Press.

Hartup, W. W. (1984). The peer context in middle childhood. In W. A. Collins (Ed.), *Development during middle childhood. The years from six to twelve.* Washington, DC: National Academy Press.

Harvard Education Letter (1986, January). Girls' math achievement: What we do and don't know. 2(1), 1–5.

Harvard Education Letter (1986, September). Early intervention for handicapped babies. 2(5), 7.

Harvard Education Letter. (1987, March). Adolescent health: Squander now, pay later. 3(2), 4–6.

Haskins, R. (1985). Public school aggression among children with varying day-care experience. *Child Development, 56,* 689–703.

Haskins, R. (1986). Social and cultural factors in risk assessment and mild mental retardation. In D. C. Farran & J. D. McKinney (Eds.), *Risk in intellectual and psychosocial development.* Orlando, FL: Academic Press.

Haskins, R., & McKinney, J. D. (1976). Relative effects of response tempo and accuracy on problem solving and academic achievement. *Child Development, 47,* 690–696.

Hawton, K. (1986). *Suicide and attempted suicide among children and adolescents.* Beverly Hills, CA: Sage.

Hay, D. R., Nash, A., & Pedersen, J. (1983). Interaction between six-month-old peers. *Child Development, 54,* 557–562.

Haynes, H., White, B. L., & Held, R. (1965). Visual accommodation in human infants. *Science, 148,* 528–530.

Heber, F. R. (1978). Sociocultural mental retardation—a longitudinal study. In D. Forgays (Ed.), *Primary prevention of psychopathology* (Vol. 2). Hanover, NH: University Press of New England.

Hechtman, L., & Weiss, G. (1983). Long-term outcome of hyperactive children. *American Journal of Orthopsychiatry, 53,* 532–541.

Hegvik, R. L., McDevitt, S. C., & Carey, W. B. (1981, August). *Longitudinal stability of temperament characteristics in the elementary school period.* Paper presented at the meeting of the International Society for the Study of Behavioral Development, Toronto.

Henley, E. D., & Altman, J. (1978). The young adult. In D. W. Smith, E. L. Bierman, & N. M. Robinson (Eds.), *The biologic ages of man.* Philadelphia: Saunders.

Henneborn, W. J., & Cogan, R. (1975). The effect of husband participation on reported pain and the probability of medication during labour and birth. *Journal of psychosomatic research, 19,* 215–222.

Hennig, M., & Jardim, A. (1976). *The managerial woman.* Garden City, NY: Doubleday.

Hess, E. H. (1972). "Imprinting" in a natural laboratory. *Scientific American, 227,* 24–31.

Hetherington, E. M. (1979). Divorce: A child's perspective. *American Psychologist, 34,* 851–858.

Hetherington, E. M. (1984). Stress and coping

in children and families. In A. Doyle, D. Gold, & D. S. Moskowitz (Eds.), Children and families under stress. *New Directions for Child Development, 24,* 7–34.

Hetherington, E. M. (1987, April). *Presidential Address.* Paper presented at the biennial meetings of the Society for Research in Child Development, Baltimore.

Hetherington, E. M., & Camara, K. A. (1984). Families in transition: The processes of dissolution and reconstitution. In R. D. Parke (Ed.), *Review of child development research: Vol. 7. The family.* Chicago: University of Chicago Press.

Hetherington, E. M., Cox, M., & Cox, R. (1978). The aftermath of divorce. In M. H. Stevens, Jr., & M. Mathews (Eds.), *Mother/child, father/child relationships.* Washington, DC: National Association for the Education of Young Children.

Higgins, A., Power, C., & Kohlberg, L. (1984). The relationship of moral atmosphere to judgments of responsibility. In W. M. Kurtines & J. L. Gewirtz (Eds.), *Morality, moral behavior, and moral development.* New York: Wiley-Interscience.

Higgins, A. T., & Turnure, J. E. (1984). Distractibility and concentration of attention in children's development. *Child Development, 55,* 1799–1810.

Higgins, E. T., & Parsons, J. E. (1983). Social cognition and the social life of the child: Stages as subcultures. In E. T. Higgins, D. N. Ruble, & W. W. Hartup (Eds.), *Social cognition and social development. A sociocultural perspective.* Cambridge, England: Cambridge University Press.

High/Scope Foundation. (1977). Can preschool education make a lasting difference? Bulletin of the High/Scope Foundation, No. 4, Fall.

Hill, J. P., Holmbeck, G. N., Marlow, L., Green, T. M., & Lynch, M. E. (1985). Menarcheal status and parent-child relations in families of seventh-grade girls. *Journal of Youth and Adolescence, 14,* 301–316.

Hinde, R. A., & Stevenson-Hinde, J. (1987). Interpersonal relationships and child development. *Developmental Review, 7,* 1–21.

Hinde, R. A., Titmus, G., Easton, D., & Tamplin, A. (1985). Incidence of "friendship" and behavior toward strong associates versus nonassociates in preschoolers. *Child Development, 56,* 234–235.

Hines, M. (1982). Prenatal gonadal hormones and sex differences in human behavior. *Psychological Bulletin, 92,* 56–80.

Hirsh-Pasek, K., Trieman, R., & Schneiderman, M. (1984). Brown and Hanlon revisited: Mothers' sensitivity to ungrammatical forms. *Journal of Child Language, 11,* 81–88.

Hittelman, J., Parekh, A., & Glass, L. (1987, April). *Developmental outcome of extremely low birth weight infants.* Paper presented at the biennial meetings of the Society for Research in Child Development, Baltimore.

Hobbs, N. (1975). *The futures of children.* San Francisco: Jossey-Bass.

Hofferth, S. L. (1985). Updating children's life course. *Journal of Marriage and the Family, 47,* 93–115.

Hofferth, S. L. (1987a). Teenage pregnancy and its resolution. In S. L. Hofferth & C. D. Hayes (Eds.), *Risking the future. Adolescent sexuality, pregnancy, and childbearing. Working papers.* Washington, DC: National Academy Press.

Hofferth, S. L. (1987b). Social and economic consequences of teenage childbearing. In S. L. Hofferth & C. D. Hayes (Eds.), *Risking the future. Adolescent sexuality, pregnancy, and childbearing. Working papers.* Washington, DC: National Academy Press.

Hoff-Ginsberg, E. (1986). Function and structure in maternal speech: Their relation to the child's development of syntax. *Developmental Psychology, 22,* 155–163.

Hoff-Ginsberg, E. (1987, April). *Why some properties of maternal speech benefit language growth (and others do not).* Paper presented at the biennial meetings of the Society for Research in Child Development, Baltimore.

Hoffman, L. W. (1984). Work, family, and the socialization of the child. In R. D. Parke (Ed.), *Review of child development research: Vol. 7. The family.* Chicago: University of Chicago Press.

Hoffman, M. L. (1982). Development of prosocial motivation: Empathy and guilt. In N. Eisenberg (Ed.), *The development of prosocial behavior.* New York: Academic Press.

Hoffman, M. L. (1984). Empathy, its limitations, and its role in a comprehensive moral theory. In W. M. Kurtines & J. L. Gewirtz (Eds.), *Morality, moral behavior, and moral development.* New York: Wiley.

Hollenbeck, A. R., Gewirtz, J. L., Sebris, L., & Scanlon, J. W. (1984). Labor and delivery medication influences parent-infant interaction in the first post-partum month. *Infant Behavior and Development, 7,* 201–210.

Holloway, S. D., & Hess, R. D. (1985). Mothers' and teachers' attributions about children's mathematics performance. In I. E. Sigel (Ed.), *Parental belief systems. The psychological consequences for children.* Hillsdale, NJ: Erlbaum.

Honzik, M. P. (1986). The role of the family in the development of mental abilities: A 50-year study. In N. Datan, A. L. Greene, & H. W. Reese (Eds.), *Life-span developmental psychology. Intergenerational relations.* Hillsdale, NJ: Erlbaum.

Horn, J. M. (1983). The Texas adoption project: Adopted children and their intellectual resemblance to biological and adoptive parents. *Child Development, 54,* 268–275.

Horn, J. M., Lochlin, J., & Willerman, L. (1979). Intellectual resemblance among adoptive and biological relatives: The Texas adoptive project. *Behavioral Genetics, 9,* 177–207.

Horowitz, F. D. (1982). The first two years of life: Factors related to thriving. In S. G. Moore & C. R. Cooper (Eds.), *The young child. Reviews of research* (Vol. 3). Washington, DC: National Association for the Education of Young Children.

Horowitz, F. D. (1987). *Exploring developmental theories: Toward a structural/behavioral model of development.* Hillsdale, NJ: Erlbaum.

Howard, J. (1978). The influence of children's developmental dysfunctions on marital quality and family interaction. In R. M. Lerner & G. B. Spanier (Eds.), *Child influences on marital and family interaction. A life-span perspective.* New York: Academic Press.

Howes, C. (1983). Patterns of friendship. *Child Development, 54,* 1041–1053.

Howes, C. (1987). Social competence with peers in young children: Developmental sequences. *Developmental Review, 7,* 252–272.

Hubbard, F. O. A., & van Ijzendoorn, M. H. (1987). Maternal unresponsiveness and infant crying. A critical replication of the Bell & Ainsworth study. In L. W. C. Tavecchio & M. H. van Ijzendoorn (Eds.), *Attachment in social networks.* Amsterdam: Elsevier/North Holland.

Hubel, D. H., & Weisel, T. N. (1963). Receptive fields of cells in striate cortex of very young, visually inexperienced kittens. *Journal of Neurophysiology, 26,* 994–1002.

Humphreys, L. G., Davey, T. C., & Park, R. K. (1985). Longitudinal correlation analysis of standing height and intelligence. *Child Development, 56,* 1465–1478.

Hunt, E., Frost, N., & Lunneborg, C. (1973). Individual differences in cognition: A new approach to intelligence. In G. H. Bower (Ed.), *The psychology of learning and motivation* (Vol. 7). New York: Academic Press.

Hunt, J. McV. (1986). The effect of variations in quality and type of early child care on development. In W. Fowler (Ed.), Early experience and the development of competence [Special issue]. *New Directions for Child Development, 32,* 31–48.

Hunt, J. V. (1981). Predicting intellectual disorders in childhood for preterm infants with birthweights below 1501 gm. In S. L. Friedman & M. Sigman (Eds.), *Preterm birth and psychological development.* New York: Academic Press.

Hunt, J. V. (1983). Environmental risks in fetal and neonatal life as biological determinants of infant intelligence. In M. Lewis (Ed.), *Origins of intelligence. Infancy and early childhood* (2nd ed.). New York: Plenum.

Hunter, F. T., & Youniss, J. (1982). Changes in functions of three relations during adolescence. *Developmental Psychology, 18,* 806–811.

Huston, A. C. (1983). Sex-typing. In E. M. Hetherington (Ed.). *Handbook of child psychology: Socialization, personality, and social development* (Vol. 4). New York: Wiley. (P. H. Mussen, General Editor)

Huston, A. C., Greer, D., Wright, J. C., Welch, R., & Ross, R. (1984). Children's comprehension of televised formal features with masculine and feminine connotations. *Developmental Psychology, 20,* 707–716.

Huston-Stein, A., & Higgens-Trenk, A. (1978). Development of females from childhood through adulthood: Career and feminine role orientations. In P. B. Baltes (Ed.), *Life-span development and behavior* (Vol. 1). New York: Academic Press.

Hutt, S. J., Lenard, H. G., & Prechtl, H. F. R. (1969). Psychophysiological studies in newborn infants. In L. P. Lipsitt & H. W. Reese (Eds.), *Advances in child development and behavior.* New York: Academic Press.

Huttenlocher, P. R., de Courten, C., Garey, L. J., & Van Der Loos, H. (1982). Synaptogenesis in human visual cortex—evidence for synapse elimination during normal development. *Neuroscience Letters, 33,* 247–252.

Hyde, J. S. (1984). How large are gender differences in aggression? A developmental meta-analysis. *Developmental Psychology, 20,* 722–736.

Ingram, D. Early patterns of grammatical development (1981). In R. E. Stark (Ed.), *Language behavior in infancy and early childhood.* New York: Elsevier/North-Holland.

Inhelder, B., & Piaget, J. (1958). *The growth of logical thinking from childhood to adolescence.* New York: Basic Books.

Jacklin, C. N., & Maccoby, E. E. (1978). Social behavior at 33 months in same-sex and mixed-sex dyads. *Child Development, 49,* 557–569.

Jackson, E., Campos, J. J., & Fischer, K. W. (1978). The question of decalage between object permanence and person permanence. *Child Development, 14,* 1–10.

Jackson, N. E. & Butterfield, E. C. (1986). A conception of giftedness designed to promote research. In R. J. Sternberg & J. E. Davidson (Eds.), *Conceptions of giftedness.* Cambridge, England: Cambridge University Press.

Jacobson, J. L., Boersma, D. C., Fields, R. B., & Olson, K. L. (1983). Paralinguistic features of adult speech to infants and small children. *Child Development, 54,* 436–442.

Jacobson, J. L., Jacobson, S. W., Fein, G. G., Schwartz, P. M., & Dowler, J. K. (1984a). Prenatal exposure to an environmental toxin: A test of the multiple effects model. *Developmental Psychology, 20,* 523–532.

Jacobson, S. W., Fein, G. G., Jacobson, J. L., Schwartz, P. M., & Dowler, J. K. (1984b). Neonatal correlates of prenatal exposure to smoking, caffeine, and alcohol. *Infant Behavior and Development, 7,* 253–265.

Jaeger, E., Weinraub, M., & Hoffman, L. (1987, April). *Prediction child outcome in families of employed and non-employed mothers.* Paper presented at the biennial meetings of the Society for Research in Child Development, Baltimore.

Janos, P. M., & Robinson, N. M. (1985). Psychosocial development in intellectually gifted children. In F. D. Horowitz & M. O'Brien (Eds.)., *The gifted and talented. Developmental perspectives.* Washington, DC: American Psychological Association.

Jensen, A. R. (1980). *Bias in mental testing.* New York: Free Press.

Jensen, K. (1932). Differential reactions to taste and temperature stimuli in newborn infants. *Genetic Psychology Monographs, 12,* 361–479.

Johnson, C., Lewis, C., Love, S., Lewis, L., & Stuckey, M. (1984). Incidence and correlates of bulimic behavior in a female high school population. *Journal of Youth and Adolescence, 13,* 15–26.

Johnson, E. S., & Meade, A. C. (1987). Developmental patterns of spatial ability: An early sex difference. *Child Development, 58,* 725–740.

Johnston, J. M. (1972). Punishment of human behavior. *American Psychologist, 27,* 1033–1054.

Johnston, J. R. (1985). Cognitive prerequisites: The evidence from children learning English. In D. I. Slobin (Ed.), *The crosslinguistic study of language acquisition: Vol. 2. Theoretical issues.* Hillsdale, NJ: Erlbaum.

Johnston, L. (1978). *Do they ever grow up?* Wayzata, MN: Meadowbrook Press.

Jones, K. L., Smith, D. W., Ulleland, C. N., & Streissguth, A. (1973). Pattern of malformation in offspring of chronic alcoholic mothers. *Lancet, 1,* 1267–1271.

Jung, C. G. (1916). *Analytical psychology.* New York: Moffat, Yard.

Jung, C. G. (1939). *The integration of personality.* New York: Holt, Rinehart and Winston.

Kagan, J. (1965). Reflection-impulsivity and reading ability in primary grade children. *Child Development, 36,* 609–628.

Kagan, J. (1971). *Change and continuity in infancy.* New York: Wiley.

Kagan, J. (1981). Discussion of cognitive development in relation to language. In R. E. Stark (Ed.), *Language behavior in infancy and early childhood.* New York: Elsevier/North-Holland.

Kagan, J. (1984). *The nature of the child.* New York: Basic Books.

Kagan, J., Kearsley, R., & Zelazo, P. (1978). *Infancy: Its place in human development.* Cambridge, MA: Harvard University Press.

Kagan, J., Lapidus, D. R., & Moore, N. (1978). Infant antecedents of cognitive functioning: A longitudinal study. *Child Development, 49,* 1005–1023.

Kagan, J., & Moss, H. A. (1962). *Birth to maturity.* New York: Wiley.

Kagan, J., Rosman, B. L., Day, D., Albert, J., & Phillips, W. (1964). Information processing in the child: Significance of analytic and reflective attitudes. *Psychological Monographs, 78* (Whole No. 578).

Kamii, C. K. (1985). *Young children reinvent arithmetic. Implications of Piaget's theory.* New York: Teachers College.

Kamin, L. J. (1974). *The science and politics of IQ.* Hillsdale, NJ: Erlbaum.

Kaye, K. (1982). *The mental and social life of*

babies. How parents create persons. Chicago: University of Chicago Press.

Keating, D. P. (1980). Thinking processes in adolescence. In J. Adelson (Ed.), *Handbook of adolescent psychology*. New York: Wiley.

Keating, D. P., & Clark, L. V. (1980). Development of physical and social reasoning in adolescence. *Developmental Psychology, 16,* 23–30.

Keating, D. P., List, J. A., & Merriman, W. E. (1985). Cognitive processing and cognitive ability: Multivariate validity investigation. *Intelligence, 9,* 149–170.

Keeney, T. J., Cannizzo, S. R., & Flavell, J. H. (1967). Spontaneous and induced verbal rehearsal in a recall task. *Child Development, 38,* 935–966.

Kegan, R. (1985). The loss of Pete's dragon: Developments of the self in the years five to seven. In R. L. Leahy (Ed.), *The development of the self*. Orlando, FL: Academic Press.

Kellam, S. G., Ensminger, M. E., & Turner, R. J. (1977). Family structure and the mental health of children: Concurrent and longitudinal community-wide studies. *Archives of General Psychiatry, 34,* 1012–1022.

Kelso, J., & Stewart, M. A. (1985). Factors which predict the persistence of aggressive conduct disorder. *Journal of Child Psychology and Psychiatry, 27,* 77–86.

Kempe, R. S., & Kempe, H. (1978). *Child abuse*. Cambridge, MA: Harvard University Press.

Kennell, J. H., Jerauld, R., Wolfe, H., Chesler, C., Kreger, N. C., McAlpine, W., Steffa, M., & Klaus, M. H. (1974). Maternal behavior one year after early and extended post-partum contact. *Developmental Medicine and Child Neurology, 16,* 172–179.

Kessner, D. M. (1973). *Infant death: An analysis by maternal risk and health care*. Washington, DC: National Academy of Sciences.

Kimmel, M. S. (1987, July). Real man redux. *Psychology Today,* pp. 48–52.

Klaus, H. M., & Kennell, J. H. (1976). *Maternal-infant bonding*. St. Louis: Mosby.

Klaus, R. A., & Gray, S. W. (1968). The early training project for disadvantaged children: A report after five years. *Monographs of the Society for Research in Child Developmet, 33* Whole No. 120).

Klinnert, M. D. (1984). The regulation of infant behavior by maternal facial expression. *Infant Behavior and Development, 7,* 447–465.

Klinnert, M. D., Emde, R. N., Butterfield, P., & Campos, J. J. (1986). Social referencing: The infant's use of emotional signals from a friendly adult with mother present. *Developmental Psychology, 22,* 427–432.

Kliot, D., & Silverstein, L. (1984). Changing maternal and newborn care. A study of the Leboyer approach to childbirth management. *New York State Journal of Medicine, 84,* 169–173.

Kogan, N. (1983). Stylistic variation in childhood and adolescence: Creativity, metaphor, and cognitive styles. In J. H. Flavell & E. M. Markman (Eds.), *Handbook of child psychology: Cognitive development* (Vol. 3). New York: Wiley.

Kohlberg, L. (1964). Development of moral character and moral ideology. In M. L. Hoffman & L. W. Hoffman (Eds.), *Review of child development research* (Vol. 1). New York: Russell Sage.

Kohlberg, L. (1966). A cognitive-developmental analysis of children's sex-role concepts and attitudes. In E. E. Maccoby (Ed.), *The development of sex differences*. Stanford, CA: Stanford University Press.

Kohlberg, L. (1969). Stage and sequence: The cognitive-developmental approach to socialization. In D. Goslin (Ed.), *Handbook of socialization theory and research*. Chicago: Rand McNally.

Kohlberg, L. (1975, June). The cognitive-developmental approach to moral education. *Phi Delta Kappan,* 670–677.

Kohlberg, L. (1976). Moral stages and moralization: The cognitive-developmental approach. In T. Lickona (Ed.), *Moral development and behavior: Theory, research, and social issues*. New York: Holt, Rinehart and Winston.

Kohlberg, L. (1978). Revisions in the theory and practice of moral development. In W. Damon (Ed.), Moral development. *New Directions for Child Development, 2,* 83–88.

Kohlberg, L. (1980). *The meaning and measurement of moral development*. Worcester, MA: Clark University Press.

Kohlberg, L. (1981). *Essays on moral development: Vol. 1. The philosophy of moral development*. New York: Harper & Row.

Kohlberg, L., & Candee, D. (1984). The relationship of moral judgment to moral action. In W. M. Kurtines & J. L. Gewirtz (Eds.), *Morality, moral behavior, and moral development*. New York: Wiley.

Kohlberg, L., & Elfenbein, D. (1975). The development of moral judgments concerning capital punishment. *American Journal of Orthopsychiatry, 54,* 614–640.

Kohlberg, L., & Ullian, D. Z. (1974). Stages in the development of psychosexual concepts and attitudes. In R. C. Friedman, R. M. Richart, & R. L. Vande Wiele (Eds.), *Sex differences in behavior.* New York: Wiley.

Kohn, M. L. (1980). Job complexity and adult personality. In N. J. Smelser & E. H. Erikson (Eds.), *Themes of work and love in adulthood.* Cambridge, MA: Harvard University Press.

Kohn, M. L., & Schooler, C. (1983). *Work and personality: An inquiry into the impact of social stratification.* Norwood, NJ: Ablex Press.

Kolbe, L., Green, L., Foreyt, J., Darnell, L., Goodrick, K., Williams, H., Ward, D., Korton, A. S., Karacan, I., Widmeyer, R., & Stainbrook, G. (1980). Appropriate functions of health education in schools: Improving health and cognitive performance. In N. Draisnegor, J. Arasteh, & M. Cataldo (Eds.), *Child health and behavior: A behavioral pediatrics perspective.* New York: Wiley.

Kopp, C. B. (1983). Risk factors in development. In M. M. Haith & J. J. Campos (Eds.), *Handbook of child psychology: Infancy and developmental psychobiology* (Vol. 3). New York: Wiley. (P. H. Mussen, General Editor)

Kopp, C. B., & McCall, R. B. (1982). Predicting later mental performance for normal, at-risk, and handicapped infants. In P. B. Baltes & O. G. Brim, Jr. (Eds.), *Life-span development and behavior* (Vol. 4). New York: Academic Press.

Kopp, C. B., & Parmelee, A. H. (1979). Prenatal and perinatal influences on infant behavior. In J. D. Osofsky (Ed.), *Handbook of infant development.* New York: Wiley.

Korn, S. J. (1984). Continuities and discontinuities in difficult/easy temperament: Infancy to young adulthood. *Merrill-Palmer Quarterly, 30,* 189–199.

Korner, A. F., Hutchinson, C. A., Koperski, J. A., Kraemer, H. C., & Schneider, P. A. (1981). Stability of individual differences of neonatal motor and crying patterns. *Child Development, 52,* 83–90.

Kremenitzer, J. P., Vaughn, H. G. Jr., Kurtzberg, D., & Dowling, K. (1979). Smooth-pursuit eye movements in the new-born infant. *Child Development, 50,* 442–448.

Kuczaj, S. A., II. (1977). The acquisition of regular and irregular past tense forms. *Journal of Verbal Learning and Verbal Behavior, 49,* 319–326.

Kuczaj, S. A., II. (1978). Children's judgments of grammatical and ungrammatical irregular past tense verbs. *Child Development, 49,* 319–326.

Kuczaj, S. A., II. (1982). On the nature of syntactic development. In S. A. Kuczaj, II (Ed.), *Language development: Vol. 1. Syntax and semantics.* Hillsdale, NJ: Erlbaum.

Kuhl, P. K. (1983). Perception of auditory equivalence classes for speech in early infancy. *Infant Behavior and Development, 6,* 263–285.

Kuhl, P. K. (1987). Perception of speech and sound in early infancy. In P. Salapatek & L. Cohen (Eds.), *Handbook of infant perception: Vol. 2. From perception to cognition.* Orlando, FL: Academic Press.

Kuhl, P. K., & Meltzoff, A. N. (1984). The intermodal representation of speech in infants. *Infant Behavior and Development, 7,* 361–381.

Kuhn, D., Nash, S. C., & Brucken, L. (1978). Sex role concepts of two- and three-year-olds. *Child Development, 49,* 445–451.

Kunkel, M. A., et al. (1986). Analysis of deletions in DNA from patients with Becker and Duchenne muscular dystrophy. *Nature, 322,* 73–77.

Kurdek, L. A., & Krile, D. (1982). A developmental analysis of the relation between peer acceptance and both interpersonal understanding and perceived social self-competence. *Child Development, 53,* 1485–1491.

La Freniere, P., Strayer, F. F., & Gauthier, R. (1984). The emergence of same-sex affiliative preferences among preschool peers: A developmental/ethological perspective. *Child Development, 55,* 1958–1965.

Lakin, M. (1957). Personality factors in mothers of excessively crying (colicky) infants. *Monographs of the Society for Research in Child Development, 22* (Whole No. 64).

Lamb, M. E. (1981). The development of father-infant relationships. In M. E. Lamb (Ed.), *The role of the father in child development* (2nd ed.). New York: Wiley.

Lamb, M. E., & Campos, J. J. (1982). *Development in infancy.* New York: Random House.

Lamb, M. E., Frodi, M., Hwang, C., & Frodi, A. M. (1983). Effects of paternal involvement on infant preferences for mothers and fathers. *Child Development, 54,* 450–458.

Lamb, M. E., Frodi, A. M., Hwang, C., Frodi, M., & Steinberg, J. (1982). Mother- and father-infant interaction involving play and holding in traditional and nontraditional Swedish families. *Developmental Psychology, 18,* 215–221.

Lamb, M. E., & Hwang, D. (1982). Maternal attachment and mother-neonate bonding: A critical review. In M. E. Lamb & A. L. Brown (Eds.), *Advances in developmental psychology* (Vol. 2). Hillsdale, NJ: Erlbaum.

Lamke, L. K. (1982a). Adjustment and sex-role orientation. *Journal of Youth and Adolescence, 11,* 247–259.

Lamke, L.K. (1982b). The impact of sex-role orientation on self-esteem in early adolescence. *Child Development, 53,* 1530–1535.

Landry, S. H., Loveland, K., Hughes, S., Hall, S., & McEvoy, R. (1987, April). *Speech acts and the pragmatic deficits of autism.* Paper presented at the biennial meetings of the Society for Research in Child Development, Baltimore.

LaVoie, J. C. (1976). Ego identity formation in middle adolescence. *Journal of Youth and Adolescence, 5,* 371–385.

Lawson, A. E. (1985). A review of research on formal reasoning and science teaching. *Journal of Research in Science Teaching, 22,* 569–617.

Lawton, J. T., & Hooper, F. H. (1978). Piagetian theory and early childhood education: A critical analysis. In L. S. Siegel & C. J. Brainerd (Eds.), *Alternatives to Piaget: Critical essays on the theory.* New York: Academic Press.

Lazar, I., & Darlington, R. (1982). Lasting effects of early education: A report from the consortium for longitudinal studies. *Monographs of the Society for Research in Child Development, 47* (Whole No. 195).

Leach, P. (1983). *Babyhood* (2nd ed., rev.). New York: Knopf.

Leadbeater, B. J., & Dionne, J. (1981). The adolescent's use of formal operational thinking in solving problems related to identity resolution. *Adolescence 16,* 111–121.

Leaf, D. A. (1982). Exercise and pregnancy compatible. *The Physician and Sports Medicine, 9,* 22, 24.

Leboyer, F. (1975). *Birth without violence.* New York: Knopf.

Lefkowitz, M. M. (1981). Smoking during pregnancy: Long-term effects on offspring. *Developmental Psychology, 17,* 192–194.

Lenneberg, E. H. (1967). *Biological foundations of language.* New York: Wiley.

Leonard, L. B., Chapman, K., Rowan, L. E., & Weiss, A. L. (1983). Three hypotheses concerning young children's imitations of lexical items. *Developmental Psychology, 19,* 591–601.

Lepper, M. R. (1980). Intrinsic and extrinsic motivation in children: Detrimental effects of superfluous social controls. In W. A. Collins (Ed.), *Minnesota symposia on child psychology* (Vol. 14). Hillsdale, NJ: Erlbaum.

Lerner, J. V., & Galambos, N. L. (1986). Child development and family change: The influences of maternal employment in infants and toddlers. In L. P. Lipsitt & C. Rovee-Collier (Eds.), *Advances in infancy research* (Vol. 4). Norwood, NJ: Ablex.

Lerner, R. M. (1985). Adolescent maturational changes and psychosocial development: A dynamic interactional perspective. *Journal of Youth and Adolescence, 14,* 355–372.

Lerner, R. M. (1986). *Concepts and theories of human development* (2nd ed.). New York: Random House.

Lerner, R. M. (1987). A life-span perspective for early adolescence. In R. M. Lerner & T. T. Foch (Eds.), *Biological-psychosocial interactions in early adolescence.* Hillsdale, NJ: Erlbaum.

Leveno, K. J., Cunningham, G., Nelson, S., Roark, M., Williams, M. L., Guzick, D., Dowling, S., Rosenfeld, C. R., & Buckley, A. (1986). A prospective comparison of selective and universal electronic fetal monitoring in 34,995 pregnancies. *New England Journal of Medicine, 315,* 615–619.

Lewin, R. (1975, September). Starved brains. *Psychology Today,* pp. 29–33.

Lewis, C. C. (1981). How adolescents approach decisions: Changes over grades seven to twelve and policy implications. *Child Development, 52,* 538–544.

Lewis, M. (1981). Self-knowledge: A social cognitive perspective on gender identity and sex-role development. In M. E. Lamb & L. R. Sherrod (Eds.), *Infant social cognition: Empirical and theoretical considerations.* Hillsdale, NJ: Erlbaum.

Lewis, M., & Brooks, J. (1978). Self-knowledge and emotional development. In M. Lewis & L. A. Rosenblum (Eds.), *The development of affect.* New York: Plenum.

Lewis, M., & Brooks-Gunn, J. (1979). *Social cognition and the acquisition of self.* New York: Plenum.

Lewis, M., Brooks-Gunn, J., & Jaskir, J. (1985).

Individual differences in visual self-recognition as a function of mother-infant attachment relationship. *Developmental Psychology, 21,* 1181–1187.

Lewis, M., Feiring, C., McGoffog, C., & Jaskir, J. (1984). Predicting psychopathology in six-year-olds from early social relations. *Child Development, 55,* 123–136.

Liben, L. S. (1978). The development of deaf children: An overview of issues. In L. S. Liben (Ed.), *Deaf children: Developmental perspectives.* New York: Academic Press.

Lickona, T. (1978). Moral development and moral education. In J. M. Gallagher & J. A. Easley, Jr. (Eds.), *Knowledge and development* (Vol. 2). New York: Plenum.

Lickona, T. (1983). *Raising good children.* Toronto: Bantam Books.

Linn, M. C., & Petersen, A. C. (1985). Emergence and characterization of sex differences in spatial ability: A meta-analysis. *Child Development, 46,* 1479–1498.

Linn, S., Reznick, J. S., Kagan, J., & Hans, S. (1982). Salience of visual patterns in the human infant. *Developmental Psychology, 18,* 651–657.

Lipsitt, L. P. (1982). Infant learning. In T. M. Field., A. Houston, H. C. Quay, L. Troll, & G. E. Finley (Eds.), *Review of human development.* New York: Wiley.

Livesley, W. J., & Bromley, D. B. (1973). *Person perception in childhood and adolescence.* London: Wiley.

Loehlin, J. C., Lindzey, G., & Spuhler, J. N. (1975). *Race differences in intelligence.* San Francisco: Freeman.

Loehlin, J. C., & Nichols, R. C. (1976). *Heredity, environment and personality.* Austin: University of Texas Press.

Londerville, S., & Main, M. (1981). Security of attachment, compliance, and maternal training methods in the second year of life. *Developmental Psychology, 17,* 289–299.

Long, F., Peters, D. L., & Garduque, L. (1985). Continuity between home and day care: A model for defining relevant dimensions of child care. In I. E. Sigel (Ed.), *Advances in applied developmental psychology* (Vol. 1). Norwood, NJ: Ablex.

Longo, D. C., & Bond, L. (1984). Families of the handicapped child: Research and practice. *Family Relations, 33,* 57–65.

Lutkenhaus, P., Grossman, K. E., & Grossman, K. (1985). Infant-mother attachment at twelve months and style of interaction with a stranger at the age of three years. *Child Development, 56,* 1538–1542.

Lytton, H. (1977). Do parents create, or respond to, differences in twins? *Developmental Psychology, 12,* 456–459.

Maccoby, E. E. (1980a). Commentary on G. R. Patterson, "Mothers: The unacknowledged victims." *Monographs of the Society for Research in Child Development, 45* (Whole No. 186).

Maccoby, E. E. (1980b). *Social development. Psychological growth and the parent-child relationship.* New York: Harcourt Brace Jovanovich.

Maccoby, E. E. (1984). Socialization and developmental change. *Child Development, 55,* 317–328.

Maccoby, E. E., Doering, C. H., Jacklin, C. N., & Kraemer, H. (1979). Concentrations of sex hormones in umbilical-cord blood: Their relation to sex and birth order of infants. *Child Development, 50,* 632–642.

Maccoby, E. E., & Jacklin, C. N. (1974). *The psychology of sex differences.* Stanford, CA: Stanford University Press.

Maccoby, E. E., & Jacklin, C. N. (1980). Sex differences in aggression: A rejoinder and reprise. *Child Development, 51,* 964–980.

Maccoby, E. E., & Martin, J. A. (1983). Socialization in the context of the family: Parent-child interaction. In E. M. Hetherington (Ed.), *Handbook of child psychology: Socialization, personality, and social development* (Vol. 4). New York: Wiley. (P. H. Mussen, General Editor)

Macfarlane, A. (1975). Olfaction in the development of social preferences in the human neonate. In *Parent-infant interaction.* Amsterdam: CIBA Foundation Symposium 33, new series, ASP.

Macfarlane, A. (1977). *The psychology of childbirth.* Cambridge, MA: Harvard University Press.

Macfarlane, J. W., Allan, L., & Honzik, M. P. (1954). A developmental study of the behavior problems of normal children between twenty-two months and fourteen years. *University of California publications in child development* (Vol. 2). Berkeley: University of California Press.

Maclean, M., Bryant, P., & Bradley, L. (1987). Rhymes, nursery rhymes, and reading in early childhood. *Merrill-Palmer Quarterly, 33,* 255–282.

Magenis, R. E. (1977). Parental origin of the

extra chromosome in Down's syndrome. *Human Genetics, 37,* 7–16.

Magnusson, D., Stattin, H., & Allen, V. L. (1986). Differential maturation among girls and its relation to social adjustment: A longitudinal perspective. In P. B. Baltes, D. L. Featherman, & R. M. Lerner (Eds.), *Life-span development and behavior* (Vol. 7). Hillsdale, NJ: Erlbaum.

Main, M., Kaplan, N., & Cassidy, J. (1985). Security in infancy, childhood, and adulthood: A move to the level of representation. In I. Bretherton & E. Waters (Eds.), Growing points of attachment theory and research. *Monographs of the Society for Research in Child Development, 50* (Whole No. 209), 66–104.

Main, M., & Solomon, J. (1985). Discovery of an insecure disorganized/disoriented attachment pattern: Procedures, findings and implications for the classification of behavior. In M. Yogman & T. B. Brazelton (Eds.), *Affective development in infancy.* Norwood, NJ: Ablex.

Malina, R. M. (1982). Motor development in the early years. In S. G. Moore & C. R. Cooper (Eds.), *The young child. Reviews of research* (Vol. 3). Washington, DC: National Association for the Education of Young Children.

Marans, H. (1979). Breast-feeding. New Evidence: It's far more than nutrition. *Medical World News, 20,* 62–78.

Maratsos, M. (1983). Some current issues in the study of the acquisition of grammar. In J. H. Flavell & E. M. Markman (Eds.), *Handbook of child psychology: Cognitive development* (Vol. 3). New York: Wiley. (P. H. Mussen, General Editor)

Marcia, J. E. (1966). Development and validation of ego identity status. *Journal of Personality and Social Psychology, 3,* 551–558.

Marcia, J. E. (1980). Identity in adolescence. In J. Adelson (Ed.), *Handbook of adolescent psychology.* New York: Wiley.

Marcus, D. E., & Overton, W. F. (1978). The development of cognitive gender constancy and sex role preferences. *Child Development, 49,* 434–444.

Marcus, R. F. (1986). Naturalistic observation of cooperation, helping, and sharing and their association with empathy and affect. In C. Zahn-Waxler, E. M. Cummings, & R. Iannotti (Eds.), *Altruism and aggression. Biological and social origins.* Cambridge, England: Cambridge University Press.

Martin, C. L., & Halverson, C. F. Jr. (1981). A schematic processing model of sex typing and stereotyping in children. *Child Development, 52,* 1119–1134.

Martin, C. L., & Halverson, C. F., Jr. (1983). The effects of sex-typing schemas on young children's memory. *Child Development, 54,* 563–574.

Martorano, S. C. (1977). A developmental analysis of performance on Piaget's formal operations tasks. *Developmental Psychology, 13,* 666–672.

Massad, C. M. (1981). Sex role identity and adjustment during adolescence. *Child Development, 52,* 1290–1298.

Masters, J. C., & Furman, W. (1981). Popularity, individual friendship selection, and specific peer interaction among children. *Developmental Psychology, 17,* 344–350.

Matas, L., Arend, R. A., & Sroufe, L. A. (1978). Continuity of adaptation in the second year: The relationship between quality of attachment and latter competence. *Child Development, 49,* 547–556.

Mather, P. L., & Black, K. N. (1984). Heredity and environmental influences on preschool twins' language skills. *Developmental Psychology, 20,* 303–308.

Mayer, J. (1975). Obesity during childhood. In M. Winick (Ed.), *Childhood obesity.* New York: Wiley.

McCabe, A. E., Siegel, L. S., Spence, I., & Wilkinson, A. (1982). Class-inclusion reasoning: Patterns of performance from three to eight years. *Child Development, 53,* 779–785.

McCall, R. B. (1979). *Infants: The new knowledge.* Cambridge, MA: Harvard University Press.

McCall, R. B. (1981). Nature-nurture and the two realms of development: A proposed integration with respect to mental development. *Child Development, 52,* 1–12.

McCall, R. B. (1984). Developmental changes in mental performance: The effect of the birth of a sibling. *Child Development, 55,* 1317–1321.

McCall, R. B., Appelbaum, M. I., & Hogarty, P. S. (1973). Developmental changes in mental performance. *Monographs of the Society for Research in Child Development, 38* (Whole No. 150).

McCord, W., McCord, J., & Zola, I. K. (1959). *Origins of crime.* New York: Columbia University Press.

McKinney, J. D., & Edgerton, M. (1983, April). Classroom adaptive behavior. Paper presented at the biennial meetings of the Society for Research in Child Development, Detroit.

McLaughlin, B. (1984). *Second-language acquisition in childhood: Vol. 1. Preschool children* (2nd ed.). Hillsdale, NJ: Erlbaum.

McNeill, D. (1970). *The acquisition of language: The study of developmental psycholinguistics.* New York: Harper & Row.

Meisels, S. J., & Anastasiow, N. J. (1982). The risks of prediction: Relationships between etiology, handicapping conditions, and development outcomes. In S. G. Moore & C. R. Cooper (Eds.), *The young child. Reviews of research* (Vol. 3). Washington, DC: National Association for the Education of Young Children.

Meltzoff, A. N. (1985). The roots of social and cognitive development: Models of man's original nature. In T. M. Field & N. A. Fox (Eds.), *Social perception in infants.* Norwood, NJ: Ablex.

Meltzoff, A. N., & Moore, M. K. (1983). Newborn infants imitate adult facial gestures. *Child Development, 54,* 702–709.

Meredith, D. (1986, February). The nine-to-five dilemma. *Psychology Today,* pp. 36–44.

Mervis, C. B., & Mervis, C. A. (1982). Leopards are kitty-cats: Object labeling by mothers for their thirteen-month-olds. *Child Development, 53,* 267–273.

Meyer-Bahlburg, H. F. L., Ehrhardt, A. A., & Feldman, J. F. (1986). Long-term implications of the prenatal endocrine milieu for sex-dimorphic behavior. In L. Erlenmeyer-Kimling & N. E. Miller (Eds.), *Life-span research on the prediction of psychopathology.* Hillsdale, NJ: Erlbaum.

Meyerhoff, M. K., & White, B. L. (1986, September). Parenting. Making the grade as parents. *Psychology Today,* pp. 38–45.

Mikkelsen, M., & Stone, J. (1970). Genetic counseling in Down's syndrome. *Human Heredity, 20,* 457–464.

Miller, G. A. (1956). The magical number seven, plus or minus two: Some limits on our capacity for processing information. *Psychological Review, 63,* 81–96.

Miller, L. B., & Bizzell, R. P. (1984). Long-term effects of four preschool programs: Ninth- and tenth-grade results. *Child Development, 55,* 1570–1587.

Miller, P. H. (1983). Theories of developmental psychology. New York: Freeman.

Minton, C., Kagan, J., & Levine, J. A. (1971).

Maternal control and obedience in the two-year-old. *Child Development, 52,* 1873–1974.

Mischel, W. (1966). A social learning view of sex differences in behavior. In E. E. Maccoby (Ed.), *The development of sex differences.* Stanford, CA: Stanford University Press.

Mischel, W. (1970). Sex typing and socialization. In P. H. Mussen (Ed.), *Carmichael's manual of child psychology* (Vol. 2). New York: Wiley.

Money, J. (1975). Ablatiopenis: Normal male infant sex-reassigned as a girl. *Archives of Sexual Behavior, 4,* 56–72.

Money, J. (1987). Sin, sickness, or status? Homosexual gender identity and psychoneuroendocrinology. *American Psychologist, 42,* 384–399.

Monkus, E., & Bancalari, E. (1981). Neonatal outcome. In K. G. Scott, T. Field, & E. G. Robertson (Eds.), *Teenage parents and their offspring.* New York: Grune & Stratton.

Montemayor, R., & Eisen, M. (1977). The development of self-conceptions for childhood to adolescence. *Developmental Psychology, 13,* 314–319.

Montpetit, R. R., Montoye, H. J., & Laeding, L. (1967). Grip strength of school children, Saginaw, Michigan—1964. *Research Quarterly, 38,* 231–240.

Moore, E. G. J. (1986). Family socialization and the IQ test performance of traditionally and transracially adopted black children. *Developmental Psychology, 22,* 317–326.

Moore, K. A., Hofferth, S. L. Wertheimer, R. F., Waite, L. J., & Caldwell, S. B. (1981). Teenage childbearing: Consequences for women, families, and government welfare expenditures. In K. G. Scott, T. Field, & E. Robertson (Eds.), *Teenage parents and their offspring.* New York: Grune & Stratton.

Moore, K. L. (1982). *The developing human. Clinically oriented embryology* (3rd ed.). Philadelphia: Saunders.

Moore, R., Pauker, J. D., & Moore, T. E. (1984). Delinquent recidivists: Vulnerable children. *Journal of Youth and Adolescence, 13,* 451–457.

Moores, D. F. (1985). Early intervention programs for hearing impaired children: A longitudinal assessment. In K. E. Nelson (Ed.), *Children's language* (Vol. 5). Hillsdale, NJ: Erlbaum.

Morrison, A. M., White, R. P., & Van Velsor, E. (1987, August). Executive women: Substance plus style. *Psychology Today,* pp. 18–26.

Morrison, D. M. (1985). Adolescent contraceptive behavior: A review. *Psychological Bulletin, 98,* 538–568.

Morrow-Tlucak, M., Liddle, C. L., Ernhart, C. B., & Haude, R. H. (1987, April). *The relationship of fetal alcohol exposure and productive speech at age 2 years.* Paper presented at the biennial meetings of the Society for Research in Child Development, Baltimore.

Morse, P. A., & Cowan, N. (1982). Infant auditory and speech perception. In T. M. Field, A. Houston, H. C. Quay, L. Troll, & G. E. Finley (Eds.), *Review of human development.* New York: Wiley.

Mosher, F. A., & Hornsby, J. R. (1966). On asking questions. In J. S. Bruner, R. R. Olver, & P. M. Greenfield (Eds.), *Studies in cognitive growth.* New York: Wiley.

Moshman, D., & Franks, B. A. (1986). Development of the concept of inferential validity. *Child Development, 57,* 153–165.

Munro, G., & Adams, G. R. (1977). Ego-identity formation in college students and working youth. *Developmental Psychology, 13,* 523–524.

Munroe, R. H., Shimmin, H. S., & Munroe, R. L. (1984). Gender understanding and sex role preference in four cultures. *Developmental Psychology, 20,* 673–682.

Murray, A. D., Dolby, R. M., Nation, R. L., & Thomas, D. B. (1981). Effects of epidural anasthesia on newborns and their mothers. *Child Development, 52,* 71–82.

Murray, J. P. (1980). *Television & youth. 25 years of research and controversy.* Stanford, CA: Boys Town Center for the Study of Youth Development.

Naeye, R. L. (1978). Relationship of cigarette smoking to congenital anomalies and perinatal death. *American Journal of Pathology, 90,* 289–293.

Nash, S. C. (1975). The relationship among sex-role stereotyping, sex-role preference, and the sex difference in spatial visualization. *Sex Roles, 1,* 15–32.

National Center for Health Statistics. (1984a, September 28). Advance report on final natality statistics, 1982. *Monthly Vital Statistics Report, 33*(6), Suppl. 28.

National Center for Health Statistics. (1984b). Annual summary of births, death, marriages, and divorces: United States, 1983. *Monthly Vital Statistics Report, 32*(13).

Neimark, E. D. (1982). Adolescent thought: Transition to formal operations. In B. B. Wolman (Ed.), *Handbook of developmental psychology.* Englewood Cliffs, NJ: Prentice-Hall.

Nelson, Katherine. (1973). Structure and strategy in learning to talk. *Monographs of the Society for Research in Child Development, 38* (Whole No. 149).

Nelson, Katherine. (1981). Individual differences in language development: Implications for development of language. *Developmental Psychology, 17,* 170–187.

Nelson, Katherine. (1982). The syntagmatics and paradigmatics of conceptual development. In S. A. Kuczaj, II (Ed.), *Language development: Vol. 2. Language, thought, and culture.* Hillsdale, NJ: Erlbaum.

Nelson, Katherine. (1985). *Making sense. The acquisition of shared meaning.* Orlando, FL: Academic Press.

Nelson, Keith. (1977). Facilitating children's syntax acquisition. *Developmental Psychology, 13,* 101–107.

Nelson, N. M., Enkin, M. W., Saigal, S., Bennett, K. J., Milner, R., & Sackett, D. L. (1980). A randomized clinical trial of the Leboyer approach to childbirth. *The New England Journal of Medicine, 302,* 655–660.

Nelson, S. A. (1980). Factors influencing young children's use of motives and outcomes as moral criteria. *Child Development, 51,* 823–829.

Newberger, C. M., & Cook, S. J. (1983). Parental awareness and child abuse: A cognitive-developmental analysis of urban and rural samples. *American Journal of Orthopsychiatry, 53,* 512–524.

Nichols, P. L. (1977). Minimal brain dysfunction: Associations with perinatal complications. Paper presented at the biennial meetings of the Society for Research in Child Development, New Orleans.

Nisan, M., & Kohlberg, L. (1982). Universality and variation in moral judgment: A longitudinal and cross-sectional study in Turkey. *Child Development, 53,* 865–876.

Norton, A. J., & Glick, P. C. (1986). One parent families: A social and economic profile. *Family Relations, 35,* 9–18.

Nottelmann, E. D., Susman, E. J., Blue, J. H., Inoff-Germain, G., Dorn, L. D., Loriaux, D. L., Cutler, G. B., Jr., & Chrousos, G. P. (1987). Gonadal and adrenal hormone correlates of adjustment in early adolescence. In R. M. Lerner & T. T. Foch (Eds.), *Biological-*

psychosocial interactions in early adolescence. Hillsdale, NJ: Erlbaum.

Nowakowski, R. S. (1987). Basic concepts of CNS development. *Child Development, 58,* 568–595.

O'Brien, M., & Huston, A. C. (1985). Development of sex-typed play behavior in toddlers. *Developmental Psychology, 21,* 866–871.

Obrzut, J. E., Hynd, G. W., & Boliek, C. A. (1986). Lateral assymetries in learning-disabled children: A review. In S. J. Ceci (Ed.), *Handbook of cognitive, social, and neuropsychological aspects of learning disabilities* (Vol. 1). Hillsdale, NJ: Erlbaum.

O'Connor, S., Vietze, P. M., Sandler, H. M., Sherrod, K. B., & Altemeier, W. A. (1980). Quality of parenting and the mother-infant relationships following rooming-in. In P. M. Taylor (Ed.), *Parent-infant relationships.* New York: Grune & Stratton.

Oden, S. (1982). Peer relationship development in childhood. In L. G. Katz (Ed.), *Current topics in early childhood education* (Vol. 4). Norwood, NJ: Ablex.

O'Donnell, M. (1966). *Around the corner.* New York: Harper & Row.

Oliver, C. M., & Oliver, G. M. (1978). Gentle birth; its safety and its effect on neonatal behavior. *Journal of Obstetrical and Gynecological Nursing, 5,* 35–40.

Oller, D. K. (1981). Infant vocalizations: Exploration and reflectivity. In R. E. Stark (Ed.), *Language behavior in infancy and early childhood.* New York: Elsevier/North-Holland.

Olsho, L. W. (1985). Infant auditory perception: Tonal masking. *Infant Behavior and Development, 8,* 371–384.

Olson, S. L., Bayles, K., & Bates, J. E. (1986). Mother-child interaction and children's speech progress: A longitudinal study of the first two years. *Merrill-Palmer Quarterly, 32,* 1–20.

O'Malley, P. M., & Bachman, J. G. (1983). Self-esteem: Change and stability between ages 13 and 23. *Developmental Psychology, 19,* 257–268.

Ornstein, P. A., Medlin, R. G., Stone, P. B., & Naus, M. J. (1985). Retrieving for rehearsal: An analysis of active rehearsal in children's memory. *Developmental Psychology, 21,* 633–641.

Ornstein, P. A., Naus, M. J., & Liberty, C. (1975). Rehearsal and organizational processes in children's memory. *Child Development, 46,* 818–830.

Overton, W. F., & Reese, H. W. (1973). Models of development: Methodological implications. In J. R. Nesselroade & H. W. Reese (Eds.), *Life-span developmental psychology. Methodological issues.* New York: Academic Press.

Overton, W. F., Ward, S. L., Noveck, I. A., Black, J., & O'Brien, D. P. (1987). Form and content in the development of deductive reasoning. *Developmental Psychology, 23,* 22–30.

Palkovitz, R. (1985). Fathers' birth attendance, early contact, and extended contact with their newborns: A critical review. *Child Development, 56,* 392–406.

Parke, R. D., & Tinsley, B. R. (1981). The father's role in infancy: Determinants of involvement in caregiving and play. In M. E. Lamb (Ed.), *The role of the father in child development* (2nd ed.). New York: Wiley.

Parke, R. D., & Tinsley, B. R. (1984). Fatherhood: Historical and contemporary perspectives. In K. A. McCluskey & H. W. Reese (Eds.), *Life-span developmental psychology. Historical and generational effects.* Orlando, FL: Academic Press.

Parke, R. D., & Tinsley, B. J. (1987). Family interaction in infancy. In J. D. Osofsky (Ed.), *Handbook of infant development* (2nd ed.). New York: Wiley.

Parmelee, A. H., Jr. (1986). Children's illnesses: Their beneficial effects on behavioral development. *Child Development, 57,* 1–10.

Parmelee, A. H., Jr., & Sigman, M. D. (1983). Perinatal brain development and behavior. In M. M. Haith & J. J. Campos (Eds.), *Handbook of child psychology: Infancy and developmental psychobiology* (Vol. 2). New York: Wiley. (P. H. Mussen, General Editor)

Parmelee, A. H., Jr., Wenner, W. H., & Schulz, H. R. (1964). Infant sleep patterns from birth to 16 weeks of age. *Journal of Pediatrics, 65,* 576–582.

Parsons, J. E., Adler, T. F., & Kaczala, C. M. (1982). Socialization of achievement attitudes and beliefs: Parental influences. *Child Development, 53,* 310–321.

Passman, R. H., & Longeway, K. P. (1982). The role of vision in maternal attachment: Giving 2-year-olds a photograph of their mother during separation. *Developmental Psychology, 18,* 530–533.

Pastor, D. L. (1981). The quality of mother-infant attachment and its relationship to toddlers' initial sociability with peers. *Developmental Psychology, 17,* 326–335.

Patterson, G. R. (1975). *Families. Applications*

of social learning to family life. Champaign, IL: Research Press.

Patterson, G. R. (1980). Mothers: The unacknowledged victims. *Monographs of the Society for Research in Child Development, 45* (Whole No. 186).

Patterson, G. R. (1986). Maternal rejection: Determinant or product for deviant child behavior? In W. W. Hartup & Z. Rubin (Eds.), *On relationships and development.* Hillsdale, NJ: Erlbaum.

Pederson, D. R., Evans, B., Bento, S., Chance, G. W., & Fox, A. M. (1987, April). *Invulnerable high risk preterm infants.* Paper presented at the biennial meetings of the Society for Research in Child Development, Baltimore.

Pederson, F. A. (1981). Father influences viewed in a family context. In M. E. Lamb (Ed.), *The role of the father in child development* (2nd ed.). New York: Wiley.

Pennington, B. F., Bender, B., Puck, M., Salbenblatt, J., & Robinson, A. (1982). Learning disabilities in children with sex chromosome anomalies. *Child Development, 53,* 1182–1192.

Perry, D. G., & Bussey, K. (1979). The social learning theory of sex differences: Imitations alive and well. *Journal of Personality and Social Psychology, 37,* 1699–1712.

Petersen, A. C. (1987a). The nature of biological-psychosocial interactions: The sample case of early adolescence. In R. M. Lerner & T. T. Foch (Eds.), *Biological-psychosocial interactions in early adolescence.* Hillsdale, NJ: Erlbaum.

Petersen, A. C. (1987b, September). Those gangly years. *Psychology Today,* pp. 28–34.

Petersen, A. C., Ebata, A., & Sarigiani, P. (1987, April). *Who expresses depressive affect in adolescence?* Paper presented at the biennial meetings of the Society for Research in Child Development, Baltimore.

Petersen, A. C., & Taylor, B. (1980). The biological approach to adolescence. In J. Adelson (Ed.), *Handbook of adolescent psychology.* New York: Wiley.

Peterson, G. H., Mehl, L. E., & Leiderman, P. H. (1979). The role of some birth-related variables in father attachment. *American Journal of Orthopsychiatry, 49,* 330–338.

Phillips, D. A. (1987, April). *Parents as socializers of children's perceived academic competence.* Paper presented at the biennial meetings of the Society for Research in Child Development, Baltimore.

Phillips, J. R. (1973). Syntax and vocabulary of mothers' speech to young children: Age and sex comparisons. *Child Development, 44,* 182–185.

Piaget, J. (1932). *The moral judgment of the child.* New York: Macmillan.

Piaget, J. (1952). *The origins of intelligence in children.* New York: International Universities Press.

Piaget, J. (1954). *The construction of reality in the child.* New York: Basic Books.

Piaget, J. (1962). *Play, dreams and imitation in childhood.* New York: Norton.

Piaget, J. (1970). Piaget's theory. In P. H. Mussen (Ed), *Carmichael's manual of child psychology* (Vol. 1, 3rd ed.). New York: Wiley.

Piaget, J. (1972). Development and learning. In C. S. Lavatelli & F. Stendler (Eds.), *Readings in child behavior and development* (3rd ed.). New York: Harcourt Brace Jovanovich. (Reprinted from R. Ripple & V. Rockcastle (Eds.), *Piaget rediscovered,* Ithaca, NY: Cornell University Press, 1964.)

Piaget, J. (1973). *To understand is to invent.* New York: Grossman. (Original work published 1948)

Piaget, J. (1977). *The development of thought. Equilibration of cognitive structures.* New York: Viking Press.

Piaget, J., & Inhelder, B. (1959). *La gènese des structures loqiques élémentaires: classifications et sériations* [The genesis of elementary logical structures: classification and seriation]. Neuchâtel: Delachaux et Niestlé.

Piaget, J., & Inhelder, B. (1969). *The psychology of the child.* New York: Basic Books.

Pick, H. L., Jr. (1986). Reflections on the data and theory of cross-modal infancy research. In L. P. Lipsitt & C. Rovee-Collier (Eds.). *Advances in infancy research* (Vol. 4). Norwood, NJ: Ablex.

Pines, M. (1981, September). The civilizing of Genie. *Psychology Today,* pp. 28–34.

Pines, M. (1982). Baby, you're incredible. *Psychology Today,* pp. 48–52.

Pitkin, R. M. (1977). Nutrition during pregnancy: The clinical approach. In M. Winick (Ed.), *Nutritional disorders of American women.* New York: Wiley.

Pleck, J. H. (1985). *Working wives/working husbands.* Beverly Hills, CA: Sage.

Plomin, R., & DeFries, J. C. (1980). Genetics and intelligence: Recent data. *Intelligence, 4,* 15–24.

Plomin, R., & DeFries, J. C. (1983). The Colorado Adoption Project. *Child Development, 54,* 276–289.

Plomin, R., & DeFries, J. C. (1985a). A parent-offspring adoption study of cognitive abilities in early childhood. *Intelligence, 9,* 341–356.

Plomin, R., & DeFries, J. C. (1985b). *Origins of individual differences in infancy. The Colorado Adoption Project.* Orlando, FL: Academic Press.

Plomin, R., & Dunn, J. (1986). *The study of temperament: Changes, continuities and challenges.* Hillsdale, NJ: Erlbaum.

Plomin, R., Loehlin, J. C., & DeFries, J. C. (1985). Genetic and environmental components of "environmental" influences. *Developmental Psychology, 21,* 391–402.

Pollitt, E., Mueller, W., & Leibel, R. L. (1982). The relation of growth to cognition in a well-nourished population. *Child Development, 53,* 1157–1163.

Powell, B., & Steelman, L. C. (1982). Testing an undertested comparison: Maternal effects on sons' and daughters' attitudes toward women in the labor force. *Journal of Marriage and the Family, 44,* 349–355.

Power, C., & Reimer, J. (1978). Moral atmosphere: An educational bridge between moral judgment and action. In W. Damon (Ed.), *Moral development.* San Francisco: Jossey-Bass.

Power, T. G., & Chapieski, M. L. (1986). Child rearing and impulse control in toddlers: A naturalistic investigation. *Developmental Psychology, 22,* 271–275.

Prader, A., Tanner, J. M., & Von Harnack, G. A. (1963). Catch-up growth following illness or starvation. *Journal of Pediatrics, 62,* 646–659.

Prechtl, H. F. R., & Beintema, D. J. (1964). The neurological examination of the full-term newborn infant. *Clinics in Developmental Medicine,* London: Heinemann.

Profiles of children. (1970). 1970 White House conference on children. Washington, DC: U.S. Government Printing Office.

Puig-Antich, J. (1983). Neuroendocrine and sleep correlates of prepubertal major depressive disorder: Current status of the evidence. In D. P. Cantwell & G. A. Carlson (Eds.), *Affective disorders in childhood and adolescence.* New York: Spectrum.

Pulkkinen, L. (1982). Self-control and continuity in childhood delayed adolescence. In P. Baltes & O. Brim (Eds.), *Life span development and behavior* (Vol. 4). New York: Academic Press.

Pyle, R., Mitchell, J., Eckert, E., Halverson, P., Neuman, P., & Goff, G. (1983). The incidence of bulimia in freshman college students. *International Journal of Eating Disorders, 2,* 75–85.

Quay, H. C. (1979). Residential treatment. In H. C. Quay & J. S. Werry (Eds.), *Psychopathological disorders of childhood* (2nd ed.). New York: Wiley.

Quay, H. C., & Werry, J. S. (1979). *Psychopathological disorders of childhood* (2nd ed.). New York: Wiley.

Radke-Yarrow, M., Cummings, E. M., Kuczynski, L., & Chapman, M. (1985). Patterns of attachment in two- and three-year-olds in normal families and families with parental depression. *Child Development, 56,* 884–893.

Ramey, C. T., & Campbell, F. A. (1987). The Carolina Abecedarian Project. An educational experiment concerning human malleability. In J. J. Gallagher & C. T. Ramey (Eds.), *The malleability of children.* Baltimore: Paul H. Brookes.

Ramey, C. T., Farran, D. C., & Campbell, F. A. (1979). Predicting IQ from mother-infant interactions. *Child Development, 50,* 804–814.

Ramey, C. T., & Haskins, R. (1981a). The modification of intelligence through early experience. *Intelligence, 5,* 5–19.

Ramey, C. T., & Haskins, R. (1981b). Early education, intellectual development, and school performance; A reply to Arthur Jensen and J. McVicker Hunt. *Intelligence, 5,* 41–48.

Ramey, C. T., & MacPhee, D. (1986). Developmental retardation: A systems theory perspective on risk and preventive intervention. In D. C. Farran & J. D. McKinney (Eds.), *Risk in intellectual and psychosocial development.* Orlando, FL: Academic Press.

Ramey, C. T., MacPhee, D., & Yeates, K. O. (1982). Preventing developmental retardation: A general systems model. In D. K. Detterman & R. J. Sternberg (Eds.), *How and how much can intelligence be increased.* Norwood, NJ: Ablex.

Ramey, C. T., Yeates, K. W., & Short, E. J. (1984). The plasticity of intellectual development: Insights from inventive intervention. *Child Development, 55,* 1913–1925.

Rank, O. (1929). *The trauma of birth.* New York: Harcourt.

Rappoport, L. (1972). *Personality development: The chronology of experience.* Glenview, IL: Scott, Foresman.

Razel, M. (1985). A reanalysis of the evidence

for the genetic nature of early motor development. In I. E. Sigel (Ed.), *Advances in applied developmental psychology* (Vol. 1). Norwood, NJ: Ablex.

Read, M. S., & Felson, D. (1976). *Malnutrition, learning, and behavior.* Bethesda, MD: National Institute of Child Health and Human Development (ERIC Document Reproduction Service No. ED 133-395).

Reed, E. W. (1975). Genetic anomalies in development. In F. D. Horowitz (Ed.), *Review of child development research* (Vol. 4). University of Chicago Press.

Reese, H. W., & Overton, W. F. (1970). Models of development and theories of development. In L. R. Goulet & P. B. Baltes (Eds.), *Lifespan developmental psychology.* New York: Academic Press.

Reisman, J. E. (1987). Touch, motion, and proprioception. In P. Salapatek & L. Cohen (Eds.), *Handbook of infant perception: Vol. 1. From sensation to perception.* Orlando, FL: Academic Press.

Reisman, J. M., & Shorr, S. I. (1978). Friendship claims and expectations among children and adults. *Child Development, 49,* 913–916.

Resnick, L. B. (1979). The future of IQ testing in education. *Intelligence, 3,* 241–254.

Rest, J. R. (1983). Morality. In J. H. Flavell & E. M. Markman (Eds.), *Handbook of child psychology: Cognitive development* (Vol. 3). New York: Wiley. (P. H. Mussen, General Editor)

Rest, J. R., & Thoma, S. J. (1985). Relation of moral judgment development to formal education. *Developmental Psychology, 21,* 709–714.

Revelle, G. L., Wellman, H. M., & Karabenick, J. D. (1985). Comprehension monitoring in preschool children. *Child Development, 56,* 654–663.

Rholes, W. S., & Ruble, D. N. (1984). Children's understanding of dispositional characteristics of others. *Child Development, 55,* 550–560.

Ricciuti, H. N. (1981). Developmental consequences of malnutrition in early childhood. In M. A. Lewis & L. A. Rosenblum (Eds.), *The uncommon child.* New York: Plenum.

Riegel, K. F. (1975). Adult life crises. A dialectic interpretation of development. In N. Datan & L. H. Ginsberg (Eds.), *Lifespan developmental psychology. Normative life crises.* New York: Academic Press.

Roberge, J. J., & Flexer, B. K. (1979). Further examination of formal reasoning abilities. *Child Development, 50,* 478–484.

Roberts, C. W., Green, R., Williams, K., & Goodman, M. (1987). Boyhood gender identity development: A statistical contrast of two family groups. *Developmental Psychology, 23,* 544–557.

Robertson, E. G. (1981). Adolescence, physiological maturity, and obstetric outcomes. In K. G. Scott, T. Field, & E. Robertson (Eds.), *Teenage parents and their offspring.* New York: Grune & Stratton.

Robinson, H. B. (1981). The uncommonly bright child. In M. Lewis & L. A. Rosenblum (Eds.), *The uncommon child.* New York: Plenum.

Robinson, N. M. (1978). Perinatal life for mother and baby. Common problems of the perinatal period. In D. W. Smith, E. L. Bierman, & N. M. Robinson (Eds.), *The biologic ages of man* (2nd ed.). Philadelphia: Saunders.

Robinson, N. M., & Janos, P. M. (1986). Psychological adjustment in a college-level program of marked academic acceleration. *Journal of Youth and Adolescence, 15,* 51–60.

Roche, A. F. (1981). The adipocyte-number hypothesis. *Child Development, 52,* 31–43.

Roffwarg, H. P., Muzio, J. N., & Dement, W. D. (1966). Ontogenetic development of the human sleep-dream cycle. *Science, 152,* 604–619.

Rogers, J. L. (1984). Confluence effects: Not here, not now! *Developmental Psychology, 20,* 321–331.

Rogoff, B. (1981). Schooling and the development of cognitive skills. In H. C. Triandis & A. Heron (Eds.), *Handbook of cross-cultural psychology: Vol. 4. Developmental psychology.* Boston: Allyn & Bacon.

Rollins, B. C., & Feldman, H. (1970). Marital satisfaction over the family life cycle. *Journal of Marriage and the Family, 32,* 20–28.

Rollins, B. C., & Galligan, R. (1978). The developing child and marital satisfaction of parents. In R. M. Lerner & G. M. Spanier (Eds.), *Child influences on marital and family interaction. A life-span perspective.* New York: Academic Press.

Rosenberg, M. (1985). Self-concept and psychological well-being in adolescence. In R. L. Leahy (Ed.), *The development of the self.* Orlando, FL: Academic Press.

Rosenthal, D., Wender, P. H., Kety, S. S., Welner, J., & Schulsinger, F. (1971). The adopted-away offspring of schizophrenics. *American Journal of Psychiatry, 128,* 87–91.

Rosenthal, R. (1966). *Experimenter effects in behavioral research.* New York: Prentice-Hall.

Rosett, H. L., & Sander, L. W. (1979). Effects of maternal drinking on neonatal morphology and state regulation. In J. D. Osofsky (Ed.), *Handbook of infant development.* New York: Wiley.

Rosner, B. S., & Doherty, N. E. (1979). The response of neonates to intra-uterine sounds. *Developmental Medicine and Child Neurology, 21,* 723–729.

Ross, G., Kagan, J., Zelazo, P., & Kotelchuck, M. (1975). Separation protest in infants in home and laboratory. *Developmental Psychology, 11,* 256–257.

Rosso, P. (1977a). Maternal nutrition, nutrient exchange, and fetal growth. In M. Winick (Ed.), *Nutritional disorders of American women.* New York: Wiley.

Rosso, P. (1977b). Maternal-fetal exchange during protein malnutrition in the rat: Placental transfer of α-amino isobutyric acid. *Journal of Nutrition, 107,* 2002–2005.

Rothbart, M. K. (1986). Longitudinal observation of infant temperament. *Developmental Psychology, 22,* 356–365.

Rovee-Collier, C. (1986). The rise and fall of infant classical conditioning research: Its promise for the study of early development. In L. P. Lipsitt & C. Rovee-Collier (Eds.), *Advances in infancy research* (Vol. 4). Norwood, NJ: Ablex.

Rovet, J., & Netley, C. (1983). The triple X chromosome syndrome in childhood: Recent empirical findings. *Child Development, 54,* 831–845.

Rowe, I., & Marcia, J. E. (1980). Ego identity status, formal operations, and moral development. *Journal of Youth and Adolescence, 9,* 87–99.

Rubin, K. H., & Everett, B. (1982). Social perspective-taking in young children. In S. G. Moore & C. R. Cooper (Eds.), *The young child. Reviews of research* (Vol. 3). Washington, DC: National Association for the Education of Young Children.

Rubin, K. H., Fein, G. G., & Vandenberg, B. (1983). Play. In E. M. Hetherington (Ed.), *Handbook of child psychology: Socialization, personality, and social development* (Vol. 4). New York: Wiley. (P. H. Mussen, General Editor)

Rubin, Z. (1980). *Children's friendships.* Cambridge, MA: Harvard University Press.

Ruble, D. N. (1987). The acquisition of self-knowledge: A self-socialization perspective. In N. Eisenberg (Ed.), *Contemporary topics in developmental psychology.* New York: Wiley-Interscience.

Ruble, D. N., Balaban, T., & Cooper, J. (1981). Gender constancy and the effects of sex-typed televised toy commercials. *Child Development, 52,* 667–673.

Ruble, T. L. (1983). Sex stereotypes: Issues of change in the 1970's. *Sex Roles, 9,* 397–402.

Ruopp, R., & Travers, J. (1982). Janus faces day care: Perspectives on quality and cost. In E. F. Zigler & E. W. Gordon (Eds.), *Day care: Scientific and social policy issues.* Boston: Auburn House.

Russell, G. (1982). Shared-caregiving families: An Australian study. In M. E. Lamb (Ed.), *Nontraditional families.* Hillsdale, NJ: Erlbaum.

Rutter, D. R., & Durkin, K. (1987). Turn-taking in mother-infant interaction: An examination of vocalizations and gaze. *Developmental Psychology, 23,* 54–61.

Rutter, M. (1971). Parent-child separation: Psychological effects on the children. *Journal of Child Psychology and Psychiatry, 12,* 233–260.

Rutter, M. (1975). *Helping troubled children.* New York: Plenum.

Rutter, M. (1978a). Family, area and school influences in the genesis of conduct disorders. In L. Hersov, M. Berber, & D. Schaffer (Eds.), *Aggression and antisocial behavior in childhood and adolescence.* Oxford: Pergamon Press.

Rutter, M. (1978b). Early sources of security and competence. In J. S. Bruner & A. Garton (Eds.), *Human growth and development.* London: Oxford University Press.

Rutter, M. (1978c). Early sources of security and competence. In J. S. Bruner & A. Garton (Eds.), *Human growth and development.* London: Oxford University Press.

Rutter, M. (1979). Maternal deprivation, 1972–1978: New findings, new concepts, new approaches. *Child Development, 50,* 283–305.

Rutter, M. (1983). School effects on pupil progress: Research findings and policy implications. *Child Development, 54,* 1–29.

Rutter, M. (1986). The developmental psychopathology of depression: Issues and perspectives. In M. Rutter, C. E. Izard, & P. B. Read (Eds.), *Depression in young people. Developmental and clinical perspectives.* New York: Guilford Press.

Rutter, M. (1987). Continuities and discontinuities from infancy. In J. D. Osofsky (Ed.), *Handbook of infant development* (2nd ed.). New York: Wiley-Interscience.

Rutter, M., & Garmezy, N. (1983). Developmental psychopathology. In E. M. Hetherington (Ed.), *Handbook of child psychology: Socialization, personality, and social development* (Vol. 4). New York: Wiley. (P. H. Mussen, General Editor)

Rutter, M., Tizard, J., & Whitmore, K. (1981). *Education, health and behaviour.* Huntington, N.Y.: Krieger. (Original work published 1970)

Rutter, M., Yule, B., Quinton, D., Rowlands, O., Yule, W., & Berger, M. (1975). Attainment and adjustment in two geographical areas: III. Some factors accounting for area differences. *British Journal of Psychiatry, 126,* 520–533.

Saario, T. N., Jacklin, C. N., & Tittle, C. K. (1973). Sex role stereo typing in the public schools. Harvard Educational Review, 43, 386–416.

Sack, W. H., Mason, R., & Higgins, J. E. (1985). The single parent family and abusive child punishment. *American Journal of Orthopsychiatry, 55,* 252–259.

Saigal, S., Nelson, N. M., Bennett, K. J., & Enkin, M. W. (1981). Observations on the behavioral state of newborn infants during the first hour of life. A comparison of infants delivered by the Leboyer and conventional methods. *American Journal of Obstetrics and Gynecology, 139,* 715–719.

Salapatek, P. (1975). Pattern perception in early infancy. (1975). In L. B. Cohen & P. Salapatek (Eds.), *Infant perception: From sensation to cognition* (Vol. 1). New York: Academic Press.

Salk, L. (1960). The effects of the normal heartbeat sound on the behavior of the newborn infant; implications for mental health. *World Mental Health, 12,* 168–175.

Sameroff, A. J. (1982). Development and the dialectic: The need for a systems approach. In W. A. Collins (Ed.), *The Minnesota symposia on child psychology* (Vol. 15). Hillsdale, NJ: Erlbaum.

Sameroff, A. J., & Cavanaugh, P. J. (1979). Learning in infancy: A developmental perspective. In J. D. Osofsky (Ed.), *Handbook of infant development.* New York: Wiley.

Sameroff, A. J., & Chandler, J. J. (1975). Reproductive risk and the continuum of caretaking casualty. In F. D. Horowitz (Ed.), *Review of*

child development research (Vol. 4). Chicago: University of Chicago Press.

Sameroff, A. J., Seifer, R., & Zax, M. (1983). Early development of children at risk for emotional disorder. *Monographs of the Society for Research in Child Development, 47*(7, Whole No. 199).

Sanders, B., & Soares, M. P. (1986). Sexual maturation and spatial ability in college students. *Developmental Psychology, 22,* 199–203.

San Francisco Chronicle (August 21, 1979).

Sattler, J. M. (1974). *Assessment of children's intelligence.* Philadelphia: Saunders.

Scafidi, F. A., Field T. M., Schanberg, S. M., Bauer, C. R., Vega-Lahr, N., Garcia, R., Poirier, J., Nystrom, G., & Kuhn, C. M. (1986). Effects of tactile/kinesthetic stimulation on the clinical course and sleep-wake behavior of preterm neonates. *Infant Behavior and Development, 9,* 91–105.

Scanlon, L. J. Savage-Rumbaugh, S., & Rumbaugh, D. M. (1982). Apes and language: An emerging perspective. In S. A. Kuczaj, II (Ed.), *Language development: Vol. 2. Language, thought, and culture.* Hillsdale, NJ: Erlbaum.

Scarr, S. (1978). From evolution to Larry P., or what shall we do about IQ tests? *Intelligence, 2,* 325–342.

Scarr, S., & Carter-Saltzman, L. (1982). Genetics and intelligence. In R. J. Sternberg (Ed.), *Handbook of human intelligence.* Cambridge, England: Cambridge University Press.

Scarr, S., & Kidd, K. K. (1983). Developmental behavior genetics. In M. M. Haith & J. J. Campos (Eds.), *Handbook of child psychology: Infancy and developmental psychobiology* (Vol. 2). New York: Wiley. (P. H. Mussen, General Editor)

Scarr, S., & McCartney, K. (1983). How people make their own environments: A theory of genotype-environment effects. *Child Development, 54,* 424–435.

Scarr, S., & Weinberg, R. A. (1977). Intellectual similarities within families of both adopted and biological children. *Intelligence, 1,* 170–191.

Scarr, S., & Weinberg, R. A. (1983). The Minnesota adoption studies: Genetic differences and maleability. *Child Development, 54,* 260–267.

Scarr-Salapatek, S. (1976). An evolutionary perspective on infant intelligence: Species patterns and individual variations. In M. Lewis (Ed.), *Origins of intelligence.* New York: Plenum.

Schachter, F. F. & Strage, A. A. (1982). Adults' talk and children's language development. In S. G. Moore & C. R. Cooper (Eds.), *The young child. Reviews of research* (Vol. 3). Washington, DC: National Association for the Education of Young Children.

Schaefli, A., Rest, J. R., & Thoma, S. J. (1985). Does moral education improve moral judgment? A meta-analysis of intervention studies using the Defining Issues Test. *Review of Educational Research, 55,* 319–352.

Schank, R. C., & Abelson, R. (1977). *Scripts, plans, goals, and understanding.* Hillsdale, NJ: Erlbaum.

Schlesinger, H. S., & Meadow, K. P. (1972). *Sound and sign.* Berkeley: University of California Press.

Schroeder, S. R., Schroeder, C. S., & Landesman, S. (1987). Psychological services in educational settings to persons with mental retardation. *American Psychologist, 42,* 805–808.

Schwartz, J. (1983, April). Infant day care: Effects at 2, 4 and 8 years. Paper presented at the biennial meetings of the Society for Research in Child Development, Detroit.

Schwartz, G. M., Izard, C. E., & Ansul, S. E. (1985). The 5-month-old's ability to discriminate facial expressions of emotion. *Infant Behavior and Development, 8,* 65–77.

Scollon, R. (1976). *Conversations with a one year old.* Honolulu: University of Hawaii Press.

Scott, K. G. (1979). Epidemiologic aspects of teenage pregnancy. In K. G. Scott, T. Field, & E. Robertson (Eds.), *Teenage parents and their offspring.* New York: Wiley.

Scott, K. G. (1981). Measuring intelligence with the Goodenough-Harris drawing test. *Psychological Bulletin, 89,* 483–505.

Sears, P. S., & Barbee, A. H. (1977). Career and life satisfactions among Terman's gifted women. In J. C. Stanley, W. C. George, & C. H. Solano (Eds.), *The gifted and the creative.* Baltimore: Johns Hopkins University Press.

Sears, R. R. Sources of life satisfactions of the Terman gifted men. (1977). *American Psychologist, 32,* 119–128.

Sears, R. R., Maccoby, E. E., & Levin, H. (1977). *Patterns of child rearing.* Stanford University Press. (Original work published 1957 by Row, Peterson)

Segal, N. L. (1985). Monozygotic and dizygotic twins: A comparative analysis of mental ability profiles. *Child Development, 56,* 1051–1058.

Segalowitz, N. S. (1981). Issues in the cross-cultural study of bilingual development. In

H. C. Triandis & A. Heron (Eds.), *Handbook of cross-cultural psychology: Vol. 4. Developmental psychology.* Boston: Allyn & Bacon.

Seibert, J. M., Hogan, A. E., & Mundy, P. C. (1986). On the specifically cognitive nature of early object and social skill domain associations. *Merrill-Palmer Quarterly, 32,* 21–36.

Selman, R. L. (1980). *The growth of interpersonal understanding.* New York: Academic Press.

Selman, R. L., & Damon, W. (1975). The necessity (but insufficiency) of social perspective taking for conceptions of justice at three early levels. In D. J. DePalma & J. M. Foley (Eds.), *Moral development: Current theory and research.* Hillsdale, NJ: Erlbaum.

Sepkoski, C. (1987, April). *A longitudinal study of the effects of obstetric medication.* Paper presented at the biennial meetings of the Society for Research in Child Development, Baltimore.

Shantz, C. U. (1983). Social cognition. In J. H. Flavell & E. M. Markman (Eds.), *Handbook of child psychology: Cognitive development* (Vol. 3). New York: Wiley. (P. H. Mussen, General Editor)

Shantz, D. W. (1986). Conflict, aggression, and peer status: An observational study. *Child Development, 57,* 1322–1332.

Sharp, D., Cole, M., & Lave, C. (1979). Education and cognitive development: The evidence from experimental research. *Monographs of the Society for Research in Child Development, 44,*(1–2, Whole No. 178).

Shatz, M., & Gelman, R. (1973). The development of communication skills: Modifications in the speech of young children as a function of the listener. *Monographs of the Society for Research in Child Development, 38* (Whole No. 152).

Sheldon, W. H. (1940). *The varieties of human physique.* New York: Harper & Row.

Sherrod, K. B., O'Connor, S., Vietze, P. M., & Altemeier, W. A., III. (1984). Child health and maltreatment. *Child Development, 55,* 1174–1183.

Shields, J. (1962). *Monozygotic twins brought up apart and brought up together.* London: Oxford University Press.

Shigetomi, C. C., Hartmann, D. P., & Gelfand, D. M. (1981). Sex differences in children's altruistic behavior and reputation for helpfulness. *Developmental Psychology, 17,* 434–437.

Shiono, P. H., Klebanoff, M. A., & Rhoads, G. G. (1986). Smoking and drinking during pregnancy. Their effects on preterm birth. *Journal of the American Medical Association, 225,* 82–84.

Shonkoff, J. P. (1984). The biological substrate and physical health in middle childhood. In W. A. Collins (Ed.), *Development during middle childhood. The years from six to twelve.* Washington, DC: National Academy Press.

Shore, C. (1986). Combinatorial play, conceptual development, and early multiword speech. *Developmental Psychology, 22,* 184–190.

Siebert, J. M., Hogan, A. E., & Mundy, P. C. (1986). On the specifically cognitive nature of early object and social skill domain associations. *Merrill-Palmer Quarterly, 32,* 21–36.

Siegal, M. (1987). Are sons and daughters treated more differently by fathers than by mothers? *Developmental Review, 7,* 183–209.

Siegel, L. J., & Griffin, N. J. (1984). Correlates of depressive symptoms in adolescents. *Journal of Youth and Adolescence, 13,* 475–487.

Siegler, R. S. (1976). Three aspects of cognitive development. *Cognitive Psychology, 8,* 431–520.

Siegler, R. S. (1978). The origins of scientific reasoning. In R. S. Siegler (Ed.), *Children's thinking: What develops?* Hillsdale, NJ: Erlbaum.

Siegler, R. S. (1981). Developmental sequences within and between concepts. *Monographs of the Society for Research in Child Development, 46*(2, Serial No. 189).

Siegler, R. S. (1986). Unities across domains in children's strategy choices. In M. Perlmutter (Ed.), *Perspectives on intellectual development. The Minnesota symposia on child psychology* (Vol. 19). Hillsdale, NJ: Erlbaum.

Siegler, R. S., & Richards, D. D. (1982). The development of intelligence. In R. J. Sternberg (Ed.), *Handbook of human intelligence.* Cambridge, England: Cambridge University Press.

Signorielli, N. (1986). Selective television viewing: A limited possibility. *Journal of Communication, 36*(3), 64–81.

Simmons, R. G., Blyth, D. A., & McKinney, K. L. (1983). The social and psychological effects of puberty on white females. In J. Brooks-Gunn & A. C. Petersen (Eds.), *Girls at puberty. Biological and psychosocial perspectives.* New York: Plenum.

Simmons, R. G., Burgeson, R., & Carlton-Ford, S. (1987). The impact of cumulative change in early adolescence. *Child Development, 58,* 1220–1234.

Simpson, A. E., & Stevenson-Hinde, J. (1985). Temperamental characteristics of three- to four-year-old boys and girls and child-family interactions. *Journal of Child Psychology and Psychiatry, 26,* 43–53.

Sirignano, S. W., & Lachman, M. E. (1985). Personality change during the transition to parenthood: The role of perceived infant temperament. *Developmental Psychology, 21,* 558–567.

Skinner, B. F. (1957). *Verbal behavior.* New York: Prentice-Hall.

Skodak, M., & Skeels, H. M. (1945). A follow-up study of children in adoptive homes. *Journal of Genetic Psychology, 66,* 21–58.

Slaby, R. G., & Frey, K. S. (1975). Development of gender constancy and selective attention to same-sex models. *Child Development, 46,* 849–856.

Slade, A. (1987). Quality of attachment and early symbolic play. *Developmental Psychology, 23,* 78–85.

Slobin, D. I. (1973). Cognitive prerequisites for the development of grammar. In C. A. Ferguson & D. I. Slobin (Eds.), *Studies of child language development.* New York: Holt, Rinehart and Winston.

Slobin, D. I. (1985). Crosslinguistic evidence for the language-making capacity. In D. I. Slobin (Ed.), *The crosslinguistic study of language acquisition: Vol. 2. Theoretical issues.* Hillsdale, NJ: Erlbaum.

Smith, A. N., & Spence, C. M. (1981). National day care study: Optimizing the day care environment. *American Journal of Orthopsychiatry, 50,* 718–721.

Smith, D. W. (1978). Prenatal life. In D. W. Smith, E. L. Bierman, & N. M. Robinson (Eds.), *The biologic ages of man* (2nd ed.). Philadelphia: Saunders.

Smith, D. W., & Stenchever, M. A. (1978). Prenatal life and the pregnant woman. In D. W. Smith, E. L. Bierman, & N. M. Robinson (Eds.), *The biologic ages of man* (2nd ed.). Philadelphia: Saunders.

Snarey, J. R., Reimer, J., & Kohlberg, L. (1985). Development of social-moral reasoning among kibbutz adolescents: A longitudinal cross-sectional study. *Developmental Psychology, 21,* 3–17.

Snow, C. E., & Ferguson, C. A. (Eds.). (1977). *Talking to children.* Cambridge, England: Cambridge University Press.

Snow, M. E., Jacklin, C. N., & Maccoby, E. E.

(1983). Sex-of-child differences in father-child interaction at one year of age. *Child Development, 54,* 227–232.

Snyder, L. (1978). Communicative and cognitive abilities and disabilities in the sensorimotor period. *Merrill-Palmer Quarterly, 24,* 161–180.

Snyder, L., Bates, E., & Bretherton, I. (1981). Content and context in early lexical development. *Journal of Child Language, 8,* 565–582.

Solnit, A. J., & Provence, S. (1979). Vulnerability and risk in early childhood. In J. D. Osofsky (Ed.), *Handbook of infant development.* New York: Wiley.

Sonnenschein, S. (1986). Development of referential communication skills: How familiarity with a listener affects a speaker's production of redundant messages. *Developmental Psychology, 22,* 549–552.

Sontag, L. W., Baker, C. T., & Nelson, V. L. (1958). Mental growth and personality development: A longitudinal study. *Monographs of the Society for Research in Child Development, 23* (Whole No. 68).

Sosa, R., Kennell, J. H., Klaus, M. H., Robertson, S., & Urrutia, J. (1980). The effect of a supportive companion on perinatal problems, length of labor and mother-infant interaction. *New England Journal of Medicine, 303,* 597–600.

Sostek, A. M., Scanlon, J. W., & Abramson, D. C. (1982). Postpartum contact and maternal confidence and anxiety: A confirmation of short-term effects. *Infant Behavior and Development, 5,* 323–330.

Spelke, E. S. (1979). Exploring audible and visible events in infancy. In A. D. Pick (Ed.), *Perception and its development: A tribute to Eleanor J. Gibson.* Hillsdale, NJ: Erlbaum.

Spelke, E. S. (1987). The development of intermodal perception. In P. Salapatek & L. Cohen (Eds.), *Handbook of infant perception: Vol. 2. From perception to cognition.* Orlando, FL: Academic Press.

Spelke, E. S., & Owsley, C. J. (1979). Intermodal exploration and knowledge in infancy. *Infant Behavior and Development, 2,* 13–27.

Spence, J. T., & Helmreich, R. L. (1978). *Masculinity and femininity.* Austin: University of Texas Press.

Spieker, S. J., & Booth, C. L. (1988). Maternal antecedents of attachment quality. In J. Belsky & T. Nezworski (Eds.), *Clinical implications of attachment.* Hillsdale, NJ: Erlbaum.

Spitz, H. H. (1986). Preventing and curing mental retardation by behavioral intervention: An evaluation of some claims. *Intelligence, 10,* 197–207.

Sroufe, L. A. (1979). The coherence of individual development: Early care, attachment, and subsequent developmental issues. *American Psychologist, 34,* 834–841.

Sroufe, L. A. (1983). Infant-caregiver attachment and patterns of adaptation in preschool: The roots of maladaption and competence. In M. Perlmutter (Ed.), *Minnesota symposium on child psychology* (Vol. 16). Hillsdale, NJ: Erlbaum.

Sroufe, L. A. (1985). Attachment classification from the perspective of infant-caregiver relationships and infant temperament. *Child Development, 56,* 1–14.

Sroufe, L. A., & Fleeson, J. (1986). Attachment and the construction of relationships. In W. W. Hartup & Z. Rubin (Eds.), *Relationships and development.* Hillsdale, NJ: Erlbaum.

Sroufe, L. A., & Rutter, M. (1984). The domain of developmental psychopathology. *Child Development, 55,* 17–29.

Sroufe, L. A., & Waters, E. (1977). Attachment as an organizational construct. *Child Development, 48,* 1184–1199.

Starfield, B., & Pless, I. B. (1980). Physical health. In O. G. Brim, Jr., & J. Kagan, *Constancy and change in human development.* Cambridge, MA: Harvard University Press.

Stark, E. (1986, October). Young, innocent and pregnant. *Psychology Today,* pp. 28–35.

Staub, E. (1979). *Positive social behavior and morality: Vol. 2. Socialization and development.* New York: Academic Press.

Steelman, L. C. (1985). A tale of two variables: A review of the intellectual consequences of sibship size and birth order. *Review of Educational Research, 55,* 353–386.

Stein, Z., Susser, M., Saenger, G., & Morolla, F. (1975). *Famine and human development: The Dutch hunger winter of 1944–1945.* New York: Oxford University Press.

Steinberg, L. D. (1981). Transformations in family relations at puberty. *Developmental Psychology, 17,* 833–840.

Steinberg, L. D. (1987a, April). *Pubertal status, hormonal levels, and family relations: The distancing hypothesis.* Paper presented at the biennial meetings of the Society for Research in Child Development, Baltimore.

Steinberg, L. D. (1987b, September). Bound to bicker. *Psychology Today,* pp. 36–39.

Steinberg, L. D., & Hill, J. P. (1978). Patterns of family interaction as a function of age, the onset of puberty, and formal thinking. *Developmental Psychology, 14,* 683–684.

Steinberg, L. D., & Silverberg, S. (1986). The vicissitudes of autonomy in early adolescence. *Child Development, 57,* 841–851.

Steiner, J. E. (1979). Human facial expressions in response to taste and smell stimulation. In H. W. Reese & L. P. Lipsitt (Eds.), *Advances in child development and behavior* (Vol. 13). New York: Academic Press.

Stenchever, M. A. (1978). Perinatal life for mother and baby. Labor and delivery. In D. W. Smith, E. L. Bierman, & N. M. Robinson (Eds.), *The biologic ages of man* (2nd ed.). Philadelphia: Saunders.

Stern, D. N., Spieker, S., Barnett, R. K., & MacKain, K. (1983). The prosody of maternal speech: Infant age and context related changes. *Journal of Child Language, 10,* 1–15.

Sternberg, R. J. (1985). *Beyond IQ: A triarchic theory of human intelligence.* New York: Cambridge University Press.

Sternberg, R. J. (1986). *Intelligence applied.* New York: Harcourt Brace Jovanovich.

Sternberg, R. J., & Davidson, J. E. (1985). Cognitive development in the gifted and talented. In F. D. Horowitz & M. O'Brien (Eds.), *The gifted and talented. Developmental perspectives.* Washington, DC: American Psychological Association.

Sternberg, R. J., & Davidson, J. E. (Eds.). (1986). *Conceptions of giftedness.* Cambridge, England: Cambridge University Press.

Sternberg, R. J., & Powell, J. S. (1983). The development of intelligence. In J. H. Flavell & E. M. Markman (Eds.), *Handbook of child psychology: Cognitive development* (Vol. 3). New York: Wiley. (P. H. Mussen, General Editor)

Sternberg, R. J., & Suben, J. G. (1986). The socialization of intelligence. In M. Perlmutter (Ed.), *Perspectives on intellectual development. The Minnesota symposia on child psychology* (Vol. 19). Hillsdale, NJ: Erlbaum.

Steuer, F. B., Applefield, J. M., & Smith, R. (1971). Televised aggression and the interpersonal aggression of preschool children. *Journal of Experimental Child Psychology, 11,* 422–447.

Stevenson, H. W., Stigler, J. W., Lee, S., Lucker, G. W., Kitamura, S., & Hsu, C. (1985). Cognitive performance and academic achievement of Japanese, Chinese, and American children. *Child Development, 56,* 718–734.

Stewart, R. B., Cluff, L. E., & Philp, R. (1977). *Drug monitoring: A requirement for responsible drug use.* Baltimore: Williams & Wilkins.

Strayer, F. F. (1980). Social ecology of the preschool peer group. In A. Collins (Ed.), *Minnesota symposia on child psychology* (Vol. 13). Hillsdale, NJ: Erlbaum.

Streissguth, A. P., Barr, H. M., Martin, D. C., & Herman, C. S. (1980a). Effects of maternal alcohol, nicotine, and caffeine use during pregnancy on infant mental and motor development at eight months. *Alcoholism: Clinical and Experimental Research, 4,* 152–164.

Streissguth, A. P., Landesman-Dwyer, S., Martin, J. C., & Smith, D. W. (1980b). Teratogenic effects of alcohol in humans and laboratory animals. *Science, 209,* 353–361.

Streissguth, A. P., Martin, D. C., Barr, H. M., Sandman, B. M., Kirchner, G. L., & Darby, B. L. (1984). Intrauterine alcohol and nicotine exposure: Attention and reaction time in 4-year-old children. *Developmental Psychology, 20,* 533–541.

Streissguth, A. P., Martin, D. C., Martin, J. C., & Barr, H. M. (1981). The Seattle longitudinal prospective study on alcohol and pregnancy. *Neurobehavioral Toxicology and Teratology, 3,* 223–233.

Striegel-Moore, R. H., Silberstein, L. R., & Rodin, J. (1986). Toward an understanding of risk factors for bulimia. *American Psychologist, 41,* 246–263.

Strobino, D. M. (1987). The health and medical consequences of adolescent sexuality and pregnancy: A review of the literature. In S. L. Hofferth & C. D. Hayes (Eds.), *Risking the future. Adolescent sexuality, pregnancy, and childbearing. Working papers.* Washington, DC: National Academy Press.

Susman, E. J., Inoff-Germain, G., Nottelmann, E. D., Loriaux, D. L., Cutler, G. B., Jr., & Chrousos, G. P. (1987). Hormones, emotional dispositions, and aggressive attributes on young adolescents. *Child Development, 58,* 1114–1134.

Taitz, L. S. (1975). Modification of weight gain by dietary changes in a population of Sheffield neonates. *Archives of Diseases of Childhood, 50,* 476–479.

Tanner, J. M. (1962). *Growth at adolescence* (2nd

ed.). Oxford: Blackwell Scientific Publications.

Tanner, J. M. (1970). Physical growth. In P. H. Mussen (Ed.), *Carmichael's manual of child psychology* (Vol. 1, 3rd ed.). New York: Wiley.

Tanner, J. M. (1975). Growth and endocrinology of the adolescent. In L. J. Gardner (Ed.), *Endocrine and genetic diseases of childhood and adolescence* (2d ed.). Philadelphia: Saunders.

Tanner, J. M. (1978). *Fetus into man. Physical growth from conception to maturity.* Cambridge, MA: Harvard University Press.

Templin, M. C. (1957). Certain language skills in children: Their development and interrelationships. *University of Minnesota Institute of Child Welfare Monograph, 26.*

Terman, L. (1925). Mental and physical traits of a thousand gifted children. *Genetic studies of genius* (Vol. 1). Stanford, CA: Stanford University Press.

Terman, L., & Merrill, M. A. (1937). *Measuring intelligence: A guide to the administration of the new revised Stanford-Binet tests.* Boston: Houghton Mifflin.

Terman, L., & Oden, M. (1947). *Genetic studies of genius: Vol. 4. The gifted child grows up.* Stanford, CA: Stanford University Press.

Terman, L., & Oden, M. (1959). *Genetic studies of genius: Vol. 5. The gifted group at mid-life.* Stanford, CA: Stanford University Press.

Terrace, H. S. (1979, November). How Nim Chimpsky changed my mind. *Psychology Today,* pp. 65–76.

Tew, M. (1985). Place of birth and perinatal mortality. *Journal of the Royal College of General Practitioners, 35,* 390–394.

Thelen, E. (1984). Learning to walk: Ecological demands and phylogenetic constraints. In L. P. Lipsitt & C. Rovee-Collier (Eds.), *Advances in infancy research* (Vol. 3). Norwood, NJ: Ablex.

Thomas, A., & Chess, S. (1977). *Temperament and development.* New York: Brunner/Mazel.

Thomas, A., & Chess, S. (1986). The New York Longitudinal Study: From infancy to early adult life. In R. Plomin & J. Dunn (Eds.), *The study of temperament: Changes, continuities and challenges.* Hillsdale, NJ: Erlbaum.

Thompson, R. A., & Lamb, M. E. (1982). Stranger sociality and its relationship to temperament and social experience during the second year. *Infant Behavior and Development, 5,* 277–287.

Thompson, R. A., Lamb, M. E., & Estes, D. (1982). Stability of infant-mother attachment and its relationship to changing life circumstances in an unselected middle-class sample. *Child Development, 53,* 144–148.

Thompson, R. A., Lamb, M. E., & Estes, D. (1983). Harmonizing discordant notes: A reply to Waters. *Child Development, 54,* 521–524.

Thompson, S. K. (1975). Gender labels and early sex role development. *Child Development, 46,* 339–347.

Thorne, B. (1986). Girls and boys together . . . but mostly apart: Gender arrangements in elementary schools. In W. W. Hartup & Z. Rubin (Eds.), *Relationships and development.* Hillsdale, NJ: Erlbaum.

Tieger, T. (1980). On the biological basis of sex differences in aggression. *Child Development, 51,* 943–963.

Tobin-Richards, M. H., Boxer, A. M., & Petersen, A. C. (1983). The psychological significance of pubertal change: Sex differences in perceptions of self during early adolescence. In J. Brooks-Gunn and A. C. Petersen (Eds.), *Girls at puberty. Biological and psychosocial perspectives.* New York: Plenum.

Tomasello, M., & Mannle, S. (1985). Pragmatics of sibling speech to one-year-olds. *Child Development, 56,* 911–917.

Tomlinson-Keasey, C., Eisert, D. C., Kahle, L. R., Hardy-Brown, K., & Keasey, B. (1978). The structure of concrete operational thought. *Child Development, 50,* 1153–1163.

Trehub, S. E., Bull, D., & Thorpe, L. A. (1984). Infants' perception of melodies: The role of melodic contour. *Child Development, 55,* 821–830.

Trehub, S. E., & Rabinovitch, M. S. (1972). Auditory-linguistic sensitivity in early infancy. *Developmental Psychology, 6,* 74–77.

Trehub, S. E., Thorpe, L. A., & Morrongiello, B. A. (1985). Infants' perception of melodies: Changes in a single tone. *Infant Behavior and Development, 8,* 213–223.

Trites, R. L., & Laprade, K. (1983). Evidence for an independent syndrome of hyperactivity. *Journal of Child Psychology and Psychiatry, 24,* 573–586.

Trotter, R. J. (1986a, July). The mystery of mastery. *Psychology Today,* pp. 32–38.

Trotter, R. J. (1986b, August). Three heads are

better than one. *Psychology Today,* pp. 56–62.

Tschann, J. M., Johnston, J. R., Wallerstein, J. S., Coysh, W. S., & Nelson, R. (1987, April). *Loss, conflict, change and psychological vulnerability: A model for predicting children's functioning at divorce.* Paper presented at the biennial meetings of the Society for Research in Child Development, Baltimore.

Turiel, E. (1966). An experimental test of the sequentiality of developmental stages in the child's moral judgment. *Journal of Personality and Social Psychology, 3,* 611–618.

Turkington, C. (1987, September). Special talents. *Psychology Today,* pp. 42–46.

Ungerer, J. A., & Sigman, M. (1984). The relation of play and sensorimotor behavior to language in the second year. *Child Development, 55,* 1448–1455.

U.S. Bureau of the Census (1985). *Statistical abstract of the United States: 1986* (106th ed.). Washington, DC: U.S. Government Printing Office.

Uzgiris, I. C. (1973). Patterns of cognitive development in infancy. *Merrill-Palmer Quarterly, 19,* 21–40.

Vandell, D. L., Anderson, L. D., Ehrhardt, G., & Wilson, K. S. (1982). Integrating hearing and deaf preschoolers: An attempt to enhance hearing children's interaction with deaf peers. *Child Development, 53,* 1354–1363.

Vandenberg, B. (1984). Developmental features of exploration. *Developmental Psychology, 20,* 3–8.

van Doorninck, W. J. Caldwell, B. M., Wright, C., & Frankenberg, W. K. (1981). The relationship between twelve-month home stimulation and school achievement. *Child Development, 52,* 1080–1083.

Vaughn, B. E., Deane, K. E., & Waters, E. (1985). The impact of out-of-home care on child-mother attachment quality: Another look at some enduring questions. In I. Bretherton & E. Waters (Eds.), Growing points of attachment theory and research. *Monographs of the Society for Research in Child Development, 50* (1-2, Whole No. 209).

Vaughn, B. E., Egeland, B., Sroufe, L. A., & Waters, E. Individual differences in infant-mother attachment at twelve and eighteen months: Stability and change in families under stress. *Child Development, 50,* 971–975.

Vaughn, B. E., Gove, F. L., & Egeland, B. (1980). The relationship between out-of-home care and the quality of infant-mother attachment in an economically disadvantaged population. *Child Development, 51,* 1203–1214.

Vellutino, F. R., & Scanlon, D. M. (1987). Phonological coding, phonological awareness, and reading ability: Evidence from a longitudinal and experimental study. *Merrill-Palmer Quarterly, 33,* 321–364.

Vernon, P. A. (1983). Speed of information processing and general intelligence. *Intelligence, 7,* 53–70.

Vernon, P. A., & Kantor, L. (1986). Reaction time correlations with intelligence test scores obtained under either timed or untimed conditions. *Intelligence, 10,* 315–330.

Vinter, A. (1986). The role of movement in eliciting early imitations. *Child Development, 57,* 66–71.

Vygotsky, L. S. (1962). *Thought and language.* New York: Wiley.

Waber, D. P. (1977). Sex differences in mental abilities, hemispheric lateralization, and rate of physical growth at adolescence. *Developmental Psychology, 13,* 29–38.

Wachs, T. D., & Gruen, G. E. (1982). *Early experience and human development.* New York: Plenum.

Waddington, C. H. (1957). *The strategy of the genes.* London: Allen & Son.

Walker, L. J. (1980). Cognitive and perspective-taking prerequisites for moral development. *Child Development, 51,* 131–139.

Walker, L. J. (1984). Sex differences in the development of moral reasoning: A critical review. *Child Development, 55,* 677–691.

Walker, L. J. (1986). Sex differences in the development of moral reasoning: A rejoinder to Baumrind. *Child Development, 57,* 522–526.

Walker, L. J. (1987, April). *Moral orientations: A comparison of two models.* Paper presented at the biennial meetings of the Society for Research in Child Development, Baltimore.

Walker, L. J., de Vries, B., & Bichard, S. L. (1984). The hierarchical nature of stages of moral development. *Developmental Psychology, 20,* 960–966.

Wallerstein, J. S. (1984). Children of divorce: Preliminary report of a ten-year follow-up of young children. *American Journal of Orthopsychiatry, 54,* 444–458.

Wallerstein, J. S., & Kelly, J. B. (1980). *Surviving the breakup. How children and parents cope with divorce.* New York: Basic Books.

Walters, R. H., & Brown, M. (1963). Studies of reinforcement of aggression. III. Transfer of responses to an interpersonal situation. *Child Development, 34,* 563–571.

Wandersman, L. P., & Unger, D. G. (1983, April). *Interaction of infant difficulty and social support in adolescent mothers.* Paper presented at the biennial meetings of the Society for Research in Child Development, Detroit.

Waterman, A. S. (1985). Identity in the context of adolescent psychology. *New Directions for Child Development, 30,* 5–24.

Waters, E. (1978). The reliability and stability of individual differences in infant-mother attachment. *Child Development, 59,* 483–494.

Watson, J. D., & Crick, F. H. C. (1953). Molecular structure of nucleic acid. A structure for deoxyribose nucleic acid. *Nature, 171,* 737–738.

Waxman, S., & Gelman, R. (1986). Preschoolers' use of superordinate relations in classification and language. *Cognitive Development, 1,* 139–156.

Wechsler, D. (1974). *Manual for the Wechsler Intelligence Scale for Children—Revised.* New York: Psychological Corporation.

Weikart, D. P. (1972). Relationship of curriculum, teaching, and learning in preschool education. In J. C. Stanley (Ed.), *Preschool programs for the disadvantaged.* Baltimore: Johns Hopkins University Press.

Weikart, D. P. (1983). A longitudinal view of a preschool research effort. In M. Perlmutter (Ed.), *Minnesota symposia on child psychology* (Vol. 16). Hillsdale, NJ: Erlbaum.

Weir, R. (1962). *Language in the crib.* The Hague: Mouton.

Wellman, H. M. (1982). The foundations of knowledge: concept development in the young child. In S. G. Moore & C. C. Cooper (Eds.), *The young child. Reviews of research* (Vol. 3). Washington, DC: National Association for the Education of Young Children.

Werker, J. F. (1987, April). *Infants prefer "parentese."* Paper presented at the biennial meetings of the Society for Research in Child Development, Baltimore.

Werker, J. F., & Tees, R. C. (1984). Cross-language speech perception: Evidence for perceptual reorganization during the first year of life. *Infant Behavior and Development, 7,* 49–63.

Werler, M. M., Pober, B. R., & Holmes, L. B. (1985). Smoking and pregnancy. *Teratology, 32,* 473–481.

Werner, E. E. (1986). A longitudinal study of perinatal risk. In D. C. Farran & J. D. McKinney (Eds.), *Risk in intellectual and psychosocial development.* Orlando, FL: Academic Press.

Werner, E. E., Bierman, J. M., & French, F. E. (1971). *The children of Kauai.* Honolulu: University of Hawaii Press.

Werner, E. E. & Smith, R. (1982). *Vulnerable but invincible.* New York: McGraw-Hill.

Werner, H. (1948). *Comparative psychology of mental development.* Chicago: Follett.

Weymouth, F. W. (1963). Visual acuity of children. In M. J. Hirsch & R. Wick (Eds.), *Vision of children: An optometric symposium.* Philadelphia: Chilton.

White, B. L. (1975). *The first three years of life.* Englewood Cliffs, NJ: Prentice-Hall.

White, K. R. (1985–1986). Efficacy of early intervention. *The Journal of Special Education, 19,* 401–416.

White, S. (1965). Evidence for a hierarchical arrangement of learning processes. In L. P. Lipsitt & C. C. Spiker (Eds.), *Advances in child development and behavior* (Vol. 2). New York: Academic Press.

Wiegerink, R., Hocutt, A., Posante-Loro, R., & Bristol, M. (1980). Parent involvement in early education programs for handicapped children. *New Directions for Exceptional Children, 1,* 67–86.

Willerman, L. (1987, April). *Where are the shared environmental influences on intelligence and personality?* Paper presented at the biennial meetings of the Society for Research in Child Development, Baltimore.

Williams, J. E., Bennett, S. M., & Best, D. L. (1975). Awareness and expression of sex stereotypes in young children. *Developmental Psychology, 11,* 635–642.

Williams, R. L. (1970). Black pride, academic relevance and individual achievement. *Counseling Psychologist, 2,* 18–22.

Williams, T. M. (Ed.). (1986). *The impact of television. A natural experiment in three communities.* Orlando, FL: Academic Press.

Willig, A. (1985). Meta-analysis of studies on bilingual education. *Review of Educational Research, 55,* 269–317.

Willows, D. M., & Ryan, E. B. (1986). The development of grammatical sensitivity and its relationship to early reading achievement. *Reading Research Quarterly, 21,* 253–266.

Wilson, J. G. (1977). Current status of teratology. General principles and mechanisms derived from animal studies. In J. G. Wilson & F. C. Fraser (Eds.), *Handbook of teratology: Vol. 1. General principles and etiology.* New York: Plenum.

Wilson, R. S. (1977). Twins and siblings: Concordance for school-age mental development. *Child Development, 48,* 211–216.

Wilson, R. S. (1978). Synchronies in mental development: An epigenetic perspective. *Science, 202,* 939–948.

Wilson, R. S. (1983). The Louisville twin study: Developmental synchronies in behavior. *Child Development, 54,* 298–316.

Winick, M. (1980). *Nutrition in health and disease.* New York: Wiley.

Winick, M., Meyer, K. K., & Harris, R. C. (1975). Malnutrition and environmental enrichment by early adoption. *Science, 190,* 1173–1175.

Witkin, H. A., Dyk, R. B., Faterson, H. F., Goodenough, D. R., & Karp, S. A. (1962). *Psychological differentiation.* New York: Wiley.

Woody, E. Z., & Costanzo, P. R. (1981). The socialization of obesity-prone behavior. In S. S. Brehm, S. M. Kassin, & F. X. Gibbons (Eds.), *Developmental social psychology. Theory and research* (pp. 211–233). New York: Oxford University Press.

Yeates, K. O., MacPhee, D., Campbell, F. A., & Ramey, C. T. (1983). Maternal IQ and home environment as determinants of early childhood intellectual competence: A developmental analysis. *Developmental Psychology, 19,* 731–739.

Zahn-Waxler, C., McKnew, D. H., Cummings, E. M., Davenport, Y. B., & Radke-Yarrow, M. (1984). Problem behaviors and peer interactions of young children with a manic-depressive parent. *American Journal of Psychiatry, 141*(2), 236–240.

Zahn-Waxler, C., & Radke-Yarrow, M. (1982). The development of altruism: Alternative research strategies. In N. Eisenberg (Ed.), *The development of prosocial behavior.* New York: Academic Press.

Zahn-Waxler, C., Radke-Yarrow, M., & King, R. A. (1979). Child-rearing and children's prosocial initiations toward victims of distress. *Child Development, 50,* 319–330.

Zajonc, R. B. (1975, January). Birth order and intelligence: Dumber by the dozen. *Psychology Today,* pp. 37–43.

Zajonc, R. B. (1983). Validating the confluence model. *Psychological Bulletin, 93,* 457–480.

Zajonc, R. B., & Marcus, G. B. (1975). Birth order and intellectual development. *Psychological Review, 82,* 74–88.

Zarbatany, L., & Lamb, M. E. (1985). Social referencing as a function of information source: Mothers versus strangers. *Infant Behavior and Development, 8,* 25–33.

Zaslow, M. J., & Hayes, C. D. (1986). Sex differences in children's responses to psychosocial stress: Toward a cross-context analysis. In M. E. Lamb, A. L. Brown, & B. Rogoff (Eds.), *Advances in developmental psychology* (Vol. 4). Hillsdale, NJ: Erlbaum.

Zeskind, P. S., & Lester, B. M. (1978). Acoustic features and auditory perceptions of the cries of newborns with prenatal and perinatal complications. *Child Development, 49,* 580–589.

Zeskind, P. S., & Lester, B. M. (1981). Analysis of cry features of newborns with differential fetal growth. *Child Development, 52,* 207–212.

Zeskind, P. S., & Ramey, C. T. (1981). Preventing intellectual and interactional sequelae of fetal malnutrition: A longitudinal, transactional, and synergistic approach to development. *Child Development, 52,* 213–218.

Zigler, E., & Freedman, J. (1987). Early experience, malleability, and Head Start. In J. J. Gallagher & C. T. Ramey (Eds.), *The malleability of children.* Baltimore: Paul H. Brookes.

Zigler, E., & Muenchow, S. (1979). Mainstreaming. The proof is in the implementation. *American Psychologist, 34,* 993–996.

Zucker, K. J. (1985). The infant's construction of his parents in the first six months of life. In T. M. Field & N. A. Fox (Eds.), *Social perception in infants.* Norwood, NJ: Ablex.

Picture Credits

Color Photo Inserts

Insert 1: p. 1 (*top*) © Petit Format/Nestle/Science Source/Photo Researchers, Inc.; (*bottom*) © John Giannicchi/Photo Researchers, Inc.   p. 2 (*top, middle, bottom*) © Petit Format/Nestle/ Science Source/Photo Researchers, Inc.   p. 3 (*top, middle, bottom*) © Petit Format/Nestle/ Science Source/Photo Researchers, Inc.   p. 4 (*top, middle*) © Petit Format/Nestle/Science Source/Photo Researchers, Inc.; (*bottom*) © 1981 Grace Moore/Taurus.

Insert 2: p. 1 (*top*) © 1985 Sandra Lousada/Woodfin Camp; (*middle*) Kasz Maciag 1986/The Stock Market; (*bottom*) © Four By Five.   p. 2 (*top left, bottom left*) © Elizabeth Crews/Image Works; (*top right*) © Townsend P. Dickinson/Photo Researchers, Inc.; (*bottom right*) © 1987 Bruce Plotkin/Image Works.   p. 3 (*upper left*) © Four By Five; (*lower right*) © A. Reininger/ Woodfin Camp.   p. 4 (*upper left*) © Four By Five; (*lower right*) Jean-Claude LeJeune/Stock, Boston.

Insert 3: p. 1 (*top left, top right*) © 1985 Sandra Lousada/Woodfin Camp; (*bottom left*) © Elizabeth Crews/Image Works; (*bottom right*) © Four By Five.   p. 2 © Four By Five. p. 3 (*top*) © 1982 Betty Vatz/Taurus; (*bottom*) © 1987 Tom McCarthy/The Stock Market. p. 4 (*top*) © Four By Five; (*middle*) © Bob Daemmrich Photos/Stock, Boston; (*bottom*) © Suzanne Goldstein/Photo Researchers, Inc.

Insert 4: p. 1 (*top*) © Four By Five; (*bottom*) © 1979 Timothy Eagan/Woodfin Camp.   p. 2 (*top*) © 1986 Will/Deni McIntyre/Photo Researchers, Inc.; (*bottom*) © Gilles Peress/Magnum.   p. 3 (*upper right*) © Four By Five; (*lower left*) © 1985 Michael Heron/Woodfin Camp. p. 4 (*top*) © 1986 Joe Bator/The Stock Market; (*bottom*) © Barbara Kirk/The Stock Market.

Text (figure numbers in italics)

Chapter 1: *1.1* © Shirley Zeiberg/Photo Researchers, Inc.; *1.3* Copyright Martha Stewart/The Picture Cube; *1.4* Michael Hayman/Stock, Boston; *1.6* (*left*) Joseph Szabo/Photo Researchers, Inc., (*right*) © 1981 Suzanne Szasz/Photo Researchers, Inc.; *1.7* Sybil Shelton/Monkmeyer.

Chapter 2: *2.1* © Erika Stone 1987/Peter Arnold, Inc.; *2.3* (*top*) Martha Bates/Stock, Boston, (*bottom*) © 1980 Erika Stone/Photo Researchers, Inc.; *2.7* Copyright Alan Carey/The Image Works.

Chapter 3: *3.3* Suzanne Szasz/Photo Researchers, Inc.; *3.4* © 1983 Joel Gordon; *3.5* © Stock, Boston, Inc., 1985; *3.6* H. F. R. Prechtl (1977). The neurological examination of the full-term newborn infant. *Clinics in Developmental Medicine* (2nd ed.), *63*. London: Heinemann. *3.7* © SUVA/DPI; *3.8* Copyright © Hella Hammid/Photo Researchers, Inc.; *3.9* L. Johnston, *Hi Mom! Hi Dad! 101 cartoons for new parents* (Meadowbrook Press).

Chapter 4: *4.1* Goodwin/Monkmeyer; *4.2* © Elizabeth Crews.

Chapter 5: *5.5* Zimbel/Monkmeyer.

Chapter 6: *6.1* Teri Leigh Stratford/Photo Researchers, Inc.; *6.3* Shelton/Monkmeyer; *6.7* Paul Conklin/Monkmeyer; *6.10* © Elizabeth Crews.

Chapter 7: 7.1 © Steve Takatsuno/The Picture Cube; 7.2 NYT Pictures; 7.4 © Elizabeth Crews/Stock, Boston; 7.7 © David M. Grossman/Photo Researchers, Inc.; 7.9 Copyright Monique Manceau/Photo Researchers, Inc.

Chapter 8: 8.1 © Susan Kuklin 1977/Photo Researchers, Inc.; 8.3 Richard W. McKenna/Taurus Photos; 8.5 Jean-Claude LeJeune/Stock, Boston.

Chapter 9: 9.1 © Ginger Chih, 1979/Peter Arnold, Inc.; 9.2 © All rights reserved, Alan Carey/ The Image Works; 9.3 © 1980 Lois Inman Engle; 9.4 © 1980 Peter Menzel/Stock, Boston; 9.5 Michael Heron/Monkmeyer.

Chapter 10: 10.1 © Arlene Collins/Monkmeyer; 10.3 © Elizabeth Crews/Stock, Boston.

Chapter 11: 11.1 The Picture Cube; 11.2 © R. Duane Cooke/DPI; 11.4 © Elizabeth Crews; 11.5 © Lynn McLaren/Photo Researchers, Inc.; 11.7 Shirley Zeiberg/Taurus Photos; 11.8 Paul Conklin/Monkmeyer.

Chapter 12: 12.1 Mark Antman/The Image Works; 12.2 © Esther Shapiro/Photo Researchers, Inc.; 12.4 (*top*) © Elizabeth Crews, (*bottom*) Collidge/Taurus.

Chapter 13: 13.1 Hays/Monkmeyer; 13.2 © Edward Lettau/Photo Researchers, Inc.; 13.6 © Elizabeth Crews/The Image Works; 13.7 © Leonard Lessin, 1986/Photo Researchers, Inc.; 13.8 © Marjorie Pickens, 1984.

Chapter 14: 14.1 L. Roger Turner/Wisconsin State Journal; 14.3 Steven Potter/Stock, Boston; 14.4 Irene Bayer/Monkmeyer; 14.5 Raimondo Borea.

Chapter 15: 15.2 Jean Shapiro; 15.4 Forsyth/Monkmeyer; 15.6 © J. Berndt, 1982/Stock, Boston; 15.8 Strix Pix (David B. Strickler)/The Picture Cube; 15.9 Bruce Roberts/Photo Researchers.

Author Index

Note: Italicized page numbers indicate names in tables and figures.

Abel, E. L., 61
Abelson, R., 436
Abramson, D. C., 395
Achenbach, T. M., 247, *511*, 512, 513, 522–524, 526, *528, 533*
Adams, G., 363
Adler, A., 334
Adler, T. F., 221
Ainsworth, M. D. S., 101, 392, 402, 403, 409, *410*
Akiyama, M. M., 303
Albert, J., *175*
Allen, H. L., 84
Allen, L., 26
Allen, V. L., 143
Allik, J., 179
Altman, J., 60
Alvarez, W. F., 488
Anderson, C. W., *496*
Anderson, D. R., 499
Andrews, S. R., 490
Ansul, S. E., 160
Antell, S. E. G., 158
Anthony, E. J., 525, *533*
Apgar, V. A., 87
Appel, M. H., 266, 267
Appelbaum, M. I., 198
Applefield, J. M., 501
Arce, S., 260
Archer, J., *145*
Arend, R. A., *413*
Arkin, A. M., 299
Arnason, L., 419
Asher, S. R., 421, *422*, 422

Bachman, J. G., 364
Badger, E., 490
Baer, D. M., 14
Baillargeon, R., 241
Baker, C. T., *200*
Balaban, T., 373, 376, 377
Baldwin, A. L., 477
Bancalari, E., 66
Bandura, A., 14, 17, 19, 22, 327–328, 330, 331, 333, 334, 348, 364, 367, 384, 475
Baraffi, G., 82, 83

Barbee, A. H., 520
Barenboim, C., 440, *441*, 442
Barglow, P., 492, 493
Barnard, K. E., 89, 91, 103, 107, 117, 210, 400, 473
Barnes, H. L., 477, *478*
Baron, P., 524
Barrett, D. E., 149
Bates, E., 279, 280, 282, 284, 297, 303, 304, 308, *309*, 548
Bates, J. E., 299
Batter, B. S., 404
Baumrind, D., 366, 416, 422, 447, 472, 477, 479–480
Bayles, K., 299
Bayley, N., 190
Bearison, D. J., 551
Becker, J. A., 296
Bee, H. L., 89, 91, 107, 117, 198, *199*, 210, 400, 473
Beintema, D. J., 98, *99*
Bell, D. C., 477
Bell, L. G., 477
Bell, S. M., 101
Bellinger, D., 63
Bellugi, U., 285
Belmont, J. M., 187, 188
Belsky, J., 106, 412, 492, 493
Bem, S. L., 381
Benbow, C. P., 520
Benn, R. K., 493
Bennett, S. M., 371
Berberian, K. E., 404
Berg, J. M., 58
Bergman, T., 157
Berk, L. E., 296
Berndt, T. J., 416, 417, 420, 426, 442, 457–459
Best, D. L., 371
Betz, N. E., 384
Bichard, S. L., 452
Bierman, J. M., 26
Bierman, K. L., 422
Bigelow, B. J., 442, *444*
Binet, A., 188, 194, 203, 226
Birch, R., 162

Birns, B., 207
Bissell, J. S., 213
Bizzell, R. P., 492
Bjorklund, D. F., 260
Black, K. N., 308
Blanchard, M., 493
Blasi, A., 458
Blewitt, P., 299
Block, J., 26, 344, 348, 375, 378, 480
Block, J. H., 344
Bloom, L., 285
Blumstein, P., 488
Blyth, D. A., 143
Bohannon, J. N., III, 518
Boliek, C. A., 518
Bond, L., 534
Booth, C. L., 409
Bornstein, M. H., *93*, 162, 163, 264
Boukydis, C. F. Z., 104
Bower, T. G. R., 162–164, 166, 170, *171*, 172–173
Bowerman, M., 288, 301, 303, 304
Bowlby, J., 392–393, 408
Boxer, A. M., *143*, 143
Boyd, E. F., 101
Brackbill, Y., 81, 117
Bradbard, M. R., 373
Bradley, L., 311
Bradley, R., 208, *209, 210*
Bradshaw, D. L., 412
Braine, M. D. S., 285
Brassard, J. A., 489
Brazelton, T. B., *398*
Breitmayer, B. J., 88, 566
Bretherton, I., 282
Brody, E. B., 196, 197
Brody, L. E., 520
Brody, N., 196, 197
Broman, S. H., 206, *207,* 485
Bromley, D. B., 439, 440
Bromwich, R. M., 401
Bronfenbrenner, U., 10, 204, 470, 487, 488
Bronson, G. W., 157
Brooks, P. H., 164
Brooks-Gunn, J., 70, 144, *144,* 354, 356, *356,* 357, *413,* 427
Broverman, I. K., 371, 372
Brown, A. L., 260–262, 264, 514
Brown, B. B., 417
Brown, J., 64
Brown, K. W., 170
Brown, M., 329
Brown, R., 277, 284–287, 298, 306, *307*
Brownell, C. A., 549
Brucken, L., 379
Brumback, R. A., 518
Brush, L. R., 221
Bryant, P., 311
Budoff, M., 537
Buehler, J. W., 63
Bull, D., 167

Bullock, D., 255
Bullock, M., 242
Bumpass, L., 482
Burgeson, R., 555
Burgess, R. L., 104
Buss, A. H., 14, 104, 323, *323,* 324, *325,* 325
Bussey, K., 374
Butterfield, E. C., 187, 188, 520

Calderon, R., 530
Caldwell, B. M., 208, *209,* 210, *210,* 492
Camaioni, L., 280
Camara, K. A., 484
Campbell, E., 366–367
Campbell, F. A., 210, 214, *216*
Campbell, S. B. G., 394
Campione, J. C., 264, *265,* 513–514
Campos, J. J., 161, 182
Candee, D., 458
Canfield, R. L., 255
Cannizzo, S. R., 259
Carey, W. B., 323, 325
Carlton-Ford, S., 555
Caron, A. J., 158, 159, *159*
Caron, R. F., 159, *159*
Carter-Salzman, L., 206
Case, R., 255, 268
Casey, M. B., 163
Cassidy, D. J., 260, 261
Cassidy, J., 411, 412
Cavanaugh, P. J., 95
Cernoch, J. M., *93,* 169
Chandler, J. J., 67
Chapieski, M. L., 475
Chase, W. P., *93*
Chase-Lansdale, L., 493
Chess, S., 14, 104–106, 323–324, 326, 327, 412
Chi, M. T., 253
Chipman, S. F., 221
Chomsky, N., 301–303
Chumlea, W. C., 124, *130, 131*
Clark, E. V., 292, 293, *293,* 294
Clark, L. V., 255
Clarke, A. D. B., 560
Clarke, A. M., 560
Clarke-Stewart, A., 299, 492, 495, *496*
Clary, E. G., 419
Clasen, D. R., 417
Clifton, R. K., *93*
Cluff, L. E., 59
Coates, S., *177*
Cochran, M. M., 489
Cogan, R., 84
Colby, A., 446, 450, *451,* 451
Cole, M., 266, 510
Colombo, J., 9
Connolly, J. A., 235

Cook, M., 162
Cook, S. J., 401
Cooper, J., 373, 376, *377*
Coopersmith, S., 366
Corrigan, R., 295
Costanzo, P. R., 139
Cowan, N., *93,* 166
Cox, M., 344, 525
Cox, R., 344, 525
Crick, F. H. C., 41
Crisafi, M. A., 262
Crnic, K. A., 489
Crockenberg, S. B., 107, 327, 350, *350,* 489, 566
Crook, C., 168
Crouter, A. C., 487
Csikszentmihalyi, M., 417
Curtiss, S., 305
Cutrona, C. E., 489

Daher, M., 168
Dale, P. S., 298
Damon, W., 371, 442, 459
Danner, F. W., 17, 252
Darling, C. A., 136
Darlington, R., 213
Davey, T. C., 142
Davidson, C. V., 404
Davidson, E. S., 380
Davidson, J. E., 519, 520
Day, D., *175*
Day, M. C., 252
Deane, K. E., 493
DeCasper, A. J., 95, 167
de Chateau, P., 394, 395
De Fries, J. C., 204, 211, 307
De Loache, J. S., 260, 261
De Meis, D. K., 488
Dement, W. D., 100
Dempster, F. N., 257, *258*
Dennis, M., 289
Dennis, S., 268
Dennis, W., 148, 179
de Regt, R. H., 85
DeStefano, L., 235
DeVries, B., 452
Diaz, R. M., 290
Di Bello, P., 326
Dickerson, J. W. T., 148
Dietrich, K. N., 63
Dionne, J., 557
DiVitto, B., 89
Dix, T., 419
Dobson, V., 156
Dodge, K. A., 421, 424
Doering, S. G., 84
Doherty, N. E., 93
Dollard, J., 423
Dominick, J. R., 501
Dornbusch, S. M., 142, 480, 484, 485
Doxsey, P. A., 164

Doyle, A., 235
Dreyer, P. H., 128, 136
Duckett, E. D., 487
Duke, P. M., 144
Dumaret, A., *205,* 206
Dunn, H. G., 60
Dunn, J., 322
Dunphy, D. C., 417, 420
Dunst, C. J., 164
Durkin, K., 295

Easterbrooks, M. A., *413,* 481
Eaton, W. O., 106
Ebata, A., 524
Eccles, J. S., 383, 384
Edelbrock, C. S., 512, 523, 524
Edgerton, M., 494
Egeland, B., 346, *347,* 411, 492
Ehrhardt, A. A., 380
Eicher, S. A., 417
Eichorn, D. H., 197
Eisen, M., 359, 360, *360,* 361
Eisenberg, N., 452–455, 457
Eisenberg-Berg, N., 458
Elardo, R., 208, *210*
Elder, G. H., Jr., 486
Elfenbein, D., 447
Eme, R. F., *533*
Emmerich, W., 371
Engel, M., 299
Enns, L. R., 106
Ensminger, M. E., 482, 484
Entwisle, D. R., 84
Erickson, M. F., 346, *347*
Erikson, E. H., 19–21, 334, 339–343, 346, 348, 361, 362, 365, 409, 417, 421, 561
Eron, L. D., 423–424, 500, 503, 523
Escalona, S. K., 552
Estes, D., 411
Evans, R. I., 341
Eyres, S. J., 103

Fagan, J. F., 264
Fagot, B. I., 372, 375
Famularo, R., 401
Fantz, R. L., 157
Farber, E. A., 411
Farber, S. L., 204
Farnham-Diggory, S., *511, 517,* 518
Farran, D. C., 207, 210, 485
Faust, M. S., 142
Fein, G. G., 234, 235
Feingold, B. F., 522
Feldman, H., 106
Feldman, J. F., 380
Felson, D., 485
Ferguson, C. A., 299
Ferguson, T. J., 446
Fernald, A., 300
Ferrara, R. A., 514
Feshbach, S., 423

Field, T. M., 103, 157, *158,* 160, 235, 400–402
Fifer, G., 167
Filardo, E. K., 551
Finkelstein, N. W., 494
Finley, G. E., *158*
Fischer, K. W., 182, 255
Fitzgerald, L. F., 384
Flavell, J. H., 230–231, 234, 236, 239, 240, 242, 253–256, 259, *259,* 262, 277, 304, 435, 549, 559
Fleeson, J., 400, 411
Flexer, B. K., 247
Fogelman, K., 60
Forbes, G. B., 124
Ford, M. E., 457
Fraiberg, S., 400, 401, 531
Frame, C. L., *424*
Franks, B. A., 250
Freedman, J., 195
Freedman, J. L., 501
Freeman, J., 520, 521
French, F. E., 26
Freud, S., 19–21, 334–339, 341, 343, 346, 354, 376, 552
Frey, K. S., 369, 376
Friedman, S. L., 100
Friedrich-Cofer, L., 501
Frost, N., 263
Frueh, T., 380
Furman, W., *422*
Furrow, D., 296

Gaensbauer, T. J., 525
Galambos, N. L., 488
Gallagher, J. J., 207, 485, *511*
Galligan, R., 558
Ganchrow, J. R., 168
Garbarino, J., 401
Garber, H., 217
Gardner, B. T., 277
Gardner, H., 201
Gardner, R. A., 277
Garduque, L., 494, 495, *496*
Garmezy, N., *511,* 528, *533,* 566
Garn, S. M., 129, *130,* 146, 147
Gauthier, R., 373, *373*
Gelfand, D. M., *426*
Gelman, R., 239–242
Gentner, D., 283, *283*
Gerbner, G., 499, *500,* 501
Gerson, R. P., 459
Gesell, A., 13, 14
Gewirtz, J. L., 101
Gibbs, J. T., 524
Gibson, E. J., 154, 155, 161, *162,* 170, 173, 309
Giele, J. Z., 63
Gilligan, C., 452, 455–456
Ginsburg, H. J., 236–237, *426*
Gjerde, P., 344

Glass, L., 89
Gleicher, N., 85
Gleitman, L. R., 298
Glick, P., 344
Glick, P. C., 344, 482
Glueck, E., 524
Glueck, S., 524
Goldberg, S., 89, 394
Goldberg, W. A., *413,* 481
Golden, M., 207
Goldman-Rakic, P. S., 125
Goldsmith, H. H., 412
Good, T. L., 497
Goodenough, F. L., *424*
Goodsitt, J. V., 166
Gottfredson, L., 383
Gottfried, A. W., 170
Gottlieb, J., 537
Gottman, J. M., 416, *422*
Gove, F. L., 492
Graham, P., *511*
Gratch, G., 164
Gray, S. W., 213
Greenberg, B. S., 501
Greenberg, J., 292, 295
Greenberg, M., 85
Greenberg, M. T., 407, 530
Greenhaus, J. H., 384
Griffin, N. J., 524
Grinker, J. A., 138
Gross, L., *500*
Grossmann, K., *413*
Grossmann, K. E., *413*
Grover, J. W., 87
Gruen, G. E., 477
Grusec, J. E., 330, 419
Guerin, D., 326
Guidubaldi, J., 344
Guralnick, M. J., 239
Gzesh, S. M., 236

Haan, N., 461
Haith, M. M., 157
Hakuta, K., 290
Halpern, D. F., *219,* 219, *220*
Halverson, C. F., Jr., 372, 377–378
Hammond, M. A., 89, 107, 117, 210, 400, 473
Hand, M., 458
Hanlon, C., 298
Hanshaw, J. B., 58, 566
Hanson, M. J., 535
Hardy-Brown, K., 307
Harley, J. P., 522
Harper, L. V., 414
Harris, P. L., 438
Harris, R. C., 561
Harter, S., 356, *357,* 357, 359, 364
Hartmann, D. P., *426*
Hartup, W. W., 421, *422, 424,* 470
Haskins, R., 515

Haskins, R., 176, 207, 214, 485, 494
Hawkins, J. A., 416
Hawton, K., 137
Hay, D. F., 414
Hayes, C. D., 70
Haynes, H., *93*
Heber, F. R., 217
Hechtman, L., 522
Hegvik, R. L., 325
Held, R., *93*
Helmreich, R. L., 381, 383
Henderson, C. R., Jr., 488
Henley, E. D., 60
Henneborn, W. J., 84
Hennig, M., 385
Hepler, N., 518
Hess, E. H., 9
Hess, R. D., 221
Hetherington, E. M., 327, 344, 484, 489, 525
Higgens-Trenk, A., 371
Higgins, A., 447, 461
Higgins, A. T., 174
Higgins, E. T., 436
Higgins, J. E., 401
Hill, J. P., 406
Hinde, R. A., 415, 481
Hines, M., 49, 50
Hirsh-Pasek, K., 298, 300
Hittelman, J., 89
Hobbs, N., *511*
Hock, E., 488
Hofferth, S. L., 136, 482, *483*
Hoff-Ginsberg, E., 300
Hoffman, L., 493
Hoffman, L. W., 383, 384, 488
Hoffman, M. L., 437, *438*
Hogan, A. E., 549, 550
Hogarty, P. S., 198
Hollenbeck, A. R., 81
Holloway, S. D., 221
Holmes, L. B., 60
Honzik, M. P., 26, 197, 198
Hooper, F. H., 267
Horn, J. M., 204
Hornsby, J. R., 243–244, *244*
Horowitz, F. D., 7, *8,* 10, 69, 88, 566
Howard, J., 534
Howes, C., 415
Hoyle, S. G., 416
Hubbard, F. O. A., 101
Hubel, D. H., 179
Huie, K. S., 414
Humphreys, L. G., 142
Hunt, E., 263
Hunt, J. McV., *496*
Hunt, J. V., 89, 197
Hunter, F. T., 406, *407*
Huston, A. C., *158,* 372, 374, 380, 501
Huston-Stein, A., 371

Hutt, S. J., *99*
Huttelocher, P. R., 125
Hwang, C., 394
Hyde, J. S., *426*
Hymel, S., 422
Hynd, G. W., 518

Ingram, D., 286, 287
Inhelder, B., 21, 237, 238, 248
Izard, C. E., 160

Jacklin, C. N., *219,* 372, 381, *426, 427*
Jackson, E., 182
Jackson, N. E., 520
Jacobson, J. L., 60, 299
Jacobson, S. W., 59
Jaeger, E., 493
James, W., 154–155
Janos, P. M., 520
Jardim, A., 385
Jaskir, J., *413*
Jensen, A. R., 206, 217
Jensen, K., *93*
Johnson, C., 138
Johnson, E. S., *219*
Johnston, J. M., 475
Johnston, J. R., 292
Johnston, L., *279*
Jones, K. L., 61
Jung, C. G., 334

Kaczala, C. M., 221
Kagan, J., 9, 26, 174, *175,* 176, 179, 404, *426,* 503–504
Kallen, D. J., 136
Kamii, C. K., 266
Kamin, L. J., 204
Kantor, L., 263
Kaplan, N., 411, 412
Kaye, K., 98, 103
Kearsley, R., 404
Keating, D. P., 252, 255, 263
Keeney, T. J., 259
Kegan, R., 552
Kellam, S. G., 482, 484
Kelly, J. B., 344, 345, 525
Kelso, J., 523
Kempe, H., 78, 401
Kempe, R. S., 78, 401
Kennedy, W. A., 206, *207,* 485
Kennell, J. H., 78, 394, 395
Kessen, W., 163
Kessner, D. M., 63, 66, *66,* 67, 71
Kidd, K. K., 41, 53, 54, 206, 217, 324, 514
King, R. A., 418
Klaus, H. M., 394, 395
Klaus, R. A., 78, 213
Klebanoff, M. A., 60
Klein, R. E., 149
Klinnert, M. D., 160, 403
Kliot, D., 87

Koewler, J. H., III, 235
Kogan, N., 177
Kohlberg, L., 376, 446, 447, *448,* 449, 450,
    451, 451, 452, 453, 456, 458, 459, 460,
    461, 462, 563
Kohn, M. L., 488
Kolbe, L., 137
Kopp, C. B., 50, 52, 53, 58, 60, 89, 147,
    198
Korn, S. J., 325, 326
Korner, A. F., 100
Koslowski, B., *398*
Kremenitzer, J. P., *93*
Krile, D., 457
Krowitz, A., 161
Kuczaj, S. A., II, 288, 292, 295, 305, 306
Kuhl, P. K., 166, 170
Kuhn, D., 379
Kunkel, M. A., 56
Kurdek, L. A., 457
Kusche, C., 530

Lachman, M. E., 106
Laeding, L., *123*
La Freniere, P., 373, *373*
La Gaipa, J., 442, *444*
Lakin, M., 68
Lamb, M. E., 160, 394, 402–404, 408, 411
Lamke, L. K., 383
Landesman, S., 536
Landry, S. H., 526
Langer, A., 161
Lapidus, D. R., 176
Laprade, K., 522
Larson, R., 417
Lave, C., 266
La Voie, J. C., *365,* 365, *366*
Lawson, A. E., 266
Lawton, J. T., 267
Lazar, I., 213
Leadbeater, B. J., 557
Leaf, D. A., 65
Leboyer, F., 85–87
Lefkowitz, M. M., 60
Leibel, R. L., 140
Leiderman, P. H., 85
Leitch, C. J., 407
Lenard, H. G., *99*
Lenneberg, E. H., 305
Leonard, L. B., 297
Lepper, M. R., 17
Lerner, J. V., 488
Lerner, R. M., 10, 12, 117, 142
Lester, B. M., 100
Leveno, K. J., 86
Levin, H., 309, 329
Levine, J. A., *426*
Lewin, R., 62
Lewis, M., 248, 354, *355,* 356, 357, *413*
Liber, L. S., 302
Liberty, C., 260

Lickona, T., *448*
Lindzey, G., 217
Linn, M. C., *219*
Linn, S., 159
Lipsitt, L. P., 96, *168*
List, J. A., 263
Livesley, W. J., 439, 440
Loehlin, J. C., 204, 210, 211
Londerville, S., *413*
Long, F., 494, 495, *496*
Longeway, K. P., 405
Longo, D. C., 534
Lonky, E., 17
Lunneborg, C., 263
Lutkenhaus, R., *413*
Lytton, H., 204

McBride, S. L., 488
McCabe, A. E., 241
McCall, R. B., 198, 211, 560
McCartney, K., 7, 350
Maccoby, E. E., 6, 16, 67, *219,* 329, 372,
    426, 427, 471, 478, *479,* 479, 480
McCord, J., 524
McCord, W., 524
McDevitt, S. C., 325
Macfarlane, A., 26, 78, 84–86
McGhee, P. E., 380
McKinney, J., 176
McKinney, J. D., 494
McKinney, K. L., 143
McLaughlin, B., 290, 291
Maclean, M., 311
McNeill, D., 303
MacPhee, D., 545
Magenis, R. E., 52
Magnusson, D., 143
Magzamen, S., 551
Main, M., *398,* 409, *410,* 411, 412, *413,* 493
Malina, R. M., 132, *145,* 148
Mannle, S., 296
Marano, H., 102
Maratsos, M., *286,* 286, 288, 303
Marcia, J. E., 361, *362,* 365, 382, 557
Marcus, D. E., 370, *370*
Marcus, G. B., 211
Marcus, R. F., 416
Martin, C. L., 372, 377–378
Martin, J. A., 478, *479,* 479, 480
Martorano, S. C., 247, 250, *251,* 252, 255
Mason, R., 401
Massad, C. M., 383
Masters, J. C., *422*
Matas, L., *413*
Mather, P. L., 308
Matthews, W. S., 70, 427
Mayer, J., 138
Meade, A. C., *219*
Meadow, K. P., 302
Mehl, L. E., 85
Meltzoff, A. N., 98, 157, 170, 233

Merrill, M. A., 189
Merriman, W. E., 263
Mervis, C. A., 294
Mervis, C. B., 294
Meyer, K. K., 561
Meyer-Bahlberg, H. F. L., 380
Mikkelsen, M., 52
Miller, G. A., 257
Miller, J., 419
Miller, L. B., 492
Miller, P. A., 457
Miller, S. M., *426*
Minton, C., *426*
Mischel, W., 374
Molitor, N., 492, 493
Money, J., 49, 50, 380
Monkus, E., 66
Montemayor, R., 359, 360, *360*, 361
Montoye, H. J., *123*
Montpetit, R. R., *123*
Moore, A. K., 98
Moore, E. G. J., 217, 218
Moore, K. A., 136
Moore, K. L., *51*
Moore, M. J., 157
Moore, M. K., 233
Moore, N., 176
Moore, R., 524
Moore, T. E., 524
Moores, D. F., 530
Morgan, N., *500*
Morris, N., 85
Morrison, A. M., 385, *385*
Morrison, D. M., 136
Morrongiello, B. A., 167
Morrow-Tlucak, M., 62
Morse, P. A., *93*, 166
Mosher, F., 243–244, *244*
Moshman, D., 250
Moss, H. A., 26
Mueller, W., 140
Muenchow, S., 537
Muir, J. E., 260
Mundy, P. C., 549, 550
Munro, G., 363
Munroe, R. H., 370
Munroe, R. L., 370
Murray, A. D., 81
Murray, J. P., 380, 501, 503
Muzio, J. N., 100

Nash, A., 414
Nash, S. C., 379
Naus, M. J., 260
Nechlin, H., 299
Neimark, E. D., 250, 252
Nelson, K., 282, 283, 292, 294, 298, 300,
    301, 308, *309*
Nelson, N. M., 87
Nelson, S. A., 446
Nelson, V. L., *200*

Netley, C., 53
Nevill, D. D., 117
Newberger, C. M., 401
Nichols, P. L., 60, 206, *207*, 485
Nichols, R. C., 204
Nisan, M., 450, 451
Nordquist, G., 326
Norton, A. J., 344, 482
Nottelmann, E. D., 127, 557
Nowakowski, R. S., 125

O'Brien, M., 372
Obrzut, J. E., 518
O'Connell, B., 279, 280, 282, 284, 304, *309*
O'Connor, S., 395, *396*
Oden, M., 520
Oden, S. L., 422
O'Donnell, M., 381
Oliver, C. M., 87
Oliver, G. M., 87
Oller, D. K., 280
Olsho, L. W., 166
Olson, D. H., 477, *478*
Olson, S. L., 299
Olthof, T., 438
O'Malley, P. M., 364
Opper, S., 236–237
Ornstein, P. A., 259, 260
Overton, W. F., 250, 252, 348, 370, *370*
Owen, M. T., 493
Owsley, C. J., 167, 170

Palkovitz, R., 85
Parasuraman, S., 384
Parekh, A., 89
Park, R. K., 142
Parke, R. D., 398, 399
Parmelee, A. H., Jr., 49, 50, *99*, 136
Parsons, J. E., 221, 436
Passman, R. H., 405
Pastor, D. L., *413*
Patterson, G. R., 18, 329, 424, 426, 472,
    475, 479
Pauker, J. D., 524
Paul-Brown, D., 239
Pedersen, J., 414
Pederson, D. R., 90
Pederson, F. A., 10
Pennington, B. F., 68
Perron, L. M., 524
Perry, D. G., 374
Peters, D. L., 494, 495, *496*
Petersen, A. C., *129*, 142, *143, 219*, 524
Peterson, G. H., 85
Phillips, D. A., 367
Phillips, J. R., 300
Phillips, W., *175*
Philp, R., 59
Piaget, J., 21–22, 95, 164, 170, 187, 188,
    226–256, 266–267, 333, 354, 434, 438,
    446, 447, 552, 563

Pick, H. L., Jr., 173
Pines, M., 305
Pipp, S. L., 255
Pitkin, R. M., 64
Pleck, J. H., 386
Pless, I. B., 137
Plomin, R., 14, 104, 204, 210, 307, 322,
    323, *323*, 324, 325, 325
Pober, B. R., 60
Pollitt, E., 140
Porter, R. H., *93*, 169
Powell, B., 379
Powell, J. S., 262
Power, C., 447, 461
Power, T. G., 475
Prader, A., 149
Prechtl, H. F. R., 98, *99*
Prescott, S., 417
Provence, S., 510
Puig-Antich, J., 525
Pulkkinen, L., 480
Pyle, R., 138

Quay, H. C., *158*, 523, 537

Rabinovitch, M. S., 166
Radke-Yarrow, M., 100, 149, 411, 416, 418
Raffaelli, M., 487
Ramey, C. T., 69, *69*, 88, 210, 214, *216*,
    494, 516, 545, 566
Rank, O., 86
Rappoport, L., 337
Razel, M., 148
Read, M. S., 485
Reed, E. W., 52
Reese, H. W., *168*, 348
Reimer, J., 450, 451, 456, 461
Reisman, J. E., 169
Reisman, J. M., 416
Renshaw, P. D., 422
Resnick, L. B., 194
Rest, J. R., 450, 452, 458, 460
Revelle, G. L., 262
Rhoads, G. G., 60
Rholes, W. S., 439
Ricciuti, H. N., 148
Richards, D. D., 188
Richards, M. H., 487
Riegel, K. F., 544
Riesser-Danner, L. A., 412
Roberge, J. J., 247
Roberts, C. W., 379
Robertson, E. G., 67
Robinson, H. B., 519–521
Robinson, N. M., *88*, 520
Roche, A. F., 138
Rodin, J., 139
Roffwarg, H. P., 100
Rogers, J. L., 211
Rogoff, B., 266
Rollins, B. C., 106, 558

Rosenberg, M., 364, *365*, 367
Rosenthal, A., 195
Rosenthal, D., 529
Rosett, H. L., 61
Rosman, B. L., *175*
Rosner, B. S., 93
Ross, G., 408
Rosso, P., 64
Rothbart, M. K., 325
Rovee-Collier, C., 95
Rovet, J., 53
Rovine, M., 106, 412, 492, 493
Rowe, I., 557
Rubin, K. H., 234, 235
Ruble, D. N., 359, 367, 373, 376, *377*, 377,
    439
Ruble, T. L., 371
Rule, B. G., 446
Rumbaugh, D. M., 277
Ruopp, R., *496*
Russell, G., 402
Rutter, D. R., 295
Rutter, M., 106, 325, *497*, 497, *511*, 524,
    525, 527, 528, *533*, 561, *562*, 564
Ryan, E. B., 311

Saario, Terry, 381
Sack, W. H., 401
Saigal, S., 87
Salapatek, P., 157
Salk, L., *93*, 93
Sameroff, A. J., 10, 67, 95, 529, 531
Sander, L. W., 61
Sanders, B., 220
Sandieson, R., 268
Sarigiani, P., 524
Sattler, J. M., 191, 196
Savage-Rumbaugh, S., 277
Scafidi, F. A., 91
Scanlon, D. M., 311, 518
Scanlon, J. W., 395
Scanlon, L. J., 277
Scarr, S., 7, 41, 53, 54, 204–206, 217, 324,
    350, 514
Scarr-Salapatek, S., 560
Schachter, F. F., 299
Schaefli, A., 460
Schank, R. C., 436
Schlesinger, H. S., 302
Schneiderman, M., 298
Schommer, M., 295
Schooler, C., 488
Schroeder, C. S., 536
Schroeder, S. R., 536
Schulz, H. R., *99*
Schwartz, G. M., 160
Schwartz, J., 494
Schwartz, P., 488
Scollon, R., 281, 282
Scott, K. G., 66
Sears, P. S., 520

Sears, R. R., 329
Segal, N. L., 204
Segalowitz, N. S., 290
Seifer, R., 529
Selman, R. L., 435, 442, *445*, 457
Sepkoski, C., 81
Shantz, C. U., 440, 462
Shantz, D. W., 421, 422
Sharp, D., 266
Shatz, M., 239
Sheldon, W. H., 117
Shepard, K., 371
Sherman, D., 401
Sherrod, K. B., 400
Shields, J., 204
Shigetomi, C. C., *426*
Shimmin, H. S., 370
Shiono, P. H., 60
Shonkoff, J. P., 127
Shore, C., 279, 280, 282, 284, 304, *309*
Shorr, S. I., 416
Short, E. J., 214
Siebert, J. M., 549, 550
Siegal, M., 374
Siegel, J. M., 407
Siegel, L. J., 524
Siegler, R. S., 188, 257, 261, 262
Sigafoos, A. D., 95
Sigman, M., 304
Sigman, M. D., 49, 264
Signorielli, N., 499, *500*
Siladi, D., 187, 188
Silberstein, L. R., 139
Silverberg, S., 417
Silverstein, L., 87
Simmons, R. G., 143, 555
Simon, T., 188, 203
Simpson, A. E., 564
Sirignano, S. W., 106
Skeels, H. M., 204, 206
Skinner, B. F., 14, 298
Skodak, M., 204, 206
Slaby, R. G., 369, 376
Slade, A., *413*
Slobin, D. I., 286, 303–305
Smith, A. N., *496*
Smith, D. W., 40, *46*, 47, 146
Smith, R., 486, 501
Snavey, J. R., 450, 451, 456
Snow, C. E., 299
Snow, M. E., 427
Snyder, L., 282, 304
Snyder, S. S., 404
Soares, M. P., 220
Solnit, A. J., 510
Solomon, J., 409, *410*
Sonnenschein, S., 296
Sontag, L. W., *200*
Sosa, R., 84
Sostek, A. M., 395
Spanier, G. B., 106

Spelke, E. S., 154, 167, 170
Spence, C. M., *496*
Spence, J. T., 381, 383
Spence, M. J., 95, 167
Spieker, S. J., 409
Spitz, H. H., 516
Spuhler, J. N., 217
Sroufe, L. A., 321, 346, *347*, 400, 409, *410*, 411, 412, *413*, 561, *562*, 562, 563
Starfield, B., 137
Stark, E., 136
Stark, R. E., 287
Staton, R. D., 518
Stattin, H., 143
Staub, E., 419
Stayton, D. J., 101
Steelman, L. C., 211, 379
Stein, Z., 62
Steinberg, L. D., 406, 417, 557
Steiner, J. E., 168, *168*
Stenchever, M. A., 40, *46*, 77, 78, 146
Stern, D. N., 300
Sternberg, R. J., 188, 201, 202, 203, 218, 221, 262, 434, 519, 520
Steuer, F. B., 501
Stevenson, H. W., 217
Stevenson-Hinde, J., 481, 564
Stewart, M. A., 523
Stewart, R. B., 59
Stone, J., 52
Strage, A. A., 299
Strayer, F. F., 373, *373*, 425
Streissguth, A. P., 61, *61*
Striegel-Moore, R. H., 139
Strobino, D. M., 67
Suben, J. G., 218
Sugar, J., 289
Surber, C. F., 236
Susman, E. J., 557

Taitz, L. S., 102
Tanner, J. M., 40, 46, 70, 89, *120*, *121*, 122, 126, 128, 129, *130*, *131*, 140, *141*, 142, *145*, 146, 149, 557
Taylor, B., *129*
Taylor, P. M., 394
Tees, R. C., 280
Teller, D. Y., *93*, 156
Templin, M. C., 283
Terman, L., 189, 520
Terwogt, M. M., 438
Tew, M., 82, 83
Thelen, E., 132
Thoma, S. J., 460
Thomas, A., 14, 104–106, 323–324, 326, 327, 412
Thompson, R. A., 404, 411
Thompson, S. K., 369
Thorne, B., 416
Thorpe, L. A., 167

Tieger, T., 427
Tinsley, B. R., 398, 399
Tittle, C. K., 381
Tizard, J., 524
Tobin-Richards, M. H., *143,* 143
Tomasello, M., 296
Tomlinson-Keasey, C., 245–246, *246,* 247
Tower, A., 380
Traupmann, K., 510
Travers, J., *496*
Trehub, S. E., 166, 167
Trieman, R., 298
Trites, R. L., 522
Troll, L., *158*
Troutman, B. R., 489
Tschann, J. M., 344
Turiel, E., 460
Turner, R. J., 482, 484
Turnure, J. E., 174

Ullian, D. Z., 376
Unger, D. G., 489
Ungerer, J. A., 304
Uzgiris, I. C., 255

Valsiner, J., 179
Vandell, D. L., 537
Vandenberg, B., 171, 234, 235
Van Doorninck, W. J., 208
Van Dusen, J. E., 136
Van Ijzendoorn, 101
Van Velsor, E., 385, *385*
Vaughn, B. E., 411, 492, 493
Vellutino, F. R., 311, 518
Vinter, A., 98
Volterra, V., 280
Von Harnack, G. A., 149
Vygotsky, L. S., 21, 292, 296

Waber, D. P., 219
Wachs, T. D., 477
Waddington, C. H., 560
Walk, R. D., 161, *162*
Walker, L. J., 452, 456, 462
Wallerstein, J. S., 344, 345, 525
Walters, R. H., 329
Wandersman, L. P., 489
Wanner, E., 298
Warren, M. P., 144, *144*
Warren-Leubecker, A., 518
Waterman, A. S., 362, *363*
Waters, E., *410,* 411, 493
Watson, J. D., 41
Waxman, S., 240

Wechsler, D., 189
Weikart, D. P., 213, 266, 267, 492
Weinberg, R. A., 204–206
Weinraub, M., 493
Weinstein, R. S., 497
Weir, R., 296
Weisel, T., 179
Weiskopf, S., 163
Weiss, G., 522
Weisz, J. R., 247
Wellman, H. M., 240
Wenner, W. H., *99*
Werker, J. F., 280, 300
Werler, M. M., 60
Werner, E. E., 7, 26, 486, 566, 568
Werner, H., 21
Werry, J. S., 523
Weymouth, F. W., *156*
Whitaker, H. A., 289
White, B. L., *93*
White, K. R., 535
White, R. P., 385, *385*
White, S., 552
Whitmore, K., 524
Wiegerink, R., 535
Willerman, L., 206
Williams, J. E., 371
Williams, R. L., 195
Williams, T. M., 501, *502*
Willig, A., 291
Willows, D. M., 311
Wilson, D. M., 221
Wilson, J. G., 59
Wilson, R. S., 204
Winick, M., 64, 65, 561
Witkin, H. A., 176
Wittig, B. A., 409
Woody, E. Z., 139

Yasuna, A., 380
Yeates, K. O., 210
Yeates, K. W., 214
Youniss, J., 406, *407*

Zahn-Waxler, C., 100, 416, 418, 525
Zajonc, R. B., 211, *212*
Zarbatany, L., 160, 403
Zaslow, M. J., 70
Zax, M., 529
Zelazo, P., 404
Zeskind, P. S., 69, *69,* 100, 566
Zigler, E., 195, 537
Zola, I. K., 524
Zucker, K. J., 160

Subject Index

Note: Italicized page numbers indicate material in tables and figures.

Abortion, 136
  prenatal testing and, 56–57
Accidents, 137
Accommodation, 22, 227–228
Achievement tests, 192–193
Activity level, temperament and, 324
Acuity
  auditory, 166
  defined, 156
  visual, 156–157
Adaptive behavior, 513
Adolescence. *See also* Puberty
  androgyny in, 382–383
  changes in body fat during, 124
  commitment in, 361–363
  conduct disorders in, 522, 523–524, 538
  depression and anxiety in, 524–525, 555
  description of others in, 439–440
  developmental stages of, 554–559
  eating disorders in, 139–140
  effect of rate of physical change on personality in, 142–145
  empathy in, 437–438, 457
  family communication patterns in, 477, 478
  formal operational thought in, 230, 247–252
  friendship in, 406–407, 417–423, 442–445
  growth spurt in, 121
  health or illness in, 136–137
  hormone changes between birth and, 126–127
  hormones in, 127–128
  identity in, 361–363, 366–367
  intimacy in, 406–407, 417, 420–421
  moral development in, 447, 449–456
  moral judgment in, 459–460
  muscle changes in, 122–124
  parent-child relationships at, 406–407
  peer relationships in, 406–407, 417–423
  physical development in, 121, 142–145, 554–559
  pregnancy in, 66–67, 136
  prenatal hormones and, 50
  psychosexual stages of, 337, 339

  psychosocial stages of, 340, 343
  schizophrenia in, 528–530
  self-definition in, 359–360
  self-esteem in, 364, 366–367
  sexual development in, 128–131, 337, 339
  sexuality in, 135–136
  shape of body in, 121
Adoption
  IQ studies and, 204–206, 217–218
  language development and, 306–308
Adrenal gland, 126–128
Age
  of child, and family functioning, 482
  language development and, 290–291
  mental versus chronological, 189, 549–550
  moral reasoning and, 450
  of mother at pregnancy, 63–67
  perceptual development and, 170–174
Aggression, 326, 331, 423–425
  as conduct disorder, 522, 523–524, 538
  day care and, 494
  hyperactivity and, 521–523
  individual differences in, 563–564
  violence on television and, 500–503
Alcohol, prenatal development and, 61–62
Altruism, 416, 418–419, 452–455
Amniocentesis, 57, 63
Analgesics, 81
Anal stage, 336–337, 337
Androgen, 379–380
Androgyny, 381–383
  occupational behavior and, 385–386
  occupational choice and, 383–385
Anesthesia, 81
Anorexia nervosa, 138, 139–140
Anoxia, 88
Antisocial behavior, 522, 523–524, 538
Anxiety, 335–336, 522, 524–525
  pregnancy and, 67–68
Apgar score, 87–88
Assimilation, 22, 227
Attachment
  of blind infants to mothers, 531
  of child to parent, 400, 402–408, 471, 531
  day care and, 404, 412, 492–493

Attachment (*Continued*)
defined, 392
individual differences in quality of, 408–414, 527
of parent to child, 394–402
social development and, 392–414
Attachment behavior
depression and, 411
described, 393
in infancy, 548–549
meshing of, 396–398
in preschool period, 404, 412, 492–493, 551
Attention-deficit hyperactivity disorder, 326, 521–523
Atypical development, 510–541
emotionally, 521–530
frequency of problems of, 511–512
impact of, on family, 533–534
interventions and treatments for, 534–538
mentally, 512–521
physically, 530–532
sex differences in, 532–533
Auditory development
acts of infants and children in, 166–167
acuity in, 166
deafness, 302, 530, 532, 534–538
detecting locations in, 166
discriminating individual voices in, 167
Australia, 402, 417
Authoritarian parental style, 366, 473–474, 479–480, 484, 485
Authoritative parental style, 366, 418, 422–423, 480, 484
Authority
in conventional morality, 449
in preconventional morality, 447–449
Autism, 54, 522, 526–528
Autonomous morality, 446
Autonomy, 341–342
early education and, 266
Autosomes, 42

Babbling, 279–280
Babinsky reflex, 91, *92*, 169
Ballet dancers, 144–145
Basic trust, 21, 365
Bayley Scales of Infant Development, 190–192, 198
Behavior
adaptive, 513
antisocial, 522, 523–524, 538
attachment, 393, 396–398, 548–549, 551
effect of television violence on, 500–503
expectations and, 117
in occupation, 385–386
physical development and, 132–136
prosocial, 416, 418–419, 452–455
social cognition and, 452–461

Behaviorism, personality development and, 328–334
Behavior problems, 521–530
anxiety, 67–68, 335–336, 522, 524–525
attention-deficit hyperactivity disorder, 326, 521–523
conduct disorders, 522, 523–524, 538
depression, 84, 401, 411, 522, 524–525, 555
interventions and treatments for, 534–538
role of short-term stress in, 525–526, 527
severe emotional disturbances, 522, 526–530
temperament and, 324, 326
Behavior therapy, 329
Bilingualism, 288, 290–291
Biological approach to personality development, 322–327
basic propositions in, 322–324
evidence to support, 324–327
strengths, weaknesses, and implications of, 327
Biological theories of development, 12–14, 23, *24*
maturation and, 13
personality development, 322–327
Birth, 76–91. *See also* Infants; Newborn; Prenatal development
cesarean-section delivery in, 85–86
conditions during, 80–85
first greeting in, 78–80
gentle methods of, 86–87
hormone changes between adolescence and, 126–127
normal process of, 76–78
problems at, 86–91
Birth centers, 82–84
Birth order, 481–482
IQ and, 211, *212*
Bisexuality, 50
Blacks, IQ tests and, 195, 217–218
Blastocyst, 46
Blindness, 530–531
infant, *171*, 172–173, 400, 401, 531
intervention for, 530, 534–538
Body type, 117, 143
Bones, changes in, 122
Books, sex-role stereotyping in, 380–381
Brain
fetal, 49
malnutrition and development of, 148
stages of development of, 124–125
thyroid hormone and, 126
Brain damage
hyperactivity and, 522
learning disability and, 518
mental retardation and, 514
Breast-feeding, 102–103, 395, 546–547
Bulimia, 138, 139

Canada, 501, *502*
Caring, ethic of, 455–456
Categorical self, 357–361
Cephalocaudal pattern of development, 147
Cerebral palsy, 532
Cesarean-section delivery, 85–86
Child abuse, 9, *396*
  as failure of attachment, 400–401
Child development
  basic theories of, 12–24
  changes in body fat in, 124
  changes in body shape in, 121
  changes in bones in, 122
  determinants of growth in, 146–149
  focus in study of, 6
  health or illness in, 136–137
  height and weight changes in, 119–121
  hormone changes in, 125–127
  individual differences in, 137–146
  major influences on, 6–11
  motor development in, 132–135
  muscle changes in, 122–124
  nature of developmental change and, 11–12
  nervous system changes in, 124–125
  perception and, 174–178
  prenatal hormones and, 50, 126, 379–380
  research on, 25–30
Childhood-onset pervasive development disorders, 526, 528
Chorionic villus sampling, 57
Chromosomes, 40
  anomalies in, 52–54, 514–515
  mental retardation and, 514–516
Classical conditioning, 15–16
  of newborn infant, 95
Classification skills
  in concrete operations stage, 243–246
  in development of word meaning, 292–294
  in preoperational stage, 238–241
Class inclusion
  in concrete operations stage, 243–244, 245–246
  in preoperational stage, 238–241
Clique, 417
Clustering strategies, 260
Cognitive development, 186–273, 559–560.
  See also IQ (intelligence quotient)
  in adolescence, 554–559
  from birth to 18 months, 545–549
  criticisms of Piaget's theory, 253–256
  day care and, 214–217, 491–492
  in the elementary-school years, 552–554
  enrichment in family and, 477
  individual differences in, 563–568
  influence of environment on, 206–217
  influence of heredity on, 203–206
  information-processing approach, 256–264
  IQ tests and, 188–201, 203, 221–222

language development and, 306–308
nature of developmental change and, 562–563
as part of developmental system, 545
Piaget's basic ideas concerning, 21–22, *23*, 226–253, 266–268
in the preschool years, 549–552
racial differences in, 195, 217–218
rate of physical development and, 140–142
sex differences in, 218–221
sex-role development and, 376–377
social cognition versus, 435, 461–462
Sternberg's triarchic theory of intelligence and, 201–203
synthesis of approaches to, 264–268
three views of intelligence and, 186–188
timing and, 560–562
Cognitive processing, language development and, 304–305
Cohort, 26
Colic, 100
College students
  identity achievement by, 362–363, 366–367
  moral education of, 460
Color constancy, 161, 163
Commitment, in adolescence, 361–363
Communication
  within the family, 476–477
  using language in, 295–296
Competence, 193, 343
Competition, 425, 457–458
Componential intelligence, 201–203, 218
Computer, human mind as, 256–264
Conception, 38–45
  genetics of, 40–45
  process of, 38–40
Conceptual tempo, 174–176, 177, 178
Concrete operations, 230, 242–247, 556
  current work on, 245–247
  overview of child in, 247
  Piaget's view of, 242–245
Conditioned stimulus, 15–16
Conduct disorders, 522, 523–524, 538
Conflict, adolescent, 406
Confluence model, 211
Conscience, 335
Conservation
  in concrete operations stage, 243, 245–246
  gender constancy and, 370, *370*
  in preoperational stage, 237–238, 240
Constraint seeking, 244
Contextual intelligence, 201–203, 218, 434
Control, methods of, in family, 471–476
Control group, 28
Conventional morality, *448*, 449, 450
Cooing, 279
Cooperation, 457–458
Correlation, 27–28

Cortex, 124–125
Crime, 524
Critical period, 9, 50, *51*
Crossing over, 41
Cross-sectional study, 26, 29
Cross-sex children, 379–381
Crowd, 420
Crying, 100–102
Cumulative deficit, 207
Cystic fibrosis, *55*, 56, 532
Cytomegalovirus (CMV), 58

Day care, *10*, 69, 491–495, *496*
    attachment behavior and, 404, 412, 492–493
    cognitive development and, 214–217, 491–492
    quality of care in, 494–495
    relationships with peers and, 414–416, 493–494
Deafness, 302, *532*
    interventions for, 530, 534–538
Deductive logic
    in concrete operations stage, 245
    in formal operations stage, 249–250
Defense mechanisms, 335–336, 347–348
Delinquent behaviors, 522, 523–524, 538
Dendrites, 49
Deoxyribonucleic acid (DNA), 41
Dependent variable, 28
Depression, 522
    in adolescence, 524–525, 555
    attachment behavior and, 411
    of parent, and child abuse, 401
    postpartum, 84
    social support and, 489
Depth perception, 161–162
Description, of other people, 438–441
Diet, 561
    eating disorders and, 137–140
    hyperactivity and, 522
    malnutrition and, 13, 62, 148–149
    physical development and, 148–149
    during pregnancy, 62, 64–65
Diethylstilbestrol (DES), 59–60
Difficult children, 104–105, 279
    temperament and, 324, 326
    vulnerability and, 527
Dilation, 76
Disability. *See also* Atypical development
    learning, 516–519, 534–538
    physical, 532
Discrimination, in visual perception, 160
Diseases
    breast-feeding and, 102
    genetic basis of, 43, 52–54
    of mother, and prenatal development, 9, 58–59
    placenta and, 47
Dishabituation, 157, 158

Divorce, 344–345
    effect on attachment behavior, 411
    influence on family functioning, 482–484
    social support and, 489
    temperament of child and, 327
Dolls, 234–235
Dominance, 425
Dominance hierarchy, 425
Dominant gene, 42
Doubt, 341–342
Down's syndrome, 52, *53*, 63, 514, 535
Drugs
    during childbirth, 81–82
    hyperactivity and, 523
    impact of, on fetus, 59–62
DSM-III-R (*Diagnostic and Statistical Manual of Mental Disorders*), 521, 522
Dyslexia, 517

Early words, in language development, 281–284
Easy child, 104
    vulnerability and, 527
Eating, 102–103
Eating disorders, 137, 138–140
Ectomorphic body type, 117
Education. *See also* Schooling
    experimental, 266–267
    moral, 460–461
    for parents of atypical child, 535
Effacement, 76
Ego, 335
Egocentrism, 434, 435
    language development and, 296
    in preoperational stage, 235–237, 239–240
    sociodramatic play and, 235
Eisenberg, Nancy, model of prosocial reasoning, 452–455
Elementary-school children
    attachment to parents, 406
    developmental stages of, 552–554
    peer relationships of, 416–417, 421–423
    self-definition by, 359, *360*
    self-esteem of, 364
    sex-role behavior of, 372–378
    sex-role stereotyping by, 371–372, 378, 380–381
Embedded Figures Test, 176, *177*
Embryo, development of, 46–48
Emotion, in family, 471
Empathy, 456–457
    development of, 437–438, *439*
Empiricism, 178, 179
Employment. *See also* Occupation
    of father, 488
    IQ test scores and, 196–198
    of mother, 486–488
Endocrine glands, 125
Endomorphic body type, 117

Environment
  changes in vulnerability and, 567–568
  giftedness and, 520–521
  heredity versus, 7–11
  IQ and, 206–217
  language development and, 297–301, 308
  mental retardation and, 515–516
  personality development and, 349–350
  prenatal development and, 55–63
  temperament and, 325–327
Epiphyses, 122
Equilibration, 228
Equilibrium, 22
Erikson, Erik, 339–343
  basic ideas of, 339–341
  impact of divorce and, 344
  psychosocial stages of development, 20–21, 339–343
  strengths and weaknesses of theories of, 346–348
Erogenous zone, 20, 336
Estradiol, 127, 128
Estrogen, 127, 128
Ethics, 450
Executive processes, 262
Exercise
  by children and adolescents, 137
  obesity and, 138–139
  during pregnancy, 65
Existential self, 354–357
Expectations
  aggression and, 424–425
  child behavior and, 117
  IQ test scores and, 195
  level of, in family, 473
  of parents, and mathematical achievement, 221
  reinforcement and, 330
Experience
  growth as determinant of, 117
  learning theory and, 14–19, 23
Experiential intelligence, 201–203
Experiment, 28–29
Experimental education, 266, 267
Experimental group, 28
Expertise, formal operations and, 252, 253–254
Expressive language, 280
Expressive style, 283–284, 308–309

Facial expression, infants and, 157–158, 233
Fallopian tube, 38
Families (Patterson), 18
Family, 471–490. *See also* Fathers; Mothers; Parents
  conduct disorders and, 524
  division of labor in, 386
  emotional tone of, 471
  giftedness and, 520–521

impact of atypical child on, 533–534
influence of institutions outside, 491–503
influences on functioning of, 481–490
IQ and, 208–213
mental retardation and, 515–516
occupational choice and, 384–385
schizophrenia in, 528–530
stepparent, 483–484
Fat, changes in body, 124
Fathers. *See also* Mothers; Parents
  attachment of child to, 407–408
  attachment to infant, 398–402
  employment of, 488
  presence in delivery room, 84–85
Fear, 522, 524–525
  of strangers, 404
Federal Education for All Handicapped Children Act (Public Law, 94-142), 535–537
Feedback, in language development, 300–301
Fetal alcohol syndrome (FAS), 61–62
Fetus. *See also* Birth
  abortion of, 56–57, 136
  alcohol and, 61–62
  amniocentesis, 57, 63
  development of, 48–49
  diet of mother and, 62, 64–65
  drugs and, 59–62
  environment and, 52–63
  prenatal hormones and, 49–50, 126, 379–380
Field dependence, 176–177, 178
Field independence, 176–177, 178
Fontanels, 122
Foreclosure, 361–362, *362, 363*
Formal operations, *230,* 247–252, 556, 557
  current work on, 250–252
  expertise and, 252, 253–254
  Piaget's view of, 247–250
France, 188–189, *205,* 206
Fraternal twins, 43
  temperament and, 324, *325*
Freud, Sigmund, 334–339
  basic ideas of, 334–336
  impact of divorce and, 344
  psychosexual stages of development, 19–20, 336–339, 340
  strengths and weaknesses of theories of, 346–348
Friendship, 425. *See also* Intimacy
  in adolescence, 406–407, 417–423, 442–445
  in childhood, 414
  developing understanding of, 441–445
  elementary school, 416–417, 421–423
  of preschool children, 415–416
  social reasoning and, 457–458
Functional invariants, of Piaget, 227–228

Games, in preschool play, 235
Gender
  atypical development and, 532–533
  differences in infant, 105–106
  eating disorders and, 139–140
  effects of parents' divorce and, 344–345
  ethic of caring and, 455–456
  genetic basis of, 42–43
  hormones in adolescence and, 127–128
  individual differences in development
    and, 564
  IQ and, 218–221
  Oedipus conflict and, 337–339
  perceptual skills and, 177–178
  personality and rate of physical develop-
    ment based on, 142–145
  physical growth and, 145–146
  prenatal development and, 70
  prenatal sexual differentiation, 49–50
  sexual development based on, 129–131
Gender concept, 368, 377–378
  development of, 369–370
Gender constancy, 370, 376–377, *377*
Gender identity, 369
  of cross-sex children, 379–381
Gender schemas, 377–378, 381
Gender stability, 369–370
Generativity, 343
Generosity, 330–331
Genes, 41–42
  differences in prenatal development and,
    70
  genetic errors, 52–57
  sexual differentiation and, 49–50
Genetic counseling, 56–57
Genital herpes, 59
Genital stage, *337*, 339
Genotype, 45
Germ cells, 41
Gestural language, 280–281, *281*
Giftedness, 191, 519–521
  characteristics of gifted children, 520
  definitions and, 519
  families of gifted children, 520–521
Gilligan, C., ethic of caring, 455–456
Gonadotropic hormones, 127, *127*
Grammar. *See* Syntax
Grasp reflex, 91, *92*
Grief, 534
Growth, 13. *See also* Physical development
Guilt, 342

Habituation, 96, 157, 158
Head Start, 213, 492
Health, patterns of, 136–137
Hearing-impaired children, 530, 532
Height and weight changes, 119–121
Helpfulness, 416, 418–419
Heredity
  giftedness and, 520–521
  influence on IQ, 203–206

language development and, 306–307
  mental retardation and, 52–54, 514–516
  physical development and, 147
  temperament and, 323, 324
Heredity versus environment, 7–11
Herpes simplex, 59
Heteronomous morality, 446
Heterosexuality, 50
Holophrases, 284
Home delivery, 82–84
HOME Inventory (Home Observation for
    Measurement of the Environment),
    208–211
Home schooling, 266, 267
Homosexuality, 50
Horizontal decalage, 247
Hormones
  in adolescence, 127–128
  between birth and adolescence, 126–127
  cross-sex preferences and, 379–380
  number of earlier pregnancies and, 67
  in prenatal development, 49–50, 126,
    379–380
Hostility, warmth versus, 471
Huntington's disease, 54, 56
Hyperactivity, 326, 521–523
Hypothalamus gland, 127
Hypothesis scanning, 244

Id, 335
Identical twins, 43
  temperament and, 324, *325*
Identification, 338–339, 347–348
  aggression and, 424
  in sex-role development, 376
  in visual perception, 158–160
Identities
  in concrete operations stage, 243, 245–
    246
  in preoperational stage, 237–238, 240
Identity achievement, 20, 343, *362*, *363*
  in adolescence, 361–363, 366–367
  formal operations stage and, 557
  gender, 369, 379–381
  individual differences in, 365
  origins of, 365–367
Identity crisis, in adolescence, 361–363
Identity diffusion, 361–362, *362*, *363*
Ideological identity, in adolescence, 361–
    363
Illness
  patterns of, 136–137
  physical development and, 149
  pregnancy and, 9, 58–59
Imitation
  of facial expressions, 157–158
  in language development, 297–298,
    304
Imprinting, 9
Impulsivity, 174–176, 177, 178

In a Different Voice: Psychological Theory and Women's Development (Gilligan), 455
Inborn error of metabolism, 514
Independence
    in adolescence, 554–559
    in preschool period, 551–552
Inductive logic
    in concrete operations stage, 244–245
    in formal operations, 249–250
Infants. *See also* Birth; Newborn; Prenatal development
    abused, 9, 400–401
    attachment of parents to, 394–402
    attachment to parents, 400, 402–408, 471, 531, 548–549
    auditory development and, 166–167
    autism and, 54, 522, 526–528
    birth and, 76–91
    blind, *171*, 172–173, 400, 401, 531
    breast-feeding versus bottle-feeding, 102–103, 395, 546–547
    combining information from several senses by, 169–170
    daily life of, 98–103
    day care and, *10*, 69, 214–217, 404, 412, 414–416, 491–495, *496*
    developmental stages of, 545–549
    development of self-concept and, 354–357
    effects on parents, 106–107
    environmental effects on IQ, 214–217
    first sentences of, 284
    first words of, 281–284
    gender differences and, 105–106
    hearing-impaired, 530
    HOME Inventory and, 208–211
    imprinting and, 9
    individual differences among, 103–106
    IQ tests for, 190–192, 198, *199*
    low-birth-weight, 7, 60, 68–69, 88–91, 102, 107, 279
    patterns of physical development of, 147
    peer relationships of, 414–416
    perception of, 174–178
    perceptual learning by, 154
    poverty and, 7
    prelinguistic phase of, 277–281
    preoperational stage and, *230*, 233–242
    psychosexual stages of, 336–337, *337*
    psychosocial stages of, *340*, 341–342
    quality of attachments and, 408–414
    recognition memory in, 263–264
    reflexes and, 91–98
    sensitive period of, 9
    sensorimotor stage of, *230*, 230–233
    smell and, 169
    taste and, 168–169
    touch and, 169
    toys and, 134–135
    visual development and, 155–166
    walking skills, 132–135, *133*

Inferiority, 343
Inflections, 284–285
Information processing, 188, 256–264
    changes in processing strategy, 262–263
    developmental approaches to, 257–262
    individual differences in, 263–264
Initiative, 342
Innateness theories, of language development, 301–304
Insecure attachment, 409–414
    day care and, 492–493
    long-term effects of, 413–414
    stability over time, 410–411
    temperament and, 412
Intellectual power, 186–187
Intelligence. *See* Cognitive development; IQ (intelligence quotient)
Interaction effect, 69
Internal working model of relationships, 408–414, 424–425
Interviews, 25
Intimacy, 456, 559. *See also* Friendship
    in adolescence, 406–407, 417, 420–421
    in elementary-school friendships, 416
Intonation pattern, 280
Intrinsic reinforcement, 17
Invulnerability, 527
    individual differences in, 564–568
IQ (intelligence quotient). *See also* Cognitive development
    adoption and, 204–206, 217–218
    birth order and, 211, *212*
    birth weight and, 7
    calculation of, 189
    day care and, 491–492
    environment and, 206–217
    family chaos and, 27–28
    giftedness and, 191, 519–521
    mental retardation and, 52–54, 61, 512–516, 534–538
    physical development and, 140–142
    punishment and, 210
    social class and, 206–208
    social reasoning and, 462
IQ tests, 188–201, 221–222
    achievement tests versus, 192–193
    blacks and, 195, 217–218
    factors influencing scores, 203
    first, 188–189
    limitations of traditional, 199–201
    memory tasks and, 263, 264
    modern, 189–192
    Piaget and, 226–227
    predictions made by, 193–198
    in the schools, 194–196
    stability of scores on, 198–199
    Sternberg's triarchic theory of intelligence versus, 201–203
Iran, 148
Israel, 450–451

Jobs, IQ test scores and success in, 196–198

Kindergarten
    IQ tests and, 194
    personality differences in, 320–321
Klinefelter's syndrome, 52–53
Knowledge, formal operations and, 252–254
Kohlberg, L., stages of moral development, 447–452, 458–461
Korea, 561

Language
    blindness and, 530–531
    deafness and, 530, 532
    reading difficulty and, 518
Language acquisition device, 303
Language development, 276–315
    auditory development and, 167
    bilingualism and, 288, 290–291
    child's role in, 301–305
    combined view of, 305–306
    communication and self-direction in, 295–297
    deafness and, 302
    definition of language, 277
    early steps in, 277–284
    explaining, 297
    grammar in, 284–289
    individual differences in, 306–309
    influence of environment on, 297–301
    learning to read and, 309–311
    major influences on, 559
    in preschool period, 551
    word meaning in, 289–295
Latency stage, 337, 339
Lead, 62–63, 69
Learning disabilities, 516–519, 534–538
Learning theories, 14–19, 24
    applications of, 18
    behaviorism and, 328–329
    classical conditioning, 15–16, 95
    language development and, 298
    operant conditioning, 16–17, 95
    personality development and, 327–334
    social-learning theory, 17–19, 23, 329–331, 344–345, 374–375, 379
Leboyer method, 86–87
Libido, 20
Listening, 476–477
Locomotor patterns, 132
Locus of gene, 41–42
Logic
    in concrete operations stage, 244–245
    in formal operations, 249–250
Longitudinal study, 26–27
Low-birth-weight infants, 7, 60, 68–69, 88–91, 102, 107, 279, 102

Mainstreaming, 536–537
Malnutrition, 13, 148–149
    prenatal development and, 62
Manipulative skills, 132
Marriage
    divorce and, 327, 344–345, 411, 482–484, 489
    influence of infant on, 106
Masturbation, 337
Mathematics, 267
    race and ability in, 217
    sex and ability in, 220–221
Maturation, 13
Mean length of utterance (MLU), 306
Medulla, 124
Meiosis, 41, 52
Memory
    recognition, 263–264, 268
    strategies for using, 259–261
Menarche, 129, *144*, 145, 147
Mental age, 189, 549–550
Mental retardation, 512–516
    assessment of, 513
    causes of, 514–516
    cognitive functioning in, 513–514
    in fetal alcohol syndrome, 61
    genetic basis of, 52–54, 514–516
    interventions and treatments for, 534–538
    IQ tests and, 191
    labels and, 513
    problem solving and, 264
Mesomorphic body type, 117, 143
Metacognition, 262
Metalinguistic knowledge, 310–311
Metamemory, 262
Midbrain, 124
Miscarriage, 40
Mistrust, 21
Mitosis, 40, 46
Modeling, 17, 330, 333, 334
    aggression and, 424
    altruism and, 419
Moral development, 446–456
    Kohlberg's stages of, 447–452, 458–461
    moral education and, 460–461
    Piaget's theories of, 446
Morality of reciprocity, 446
Moral judgment, 446, 458–461
Moral realism, 446
Moratorium, 361–362, *362*, *363*, 365
Moro reflex, 91, *92*, *96*
Mother-child interaction
    in breast-feeding, 103
    low birth weight and, 107
    quality of, 343–346
    trust in, 341
Motherese, 299–300
Mothers. *See also* Family; Fathers; Parents; Pregnancy; Prenatal development
    attachment of child to, 407–408

attachment to infant, 394–402
  childbirth and, 76–91
  depression of, 525
  employment of, 486–488
  talking to children by, 298–301
Motor development, 132–135
Motor skills, of newborn infants, 94–95
Multiple sclerosis, 125
Muscles, changes in, 122–124
Muscular dystrophy, *55, 56*, 532
Music, infants and, 167
Muttering, 296
Mutuality, 397
  child abuse as failure of, 400–401
Myelin, 125
Myelinization, 125, 134, 148

Nativism, 178–179
  language development and, 301–304
Nature/nurture controversy, 7–11
Negative reinforcement, 16
Negative social interactions, 423–425
  aggression, 326, *331*, 423–425, 494, 500–
    503, 521–524, 538, 563–564
  competition and dominance, 425, 457–
    458
  sex differences in, 425–427
Neglecting parental style, 480–481, 485
Nervous system
  changes in, with growth, 124–125
  fetal, 49, 62
Neurons, 49
Newborn. *See also* Birth; Infants; Prenatal
    development
  attachment of parents to, 394–396
  attachment to parents, 400, 402–408
  birth, 76–91
  breast-feeding versus bottle-feeding, 102–
    103, 395, 546–547
  daily life of, 98–103
  developmental stages of, 545–547
  operant conditioning of, 95
  reflexes and skills of, 91–98
Nonlocomotor patterns, 132

Obesity, 137–139
Object concept, 163–166
Object constancy, 160–163
Object identity, 164–166
Object permanence, 163, 164, *165*, 403
Observation, in research, 25
Observational learning, 17
Occupation
  behavior in, 385–386
  influences on choice of, 383–385
  IQ test scores and, 196–198
Occupational identity, 361–363
Oedipus conflict, 337–339, 376
Operant conditioning, 16–17
  of newborn infant, 95
Operation, 242–243

Operational thinking, 552
Oral stage, 336, *337*
Organizing relationships, 440, *441*
Organizing strategies, 260
Orphans, 561
Ossification, 122
Ovaries, 126–128, *127*
Overextension, in language, 293–294
Overregularization, 288
Ovum, 38–40
  in prenatal development, 46
  twins and, 43

Parent Child Development Centers
    (PCDCs), 490
Parents. *See also* Family; Fathers; Mothers
  altruistic behavior and, 418–419
  attachment of, to child, 394–402
  attachment of child to, 400, 402–408, 471,
    531, 548–549
  authoritarian parental style, 366, 473–
    474, 479–480, 484, 485
  authoritative parental style, 366, 418,
    422–423, 480, 484
  characteristics of child and, 481–482
  child abuse by, 9, *396*, 400–401
  cognitive enrichment and, 477
  communication patterns and, 476–477
  effects of infant on, 106–107
  first greeting of newborn by, 78–80
  impact of atypical child on, 533–534
  influence on self-esteem and identity,
    365–367
  methods of control used by, 471–476
  neglecting parental style, 480–481, 485
  permissive parental style, 366, 473–480
  quality of attachments and, 408–414
  schizophrenia in children and, 526, 528–
    530
  sex-role behavior and, 374–375
  short-term family stress and, 486
  social class and, 484–485
  social support for, 488–489
  structure of family and, 482–484
  warmth versus hostility of, 471
  work roles of, 486–488
Parents Anonymous (PA), 490
Partial reinforcement, 16–18, 329
Peers
  adolescent relationships with, 406–407,
    417–423
  day care and relationships with, 414–416,
    493–494
  early interaction with, 414–416
  elementary-school interactions, 416–417,
    421–423
  moral judgment and, 459–460
  positive social interactions among, 414–
    423
  sex-role behavior and, 375

Perception, 154
  individual differences in, 174–178
  of newborn infant, 91–94
  in prelinguistic phase, 277–281
Perceptual constancies, 160–163
Perceptual development, 154–182
  auditory development, 166–167
  basic characteristics of, 154–155, 170–
    174
  combining information from several
    senses in, 169–170
  explanations of, 178–179
  individual differences in, 174–178
  smell and taste, 168–169
  touch, 169
  visual development, 155–166
Perceptual learning, 154
Performance, 193
Permissive parental style, 366, 473–480
Personality, 13–14, 320–352. *See also* Tem-
    perament
  biological approach to, 322–327
  defined, 321–322
  effect of rate of physical development on,
    142–145
  learning approaches to, 327–334
  psychoanalytic theory and, 19–21, 334–
    348
  self-concept in, 364–367
  synthesis of theories of, 348–351
Perspective taking, in preoperational stage,
    235–237, 239–240
Pervasive developmental disorders, 522,
    526–530
Phallic stage, *337*, 337–339
Phenotype, 45
Phenylketonuria (PKU), 45, *55*, 514, 515
Physical development
  in adolescence, 121, 142–145, 554–559
  basic sequences and patterns in, 119–128
  from birth to 18 months, 545–549
  determinants of growth in, 146–149
  effect of, on behavior, 132–136
  in the elementary-school years, 552–554
  health and illness and, 136–137
  individual differences in, 137–146, 563–
    568
  major influences on, 559
  nature of developmental change and,
    562–563
  as part of developmental system, 545
  in the preschool years, 549–552
  reasons for studying, 116–119
  sexual maturity and, 128–131
  timing and, 560–562
Physical disabilities, 532
Piaget, Jean, 21–22, 23
  basic ideas of, 226–230, *230*
  concrete operations and, *230*, 242–247,
    556
  criticisms of, 253–256

early education and theory of, 266–267
  formal operations and, *230*, 247–250, 556,
    557
  moral judgments and, 446
  overview of stages of cognitive develop-
    ment, 252–253
  preoperational stage and, *230*, 233–242
  sensorimotor stage and, *230*, 230–233,
    234
Piaget, Lucienne, 232
Pituitary gland, 125–127
Placenta, 47, 78
Plasticity, 9
Play
  in language development, 304
  of parents with infants, 398–399
  in preschool period, 234–235, 372–374,
    375, 551
  sex segregation in, 416–417
  toys in, 134–135, 234–235, 371–372, 374,
    376–377, 380–381
Polygenic, 42
Popularity, 421–423, 425
Positive reinforcement, 16
Positive social interactions, 414–423
  in adolescence, 417–421
  altruism, 416, 418–419, 452–455
  in infancy and early childhood, 414–416
  popularity and, 421–423, 425
  at school age, 416–417
  sex differences in, 425–427
Poverty
  adequacy of parenting and, 395–396
  age at pregnancy and, 63–67
  conduct disorders and, 524
  day care and, 492
  impact on development, 7, 9, *11*
  influence on family functioning, 484–485
  IQ and, 213, 214–217
  IQ test scores and, 206
  physical development and, 146
  professional advice and support for par-
    ents, 490
  vulnerability and, 566
Practice, 147–149
Pragmatics, 295–296
Preconventional morality, 447–450
Preference technique, 157
Pregnancy. *See also* Birth; Prenatal develop-
    ment
  adolescent, 66–67, 136
  age of mother and, 63–67
  childbirth and, 76–91
  diet and exercise during, 62, 64–65
  diseases of mother during, 9, 58–59
  drugs taken by mother during, 59–62
  emotional state of mother and, 67–68
  genetic counseling and, 56–57
  number of earlier pregnancies and, 67
Prelinguistic phase, 277–281
Premature infants, 400

Prenatal development
  conception, 38–45
  embryonic period in, 46–48
  environmental influences on, 55–63
  explanations of normal sequence of, 50–52
  fetal period in, 48–49, 56–65, 136
  genetic errors in, 52–57
  hormones in, 49–50, 126, 379–380
  other characteristics of mother and, 63–68
  period of the ovum in, 38–40, 43, 46
  risks and consequences of problems in, 68–69
  sex differences in, 70
  sexual differentiation in, 49–50
  social class differences in, 70–71
Preoperational stage, *230*, 233–242
  current work on, 239–242
  independence in, 551–552
  overview of child in, 242
  Piaget's view of, 235–239
Preschool. *See also* Day care
  attachment to parents, 405–406, 551
  bilingualism and, 290–291
  developmental stages of, 549–552
  Head Start program, 213, 492
  independence in, 551–552
  interventions in, and IQ, 213–214, *215*
  IQ tests and, 194
  peer relationships in, 414–416
  play in, 234–235, 372–374, 375, 551
  preoperational stage and, *230*, 233–242
Preterm infants, 89
Primary sex characteristics, 128–131
Principled morality, *448*, 449, 450
Problem solving
  in formal operations, 248–249
  in information processing, 261, 264
Projection, 335
Prosocial behavior, 416, 418–419, 452–455
Prototypes, 295
Proximodistal pattern of development, 147
Psychoanalysis, 334
Psychoanalytic theory
  personality development and, 19–21, *23*, *24*, 334–348
  of sex-role development, 376
Psychological constructs, 440, *441*
Psychopathic delinquency, 524
Psychosexual stages, 19–20, 336–339, 340
Psychosocial stages, 20–21, 339–343
Puberty, 116, 128–132, 554. *See also* Adolescence
  hormone changes and, 127–128
  late, and spatial abilities, 219–220
  personality and changes during, 142–145
  psychosexual stages and, *337*, 339
  psychosocial stages of, *340*, 343
Punishment, 16
  effects of, 474–476

IQ and, 210
spanking as, 474–475

Quasi experiments, 29
Questionnaires, 25

Race
  IQ and, 195, 217–218
  physical development and, 146
Rapid eye movement (REM) sleep, 100
Reading
  basic steps in, 309–310
  conceptual tempo and, 176
  effect of language skills in, 310–311
  learning disability involving, 517–519
  unlearning shape constancy in, 163
Reasoning
  moral, 450
  in preoperational stage, 239, 241–242
  social, 457–458
  verbal, 220–221
Receptive language, 280
Recessive gene, 42
Reciprocal trust, 442
Recognition memory, 263–264, 268
Referential style, 284, 308–309
Reflection, 174–178
Reflexes, 91, *92*
Rehearsal, 259–260
Reinforcement
  in language development, 298
  negative, 16
  partial, 16–17, 18, 329
  personality development and, 328–334
  positive, 16
  vicarious, 17
Repetition, in motherese, 299–300
Residential treatment, 537–538
Resilience, 527
  individual differences in, 564–568
Responses, of others, and child growth, 117
Restrictiveness, 473–474
Reversibility, 243
Role confusion, 343
Rooting reflex, *92*, 169
Rubella (German measles), 9, 58
Rules
  clarity and consistency of, 472
  in gender identity, 377–378, 381
Runner's World, 65

Schemas, in gender identity, 377–378, 381
Schematic learning, of newborn infants, 95–96
Schemes, 227–228, *229*
Schizophrenia, 526, 528–530
Scholastic Aptitude Tests (SATs), 193
Schooling, 495–499. *See also* Preschool
  beginning of, 552–554
  for blindness, 530–531
  for deafness, 530

Schooling (*Continued*)
  mainstreaming versus special classes in, 535–537
  Piaget's theory and early education, 266–267
Science, 267
Secondary sex characteristics, 128–131
Secure attachment, 409–414
  day care and, 404, 412, 492–493
  formation of, 411–412
  long-term effects of, 413–414
  stability over time, 410–411
  temperament and, 412
  vulnerability and, 527
Sedatives, 81
Self-concept, 349, 354–390
  defined, 357
  developmental patterns and, 354–364
  effect of growth on, 118–119
  gender concept in, 368, 369–370, 377–378
  individual differences in, 364–367
  occupational choices and, 383–385
  personality development and, 333–334
  sex-role behavior in, 369, 372–383
  sex-role concept in, 368, 371–372, 374–377
  sex-role stereotyping in, 369, 371–372, 378–383
  social development and, 392
  summary of, 363–364, 367–368
Self-definition, in adolescence, 359–360
Self-efficacy, 330–331
  occupational choice and, 384
Self-esteem
  androgyny and, 383
  authoritarian parental style and, 473–474, 479–480
  defined, 364
  employment of mother and, 487–488
  individual differences in, 364–367
  occupational choice and, 384
  origins of, 365–367
  popularity and, 421–423
Self-regulation, in language use, 296
Self-scheme, 331
Semantics
  defined, 276
  development of, 289–295
  early stages in, 277–284
Sensitive period, 9, 50, 51, 149
Sensorimotor stage, 230, 230–233
  current work on, 232–233
  overview of, 233
  Piaget's view of, 230–232
  play in, 234
  substages of, 231
Sentences
  first, 284
  syntax of early, 284–289
Separation protest, 404

Sex chromosomes, 42–43
Sex-linked inheritance patterns, 43, 49–50, 52–54, 55
Sex-role behavior, 369
  androgyny and, 381–383
  cross-sex children and, 379–381
  development of, 372–374
  theories of development of, 374–378
Sex-role concept, 368
  androgyny and, 381–383
  cross-sex children and, 379–381
  development of, 371–372
  occupational choices and, 383–385
  theories of development of, 374–378
Sex roles, defined, 368
Sex-role stereotyping, 369
  development of, 371–372
  individual differences in, 378–383
  occupational choices and, 383–385
  social interactions and, 425–427
  in television and books, 380–381
Sexual identity, in adolescence, 361–363
Sexuality
  adolescent, 135–136
  development of sexual maturity, 128–131
  Freud's psychosexual stages and, 19–20, 336–340
  prenatal hormones and, 49–50
Shame, 341–342
Shape, changes in body, 121
Shape constancy, 161–163
Shyness, individual differences in, 564
Siblings, 43
Sickle-cell anemia, 55, 56
Sign language, 277, 278
  deafness and, 302
Size constancy, 160, 161–162
Sleeping, 99, 99–100
Slow-to-warm-up child, 104
Small-for-date infants, 89
Smell, 169
Smiling, 531
  temperament and, 324–325
Smoking, prenatal development and, 60–61
Sociability, temperament and, 324
Social class. *See also* Poverty
  conduct disorders and, 524
  differences in infant according to, 106
  impact on secure and insecure attach-
    ments, 409, 411
  influence on family functioning, 484–485
  IQ and, 206–208
  perceptual skills and, 178
  physical development and, 146
  prenatal development and, 70–71
  vulnerability of children and, 566
Social cognition, 434–462
  behavior and, 452–461
  cognitive side of, 434–435
  defined, 434
  describing people in, 438–441

development of empathy in, 437–438, *439*
general cognitive development and, 435, 461–462
social side of, 435–437
theories of, 445–456
thinking about relationships in, 441–445
Social development, 392–431
  in adolescence, 554–559
  attachment and, 392–414
  from birth to 18 months, 545–549
  in the elementary-school years, 552–554
  giftedness and, 520
  individual differences in, 563–568
  major influences on, 560
  nature of developmental change and, 562–563
  negative social interactions and, 423–425
  as part of developmental system, 545
  positive social interactions and, 414–423
  in preschool years, 549–552
  sex differences and, 425–427
  timing and, 560–562
Social-learning theory, 17–19, *23*
  impact of divorce and, 344–345
  personality development and, 329–331
  of sex-role development, 374–375, 379
Social reasoning, 457–458
Social referencing, 160, 403–404
Social skills, of newborn infants, 96–98
Social support
  attachment of infant and, 350, *350*
  for parents, 488–489
Spanking, 474–475
Spatial ability, 219–220, *220*
Specific learning disability (SLD), 516–519
  intervention and treatment of, 534–538
  possible causes of, 518–519
  problems of definition of, 517–518
Stages of development, 12, 544–559
  in adolescence, 554–559
  from birth to 18 months, 545–549
  during elementary-school years, 552–554
  individual differences and, 563–568
  major influences on, 559–560
  nature of developmental change and, 562–563
  during preschool years, 549–552
  system of, 545
  timing and, 560–562
  transitions and consolidations in, 544–545
Stanford-Binet, 189, 195, 198, 207
States of consciousness, 98–103, *99*
Stepparent families, 483–484
Stepping reflex, *92*
Stereotyping. *See* Sex-role stereotyping
Sternberg, Robert, triarchic theory of intelligence, 201–203
Strange situation, 409, *410*
Stress
  behavior problems and, 525–526, 527

child abuse and, 401
divorce and, 483–484
short-term family, 486
social support and, 489
vulnerability and, 527
Structures, cognitive, 187–188
Style, differences in language, 308–309
Subcutaneous fat, 124
Subnutrition, 148–149
Sucking reflex, *92*, 169
Suicide, 137
Superego, 335
Swallowing reflex, *92*
Sweden, 399–402
Symbiotic relationship, 354
Symbolic play, in language development, 304
Symbols, language as system of, 277, 282
Synapses, 49
Syntax
  defined, 276
  development of, 284–289

Taste, 168–169
Tay-Sachs disease, *55*, 56
Telegraphic speech, 285
Television
  nonviolent, 503
  sex-role stereotyping in, 380–381
  violence on, 499–503
Temperament, 13–14, 322–327. *See also* Personality
  behavior problems and, 324, 326
  defined, 323
  developmental change and, 563
  infant, 104–107
  personality development and, 348–350
  and security of attachment, 412
Teratogens, in prenatal development, 55–63
Testes, 126–128, *127*
Testosterone, 49, 127, 128
Tests and testing. *See also* IQ tests
  achievement, 192–193
  amniocentesis, 57, 63
  Apgar score, 87–88
  Bayley Scales of Infant Development, 190–192, 198
  Embedded Figures Test, 176, *177*
  prenatal, 56–57
  Stanford-Binet, 189, 195, 198, 207
Thalidomide, 59
Theories of development, 12–24
  biological, 12–14, *23*, 24
  cognitive-developmental, 21–22, *23*, 226–253, 266–268
  contrasting of, 22–24
  learning, 14–19, *23*, *24*, 95, 329–331, 344–345, 374–375, 379
  psychoanalytic, 19–21, *23*, *24*, 334–348, 376

Thyroid gland, 125–126
Timing, development and, 560–562
Touch, 169
Toys
 commercials for, 380–381
 dolls, 234–235
 motor development and, 134–135
 sex-role behavior and, 374, 376–377
 sex-role stereotyping and, 371–372
Tranquilizers, 81
Transductive reasoning, in preoperational
 stage, 239, 241–242
Triarchic theory of intelligence, 201–203
Trust, 21, 341, 349, 365, 409, 442
Turkey, 450–451
Turner's syndrome, 53
Twins, 43
 IQ scores of, 204
 language development and, 306–308
 temperament and, 324, *325*

Ultrasound, 56–57
Unconditioned responses, 15–16
Unconditioned stimulus, 15–16
Underextension, in language, 293
Universal ethical principles, 450
Uterus, 38

Verbal reasoning, sex and ability in, 220–
 221
Very low birth weight, 88, *90*
Vicarious reinforcement, 17
Visual cliff, 161, *162*

Visual development, 155–166
 acts of babies and children in, 157–160
 acuity in, 156–157
 blindness, *171,* 172–173, 530–531, 534–
 538
 ignoring visual cues in, 160–163
 making discriminations in, 160
 object concept in, 163–166
Vocabulary
 development of word meanings and, 289–
 295
 first words in, 281–284
 of motherese, 299–300
 talking to child and, 298–301
Volunteers, 419
Vulnerability, 7, *8,* 527
 individual differences in, 564–568

Walking
 development of, 132–135, *133*
 importance of practice and, 147–148
Warmth versus hostility, in family, 471
Wealth, influence on family functioning,
 484–485
Weight and height changes, 119–121
WISC-R (Wechsler Intelligence Scale for
 Children—Revised), 189–191, 194, 198
Words
 development of meanings of, 289–295
 early use of, 281–284
 in later grammar development, 288–289
Working Wives/Working Husbands (Pleck),
 386

MULTIMEDIA LEARNING CENTRE
DEESIDE COLLEGE

MULTIMEDIA LEARNING CENTRE
DEESIDE COLLEGE